Love

Without

Borders

From Inca Lands to Iraqi Sands

Cameron Powers

Love Without Borders
From Inca Lands to Iraqi Sands

First Edition

Original Copyright © 2015 by Cameron Powers
Published by GL Design, Boulder, Colorado, USA

All rights reserved. No part of this book may be reproduced in any form or by any electronic or mechanical means including information storage and retrieval systems without permission in writing from the publisher, except by a reviewer, who may quote brief passages in a review.

ISBN: 1-933983-22-1
ISBN Complete: 978-1-933983-22-6
Library of Congress Control Number: 2019901347

I have included quite a few photos in this book.
There are a lot more online.
To see them go to https://www.cameronpowers.com
Look under the Biography Menu Tab and you will find the photo histories organized loosely by year and by location.

Cover design by Ariana Saraha
Photo of author playing oud on cover
by Eva Soltes
Photo of Dawn Hurlburt (dancer in the dunes on cover)
by Jodajen

Foreword

If I ever got even a glimpse of a place called Love Without Borders then I can count myself as a very lucky person. Hopefully these adventures will inspire others to enter even more deeply.

I don't think I ever really existed... at least not in the ways that many people do. My identity remains elusive but I did discover, reading beat poetry in bookstores at age sixteen, that simply chronicling one's path might be existence enough... If, of course, one's path was an interesting one...

What determines the path? From a very young age I was strongly magnetized by the beautiful girls I saw all around me. And because I had been fortunate to have a warm and loving mother, I trusted women and have partnered deeply with quite a few.

Fascinated by cultures far-flung from my own, I worked to learn other languages and explore other worlds. This book describes my adventures along the paths of exploration into the Inca, Greek and Arabic worlds which graciously revealed a few precious ancient secrets.

Partnering with the beloved women in my life has been no less of an adventure into exploring other worlds... each woman an amazing magical mysterious world... each one another enticing landscape through which I have been drawn to eagerly wander. I am so grateful to them all!

Sacred flirtation is our most primal activity. We flirt with every possibility in life and love until we dissolve into the huge family of beloved souls which magically appear around us and with whom we live our lives.

One's "public life" and "private life" should be the same, it seems to me. If we don't even dare to tell the truth to each other how in the world will we ever learn to get along? At the same time that I say this I must also admit that I have omitted some details about my partnerships with certain women out of deference to my knowledge about their sensitivities.

I know that readers who have been continuously subjected to the English-language journalism of the last few decades have developed almost iron-clad belief systems which paint Arab-world culture in negative terms. And I know that my descriptions of the beauty and hospitality I have experienced in places like Syria will fall on skeptical ears. So I want to emphasize that my faith in the beauties of the Arab-world cultures as I experienced them no doubt remain unchanged even after so many years now of war in Syria. Anyone who, like myself, followed the unfolding of those violent events closely and with deep background knowledge, knows that there was never really a civil war in Syria. The violent elements were cultivated and imported from the outside with sponsorship from immensely wealthy and powerful entities. Syrian people, I'm sure, remain generous and tolerant and still are as I have described them after my travels back in 2004-2010.
-Cameron Powers - 2019

****

A Timeless Quote You've Probably Seen Before

The real treasure, that which can put an end to our poverty and all our trials, is never very far, there is no need to seek it in a distant country. It lies buried in the most intimate parts of our own house;that is, of our own being. It is behind the stove, the center of the life and warmth that rule our existence,the heart of our heart, if only we knew how to unearth it.

And yet -- there is this strange and persistent fact that only after a pious journey into a distant region, in a new land, that the meaning of that inner voice guiding us on our search can make itself understood by us. And to this strange and persistent fact is added another: that he who reveals to us the meaning of our mysterious inward pilgrimage must himself be a stranger of another belief and another race.

- Heinrich Zimmer as quoted by Miriea Eleade
in Myths, Dreams, and Mysteries

****

Sacred Flirtation

This book is about Sacred Flirtation. We humans are attracted to one another and it is through our flirtations that we renew our connectedness.

Sacred Flirtation is pure playfulness which pushes no agenda and does not feel invasive. It is a beautiful thing and people all over the world love to engage in it to express our mutual attractions. Everything from friendships to romances to business partnerships result from our sacred flirtations.

Egyptians have their ways... Greeks have theirs... Peruvians theirs... And of course Westerners in Europe and America have theirs. Learning different styles of expressing our attractions can broaden our communication skills on deep pre-verbal levels.

****

Lonely Planet Article about Cameron and Kristina

Cameron's lifestyle led to an article about his adventures with his wife, Kristina, being included in the May, 2009 Lonely Planet Guide to the Middle East. The article was entitled "Musicians for Peace" and was written by Anthony Ham.

"It's not every American musician who can claim to have learned to play the oud (Middle Eastern lute) like an Iraqi, mastered the complexity of the maqam scale system and played love songs on a Baghdad street in the dangerous aftermath of the US invasion of Iraq. But then Cameron Powers is not your ordinary musician.

Together with his partner, singer Kristina Sophia, Powers was seriously disillusioned with his country's response to the terrorist attack on 11 September 2001. When we caught up with them in Latakia, Syria, in May 2008 on their fifth visit to the region, Powers and Sophia spoke of how they performed with a Palestinian musician in Boulder, Colorado two weeks after the attacks, a concert that only went ahead when the word "Palestinian" was removed from the promotional material. Experiences such as these prompted the couple to make their first trip to the Middle East in November 2002, hoping to build bridges between Western and Arab cultures through what they call "the warmth, beauty and sensuality of Arab music."

The welcome they received from ordinary Arabs convinced them to return. In Spring 2003, impromptu performances for the Iraqi visa-issuing authorities and border officials saw Powers and Sophia granted permission to enter Iraq - "music is an instant passport" is his explanation. Unable to find any functioning concert venues in post-invasion Baghdad, they simply began performing on the streets. "The fact that we were on the streets of Baghdad singing Iraqi love songs, showed the Iraqi people that Americans could also invade with music," Powers told us. A performance before 60,000 people in Cairo followed the same year.

Struck by the warmth of the welcome they received in the Middle East, the couple realized that American audiences needed to hear an alternative vision of the Middle East as much as ordinary Arabs needed to feel their solidarity. Since then, the couple has covered more than 60,000 km and performed at over 200 presentations in universities, schools and churches across the US. Nonetheless, they still find themselves confronted with the suspicions of post-9/11 America: "We encounter fear first and then openness to the music. It used to be the other way around."

Not content with the power of performance, Powers and Sophia have set up a secular NGO, Musical Missions of Peace, also known as Musical Ambassadors of Peace, which is based around the premise that "People who have learned and sung each others' popular love songs together are less likely to war with one another than those who have not." The NGO provides support to Iraqi musicians and refugees in exile in Jordan and Syria and promotes education and performance of international music in the US.

- Anthony Ham - Lonely Planet Guide to the Middle East.

****

Musical Ambassadors of Peace - Deep Origins

Although I have helped create principles which can be followed to help facilitate loving cross-cultural friendships and communications, I would guess that the roots of my behavior and attitudes came from my mother. She had a deep admiration and sympathy for African-American people and kept cherished friendships alive with several women. She always went into conflict-solving by assuming that the problems were not a big deal and were the results of simple mis-understandings. She saw 'good people' everywhere and when I was around her as a child I don't recall ever having to listen to angry complaints. She would express general concern but without blame.

So for me to have wandered the world and discovered so many wonderful people to befriend was the natural emulation of my mother's style.

I could say something similar about my father who was eternally occupied with his high-tech business of saving the world by creating what he thought was the relatively clean energy of nuclear power. His was very much the purely scientific mind but he did love to listen to music... Western classical music. He seemed to have a calm and meditative mind and would lean back in his reclining living room chair to listen to the speakers of his 'hi-fi' vinyl record player. But it had been my mother who used to put on the dance music and scoop my little three-year-old self up and whirl us around the room. And it was she who had encouraged me at around the age of nine to bring home and play the latest 45 rpm vinyl discs which contained the latest hits from that new genre which was becoming known as 'rock and roll.'

As it turned out, music and dance took me further than anything else. It feels good to me that "Musical Ambassadors of Peace" has been created to commemorate and continue the legacy of our musical bridge-building adventures around the world.

****

Dedication

To my son and daughter: Loren and Melina. I just hope that if you ever read the stories in this autobiography that you will find them fun and useful and perhaps oddly familiar.

✳✳✳

Text Border Key

Certain blocks of text are surrounded by borders of two different appearances.

Much of this autobiography has been extracted from journals which I kept periodically throughout my life. Certain journal entries are not just narrative but rather more like poetry or flights of fantasy which I had written at the time.

> *These are distinguished by a border which looks like this.*

Other blocks of text were extracted from journals or emailed communications written by two of the women who have accompanied me: Lisa and Kristina. I value their descriptions highly as they offer insights which vary considerably from my own.

> *The entries from these women are distinguished by a border which looks like this.*

Contents
Love Without Borders

Foreword	3
A Timeless Quote You've Probably Seen Before	4
Sacred Flirtation	5
Lonely Planet Article about Cameron and Kristina	5
Musical Ambassadors of Peace - Deep Origins	7
Dedication	8
Text Border Key	8
Contents	9
Birdie: Feeling the Magic	27
My Family Dissolves	29
Bonnie: Exploration of Love	31
Ike and Tina Turner	32
Turn Off the TV - Jail in Florida	33
I Don't Really Like To Fight, But...	34
African Americans	36
Bob Eagle and Me at Age 14	36
First Rock Band	37
Kay	37
Do Girls Have Inverted Penises Called Vaginas?	38
Women of the Night	39
Monterrey, Mexico	40
Drive Drive Drive	41
Map: 1960 Road Trip	41
Western Military Academy - Alton, Illinois	42
French Existentialism, Beat Poetry	42
A Commissioned Portrait	44
Paranoid Fear Vibes of the Big City	47
Wild Blackberry Countryside	48
Falling in Love with Bonnie	50
Family Disasters in Texas and Missouri	50
On the Beach in Mazatlan, Mexico	51
Map: Hitch-hiking Portland to Mazatlan and Back	53
I Rented a Little Cabin in the Forest	54

Bonnie Also Moves to Colorado ... 56
   Bonnie on our Porch in Manitou Springs ... 56
First Trip to Peru ... 57
   On Ranrapalca in the Cordillera Blanca ... 59
   Rappelling off Ocshapalca Ridge ... 60
   Map: Climbing Peaks Above Quebrada Ischinca ... 60
   No Buses... Just Trucks... ... 61
   Mysteriously Precise Inca Stonework above Cusco ... 62
   Train to Machu Picchu ... 62
   In the Back of Another Truck ... 63
   Map: Wandering Through Inca Lands ... 63
   But Not Ready for More School ... 64

Lisa: Into the Inca Lands ... 65
   Camille ... 67
   Up into the Mountains again with Camille ... 67
Search and Not Rescue but Confuse ... 69
   Ten Mile Peak ... 69
Back to South America ... 70
   Bogotá, Colombia ... 71
   Some Kind of Rape? ... 74
Drunk Police Detective ... 76
Some Other Kind of Music ... 77
When All Else Fails - Back to School ... 78
   Robin Painting ... 79
   Robin in Her Remodeled Carriage House ... 80
   Robin Cross-Country Skiing ... 82
How-ya Doin' Big Boy? ... 82
   Lisa - The Girl who Lived on the Back Porch ... 83
Robin Back from Cambodia ... 84
Winter Wilderness on Skis ... 86
Inca Language Intensive at Cornell ... 88
I Decided to Go to Peru with Cameron ... 90
Iquitos on the Amazon ... 92
   Ready to Dip Into the Amazon River ... 93
   Lisa Sitting on the Bardales in Iquitos ... 94
   Lisa in Our Hammock on the Adolfo ... 96
Lima, Peru ... 99
Cusco and Machu Picchu ... 100
Typhoid ... 102

A Mobile Gold Mine	102
Walking to Sina	105
Lisa on Pampa Blanca	105
On His Floor with his Seven Children	109
Valley Walls above Sina	109
Lisa Bonding with the Village Girls	111
Drink until Dawn	111
Nemia - A Six-Year-Old Woman	114
The Other Side of the River	115
Amalia and Ilateria Weaving	116
Wish I Was a Doctor	117
And With You, Thirty-One!	118
Market Day Back Up at 16,000 Feet	119
Chasing the Chicken	121
Guinea Pigs or Music	122
Potatoes, Gratitude and Flying Too High	125
Going to School	126
Ghosts, Money-Making and Our Last Antibiotics	127
Women and Wool	130
She's Over a Hundred Years Old	131
A New Owner for My Guitar	132
Ah Mi Compadre!	134
Lisa Gets to Ride	136
Leaving Sina	136
La Paz, Bolivia and Back to Peru	137
Nasty Catholic Priests and a Dissertation on Conflict	138
Cusco and the Mummies	140
Me and Lisa	141
Lisa Departs; Hitch-Hiking For Me	141
Tito	143
Tito	143
Drunks in a Chinese Bar	146
A Coup in Panama	147
South American Routes in 1968-1969	148
Tonsils, Steamboat Springs, A Message from Robin	148
Lisa at The Barn in Steamboat Springs	149
Cataract Canyon	149
Resting On One of Our Rafts	150
Grays, Desolation and Cataract Canyons	151

Climbing the Grand Teton and Blanca Peak	151
Grand Teton Complete Exum Ridge Route	152
North Face of Blanca Peak in Sangre De Cristo Range	152
Linguistics, Robin, Yosemite	154
Carp's Cabin Again	155
More Rivers and Roofs	160
Terrible Tours in Mexico	160
Friendly Crabs and Creating Canyons	161
Musical Wandering	162
Pablo, a Student from Thailand, Sings 'Here Comes the Sun'	163
Singing in Patzcuaro	164
A Good Field in which to Rest	165
Guitar and Drum	165
Whatever You Do, Don't Go into That Area!	166
School Children with Rafael	167
A Horse from Jesus	167
On the Trail with Jesus Fernandez	168
Bruce Climbs Part Way Up a Palm Tree	169
Our Music Flowed Through Us As Never Before	173
Hanging Out with Rafael Cisneros	173
On the Trail to La Ticla	174
Wandering South from Aquila to Coalcoman River Valley	176
Fish in Our Pants	176
Saving Chicki from the Red Light District	177
Sailing South	178
On the Loose in Acapulco	180
Dancing in La Zona Roja	182
Itchy Feet: on to Mexico City	184
Onward to Veracruz	186
Crazy but Lucky	187
Pedro - Mexican Hippie	189
Escárcega and the Girl in the Yellow Dress	191
Chetumal, Belize, Guatemala: Psychic Sexual Energy	194
Manzanillo to Guatemala City	198
Gypsies in Lima	198
A Rock Laughs Back at Me in Machu Picchu	199
Back Home into Sina	200
Lisa, Edwin, Pastor in Sina	200
Lisa with the Girls	201

Ancient Stone Wisdom and Climber Dreams	202
Pampa Qarqa - New Friends	203
Bad Weather and Exhaustion	206
Trucks Every Saturday at Iskay Cruz	207
Gregorio, Eusevio and Their Mother in Pampa Qarqa	209
Where is My Sheep?	209
Lisa Washing Fleece	210
Finding Pastor's Cows - Down to the Jungle	211
Bear Killed for Eating the Corn	212
1970 Journey Through Sina	213
Lucio Gonza and Friends in Sina Playing Panpipes	213
Inca Elders at Inti Raymi in Cusco	214
1970 Travels in Peru	215
Colorado, New Mexico and Texas	215

Leda: Greek Odyssey   221

Linguistics at University of California in Berkeley	221
Grand Canyon - Communal Life in Boulder	225
Down the Upper Half of the Grand Canyon	226
Extreme Tragedy	228
Terrible Tour to Peru	228
Back into Sina with a Different Woman	230
Descent into Sina	230
Anna and Charlie; John and Norma	231
Leda and Pastor	232
Lucio Gonza and Wife Patrunila with Natilminda and Gladys	232
Idelsa and Emilio	233
Me and Idelsa	234
Climbing on the Glaciers of Ananea	236
Ananea Summit	237
Stone Hut at Iskay Cruz	238
What a Beautiful Woman!	238
Daily Life in Sina Unfolding	239
Benito and Irene	240
Down the Valley Toward the Jungle	243
Sea of Clouds over Amazon Jungle Below	243
Mouse Plague in San Lorenzo	245
Bridge at San Lorenzo	247
Washing Each Other's Backs	247
Onward to Yanawaya	248

Cooked Corn and A Pineapple!	250
Way Too Much Food	251
Barker, Victor, John, Charlie, Pastor, Me, Mauro, Placida, Leda	252
How Many Oranges Can I Eat?	254
Walking Through Sina into Jungle Below in 1972	255
Back to the Altiplano	255
Pastor's Family in Juliaca	256
Cristobal's Children in Puno	258
La Paz, Bolivia - Hanging with the Rich Folks	258
1972 Route Through Peru and Bolivia	262

Feeling Our Way in Colorado — 262

View from Long's Peak	263
Mt Holy Cross: The Buzzing Summit	264
Mt Holy Cross	266
Our Tent on Melvina Hill	266
Happy Campers	267
Paradise in the Mount Zirkel Wilderness	267
Dancing Naked in the Living Room	269
John Link	269

Another Terrible Tour to Peru — 272

Martin, Graham, Chris, Spectra, Sue	274
I Just Like This	275

DNA: Deep Natural Awareness — 280

Sexual Repression and Human Violence — 283

Onward Towards Home in Sina — 284

Feeling at Home in Sina with Laura and Edwin	285
Laura, Sue, Edwin	286
My Magic Rock	286
Fever Strikes; La Jesusa Strikes; Dreamworlds Reign	287
I must go and see Lucio!	290
Alberto	291
Potato Field Work and Climbing Ananea	293
Ridge on Ananea	295
Cordillera Apolobamba to the East in Bolivia	296
Ananea Summit	297
Iskay Cruz and Entrance to Sina Valley Below	298
Down Through Rinconada: Highest Town in the World	298
Rinconada: Highest Town in the World	298
Natural Ancient Ways of Life in Sina	299

Patrunila	303
Walking into Bolivia	303
Into Bolivia with Horses	304
Walking Route Through Sina in 1973	305
Festival in La Paz	305
Disaster with the Ladies of the Night	308
These Miraculous Little Visits	309
Sailing to the Island of Taquile	311
Island Sunrise	314
A Translator's Paradise	315
Our Tales Turned Toward the Spooky	318
Labyrinths of Lima	320
1973 Routes Through Peru and Bolivia	322
Tito Again - by Chance	322
Magic Piles of Lettuce	326
She Allowed Herself to be Led Out	329
His Eyes Shone Warm Sickness and Hate	331
You Will Have to Pay!	335
Leave Me One of Those Two Girls	337
Sittin' on the Jet Plane	340
Colorado: Man Came Home to Woman	343
Who Was That Person...?	343
Whoops... Born Again	345
On Our Way to Oaxaca	345
Señorita, Look What Mexico City Has Done to You!	347
Back to the Mescal Bar	348
The Colored Threads of Energetic Connection	350
Guitar Heaven in Paracho	351
Wandering with Leda Through Mexico	354
The Most Terrible Place We Have Yet Found!	355
Friends and Greeks in Albuquerque	356
Boulder to Athens	359
Leda, Tassos, Elli, Costis	360
Elli, Leda, Cameron, Tassos	361
Taking a Break	363
Grab the Erect Wooden Penis and Push Down	364
Yorgos	365
To Mani with Yorgos Maniatis	366
Valendini and Yorgos	366

Athens to Mani with Yorgos Maniatis	367
She Deserves To Stay and Be Greek	368
November 17th Revolution	368
North to Ioannina	371
From Athens to Ioannina with Spyros and Dorothea	373
Moving to Crete	374
Yannis	376
Nikos - The Gentle-Looking One	377
Yannis and Angela	377
Finding our way to Kokkinos Pirgos in Crete	378
A Man in Love Kills for His Woman	379
We Began a Slow and Sensual Dance	380
He Had Brought His Guitar	382
The Athenians Retreated, Jumping into Their Car	384
Swimming Towards the Moon	387
Get Death on the Run	389
Steal One Day from Death	392
I Felt Like an Intruder	394
Yannis and Me	395
No Fifth Plate Was Forthcoming	398
Alexandros with Bouzouki	403
Yannis' Place in Kokkinos Pirghos	404
You're on the Run	404
Translating One of Yorgos' Books, into English	407
Exchange Energies Only Through the Eyes	408
More Painful... but Much Richer	411
Busy Making Money in Colorado	413
Birdie, Music, Skiing, Rivers	414
Silk Route: Mona, Margie, Leda, Me, Steve, Bob, Mark	415
Melinda, Lindy, Claire, Jeannie, Others	416
Pearl Pass Between Aspen and Crested Butte	416
Colorado River: More Grand Canyon	417
On the River Again	417
Magnificent Plunge into the Pool Below	419
Bill Chase and the Cactus	420
Chase Dancing on the Rocks	421
Mike, Rebecca, Andy	422
The Scorpion Did Not Seem to Mind	423
Connection Through the Dance	424

I Forcefully Repossessed My Soul	425
Lower Havasu Canyon	427
We Don't Welcome White Trash!	428
Havasu Falls	428
We Watched Person After Person Tumble Off into the River	430
Wayne's Boat Enters Lava Falls	431
Spun Around Backwards in Lava Falls	432
We Were in Exactly the Right Place	433
An Indian Was Huddled Against Me For Warmth	435
Time for Relaxation Above Diamond Creek	435

Wild Dance Parties … 439

Lindy, Leda, Josie, Bob, Cameron on Idaho Tour	440
The Silk Route with Our Dancers	440
Steve Fundingsland and Lindy	441
The Leda Guitar	442

Wedding … 443

Leda and I Get Married	445
Bonnie and Lisa at Wedding	446
Leda's Belly Was Growing	447
Astrometer	448
Guitar and Bouzouki Making	449
Loren Arrives	449
Steve and Margie	451
Athens and Naxos	451
Taking Loren to Athens and Naxos in 1978	452
Stonework Stairs	452
Stonework Walkways	453
Becoming a Home Owner	453
It's a House in North Boulder	454
A Son and a Daughter and More Time in Athens	454
Melina Arrives	455
Back to Athens, Delphi and Zakynthos in 1982	456

Deeper into Music and Dance … 457

Loren and I in Colorado Mountains	458
Greek Music in Nebraska - Melina Dancing Back to Leda	458
Melina and Loren	459
Boulder Bouzouki Band	460

Boulder Concrete Sawing … 461

Loren on Clarinet	461

Melina on Violin	461
Boulder Concrete Sawing	462
Managing Sexual Energy in Iraq	463
Taverna Terzakis	465
Eva, Me, Kathleen, Dave	465
Loren and Melina - Halloween	466
Kathleen	467
Sol Spice	469
Solspice at Zenobia's	469
Me and SlideRay	470
Costa Rica	470
Melina in Costa Rica in 1994	471
Melina in the Jungle	471
Exploring Manuel Antonio, Volcan Arenal, Nicoya Penninsula	472
Children's Television and Bilingual Teaching Programs	472
Loren Graduates from Boulder High	473
An Albanian Gypsy in the Band	474
Me, Kathleen, Joffer	474
Saadoun al Bayati	475
Deeper and Deeper into Imsak	475

Kristina: Crossing the Iraqi Sands . . . 479

Eleanor, Camille, Melina, Loren	480
Off to Egypt with Eva	480
The Mizmar Band Continued Until Dawn	481
Eva	481
Eva and Me	482
Felucca on the Nile	484
Mizmar and Taktib Party	485
Energetic Connection Through A Stick - Eva	486
Eva Uses Bench for Stage	487
Asata and Ibrahim	488
Egypt with Eva in 1996	488
Hitting Bottom in Pennsylvania	489
Playing with a New Band Called Sherefe	489
New Musician Friends	490
Enjoying Time with Camille	491
Loren and I in Victoria, Canada	492
Demystifying Turkey and Alexandria, Egypt	493
Birgul and I - And Miramar	493

Playing in Kusadasi	494
Turkey with Eva and Friends in 1999	496
Asata and Adil	496
Cairo to Alexandria in Search of Giant Oud	497
Egyptian Dervish	498
California, Mexico, Music Music Music	498
Melina Graduates from Boulder High	499
Early Sherefe Fun	500
And Excellent Musicianship Makes for a Good Band	500
Sacred Music in Morocco	501
Playing in Fes, Morocco	502
Playing with Nabil's Father, Abdrafie	503
Southern Spain, Gypsies, Moroccans	504
Barcelona Thievery	506
Greece: Corfu, Athens, Samos	510
Dance Party on Samos	512
Morocco to Spain to Greece in 2000	513
Chorus of Female Singers	513
Sherefe and the Habibis	514
Kristina and I - Halloween	515
Puerto Vallarta and Southern Utah	516
The Habibis in Front	517
Boulder Theater	518
Sherefe and the Habibis in a Pile	518
No Palestinians Allowed at Boulder Theater	519
Kristina and Nabil	520
Middle Eastern Moods CD	520
Long Drive Down the West Coast of Mexico	521
Myra	522
Alamos Music Festival	525
Cute Little Dangerous Mexican Bandito Families	528
Paracho - Thirty Years and Five Thousand Guitars Later	529
Mexico by Van 2002	530
Boulder to Santa Cruz, California	530
Me, Eleanor, Bonnie	531
Melina and Kristina in Santa Cruz	532
Melina at Botanical College in Santa Cruz	532
As Lovers of Arabic Music We Head for Jordan	532
Ali Picks us up and Takes us Home	535

No, I am not an Admirer of Saddam 537
Are You Afraid to Come Here? 539
   Kristina and Ali 540
It Was Very Passionate Playing 540
We Had to Leave Haifa in 1947 541
Red, Blue and Green Pigeons 543
   Playing in Roman Theater in Amman 544
More Nightclub Shows 545
   Jihad's Music Shop 545
Baghdad Had Come to Us 547
   Lisa and Kristina 547
   Playing in Public Park in Amman 549
   Family in Park Appreciating Our Music 549
Our Favorite Late-Night Spot 550
Suad Told Stories for Hours 551
   Kristina and Suad 552
   Kristina in Suad's Dress 555
Aqaba 556
   Butcher Shop in Aqaba 557
   Playing at Night by the Red Sea 557
   A Bedouin Guy Approached 558
   Hussein 559
   Jafar's 'Camel' with Hussein and Kids on Top 559
   Bedouin Road 560
   Desert Arch in Southern Jordan 560
   Camped in Desert Canyon 561
   Jafar and Zeinab 562
   Kristina and Hussein - Music All Evening 562
   Taif and Hussein 565
   Hussein and Zeinab 565
Jafar Has to Confess Something 566
   Kristina on a Camel 566
   Carved Nabatean City of Petra 567
   Jafar 568
Ramallah, Palestine 569
   Mataam Ziryab - Ramallah 570
   Me, Raja, Tayseer in Mataam Ziryab 571
   Hotel Clerks and Friends in Ramallah 572
   Yaser Arafat's Government Offices 573

- 2002 - Amman, Aqaba, Al Quwayra, Petra, Ramallah ... 574
  - Colorado Friends Want to Know ... 575
    - MESTO Performing in Los Angeles ... 575
    - Kristina and Nabil ... 576
- Back Across the Ocean To Egypt ... 577
  - Cairo Anti-War Demonstration ... 580
  - Me in Center Playing Oud ... 581
  - Egyptian Girls in Central Cairo Square ... 581
  - Kristina and Crowd ... 582
  - Playing Music in Cairo Bar ... 583
- Magnetized Toward the North: Back to Jordan ... 585
  - Music at Night in Aqaba Park ... 586
  - Me Playing Nay ... 586
  - Kristina Dancing ... 587
  - Warm Feelings from the Music ... 588
  - More Dancing with Kristina ... 588
  - Dead Bodies of Many Civilians ... 592
  - Preparing for the Trip to Baghdad ... 594
- Crossing Into Iraq ... 598
  - Bombed Highways ... 599
  - Blood-Filled Bus ... 600
  - Bombed Bridge ... 600
  - Remains of Truck ... 601
  - Baghdad ... 601
    - Baghdad Buildings Burning ... 602
    - Passing the Oud Around on Streets of Baghdad ... 604
    - Playing for Appreciative Iraqis ... 605
    - Shishkabob Vendors Feed Us a Bite ... 605
    - More Burning Buildings ... 607
    - Playing for Iraqi Musician in Front of Saddam Statue Pedestal ... 608
    - Marine Can't Talk to Us ... 610
- Out of the War Zone and Back to Amman ... 612
- Settling Back into Cairo - Time for Reflections ... 614
  - 2003 - Cairo, Aqaba, Amman, Baghdad ... 615
- Back to the USA - Culture Shock ... 615
- Arabs Are Not From India ... 616
  - We Quickly Constructed a Tour ... 620
    - Baghdad and Beyond CD ... 620
    - One of Hundreds of Venues in which We Performed ... 621

These American Audiences are Hungry for Information	621
Our Diesel Van and Travel Trailer	622
Summer 2003 Singing in Baghdad Tour Through USA	622

Egypt - The Cairo Stadium — 623
Audience of 60,000 in the Cairo Stadium	624
Kristina and I Singing in Cairo Stadium	624
Kristina and I on Egyptian TV	627

Palestinian Refugee Camp in Syria — 627
Singing in Palestinian Refugee Camp in Damascus	628
Palestinian Refugee Children Gather	628
Umayyad Palace Restaurant	629
Down to the Mediterranean Coast	629
Mohammad's Family in Latakia	630
North to Aleppo by Train	631
Ibrahim Sukar - Oud-Maker in Aleppo	633
He Gave us our Midnight 'Lunch' for Free	635
Summer 2003 - After Cairo Concert - First Visit to Syria	638

Colorado and Touring the USA — 638
Lots of Coverage	639
Quick Swing through Southern California	642
Touring Through USA 2003 - 2004	644

Syria Calls us Back — 644
Aleppo, Syria Again — 646
Ibrahim Sukar Oud Factory	646
Restaurant Audience in Latakia	648
Enthusiasm in the Restaurant Crowd	649
Kristina and I Sing	649
Finishing another Song	650
Kristina Dancing	650
Mohammad and I	651
Mohammad and Friends	651
Restaurant Friends	652
More of Mohammad's Family	652
Two Syrian Women Discuss Lifestyles with Kristina	653
More Singing with Mohammad's Family	653
Me and Mohammad's Crazy Uncle	654
All We Want to Do in Life is to Dance	654
Muhsin and I	655

New Years Eve with Cairo Bedouins — 656

      Me and Sabry at Bedouin Party 657
      Kristina Dancing - New Years Eve 657
      Children Dancing 658
      Sabry and Friend 658
   Egyptians playing for Egyptians 658
      Kristen, Lauren and Kristina 659
      Crossing the Nile 659
      Lauren Steering 660
      Street Band - West Bank of Luxor 660
   More Dancing on the Red Sea Coast 660
      Lauren Dancing 661
      Kristina and Friend 661
      Dancing Fun in Hurghada 663
   Making Flutes and Human Rights Concert 663
      Qadry Sorour Making a Nay 664
      Performing for Human Rights Center 664
      They Want More Music 665
      Kristen, Lauren, Ahmad 665
      2004 - 2005 Syria and Egypt 666
Surgery in France 666
Louisiana, Paris, California Disaster 667
   2005 - 2006 in the USA 670
Belly Dancers in Venezuela 671
   Angy Najla and Her Belly Dance Class 671
   Me and Loren 672
   Green Andean Valleys 672
      Stop Smoking! 673
      Venezuela Street Musicians 674
      Very Free and Happy Dogs 675
      Happy Venezuelans on the Beach 675
      Venezuela - 2006 676
Telepathic Plant Communication in Mexico 676
   Tolontongo Hot Springs 677
   Mexica Feathers 677
   Arabic Musical Scales 678
Huichol Indian Refuge in Guadalajara 678
   Huichol Friend 679
   Huichol Child 680
   Antonio - Master Keyboard Artist 680

Playing for Aisha at the Arabian Corner	681
Aisha	681
2006 - Mexico	682
Boulder - Visit from Robin	682
Seven Hundred Voices	683
Expanding My Colorado Band	684
Lots of Dance Parties	685
Cameron Powers Project Band	685
More Hot Pools and Green Leaves in Mexico	686
Back in Tolontongo Hot Springs	686
Mexica Friends in Tolontongo	687
Iraqi Music Party in Jordan	688
Muhsin with Violin in Jordan	688
We Sing for Iraqi Refugees in Jordan	689
Kristina Sings at Muhsin's Party	689
Musical Missions of Peace Project in Jordan and Syria	690
Famous Female Singers Performing in Syria	692
Aramaic Speakers in Ma'alula and Networking in Latakia	692
Aramaic Speaking Christians Still Live in Ma'alula	693
Fadhil and Me	694
Mediterranean Beach in Northern Syria	695
Jewish to Iraqi to Sabaean to Palestinian Neighborhoods	695
Little Iraq Street in Saida Zeinab	696
Saida Zeinab Mosque	696
Millions of Iraqis in Syria	697
The Exact Opposite of War	698
Just Give this Hundred Dollars to some Iraqi Refugee!	699
Greece Island of Rhodes: Finding the Music	700
Greek Music on the Island of Rhodes	701
My Kids' Athenian Grandmother is Ninety-Nine	702
2008 - Syria, Jordan, Rhodes and Athens	703
Iraqi Refugee Musicians Begin Teaching	704
Iraqi Music Lessons in Syria	704
Musical Detective Work	704
Losing my Mom in Colorado	705
New Mexico; Alone in California	706
Moving Slow in Panama	707
Music Festival in Azuero Peninsula in Panama	707
2009 Panama	708

Robin Calling Through the Ether ... 709
   West Coast: Healing The World Through Music ... 710
   2009 - Arizona, California, Washington ... 712
My Musical Dreams Deepened ... 713
   Playing with Lunar Fire in Denver ... 713
Bedouin Eye Contact in Jordan ... 714
   The Western 'Bankster' Problem ... 715
   Held Captive for Eight Hours in a Palestinian Restaurant ... 716
   Young Iraqis Now Hate America ... 717
Gaza-bound Palestinian Relief Convoy Parked in Syria ... 719
   Sexy Lingerie Shops and Glittering Mosques ... 721
      Saida Zeinab Mosque ... 722
      The Kaaba Inside the Mosque ... 722
   Singing in Latakia for the Convoy to Gaza ... 723
      Guy and Me in Latakia Beside Donated Ambulance ... 724
      Kristina and I Perform for Gaza Relief Convoy ... 724
      Performing at the Nay Cafe ... 725
      Mohammad's Cousin Judy Misto ... 726
Back to Beirut, Lebanon ... 727
Little Iraq Street in Saida Zeinab ... 727
   Zahara and Kristina ... 728
   Iraqi Refugees in Damascus - Saida Zeinab Neighborhood ... 730
   Love is My Religion ... 731
Back into the Arms of Palestinian Friends ... 734
   2010 - Jordan, Syria, Lebanon ... 735
   Harmonic Secrets of Arabic Music Scales ... 736
Connecting our Love Bridge in the USA ... 736
I Finally Meet Saadoun ... 738
Iraqi Refugees in California ... 738
   Kristina with Iraqi Refugee Women in El Cajon ... 739
   Musical Ambassadors of Peace Program Ongoing in El Cajon ... 739
   2010 - 2011 West Coast ... 741
More Ecstatic Trance Dances in Colorado ... 742
Can I Compose Egyptian Songs? ... 745
   2011 -2012 Southern California Artist Residency and Tour ... 747
Earth Dance and Gigs and Workshops ... 747
Health Catastrophes: Life Gets Stark ... 749
Agony into Ecstasy: Dancing with Our Shadow ... 752
   Seemie Xavier ... 753

      Cameron Powers Project Band 754
Ecuador: Back to South America At Last 754
    Oscar Santillan in Otavalo, Ecuador 754
    Inca Traditional Music - Oscar's Brother Rumi 755
    Rumi and His Wife 755
    Fishermen Carry in Their Bags of Fish 756
    2013 - Ecuador 757
Mexican Village with Turkish Friend 758
Colorado, Washington and California 758
    Soulscapes - Five CD's of Perfectly Harmonious Music 759
    Rainbow with Lightning Over My Head in Pagosa Springs 760
    My Son's Wedding - James, Gilly, Loren, Alison 760
Dumping Our Belief Systems 761
    Dancers and Musicians in Sadie Fundraiser 762
    Sadie Fundraiser 763
    Ari Honarvar's Rumi Show 763
  Our Loving Has Survived and Deepened 764
Do Lovers Amplify Each Other? 765
Musical Ambassadors of Peace 765
Other Books and CD's by Cameron Powers 766
  Harmonic Secrets of Arabic Music Scales 766
  Arabic Musical Scales 767
  Maqam Practice Tracks 768
  Soulscapes 769
  Middle Eastern Flute Magic: Play the Nay 770
  Singing in Baghdad 771
  Spiritual Traveler 772
  Naked Wild and Free in the Grand Canyon 773
  Cameron Powers Project CD 774
  Baghdad & Beyond CD 775
  Middle Eastern Moods 776
  Dancing with Your Soul 777

Birdie: Feeling the Magic

I don't think I remember the first kiss. But I remember the kisses. We were surrounded by the singing cicada wilderness of the Missouri countryside. It was 1952. I was eight and Roberta was ten. I called her Birdie. Her family was Armenian. When our lips touched it felt like velvet magic. I wanted more. We were playing hide and seek with our friends, but we would be clever and go hide together where we could decide on the next kiss. Would it be on the cheek or on the lips? The lips were definitely more exciting. The lower dragons in my sexuality had not yet awakened, but our lips were channeling something amazing. Our kisses sent me into a cool and refreshing new world... a world from which I could endlessly drink.

We were in love. She liked to whisper "my future husband!" into my ear and I would murmur: "my future wife!" There was something very exciting about that. And we loved to wrestle. She was two years older than I and it took some work, but I could pin her shoulders to the ground and hold her down.

We explored the leafy trails which led to the Old Mill and the old Quarry. We ran from stone to stone up the creeks. We squirmed into limestone caves and admired the salamanders. We befriended the snakes and turtles. We dug holes in the ground and called them "forts." We nailed boards up high in the catalpa trees, constructed rope ladders and rested in our tree house homes.

Sometimes as the daylight faded and the darkness of the night gathered we felt the chilly fearfulness which comes with no longer being able to see clearly in the forests. I remember deliberately getting on my hands and knees and crawling into the darkest places under the bushes to discover that in reality there was nothing to fear. My hands reached into the scary shadows and only found the familiar warm beds of leaves and dirt. I was learning again and again that the natural world was a friendly and fun place.

We rode our bikes through back roads down by the Meramec River past little wooden shack taverns with names like "Pass-Out Palace" and absorbed mysterious hints coming from the more adult and alcoholic world we had not yet entered. Some folks had threatening vibes... confusing to us.

The neighborhood gang was largely friendly. We weren't wrestling to hurt each other, we just liked the wild chasing and tumbling. It was a dance we did. Our fondness for wrestling brought us into close contact. But occasionally the fun would end when our friend Bill seemed to take pleasure in getting too rough and would actually try and hurt someone. There was another kid who liked to torture animals. We couldn't imagine wanting to do that.

By our second summer of playful romance I couldn't help but notice when her shirt brushed upwards as we wrestled that something was happening to her nipples. We went to her house next door so I could see her older sister's nipples and have an idea about changes to come. They were larger and darker and more mysterious.

Something dramatic happened when another neighbor's family bought a little black and white TV. Suddenly our endless running in the woods tapered off: "Hey Patrick!" I would shout into his front door... "Let's go to the Quarry!"

"I wanna watch 'Sky King!' And then comes 'The Cisco Kid!'... And then 'The Lone Ranger!'" he would say.

I tried watching a few shows but my feet kept itching to be running up the creeks in the woods, jumping from stone to stone. I also loved riding my bicycle through the back roads and remember occasionally experiencing what others would later describe as "kundalini awakenings." The physical movements involved with pedaling the bicycle for long distances would create sudden floods of ecstatic feelings rushing up and down my spine. It was like a cool spinal drink of delicious electricity.

I gave up on the TV and stayed on the roads and in the woods by day and I would lie on the ground on my back staring into the awesome and obviously infinite array of stars above by night. But Patrick's family's house with its TV had a big draw and was therefore a big drain on my playmates.

Birdie's and my romance had begun when she was in the fifth grade and I was in the fourth grade at Robinson School in Kirkwood, Missouri. It continued through her sixth grade year, but when she moved on to seventh grade and Junior High School that was the end of that. Her social life had begun in earnest and I, two years younger, could not be in the running. Occasionally she would come over to practice dance steps but she gradually vanished from my life.

Her eighth grade year was spent in India with her Armenian family. I remember signing "love" at the ends of the letters I wrote to her. The voltage set running through my body as I wrote that magic word was as thick as apple sauce.

By the time she got back from India the great wide world had intruded and taken her well beyond the grasp of the boy next door. I heard through the grapevine that she had studied Indian dance and could be seen performing at the local schools. I never got to see her dance and she and I never got to wander the world together, we did find each other and re-affirm our deep friendship again some twenty years later. She and I had discovered love.

My Family Dissolves

I had been very lucky. I was born into a small but very peaceful family. It was just me and my mom and dad. They were both gentle and loving and concerned with helping to make the world a better place. Absolutist belief systems like religion were never even mentioned. My father honored my interests in science and mechanics and approved of my "chemistry lab" which I assembled in the basement from components I had found in the trash. I fell asleep at night listening to mysterious signals made audible by a large short wave radio which I had also found in the trash. I bought some lenses and with my father's help built a telescope with which to admire the night sky. My father also went with me to a junk yard when I was twelve years old and bought me a 1949 Ford so that I could keep it in the driveway, take it apart and figure out how it worked. Amazingly enough it seemed to run just fine and I soon learned to drive by taking it out on the country roads.

But sometime during my twelfth year, big changes were happening. My father had been working in France to develop their nuclear power industry. He fell in love with a woman in Paris. He returned one day to our house in Missouri and something was not right. I sat with him and my mom in a car in our driveway. My mom was crying and my dad seemed cold and distant. I remember telling him, "Dad, just tell her you love her and everything will be fine!"

But he did not respond and remained silent. Soon he was gone... back to France. My mother could be seen crying in the kitchen. She blamed herself for the failed marriage and attempted suicide. A friend found her in the garage with the car running hoping that the exhaust fumes would end her life. Soon she was living in a mental hospital in downtown St. Louis.

I moved in with one of my school friends, Steve Black. I became the youngest of four boys in that family. Steve's mom was loving and tried to help me from time to time with my homework. Steve's Dad, whose job was to help make Budweiser beer, snored every night in front of his TV set.

Soon I was struggling to keep up with schoolwork, social life and the expectations of team sports. It didn't help that I was still the youngest one in my class. I had done well on some silly IQ test when I was four years old and, largely based on the enthusiasm of my proudly intellectual father, it was decided that I should skip kindergarten and enter first grade a year ahead of schedule. Now, as all my classmates began sprouting hair and charging forward into full-fledged puberty, I was still more like a little kid. But I was a thirteen-year-old kid with curiosity.

Bonnie: Exploration of Love

    I created some new habits around school. Steve's older brother would drop us off in front of the school every morning. I would go in and deposit my books in my locker and slip back out the door, walk down the hill to the bus stop and head into downtown St. Louis. I would be back in time to be picked up and driven back home to Steve's house late in the afternoon, but in the meantime I had found time to explore the city.

    I wore a leather jacket and soon learned that cool kids like me walked with shoulders hunched forward so that our heart chakras were closed and protected. I hung out and played pool and snooker and billiards with old men who could spit handily into brass spittoons on the floor.

    I became a fan of Virginia 'ding dong' Bell and Evelyn West with her 'million dollar treasure chest'. They both performed regularly in the 'Grand' and the 'World' burlesque houses. I was mildly interested in their bodies and in their dances which were performed to live music. I can still replay the drums and clarinets in my memory! I wondered about the musicians' lifestyles… what did they do when not playing their music? And I kept hoping that the sleazy old comedians would someday actually get funny. They never did but it was still more interesting to watch them than to go to school.

I learned how to shoplift and soon had a collection of guns, switchblade knives, black leather jackets and mechanic's tools pilfered from the pawn shops and hardware stores so I could actually begin to take my Ford apart and re-assemble it as a prelude to learning how to fix it.

Ike and Tina Turner

Ike and Tina Turner were emerging in the music scene. Now that was *real* dance music. I would never be confused about that again. They weren't called Ike and Tina Turner back then. The band was called "Kings of Rhythm: Ike Turner and the Ikettes." Tina, whose real name was Anna Mae Bullock was introduced as "Little Ann…" She was in love with the Saxophone player at the time… had her first baby with him. The two of them did sexy things on stage that were amazing to see. They rocked the house. I was frequently one of the few white folks in the audience and my body and soul sucked in that amazing energy. That music was so sexy it launched me into a brand new world. I was forming my lifelong musical tastes.

I moved out of Steve's house into a room in Minna Elman's house. She was a friend of my mother's who was an artist and who lived on Gaslight Square, a newly-constructed neighborhood of art galleries resurrected from the destruction wrought by a nasty tornado. There was a gay painter named Sam who also lived in the house. I was nervous around gay people but Minna assured me that Sam wouldn't try anything sexual. He was a gentle and friendly artist. Now, free by night, I made use of the 1949 Ford. I would park my Ford in Wellston next to the Lindy Ballroom where Ike Turner was playing and let myself soak it all in. I hadn't been to school for months.

My mother was still a part-time resident in two mental hospitals: one in St Louis and one up in New England. She was juggling a mild alcohol problem, receiving regular electro-shock therapy and had a pressing need to find a new husband. Eventually she rented an apartment and I moved out of Minna's house.

Turn Off the TV - Jail in Florida

I bought something new which I had never had in my own house before: a TV. I tried watching it for a few weeks but noticed that it wasn't as fun as my real-life adventures. I also began to feel weirdly disconnected from myself and after having the disquieting experience one evening of being suddenly afraid of my own reflection in the mirror, I grasped the knob on the TV and turned it off forever. I noticed that my feelings of isolation and dis-orientation simultaneously vanished. I was back on the streets full time again.

I started inviting whatever kids I met on the streets to parties at the new apartment. Bottles of bourbon and rum and cases of beer were always on the tables. I got good at playing poker. My mother was seldom actually there but when she was home she joined in the fun and drank bourbon with us.

My father, back in Missouri briefly from France, announced that he would come by the next morning and personally deliver me back to school. I couldn't even imagine setting foot back in that place. I needed to vanish. So I was on a bus by 4:00 AM headed across the river to Illinois.

I was fourteen-years-old. I had a gun, a switchblade knife and a twenty-dollar bill in my pockets and by dawn I had my thumb out on a south-bound highway. I declined a 'friendly' overture from a truck driver who 'just wanted to feel me up.' I told him that I had changed my mind about my destination and he complied with my request to be dropped off at the next highway intersection. After his truck disappeared I stuck out my thumb again and rode on down into Alabama with two younger truckers. They parked at a truck stop to go in and "take showers." They came back out after a couple of hours describing the delights they had found with the newest ladies who worked as prostitutes for the truckers. The world was feeling very big and sometimes frighteningly adult to me. But soon I would be diving in deeper.

Arriving in Sarasota, Florida, where it felt warm enough to sleep out on the beach, I began looking for a job until I was picked up after a few days by the local police. They kept me in a jail cell until I finally gave them a phone number. My father talked to them and assured them that I was a good kid and he suggested that I should not just be left with nothing to do in jail. Soon the cops began carrying me around in their squad cars to offer me a little entertainment.

My mother rode down on a train and she and I headed back to Missouri together. We made a deal. I would find a job and stay there in the apartment as long as no one made any further efforts to make me go back to school.

I found a job washing test tubes in a laboratory at the Washington University Medical School. I was offered an initial salary of $100/month and was soon raised to $250/month.

I got very little sleep. I worked by day at the Medical School, eventually becoming skilled at performing various lab technician procedures. My hands were young and steady. I was good with microscopes and could weigh single cells on quartz-hair balances.

I kept that job for two years, until I was sixteen years old and had decided that I actually did want to go back to school. I did make an attempt to begin classes at another high school at one point but my interest flagged and I soon gave up on it.

I had met Bill Sneed playing pinball machines in a local bowling alley. He also had acquired a Ford. We practiced swapping transmissions, engine parts, clutches and axles until we began to know a little more about mechanicing.

I upgraded my 1949 Ford to a 1953 Mercury and set about turning it into a hot street machine. I carried a fifth of bourbon in my glove compartment and seldom got home before 4:00 AM. Occasionally exhaustion would overwhelm me and I would take a night off from my explorations.

I learned to function at high speed with my belly full of bourbon or rum. We raced our hot rods through rural Missouri passing through tight turns at high speeds. But being proud of rolling your car and surviving, as many of my friends seemed to feel, was not one of my goals. I learned to use my conscious intention to burn through the various states of drunkenness and never make a mistake. Driving through tiny back roads at a-hundred-miles-an-hour became a training ground for maintaining high focus and concentration: either burn through the alcohol with an unwavering alertness or end up, like my friend, Bill Cortis, paralyzed in a hospital bed for life.

I Don't Really Like To Fight, But...

I didn't like to fight, but our nights were filled with suspense. If 'Tiny' was in the other car, we would have to watch out. Knowing when we were outnumbered we had to make choices: fight and lose but preserve our honor or find a way to flee. We struggled and held our ground. We really just wanted to find the next party and dance.

Loner personalities like Monte Byers and Frank Mullins would invite friendship when sober and then turn mean with alcohol. Armed with a nasty tool called a 'frog gig,' Frank Mullins attacked me in a remote abandoned farmhouse one night. I was agile enough to stay out of the weapon's reach. A few days later, Frank treated me again as 'friend.' Monte Byers kept his hair bleached blond. This was 1958 or so, well before the California surfer look became popular. His goal was to drink a case of beer every night. I learned to recognize the look in his eyes as he would gradually turn from friendly comedian to aggressive and mean. But there were others who were even meaner.

Bill Sneed, with whom I had spent so many nights covered with grease as we practiced our fighting techniques and our mechanicing skills, ended up under the pummeling blows from a rival group of aggressive drunk kids led by a nasty guy who had been threatening us for months. There were about five of them and only two of us. Hopelessly outnumbered, we were at their mercy. The unspoken code of ethics implied that if we fought them hard enough we would qualify to become one of them. Bill Sneed's efforts eventually earned our freedom. I remained a future target because I had been less willing to fight. The real ages of some of these kids were hard to guess. Their eyes and faces were hardened into meanness even from childhood. They looked older than they actually were.

Bill Sneed joined the Marines as soon as he turned sixteen. I went with him to the airport and watched him disappear, along with many other young recruits, onto a military plane. One of the others had a bottle of liquor which would alternately drain and refill from the contents of his stomach as he guzzled away his last few minutes of freedom.

The laws in Missouri back in the late 1950's were loose. We drank in the bars, we carried our bottles of liquor in our glove compartments and the cops who occasionally pulled us over told us to party in the woods and stay off the highways for a couple of hours. Sometimes they lamented that they couldn't take away our drivers licenses because we didn't have any. The cops were just more of us street kids but with badges. We were easy on each other.

African Americans

I kept discovering that I felt a warmer connection with my music-loving African-American friends. It seemed that the backwoods Missouri white folks were the ones with seriously aggressive mean streaks.

I found myself showing up on my African-American friends' behalf at various civil rights events. I went to some CORE meetings (Congress of Racial Equality) and reiterated that 'we are all the same' and that 'some of my best friends are black people.'

My friend Doug Chaudron sometimes attended those meetings with me. He and I were amazed at the world we were growing up in. We saw organized religion as the perpetual culprit. Doug has remained a lifelong friend.

I remember attending a huge event at Kiel Auditorium when Elijah Mohammad, whose work facilitated the rise in popularity of Black Muslims and Malcolm X, first came to St. Louis. I felt proud to be one of the very few white folks in that huge crowd. As we exited the auditorium we walked past the city jail. The African-American prisoners were audible behind certain barred windows as they screamed for their freedoms. I felt the enormity of social injustices in American culture and felt drawn to become part of the needed changes.

My twin brother friends, Tim and Terry Holmes, were still struggling to stay in school... not so easy with a father who would beat them if he caught them wasting their time 'reading books.' Tim was a natural master of the African-American dance moves and I would practice imitating him. Terry was a natural acrobat and we would hang out at the newly popular trampoline parks.

Bob Eagle and Me at Age 14

First Rock Band

I bought a guitar and began to learn to play the blues. Soon my friend Bob Eagle and I had a small band and people hired us to play for dance events and would tip us with $20 bills. The fact that we played the same few songs over and over again didn't seem to be a problem. I was amazed.

I played the bottom lines of the blues on my guitar to my Dad over the phone. No comment from him... He didn't get it...

My mom went back into the mental hospital and left me the apartment to myself. Endless parties materialized. Drunk teenagers plowed their cars into the corner of the apartment building which, fortunately, was made of stone. We kept the blues flowing on the record player and we danced 'the slop' just like the guys at the Lindy Ballroom in Wellston... or at the Imperial Club... all African-American moves. There were some beautiful young girls who liked to come to my parties. We would dance but I hardly knew their names or where they had come from. They were friends of friends of friends.

My mom re-appeared for my fifteenth birthday and gave me a bottle of rum as a present. She was around again for some of our parties. A psychiatrist finally convinced her that she should just move forward with her life and that she would discover that she wasn't really crazy after all. She began bringing her new boyfriends home. Sometimes she forgot to close the door to the bedroom and I would get glimpses of her making love with men I didn't know.

My attempts to get really close to girls were still confusing and frustrating. I had an ongoing flirtation with a cute girl at work who came up from Texas during the summers. Her name was Kay and occasionally she would sit close... snuggle up to me at work... and... what was the meaning of her smile?

Kay

But she didn't really fit into my late night lifestyle. She didn't seem to be a dancer. I invited her to my apartment for a date. I lit dozens of candles which I had bought for the occasion and put on the music. We sat on the couch and flirted until I spilled hot candle wax all over her dress.

At some point I drove down to Ft. Worth, Texas to visit her in her home territory and realized what vastly different worlds we came from. Her house was the size of a school building... surrounded by groomed green lawns with gardens and walkways. I felt terrified by her house and its mysterious occupants, her parents and brother. They seemed to have no idea of what to make of me. After spending one night in a sterile bedroom alone, I excused myself and departed.

Do Girls Have Inverted Penises Called Vaginas?

Back in St Louis, the flirtation with Kay persisted. But there was a fatal flaw: I had no realizations about the differences between male and female sexuality. I erroneously assumed that girls were just like boys but with inverted penises called vaginas.

Our attempts to go out at night were filled with confusion. It never occurred to me that Kay wasn't burning inside with the same desires I was experiencing.

One night I drove us out the highway into the remote Missouri farmlands. We were sipping from my ever-present bottle of bourbon. Convinced that we must both be feeling what I was feeling, I parked the car on a country road and we began to snuggle and kiss. Once again I discovered that she was wearing armor-plated underclothing: some kind of 'girdle' designed to make it almost impossible to gain access. I just didn't understand how she could not be raging inside with desire. I would struggle to get my fingers underneath the armor with no real help from her.

Frustration took the upper hand. I did not know what to say or what to do. I started the car and swerved into a nearby field to turn around and head back for the city. Sensing the muddiness under the wheels, I spun the tires until we were good and stuck in the middle of that field: some kind of crazy expression of desperation.

"Just wait here," I told her and strode off across the fields towards the highway still in some kind of confused rage. Sticking my thumb out I enticed a passing trucker to stop. The tractor was a single cab with room only for the driver.

"You can ride on the hood," he yelled at me through the window.

Ten miles down the road we pulled into an all night diner where I aired my predicament sufficiently to enlist the help of a guy with a truck and a long tow chain.

Kay must have been waiting for more than two hours by the time we made it back and wrenched the car out of the muddy field.

We had no way to explain ourselves to each other and that night's adventure marked the end of our romance. I don't know if things would have been different if there had been someone... an elder brother or sister perhaps... who could have explained women to me just a little bit...? I am sorry that I couldn't honor her with more awareness and have been better able to give her more space to show me who she was. I had been coming from a deeply "clueless" place.

I found it much easier to find girls in bars like 'Gus's Nuthouse' in downtown St. Louis, or over in East St Louis on the Illinois side, who were happy to retire to rented hotel rooms where they would give me basic sexual instructions. Sometimes they were African-American and sometimes they were white women.

I gradually became aware of the power of eye attraction. Sometimes when a woman and I looked at each other, if our gaze was direct enough, I could feel a powerful honey-sweet spark of energy leap between the pupils of our eyes and connect us. When I looked into the eyes of women I began to search and stay open for that energy. The amazing thing was that when I felt it I could see that they felt it too! I used it as an energetic divining rod.

Women whom I would meet in downtown St. Louis were sometimes older than I. They seemed to understand that teenage boys were very sexually driven and they found their own ways to enjoy that intensity. They were tender with me and I was tender with them. We didn't even need to know each other's names.

Women of the Night

Monterrey, Mexico

Driving down through Texas to the border, I crossed into Mexico and immediately sensed a warm and friendly atmosphere. This was not the aggressive Germanic rural Missouri feeling. Exploring Monterrey, Mexico by night I found places where teenagers my age would take the opportunities to flirt and check out each others' vibes before deciding to rent little cots for love-making outdoors under the night sky. It felt genuine, natural, healthy, easy and real to me. Mexican culture seemed to understand that flirtation and love-making need to happen or people get bottled-up with neurotic starvation. I felt satisfied that I was fully human. And I felt a lot of love for my first 'Mexican girlfriend.'

Meanwhile, my father brought his new wife back home from France. She distanced herself from me by announcing that I would "spend the rest of my life living in the gutter."

My mother selected a new husband who privately told me one night that "he and I would never get along." He bought a house and my apartment vanished. I needed to make a major change. I moved back into Minna Elman's house.

I explored the bars and coffee shops and discovered a young mulatto folk singer named Don Crawford who was regularly performing. I wanted to be like him. I could see that he was expressing himself in deep musical ways which didn't depend on having a huge blues band like Ike Turner. I began to work on learning some of those folk songs which expressed the loves and the hardships of life. When he would take his breaks I would have to struggle to resist the urge to run up and grab his guitar and play and sing. I knew I could do it.

And when the sexual pressures reached certain heights inside my body I would go find more friendly women of the night. Life was exciting and sweet.

We now live in another era. We all know that women have been victimized and that the patriarchy still rides roughshod through our culture. Polarized viewpoints abound and many would conclude that "women of the night" are always either 'victims' or 'bad women.' My experiences led me to see that men and women have actually frequently found amazing ways to bring gentle and loving energies into their casual sexual connections. These magic moments are difficult to capture and express with words and most writers would not even try. But I will attempt to share what I can in ways which honor both women and men and which can help us to discover the fleeting but genuine beautiful moments which glisten like silver threads in a mysterious fabric.

Drive Drive Drive

I loved to drive and cover vast distances. After leaving Mexico I headed to New Orleans to drink bourbon on Bourbon Street and listen to "dixieland jazz". From there I drove down into Florida to revisit the beaches... then north to see my dad who was up in Indiana and from there back down to St Louis. I remember going for sixty hours on the road with no sleep.

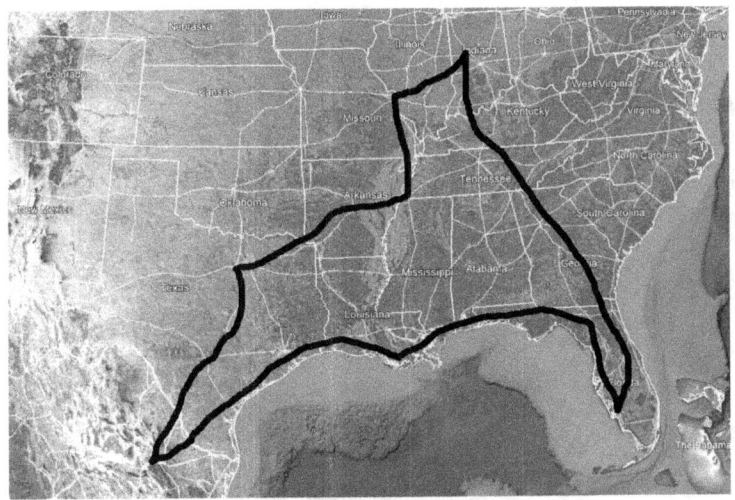

Map: 1960 Road Trip

But part of my long-term vision for myself included finishing high school somehow somewhere. At age sixteen I quit my job and enrolled in the only school I could find which would still accept me: Western Military Academy across the river in Alton, Illinois. I learned to march like a soldier, keep my M1 rifle polished and ride half-wild horses through the freezing winter landscape. I kept my car parked at the school so I could return to Missouri on the weekends or occasionally visit my Dad who had eventually settled in Indiana.

My weekends in St Louis enabled me to continue my alcohol-driven social life and my occasional flirtations with the ladies of the night, but basically I was leaving it all behind. I had no further interest in testing the limits of my bourbon-shrouded awareness. I had been there and done that. For the rest of my life drinking alcoholic beverages became less and less interesting and rapidly reached a point where I hardly drank at all.

Many of the kids who, like me, had ended up at Military school had likewise explored the limits of street life and were seeking pathways back into more sober lifestyles. But my friends back home were still my friends. We would drive out into the remote Missouri countryside in search of the ever-promising next party. We would drink our liquor and, if harassed by the highway patrol, I would teach my friends how to march through the woodlands until we had fulfilled our promises to the police to stay off the roads for a few hours. I found that wearing my military uniform bought me additional sympathy from the police.

Driving up to Indiana to visit my Dad I was brought to a halt by a highway patrol roadblock.

"We've been chasing you and clocking you at up to a hundred-and-twenty miles-an-hour for the last fifty miles!" they informed me. But my military uniform gained me a mere casual warning.

"Try and keep the speed down!" I was told and went on my merry way.

Western Military Academy - Alton, Illinois

French Existentialism, Beat Poetry

The following year, with my mother's help, I found another school which, thanks to the good grades I had achieved at the Military school, accepted me. I moved to Colorado Springs and endured another two years of what felt like prison to me but I succeeded in finishing high school. I finally graduated shortly after my nineteenth birthday.

Time spent in St Louis during the summer between my junior and senior year was difficult. My mother was becoming her new husband's faithful wife and our old connection had to go underground. I had acquired three step-brothers and a step-sister in the process but they had never shared my explorations of life and largely lived in a different world. Watching my step-sister hone her adolescent skills at being distantly unavailable for any real friendship somehow triggered my frustrations one hot summer night and I took it out by punching trees and barbed-wire fences in the woods until my hands and arms were covered with blood. I was filled with passions which needed expression but all the avenues were blocked.

I felt like I was ready to re-create life on my own, but the school in Colorado Springs was a boys' boarding school and most of my classmates came from wealthy suburban backgrounds and seemed hopelessly naive to me. I couldn't share life's adventures with them in the same deep ways I had explored with my street friends back in Missouri. And I was experienced enough at love-making to be ready for a real sexual relationship with some loving female. But I was basically doomed to a nearly two-year prison stint for the sake of a high school diploma.

I found ways to escape from Colorado Springs to Denver on the weekends and managed to have brief moments of closeness with a few girls who were friends of friends. It was not possible to really feel much connection although I would regularly play my guitar and wail out the tragic folk tales bemoaning the legacies of slavery learned at Don Crawford's inspiration back in Gaslight Square.

I discovered French Existentialism, Beat Poetry; I found a resonance in the 'theater of the absurd' and played electric guitar in a little blues band I started at the school. But there was no dancing audience to play for so the satisfaction was not great.

I made extra cash by copying images of women from magazine photos onto canvases with oil paints and selling them to my fellow students who sometimes paid me quite handsomely to try and match some fantasy vision of theirs. The painting below was my attempt to capture "a beat chick with blue hair and an expression of horror on her face."

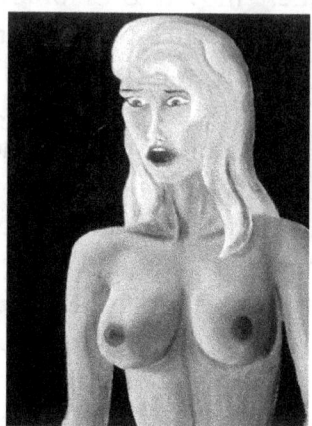

A Commissioned Portrait

I wrote stories about girls who existed only in my fantasies. The arroyos surrounding the school were filled with giant cottonwood trees and sometimes by night I would wander under the moonlight exploring both the inner and outer worlds. The primary driving obsession was "Where is she? What does she look like? Who is she?" I created my own personal moon goddesses to keep me company while I did my two years of confinement. I made up stories about them.

> Somewhere at night, somewhere in the crook of a cottonwood tree sat an owl. Now this owl knew about the presence of an egg. But being a very wise owl, he knew that the men who walk the earth should not know of this egg nor of the wonderful creature which would one evening emerge from that egg.
> And so the owl sat, guarding the secret of that egg in the way that owls do. Night after night, as he watched the moon wax and wane, he nursed the spirit of the egg in his mind, warmly chuckling over the adventures in freedom he knew were in store for the beautiful creature which would emerge one night to sleep briefly bathed in starlight and then begin its life...
> It so happened, however, that a young man named Anselm, a child of loneliness as so many of this modern age are, was out wandering alone one night of the full moon and was struck by the sight of this owl sitting silhouetted against the moon in the crook of his tree.
> Seeing this owl sitting so comfortably in his loneliness, Anselm raised his voice against the sky and begged the owl to know one thing: "Of what are you thinking, Owl, that rings so harmoniously through your soul that it enables you to tolerate the incredible loneliness night after night after night?"

The owl, it seems, was so moved by the earnest plea in Anselm's voice that almost without hesitation he began to softly explain: "I have a most marvelous thing to tell you, an image which gives rise to such excitingly marvelous dances in the theater of my imagination, that I can only hope to give you a glimpse of the endless joy which pervades my solitary contemplation. Only very seldom is one of the woodland folk of such humble stature as myself privileged to have born witness, quite by fortunate chance, to the appearance of an egg from which is destined to emerge a genuine nymph of the woodlands. It is a pair of trees which has miraculously produced this egg, and it so happened that I caught sight of a pair of chipmunks bearing this egg to its place of ripening. The chipmunks, you know, are safe conveyors of sacred objects since they are so incredibly short in memory that no possibility of their letting escape a secret exists. They do something and then they have forgotten it!"

At this point it suddenly occurred to the owl that he himself was divulging a woodland secret which perhaps he had best not continue to reveal in any more elaborate detail in spite of the fact that it was Anselm's earnestness of request which had made him respond so easily at the outset. So he concluded his words with the following: "So you see... it is by passing my time with such dreams as these that I keep myself warm and content inside..."

Anselm of course wondered the next day if he had met the owl in a dream and whether, if in fact he had heard an owl speaking to him, the owl's dreams were to be trusted any more than his own? But during the quiet hours of the night the conviction would steal upon him that the most ravishingly beautiful maiden he would ever be likely to set eyes on might be emerging any night from an egg somewhere in the forest. And his curiosity drove him night after night to frequent the habitation of the owl in the crook of his tree. But the owl, fearing the consequence of having let escape this marvelous secret, secreted himself in a higher crook and Anselm only caught sight of him once in his previously preferred spot, at which discovery the owl only ruffled his feathers and shuffled his feet in a disgruntled sort of a way.

Meanwhile, inside of the egg, the tiny hands and feet of Daphne, forming once again in her long series of incarnations, began to assume their lovely shape. And one night, exactly as the owl had predicted, she found the shell in which she had been blissfully encased falling open. She opened her eyes and spread her tiny fingers and her tiny toes just once before dozing off once again. But she was bathed now in the light of the stars which soaked her through and through and gifted her with a love for sparkling motion.

> *Quite early, and before dawn had laid his pink tongue on the edge of the horizon, she sprang loose from her sleep and found herself filled with a tingling delight which can be seen only in the twinkling of the stars and the reflections of the sun in the splashing water droplets of the falling streams.*
>
> *The owl saw her depart from her nest and stretched and re-stretched the muscles in the backs of his wings so filled was he by the delightful anticipation of flying through the forest to quietly observe the glorious emanations from this light-filled maiden.*
>
> *And Anselm, during one of his nightly explorations of the forest, suddenly caught sight of Daphne's newborn ankles pattering up over fallen logs and down through underground holes, driven by the ecstasy of starlight to run and run and run unthinking through the dawn of the forest.*
>
> *Even the owl's delighted anticipation was nothing compared to the cool shivers which streaked up and down the innards of Anselm's velvety spine at catching this brief glimpse of her. Breathless, he felt his stomach draw itself smoothly inward in spasms of helpless wonder.*
>
> *Two hundred and fifty years and eight incarnations later, Daphne and Anselm, quite seemingly by chance, found each other again in the forest and began to develop a deep friendship.*

During school vacations and parts of the summer I would sometimes drive to New York City and begin to explore. I procured a source for marijuana and for amphetamines and brought those substances back to share with a few classmates in Colorado.

I lost two friends at that school... Ballard Peabody went home for Christmas and died in a car crash. He and I both liked to go without sleep and we would drink coffee together in the study lounge at 4:00 AM. The last night before he left for vacation he was too tired to meet me and he left me a note saying, prophetically, "Am Dead."

Hank Taylor went rock climbing in the Garden of the Gods with my room-mate Lew and with the math teacher, Bill Buckingham, and fell two-hundred-and-seventy feet to his death. Hank's bereaved parents came to the school and his mother, in her drunken stupor, kept thinking that I was Hank... still alive... She hugged me and held onto me screaming, "Hank! Hank!" until someone pulled her away... We were overwhelmingly aware of the drama of death but were too young to fully feel and comprehend it.

Paranoid Fear Vibes of the Big City

After graduation in the spring of 1963 I headed for New York City and moved in with Errol Sawyer, an African-American kid from the Bronx who had never ever left the city... not even once in his eighteen years of life. I had a job working for a sleazy organization which made its money ferreting out slanderous comments made by one politician about another. I would smoke pot all day and type up indexes based on recorded radio programs which I would listen to through headphones. By late afternoon I would be on the streets exploring the city. I followed Errol through the city and we sold pounds of 'boo'... marijuana. I ate way too many strange drugs offered by way too many strange people I didn't even know and nearly died from overdoses of who-knows-what a couple of times.

I managed to check out the music scenes in Greenwich Village and I soaked in the vibes from Herbie Mann, Ornette Coleman and others. None of that music made me feel good the way Ike and Tina Turner had.

Exploring the city by night gave me an opportunity to join a gang, apparently in order to save my own life, and then find a way to escape later on. I discovered the homeless world of misfits from all over the country who inhabited the vast semi-truck-trailer-parking-lots down by the East River. They built fires to warm their food and were kicked and beaten endlessly by the police for no reason. When I accompanied Errol on his drug-dealing expeditions I would get a glimpse of the networks of neighborhood watchers who would warn of law-enforcement or gang-related territorial dangers. Sometimes an older woman sitting on her steps would give us the nod that meant it was safe to proceed.

We spent our time in the Bronx and on Manhattan, sometimes in the African-American and sometimes in the Puerto-Rican neighborhoods. When we rode the subways we would double back by running across the platforms to catch the opposite-moving trains in order to make certain we couldn't be followed. We smoked our marijuana out of large 'boo-pipes' from the moment we awoke until the last moments before sleep. The paranoid fear vibes of the city slipped into me. Smoking pot in Colorado had been a spiritual exploration. Here it became a mindless habit.

As a logical consequence of graduating from high school, I applied to some college and was both accepted and given some kind of financial support. I really had no idea of what kind of college I was headed for, but at the end of a summer in Greenwich Village, I dragged my drug-soaked consciousness to Portland, Oregon. My New York City friends told me that I would be back soon because "no one ever leaves New York City."

Wild Blackberry Countryside

Arriving in Oregon in the fall, I rented a hotel room in downtown Portland, bought a bicycle and delayed going to see the college until the last possible moment. I had acquired a love for mountains while living in Colorado and the towering glacier-covered volcanoes of the Pacific Northwest were beckoning. Little did I suspect that they would soon all be enshrouded in chilly fog. I rode the bicycle through the amazing wild blackberry countryside and distanced myself from the drugs. It was the fall of 1963 and I was still nineteen-years-old.

The school year at Reed College started and I found myself hanging out in the girls' dormitory. I had searched among the guys for some semblance of the street camaraderie I had known back in St. Louis. I had heard that this college was popular with young adventurers and artists but I felt alone. I was looking for some shared fascination with the Beat generation poetry and the theaters of the absurd, but connections were not happening. Perhaps the girls would be more available? And of course they were more enticing just because they were girls.

At a party in the girls' dorm, where it seemed the kids were experimenting with their first tastes of wine and their first puffs of tobacco and marijuana, I tried some kind of expressive experiment. I don't know exactly why, because it really wasn't my habit, but I pounded my fists on the wall and made primal sounds. I had drunk some bourbon at the time but I remember the feeling of deliberately putting on some kind of show of animal energy. We were in Laura's room. Natalie and Bonnie were also there. Laura had red hair like mine.

"We kind of look alike!" I mentioned to her. I sensed that I had her attention because of my animal act.

"Yes," she replied.

"I wonder in how many other ways we might be alike?" I suggested.

She was curious about that too. She took me out onto the grass and we made love. It was her idea. For the next week or so we made love every night and I discovered that yes, we made love alike, we talked alike and believed alike. This was so easy. Too easy. My fascination was anchored to a couple of the other girls who had been in her room at the party who seemed more mysterious.

I signed up to ride the bus down to the Oregon coast for the following weekend. Natalie was on the bus. She went down to the beach, pulled out a small flute and began to play. I felt the enchantment. She remembered my animal act and we made love in her tent on the beach that night. Returning to the school on Sunday night I spent the night in the girls' dormitory and slept again with Natalie. Bonnie, who had also captured my fascination was in the upper bunk. I hope she enjoyed the rocking of the bed.

After a few nights with Natalie, Laura chastised me for not letting her know that something had changed. I explained something about "just wanting to be friends with a lot of people" and Laura seemed to understand. She took me back outside to make love on the grass again.

But I was thinking more and more about Bonnie. I didn't know why, but I felt more and more attraction in her direction. She was already supposedly 'going with' my friend Ron, but after sitting up most of the night talking, we made love. After that I lost interest in both Laura and Natalie and they both moved out of my intimate world. We never talked about it.

Bonnie and I began planning adventures together. She was from Austin, Texas, and equally naive about the Pacific Northwest. We took sleeping bags and a tent and hitch-hiked up to Mt Rainier. Our hiking plans were interrupted by all-night rains which soaked us and made us chilly while some bears were foraging through the trash containers next to our tent. After another rained-out attempt to explore the glorious mountain range we had both seen when first arriving in early September, we gave up on the wilderness and hitch-hiked down to San Francisco where she had lived the previous summer.

Bonnie was seventeen and I was nineteen. We weren't diving hungrily just into sex the way Laura and I had. There was a big difference. We were falling in love.

We played 'do-gooders' in her friends' San Francisco apartment and washed six-months-worth of dirty dishes which we found stacked in the corner. At the end of the long Thanksgiving weekend we stuck out our thumbs and returned to Reed College.

I was finally exercising my pent-up desires to create a real life and family of my own. I hadn't known what it felt like to really have a family since I had been twelve years old so Bonnie was very precious to me. She was also an only child and perhaps in need of creating family.

Falling in Love with Bonnie

I approached our lovemaking very tenderly and tried to discover her secrets. Whatever we were doing, it was working and the feelings of love grew between us.

Family Disasters in Texas and Missouri

She traveled back to Austin and I to St Louis for Christmas. I received a phone call from her after a few days.

"My parents kicked me out of their house. They told the police to keep me in jail, but the police have no reason to keep me in jail. Can I come up to St. Louis?"

Bonnie and her mother had been at odds for a long time and it had come to a head again. Her father was nicer to her but was not a powerful player in their family dynamics. I told her to come on up, trusting that my own mother, with whom I had a frictionless history, would be supportive. The wild card was my new step-father.

Soon Bonnie was with us in St. Louis and I was excited and happy to be available to be a port in her storm and my feelings of love for her were being validated. But with my new step-father in the mix it seemed that the long-standing relationship of essential freedom which I had enjoyed with my mother since my return from Florida, now six years in the past, had come to an end. I expected that my desire to offer my young lover a haven would be honored. But my step-father had different ideas. He didn't want us to sleep together in his house. After an uncomfortable night being forced to sleep in separate rooms, it was agreed that Bonnie and I should drive out to stay in the cabin which my step-father owned further out in the country. But after our first night in the cabin my step-father drove up the driveway quietly, burst into our bedroom just at a moment when we were making love and let fly some nasty language. Later he claimed that he regretted his words but I never really forgave him and Bonnie felt traumatized by that invasion. We took my car and headed back toward Portland the next day feeling bruised on deep core levels.

Back on the road we could breath back into our freedom and our adventure. The heater hardly worked as we rolled through Wyoming in mid-winter. We kept blankets wrapped around our legs and stopped frequently to warm up in little cafes. When we descended into the Columbia River gorge the rain began but our windshield wipers didn't. We tied a rope to them and ran each end through slightly open windows in the car doors. We pulled by turns and managed to make the wipers work manually as we drove along through the rain.

Our love-making was poisoned for the next few weeks with memories of my step-father's violent accusations. Back in Portland at Reed College we found a small room in a house rented by three students who were juniors and seniors and moved in with them. We were free of the dormitories. Bonnie no longer had to ask Natalie to find another place to sleep when I was spending the night. Actually, we were pretty free of the school altogether. My interest in the history of Europe, which formed the backbone of the freshman year humanities program had never been very high. Now that interest plunged to zero and I basically dropped out. Bonnie succeeded much better than I did at attending classes, studying and earning decent grades. As the months passed I felt a deepening guilt about my lack of interest in the school and eventually reconciled to the idea of calling it quits at year's end. I became even more focused on deepening our love-making by trying to track what made her feel good and what didn't. I kept a written journal on the subject and that became my passion and fascination.

On the Beach in Mazatlan, Mexico
As spring vacation approached we made plans to travel south.

Hitch-hiking was a bigger adventure than driving so we went to the highway and stuck out our thumbs. We were picked up by the usual motley assortment of crazy humans. There was the guy in northern California who couldn't drive at a steady speed. His foot kept pumping the accelerator up and down. "I've got to get a divorce from my wife," he moaned.

"Really?" I asked. "How long have you been married?"

"Two weeks!"

Nothing he said made any sense.

We passed through San Francisco and kept moving south. Somewhere outside San Diego we had to flee a religious fanatic who was trying to entice us into his car "to help us" because he "knew we were in trouble..." We smelled something very fishy and refused to get in.

We kept going south into Mexico. Bonnie was still seventeen and I was nineteen but no one was asking. We put up a tent on the beach in Mazatlan and felt like we had arrived. We were warm at last. I had studied some Latin in high school and I was realizing that learning Spanish was a lot like learning Latin. Bonnie, being from Texas, already knew some Spanish. After a couple of days our skin was bright red and painful. Enough sun.

On the way back north we visited a friend of mine in Tucson, Arizona whom I had shared fascinations about beat poetry and French existentialism at school in Colorado Springs and then later in New York City. Peter Botsford offered us shelter and some peyote. Shortly after consuming the peyote I came down with Montezuma's revenge, a Mexican dysentery which threw me into a high fever of 104 degrees. Between the fever and the hallucinations I was not doing well. A trip to the doctor confirmed that I would recover but that for the next four days I should eat no solid food and only drink liquids which I could see through... clear liquids... no pulp allowed.

Miraculously, the fever went down the next day and we stuck out our thumbs on the highway toward Phoenix. After a few short rides we were picked up by Michael Culbertson and Penelope Galitzke. They took us to their house in Mesa, Arizona and offered freshly made lasagna. It looked good to me so I ate it long before my four days of fasting were complete. Michael and Penelope offered, after dinner, to take us to the nearest highway entrance ramp. But as we approached they began to reminisce about their previous Northern California home and they announced that they would drive us to

San Francisco. They had left the door unlocked and the lights on but once the idea took hold there was no turning back. Sometime later the next day they dropped us off at another entry ramp outside San Francisco. We had exchanged contact information and we still stay in touch and share networks of mutual friends.

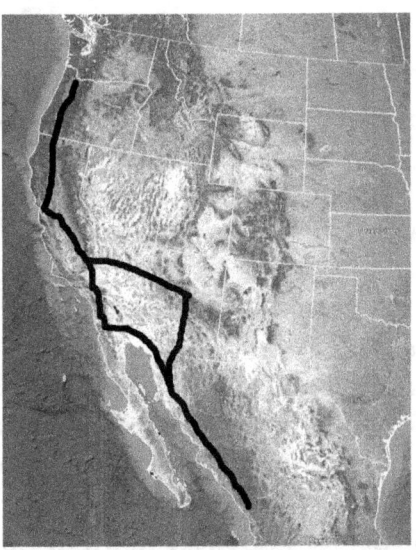

Map: Hitch-hiking Portland to Mazatlan and Back

Bonnie and I finished our hitch-hiking back north to Portland through seriously cold weather. Not fun for Bonnie's freezing toes. My shipment of peyote from the Texas Cactus Ranch had arrived. Our first adventure together into the psychedelic realms was mixed. We enjoyed the hallucinogenic gardens in the lush green Oregon landscape but hints of my step-father's frightening presence tainted the edges of our consciousness.

Every other night we would hear a quiet knock on our bedroom door. One of our house-mates, Nick Tideman, an Economics major in his third year at Reed had fallen in love with us. He loved to sit beside our bed and admire us. He thought our love affair was very beautiful and just wanted to absorb the energy. It was OK with us.

We finished the year. I took my F's and D's and said goodbye forever to Reed College. We moved up to Seattle where, after failing to find a logging job in the woods, I began working as a copy editor for the Seattle Post Intelligencer, a local newspaper. We rented a little house and Bonnie worked all summer with a temporary office help agency as a "Kelly Girl." We adopted a kitten and named her 'Snohomish.' We had time to play our guitars together and learn some Irish songs. I bought a used 1948 Harley Davidson motorcycle and enjoyed the late summer respite from the rain out cruising the highways. I felt like I had a real family: me and Bonnie and our kitty.

I Rented a Little Cabin in the Forest

The summer of 1964 ended. Bonnie returned to Reed College and I moved back to Colorado. I had it in mind to study creative writing in Boulder but had to prove myself academically for a year by taking night school courses first in Denver and then back down in Colorado Springs. My father agreed to help me with money if I tried to meet his terms. The deal was that I would not have to pay the money back if I earned all A's and B's. I enjoyed the writing classes. I would clip out strange little articles from the local newspaper and then make up an even stranger fiction and hand them in. The professors liked what I created and gave me good grades. I rented a little cabin in the forest up in Coal Creek canyon and built fires in the wood stove for heat while I wrote.

I had a friend at Colorado College down in Colorado Springs. I began driving to visit him over the weekends and enjoyed meeting some of his house-mates.

I ordered more peyote from the Texas Cactus Ranch and we perfected a method for preparing it in a way which allowed ingesting extremely large dosages. One of my new friends, John Fernie, came up to visit me in Coal Creek Canyon over another weekend and we lay on our backs in the snow admiring the magical lights streaming up from the eastern horizon many hours before sunrise. We could see little blue lights glowing inside the hearts and souls of the trees in the surrounding pine forest. Our bodies were impervious to the cold and we sailed in and out of near death experiences with wide-eyed wonder. I discovered that I could actually feel and see the rhythms I developed on my guitar as if they were live elastic muscular tissues. As decades passed later in life I discovered and re-discovered that same peyote connection to rhythm and used it to lead people into ecstatic dance.

My mother came to visit me in my little cabin. I was glad to see her but we had no activities to share and I found her presence de-energizing. My daily adventures had to be put on hold... but only for the couple of days of her visit. It was sweet of her to come and check on me.

Soon the snow had accumulated and it was too hard to get in and out of the little cabin so I moved into an apartment in downtown Denver on Clarkson street but my Denver social life was slow to start. I kept driving down to Colorado Springs over the weekends and was soon integrated into the social life down there.

Their English department was actively inviting young writers whom I could admire and from whom I could learn. I attended a poetry workshop given by Robert Bly when he was first beginning to travel and teach. I sat up all night with Ken Kesey playing marijuana-enhanced games and sensed the flavors of the counter-culture revolution which was soon to go mainstream in San Francisco's 1967 summer of love.

I continued writing short stories for my classes. I was singing and playing for people to dance at parties. I took on six guys who were taunting me and my friend, Wick Havens, in a local bar. The fact that Wick was wearing sunglasses was enough to attract streams of verbal abuse. These guys didn't like 'hippies.'

"Assholes!" came the challenging jeers from a whole line of guys who had followed us out of the bar. I turned around and landed a solid punch on one of their noses. After a bloody fist-fight in the middle of a busy downtown street, the flashing red lights of arriving squad cars put an end to our fight. We were surrounded by broken beer bottles on the pavement.

The cops put me and one of our taunters in the back seat of a squad car. It turned out that I had broken his nose, but at that moment, contained in the police car, we looked at each other and found the whole thing funny. We burst out laughing. He told me his name was John and it turned out that he was the cousin of a friend of mine. The cops in the front seat were soon overcome by our infectious laughter.

Some kind of bonding experience which followed the laws of the St Louis teen-age street jungle I had grown up in had occurred. I was not surprised. The cops took us to their station but never charged us with any crimes. Our laughter had by now taken over the whole office. They decided to release us. We began walking back toward the bar. A group of John's friends appeared from the shadows ready to attack me again.

"Forget it, you guys," he told them. "We're friends now." I never had felt the fears I had experienced with the New York City gangs where knives had been involved.

Still thinking fondly of Bonnie, I made a deal with a friend. He would help me drive to Portland one weekend so I could visit her if I would help him drive to St. Louis over another weekend so he could visit a girl named Cathy.

When I arrived in Portland, exhausted from the twelve-hundred-mile drive, Bonnie greeted me and we made love. We were feeling the same strong connection so she made plans to leave Reed College and move to Colorado at the end of the semester. After only a few hours of visiting I was headed back on the long drive to Colorado.

Bonnie Also Moves to Colorado

My secret wish would come true: after the first semester was over, Bonnie got a ride to Cheyenne, Wyoming where I picked her up and brought her home with me. We both signed up for night school classes in Colorado Springs and we rented a little house perched high on the Manitou Springs hillside, just west of Colorado Springs in the foothills below Pikes Peak.

Bonnie on our Porch in Manitou Springs

We were deepening our new friendships with students at Colorado College. My short stories were being published in the Colorado College literary magazine, photos of me were being prepared for inclusion in the Colorado College yearbook, and many thought that I was actually enrolled there as a student.

It was the spring of 1964. LSD was arriving in the neighborhood and I traveled alone on foot by night through the Garden of the Gods and high up into the surrounding foothills high on 'acid' to renew my communions with the birds, the deer and the trees. It felt like my personal adventure was moving forward. I was having fun. I had my tools with me and was making and saving money as a free-lance car mechanic. And most importantly, I had successfully flirted my way into this new extended family of student friends.

The trails up Pike's Peak began almost right outside our door. I made friends with a rock climber named James who nurtured my rock climbing skills with patience and kindness. I was gradually hiking and climbing my way into greater physical strength. As the Spring semester came to an end, another new friend named Gary Ziegler invited me to join a mountaineering expedition to climb in the Peruvian Andes. Bonnie and I completed the necessary applications to enroll as in-state students in Boulder the next fall and we were free for the summer. I had managed to bring my grade average back up and to also become a legal Colorado resident. So I said yes to the opportunity to travel to Peru.

First Trip to Peru

We hiked and climbed to get into better shape so we would hopefully be able to function in the 20,000 ft Andean altitudes. We assembled rock and ice climbing gear. Gary insisted that we carry pistols in our pockets to protect ourselves from the 'untrustworthy back-stabbing Indians.' He had been there before and claimed he knew what he was talking about. Soon we were on a propeller-driven aircraft headed for Lima, Peru.

We rested for a couple of days at the hotel Manco Capac, surely the cheapest hotel in downtown Lima and then headed for Huaraz, the biggest town near the Cordillera Blanca. We had our sights set on climbing two 20,000 foot peaks, Ranrapalca and Ocshapalca. We didn't make the summits of either, but we spent two weeks navigating ice and rock obstacles high in the Andean glaciers and got close.

Gary had hired a few local porters to help us carry our gear up to the base camp at sixteen-thousand feet where the edges of the glaciers began. He warned us again that these Indians were not trustworthy and that we should keep our eyes on them and our pistols ready. I found these instructions confusing because when I looked at our hired porters I saw incredibly strong and amazing beings. I wanted to be able to talk to them and get to know them. I saw no signs whatsoever of untrustworthiness and enjoyed walking along with them up the Quebrada Ischinca toward our base camp. But I knew so little Spanish that conversation was ridiculously minimal. Soon I realized that they weren't even speaking Spanish. They, along with six million other indigenous Peruvian survivors of the Inca empire, were speaking Quechua, the Inca language.

We set up our base camp and spent a few days moving equipment slowly uphill and establishing higher camps up on the glaciers. We needed to move slowly and acclimatize to the altitude. I was envious of our porters who were obviously perfectly happy breathing in these heights.

We shared the base camp area with a team of Japanese climbers but, again, we were frustrated by lack of language skills. It seemed that they also had their sights set on climbing Ocshapalca, at that time still a virgin unclimbed peak.

I felt fairly strong and moved ahead, sometimes alone, to carry our equipment higher. My new friend, a physicist named Joe Ball, and I climbed a nearby unnamed summit just for practice. A high altitude humming bird hovered in front of my eyes for a few seconds checking me out. Was I some kind of strange walking flower? We heard the sound of an airplane. We looked up to spot it but saw nothing. Confused, we looked thousands of feet down into the valley below. There it was, barely able to attain enough altitude to skim over the sixteen-thousand foot pass far below us.

Soon we began working our way up Ranrapalca and I led our team up a steep ice wall during part of the climb. Using my ice ax to chop hand-holds I began working my way up. The ice had layers created by the history of annual snowfalls, like tree rings. I kicked my boots in between the layers and found a system for feeling secure. Every so often I would reach over my shoulder and extract another three-foot-long section of aluminum tubing, snow pickets which protruded in a cluster from my pack like arrows in a quiver. I was being belayed from below so I could anchor the rope through carabiners to the pickets as I ascended. I suddenly remembered the hardware store back in Colorado with its long ordered rows of nuts and bolts where I had bought the aluminum tubing two months ago. My body worked smoothly like gears in a bucket of oil. I suddenly realized that back in Colorado I would probably have been afraid. Here, now I was free of that feeling. Four thousand miles away were the closest people caring and worrying about me. Miles below were people who spoke a different language. As I thrust myself up between the pinnacles of ice guarding the top of the wall I felt the exhilaration of a new kind of greater freedom. But the next step up gave me the ultimate surprise.

"What the hell?" Nearly at the top, I had expected to be able to step onto a higher snow field, but no...

"Holy Christ!" I yelled down. "This wall is only two feet thick and overhanging!"

"How far down is it?" Gary cried.

"Farther down than you are!" I had to reply.

"You'd better get down off that thing!"

"We can't get anywhere this way!" Plunging my ice ax deep into the wall, I peered over the edge again and saw its tip emerge through the other side. We were climbing a wafer-thin slice of ice. Placing another snow picket on the top, I had Joe lower me with the rope. That was as high as we managed to climb on Ranrapalca.

On Ranrapalca in the Cordillera Blanca

We spent another week climbing up the ridge on Ocshapalca but difficult sections of rock stopped us.

Rappelling off Ocshapalca Ridge

With faces blistered from high altitude solar radiation, dwindling supplies of food and energy we called it quits and began our descent. We felt like our adventure had been a success.

Map: Climbing Peaks Above Quebrada Ischinca

A few days later, back down in Huaraz, Joe Ball and I decided to re-schedule our return to Colorado. We lightened our loads to include only sleeping bags and a few other basic back-packing supplies, bade adieu to our climbing buddies in Lima and stuck out our thumbs heading south along the Pacific coast through the Atacama desert. I wasn't aware that the real adventure was now beginning.

We stood for hours waiting for rides in the desolate desert environment with the mysterious Nazca lines surrounding us. We climbed onto the flat greasy top of a gasoline truck and rode for hours through the night. Goblin-like rock crags formed silhouettes against the night sky as we gained altitude somewhere on the way to Arequipa. Two young Peruvian Indians were chewing their coca leaves beside us as we struggled to create pockets of warmth in the freezing cold. Peru is approximately the size of the western third of the United States and the vastness of the landscape was sinking in. There was only one paved road in the whole country at that time, the pan-American highway on the coast, so travel was interminably slow.

No Buses... Just Trucks...

I thought I was learning a bit of Spanish but my friend Joe was way ahead of me. He was much better at deciphering restaurant menus, comprehending directions and keeping us oriented. If I introduced myself as "Cameron," people looked at me quizzically. There was no equivalent name in Spanish or Quechua and the nearest word, "Camarón," meant "shrimp." So I began using "Felipe," the equivalent of my legal first name in English, "Philip." In Spanish-speaking countries I am always known as "Felipe."

We made our way up to Lake Titicaca and across to La Paz, Bolivia. I realized that I was getting a peek at a completely different world. I wanted to find an entry point for future adventures so I looked for and found English-teaching job opportunities.

Mysteriously Precise Inca Stonework above Cusco

We turned around in Bolivia and traveled back across the Lake and then through Puno and up to Cusco, Machu Picchu, and then north over the rugged narrow highway through Abancay, Andahuaylas, Ayacucho and Huancavelica to Huancayo.

Train to Machu Picchu

The highway traffic opened on alternate days to north-bound and south-bound vehicles as it was not possible for trucks traveling in opposite directions to pass. We rode in the backs of trucks. I don't remember seeing any buses.

In the Back of Another Truck

Looking back on these adventures after returning to Colorado I realized that it was the Inca people, even more than the mountains, who were going to call me back.

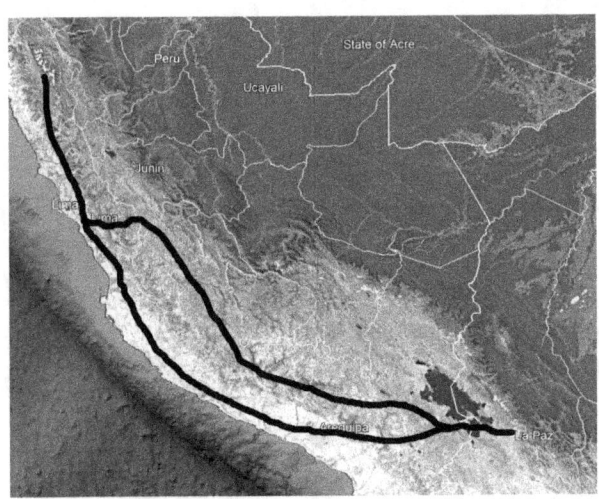

Map: Wandering Through Inca Lands

But Not Ready for More School

I moved from Manitou Springs to Boulder and rented an apartment. The school year was about to begin when I realized that something wasn't right. I was confused about what to do. I was about to resume classes in creative writing but I felt like I had shifted, changed, moved on. Bonnie was in the process of moving in with me but I couldn't feel settled with the idea. I needed more space to digest it all. I went to the admissions office and postponed the resumption of my school career for a year and drove up into the mountains.

Lisa: Into the Inca Lands

I drove up to Leadville, Colorado and got a job at the Climax molybdenum mine. That was the highest paying labor job in the state and I determined to work, save my money and return to Peru or Bolivia. In order to qualify for the mining job I had to weigh at least one-hundred-sixty pounds, spend a week shoveling rocks eight-hours-a-day into ore cars and demonstrate claustrophobia-free comfort with working a thousand feet underground.

I got the job and began working to drill deep holes, load them with explosives, lay tracks and build timber scaffolding to prevent cave-ins. My partner underground was an experienced Hispanic guy named Oakie. We got along well and I visited him in the neighboring mining town of Redcliff where he was the local boy scout master. I brought photos from Peru to show the boys and felt welcomed into the Colorado mining world.

We worked seven days on day shift and took two days off; seven days on swing shift and took one day off, and then seven days on graveyard shift and took five days off. I told James and Kevin and Kendall Smith, friends from Colorado Springs, about the high wages and they all moved up to Leadville too. The twin Smith brothers and I rented an apartment and ignored the fact that there was no heat or hot water. James chose to live in the company hotel. We hardly ever saw the sun. We were endlessly working underground or catching up on sleep. Monica Beck, who had been a student at Colorado College came up, slept on the couch and practiced levitating. We worked hard underground in freezing cold tunnels and ate incredible quantities of food provided in the form of breakfast at the company store. I saved my money for a ticket back to Bolivia.

Driving down to either Boulder or Colorado Springs didn't take long, so during those breaks when I had one or two or even five days off I would sometimes drive down out of the mountains. Leadville was at ten thousand feet; the entrance to the mine at the top of Fremont Pass was at eleven thousand feet. Driving down to six thousand feet was a bit like heading down to the tropics, even in mid-winter.

I received a letter ordering me to get a physical exam for the US military draft. I drove down to Boulder where a nurse at the University of Colorado health clinic exaggerated my height measurement and kept me from going to Viet Nam. It was entirely her idea. Thank you, whoever you are!

Visiting Bonnie in Boulder was always sweet although she was hinting that yes, she was getting closer to some new boyfriends.

"But I think it will always be OK for us to make love, don't you?" she asked me. I liked that idea and we did continue to make love when I visited... or when she visited.

Hunkered down in a ditch to stay out of the freezing winds while hitch-hiking up into the mountains to see me she was spotted by a passing snow plow driver. "You're likely to freeze to death out here! Climb in! I'll give you a ride!"

But our visits were short. She was involved with school and I with working underground.

More than fifty years later, Bonnie and I are still enjoying a wonderful quality of loving friendship but somewhere back there the deep intimacy of love-making vanished from our connection.

I had also grown close to some of the young women at Colorado College. Sometimes I would drive down to Colorado Springs and visit them and there were several with whom I would occasionally get sexy.

Camille

My friend Camille loved to hike with me in the mountains during those autumn months. We would explore southern Colorado and rent little motel cabins for the night. We would make love, sometimes out on the rocks in the trees... we would take showers and spend our time together very quietly. We never had a whole lot to say. Our connection wasn't fueled by words. There was a sweet and magical mist in the air between us.

Up into the Mountains again with Camille

I would receive letters in Leadville from her nearly every week. She would dye the letters with juices from purple berries she had picked on our mountain hikes.

"For the next two years it will be difficult, not being able to see each other much," she wrote to me in December. "For we must both get on with our lives and I have applied to work for the Red Cross in Viet Nam. But after that..."

'For the next two years?' I thought. 'With whom is she in love and wanting to wait for two years? Surely it is not I whom she plans to love for so long: It must be someone else...'

I drove down and went to see her. I said, "I will be your very dear friend, but I can not pretend to promise that I am your lifelong lover."

"I could not bear to see you and be only your friend. I would sooner never see you again," she whispered.

But we sat in a bar talking of other things and after an hour she said, "Okay, I will be your very good friend..." And when I took her home that night she asked, "And with your very good friends, do you... ...still make love?"

"I will be happy to make love with my very good friends," I told her.

But late the next night she was angry. That morning I had gone horseback riding with Josie; and that evening I had danced at the party with Eleanor, and so Camille, with her back toward me in bed, said, "...and I think I would just as soon go to sleep..."

But no, at four o'clock in the morning she was sitting up in bed smoking a cigarette. I was patting her on the back to let her know that I sympathized. Finally she put her head on my shoulder, and in another moment we made love, perhaps more beautifully than ever before. I fell asleep on top of her.

Late the next morning I awoke to a cold finger, still wet from the bathroom, being passed along my cheek. Camille stood by the door, dressed and ready to go.

"Goodbye," she said and closed the door. My eyes remained open wide as I stared at the wall.

But during the coming decades, as we shall see as these adventures unfold, Camille would miraculously float in and out of my life, almost always ready to resume our love connection. We remain, more than fifty years later, bonded in deep friendship.

Search and Not Rescue but Confuse

Back up in Leadville I continued to work and save my money. During another of our five-day breaks, Kevin, Kendall and I headed up into the nearby peaks on snowshoes. We set our sights on climbing Ten Mile Peak at the northern end of the Ten Mile Range above Breckenridge.

Ten Mile Peak

Struck by a major snowstorm, we dug ourselves a snow cave high on the ridge near the summit. But our body heat melted the snow until our sleeping bags were soaking wet. At three in the morning we gave up, rolled up our sleeping bags allowing them to freeze into solid cylinders of ice, and headed back down the mountain. The temperatures were dropping and our hands and feet were becoming numb. As the ridge leveled out we began relying on detecting the divots of our own still-barely-visible snow-shoe tracks for navigation. The blizzard was obscuring the view.

As we descended further we began to be unable to distinguish the remnants of our own tracks from a plethora of newer tracks which seemed to curl and circle everywhere through the wilderness. After many hours of slogging we had to admit that we were lost. We were, in fact, passing the same places more than once - traveling in circles.

Now the situation was serious. Our hands and feet had long ago succumbed to the numbness of impending frostbite. But the next time around the circle we made a different choice and finally emerged beside the highway and found my parked car.

Eager for warmth and food, we drove until we found an open gas station and convenience store which offered something minimal like coffee and dough-nuts. We stood shivering inside the store and listened as the attendant shared the latest local news. It seemed that the sheriff's department had deployed a rescue crew with snowmobiles to try and find a lost party of climbers. Unsuccessful, they had given up and retreated.

We now knew the origin of all those confusing tracks. We said nothing about having been the object of their failed search and went on our way.

Back to South America

Having saved enough money, I was ready to buy a ticket back to South America. I had written to the director of a language institute whom I had met in Bolivia and he promised me a job. I received the surprising news that my mother and step-father wanted to travel to Mexico City and see me off from there. The cheapest flight would take me from Denver to Mexico City and then to Bogotá, Colombia. I planned to travel overland from there through Ecuador and Peru and down to Bolivia.

The whole trip did not go well for me. In Mexico City my step-father offered to pay my way in a house of prostitution. He was trying to do me some kind of favor but he was the last person I wanted to have involved in my sex life. I told him I wasn't really interested, which was the truth anyway, and we dropped that idea. I couldn't help but wonder if he was trying to follow up and mend the awkwardness he had created a couple of years earlier when Bonnie had come up from Texas to stay with me. His approach seemed strange and I felt mildly insulted.

We stayed in a fancy hotel and sampled delicacies like 'marinated baby eels' and 'baby octopus cooked in their own ink.' There was a flamenco guitar player performing there who sounded so good to me that I wondered if I should perhaps cancel the rest of the trip and just stay in Mexico and study music with him.

It was Easter time and we happened to be in the silver-smithing town of Taxco for the candle-light parade. As evening approached the streets and central plaza filled with silent worshipers. Thousands of Mexicans stood with candles. Not a sound was being made. Even the babies in their parents' arms were in a state of wide-eyed silent wonder. The silence itself became audible. I was impressed. No, I had never seen a mood of reverence shared by a giant crowd like that!

As the evening progressed I began to see groups of passing penitentes. Young men with blood running down their bare backs carried huge bundles of sharp thorns or heavy crosses. Some lashed themselves with sharpened crosses whenever the procession paused. Blood was also running down the skin on their backs. Yes, this was some kind of serious devotion. The penitentes faces were covered with black cloths but I guessed that their identities were given away to close friends and family members by the recognizably detailed shapes of their bare feet. I knew I was an outsider getting a peek into some other kind of world. I was mystified and intrigued.

But the few days spent with my mother and step-father somehow interrupted my own personal flow. By the time my plane landed in Bogotá, Colombia, I felt de-energized and confused. I rented a hotel room and explored the city. But as I wandered I felt isolated. Had I been relying on the Spanish-speaking skills of my friend, Joe Ball, the year before in Peru more than I had realized?

I had wanted to travel alone. I wanted to learn to be 'alone but not lonely' so that I could learn to stay focused on my writing. I had a job teaching English waiting for me in La Paz, Bolivia. I had researched and found an apparently un-mapped area in Southern Peru and North-western Bolivia which I was going to explore. I had planned to hitch-hike south toward Bolivia after just a few days in Colombia.

Bogotá, Colombia

I found a room with breakfast, lunch and dinner included in central Bogotá for $2 a day. Not a bad price. The very first time I entered the room on the afternoon of my arrival, as I was taking my pack off my back, a young man had burst into the room. He looked immensely startled to me there. Nevertheless, he succeeded in placing a used bar of soap on the dresser and, muttering in a strange voice incomprehensible apologies and explanations, withdrew from the room. I had only managed to briefly say "thank you" before he rushed out.

Soon I went to the shared bathroom down the hall and there he was, mopping the floor. He beamed apologetically at me and again resumed his incomprehensible talk. I told him I wasn't able to understand. The young man's face, which had been as bright and exuberant as that of a child, underwent a slow transformation. His look got darker and darker until he darted out the door in a sudden panic. As I re-entered my room I saw his face peering at me from around the corner. The storm seemed to have passed and he now looked quite gleeful. I leaned backward out of my door to look again. His face disappeared and then re-appeared. Our eyes met with a startled clash. I smiled but he looked a little uncertain and he withdrew from sight again. I began to re-enter my room but something made me want to look again. His face had re-appeared but he still looked very uncertain. So I smiled again. We remained frozen in a strange mutual stare until he flashed a quick smile and released us. I plunged into my room and closed the door. 'Must be some kind of an idiot,' I thought to myself.

After a bit I headed out to explore the city. Bogotá was nothing like the colorful capitol of Bolivia. Instead of the endless color of indigenous life, I encountered a city full of men wearing gray business suits and carrying brief cases. Not warm and inviting to me. I returned to my room and about midnight there was a very timid knock on the door and it opened a bit. "Come in!" I said.

The young man stood in the entrance to my room grinning madly at me. He looked almost desperate. "I saw your light on so... so..." he said.

I could understand his words now. I beckoned him in, offered him a glass of water and we pulled up two chairs to sit very close together.

"I saw you this afternoon when you arrived!" he whispered. He was grinning and looking very happy about this.

"Yes, you came to return the soap you had borrowed from the room," I volunteered.

"Yes!" He looked at me intently. He was ecstatically clenching his teeth. He said something else but it was very jumbled and spoken in a hee-hawing donkey-like voice.

I shook my head to indicate that I had not understood.

"You didn't understand?" he queried. This seemed to strike him as very funny and he leaned toward the wall giggling hysterically.

"No, I didn't understand!" I reiterated slapping him on the knee. I suddenly found myself infected with the laughter too. Something relaxed inside of me. Everything now appeared gleefully, ridiculously and absolutely funny!

The young man shrugged as if to say, 'It doesn't matter in the least whether you understand or not!' We both rocked in an ocean of giggles.

So it went for nearly an hour. I started spouting stories in my best Spanish. It didn't matter in the least what I said. I talked about how there were so many lands and countries with so many different languages being spoken. There were mountains in some, deserts or jungles in others. There were oceans. The young man seemed to not understand most of what I was saying but that didn't matter. All that mattered was that we were sitting there and that this was deliriously funny.

"We are in Bogotá, Colombia!" the young man explained.

I understood what he said and repeated, "Yes, in Bogotá, Colombia!" The fact that I had understood became even more hilariously funny to us both. But when I didn't understand his words that was just as funny too.

Finally we decided that it was late and that we should go to sleep. We said goodnight and the young man left. I went to sleep feeling glad that I had been an apparently desperately-needed friend.

The next two nights, at a very late hour, he tapped on my door again and the whole hilariously funny exchange was repeated.

I also met a middle-aged artist from France who had been living in Colombia for the last ten years and who had made a few travels down into the jungle. We spent an entire day together and he told me many stories. He told me of a variety of giant snake which was like an Anaconda but not an Anaconda. This snake, he said, could swallow an entire cow.

"Are they extremely dangerous?" I inquired.

"It depends on the length of the cow's horns," he replied.

"The length?"

"Yes," and he began drawing me a picture on a handy napkin.

"You see, when these snakes begin swallowing a cow, they succeed in swallowing the whole body, tail first, until they get to the horns. Then, if the horns are too long, they can't finish passing through the jaws into the snake's stomach. He sits there, unable to move, with a partially-swallowed cow in it's throat." He finished sketching a hilarious picture of a snake in this situation. "So, when this has happened, the snake is no longer dangerous and you can safely pass in front of it!"

Georges, my French artist friend, also told me of a young couple from North America who had vanished into the jungle. The Colombian government became concerned because that region of jungle was dangerous with quicksand.

"After about a month," Georges explained, "a search party was sent to find the young couple but they also disappeared… and within the next months two more search parties were dispatched. Finally, the surviving members of all three search parties had found each other and they emerged from the jungle together. They had become lost; some had died from snake-bites... the survivors all had to be hospitalized because of the horrible diseases they had contracted.

"Well, another month passed. A helicopter finally spotted the young couple playing in a river. They seemed to be happily splashing in the water and were eating fruits from the nearby trees. They looked like Adam and Eve in the garden of Eden!

"A few weeks later they finally emerged from the edge of the jungle. The Colombian government invited them to come tell their stories to a group of assembled anthropologists but when they disclosed that they weren't legally married the government officials became upset. You know how they can feel about that down here!

"Apparently no longer feeling welcome in civilization, the young couple vanished again into the jungle... this time for good! Perhaps they had been hippies back home in North America! Have you ever met a hippie?"

"A few," I replied.

"Are they learning to live more like animals again?" Georges inquired.

"Yes, I think so."

"And they don't need to get married to have sex?"

"No, I don't think so..."

I was spending hours every day walking the streets of Bogotá, exploring the city on foot. In the evenings I would return to the hotel to claim my free meals. I would write of my adventures sitting in the lobby.

Some Kind of Rape?

Another young man offered to guide me through remote parts of the city to show me where the Inca people lived. "There aren't many Indians in Bogotá, but they live near to where I have an apartment."

I was getting closer to deciding how I would proceed on to La Paz, Bolivia, but I had no other plan for that evening so we began riding buses. We rode bus after bus into remote suburbs of the city. I had no idea where we were. Long after dark it began to seem strange to me that we apparently still hadn't arrived yet. "I am so happy to have met you and to have a new friend!" he told me.

I wondered at his apparent isolation and loneliness but remained on the lookout for our entry into 'the Inca part of the city.'

"You know the buses are going to quit running soon," he told me. "But my apartment is near here. I want to show you where I live."

"I need to get back to my hotel..."

"No, my apartment is right here... We should just spend the night here and then go back to your hotel tomorrow..."

The buses quit running and I finally agreed. We entered his apartment to sleep. He offered me the bed in the one-room space. He curled up on some blankets in the corner of the room and we went to sleep. At least I did. Next thing I knew he was slithering into the bed with me. I kept pushing him away. "I really just want to sleep!" I told him.

By four o'clock in the morning he had again crept under my blanket from way down by my feet and was relentlessly trying to suck on my cock. I finally just let him suck on it and I guess he must have masturbated down there under the sheets. After that he stayed on the other side of the room and I slept for a few hours. The sun came up and the buses started running again. I escaped. He wanted to accompany me back to the city center but I just got on a bus, any bus. As the bus pulled away from the curb I could hear him pleading, "Write me a letter! Write me a letter!" What was he thinking!? I was finally free of him.

I spent another afternoon a couple of days later with Georges, the French artist, but most of my time was spent walking the streets alone. I was feeling that hitch-hiking overland all the way to Bolivia was a long way. And something deep in my psyche was making a clamor. It wasn't really located in my mind. When I talked to others I was rational and even cheerful. But the buildings and sidewalks were beginning to spin before my eyes. Objects in my field of vision would fade in and out. I didn't stumble or fall but I was being invaded by a private, overwhelming giddiness... and dizziness. There was a wrenching and hurting in my chest. No real nausea entered my stomach and I appeared to myself and to the world to be functioning quite well.

I went to the airport and found that I had just enough money left to fly to Bolivia. I had the English-teaching job lined up there and would supposedly be able to begin making money. But I didn't buy the ticket. I spent another day walking the streets to think about it. Deep inside something trembled and shook. I went back to the airport with my things packed. I would purchase the ticket to Bolivia and wait in the airport for the plane to leave. Arriving at the airport I was drawn to just inquire about the price of a ticket to Miami. It turned out to be the same price as the ticket to Bolivia.

Exactly how the decision came to be made remained a mystery. Soon I was on the plane to Miami. And it was dark and it was raining. Rivulets of water ran down the outside of the glass as I stared out the window. The plane gathered speed for take-off and the rivulets streamed sideways. My mind took a photograph of that moment: a moment which remains engraved in my memory as a relic of a terrible mistake. I should have been on the plane to Bolivia!

Drunk Police Detective

Landing in Miami, I hitch-hiked up to New York City. I wanted to visit my old St. Louis friend, Doug. He was working for the welfare department in Harlem as an alternative service which supposedly qualified him, as a conscientious objector, to not go to war in Viet Nam.

Doug and I and his good friend Hans, whom he had met at Wabash College in Indiana, stopped in a bar for a few beers. After a half hour or so the bartender leaned over to me and said, "You better get out of here!" He pointed toward the side door which led out of the bar into the alley.

"Why?" I inquired.

"Someone wants to kill you," he whispered.

I exited the bar into the alley but, turning around and looking behind me, I saw a pudgy middle-aged man leveling his pistol at my back.

"I'm gonna take care of you, Red!" I kept hearing him mutter. Doug and Hans were exiting the bar right behind him and some pushing and shoving ensued which gave me the chance to run out of the alley to the nearby street.

I stopped under a street light vaguely hoping that I would be less likely murdered if I was more in public. My attacker emerged and began trying to drag me back into the darkness of the alley. But he could not drag me out from under that street light. I saw him draw the gun a number of times. He seemed to be drunkenly trying to make up his mind whether to go ahead and shoot me under the street light.

Seeking any refuge, I struggled over to the front door of the bar but by now, of course, it was locked and lights inside the bar had been turned off.

There was very little traffic on that street but a police car was passing and I made enough noise to attract their attention.

They put me in the back seat and I felt a moment of immense relief... until my attacker slid into the seat beside me. The two police got back in their front seats and we started driving. They all knew each other! It seemed that my pistol-wielding attacker was a local drunk off-duty police detective! We left my friends Doug and Hans on the sidewalk.

I was having visions of being murdered and dumped into the East River, which wasn't far away. But we arrived at the local precinct station and went inside.

"Detective McWalters," my attacker muttered at me, opening his wallet to show a badge. "You're under arrest for..." But the other officers told him they wanted to discuss the situation with him and they all disappeared into a room. I was escorted to another room where I was soon joined by my friends Doug and Hans who had found their way on foot to the station. After a half hour or so another officer appeared and told us we could go.

Doug inquired and found an American Civil Liberties Union lawyer to talk to and filed some kind of complaint. Years later someone sent me a book called *'Police Power: Police Abuses in New York City'* which told the story of how Detective McWalters was demoted after that from Detective to Patrolman. The book got most of the story right about what had happened that night.

I left New York City and headed back west. I stopped for one night in St. Louis and made love to a friendly slender girl who was a room-mate of a friend. "I want to keep you!" she told me the next morning, but I was headed back home to Colorado.

On my way out of the city I stopped in Richmond Heights and found my old friend Tim Holmes. He had become a cop and was driving a fancy squad car wearing a uniform. "Moving to Colorado is not a good idea," he told me. "You should stay here in St Louis with your friends!" He said that his twin brother Terry had moved to Sacramento, California.

Some Other Kind of Music

Back in Boulder, I rented a basement coal bin to sleep in for $15 a month, got an additional job mopping the kitchen floor at a girls' rooming house called the Cameo in exchange for meals, and I made extra cash from time to time with my free-lance auto repair business.

It was late springtime in 1966. I also began working for Nuzum's, a landscape company in Boulder. The job was to dig ditches for underground sprinkler systems in peoples' yards. My partner was an ex-convict who had been recently released from the prison in Canon City and he had nothing to say except "huerfano motherfucker!"

"They don't call these the Rocky Mountains for nothing!" I would add as we tried to dig trenches in the exposed granite bedrock.

My guitar was a frequent friend. It would leap into my hands and I began hearing some other kind of music in my head. There was something of the night sky in this music... the eerie music of great distances... the music seen in the passionate flashes from the dancers' eyes... single string music plucked high on the neck of a very electric guitar... piercing... I could feel an inner undulation as my inner drummer played rhythms which surged along on the crests of waves... always a surprise because they never stopped... were almost painful in their relentless flow... like the thumping of the waves of the sea at night... yet strung through with the grand tranquility of the universe. I could hear this music inside me and I could see the dancers dancing...

Bonnie was in Boulder and she would stop by to try and entice me back into the local folk-singers scene. But the music in my head now was different. We would catch up from time to time to offer each other encouragement, but we were no longer drawn to want to live together.

When All Else Fails - Back to School

I had no other plans so I began school again. Now I announced that I wanted to major in anthropology. If I couldn't yet make it back to Peru and Bolivia in person, I could at least learn something about the amazing world of indigenous peoples.

I began school classes. My father was willing to resume helping me with the $250-per-semester tuition and again agreed that I wouldn't have to repay him if I made all A's and B's.

My friend, Jim Sharp, moved into the other underground sleeping space with me in that basement. We took showers at the university gym and settled into the rhythm of the two short summer semesters.

I loved it. I never missed a class. I sat in the front row and never took my eyes off the professors. I learned about cultural relativity... how people see the world through the eyes of their cultures and make sense of the world in so many different ways. I took courses about Central Asia, the Middle East, Ancient Greece, Native North American tribes, physical anthropology, archaeology, geology. I covered my basement walls with time charts so I could see and understand the differences between a thousand years... a million years... a billion years...

Camille didn't go to Viet Nam after she graduated from Colorado College in the spring. She went ninety miles north to work for Shell Oil and to live in an apartment by herself. In August I heard she was planning to get married to a guy she had met during the summer. Two weeks later I saw her. We spent the evening talking with four other mutual friends and were never alone together.

"He works to supply the Army with equipment, which doesn't sound very exciting, I suppose..." she told us. "...yes, in Rock Island, Illinois, but...we hope to move after a year."

At three in the morning we drove Camille to her car, beautiful Camille, always misty-eyed Camille. My friend Joe said he thought she had tears in her eyes.

She stood in the dark looking at us longer than any of us expected. She finally climbed into her car and drove away.

A few weeks later I was at a dance at the University Memorial Center. The tall and lovely blond girl with whom I was dancing seemed to like me. She gave me her address and I began stopping by to visit. Her room-mates seemed to like me too. She was an art major and loved to go up in the mountains with large canvases, take off all her clothes and paint.

Robin Painting

She was friendly, strong and adventurous. She was endlessly cheerful and we loved to dance acrobatically together. We would go out to Rocky Flats Lounge, otherwise known as the 'Hummer Club,' put a quarter in the juke box and take over the entire dance floor.

We deepened our dance connection at local drum circles. The threads which bound us were more elaborate than the webs of the spider. We became willow tree lovers, swaying to the same breezes. We became high altitude tree roots as the musical storms would grow into powerful gusts and we would cling to the cracks on the exposed rock ridges.

"Cameron?!!!" she would exclaim if I missed catching her as she flew through the air in some amazing dance move which she could see perfectly in her mind.

She told me later that she had wanted me to move much faster toward ending her virginity. But soon enough we were lovers. She moved out of her shared apartment into a remodeled carriage house in an alley where she could set up an artist's residence and I moved in with her part time.

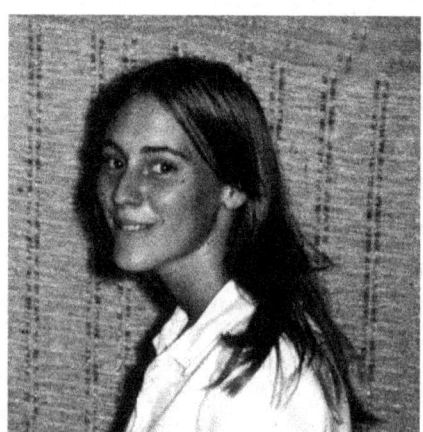

Robin in Her Remodeled Carriage House

We began sharing outdoor adventures cross-country skiing and hiking together in the mountains. Robin saw the world as a big moving picture filled with wonderful colors. Losing ourselves mid-winter on cross-country skis in the wrong drainage descending from the top of Rabbit Ears Pass we nearly skied off cliffs accidentally in the pitch dark cloud cover. These were the adventures which Robin loved. Still it was up to me to succeed with making emergency repairs to her wired-together ski bindings at midnight in the dark.

"Cameron?!!!" she would exclaim again. An artist with few words, she communicated with tones of voice. In just the way she was saying my name I could feel her meaning: 'Wow isn't it kind of crazy that we're doing this? Isn't it wonderful that we're doing this? I love you! I hope you get my ski binding fixed soon! I'm having a hard time balancing on one leg! It's freezing out here! Do we have any idea where we are?' All this and more was contained in just the way she pronounced my name... and always with a smile. We never disagreed or fought or argued.

She carved an elaborate leaf sculpture from a piece of brown hardwood and hid a small paper scroll inside of it on which she had written a poem for me:

> *What is brown?*
> *Brown is the color of a country road*
> *Back of a turtle*
> *Back of a toad*
> *Brown is cinnamon and morning toast*
> *And the good smell of the Sunday roast*
> *Brown is the color of work*
> *And the sound of a river*
> *Brown is bronze*
> *And a bow and a quiver*
> *Brown is the house on the edge of town*
> *Where the wind is tearing the shingles down*
> *Brown is a freckle*
> *Brown is a mole*
> *Brown is the Earth when you dig a hole*
> *Brown is the hair on many a head*
> *Brown is chocolate and ginger*
> *Brown is a feeling you get inside*
> *When wondering makes your mind grow wide*
> *Brown is a guitar and Cameron's eyes*
> *Brown is the odor of falling leaves*
> *Brown is a leather shoe and a good glove*
> *Brown is as comfortable as love*

Robin was an adventuress.

Robin Cross-Country Skiing

I told her about the wonderful big wide South American world and she listened eagerly to my tales of adventure.

After only a few months of sharing the warmth of our love, something happened: she graduated from the Art department in June of 1967. She took my advice and headed for South America.

How-ya Doin' Big Boy?

Robin had been gone for a while. I was down having a hamburger and a beer in The Sink... Wow! 'Look at all these bare-legged chicks; just the place a college man needs to come to when the going gets rough. Meet her here... greet her here... in the mysterious depths of The Sink!'

Blonde girl approached me... "How-ya doin' big boy?"

"Heh heh."

"Why don't you come over for dinner at my house? I think we might have a little party. Come on!"

I followed her to her house.

"I think I'll slip into something a little bit more comfortable if you don't mind." She said her name was Linda.

This led up to orgasm and then dropped off into silence.

I opened my eyes. It was morning. Another girl was in the room with us.

"Good morning," she said. "I'm her room-mate. She doesn't like to get up early. It's impossible to wake her up."

I got up... got dressed... looked at her sleeping face. Was she really asleep? Or just avoiding eye contact...? I went out the door feeling strange...

I began feeling an attraction to the girl on the back porch. She was quiet and definitely a mystery, but I kept noticing her. I was busy studying and making my good grades but there was some time for climbing, cross-country skiing, repairing cars and hosting a stream of friends of friends who would camp out in various nooks and crannies of our basement commune.

Lisa - The Girl who Lived on the Back Porch

The mountains were our playground and every once in a while we would drop acid as a tribe and spend the day in the high country. Lifelong friendships were born. Lisa, since she happened to live on the back porch, shared the use of the toilet and the laundry sink which happened to be in the basement. She was a very familiar face. Little by little we became friends.

The summer sessions of classes ended in early August of 1967. I had a few weeks before classes began again. Lisa had said something about wanting to go to San Francisco. I said, "I could give you a ride."

We stopped in Steamboat Springs along the way. I spotted Charlie's can parked near the top of Rabbit Ears pass. He later told us he had been flying a kite nearby. We gave up on hoping to find him and descended down into Strawberry Park to The Barn where we were invited to join friends for an evening sauna down by the creek. Lisa was enamored. The scene at The Barn looked enormously attractive to her.

We continued westward through Utah and stopped in Nevada at

Sand Mountain and climbed the huge dune. We took our clothes off and tumbled naked in the sand. We were getting slowly more comfortable with our attraction.

Arriving in San Francisco, we drove into the Haight-Ashbury district and found my friends, Joe Sharp and Skip Archer. Lisa later confided in me that she was impressed and relieved when we slept together in the same bed in Joe's apartment. I hadn't insisted on sexually attacking her. She remembers that as a positive thing which enabled her to continue to feel more and more comfortable in my presence. I did, in fact, wait until another moment a few months later back in Boulder when I could tell she was ready to make love.

It seemed to me that Joe and Skip were being drained of their vitality by soaking themselves too deeply in the 'summer of love' there in San Francisco. It had of course become a 'summer of drugs.' I suggested we drive north to climb Mt Rainier, a fourteen-thousand-foot glacier-covered volcano in Washington state, and they thought that a fine idea. We left San Francisco and the rest of my free time before classes started again in Boulder was spent climbing up onto the glaciers. Lisa had already taken a plane back to Colorado.

Robin Back from Cambodia

I returned to Boulder after delivering my friends back to San Francisco and Robin came for a visit. She had easily become 'the beautiful wandering blond artist' and she had already traveled through much of Latin America working her magic. Eventually she had joined with an Argentine adventurer and together they had explored Southeast Asia, especially Cambodia. Now she was traveling with a little monkey, a gibbon, as a constant companion. She said that if the monkey didn't bite you, then you were cool. That was the test.

Now obsessed with spreading the word about the genocides and deep social injustices committed by the USA all over the world, Robin had become a political activist. We spent a week in the mountains at Carp's Cabin to make love and reconnect. My friend James, who had followed me up to Leadville to work in the mine, was also there. We played conga drums, guitars and sang out our primal energies for days. We were all powerful personalities, including the monkey. I could feel underground forces of attraction between her and James. I could feel her deep frustration with the fact that America had become a powerful destructive force with its crazy foreign wars and I could feel her desperation for us to rise to the occasion and do something about it.

"Cameron!!!" she would exclaim, hoping that I could manifest as another Che Guevara... or... who knows. I felt a strong call to move deeply with her in these passionate adventures... but how? Neither one of us seemed to know... exactly. We would somehow be flying in parallel formation, but not together.

Back in Boulder I felt a different feeling evolving between me and Lisa. The girl who lived on the back porch was now someone with whom I had shared warm adventures and quiet cheerful times. At some point our eyes locked in telepathic unison and we both knew that the time had come. I scooped her up in my arms and carried her into my private coal bin to make love.

Lisa was an education major. She planned to create a career working with young children. Our interests and social life didn't really overlap except in the small world of the basement commune. She began accompanying me and my basement room-mate, Jim, to Steamboat Springs for cross-country ski adventures. I was gradually deepening my new friendships with Wayne and Linda who ran The Barn Lodge in Strawberry Park and with Charlie Bates, a friend from Colorado College and a champion cross-country ski racer, who had introduced me to Wayne and Linda. Lisa gradually became a friendly and familiar face among my friends.

Lisa loved our adventures but she was not a public personality. Her inner nature was gentle and delicate. Making love to her required a certain surrender. If I followed my own rhythms it could backfire.

"Meanie!" I remember her telling me. "You push too much!"

"I give up! I'm in the doghouse!" I replied. "You need to show me what to do!"

Then, sometimes with her on top she would lead us into just the right sexual places and we would happily fall asleep bathed in the ecstasy of the magical outcomes.

Identifying as a couple was a gradual thing. We didn't try to put words to it. She had confided that the relationship with her very first boyfriend, Jim, who was the manager of our student rooming house, had felt abusive. I didn't know what had happened between them but when he mentioned her to me one afternoon with some underlying patriarchal attitude I punched him in the jaw. He didn't fight back. Maybe he understood something. The lukewarm friendship I had with him continued more or less unaffected. Maybe it was my way of announcing to the world that Lisa and I were now connected. And it was true: amazing adventures lay ahead for me and Lisa.

Winter Wilderness on Skis

Charlie had a plan for introducing me much more deeply into the winter magic of cross-county skiing. Thinking to ski from Clark, which is as far as the snow plows go up the Elk River road, into the Mt Zirkel Wilderness we prepared for being out in the winter wilderness for a few days. I was recovering from a cold, so we delayed departure for a day.

Thinking it might get steep, we added ropes and ice axes to our packs. Food, tent, sleeping bags, a primus stove and fuel; layers of clothing and of course, waxes to spread on the pine tar coatings we had torched onto the bottoms of our skis: we had everything we might need. We shouldered our giant packs and headed up the valley. Charlie was the experienced cross-country ski racer so he broke the track ahead of me through the deep snow. In spite of that extra exertion required to break track, his greater strength kicked in and eventually, by the time we were six or eight miles into the wilderness forest, he was probably about two miles ahead of me.

Suddenly, I felt a great shudder and heard a big 'Whumpf!' I stopped and looked around and I figured a big section of the snow crust I was standing on must have given way and settled. So I went on ahead. But pretty soon I thought I heard a sound like something crashing through the brush on the mountainside above me. The whole valley and mountain started to shudder and rumble again. It got louder and louder. I looked up the mountainside and saw the white cloud of snow spewing up above the trees. It looked like it was a little behind me, so I skied ahead as fast as I could. The full force of the avalanche landed behind me.

A bit later I heard another noise on the mountainside above to my right. An large elk was using the amazing muscles in its hind quarters to literally bound up the steep slope through unfathomably deep snow.

I began to wear out. Suddenly I felt the last of my strength ebb away. I lost my balance and the weight of my sixty-pound pack pinned me face-down in the deep snow. It took the last of my energy to upright myself and I found a rock on which to rest. I pulled a plastic bottle of honey out of my pack and bit off a big hunk. I felt the sweet taste melt into my throat. Fifteen minutes later, maybe even sooner, I could feel my energy suddenly recharged by the sugar! I began skiing again. My toes hurt because my ski boots were a little too small but I ignored the slight pain. Catching up to Charlie was the new name of the game. At some point an hour or so later I found him where he was waiting for me.

We skied a little farther and came across a forest service cabin -- completely closed up for the winter of course. Using knives to carefully carve out the putty around a pane of glass, we managed to get in. This would be an added luxury and we would replace the window pane and no harm would be done.

We built a fire in the stove and then we noticed a couple of Coleman lanterns... you know the kind you fill with white gas and pump up and then light the flimsy white mantles for bright light? Well, nether of us had ever run one before, but we decided to try and light them.

Meanwhile we had a candle burning on the table for a little light. As I was pumping up one of the lanterns, something came loose -- I don't know what -- and it sprayed gas all over the place!

In a split second the whole room was a burning orange ball of flames! I remember standing there beating at the flames on my jacket and realizing with absolute certainty that the cabin was going to burn to the ground! Neither of us even had our boots on! In what must have been a half a second I pictured everything that would happen: the long trek back without sleeping bags, skis or boots -- walking on frozen feet and probably being overtaken by death before we made it the ten miles back.

But then I looked around and Charlie was frantically wrestling with a fire extinguisher. *A fire extinguisher!* Can you imagine that? He had noticed one by the door as we had carried in some firewood! But he couldn't get the pin out. Then I was behind him pulling on the pin while he held it. It came out and there we were, somehow both holding the fire extinguisher, aiming it with our arms and legs all tangled together.

The fire was out just as suddenly as it had begun! A half inch of white powder from the extinguisher coated everything! The walls were scorched and brown. For at least a full minute we stood frozen, without daring to even look at each other. We both felt terrible!

Then simultaneously it occurred to both of us. The only thing to do then... the only thing... was to laugh! We both started laughing and finally looking at each other, we laughed all the harder!

We went about cooking our dinner and preparing for sleep. We would spend the next morning renovating the cabin as best as we could.

But I could not get to sleep. My foot had started to hurt. For the first couple of hours I thought it was a cramp that wouldn't go away and I kept getting up to walk around. Finally about two o'clock in the morning I got up to take some pain pills. An hour later I got up to take some more. Thinking that I might be bleeding under my toenails I took a needle and poked holes under the nails to relieve any pressure. That didn't help. About four o'clock I got up, went outside and stuck my bare feet in the snow for about half an hour until they were numb and I could no longer feel them. Then I quickly went to sleep before they thawed out.

Morning came and I could hardly walk! And ski? Skiing was excruciating! But ski I must, so in the early afternoon after we had done what we could to clean the cabin, we headed back down the valley. We made it back out late that night. So much for our extended winter climbing expedition! I drove back down to Boulder to live the quiet life with school and Lisa. My toes continued to hurt for days and then for weeks. Eventually both big toenails turned purple and finally fell off completely, revealing fresh but very wrinkled new little toenails underneath. They've been wrinkled ever since.

Inca Language Intensive at Cornell

I was studying anthropology with the same fervor I had felt a year earlier when I had begun. By taking full course loads through the summer as well as the fall, winter and spring, I was speeding toward graduation. I created special studies courses for myself with the help of my favorite professor, Gordon Hewes, and focused on learning as much as I could about the Inca culture and their language, Quechua. I realized that language carried almost all of culture. You will never really get to know another person unless you speak their language. I took every linguistics course offered at the University of Colorado and thrived.

I graduated in the spring of 1968 with a bachelor's degree in anthropology, a minor in linguistics and an almost perfect grade point average. The University added the 'phi beta kappa' and the 'summa cum laude.' I had discovered that an intensive two month summer program in the Inca language was being taught at Cornell University. I was accepted and given a full scholarship.

Lisa made arrangements to attend a weaving school nearby in New York state. She kept this a secret and, after I had rented an apartment near the Cornell campus, she surprised me by walking in. I gave her a ride down to the weaving school and it was on that journey that we mastered the art of making love while driving on the highways. She was small and could sit on my lap while I kept the car under control. Passing truckers might look down from their cabs and wonder. Fifty years later, while sifting through shared fond memories, Lisa made a point of reminding me how much she had enjoyed what we had called our "acrobatic sex."

I was persistent in my Inca language studies but I was anything but a natural at learning languages. Lisa was at weaving school a few hundred miles away and I was pacing the streets night after night trying to finish memorizing the phrases, grammar and vocabularies for the next day in class. This went on for two months. It was supposed to be an intensive immersion in the Inca language and it definitely was. It was taught in Spanish so I was actually learning two languages at once.

Lisa and I meandered back to Colorado at the end of the summer. I was now ready to return to Peru and Bolivia. Lisa wanted to go with me.

Friends from Steamboat wanted us to accompany them down to Taos, New Mexico where we admired the communal adobe architecture being created at Morningstar and New Buffalo by tribes of happy naked hippies. We attended a peyote meeting with the local Pueblo Indians and were welcomed and included by John Pedro and Little Joe, known locally as 'magic Indians,' and by hippie visionary Justin Case who had devoted his life to helping all and everyone 'just in case' he was needed. My friend Joe Sharp had migrated from San Francisco to Santa Fe and helped us find our way. A lot of time was spent standing around with our hands in our pockets waiting to find out what actually might be happening next. It was a slow-moving life style.

I Decided to Go to Peru with Cameron

I arranged for us to deliver a drive-away car to Miami, Florida. An African-American lady in a hotel there told Lisa that she certainly was "a wimmin among wimmins" if she was willing to follow me down to "where all them snakes and vampire bats is."

> *Lisa writes: I can't remember when it was that I decided to go to Peru with Cameron. It just happened that one day I found myself packing to go with him. It hadn't been an inevitable move at all, my joining him. For months I happily dreamed of going off to England and joining the wonderful group in Leicestershire who were doing important new work in the area of teaching young children. And being myself a teacher involved in the birth of an experimental school in Boulder and full of boredom for the old ways, I looked with excitement at the prospect of joining them.*
>
> *While I was becoming increasingly involved with my thoughts of England, our friend Hans Heinzerling expressed his interest in Cam's proposed trip to South America. Gail was Hans' girlfriend. I remember one day when Gail and I were out biking around on a regular (which means spectacular) Colorado afternoon. We both expressed secret annoyance at being left out of a trip that was bound to be history-making in one way or another. We bravely agreed to accompany each other to Peru if worse came to worse (what we would do once we got there we didn't know).*
>
> *Apparently the day came when I had to decide between England and Peru. As I said, I can't remember when it was, but the trip had to get rolling, me or no me. The way I figured it finally was that I could always go to England -- even after years had passed, but a trip to Peru was something to be grabbed at and if I didn't I would have lost something enormously valuable and fun. And even from the beginning, when I first met Cam and over the months hearing bit by bit of his Peru plans, I had pictured myself, in fantasy, there participating, too. Hans slipped out of the plans for some reason. Besides, why not take your girlfriend?*
>
> *Sometime during the end of September I gave away my cat Floyd, to whom I was fiercely devoted. Her grandchild, Little Stupid (who had just produced kittens), also went. Big Stupid, Little Stupid's mother, had wandered away several months previously which solved THAT problem. I prepared to leave my apricot-col-*

ored one-room apartment in which I had so joyously and securely lived for two years. It had been a haven, airy and light, where I could play with the cats or make bread after returning home at 3:30 from the most wonderful job conceivable: teaching at a tiny school for seven and eight-year-olds. And it was a school I myself had helped to start. As much as I wanted to go with Cameron, 1 had to rip myself away from that life.

Once down in Florida we killed time by stopping to swim at beaches along the road. This is an unusual treat for two people from Colorado and we soaked it all in. I liked having all the seaweed I wanted to smell and all the warm sand I wanted to dig my toes into. I made castles and did all the other things I dream about doing with a deserted beach. The most pleasant aspect was that the beach really was deserted and red polka-dot underwear offended no one.

At the gleaming, lighted airport we were met by a man who drove us out to a cargo shed where our plane was waiting. The Amazonian-looking necklace hanging from his rear view mirror caught my eye and prompted my mind to begin picturing where I would be in the morning. It was quiet near the plane. A few people were milling around. I couldn't help but feel like a participant in a smuggling plot out there in the dark with muffled voices that spoke with Spanish accents. Out here in this remote part of the airport there were no gleaming corridors, black upholstered seats, glaring lights, arrival announcements, or stewardesses with red suits.

About 2:00 AM we got on with the eight or so other passengers. Some were missionaries with their white transparent hands, immaculate bodies and expensive-looking luggage. The whole front part of this plane was jammed with a cargo of jungle animals who had been denied entry into the USA.

This was to mark the beginning of a whole series of odd, macabre, nutty, and funny things I was to encounter in Peru. In the same category I will put the time a train we were on stopped and a woman shoved a gargantuan hog's head in through my open window to ask if I would like to buy it. The tongue, the life-less eyes and hanging entrails moved my mind to an unfamiliar realm.

Iquitos on the Amazon

Through the night we flew. The next day, October 2nd, 1968, Cameron and I landed in Iquitos, a city in northern Peru on the Amazon River. We were far away from our final destination in southern Peru, but we were in Peru. All I had been able to see for the longest time when I looked out the airplane window was tangled green and a muddy snake-like river cutting through it.

We were to be in Iquitos a week. During that time we slept in two cheap hotels (one of which had cute little lizards on the ceiling and termites in the walls) and on the deck of the Bardales an African Queen kind of boat tied up at the river.

No roads lead to Iquitos. To get there you have to be born there, fly there or come down the Amazon. Besides the city, which is up on high ground, there's a river village of shacks on stilts called Belen. Down there are boats and canoes tied up edge to edge along the muddy oozy bank. Down there most people are up by 4:00 AM carrying around big crates of monkeys and birds, loads of bananas, melons, charcoal, giant turtles, babies, or small goods to be sold up at the market. The nights we slept on the Bardales we, too, would wake up at this time. With dozens of roosters crowing at fifteen-second-intervals all over the village, sleep was out of the question. After having coffee with the captain we would walk fifteen minutes up to the main part of the city for a big breakfast. By this time the market up there would really be buzzing.

This market filled me with terror and amazement. A thousand unfamiliar smells and noises and sights bombarded me at once. There were stalls for monkey meat. Food was frying, boiling, smoking, crackling or rotting everywhere. Peelings and skins were piled up under and around the stalls. Greasy smoke billowed up. We would make our way down the crowded street past the piles of food. On one corner men and boys of all ages were assembled reading Spanish comics. On another, a pig almost too fat to walk was sleeping and grunting. All day we bought snacks. Sometimes they were foot-long plastic containers filled with cherry, lemon, or raspberry flavored ice. Once we sampled some sweetened raw egg-white whipped to a froth. It was good. For lunch, in the fancier restaurants above, we'd have fish, salads made of palm hearts, papaya, and fresh juices. Lunch on the Bardales was sweet coffee, rolls, and chicken soup that contained not only rice but sometimes a chicken foot. Water for these meals invariably came from the very brown and often oily river alongside the boat. Here, both night and day garbage was dumped in. Women washed their clothes in it, children pissed in it, hogs cooled off in it, and everyone drank it. I must openly confess here that the thought of drinking this water frightened me. But I think it was the even greater fear of offending the captain of the Bardales, when he so graciously handed me a cup of coffee, that made me swallow it enthusiastically. I did manage to dunk my hot body in the water briefly one day when we did some canoing on another part of the river.

Ready to Dip Into the Amazon River

We had settled upon the Bardales as a base there in Iquitos because it was eventually headed south towards Pucallpa, the town from where we could begin traveling overland to an area Cam had previously picked out as a likely spot for remote Quechua villages. We hoped to find one of these villages and stay awhile to get to know the Indians. We were not to reach such a village until about five weeks later. The Bardales was step number one in getting there. Eventually the captain was ready and the little boat moved south. Night number one was spent in the bottom of a little rowboat tied along side the Bardales... no room anywhere else that night. It was clammy and drizzly, but I remember sleeping well.

Lisa Sitting on the Bardales in Iquitos

Lisa nicknamed our captain 'mustache.' He ruled the heroic Indian boys with whom Lisa fell so passionately in love. Night and day five fine young Indians slept in the grease of the engine and doused in and out of the river tying and untying the boat while the other passengers lazily sagged in their hammocks on the deck. The young Indians knew they were river gods.

The second night out on the river was in our own multi-colored hammock we had bought in Iquitos. That night it rained hard and the visibility became too poor to proceed, so we tied up along the shore under a mass of overhanging trees. Instantly the mosquitoes closed in on us.

Cam and I had developed an uncontrollable hatred of mosquitoes in Florida when one night, while we were asleep in the car, they tortured us for hours. If we closed the windows it got too hot. If we opened them even a quarter of an inch they came in.

This night on the Bardales we set out with tight-lipped determination to make an impenetrable sleeping compartment by rigging our blue mosquito net over the hammock. Everything we tried failed. The mosquitoes would bite us from beneath or fly through the holes we had torn in it from trying to pin it in place. Finally, wrapped in ponchos and other odds and ends, we slept while the mosquitoes bit at my ankles and buzzed in Cameron's ears.

During the day on the Bardales I would read, knit or just watch the goings on. Cam and the captain would discuss our plans. We were to get off the boat during the night, they decided, at a particular point on the river, as the Bardales would soon be branching off on another tributary and go up the Marañón. Another, bigger boat would be passing by. Pucallpa was still about two-hundred miles away. I pictured us climbing off into a thick mess of snake-infested jungle in the middle of the night, and was terrified. We would not be able to see. We would never find the other boat. We would run out of food. My hair would get tangled in the branches. This had to be the ultimate in danger, I thought.

As it was, the captain let us off towards the end of the second night. There was a clear area. Not one minute had elapsed when I saw through the darkness little houses on stilts and a few people. At least we would not be alone. A nice man brought us to his house and we climbed up into it to sleep the few remaining hours of night. Again, up went the blue mosquito net. I was greatly relieved. When morning came we heard a woman crying and woke up. As it turned out, there was a terrible diarrhea epidemic in the village and most of the children were sick. What could we do for them but give from our supply of diarrhea pills? We did.

Later that day we paid a small wily-looking man with a gold tooth to take us in his motor boat down to the little village of Yucurruchi where the big fast boat would come. It took an hour. We were greeted at the bank by a nice woman and a boy who took us to the local Guardia (police) station. Here, again, we were enthusiastically greeted. For several days we stayed there and it was the hungriest few days I have ever experienced. The Guardias lent us their beds but never offered us any food so we were forced to eat what the local store could provide. This turned out to be cans of very greasy, strong-flavored tuna fish filled with little pieces of bone and cartilage, and sweet orange pop. This diet made me very crabby. It was disgusting. We were both very dirty and sweaty too. When shown where the Guardias bathed. I recoiled in horror. Or at least I didn't like the looks of it one bit. A steep slippery muddy bank led down to the same old muddy water I'd been looking at for a week. Cameron jumped in eagerly and soaped himself up. I stood there revolted. When one of the Guardias asked why I didn't go in and wash myself and my hair I became furious. I wouldn't have considered putting my big toe in that slime, much less coating my hair with it. Needless to say I kept my mouth politely shut.

Here at Yucurruchi were insects almost as infuriating as mosquitoes. Each looked like a grain of paprika. When one got in your bed or clothes and bit you it was as though someone had pushed you against a hot stove. A square foot of your body would get red and sting like a burn.

The tuna and pop diet abruptly ended when the Adolfo came in a few days later. Once on board we went straight to the bar and wolfed down big hunks of cake and cups of coffee. Although not nutritious, they temporarily filled our stomachs and satisfied our taste buds.

I liked our week on the Adolfo. It was many times bigger than the Bardales. We got three hot meals a day, could buy fruit cheaply from the natives on shore, and even adopted a system whereby we both could sleep comfortably in the single hammock. During the day we'd take turns lying in it and reading. I'd knit, take photographs, drink beer, or munch some papaya. There was a shower, which we took advantage of, and a john that was more than a hole. At every meal we ate the same thing: beans, a little meat, and boiled potatoes... for a side dish we had boiled bananas... for breakfast there was coffee and rolls but with only two table-spoons of butter for eight people. This, supplemented by fruit eaten in between meals, suited me just fine. Cam does not like being inactive for so long, though, and began getting bored.

Lisa in Our Hammock on the Adolfo

The most exciting thing about the Adolfo was that it was a real feast for the eyes. There were so many humorous and interesting things to look at. Halfway through the week a man tied his large rooster RIGHT underneath our hammock. Besides letting out ear-splitting crows it went to the bathroom all over everything. There was a man with nothing but a bundle of about fifty brooms. There was the matter of the loretos on the deck below -- thousands of parakeet-like birds crated up and making a racket. There were charming-looking children and babies of every age to watch and make friends with. Mothers nursed, husbands and wives squabbled, and men played cards and got drunk. With fifty or sixty people up there I could always count on entertainment.

When the boat landed in Pucallpa finally we walked a hot half mile into town and chanced upon a man wheeling a cart full of ice cream sandwiches. I slurped this delicious cool substance down my throat and felt truly wonderful.

In Pucallpa we visited a group of missionaries. The girl that came over on the plane with us was supposed to be there, although we never saw her. The thing that struck me about this particular group was the setting in which they lived. It was as though they had lifted a neat little upper-middle-class suburb right out of somewhere in Connecticut and placed it gently down in the midst of this wild jungle. The lawns were neatly mowed and hedges clipped (by Indians brought in from nearby jungle). The houses were low rambling ranch style. They had their bay windows, driveways, and backyard barbecue rotisseries. The children had two wheelers, piano lessons, and dogs. There was a lake nearby where they all swam in country club fashion. We swam too and would have really liked it except that it was HOT. The heat of the sun is so intense that this lake never cools.

To get out of Pucallpa we waited practically one whole day on the outskirts of the city for a truck headed for Lima. We waited for hours and relieved the boredom we felt by eating an entire pineapple and letting the juice slowly trickle down our throats. Finally, towards the end of the afternoon, a man with a gasoline truck came by and we hopped in. This man was a horrible driver. He went twice as fast as the conditions allowed. The roads were rutted and curvy, but most terrifying of all was that this man's eyes were all clouded. Could he have had cataracts? We went on and on and after dark and I discovered something new about Peruvian truck drivers. Whenever another vehicle passes they honk furiously and flick their headlights to all different intensities (including off). Honking and flicking like this leaves very little time for steering. And when the headlights are off, the road cannot be seen. About midnight we stopped at a restaurant and Cam and the driver got out. I stretched out on the seat meanwhile and got five minutes of sleep. When Cam came back he told me we were to change trucks. The new one was a little uncovered pickup that was half filled with pineapples, a sewing machine, and a spare tire. Trying to stretch out and sleep on these things with three other people was not an easy trick. Night is endless when you want morning to come. When it did, we were arriving at Tingo Maria where we ate well and slept one night. I saw a funeral procession in the street.

From Tingo we boarded a bus whose destination was Lima. This ride was to be harrowing for us both. It was to last twenty-eight hours. Needless to say, it never stopped when we had to go to the bathroom. After the first three hours on the road we stopped for five hours while, in the pouring rain and darkness of night, men and bulldozers tried to clear a series of huge muddy landslides off the road. We finally continued on our way hour after hour, jiggling, jogging, bumping and lurching along until our intestines were all in the wrong places. It was impossible to get even a minute's sleep at night. I tried it several times, having an entire seat to myself, but my head knocked against everything. My whole body was flung up and down a thousand times and I became even more tired trying to brace myself against this rough movement. I preferred sitting there in a stupor to anything else. Cam, being too large to sleep comfortably on his seat, rested his head on the hard metal back of the seat in front of him. Hour after hour it bumped up and down as he tried to sleep.

I actually began to feel on the verge of death. No one on the bus had been on as long as we. The second afternoon a woman got on and sat in back of me. Soon she began depositing large globules of spit every sixty seconds on the floor. They landed with a big splat. Pretty soon there was something close to a puddle down there. My sneakers started slipping around in it. I remember getting some relief later when the bus made a food stop at a little restaurant. I ordered an orange pop and sat down across the street to drink it. We were now only about six hours from Lima, and another step closer to our destination. Soon we began climbing higher and higher.

Although the view from the windows got more exciting with every thousand feet we gained, my stomach and head began to feel more and more uncomfortable. This at last was the Peru I had always imagined. The terrain was bare, brown, and rocky. Men with herds of sheep and alpacas stood in nearby fields. Their knitted hats were brightly colored and had ear-flaps (which never seemed to cover their ears, but were nice anyway). We could see white peaks in the distance, and little stone huts close by. Women in long skirts were on the road. Once over this pass we began descending at a dizzy speed. The altitude (sixteen thousand feet) combined with the shattering bumps (caused by four-foot wide potholes) and curvy road made our bodies rebel. I soon knew I was going to throw up because my mouth got watery. We got out the blue Penney's towel I had bought back in Boulder and I threw up in it six times. It was all colored bright orange from the pop. Finally we threw the towel out the window.

Lima, Peru

Lima was not the glistening city I had expected. The image I had formed fell away when I saw the solid gray sky and dirty streets and buildings. I also could not seem to find anything I liked to eat there. Cameron never got tired of 'lomos' which I describe as big piles of greasy white rice and he describes as a fine fluffy serving of rice mixed with vegetables and chopped steak. I remember liking the first one he ordered for me but thereafter stuck to cheese sandwiches (which every restaurant seemed to have) and tea. One night he took us to an expensive German restaurant where I stuffed with roast duck and applesauce.

Our week in Lima would have been uneventful if it had not been for the younger brother of a person Cam had met in the Quechua class the summer before at Cornell. He was a fine, very pink-cheeked fourteen-year-old with all the straightforwardness of a grown man. He brought us many places. In the barriadas (unbelievable slums encircling Lima) I saw a ragged dog chase after and bite a little child. In the main produce center of Lima, where all the vegetables come in from the country, he showed us acres of neatly bagged up, in infinite variety, corn, potatoes, beans, carrots, lettuce and all kinds of unfamiliar roots and tubers. Trucks were unloading everywhere. Men carried bulging sacks on their backs. There was a small street for each variety of food. In a poor country such as Peru it was enigmatic to see such masses of food assembled. Bags and bags of pure solid food. This was to be the case, I discovered, almost wherever food was sold in Peru. There was always a lot of it. Cubic yards stacked up until one almost tired of looking at its sheer bulk. The immediacy of its smell, color, and texture soon overwhelms one used to the neatly packaged non-foods we see in orderly rows on supermarket shelves.

Louis Felipe, the young boy, took us to a variety of museums, several of which displayed those partially decomposed bodies known as 'mummy bundles.' The ancient Incas, when a person died, stuffed him, knees pressed to chest, into a rope basket. The bodies are dried up but still look like people. It was fascinating to examine them in detail. They still had their toenails, teeth, and hair. Although each was enclosed in a glass case I could get very close and if the rope bundle had been removed, even look into the stomachs. Sometimes the mummy of a cat or baby (even now with evidences of pudginess) would be included in the same bundle as an adult.

Cusco and Machu Picchu

Having tired of Lima and having had our fill temporarily of overland transportation, we decided to fly to Cusco by jet. This way, Cam said, we could cover a lot of ground in a short time and we would be a lot closer to the Quechua area he had in mind. In the airport we felt, once again, in touch with the other world where coffee shops, fancy luggage and red carpets are commonplace. Once there in Cusco we wandered around for a day or two, looked at ruins, and played countless games of checkers while waiting for a train to Machu Picchu. We enthusiastically took in those mysteri-

ous carved stones in Cusco, but they were nothing compared with the mysteries that confronted us at Machu Picchu .

We arrived at the station just as the train was pulling out. We both ran and Cam managed to jump on. I couldn't make it. Right away I began blubbering, and a group of perhaps fifteen individuals assembled around me and began offering condolences and suggestions. My frustration rose fast. Everyone was talking at once. One man seemed to have a real idea about how I could get back on the train. He was pointing and gesturing. Having no money with me, I felt completely helpless. People had started to leave. I began trying to think what I would do. I sat there in the station, seething with frustration and embarrassment. The man was trying to arrange something, but I knew I would never understand what he wanted me to do. But inside of five minutes there was Cameron back at the station. He had jumped off the train. Quickly we got in a truck and we met the train again at the first stop above the city. I sat there feeling dumb, ridiculous, and ashamed simultaneously. I had completely lost my cool for no reason at all. I didn't speak for an hour.

At Machu Picchu we were able to spend three relaxed days wandering around the ruins, taking photographs, revisiting favorite spots, watching the baby alpacas play, and meditating about what could have possibly gone on here centuries ago. After our wanderings we would return to the bare stone house with its reconstructed roof of thatch that we had claimed as our own. Here, for free, we could lie on our sleeping bags and look out directly into the wide sky or over to the craggy peaks all covered with hairy green jungle growth. For days we watched the frantic tourists come in droves to rush around for one hour and see only a quarter of the whole. Then they'd have to rush down again so as not to get behind their pre-determined schedule. We cooked and ate in the little house and set candles about at night. We really had a successful time. One afternoon in the rain we made a triumphant ascent of Huayna Picchu, a neighboring peak. The view and the height and the plunging sheer rock walls practically made my eyes cross. And the thought that at one time real people inhabited that inaccessible, steep, and exposed place made my mind reel with excitement.

Typhoid

Juliaca, our next stop by train, was a dismal spot but at last we could begin to feel close to Cam's village. We stayed in a hotel where there was supposed to be hot water. But fifteen seconds under an ice cold shower convinced us differently. Right after we got there I began feeling very tired and wouldn't go out and eat with Cam. Before long I couldn't eat at all or even sleep because of a persistent general ache in my body that made me toss and come out with a few genuine groans. I threw up and had the trots. We began talking about going to the little clinic there to be looked at and possibly tested. In the morning I wobbled the few blocks to the clinic where, in the midst of a blood test I threw up what was left in my stomach. Cam translated for the doctor. The tests showed I had typhoid and anemia. After being given a brand new roll of toilet paper I was brought upstairs and stuffed into a most comfortable clean bed with a hot water bottle at my feet. At last I was warm. The strange surroundings and long needle I saw being brought in left me mildly hysterical, though, and I felt great relief knowing that Cam could sleep in the other bed (free).

For three days I lay there, six hours of each day with a needle in my arm squirting in an antibiotic. The eight or so people that seemed to be taking care of me were wonderful. They brought delicious food and were patient when I couldn't understand them. I am convinced that no big hospital could match the care they took of me. When the time came for me to leave we went to the house of a Peace Corps guy Cam had met while I was sick. We stayed with Jeff three to four days while I recuperated more and practiced spinning wool like the Indian women.

A Mobile Gold Mine

After a few days at Jeff's, I was rested enough for the ride we had planned to Ananea. Cam had heard that there was a good possibility of finding a small village within walking distance of this spot. There was also a gold mine in Ananea. We piled into a truck one afternoon with many others and their belongings. This ride we had along some pigs in a big sack. We drove along and towards evening it began to get cold. We were climbing high. Cam and I were seated on two oil drums towards the cab. I was glad that when we stopped for supper the driver pulled a tarp over the top. About midnight it began to snow lightly. The zipper to my parka refused to move.

At what seemed like about 1:00 AM (although I hardly ever had any way of knowing what time it was in Peru) the driver stopped at a fork in the road, came around to the back of the truck to indicate that this was our getting off point. This was the closest to Ananea that he was going. It was only a short walk from there. With difficulty we picked our way towards the open part of the truck -- over lumps of sleeping babies, and around bent-over adults. Cam paid the driver and he drove off leaving us alone in the midst of a VAST empty plain. The headlights disappeared completely after about fifteen minutes. We walked away from the road and pitched our tent. It seemed to me at the time so completely insane to be out there at all, but I mechanically helped set things up. During the night it snowed and we awoke to a 'pampa blanca,' or a high plain dusted with snow. For breakfast there at 16,000 feet I cooked a pot of chocolate pudding, then collapsed. The altitude finally got me. I could offer Cam no help at all in packing up our things. All I could do was lie there and look dumb.

When morning came I jubilantly spied glacier ice through a hole in the clouds. Part of a line of twenty-thousand-foot peaks stood just to the northeast of us. We walked down the road toward a gold mine about which we had been told some weeks before. We had met a Bolivian lady who had given us directions and the name of the mine explaining that she had a Canadian husband who worked there. We therefore anticipated finding one more English-speaking contact before setting off toward a small Indian village. A yellow pickup truck came jouncing down the road and a man with a British accent hailed us from the driver's seat. He turned out to be the chief operator of the mine. Later he told us that at the time he had met us he had been transporting a gold brick between his feet. He unhesitatingly gave us instructions to set ourselves up in style in the mine quarters for a few days.

Mr. Williams, the chief operator of the dredge, returned after a day and a half. In the meantime we had been enjoying breakfasts of bacon and eggs, jam, butter and salads, all of which, except for the eggs, were practically unheard of by the Indians.

So we stuffed ourselves for four languid days there at sixteen-thousand feet and at night we had an entire room with a big bed in it to ourselves. Slowly we began to get to know Mr. Williams. He was in his fifties. He had operated mines of various sorts in thirty-four different countries around the world. He was a colonial-style Englishman.

"A little alcohol in them and they revert right back to savagery, these Indians. You can dress 'em up in a suit of clothes, but they're never very far away from being animals. You gotta watch 'em all the time."

He had a Bolivian wife whom he had acquired only five years earlier, and he had a little daughter who spoke Spanish instead of English, much to his disgust. "We're going to Canada for the rest of our lives in another year," he told me. "I can't have my daughter growing up and marrying a South American man. These South Americans cannot be faithful husbands," he explained. "I don't even want my daughter growing up around the savages."

The next night he and I sat up around the dinner table after Lisa had gone to bed. It was clear that he was starved for English conversation. He began telling me of his latest exploits. He told me about the eighteen-year-old girl he'd fucked in San Francisco a few months back. He'd also managed to fuck a few of the wives on a cruise ship, getting cleverly away with this not only behind his own wife's back, but behind the backs of the other womens' husbands. I listened to his tales of conquest for nearly two hours before we finally climbed away from the dinner table and waddled off to our respective mates.

For four days we ate and rested and listened to the tales of Mr. Williams. We spent an entire day climbing around through the dredge itself, seeing just how the monster managed to digest gold out of the earth. It literally ate its way along through the high Andean plain floating in its own little pond which it constantly filled in behind itself. It looked just like a huge misplaced organ supported greasily in its own insidious bodily fluid, a parasite on its earthen host. Every ten days Mr. Williams drove his pickup down to Juliaca with another gold brick worth $26,000.

I was summoned to check in with the local civil guard post. I was surprised at its existence in such an out-of-the-way place. It was a little shack on the edge of the mining camp. The Sargent was at his table flanked by two younger civil guards. He was not friendly and kept insisting that, if there was a village called Sina, it lay in the other direction from which I thought. Unfortunately for him, the younger civil guards were friendly and encouraging to me and agreed with my understanding of the geography. After an hour or so I continued on my way. My papers seemed to be in order.

Walking to Sina

Lisa on Pampa Blanca

Saturday it snowed on Pampa Blanca, where the mine was located, making it all blanca. Sunday was nicer, so we set off from the mine carrying the slab of bacon and the pound of butter which Mr. Williams had kindly given us. He drove us from the dining room up to the dredge after breakfast. On the way we passed an alpaca which for some superstitious reason the Indians had never sheared in its whole life long. Its hair hung in a straight and flowing curtain all the way to the ground beneath its feet.

After a prolonged series of good-byes and good-lucks (I believe he was overwhelmed at our courage and optimism) we left him and began walking towards a Quechua Indian village called Sina which Cam had been collecting information about for a few weeks. Taking all estimates into account, it was anywhere from eight hours to eight days away.

This was what we had come for. I was filled with a vague ter-

ror at what we were about to do. We would surely become hopelessly lost. Our food supply would run out. No one would be able to find us, etc. Not one thought did I give to what we'd find in Sina. It was simply too far away to worry about. At hand we had a sort of puzzle that had to be carefully completed. We would be walking at high altitudes over unfamiliar territory with only a roughly drawn map. We might not see anyone else the whole way. Any kind of unexpected problem could pop up. I was acutely aware of our vulnerability. Cameron moved towards Sina with relaxed confidence. I, though, remember having the feeling that we were on an endless journey to nowhere. But at the same time I was amused and excited. The challenges and strange things would be truly fun. If we ever made it, we would find at the far away end a bunch of little surprises: Sina.

The dredge sank out of sight and we moved like microscopic specks to the right around an immense snowy peak. It rose to over twenty thousand feet. Here right away was a new experience: being close to one of those. On and on we went for three complete days. The land we passed over was as eerie as any in a science fiction film. My state of mind was coloring all that I saw. It was simply that I was afraid. The fear felt like the kind I used to feel when I was a child. It was a basic fear, not one having to do with a social situation. It was like walking in the dark when I was a child or looking into the darkness of my room at night. The shapes looked menacing. The continual mist wouldn't let my eyes see anything clearly. We couldn't see very far ahead of us. It was like running very fast and not knowing what was ahead. The alpacas we'd see in the distance looked floating. There were no noises. I was too alone to feel good anymore. The occasional stone houses along the path were crumbling and deserted. Boulders taller than Cam or any elephant for that matter were strewn along the path. They were smooth and rounded. Big white birds swooped around and made noises. Lizards were on the path. The mist moved like smoke does from a cigarette.

For three days I went on with Cam seeing things in this way. Cam was carrying eighty pounds and I forty pounds. We were walking at altitudes up to seventeen-thousand feet and there were obstacles. Every half hour a fast deep stream crossed our path. Sometimes there were stepping stones, sometimes not. It took time *to get across these. At times we had to find large rocks to put in the water. Cam would always have to carry one pack over, then the other, and come back to help me. I never could balance too well with that pack.*

We ate a lot on the trail. Every now and then we'd stop and munch some bread or cheese. Williams had kindly supplied us with a slab of bacon, bread, a pound of butter, jelly, and cheese. In a Cusco supermarket I had found dry soups, canned peaches, chocolate bars, prunes, tea, kool-aid and nuts. I used up food fast. In some places it was so much work to walk that we were stopping to rest and eat every five or ten minutes. I could not believe this as it was happening. Each of my steps were only a few inches apart. My chest had a pain in it. I was always hungry.

We passed some cattle. Fat cattle, which surprised me. I didn't know cattle could grow fat at sixteen-thousand feet. A young man appeared ahead of us. He rode a white pony and drove two mules ahead of him. The sight of two strange gringos frightened his mules and it took him a moment to get them back under control. He then came over to us and asked where we were going. We told him Sina, and he said that Sina was where he was from.

"Why are you going?" he asked.

"Oh, I want to study Quechua," I replied.

"You're off adventuring then," he said and he smiled.

"That's right."

He spoke good Spanish and was about the same age as we.

The rainy season had begun, and although the next day kept itself shrouded in clouds, we got a few peeks at the twenty-thousand-foot summit we were passing. We traveled quite well that day. We climbed up perhaps a thousand feet that morning, and finally reached a pair of huge cairns at about noon which marked the high point of the pass. We must have been up to at least seventeen-thousand feet before we plunged down the swampy tundra on the other side into the mist toward a nice place for lunch. The afternoon was spent descending.

The sides of the valley were still steep. We met a few people on the trail in the early part of the day. They spoke no Spanish and seemed pretty surprised to see us, and were pretty mystified as to what to try and tell us. I was trying out speaking in Quechua, young and innocent as a newborn Indian babe.

We passed a graveyard and Lisa said, "How interesting! Let's go look at the graves!"

But I thought about some of the things I had read in my anthropology courses about how Indians generally think gringos are all size, shape and variety of devils, body snatchers and rapists. I said, "Hmmm, better not. Respect for the dead and all. Never know what they might think if they saw us poking around in a graveyard."

And then there was a swamp. We lost the trail part way through it. There were steep mounds of rock too. The terrain itself, even in the flatter places, was uneven and difficult to walk on. Deep grooves made by horses, tufts of hard moss, squishy wet places, and steep pebbly surfaces were a hindrance to fast smooth traveling.

> *The next night we camped off the trail on a high unprotected spot. It rained and we had to rig up rubber ponchos outside to keep the tent from leaking. We cooked supper inside on Cam's primus stove. When morning came it was still wet so we cooked bacon in there and opened a can of peaches.*
>
> *We kept walking, sometimes up and sometimes down. We saw two Indian women sitting on the side of a hill tending alpacas. Halfway through the third day, during a downpour, a man in a house down below the path yelled for us to come in for a cup of coffee. We did and it felt good. My fear this day was replaced by misery. The problem was that my knees hurt. We had been walking downhill since the day before and the weight was putting a strain on them.*
>
> *The man told us that there was only an hour or two 'till Sina. I had noticed that the houses along the way were beginning to look lived in. More and more land was planted. As we dropped slowly to ten-thousand feet the plants became leafier. There were bushes finally. Things were growing taller. It even felt the smallest bit like jungle, but nothing grew high. Cam told me that we had passed a couple of Indians hiding behind bushes. I had seen no one. Can you blame them for being afraid of us the way we looked? Rubber ponchos over high green packs. Hunchbacks. A woman in strange boots, wool hat, and pants. I looked way down the path ahead to find more evidences of a village ahead. What I saw was two Indian men running furiously down the path away from us.*
>
> *"Cam, did you see those men, look!" He hadn't seen them,*

so I couldn't be sure. But to me they looked absolutely panicked. They had seen us. Oh God.

On His Floor with his Seven Children

In a few minutes we walked into Sina. Evening had arrived and the weather was breaking up. Everything ceased being mysterious. I was transferred to the world of the three little pigs. Here before us was a soft green valley dotted with clusters of tiny stone houses. The mist had lifted and for the first time that day I saw evidences of the sun. The wet shaggy thatch roofs steamed. Cows bellowed on the hillsides. But where were the inhabitants? An empty village. Not a single being walked in the courtyard.

Ah yes, there was someone. A man approached nervously. He and Cam greeted each other. I did not understand. The man pointed to the houses. Right then men's heads began appearing above stone walls and around corners. I saw a couple of embarrassed smiles. The men came out and walked over to us. They saw the guitar. He showed it to them and played, 'Ghost Riders in the Sky' and 'Johnny B Goode.'

After this, things relaxed. We were escorted to the home of the village 'mayor.' Teofilo invited us to sleep right there on his floor with his seven children and handed me a bottle of liquid for my knees.

Valley Walls above Sina

Pre-dawn rooster right outside the door. No more time for sleep. The kids were getting up. Out of our sleeping bags.

Here came a kid with coffee and bread. No one came to join us. Everyone was busy. We ate our bread and coffee and wandered out through the chickens. Did I see a woman through the smoke in the next room? Was she the governor's wife? Should I go inside and say hello? No, she was very shy.

"Well, Lisa, let's wander down this way." The sun came out. A flood of little girls stopped, standing in clusters, each with her finger stuck pensively in the corner of her mouth. The little girls watched us uncertainly. Then one came winding her way through the tall greenery and shyly handed Lisa a flower. Oh my god! *A flower!* Every one of them had now to make her donation of flowers to Lisa until Lisa had such fist-fulls that the danger of dropping some made it difficult to receive more. Finally the smallest and shyest little girl tiptoed over and contributed her flower.

> *The little girls knew what I was all about the moment they saw me. Loading my arms with flowers was only a little bit scary for them. But it was fun, too, because they knew I would love it. I almost sank into the ground with joy and the weight of the flowers they heaped into my arms -- a million varieties of painfully fragrant blossoms on long stems and in short squat bunches. Nothing so beautiful has ever happened to me. They were not afraid, how absurd. They knew me already.*
>
> *And. I knew them, too. Every one, with her face full of excitement and shyness. Right down to the sets of brown stubby toes I knew them. If I picked one out with my eyes she would melt away behind some bigger girls with a soft frightened laugh. I had to react to them as a group. No one at that point wanted to be the sole object of my attention. But later they didn't mind so much. Later they let me put flowers under the strings that tied their pigtails.*

Lisa Bonding with the Village Girls

Drink until Dawn

Lisa smiled and opened and closed her eyes with each additional fistful of flowers, for that was all she could do.

Along came the village head, Teofilo. "These people need a house to stay in," he announced to a couple of passing men, and soon it was decided that Roberto would be the person to ask. Before much of the afternoon was out, Roberto had appeared and we had a house. He said we could have it for a month, as he was staying in his other house in another village two-and-a-half hours walk up an adjoining valley. So we gave him the equivalent of a dollar which others later told us had been unnecessarily extravagant.

Our house was the same as all the others with its stone walls loosely but cleverly fitted together; its earth floor, and its raised sleeping platform of bamboo slats - no wider than a narrow single bed.

While Lisa set about preparing our first home-cooked meal, I walked over to a spot on the edge of the plaza where ten or fifteen men were finishing digging out the square foundation for a new house. A trench about a foot and a half wide had been dug around the small perimeter and I realized that a cornerstone had just been placed in the trench. A bottle of drink and a pile of coca leaves were placed on the cornerstone and people began picking up the coca leaves and counting out a specific number of them - a dozen or so. They arranged the leaves carefully in their hands, as though they were playing cards, and once they were counted and arranged, they were placed in a tin cup and some of the drink was added. Then the cup would be given to one of the men who had no doubt dug the trench

- the ones whose pants and shirts were rough-woven of a cloth that looked like burlap, and who spoke no Spanish at all. The cup would be handed to one of them, and they would throw it down the length of the trench while the others yelled, "hueyfalalay," and "q'intukuy, taytay." The bottle was passed around to the rest of us along with coca leaves and cigarettes.

It was about that time that I learned whose house it was going to be: Alberto's... was he the village drunk and buffoon? Alberto told me that we would sit on the ground and drink until dawn. I assumed he was either joking or wishfully thinking. I was already late for Lisa's supper; it was getting dark and everyone seemed to have melted away, so I melted away to dinner too.

An hour or two later it was raining. I decided that the very least I could do would be to contribute our two ponchos for a roof, so I carried them out to Alberto's new house and helped set them up. I began to realize that Alberto hadn't been kidding about his vigil. The idea of sitting outside drinking in the cold 'till dawn didn't attract me but other people began to return from their dinners. We sat down under the ponchos. Talk was going pretty slowly. Alberto was officiating, pouring out the warm anise-flavored alcohol.

A few candles burned bravely against the night wind. Alberto was nursing a little plastic Japanese portable transistor record player so by god we had music. Out of tune and tinny-sounding as the music was, it cut a little festivity into the night. We drank a few bottles of the alcohol. A few of the men who had helped move the stone foundation into place took small sips of drink when it was passed their way. It was clearly not really their night for celebration. They were very quiet and looked infinitely patient while Alberto expressed increasingly drunken appreciation.

Before long I found myself feeling warm and cozy under the poncho. People talked over the scratchy huayños, as the Indian music is called, and I found it very easy to just sit and try to listen. Nothing was being demanded of me. The candle flames grew warmer and warmer.

Alberto was talking of people... names I didn't know: Humberto, Santiago, Policarpio and dozens of others... I listened and eventually figured out one or two relationships. So-and-so is brother of so-and-so...

"And he is not here!" exclaimed Alberto. "How can I thank him if he is not even here with us!" I suddenly realized that Teofilo, the governor was not among those present. He had apparently been the one to lay the cornerstone during the afternoon.

"I'm so glad, so very happy that you all are here now... here now to help me begin this house on this night in such a fine way. My fiancée, who lives in Bolivia will one day be here and we will live here together so happily, because of all you wonderful people who have come here tonight when even my own brothers have not come. Yes, that is why I'm crying now. Because on this night, this one night which is so very important to me, my own brothers have deserted me. Yes, left me unhappy and completely deserted. Yes, so that is why Don Cristobal, I am so grateful that you have come tonight. Salud! Don Cristobal mi amigo!" he sobbed, now standing.

Cristobal told him that he was most honored to be there and that it was truly wonderful to be able to contribute to Alberto's so well-deserved happiness!

"And you, Emilio!" Alberto continued toasting and thanking each person individually which gave me a golden opportunity and I learned all their names... almost, anyway. Alberto's speech soared on for half an hour. I was swept in. I was truly in Sina. The emotions made me all sticky and then warm inside.

So before long I stood up and said, "I have only one thing to say. I would like to say only one thing! Alberto... here Alberto you are having your house opened in such a perfect way with the help of such fine friends, yes I would like to say only one thing!"

"Como las onzas de oro!" someone toasted.

My voice tightened with emotion, "I would like to say that you, Alberto, who live here in Sina, if you have one or two friends... ...even if you have only two friends! Then you have something more valuable even than money! With only two friends then you have more here in Sina than the wealthy people I have seen, because, no, you cannot buy friends with money!"

Alberto thanked me from the bottom of his heart and I knew I had been a success. I began to feel sleepy. The speeches died down, and soon it was time to stand up and leave. I promised that I would begin helping with the construction of the house the very next day. I didn't know that it would be months before more work would actually begin.

Nemia - A Six-Year-Old Woman

We were to live in Sina two-and-a-half weeks. I value the time I spent there because of any place I have ever seen, it comes closest to my idea of what life for me should be like. It comes closest to my dream. In Sina the noise of a vacuum cleaner never intrudes. In Sina time to take out the trash never comes. Sina was where Cam and I supported each other in our respective adventures. It was where we slept side by side at night in a house with a dirt floor and no furniture except a bench and a table and a bamboo platform to sleep on. We could have very easily smiled in our sleep during those nights. We were a success from the moment we walked in there. We had wanted it so badly, and they liked us, they really did.

During those days I wanted very badly to be liked. I wanted it so much from the moment I walked into the midst of them that I sort of became tuned in to being liked. I responded with smiles and shy looks to being liked. The first thing I remember doing when the men of the village surrounded us was to play gently with their dogs. "See, I know about dogs, too. Your dog likes me -- we're friends," I beamed. Of course Cameron was doing the hard part -- talking -- but this was my way of helping. And I continued for a long time this way, exposing my vulnerability, smiling, stumbling over words, and exhibiting my ignorance at every step. All this was really there. I did not have to pretend, just resist the impulse to hide it. I wanted them to know that they need not fear a gringa lady like me.

Nemia was a six year old woman and became our confidante after a few days. She lived alone with her father, Cristobal, our kind neighbor who, along with one other man, taught school in the village. His wife lived in Puno with their older children where they were continuing school. (Sina's school only went up to third grade.) Nemia tended the fire, cooked soup, swept and tidied their house. She was a capable and beautiful child with long cheerful hair and sturdy coltish legs. She seemed always to wear dark blue and red. When her father took the day to go to the market, she would get up at 2:00 AM to cook him a hot soup. She expertly taught Cam how to make a good fire out of wet wood by blowing through a long tube.

The other little girls were equally as capable. They wore faded cotton skirts or dresses to below their knees. Each had a wool shawl called a lliklla, fastened with a big pin. When they became mothers, the lliklla would be used to carry their baby or firewood or potatoes. Now it kept them warm. They went barefoot or wore plastic shoes which I have since heard are being sent to various countries (in Africa too) by the United Nations. These shoes are horrible. They tear easily, are stiff, and don't breathe. You can buy them from huge sacks, in any color or style, all over Peru.

The Other Side of the River

The next day we decided to go and see who lived on the other side of the big green valley. We found an elegant little bridge made from a perfectly rectangular slab of stone laid across the top of a miniature canyon some fifteen-feet deep.

We began climbing the trails and passed two households where we saw no one. At the third and highest, we found two women at work weaving a rug. One was nervous and reluctant to try and communicate. The other, a thin wiry and seemingly old woman, was playful and vivacious. Neither woman knew any Spanish at all, so communication struck sporadically, like lightening in a forest. When we missed altogether, the playful lady would look up at me and laugh, her eyes chock full of happy electricity. Ilateria was her name. Her mother was still living and was said to be over a hundred years old.

Ilateria spoke a crisp and clean Quechua that was pure joy for me to listen to. I could at least make out her words. Except she spoke so rapidly and excitedly that by the time I would have a single word finally nailed down wriggling in my head, she would have changed the subject. She found my hopeless ineptitude just plain funny. I don't think she could believe that anyone could miss the point so completely. But it didn't matter.

Lisa sat down between the two women and watched them pass balls of yarn back and forth. They were stringing a web on a rack held between four sticks jammed in the ground. And if one of them dropped the ball, Lisa would retrieve it.

Amalia and Ilateria Weaving

I figured women should inevitably be able to find their own way to get along, so I trotted down across a smaller side stream and up the other side to a large and quite isolated household where I met Amalia who spoke fluent Spanish, and although I had studied Quechua for a year and a half, I could of course communicate infinitely better in Spanish. It was easy after talking with Ilateria in Quechua, although not half so enticing. Amalia asked me to sit down, and soon she had me trying to explain to her all the reasons I had for being there, and she seemed to approve of all of them. I felt like a son talking to his mother. I could tell by the look in her eye that she understood me.

Amalia and her brother Jacob were the only two residents of Sina who had not either been born right there in the village or within a hundred miles or so, that being the apparent radius within which Sineños found their spouses. Amalia and Jacob had come from an entirely different region of Peru. Amalia was always ready to give us some lettuce from her lettuce patch, or to fry up a guinea pig. After my first visit of an hour or so, I knew I had found a good friend in this fifty-year-old little lady who perked around under her black felt hat. She made me promise to bring Lisa over as soon as possible, gave me a handful of lettuce, and I wandered off feeling very successful.

Wish I Was a Doctor

Back on the other side, out in front of our house, a very worried looking little boy came up to me and said, "I bring you," in Spanish and looked at my kneecaps.

"Who?" I asked.

"You," he said.

"What for?" I asked.

"In order to cook," he replied somewhat dubiously.

Knowing that we weren't living with any cannibals, I thought, 'Oh my, we've just been invited to dinner. Why this is our first invitation to dinner!'

I fell in behind the little fellow and we set off to his house. Along the way I prepared myself by thinking all the most polite things I knew how to say. In the house lay a very sick man. He was lying by his stove which his wife was worriedly tending, and he held his stomach and sounded very miserable indeed.

"Stomach ache, diarrhea, cough, everything!" he told me. "Do you have any remedies, Señor? I have good dry firewood I can give you in order to cook with!" So that's what his little son meant by "in order to cook!"

"I do not think I have much," I told him. "In fact I am afraid that I have nothing at all. But perhaps the Señora has something. I will go and ask her," I said knowing that I could then go sort through my pill collection and see what I had.

"Some remedy, please Señor."

"Yes, I will go and ask the Señora."

Up in our house I found a bottle of antibiotics which a doctor in St. Louis, Missouri had prescribed for me so I wrapped up ten of the large pink capsules, carried them down to the sick man's house, and explained to him how to take them.

"I don't know whether they will help or not," I said, "but you can try it."

"Thank you very much, Señor."

"His kidneys. His kidneys hurt too," his frightened wife added.

'If only I were a Doctor,' I thought as I walked back through the darkness up to our house.

Alberto and two of his brothers, Roberto and Santiago, were again gathered to celebrate the eventual construction of the new house. I sat down with them and soon we were crying and singing at the sky.

The alcohol with anise with sugar mixture was appearing from somewhere.

And With You, Thirty-One!

Suddenly a civil guard Sargent who had just arrived in the village appeared in our midst. Like his compatriot up on the altiplano above, he seemed suspicious and unfriendly. And, also like his compatriot above, he was accompanied by two younger civil guards who hadn't lost their friendly smiles. Perhaps the fact that Che Guevara, one of the prime symbols of the Cuban Revolution, had, with CIA backing, just been tracked down and executed across the border in Bolivia had something to do with these Sargents' reactions.

The Sargent began to drink and soon was boasting that he had killed over thirty men. He kept looking at me in an unfriendly way and was insisting that I 'check in' with him by showing my passport and visa. We all agreed that tomorrow would be soon enough for this but the Sargent still looked unhappy and was rapidly getting drunker on the powerful alcohol mixture.

"And with you it will be thirty-one!" he eventually snarled at me.

I left the party after a while and went back home to Lisa and to bed. But I woke up sometime in the early morning before dawn to the sounds of someone outside my door. I very quietly climbed up into the wooden rafters under our grass roof and peeked out through a gap in the stone wall to see who it was. I had my pistol in my hand. I was still in the habit of carrying it with me.

I could make out the Sargent's shape. He was standing outside the door with his large automatic weapon. He was by now extremely drunk and wobbling on his feet. How could my little pistol be a match against that huge assault rifle? I would have to disable him with one shot... what if I just wounded him? What would happen next? What would the younger civil guards do? Nothing seemed like a good idea. And the idea of actually shooting someone? Not at all sure about that either...

"Mi Sargento..." I heard one of my village friends call to him. "Felipe is asleep! Come back and have another drink with us!" The Sargent staggered off back to the little party. I climbed back down out of the rafters and went back to sleep. Lisa hadn't even woken up.

The next day I went and showed him my papers. He was seriously hung over and not looking happy. He still didn't seem to like me but he could tell that the villagers did. The following day he continued on his way and during the next few years I never saw crazy police in Sina again.

Although anyone could put a pistol in his pocket and travel freely by airplane in those days, after thinking about it, I decided to quit carrying it. It felt like the escalations of violence which would occur, even if one were to 'save oneself,' would be so overwhelming that it would be smarter to just trust to fate and hope for the best.

Also it seemed to me that by carrying a weapon I was accidentally signing on to having to become some kind of judge of good and evil which would not serve in the long run. Better to just always project a hundred-per-cent confidence in everyone's basic goodness and let that attitude soak into every situation. So I never carried a weapon again and I later threw that pistol into the mud beside a creek back in Colorado.

Market Day Back Up at 16,000 Feet

Every Saturday was market day for Sina. Four trucks came to the top of the sixteen-thousand-foot pass which marked the entrance to the valley which descended to Sina. A road ended there at a spot called Iskay Cruz, which means 'Two Crosses.' At the end of the road were two piles of stone each with a wooden cross implanted. This pass was also known as the 'Apacheta,' a magical spot. So every Saturday the trucks would bring soap, flower, alcohol, cookies and dozens of other items to the lonely and icy spot at Iskay Cruz while the villagers from Sina trudged eight miles up from ten-thousand feet to sixteen-thousand feet to meet them. Usually they brought potatoes with which to trade.

Lorenzo knocked on my door at 3:00 AM according to our plan. I had decided to go to market, and Lorenzo had offered to travel with me. There was no moon behind the clouds, so the night was a very black one. Lorenzo already had four horses loaded with potatoes and ready to go. Driving the horses in front of us, with a cold and misty near-rain hanging close about us, we stumbled up the trail above the village. Lorenzo had a carbide miner's lamp which seemed in no way inferior to my battery-powered lamp.

We walked along as fast as we could, shushing the horses along in the darkness ahead of us. Peruvian horses know a completely different language. Our cluckings and 'Whoa Boys' would be completely lost on them. The way to get them to go forward is to walk behind vigorously whispering "Pasa pasa!" and "Shh! Shh!" while twirling a rope or a stick just within their range of vision behind them.

Lorenzo and I spoke hurriedly and quietly as we walked along. Our walk was brisk and our talk was brisk. Our minds seemed stiffer than our limbs in the pre-dawn blackness. I settled into asking questions about Quechua. Lorenzo became my teacher, and I hardened up my brain and learned as much as I could while my soul had trouble unbending itself and crawling out from underneath its early morning stone.

About 7:00 AM we began walking along with some other Indians. They gave us some boiled potatoes and I gave them some hard candy. One of them asked me if I had pills I swallowed to teach me Quechua. The others looked at him as though he were not very bright.

By 9:00 we reached the top and there were the trucks. Goods were spread out on blankets on the ground. Many of the Indian women who had come with the trucks nursed their primus stoves inside tin cans and came up with hot coffee despite the stiff wind and below-freezing temperatures. Some huddled behind the trucks or lay on the ground behind their sacks while others hurriedly bargained to conclude their business. Someone asked Lorenzo who I was and he told them I was living in Sina.

"He knows Quechua," he added and I cleverly spouted a few words. "He's a Sineño," he laughed and I felt glad that soon we would be walking back down the trail toward my new home.

'These lousy trucks don't have any claim on me now,' I happily thought. I spent an hour or so examining the available goods. I had come ostensibly to buy some butter and jam. Neither was to be found. I did buy a handsome pile of goodies, however, which we eventually loaded on the horses which had carried Lorenzo's potatoes. Lorenzo had brought two-hundred pounds of potatoes which he sent to his wife in Juliaca. He told me that they were worth four-hundred soles, which is $8.80 dollars. Not bad.

I was surprised and delighted to find Amalia. She and her white-haired brother, Jacob, had left the night before and slept under the overhang of a rock along the way. She had come to see if an item which she had requested had arrived. It hadn't. But she had some potatoes to sell and I was pleased to see that she had no doubts about their quality and the price that she was to be paid. Jacob had brought up some wooden boxes which he had made to sell. Jacob was one of Sina's two carpenters. Amalia did say that the old fellow had been pretty tired out by the climb, however, so he'd already begun the descent.

A ten or twelve-year-old kid walked over to me and slyly informed me that he had some trout to sell. He said he had just caught them in one of the nearby lakes. A little crowd gathered. Everyone wanted his trout.

"Six soles apiece," he announced, and we all began to reach into our pockets, anxious not to miss out on the fine looking fish. Suddenly Amalia appeared on the scene and announced that the fish were only worth three soles apiece. Unfortunately for the young fisherman, Amalia's tone of voice had left no doubt whatsoever about how much the fish were worth: three soles or 6.6 cents. The poor fellow asked for four soles, but the question had already been settled. We all returned some of our money to our pockets and quietly paid only three soles apiece for the fish. I bought two fish and gave one to Amalia.

By about 11:30 AM our horses were packed and we scurried off back down into the valley towards Sina. Lorenzo and I ran for a mile or so, until the sides of the valley, the wonderful protective valley in which Sina lay, shielded us from the winds and the sun fell warmly upon us. A very poor-looking Indian sat panting upon a rock. Lorenzo told him he'd better hurry if he was to catch the trucks, so off he went, churning up the rocky valley with his bare toes, with two hand-carved boards across his shoulders. Lorenzo explained that he had left two days earlier from forty miles below in order that he might sell those two shaggy boards. I had understood Lorenzo tell the fellow that he didn't know whether anyone was up there who would buy the boards or not.

Chasing the Chicken

Soon we caught up with Amalia who was steaming along jumping from rock to rock over the water and mud. We quit running and for the next three hours we talked and talked and basked in the ease of tumbling homeward, while I happily showed off my new acquisitions from the morning's language lesson. Eventually we met with someone who explained that Jacob had apparently taken a side trip of some kind, so Amalia decided to wait for him. Lorenzo and I and another man continued onward. My conversational energy was used up. Lorenzo discussed important issues with the other man, while I remained silent. Lorenzo, you see, was Sina's alcalde - one of the three officials of the town - and therefore actually quite an important man.

Every six months he was the recipient of Peruvian government money to which Sina, as an acknowledged and represented Peruvian village, had a right. The sum was either 1500 or 15000 soles which means either $33.30 or $330.00. Unfortunately I didn't get it straight. But Lorenzo, as alcalde - a position which he would fill for three years - had the responsibility of representing Sina in the nearest district capitol, receiving the money, and seeing to it that it was used to benefit the town as a whole.

Suddenly a chicken appeared ahead of us on the trail. "Where's the owner?" asked the alcalde.

"I don't see any," replied the other man, and Lorenzo was off in a flash. For several minutes our somewhat stiff and respectable alcalde pursued that chicken as it climbed higher and higher up the side of the valley. Finally he came back down.

"It was too fast for me," he said.

We wandered into Sina late in the afternoon and I triumphantly laid my spoils before Lisa: cans of peaches, dried corn and a wonderful Peruvian grain called quinoa.

The next the day Lisa and I spent down the valley - after a twisted wet and green and slippery walk - looking at Cristobal's new calf. With us came Cristobal, his lovely six-year-old daughter Nemia, and Idelsa, Emilio's sexy fifteen-year-old wife who made Lisa nervous because she was always examining and feeling Lisa's clothes. Idelsa milked the cow and then we sat under our ponchos waiting for it to stop raining, which it didn't.

Guinea Pigs or Music

It was about that time that Lisa fell in love with Santiago. He was one of Roberto's brothers. And it was about that time that I realized that Santiago had only one arm. The other one was gone. He had been around every other day for a week and I had never noticed, although I remember being surprised at shaking someone's left hand instead of his right hand shortly after we had arrived. Santiago had fallen on a rock while playing soccer when he was only about twelve years old. His right arm simply dried up and came off, all right there in Sina. So the story goes.

Monday after market day, like Sunday after market day, everything was quiet and settled in Sina. We had wandered across the valley over to Amalia's house and were admiring her scurry of patchwork long-haired guinea pigs. Peruvian guinea pigs have extremely long hair which grows out at entirely unpredictable angles all over their bodies. They look like little walking thatches of cowlick which chitter all over the floors of the Indian houses looking for all the world as though they might be on minute racing wheels, so obscured by their ridiculous cowlicks are their legs. They eat the garbage and their own poop, so there's nothing to do but let 'em be. We told Amalia that we'd never had one.

"Broiled or fried?" she asked. "I'll have one cooked up by four o'clock." We decided on fried.

Back on our own side of the river the kids had all come over to visit us. "Play!" one said and immediately hid her face laughing behind her hands.

"Play!" another one said and shyly giggled.

So I got my guitar and played them some songs. I sang 'Streets of Laredo,' and 'Old Paint.' We had lots of time. "Now you sing us a song," I said jokingly. About fifteen children were standing in our house. They jiggled and jittered a bit, so I sang another song.

By the time I had finished, the older girls had somehow organized themselves and were diligently singing us a song: 'Los Trigales,' (The Wheatfields). Nemia, sang with them, only, unlike the others, she wasn't really shy at all. She hid her face and giggled only because she felt she had to. Six-year-old custom demanded it. "Oh Nemia, don't be ridiculous!" Lisa would say in English. And the boys sang too. And before long they had sung the song through quite a few times and I wanted to sing again, so I sang 'em 'Johnny B. Goode' by Chuck Berry. "Go Johnny go!" One of the boys laughed and imitated the way the funny gringo was stomping his foot up and down: "Well down in Looziana close to New Orleans..." So I stomped my foot even more and they stomped their feet even more and sang, "Go Johnny Go Johnny Go Johnny Go Johnny" and I looked out and saw that every kid in the place was jumping up and down as hard as he could with both feet shouting "Go Johnny Go!"

I thought the music of the Andes was neat, but I could not yet find the rhythm and I could not yet learn the tunes. I'm sure the Indians had enjoyed my singing, but they always asked: "But don't you know such and such?"

"No, I don't," I would reply. "Your music and mine are very different and I still cannot learn it." And I would see that they were very frustrated, for they found nothing familiar in my rhythms and tunes - until I played 'Johnny B. Goode.'

So there we were, trying to learn the tune and words to 'Los Trigales,' when in walked a little boy with two plates heaped high with potatoes and fried guinea pig.

"Oh my God! I wonder what time it is?" Of course we didn't know, 'cause we never did, 'cause we didn't have a watch. Well we quit playing and started eating. Guinea pigs taste sort of like tough chicken. The kids eventually drifted off. We took our empty plates back to Amalia and told her we were sorry and asked her what time it was. It was about 5:30. We told her we had been playing music with the kids. She said her brother Jacob could play the harp.

"Oh, that one I saw inside?" I asked.

"That's the one." Before long Jacob himself came by. He played the harp outside while Amalia took turns dancing with me and Lisa 'to show us how to dance.' Jacob played with terrific precision. It was terrific music: Andean music or 'huayños,' as they are called. With the sun still in the sky, we drank toasts to each other after each dance. Amalia had run inside and fetched a bottle of alcohol.

"Salud!"

"Salud!"

The next day people from our own side of the valley told me they had seen us dancing. After it grew dark in the valley outside, we moved into Amalia's house. We danced and drank, and I could feel Peruvian music slowly creeping into my soul. But it would have to creep quite a bit further before I would actually be able to play any of it.

Late at night, at ten or eleven we finally finished dancing, and I left feeling we had enjoyed quite a successful fried guinea pig. I placed my foot on the lower stepping stone in Amalia's stone wall and the wall collapsed on my foot. I stumbled home wishing my left big toe would quit hurting, but it didn't. My toe kept me confined to Sina for the next week when otherwise I might have wandered down to the next village to have a look at it before leaving the valley. But there would be plenty of time to do that.

> *Along with Cristobal and Nemia, Amalia and her brother Jacob became our special friends. Amalia was the only one in Sina who had a garden patch growing lettuce, radishes, and onions. At night for supper we made delicious salads from what she gave us. From Amalia Cam found out many things about Sina and Quechua. She seemed to really understand his interests and could explain things in a way that many others couldn't. Amalia was always cheerful and warm with us. She was a tough, animated woman in her fifties who could walk the five hours to market and never need a rest. She wore a black felt hat and her eyes always sparkled.*
>
> *The moment I found myself most at-one with the life in Sina's valley was one musical night when she and I danced ourselves dizzy in her front yard while Jacob sang and played raucously on his harp. The music was like that of a carousel and as we spun so did the stars and my orange skirt and the whole green valley of Sina until it became one big flying cyclone of joy with me in the center of it. Amalia lived high up on one side of the valley where we could look down and in one glance see and feel the whole of Sina.*

Potatoes, Gratitude and Flying Too High

The next morning we slept late. We cooked a leisurely breakfast of rice and butter and salt with bacon and three eggs, canned peaches and boiled corn thrown in as well. Then I had a coffee while Lisa enjoyed her ovaltine. Then I began to boil potatoes, the only obvious thing to do in Sina.

I felt good. I added more water to the potatoes. No matter how many potatoes we boiled, they always seemed to be gone within an hour. For once I was determined to boil up enough. I wanted to be able to feel that I could eat as many as I wanted and still have some left over. So I sat on the floor boiling potatoes and peacefully writing in my journal.

> *I became a balloon. A helium balloon. The kind of balloon that tugs toward nothingness: toward the black space that lies behind the twigs of brittle trees at night. The black space that a man can depend on when all else fails: the space will still be there. I tugged toward the stars, old friends, twinkling their cold and honest light down*

and through the twigs. I tugged out there toward loneliness, that black place of no doubt where I can see the darkness as it sees me. And I thought, 'By God I'm glad that Lisa's down there holding me by my string!'

I bobbed my orange balloon head and said, 'It may be true I'm out beyond the step and fetch of homely bound-ward wings It may be true I've gone too far to rest my head on the green grass bosom of familiar hills I could dare to call my own. And cats and mats and all of that. (But hang on down there!) Maybe up here's the only place I can face the view of all and everything... that infinite circus of life with its elephants and baboons... (Don't let me go too high!) Hang on to your balloon, dear Lisa!

'I must not forget to thank these people,' I thought as I sat before my little stove. What a fine little potato I have here now all boiled by me for me to eat - with a little salt! 'I must not forget to thank these people; to tell them how valuable they are in their crystal world of potatoes and no kings! That's it! Here in Sina there are no kings! Only an alcalde with a fiendish grin for capturing stray chickens.

'Potatoes and children. Potatoes and children. Where's Jacob and his harp? Cristobal's teaching school. So is Emilio. How's Ilateria? How's her blanket coming? I miss hearing her crisp, energetic speech! What is the Governor, Don Teofilo, doing these days? Why his wife has had her eighth child two days ago! Congratulations, Don Teofilo!

Going to School

Cristobal and Emilio had invited us from the very beginning to come down and visit the school. By now we felt that we knew the kids well enough so that we could come and visit without making everyone hopelessly nervous. We asked Cristobal and he told us that the following morning would be just fine. So we arrived bright and early and in time for me to play a bit of soccer with the boys in front of the schoolhouse. While the remainder of Sina's hundred-or-so inhabitants were quietly hilling potatoes, washing clothes or maybe taking a trip somewhere - the village activities to which we had become accustomed - we thirty or so in the schoolhouse were about to conduct some separate business. That was why all these little pairs of feet were all lined up so purposefully. Cristobal announced very matter-of-factly that the school was going to have two visitors today, Don Felipe and Doña Lisa, and we all filed into two classrooms. Emilio had the six and seven-year-olds and Cristobal had the eight and nine-year-olds. Lisa went in with the younger ones and I went in with Cristobal's group.

Unfortunately as it turned out, Emilio had been embroiled in an argument with his fifteen-year-old wife the night before and had stayed up all night drinking, so he was a little under the weather. He told Lisa to take over the class for him and disappeared.

Cristobal ran through some Spanish grammar and long division, but soon he got me to start talking, and once started, I didn't feel like shutting up. I stood up beside the map of the world which was hanging on the wall and began spewing out anthropological theories. I explained about how their ancestors had been separated from us white men's ancestors for fifty-thousand years, so we were just like old friends meeting who hadn't seen each other for a long time. I explained about how their ancestors had migrated across the Bering Straits maybe twenty-thousand years ago. I had a wonderful time rattling out what I thought I knew in Spanish.

After recess, Cristobal resumed with the arithmetic, so I wandered over to visit Lisa. The kids said they wanted to speak English, so we started in on some kind of English lesson, but it was soon time for lunch. Emilio returned after lunch, so Lisa and I both took up our English instruction back in Cristobal's class with the older kids. We spent the whole afternoon at it. I managed to utilize some words that I knew in Quechua as well as in Spanish. No one got bored.

Ghosts, Money-Making and Our Last Antibiotics

That night about midnight, just after I had blown out my Quechua-studying candle and slipped into my sleeping bag, Lisa heard some noises outside. I listened and didn't hear anything, but shortly thereafter I felt something like a little clod of dirt land on my feet. I started sneaking out of my sleeping bag. It took a good five minutes for me to creep out and slide on my pants without making a sound. I snuck over to the door and after listening for a minute I flung it open and stepped outside. No one was there, but quite a ways away I heard someone whistle. I looked around a few obvious hiding places that were close by and decided to take a piss.

"Don Felipe?"

I looked up and Cristobal was hanging out of his window. "I heard some noises," I explained, "but there's no one here."

"Probably some kids," Cristobal said.

"Well goodnight, Don Cristobal."

"Goodnight, Don Felipe," and we went back to bed.

A couple of days later, late in the afternoon, I went over to the tiny little thatched cooking hut which adjoined Cristobal's house. Nemia and her friend Julia were inside boiling potatoes and frying them for Cristobal's dinner. So I sat down for a minute to watch their expert little six-year-old hands tending the fire. Cristobal came in and soon we were all eating a pan of fried potatoes.

"We have business," said Cristobal.

"Oh yeah? What business?" I asked.

"A machine," he explained. And he went on to explain that if I would simply bring him the appropriate machine next time I came, he would print money with it and, since we were only a few miles from Bolivia, simply take it to La Paz. There it would be used to buy things for Sina, and Sina's problems would be solved! It is a common Andean belief that all gringos have these machines with which we literally 'make' money - I suppose because we always seem to have all we need. Cristobal explained that once in his childhood a German had come through his village offering to sell just such a machine but no one had been able to come up with enough money to buy it.

I explained to Cristobal that I had no idea where to buy such a machine; that I expected such machines to be almost impossibly dangerous to try and obtain and that I was the last person in the world who would be likely to run into somebody who had one. Cristobal remained unconvinced however, for up until the last day I was there, he referred continually hopefully to 'our business' and 'the machine.'

But before Cristobal and I had gotten all the details worked out over our fried potatoes that night, a middle-aged woman had come in, sat down, and proceeded to tearfully explain in the sobbing Quechua style which is adopted whenever a favor of any kind is being requested. I didn't know what favor was being asked until Cristobal told me later, because the sobbing obscured the nice sharp consonants on which I depend for understanding. And when there are eight sounds which are distinct in Quechua yet which to an English speaker all sound like "K's", the English speaker learns to appreciate crisp speech. But as it was explained to me after she left, the lady was Idelsa's mother - Idelsa being Emilio's fifteen-year-old wife - and Cristobal was being asked to please persuade Emilio to patch things up with Idelsa, as Cristobal was a compadre of Emilio's, as well as being a native of the same town (a village about a hundred miles away). Cristobal assured her that he would discuss it with Emilio the next day at school and didn't seem to take the problem very seriously himself. This said, Idelsa's mother's tears evaporated, her Quechua cleaned up and her toes stretched themselves happily as she turned herself to subjects I could understand.

Shortly thereafter I went over to my house to get a little more cooking oil (a very valuable commodity in Sina) and while I was getting it, a little boy timidly approached and said something which I understood as "My father is crying you." A look in my dictionary showed me that I had mistaken one K for another as usual and that the real message was, "My father is calling you."

So I said, "Let's go," and followed the little boy down to his father's house. His father turned out to be the same man to whom I had first given antibiotics when he had told me that "everything was wrong" with him. I had visited him since and discovered that he seemed to have recovered, but now he told me that his wife seemed to be sick. Her kidneys hurt. And she held her back over her kidneys to show where it hurt. So I returned to my house and got the last of our antibiotics and brought them down. I had already given the rest away to another man whose throat was so swollen shut he hadn't been able to eat for a week.

After I gave him the pills for his wife and explained again how to take them, we sat talking for a bit. He was a man who felt his Spanish was so poor that he preferred to communicate in Quechua with me. He said, "I understand that you heard some noises outside the other night."

"Why yes, that is so," I replied.

"Tell me," he asked, "just what time of night was this?"

"Oh, about midnight. It must have been some schoolboys looking through our window," I explained.

"At that hour of the night, sir, it could have been neither boy nor man. It was surely a..." And here he used a Quechua word I didn't know.

"What is that?" I inquired.

"A skull," he replied in Spanish. "You know, the Dead."

"Ohhhhh!"

"They often make noises and throw stones," he explained.

When I asked Cristobal about the possibility of skulls and ghosts, he laughed and said that it had surely been a couple of boys looking through our window.

Women and Wool

Lisa suggested that we go on a wool-buying expedition. She had learned to spin wool - both sheep's and alpaca's - using the little top-like contraption which the Indians called a *puchka*. Lisa was starting to look like a little Indian herself. She wore hand woven skirts which she had bought in the market in Juliaca, and for a few days she wore a beautifully woven *lliklla* which Idelsa and Emilio had lent her. It was so beautifully woven of such fine colors that we offered more and more money for it... just as we were trying to buy the blanket which Lisa had helped to weave. In the end we got neither one. They were simply not for sale at any price.

The longer we stayed in Sina the less satisfied I became with relying on Cam for everything. It seemed that whatever house we visited, I would be left out of things because I couldn't say anything. He invariably made a gallant effort to include me but I was not satisfied with second-hand relationships with the people of Sina. Little by little I ventured forth alone to the houses and found that I could make my own contacts without language. It was triply exciting being alone. As an excuse for going (and partly because I needed it) I would ask to buy some wool for my spinning. Using the few words I did know I could ask a question about some article hanging on the wall or indicate that I liked something and had never seen one before. If the little girl was home the two of us could show the adults that we already knew each other. When my supply of words and ideas was exhausted I could leave with the wool feeling as though I had taken a step in getting to know them. I could go back to our house and, while I was spinning, carefully think over everything that had happened.

It must have seemed odd from the Sineños point of view to look over at our house and see the gringo lady hour-after-hour sitting there engrossed in the work of a Peruvian woman. But she, unlike I, could walk, talk, cook, and mind children while she spun. All I could do was plant myself in one spot and concentrate on making the yarn come out lump-less. Spinning wool into yarn on this simple stick relaxed my mind and provided a kind of escape when I needed it. It provided a time when I could think over all that was happening to me and it was a useful tool for starting conversations with other women.

> *It is hard to remember now exactly how our days went in Sina. I know that in the evening Cam lit candles and wrote at the table while I lay in my sleeping bag asleep. In the morning we would be the last ones in the village awake. In the middle of each afternoon we made a delicious pan of fudge from the chocolate and sugar sold at the mayor's store. Sometimes during the school recess the children would come over and we'd take turns singing songs. Most clearly I remember the small things: the way the potatoes looked in the morning when I washed them... lying in the pan of water, their skins were all shades of purple and pink... how the ground inside our house by the front door got muddier and muddier as the rainy season progressed... the red and black pattern on Julia's lliklla... she was the oldest of the girls and the most beautiful... how the clouds of smoky mist pumped up the valley and tucked themselves beneath and around every potato plant... the day we finished off the butter... the time I made potato pancakes... the clay jug we used for carrying water... the brilliantly colored yarns Ilateria used to make the blanket... the delicious warmth of my sleeping bag on cold nights.*

She's Over a Hundred Years Old

We hadn't seen Ilateria, nor had the pleasure of listening to her crisp glottalized Quechua consonants for quite some time, so we climbed up to the very highest house on our side of the valley, where she lived. Sitting cross-legged in the doorway was the oldest lady I had ever seen. She had only a few wisps of hair left on her head, and one eyelid was swollen out and drooped down below the bottom of her nose. The whole lower half of her body was swollen and a putrid yellow color.

"Hello, how are you?" we said. "We're looking for Ilateria!" But we got no response. I was irresistibly drawn into retreat, and was just about to bolt back down the hill, when one of Ilateria's daughters came out of the house. She was only about nine but had the same spontaneous vivaciousness which her mother had. I recognized her as having been one of the children who frequented our house for visits and song-singing. In her mother's absence, she was assuming the role of responsible adult of the household, which most other nine-year-olds in the village would have been too shy to do. Looking at

Ilateria's house, I realized that she was perhaps the poorest person in the village.

A few minutes later, back down in the center of the village, I ran into someone I knew and said, "My God, there sure is a sick looking old lady up at Ilateria's house!"

He laughed and said, "There's nothing you can do for her now! That's Ilateria's mother and she's over a hundred years old! She's already lived her life."

A New Owner for My Guitar

In the afternoon I went up to Edwin's store to join the little congregation of menfolk who gathered there every afternoon to exchange the latest news. Edwin was the same fellow whom we had met riding on his white horse when we were first walking toward Sina. I liked him. He and his kind and lovely young wife Laura ran a store just like the governor's and we usually bought our chocolate there. She had also given Lisa some good quality brown alpaca wool to spin. Edwin had expressed an interest in buying my guitar so after a while the congregation moved down to my house in order to look at the guitar.

A young guy from Bolivia was there who also claimed he might be interested in buying the guitar. So I sang a few songs and Alberto sang a few songs. I even began to feel that huayños had sunk far enough into my blood that I might soon begin to be able to learn one. But while we were singing and talking, someone came down and informed us that we were all invited to dinner. A man named Florentino was giving a feast for many of the people in the community to honor his father who had died exactly one year before.

Two candles burned solemnly on a table draped with black cloth inside Florentino's house, and everyone crossed himself upon entering. I sent Nemia back to get Lisa, and we had a fine dinner. A cow had been butchered for the occasion. This was the first time we had seen anyone in Sina eating any kind of meat except guinea pigs. I had brought my guitar simply because I had been holding it in my hand, so after dinner Alberto and I began singing songs again. Alcohol, cigarettes and coca leaves were passed around and the occasion became less solemn. I sang *'Johnny B. Goode'* again.

Before long the subject of the guitar came up again. It seemed that five or six wanted to buy it. Having no way to select to whom I would sell it, I finally said, "I will simply leave it here in Sina and let all of you decide what to do with it. Then all of you will be able to play it. Or if you decide you want to sell it, you can do that too. I simply leave it as a remembrance."

No one looked happy about that idea. Thoughtful silence. Finally Alberto said. "A magnificent thing has done the Señor!" They all nodded gravely and began discussing it among themselves.

"Why don't we let Don Cristobal decide who will be its custodian then?" I suggested. "He is a man who works hard every day in the school. He will make a fair decision."

Cristobal looked flustered and nervous, not happy at all with his new role. Alberto laughed and said, "I'll tell him to give it to me and he'll give it to me."

At last Cristobal said, "In the house later we will talk," and laughed from embarrassment. Emilio surprised me by making a little speech to the effect that everyone should keep in mind how valuable an instrument the guitar was. He claimed that they were unobtainable anywhere nearby, even in La Paz, Bolivia, and that Iquitos, where I had bought it for $15, was probably the only place where they could be obtained.

Alberto laughed again and said, "Only one of us had better buy it. That would be better. Otherwise we'll have a civil war in Sina!"

"That's the way life is amongst us here in Sina," someone lamented.

"No we're better than that," corrected Cristobal.

"Very well," I said, "but I don't want much for it."

I was amazed and gratified to hear Humberto, one of Roberto's brothers, remark that I myself might need money for the remainder of my trip. Suddenly it was agreed that I should receive 600 soles - about $14 - for it.

"Less," I said.

So we agreed upon 500 soles and both Humberto and the guy from Bolivia left to get the money. The guy from Bolivia didn't come back. Humberto did. The guitar was his.

"Is this OK with everyone?" I was curious to know, because I really didn't have any idea of what was going on at all. As far as I knew, Humberto didn't even know how to play a guitar. Everyone, including Edwin, expressed his satisfaction, so that was that.

The next day Humberto invited us over for lunch. Perhaps that was the appropriate thing for him to do as a consequence of buying the guitar. I didn't understand, but I didn't need to. Lunch was elaborate with some of the recently slaughtered beef making it extra special.

After Humberto's delicious lunch we ascended again to Ilateria's house. This time we found her home. She immediately launched into a dramatic and tearful tale about how she had been up the valley for several days mourning a friend who had just passed away. Once again I had the pleasure of being able to understand enough of what she was saying in Quechua to understand a running tale. Otherwise my conversations in Quechua were generally limited to such as the following complex exchange:

"Hello, how are you?"

"Fine, how are you? Are you going to the other side?"

"No, I'm just going down to the stream for water."

"Oh, goodbye."

"Goodbye."

Humberto had actually invited us back for lunch the following day. We had told him that inviting us again was too much, but he still insisted. As it turned out, however, Emilio gave us lunch instead. Cristobal was invited too, along with Nemia. Time was running out. We had decided to leave on the following Saturday which was only a day or two away. The rainy season was getting rainier, and this was to be the last Saturday on which the trucks would be certain of being able to arrive. If they didn't, we would have an additional forty miles to walk.

Lunch with Emilio, which Idelsa had cooked, was very relaxed indeed. We ate and talked for two hours until they both had to go and start the afternoon session down at the little school.

Ah Mi Compadre!

Finally the Friday evening came. We had given away everything we didn't want and had packed up the remainder to take with us up to Iskay Cruz at 3:00 in the morning. Cristobal had agreed to accompany us. He had five fine horses of which we were to use two for cargo and one for Lisa to ride. I went over to say goodbye to the governor and buy a sack of bread to take along with us. While I was buying the bread, he asked me something I didn't understand.

"What?" I asked. He repeated himself and I still didn't understand. The third time around I suddenly realized that he was asking me to baptize his new child!

'Oh my God,' I thought, 'how am I to do that?'

We went back into the same hut where we had spent our first night in Sina. The governor's wife brought over the child while the governor, Don Teofilo, explained that children must be baptized so that they wouldn't die without a name.

"But he won't die, will he?" I asked.

Don Teofilo smiled and said he didn't think so. He explained that they always asked a very special person to baptize their children for them. "A very special person," he repeated and smiled again.

'Oh my goodness,' I thought, 'I don't know how to baptize someone!'

But Don Teofilo explained exactly what I was to do. He told me to hold the child in my arms and say, "I baptize you in the name of God, the Son and the Holy Ghost, with the name of Juan de la Cruz."

"Juan de la Cruz! That is to be his name?" I asked.

"Juan de la Cruz." Then he explained that I must make a cross over him as I said it and then put a little salt in his mouth.

"Ok," I said and took the child. "Yo te bautizo en el nombre del Dios, del Hijo y del Espiritu Santu, con el nombre de Juan de la Cruz!" I said gloriously, all the while describing a slow and important cross over him. Then I took a little salt and put it in the baby's mouth.

"A little more," said Don Teofilo.

So I put a little more in his mouth and then handed the baby back to his mother. Happily he hadn't cried. Then Don Teofilo embraced me and said, "What a good hour!"

"What a good hour!" I said.

His wife came over and embraced me. "What a good hour!"

"What a good hour!"

Then Don Teofilo explained that we were Compadres henceforth, and I was amazed. Compadres! "Ah mi Compadre!" And that I was the child's godfather. Then Don Teofilo gave me the bread for our trip and told me not to pay him. Compadres must help each other out, after all. So I took the bread back to Lisa and casually announced that I was a godfather.

Lisa Gets to Ride

Leaving Sina

It was horrible to leave Sina. We had to, though, because the height of the rainy season was approaching and at that time travel was next to impossible. We would go to a market place five hour's walk up the valley. Here would be trucks to take us to Cojata, the nearest town by vehicle. It happened one night when all was packed up except ourselves and our sleeping bags. We were asleep and there was a knock at the door. Cristobal was going to accompany us and offered to let me ride one of his horses. The other horse would carry the packs and his potatoes. Nemia was up making soup for everyone. The sun was about to rise as we started off. The day was a sparkling one. We retraced for a few miles the path that brought us to Sina. What once was mysteriously covered with mist and lurking with frightening shapes was that day revealed in sunshine.

At the top of the pass the Indian women, with their voluminous red, orange and brown skirts tucked beneath them, were sitting around selling all sorts of food and supplies: soap, macaroni, plastic shoes, corn, wool, cloth, candy, hot meals, yarn, coffee, beans, little mirrors, and cookies. Three trucks were up there. We wandered around until it began snowing. A sharp wind blew.

A wool dealer there with a small turquoise pickup agreed to take us to Cojata. Time passed and the weather became more uncomfortable. Women huddled under their shawls. People began to pack up. Slowly it began to dawn on me that the sixty or so people still left up there at Iskay Cruz were counting on that turquoise pickup to carry them to Cojata. The other two trucks had left. As people got ready to leave, the tempo among us got gradually faster until at the last minute the whole horde made a movement to board the truck. It was filled comfortably after the first ten and their bags of goods had gotten in. Faster and faster people boarded with their enormous sacks, throwing them on top of those already seated. Cam and I watched with rising awe and anger. Within seconds I was absolutely furious. We had to get out of that area that day, or would be forced by the coming rains to stay on for months. And this we weren't prepared to do. I felt as though the truck driver had tricked us. I lost all cool and exploded rudely to the driver. Although Cam showed a moment of disbelief and anger, it passed quickly. All we could do now was fling ourselves at the truck and find a hand hold on the outside.

We had gone two miles when the driver stopped and ordered everybody off for a general reorganizing of the load. It was decided that certain barrels and many bags of goods would have to be left and picked up at a later date. This way everyone would at least get a seat inside. It was to be another grueling ride. Cam joked and laughed heartily with the Peruvians about too many children and birth control pills. I sat there feeling wretched and sort of embarrassed (partly because of the pills and partly because I knew I should be joining in the fun). Once in Cojata that evening we were a long hard thirty miles from the entrance to Sina's valley. From there, after five more days of waiting for another truck, it was on to La Paz, Bolivia.

La Paz, Bolivia and Back to Peru

Our first evening in La Paz Cam and I joyously celebrated our wonderful time in Sina at a fancy Chinese restaurant. We feasted over a large, tasty dinner while Christmas carols played and the lights of a decorated tree blinked merrily. We walked back to our hotel afterwards ridiculously stuffed and laughing the whole way.

We spent a week in La Paz and then took a fancy steamer back across Lake Titicaca to Puno, back in Peru. There we met Cristobal as planned. He was somewhat transformed. In Sina he was one of the most respectable men in the village but in Puno he was just another poor Indian. His wife was a very strong and healthy-looking woman who sold goods every day from her little table in the Indian market. She was very receptive to us while in her house but nearly died of embarrassment when I invited her to a movie in public.

The other five children seemed as brilliant as was Nemia. Grimosna, Florinda, Nila, Dimas, and Rinaldi. I swear I almost felt like one of the family what with them looking over Grimosna's report card right there with me included. Cristobal did agree to come see a movie with me at the local theater. He brought two of his children but would cover their eyes with his hands whenever he thought the movie might be getting too dramatic. We prepared to leave and in the last moments of saying goodbye, the first thing on his mind was to ask again for a money-making machine!

Nasty Catholic Priests and a Dissertation on Conflict

From Puno we took a small boat north into the lake up to the Capachica Peninsula where we hoped to find a young couple whom I had met at Cornell. We arrived on the peninsula after dark on Christmas eve and Lisa promptly got bitten by a dog thus proving that I had been wrong to poo-poo her fear of them. We walked a couple of miles into town and were conducted straight into the compound of a gaggle of Catholic priests. They were young guys and greeted us heartily. They wore army caps and sat smoking cigars and writing Christmas cards in their luxurious compound all lit up with their own private generator. A Christmas Eve party was going on. The Indians were all in one of the church buildings dancing to their own music. The padres had supplied the place and perhaps the idea, since Christmas wasn't generally a particularly important occasion to the Indians. We joined in the party for a while and danced around in circles until we couldn't go on any longer.

The astronauts on Apollo 8 happened to be circling the moon at the time, so we went out and looked at the moon and explained to the Indians that there were men up there right then. One of the Padres thought it would be clever to announce to the Indians that Lisa and I had just arrived from the moon. He thought it was funny because the

Indians didn't know what to believe.

We went back into the private reaches of the compound and listened to the Padres tell about what stupid people the Indians were; about how they were such thieves and about how much they all hated it there.

I tried to explain to the Padres that no matter where in the world they might live in such utter luxury among poor people, they would be bound to inspire people to steal from them. One of the priests explained, with great relish, about how he had beaten and punched an Indian whom he had supposedly caught trying to steal some clothes. I later heard in the town that the Indian was still suffering black eyes from the blows.

On that same Christmas Eve, to top it all off, after Lisa and I had listened to some of the Padres' complaints, 'lo and behold it was time for midnight mass. 'I'd better not miss this,' I thought to myself, so I went over.

The three priests were all decked out in robes and finery with tall golden pointed hats and were chastising the Indians from the pulpit: "Can you really in your innermost heart," they were saying, "feel that you are living like brothers, true brothers with each and every fellow human being?" Meanwhile, the Indians, I was glad to see, were mostly talking or sleeping.

Fortunately our long shot had paid off and our friends were indeed at their new home on the peninsula. They lived about two hours' walk away from the town and had only moved in a couple of weeks earlier. They planned to stay there for a year and then move to another community for another year in order that Ralph might write his Doctoral thesis for a degree from Cornell in anthropology. His house was filled with piles of books and papers.

Unfortunately, a potato crop failure was just occurring. No rain had fallen during the two weeks since our friends had arrived and fifteen-hundred Indians who lived on the peninsula seemed fairly unanimously convinced that it was because of the gringos' presence. It seemed that they were planning to ask the Guardias from the town to come out and expel them. The fishermen claimed they had seen the gringos climbing the mountain behind the beach at night with red and white lights to scare away the rain gods. The orphans on the peninsula would wail piteously at night to plead for rain. We visited for a week but Ralph discouraged us from going out to look for musical opportunities to connect with the villagers. I had the guitar with me but he insisted it would set a bad precedent. I didn't understand his thinking but he had come to write his dissertation about 'conflict' so it made sense that he would be finding evidence of conflict.

Cusco and the Mummies

Eventually we jammed ourselves into another truck and continued homeward. Two days here, two days there. A train ride here, a truck ride there. We spent a day or two or three or four back in Cusco, waiting for a plane back to Lima.

We went to the Cusco museum of archaeology while we were there and saw a fine roomful of dried cadavers. When the jaw muscles dry out they contract and open wide the mouth. They all look as if caught dead in the act of a final scream.

Bones always make one think. Someday that may be my skull sitting in the museum case. An archaeologist will dig me up, put a little ink number on me and pilot me off to the museum case for people like me to come and see. They'll wonder, staring unabashedly into my eyes: "Did that person indeed have the same silly hopes for himself as I? And is this, then, all he's got to show for it? Is it really possible that life is so incredibly cheap?"

> "Say, mister, how much is that skull worth?"
> "I dunno. It was given to the museum."
> "But that's my skull! Whadaya mean it was just given to the museum! Don't you realize how many hours, how many years went into that?"

While in Cusco we spent a good deal of time wandering about the market trying to buy alpaca wool for Lisa to spin. There was a lady selling the following things: a small empty cold cream jar without the top, a broken cork, cover-less manuals for a Sony TV, a light-bulb in doubtful health, the arm of a plastic doll, a rusty connecting rod, broken plastic jacks and old transmission gears.

Fleas again. While I was reading: bite! Run run run run -- out from my shirt sleeve onto my wrist in broad daylight! A stupid flea. A mutation from its otherwise clever race. Smash! I caught him under my finger. Whoops! Still alive I see. I pinned him down again and wondered how I should manage to kill the little feller -- I mean the odious little body -- but; when I looked again: ? Gone!

Me and Lisa

Eventually we got on a plane to take us back to Lima. There we decided that Lisa would fly directly back to Miami in order that she might visit her parents while I planned to hitch-hike north, perhaps returning to Colorado via Mexico.

Lisa Departs; Hitch-Hiking For Me

After a final few days in Lima, the time came and Lisa and I went together to the airport. Her plane was announced and it was time for her to go. She waited in line to have her passport stamped and then as she walked down the long hall past the closed doors marked 'Immigration For Authorized Persons Only.' I waved and waved and started to cry as she walked out to the airplane and I waved some more from the observation deck. My throat began to dry and shrink. As the plane taxied off I felt another surge of emotion and had to quickly walk out to the end of the platform in order to not feel conspicuous. Lisa had waved from the window. As the plane took off I began waving and soon everybody else on the platform was waving too. We all had loved ones on the plane. As I walked away, the plane having shrunk into the morning gray, my eyes were as dry as I could keep them, but nevertheless wet, and my throat was locked tight in an unrelenting sob. I had a cup of coffee and went back downtown.

The next day I set off hitch-hiking north. I traveled all day and just as it got dark I got a ride in a big shiny new 1969 red Mack truck.

I just sat way up in that huge truck looking out over that big red hood and watching the little bitty cars way down there below us as we passed them. There was some absurdity of riding in that big truck after all the tiny ones we'd been crammed into in the mountains. It made the donkeys look like mice. So I rode on and on.

I planned to get out about 2:00 AM and sleep in a field but I missed my hour and found myself on the south edge of a town with the roosters already crowing. I walked a fast two miles through the town, extremely tired.

If only I had gotten off at a nice secluded spot between the sand dunes half an hour earlier! At last I came to open fields on the north side of town and spread out my pad and lay down. I felt something light and insidious land on my neck: mosquito! Shortly I had one crooning in my ear and had swatted a couple on the backs of my hands.

I smiled and got up. Maybe they're *very* local, I flung out a long distance hope. I walked until it was definitely beginning to get light and, in addition to the crowing of the roosters and the barking of the dogs, a man had walked by on his way to work. The day had begun. But I was so tired. I saw another dry field 'midst the planted ones and plunked down my pad. My ears soon filled with mosquitoes. I don't know why they always insist on congregating in your ear and singing you their dreadful songs. I put my poncho over the top half of my body and, about the time I was wondering when some passerby would come to see if I was a corpse, the mosquitoes came in anyway. They sang louder in my ear.

So I got up and hitch-hiked for the rest of that day and finally about 6:00 PM I rolled into Talara, the oilfield which the Peruvian government had just nationalized from Standard Oil of New Jersey.

I got a hotel room and took a shower and went out and sat in a little tea shop. Pretty soon some Americans with flat-top haircuts came in. Middle-aged women with tightly curled hair were speaking in a heavy Texas accent. Maybe they were nice people.

A fellow came in and said he was flying up to the States the next day in a private plane. "Why don't you take him?" said a young Frenchman with whom I had been talking, indicating me. The fellow looked at me and said, "Well... I don't think I'd better..."

The next morning I was off again. There didn't seem to be any traffic so when a bus came along I climbed on. I must have looked so down and out that a ten-year-old kid bought me an empanada to eat and when we arrived I was told not to bother to pay for the bus ride.

By afternoon I was at the northern Peruvian border. The border was closed for the weekend so there I was stuck. When I'm alone after a while I have trouble being friendly. I begin to feel like an ugly and persecuted -- or rather persecute-able -- bum.

Tito

Monday morning I was standing in Ecuadorian customs, and there was a young black-bearded fellow with hair down to his shoulders, a pack on his back with a big bayonet sticking out of it, so I thought, 'Oh great! A guerrilla.' Now he'll come over and want to team up with me and I'll be in jail before long. That was Tito. He came over and said, "Let's travel together..."

"Ok," I said.

Tito

Surprisingly enough we were soon through customs and on our way north. We walked on down the road into Ecuador, and I saw a big police post beside the road. Walking eyes front, I'm thinking, 'if they call us over I'll talk to them but otherwise I haven't even noticed them.' My natural U.S.-born fear of police was coming through. Tito said, "Let's go over and ask these guys to help us get a ride."

"Oh, we'll do alright by ourselves," I said.

"But they'll help us out," Tito said.

"Ok," I said, "you're a Peruvian and you know more about this than I do."

"We'll just go over and ask them to 'hablar' (talk) with the truck drivers that come along, and we'll get a ride faster," he said. So we went over and not a suspicious look was cast on us. Not a question asked. We talked about soccer teams. And soon one of the policemen 'hablar'ed' with a bus driver and we had a free ride. I had a lot to learn in the next four days traveling with Tito the authentic Peruvian hippie.

After a couple more free bus rides, we got to a ferry boat which would take us all night, so that in the morning we would be in Guayaquil. The situation looked clear to me. There were ticket sellers and ticket collectors and a big sign saying that the price was the equivalent of 26 cents. But Tito was determined to 'hablar' with the captain so we stomped right onto the boat. We climbed up to the third deck to where passengers were not allowed and waited for the captain to finish his conversation. Tito explained that we were traveling and that we were low on money. Eventually the captain nodded gravely and understandingly and said we could stay on the boat.

In Guayaquil the next day I learned about the Cuartel de la Policia. It seems that in every large city the police run a kind of free hostel and anyone who wants to can find free lodging there for the night. Again the police had no suspicions and no questions for us. I was learning. They invited us courteously to spend the night in their Cuartel but soon we found a bus which was leaving for Quito, the next city north.

Tito 'hablar'ed' a bit and the owner said he would take us for 30 sucres (Ecuadorian currency before they adopted the dollar) instead of the usual 50. We rushed back to the cuartel to get our packs but arrived ten minutes after the bus had already left. But the owner, the big cheese himself, was still there. He told us to hop in his green pick-up truck and we roared out of the city breaking all speed limits. After about twenty minutes we caught the bus. The deal was still on. We paid only 30 sucres!

When we got to Quito about 2:00 AM, the driver said he knew we were low on money, so why didn't we just go ahead and sleep the rest of the night in the bus? So sleep we did, freezing our asses off there at nine-thousand feet or so, only thirty miles from the equator. And when the driver came out the next morning he asked us where in the city would we like to go? "Cuartel de la Policia," we told him.

We walked into the police station. "Welcome to Ecuador," a policeman said. "What can we do for you?" The cuartel was full, but the police drove us around for half an hour trying various places and finally arranged for us to stay free in another lodging.

And so it went. We traveled by train, by bus and by truck. We spent one night with some American Peace Corps volunteers. Meanwhile, Tito and I had some intense conversations. He had the same eye-power commonly referred to in the U.S. as 'intensity.' He explained that a hippy could never tell someone else what to do; that a hippy could not have any doctrine, for if he did, he would no longer be free. He had his translation of the Tibetan Book of the Dead and could tell me all about Timothy Leary and various Oriental philosophers.

But I was traveling too fast and too slow: too fast to really connect with the people and towns through which we were passing and too slow to arrive in Colorado at any time in the foreseeable future.

Eventually we arrived in Cali, Colombia, where Tito had some friends with whom he planned to stay for a few days. We passed through a crowd and learned that fifteen people had just been killed in a battle between the public transportation authorities and the police. That was eleven more than had been killed in Peru's military 'revolution' of last October 2, 1968 the day we had arrived in Iquitos. Colombians, I had been told quite a few times, had a different and more violent way of doing things. Of course everyone I met there was nice. But the brand of Spanish was getting very different from Peruvian. I was having quite a difficult time understanding what was being said.

My head was ringing with the effort of trying to live up to Tito's expectations so I decided not to tarry and to move on. I had spent $6 in the last four days traveling with Tito. That was largely because I had snuck off while we were in Quito and indulged in a Chinese restaurant.

Drunks in a Chinese Bar

My total bill since Lima was still less than $20 so I decided to spend some money and fly from Medellin, the next city north, on to Panama. It took me two days of hitch-hiking to get to Medellin, during which time I stopped for most of a day and night to visit an American Peace Corps Volunteer who was trying to introduce fish which could be bred in home-dug artificial ponds.

I was in a hurry but I was tired. My patience was wearing thin and dreams of the snows of Colorado were beginning to assail me. I started out in a truck one night with a super macho guy whose local slang dialect of Spanish was almost impossible for me to understand. After a short while, he dismissed me as someone impossible to talk with and assailed the empty cab with all kinds of very 'macho' hacking and spitting and coughing followed by some ear-splitting whistling and soul-bending singing. I liked him best as a singer.

But I was tired, so when he stopped to change a tire, I told him I was going to stay there and sleep. I got a room and went into a restaurant to write. Sitting by myself again was a real pleasure! The waiter told me after I'd finished my meal that if I wanted to sit and write a bit, he'd go out and bring me some coffee from somewhere else, even though he didn't have any there. I said yes.

I figured I'd better change some dollars into Colombian pesos if I could that night, so I started asking around. I tried here and I tried there, and finally was directed to a Chinese bar. Inside, I announced that I wanted to sell $4. Someone invited me to have a beer, so I sat down for a little quiet conversation and twenty people drew up their chairs. One of them was a real drunk personality who was going to do everything for me. He decided that I was a guerrilla and wrote me a little secret note to that effect. I managed to get my $4 changed and soon about three people had quietly warned me that I'd better watch my step on my way home for someone was sure to try and steal it. The first drunk was trying to tell me he'd take me to his house in his car so I finally had to tell him no and physically push him out of my way. I took a devious route home, and went in and got the good night's sleep for which I had stopped.

A Coup in Panama

Eighteen hours later I was in Medellin and went straight to the airport. They did indeed have a flight to Panama and it was only $33 but it wouldn't be taking off for a week.

I wanted to spend some money for a change. I'd been on the road for two weeks since Lima, so I took $20 and spent it for a flight to the port of Cartagena on the northern coast of Colombia.

No sooner was I downtown walking around looking for a room for the night in Cartagena when I met a young fellow from New Zealand who was trying to get to Panama too. We spent the next day going more places and seeing more people than I had ever crammed into a single day in my entire life. All of our efforts were aimed at finding a way to get to Panama and the best we finally came up with was a little boat which promised to start us off on a two-week binge of fishing and boat-riding all for the sake of getting about three-hundred miles. No planes to Panama either. The airports in Panama were closed due to some internal disturbances. An attempted coup against Torrijos, the General in charge of the government, had just been thwarted.

I thought I had seen some noisy market places in Peru but they were nothing compared to the roaring Caribbean waterfront in Cartagena. The African exuberance was powerful.

While standing by the docks we saw two young gringo couples. I cheerily asked, "Speak English?" No answer. "Hablan Ingles?"

"Where are you from?" came the sullen reply in a heavily accented English. (French perhaps?)

"I'm an American and..."

"Oh, well, we don't like Americans."

"Oh is that right!" Instead of punching him, I walked away.

I saw him again later on. I swelled myself up in front of him and challenged: "Where do you live, heaven?"

"No, Alabama," came the clever reply. I again managed to contain my urge to flatten his nose.

That same night the New Zealand fellow and I got on a bus to the nearby city of Barranquilla. There he introduced me to three young English fellows, two of whom had been there for a couple of years. They were in the fishing business. That is, they had gotten enough money to buy two boats and were learning how to fish from local folk whom they had hired to help them. Nice guys. Played guitars. Could have been a nice place to stay for a while, but I was on my way.

I found out that I could fly from there to Miami for only $65, so I hoped my clothes wouldn't stink the poor folks off the plane and decided to go. At least I could keep my socks caged in my shoes.

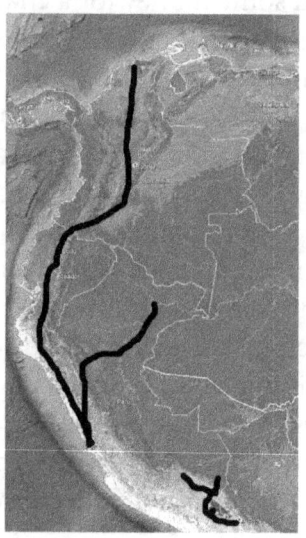

South American Routes in 1968-1969

Tonsils, Steamboat Springs, A Message from Robin

Landing in Miami, I made my way to St Louis and then to Albany, New York. My uncle Sam, the surgeon, arranged to have my chronically infected tonsils removed by one of his expert Doctor friends. Recovery took a few days more than I had expected but the long term benefits of that surgery were wonderful.

I visited a cousin in Chicago, my father in Indiana, my mother again in Missouri and finally arrived back home in Steamboat Springs and moved into Wayne and Linda's communal Barn Lodge. I played and sang the live music for the wild dance parties and washed the dishes in exchange for my keep. My friend Charlie Bates was living there too and together we procured roofing jobs and made our money.

I received a letter from Robin telling me that what she would decide to do in life depended on me! I wasn't sure exactly what she meant by that and I wasn't sure how to respond. But soon, as it turned out, I would have a chance to re-connect with her.

Lisa came up to visit on the weekends and we maintained our

happy connection. During the late spring and early summer Wayne and Linda departed for an extended trip and Lisa and I took over the logistics of running the Lodge.

Lisa at The Barn in Steamboat Springs

Cataract Canyon

I set my typewriter out on the hay-wagon in the pasture and wrote about our adventures in Peru until Wayne and Linda were back and we set off on a river trip down the Green River through Grays, Desolation and Cataract canyons. Our rafts were assembled from inflatable pontoons called 'J-tubes,' wooden infrastructures which provided room for lots of beer and gear and upon which we could mount five twelve-to-fourteen-foot sweep oars. Weeks spent naked on the river brought out deep and primal friendships. It wasn't until we reached Cataract Canyon that the excitement peaked. I loved it. I became the natural captain of one of our three boats because I apparently had the knack for staying focused on reading the river and threading a safe course through rapids like the 'Devil's Gut' in 'The Big Drop.'

Resting On One of Our Rafts

Somewhere in the slick sculpted white rim sandstones above the Green River in Canyonlands we had managed to rappel to safety from another high lip of stone. About six of us had set off to climb up and over from one side canyon to another. But the descent was a mystery. We had no idea of what lay ahead. …or rather, below…

Choosing a cleft in the top of the cliffs we began a descent which took us hundreds of feet down through the secret canyon wall waterways. Time and time again we leapt off rock lips into pools of water below. It became obvious that even with our best rock climbing skills, which were considerable in that crowd, we were committed. We would not be able to climb back up those slick sculpted walls.

Finally we peered over the last lip in the system of eroded cracks. The floor of the canyon was visible below. We were perched in an overhanging notch. The descent was not possible to down-climb. It was beyond the vertical in a canyon wall with no hand or foot holds. Treading water in a pool we finally found a crack into which to drive an anchor for our ropes. But how far down was it? We had enough rope with us to descend a hundred-and-fifty feet. Peering over the lip it looked like the vertical distance might easily be much more than that... What to do? Rappel down a hundred-and-fifty feet and let go and fall the remaining distance? To our amazed relief the ropes almost reached the bottom and we lowered ourselves one-at-a-time like spiders and had only to let go and free-fall the last five feet or so.

A couple of days later, after a long hike up and over the ridge from one canyon to another, my friend Byron and I found no one at our agreed-upon rendezvous camp spot. Gambling that our boats must have missed the landing, the two of us rode driftwood logs after dark down the river for half an hour and caught up to our boats.

After that immersion in those beautiful canyons, during the next few years I joined every river trip I could manage to squeeze in.

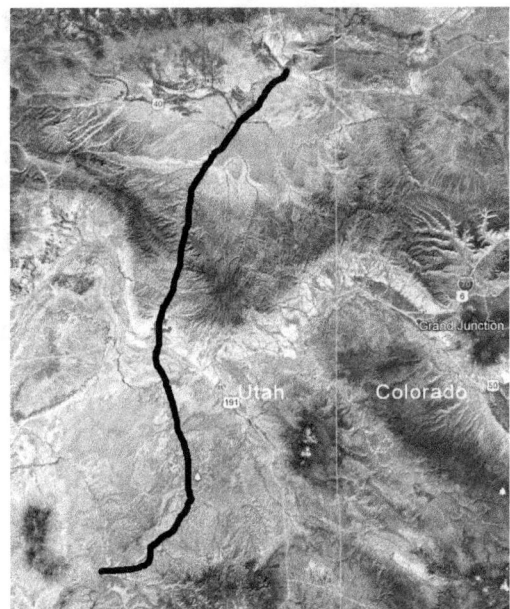

Grays, Desolation and Cataract Canyons

Climbing the Grand Teton and Blanca Peak

Charlie, I and another friend, Gordon Norton, also took time to go up to Wyoming and climb the complete Exum route on the Grand Teton and then we went down to Southern Colorado to climb the north face of Blanca Peak. Both climbs required several days of living and sleeping on steep rock with midnight rappel descents in pitch-black chimneys and horrendously long avenues of approach.

Grand Teton Complete Exum Ridge Route

Our second day on the north face of Blanca peak was so arduous that we never even stopped once, not even for a bite or a drink until after dark when we finally reached the ridge above and got off the face and ate our last two cans of sardines and a can of mincemeat. The climb had been about twenty-five-hundred vertical feet which we had divided into about twenty-five separate roped pitches. I was able to make the climbs, but it was Charlie and Gordon who led the hardest parts. If we knocked a rock off near the top it would take nine seconds of falling before we would hear it land.

North Face of Blanca Peak in Sangre De Cristo Range

That climb had truly seemed like it would never end. I began imagining that I had passed through some kind of space warp into another universe wherein all the land was permanently nearly vertical. I decided that life would be bearable under those circumstances but certainly lacking in some of the basic pleasures like food, water and being able to get from one place to the next. The strata in that rock face emerged in down-sloping little ledges so it was never possible to find a good hand or foot-hold. The face was always trying to dump us off... to get rid of us... Climbing the Grand Teton, a five-thousand-foot vertical ascent, had been even more vertical but actually much easier with its much friendlier and more available hand-holds and foot-holds.

After finishing the last of our food at the top of the climb up the north face of Blanca Peak we still had a four-thousand-foot descent and then a hundred miles of hitch-hiking on little dirt roads to make it back to our car. We must have been given some food along the way. A young Hispanic guy we passed showed us how easy it could be to catch trout by simply reaching into holes in the bottoms of streams and pulling them out by hand. I developed that skill back home in Steamboat Springs. No more need for fancy fishing equipment.

Charlie and I had landed a huge job re-roofing the multiple buildings of an entire school so we kept pushing to get the job completed. A baby raccoon had befriended me and rode on my shoulder up and down the ladders and scampered around the rooftops as we worked. Steamboat Springs, then a ranching community of five-thousand people, was a man's world. Women were few and far between and the ones who came to visit had to deal with our rough, barbarian attitudes. Some of them seemed to like us; others found ways to keep their distance.

I don't remember exactly how, but it was during this summer that Bill Chase entered my life. Hair grown halfway down his back, and with a face which could instantaneously switch from insane laughter to vicious aggression, the man appeared to be completely mad. Having grown up in Wichita, Kansas, he and his brother Tom had built the muscles in their bodies by climbing hand-over-hand up the guy wires to the tops of the local transmission towers. Bill made his way through college in Hays, Kansas as the undefeated wrestling champion. Ninety percent of what Bill said was incomprehensible. But his endless joviality seemed un-match-able.

No, I had never met anyone like Bill. I never suspected that we would remain friends for life, but that's what happened. Somehow through the quarts of Wayne's home brew which we imbibed and in between shoving whole pickled jalapeño peppers into each other's mouths I did my best to follow his tales of favorite bar fights. Bill absolutely loved to fight. "Just protect your teeth and there's no problem," he insisted. He had endeared himself to the local cowboy and rancher population, not a group which was particularly fond of hippies, by personally defeating them all with his fists and his wrestling moves. I had never met anyone who communicated with such pure projections of energy... something way beyond the realms of words. It was like being exposed to solar flares from close up.

Bill was making trips to Africa and I to South America and we were comparing notes. I was drawn to spend hours with the guy when he would come to hang with us at the Barn. We seemed to almost know what we were talking about although it was all conducted in uproarious gibberish. A few years later I would get married in his back yard down in Boulder and I would be some kind of "best man" at his wedding at the "difficult creek" campground near Aspen.

Linguistics, Robin, Yosemite

I continued to study Quechua, the Inca language and felt like I had only scratched the surface of being able to converse with my new friends in Sina. Acknowledging that my successes were largely thanks to the linguistics training I had received in Boulder and at Cornell, I decided to dive in deeper. I sent letters of inquiry to Harvard, the University of Chicago, Berkeley, Stanford and UCLA. I received positive replies from all five universities and determined to visit them.

I drove east with Harvard in Boston as my goal. Robin was in her home town of Cincinnati and she was excited to have me stop and visit. She greeted me at the door of her apartment. Few words were necessary. She led me down to a sheltered spot on the bank of the Ohio river and we made love. I felt like we were both at the mercy of a powerful goddess who was using us as the brush strokes in her never-ending work of art.

Wandering back to her apartment she informed me that her Argentine lover was also visiting. He was upstairs. Telling me she would be right back, she headed up the stairs to let him know something... I don't know what... A couple of hours passed. I felt like something must be stuck... Some energy was feeling like a log trapped sideways in a stream in a flood. I didn't know what it was, but I went out the door without saying goodbye, started my car and continued on my way to Boston.

I spent a day absorbing the feel of the Linguistics department at Harvard. Then I headed back west and did the same at the University of Chicago, then Stanford and the Universities of California in both Los Angeles and Berkeley.

Joe Sharp and Charlie Bates were in California at that time too, so we met up in Yosemite and climbed up to 'lunch ledge' on Washington Column. It took us until after dinner time to reach 'lunch ledge' so we rappelled back down from there in the dark. Yosemite rock is challenging: tiny hand and foot holds with a lot of acrobatic crack climbing required. Joe and Charlie were my heroes. They led the hard pitches... which was all of them...

I felt most at home at UC Berkeley so I finished the application process and soon was offered a full scholarship with all expenses paid to complete a doctorate. I was scheduled to begin classes in the fall of 1970, the next year. I could not guess that I was about to enter into some of the most kaleidoscopically tumultuous adventures of my life.

I was offered a job teaching anthropology at the private high school we were roofing in Steamboat Springs. I couldn't imagine assuming the full-fledged role demanded by actually joining the faculty which would have also required playing policeman and disciplinarian, but I agreed to teach a few classes in an informal way.

The school was planning to move to Mexico for two months later in the spring and they offered me a job teaching Spanish and taking the students on tours to remote local villages near their temporary home base in Manzanillo on the Pacific coast. If I could find marvelous little villages in Peru then I could do that in Mexico. I agreed to head south with them when the time came.

Lisa and I decided to meet in Peru sometime after that and return for another visit to our new friends in Sina.

Carp's Cabin Again

I learned that my friend James was back at Carp's cabin for another winter alone. I worried about his poverty and isolation and decided to drive down for a visit. I hadn't forgotten the kindness he had shown me five years earlier as he coaxed me up rock climbing routes near Manitou Springs. Something told me he might need a friendly visit.

I stopped my car and opened the gate somewhat apprehensively. I remembered that the old miner who lived between the highway and Carp's place didn't welcome strangers. I had been told that the best thing to do was to drive through as rapidly as possible, hopefully avoiding the old miner, for he would supposedly do everything he could to discourage people from passing through. The old guy was supposedly off his nut and might not only deny that I was on the right road but perhaps even take a few shots at the car.

I proceeded until I came to a fork in the road. Uh Oh! It had been so long since I had been there I couldn't remember which way to go. I chose the fork on the right-hand side and drove across the ice which covered a shallow creek.

Driving up a hill to another gate, which was open, I spied an old green jeep coming down the road toward me. I stopped on my side of the gate. The jeep stopped on the other side of the gate. I waited. The jeep waited. I started forward again just as the jeep did. The jeep stopped and I went on through and stopped beside it.

The driver was a very old and very small wrinkled man who looked at me with the reddest pair of eyes I had ever seen. I don't know whether they were bloodshot from his days in the mine or from some subsequent vice, but they were unlike the eyes of a drunk. Something keen shone out through them. He looked at me and said, "Where ya headed mister?"

"I'm lookin' for Carp's place," I said.

"Well Carp's not up there, ya know, but James is."

"Yeah, James is? Well good!"

"1 just drove him up there," he said. "Just keep goin' on this road and take the left fork before you get there."

"Well good," I said, "James is up there. Thanks a lot."

"If this arthritis gets any worse I'm gonna go down and drown myself in the creek!" he laughed.

"Good luck with that!" I told him.

"Fine and dandy, then," he said, putting his jeep into gear.

"Thanks," I said and drove on up the road. So much for a scary encounter with the supposedly nasty old miner.

Around the next corner I stopped and watched a herd of twenty-five mountain sheep who were standing petrified about fifty yards from the road. I took the left fork when I came to it and saw James' old black panel truck with its stove pipe sticking out of the side.

"Well I'll be damned," James shouted. "It's Cameron!"

We went on into his cabin. I spied two conga drums sitting in the corner.

"I've eaten over a thousand eggs in the last two months," James laughed. He showed me a bucket half-filled with pulverized egg shells. "I've filled that bucket one and a half times," he said.

"I used to have some flour," he explained. "...different kinds of flour that I used to make all kinds of baked goods out of. I found you don't even need baking soda, man, all you need is the flour to make the most delicious kinds of bread! Good, solid bread. Oh, I used to spend whole days doing nothing but baking the shit up. But what I really miss is oats! Steel cut oats! I could live off those things. I've got some oats for the animals, and I tried to use 'em, but I couldn't get the husks off. I can't figure out how they do it! So it's been eggs. Just eggs and eggs and eggs."

"Where do you get all the eggs?" I asked.

"Oh, I've got chickens. Twenty-six chickens. Come on, we'll go and feed the animals and I'll show ya."

We went outside again and James walked up to a donkey whom I hadn't noticed before. "Hello Sue," he said. "Cameron come on over and meet Sue."

I walked up and met the nicest donkey I'd ever met in my life: the kind of donkey I'd always wanted to meet. She had long bangs down over her eyes so when she looked at you she had to tilt her head back.

"She really likes to be ridden," James said, climbing on her. Then I climbed on her and she walked around a little bit. I couldn't tell whether she was really enjoying it or not but I was willing to take James' word for it.

We fed two horses and the chickens and went back inside. James brought some of the cracked dried corn with which he had fed the chickens.

"And I do have some venison," he added. "Carp and most of his friends are eating only vegetables but I still have got to have some meat so finally I went out and poached a deer. Oh by the way, this is just between you and me, 'cause if old Ed... -- you met him on the way in didn'tcha?"

"Yeah, I met him in his jeep and stopped and talked to him."

"If he ever found out, boy, that someone was poaching on his land -- I had to go onto his land to get the deer -- boy, would he raise a stink. You can stay for three or four days, can't ya? Or a week, stay as long as you want. There's all kinds of neat things to do around here. I get stoned and go ice skating up at the pond at night, and it's really neat!" James exclaimed.

He took me outside again and showed me through some binoculars where he had been doing some climbing. The ranch was surrounded by granite pinnacles and walls, all about four-hundred feet high. We were far enough south in Colorado so that even in mid-winter some days were warm enough to allow climbing on the rock. I looked at the routes through the binoculars with amazement. What a place to be doing such difficult solo climbing!

Back inside James cooked us a delicious dinner of fried egg yolks overlaid with brown rice overlaid with venison. Meanwhile, as the sun went down, we drank three six-packs of beer which I had saved in the trunk of my car. "I don't have any gasoline left for the truck, and it doesn't work very well anyway," he added.

"I remember hearing that old Ed sometimes gives people a really hard time when they tried to pass through his place," I said.

"That's right, he does. He's even been known to shoot at people who haven't stopped to talk to him. It depends on his mood. But all you have to do is stop and talk with him to make him happy."

We ate dinner and both immediately started farting sulfur dioxide. I suggested that we smoke some more of the grass I had in the car which I had gotten in California. So we did. We sat in front of the fireplace and smoked one joint.

Fifteen minutes later James stood up and said, "Uh oh, I've gotta get out of here!" He rushed out the door leaving me sitting on a stool in front of the fire.

I stood up and I went outside. James was sitting on the ground, leaning against a barrel. "Jesus Christ, Cameron! What has that shit got in it? That's not like any grass or hash I've ever smoked."

I laughed and looked up at the stars. I milled around a little bit and James finally got up and we went back into the cabin. "Jesus Christ, that shit is too much!" James exclaimed.

I laughed again. I started babbling about something, but James wasn't listening. He suddenly turned around and looked behind him and said, "Uh oh, here it comes again. I've gotta get outa here..." He rushed towards the door.

I sat down on my stool again in front of the fire. I felt suddenly empty. I sat there for a long time with nothing but vague confusion. Then I heard a noise outside the window. Everything inside me jumped and I glared at the window.

I suddenly put two and two together. James, the gravedigger. When I had first known James he had been a gravedigger. That was why he always wore black. That was why he drove a black panel truck. That was why old Ed was there to guard the entrance. That was why the ranch was surrounded by granite crags. The only hope left was to rush out, jump in the car and drive out as fast as I could. I budged on my seat but stayed put.

'But what if James is just sitting out in his outhouse?' I thought. 'Poor guy. What if I run out, tell him I've gotta get out of here, and tear off down the road. That could be the final stroke! The final event which would make James put two and two together in the way I had, and what a thing to do to a friend! I would be creating a James which James himself would not want to be! And what would happen to the next person who came out to visit?'

'Oh my God, help,' I thought and shook my head. 'Help me get this Shit out of my head, James, for Chrissakes!'

I stood up and went outside. I could see a light glowing in the outhouse. I stood and waited in front of the cabin until James came striding toward it. He had only one thing to say. He looked at me out of the corner of his eye, shook his head and said, "Heavy Shit."

We were telepathically connected. We could feel each others' fears and anguish. I stood looking up at the stars. I was actually seeing them moving and swirling around.

After about five minutes we started heading back toward the cabin. "I've got to go to bed, or something," James announced.

"I was thinking, ever since I came in here, though, that we really ought to try playing those drums," I said.

"Yeah, OK," James said.

We sat down in front of the fire with the drums. We played and played and played. It worked beautifully. We found a way to release an overwhelming quantity of strange mental energy that was floating around that night. Finally my hands began to lag behind. I was all played out.

"I don't know what kind of drumming you're used to," I said, "but I thought that was mighty fine."

"Yeah," James smiled, "That was good."

The next morning we ground the cracked corn up in a coffee grinder and mixed it with eggs and fried it for an experiment. Eggy, but good. I headed back up toward Steamboat Springs. I would see

James again in a few months and my intuition would again register confusing signals of an impending disaster.

More Rivers and Roofs

Back at the Barn Lodge in Steamboat Springs I discovered that we had time for one more river trip before leaving for Mexico with the school. We took our boats to run the 'Gates of Lodor' on the Green River above the confluence with the Yampa. It was springtime and the water was running high. Upper and Lower Disaster Falls and Hell's Half Mile were wild rides. I was bonding more and more deeply with a group of about sixty 'river rats.' We had three boats, each one with five oars. One man on each oar provided enough strength to pilot those craft and in coming years we explored the Yampa, the Green and Colorado rivers all the way down through the Grand Canyon.

But Charlie and I still had a huge roofing job to finish back in Steamboat.

"Thwack Thwack Thwack!"

"Hey! Would you guys hold off for a while? We're trying to have study hall down here."

"OK. We'll try and hammer more quietly."

Thus the roofing progressed on through the school year.

"Hey, Charlie! How much longer you reckon it'll take us to finish the other side of this roof?"

"I don't know. We'll shovel the snow off it tomorrow and then we can see."

And so it was that Charlie and I worked our way up in the school from the top down. Several months later, in March to be exact, I woke up one morning at The Barn in Steamboat at the stone cold hour of 3:00 AM and went outside to climb into the school's Checker Airport Limousine with about fourteen other sleepy people and off we went to Manzanillo in Colima, Mexico.

Terrible Tours in Mexico

The headmaster of the school liked the idea that I could take students into remote places traveling by bumping over roads in buses or on horses or on foot... "Of course I imagine you'll have trouble finding any places as terrible to travel through as you have found in Peru..."

"Oh, I don't know," replied. "I imagine there's some pretty terrible places around; we'll certainly make these tours as terrible as possible." He seemed satisfied with that prospect so I felt free to follow my instincts and the name, which I would employ later in Peru, "Terrible Tours" was born.

I was told to go see Mr. Halsey who was an American who owned a store in the vicinity. He reputedly had been getting to know that part of Mexico (Colima and Michoacan) for fifteen years and he might understand what kinds of 'terrible places' I was looking for and be able to direct me to them. I went into his store with a map and explained my quest.

"Sure, I know just the places your looking for," he said. "You can go here, or here, or here..." None of the places he was describing seemed interesting to me.

Finally I asked, "What about this big region on the coast of Michoacan? It doesn't seem to have any roads built into it yet."

"Whatever you do," said Mr. Halsey, "don't go into that region. I have a friend who has lived on a mountain on the edge of that area for twenty years now. He's never gone over to the other side of that mountain 'cause if he did, God only knows what might happen."

I now knew exactly where to lead my Terrible Tours.

"Well, thank you very much," I said to Mr. Halsey. "I think I've got some pretty good ideas now, anyway. See you later."

Friendly Crabs and Creating Canyons

The first 'terrible tour' sent us scampering around a deserted beach at the northern end of the forbidden area. We didn't have more than a couple of days for that first trip but we got to know the crabs.

If you ever want to meet one, here's how you do it. Chase one around the beach for a while until you're both exhausted. You have to prevent him from getting down one of his holes, but if you both scuttle around frantically for a long enough time, you can come to some kind of terms whereby you both just sit worn out and stare at each other. That's what you want to accomplish.

Then, if his great long windshield-wiper eyes haven't gotten accidentally covered with sand, you can bend over, pick him up from behind, and stare deep into those big luminous globes he's got for eyeballs, and whamo! You'll suddenly realize he's just like you are. Getting the right angle is important. First of all, his eyes have to be standing straight up and looking. It's difficult to really get much going when they're in the off position. Then you have to look from absolutely dead center in front of him. Then you'll discover that he has long narrow vertical pupils in his eyes behind which is that same profundity of black and infinite space you'll find in your own very most magical girlfriend's eyes. Before he dries out too much, set him down and let him run off to cool off in the ocean or in one of his holes while you strike up a friendship with another one.

A short way up the hill behind the beach I found an instant Grand Canyon kit built right into the hillside. The moisture content of this sand bank was just exactly right so that, once set in motion by the removal of a handful of sand from the bottom of the bank, mountains and canyons would automatically form as the streams of liquid sand collapsed. Millions of years of dramatic erosion would happen in five minutes before your very eyes.

On our journey to that remote beach we had stopped in Cerro de Ortega and met Antonio Castrejon and his family, including his lovely daughter Josefina. We met Antonio in a restaurant. He very kindly let us spend the night on the floor of his barbershop. We continued to visit him and his children and their friends on later trips and learned to play some great popular Mexican songs from them.

But our most important connections were with the local grade school teacher and his lovable little wife at the end of the road in Aquila. I had inquired about going further and we were directed to a small hunch-backed and somewhat crippled schoolteacher.

This was Rafael Cisneros, who had lived there in Aquila for the last few years. But he had spent his younger years teaching in villages in the vast Nahuatl and Tarascan-speaking region to the south and he knew that territory all the way down to a remote village called Pomaro. We spent the afternoon talking with him and recording some sentences in Nahuatl. He told us that he would be only too happy to help us rent pack animals or whatever we might need to continue south. We left it as a plan for a subsequent Terrible Tour when we would have more time.

Musical Wandering

For the next Tour we decided to go quite a ways up to Lake Patzcuaro. We rode all afternoon and 'till midnight on the bus and still hadn't arrived, so we got off just west of Carapan and camped in a creek bottom. It seemed we were being spied upon from the bushes by a donkey -- or perhaps by some people -- which sent Peggy into the bottom of her sleeping bag from which she absolutely refused to budge. Presumably she eventually fell asleep, because the next day she was in pretty good shape. The next day we got up in time for Pablo, who had brought his guitar with him, to sing us 'Here Comes the Sun,' discover that we had in fact spent the night in somebody's brick factory, and set off for Paracho.

Pablo, a Student from Thailand, Sings 'Here Comes the Sun'

Paracho is a famous guitar-making center. I would return there more than once in later years. In fact the entire town is filled with shops which are filled with practically nothing but guitars. At least half the population of the town makes its living from musical carpentry.

Right off the bat Pam bought a good twelve-string guitar while I combed the stores for a conga drum. It was market day and the plaza was filled with the stalls of vendors. There sat Jim, right in the middle of the plaza, right beside the circular structure which marked the very center of town, underneath the tall tower of an adobe church whose clock face had gone haywire and come hanging crooked out of its hole presumably on the end of a long spring -- there sat Jim at the bottom of all this, throwing up...

"Must have been something I ate," he said. One of the girls brought him some flowers to make him feel better, and pretty soon all eight of us were sitting around him. The shops had closed. It was siesta hour. Pablo decided to sing him a song with his guitar. Maybe it would make him feel better. Two hours later, Jim had completely recovered and was singing at the top of his lungs with the rest of us to a crowd of about two-hundred people who had gathered quietly to hear our musical noises which were getting better all the time.

Singing in Patzcuaro

Eventually, at 3:00 PM or so, when the shops reopened, I decided that $32 wasn't too much for a good conga drum after all, and that besides, it was either now or never. I retraced my steps to where I had seen the drum for sale, wandered into the shop and said, "I'll buy it!" Now we had two guitars, maracas, a guiro, and a conga drum. Cumbersome, but nice.

We left Paracho, passed briefly through Uruapan, decided not to go see the volcano which had been born in somebody's cornfield nearby, and proceeded to the town of Patzcuaro on the edge of a large lake. We walked for a long time through the night looking for an empty field in which to rest.

A Good Field in which to Rest

The next morning the sun was shining pleasantly. Along came a friendly Indian carrying his hoe over his shoulder who spoke Tarascan. We began chatting in Spanish and I asked him to help us learn to speak Tarascan. I brought out my cassette recorder and we filled up a few tapes with his translations and made good headway into being able to say a few words in Tarascan. Then he went on his way back from whence he had come, for by that time we had used up his hoeing time. We called after him and invited him to a lunch in town.

Guitar and Drum

After lunch there was nothing else to do but find the central town plaza, break out our new instruments and keep ourselves awake with a little music. Then the local schools let out and two or three hundred people joined us. I think we were getting better at the music, although we were also getting tired. The females in our group, Peggy, Pamela, Sarah and Clarents were quite an attraction all by themselves.

That night Pablo and I went up to Tzintzuntzan because an American anthropologist from Berkeley named George Foster had written an ethnography of that village. We visited a few people and recorded some more Tarascan phrases and then caught the bus back to Patzcuaro. I was disappointed because, although I had ordered Mr. Foster's book in order to have it for our visit, I didn't end up actually receiving it 'till some eight months later. Anyway, I was glad to see that the Terrible Tours were proceeding from bad to worse. It took us a good sixteen hours on the bus the next day to get back to Manzanillo.

My birthday came up in the next couple of days and the Terrible Tourers, aside from getting me a cake and singing me happy birthday, gave me the money I had spent for the drum, thereby transforming it into a present from them. I suddenly realized that I felt younger on my 26th birthday than I had on my 24th! I had a hunch that if I could just make life more Terrible each year, I would feel younger and younger!

Whatever You Do, Don't Go into That Area!

The next Terrible Tour was the Big Terrible Tour. The Really Terrible Terrible Tour. The Five-Day-Terrible-Tour. Who was going to go? This would be the longest trip we would make. Most of the kids were going to go to the bright lights of Guadalajara or to the champagne and milkshakes of Mexico City.

Who wants to go drag-ass along behind a hot dusty mule down there in the unknown territory south of Aquila somewhere? Even I was becoming envious of the others who were combing their hair or dashing perfume behind their ears to head for the big cities.

But now was the chance to get into Mr. Halsey's promised land south of Aquila. ("Whatever you do, don't go into that area!" echo echo echo). Most of the kids were smart and went elsewhere. But Pablo and his famous guitar came along. Bruce Burrow (el burro) and his bag of Corpus Christi tricks came along. Faithful Pamela came along. And me. That was just about it.

We spent the first afternoon pausing to make and learn music in Cerro de Ortega with Antonio's daughter Josefina and her friends and we then spent the night with Rafael and his wife Rosa Ramos and their two daughters Felipa and Luisa in Aquila. The next morning we all woke up years younger, so off we went with Rafael to grade school. Pablo, Pam and I made pretty good second graders, but El Burro was either goofing off or dozing at his desk.

School Children with Rafael

A fifth grader, El Chui, said he would come with us on our walk south. He went to check it out with his mother, Agapita Garcia, who agreed it would be a good idea. Jesus Fernandez, an old gray-headed man whose business has been the transport of goods by mule for some fifty years, decided he would come with us to provide a pack animal and a horse, but for only as far as La Cofradia, the first village.

A Horse from Jesus

We got off to a rather late start and ended up walking into La Cofradia about midnight. We offered Jesus some of our food but he turned it all down and stuck with his simple diet of tortillas and salt. It had been nice to have the coolness of the night for walking but arriving at midnight didn't lead to any fun with the villagers.

On the Trail with Jesus Fernandez

The next morning we had a nice talk with the local teacher, a young man from Nayarit, but nothing held us there, so we wandered on off down the trail again but without Jesus and his pack animal.

Luck was with us. A third-grader decided to come along with us with one of his daddy's mules. The mule carried our sleeping bags, some food and Pablo's guitar. So we took it easy while the heat of the day grew and we felt more and more thankful for the mule, which allowed us to saunter along unencumbered. But we never made it to the next village.

Pam had begun the day by saying that she didn't feel too well and that furthermore, she hadn't felt well all night. Being the incurable optimist that she was, however, she kept assuming that she would feel better as the day wore on. But by noon fever overtook her and she lay in semi-sleep in a handy shadow under a tree by the river Coalcomán.

This wasn't a bad place to get hung up, right next to a grove of coconut palms. El Chui proved to be the only one among us who dared climb all the way up into the top of one of the palms and throw us down a coconut. Our little nine-year-old friend, who had brought his daddy's mule, went off to find the owner of the palms and give him 50 centavos for the coconut but he couldn't find anyone. El Chui instructed us in the art of opening coconuts with only a small pocket knife, so we spent the next two or three hours opening two or three coconuts. And we practiced climbing more coconut palms.

Bruce Climbs Part Way Up a Palm Tree

And we threw sticks at little edible buds to knock them off the branch tips of the high trees on which they grew. We ate buds and coconuts until we were overstretched on the inside and needed something else to do. But Pamela lay in the shade making it very apparent that, since we were Westerners, we'd better get to some Western medicine as soon as possible.

A few men came by with a long train of donkeys, all loaded with firewood. We conferred and planned. It seemed that there was a shorter way out than the way we had come in. So we decided to head back to Aquila. But Pamela could only walk a few hundred yards. We settled her down on her sleeping bag under a tree, tended to her food and water needs, and went over and spent the remaining three hours of the bright afternoon daylight sitting in the middle of the river playing with the currents and the fish while we hoped that Pamela would be stronger the next morning. The little third-grader went on back to La Cofradia with his mule. That night I was still deep into playing the guitar long after everyone else had fallen asleep. Some kind of animal was scuttling and crashing around the periphery of our camp. I could only imagine that it must be some kind of pig, but when it eventually came close enough for me to lay the beam of a flashlight on it, I saw that it was an armadillo.

The next morning Pam said she felt some better, but before long she was weak and feverish again. El Chui kept assuring us that we were not far from a place called La Laguna, but it took Pam perhaps an hour to walk the last half mile to get there.

La Laguna seemed to be composed of about three houses. There didn't seem to be any 'laguna' around; in fact we had climbed up to the top of a high ridge out of the river valley in which we lad spent the last day. We had drunk all the water we had been able to carry and Pam was desperately thirsty. El Chui had gone over to one of the houses to ask if there was perhaps a horse or mule on which Pam could ride but came back saying that there didn't seem to be any animals available.

The truth of the matter was that El Chui was, even at the age of eleven or twelve, such a shy loner that he hardly ever dared to ask for anything, and if he did, he always managed to ask in such a way as to practically assure a refusal. He had told me that his father had been shot by another man a few years earlier and it seemed that El Chui was growing up chained tightly to the karma which he had acquired from that murder.

Suspecting that I might do better myself, I went up to another one of the houses in La Laguna. We were immediately invited into the shade and offered water in the house of Trino Magaña Fernandez, father of a dramatically handsome family.

His two daughters, Carlota and Teresa, dominated the conversation from the very beginning. They were ready and anxious to talk about everything and anything while they and their mother, Victoria Garcia, ministered tenderly to Pamela's and our food and juice needs. Carlota and Teresa were both in their mid-twenties, it seemed to me, yet still single, and still at home. I supposed that this was because they were both so incredibly beautiful that it could only happen once in a decade or so that a man of suitable prospect could wander into their midst.

Their somewhat younger brother, Josemaria, who told me later that he was nineteen -- sat calmly watching the activity. He didn't say a word but his attention was completely entwined in what was going on around him. He did not suffer from the typical adolescent habit of lapsing into inattentiveness and distraction. Perhaps it was because, as he told me later, he had never been to school for even a day in his life. Nor had his sisters. He said that he would come down to Aquila with us with a horse for Pamela to ride on although his sisters cautioned him about using his left foot too much. He had a deep machete wound on the top of his ankle which he had accidentally inflicted on himself while working in the cornfield -- a cornfield, incidentally, which was surely one of the driest and dustiest pieces of ground which I had ever seen sprouting food. It seemed that the nearest water source for La Laguna was a fifteen-minute walk away.

Across the way, in the third house, a woman offered to cook us up some eggs and beans and tortillas. She used her house as a sort of restaurant for the feeding of passersby. There I met a tall middle-aged man whose name I cannot remember. He was of striking appearance because he clearly had a good deal of gringo blood in him although he was clearly as poor as any Indian who had chosen La Laguna for home. I asked him why La Laguna had been settled on such a dry and dusty spot? How was it that they could live there where they had to walk fifteen minutes just for a bottle of water when just two miles down the trail the river valley was relatively green and lush? He explained that he had been among the first to settle there in La Laguna. I was astonished to notice that his feet were apparently as large as my own. He explained that the river valley below was all owned by other people; that there was no room for them down in the valley. "But above all," he added, "here we can live a free life; we can live exactly as we want to here, no?" I agreed. That was certainly clearly true.

Eventually we got ourselves together, put Pamela on a horse, and wandered on down toward Aquila. Josemaria prepared himself for going down to town by having one of his sisters tie a fresh batch of herbs over the wound on his ankle, and by strapping on his fancy holster and shiny six-gun. I asked him what he needed the gun for and he said that it was just part of getting dressed up. He had a girlfriend to visit down in Aquila.

Once back in Aquila I decided to take advantage of the availability of Western medicine -- something for which it seems Pamela may never forgive me. I said, "Let's go to the clinic and see what the Doctor thinks should be done."

"I hope they don't want to give me a shot!" Pamela pleaded into whatever winds of fate might have been passing by.

"Well, let's go see," I said knowing full well that there's only one thing Latin American doctors all swear by: injections. So they took poor Pamela who was, incidentally, apparently already on the road to recovery, into the adjacent room and closed the door.

"Put it in my arm please," she said.

"But it's too big to put in your arm," the nurse kindly explained.

"Please can't you put it in my arm?"

"Really, it will be better for you if we put it in behind."

So they gave her a great big shot in the ass, something for which, as I said, I guess she will never quite forgive me. I remember the way she looked at me when she came out of the adjacent room with a few tear streaks running down the dust on her cheeks.

Rafael and Rosa Cisneros, however, had just the thing for Pamela. They gave her a little green bird called a cotorita. And they saw to it that the four of us spent a comfortable night on the floor of their home. The next day we rose early and all six of us caught the 6:00 AM bus.

Rafael arranged to have someone take care of his schoolroom for a few days and he and Rosa came back to Manzanillo with us. We had taken advantage of multiple opportunities to see his school and to learn from him. Now he was curious to see how we gringos operated things in our school.

Pamela continued to be sick for the next few days, so Rosa helped her keep the bird well-fed. Rafael helped us with our Spanish and gave us some more Nahuatl sentences. I tried to introduce Rafael and his wife to other teachers at our school but none of them would take the time from their schedules to meet with us. I felt embarrassed since

Rafael and Rosa had taken so much time to welcome us into their world. But I had no real power in the school to draw more attention to our new friends and I had to give up. I felt like I was witnessing just one more example of the unconscious arrogance buried in our Northern European culture.

Our Music Flowed Through Us As Never Before

In a few days it was time for another Terrible Tour and we were all back in Aquila again. I was beginning to feel at home in Aquila and it seemed natural to eat at Agapita's and to spend the night at Rafael and Rosa's house.

Hanging Out with Rafael Cisneros

It's always nice to rest in familiar places. The next morning we got a chance to be eight-year-olds again for an hour or two while we sat in the local Aquila school house soaking in a bit of arithmetic. Just as we were getting deep into the multiplication tables however, Father Time put the scrunch on us and said: 'If you-all ever expect to get to where you're planning to go these few days you'd better get going!'

So up we stood up right in the middle of the school-day morning and off we went. El Chui brought his slingshot and came with us. We ran real fast and just had time to say goodbye and get on the noon bus back out of Aquila... which we rode for an hour and then got off of in

La Placita. We had determined to enter the vast road-less area from a different village.

We wandered into a restaurant -- all six of us -- piled all our belongings around us like a fortress and waited for half an hour before discovering that they weren't serving any food there at the moment.

It seemed that there were no mules or horses to be had. Perhaps they were all already out in the fields working. Or perhaps their owners had decided that the afternoon was just too hot to be sending their gently dozing animals out with a bunch of crazy slave-driving gringos anyway!

So I cheerfully announced that we would simply have to carry all our stuff and that La Ticla wasn't that far away anyway. Sara and Peggy were back with us this time. They both had a good natured manner and made jokes abut the apparent impossibility of getting anywhere.

We set off on foot and, just as I was beginning to be afraid that the sun might really be getting to us, we were overtaken by a quiet Mexican family: a man with a woman and child on a horse. It seemed that putting Peggy's and Sara's packs onto the horse with the woman and child was not so difficult after all which freed Peggy and Sara to float effortlessly along the trail.

On the Trail to La Ticla

El Chui was joined by another friend with a slingshot. The two of them amused or perturbed us all by shooting birds down out of trees and then presenting them to us as pets -- as soon, that is, as they might regain consciousness.

But anyway, Kiko, as Chui's friend was named, made things easier for all of us. Kiko and El Chui led our fastest hikers along the edge of the cliffs above the ocean while I led the rest of us down the hot inland trail behind the man, woman and child who were headed back to their home in La Ticla. Sara even got to ride the horse for a while.

Eventually our trail emerged back onto the beach and soon entered La Ticla. Our new friends invited us into their home to sit for a bit while we ate a banana or two and they then let us leave our belongings there while we set off for a swim. Coconut palms lined the edges of the warm fresh water which runs into the ocean at La Ticla. La Cofradia, the town to which we had walked the previous week just before Pamela got sick, was one to two days walk up that same river.

Now on the beach we climbed into the cold salt water. It was a beautiful spot except for one edge of the river's mouth where the ocean current was so strong that, when I inadvertently ventured into the edge of it, I suddenly found myself having to use all my strength to cling to the rocks below while the water rushed tugging past me in a rapidly moving crescent trying to pull me far out into the ocean. I clambered back up the beach somewhat frightened by the idea of what might have happened had I let myself go even one or two yards further along that current. I asked one of the people who lived there what happened to someone who got caught in that current. "The sharks finish you off far out in the sea," he said. So I began shouting and screaming about, yelling to my students not to get too far out into that current.

Then I lay down in the very mouth of the river where the warm fresh water ran over my shoulders from above while at fifteen second intervals the cold ocean poured up under me from below and floated me up the river a way before gently setting me back down on the rocks where the warm fresh river water would run over me from above once again. It was kind of like lying in nature's washing machine.

We stayed by ourselves down on the beach for the night. We built a fire and our music flowed through us as never before as we sat by the luminous crested, crashing, splendor of the sea and let our rhythm section grow and grow there all alone on the rocks.

I felt we were being a little selfish keeping all that good music just to ourselves. I would have preferred to set us up in the village of La Ticla in order that we might be with the people who lived there, but our popular consensus ruled the choice of the private beach site. I certainly couldn't say it was a wasted evening... the sea never forgets...

The next day some local folks showed us how to handle throw nets, but I couldn't ever see the fish as they swam by so I had to be content with gracefully netting a few rocks.

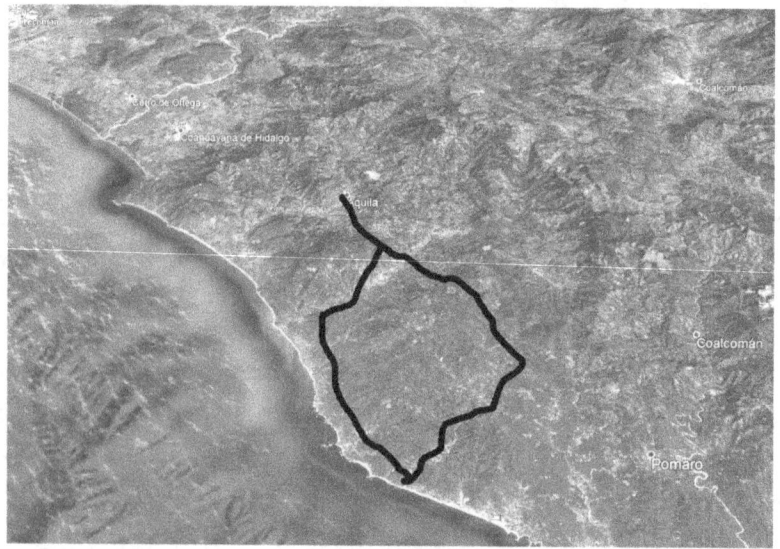

Wandering South from Aquila to Coalcoman River Valley

Fish in Our Pants

Terrible Tour number Five was a waterless and hot dusty venture where we parched our brains until at last we found ourselves outside of Tomatlan.

We had set out for Puerto Vallarta -- our first trip north. We'd gone east; we'd gone south; it seemed incomplete not to go north. But we drew a hot dusty zero from trucks and buses that never came.

We sought refuge from the heat of the second day out in big sections of giant concrete drainage pipes which lay beside the road. We eventually turned around and shifted our hopes that a vehicle would come from the opposite direction. We finally arrived some fifty or so kilometers north of Barra de Navidad and gratefully bedded down on the beach with a fire and some friendly scorpions and mosquitoes.

The next morning we took a long run down the beach around to the cliffs on the other side of the bay where starfish moved imperceptibly over rocks and a city full of crabs scuttled in busy hordes. Entering the water we swam into tens of thousands of silver squirming finger-sized fish which created the ultimate tickle. There were fish in our pants. There were fish in the water everywhere. Who would dare to completely immerse himself in the electric school? Throwing hands-fulls of fish out of the water into the air we were standing in a rain of fish, letting them flash down and slip through our hair and wriggle off our backs all the while standing in that incredible electric mess of silver life. Or why not throw a handful at your friend?

We made our way back to Manzanillo. That was the last Terrible Tour of the season, but I continued teaching a second-year level Spanish class every day at the school. I enlisted local Mexican kids to come and help by giving us opportunities for real communication in the local Mexican Spanish dialect.

I finished studying with Dr. Greenwood, the school's medical Doctor, who had told me that he could teach me in a couple of months everything of practical value he had learned in medical school. I had taken him up on it and we had used *Medicine for Mountaineering* as a textbook.

Saving Chicki from the Red Light District

The Spanish teacher asked me to accompany him to the local red light district. He was a Spaniard and suffered from the traditional European disease of seeing everything as good or evil. Señor Egues, as we called him, was suffering from this confusion. I don't know exactly how he got himself into this mess, especially since his wife was there in Manzanillo with us also, but he had fallen in love with a young lady of the night there in the red light district.

Chicki was her name and Señor Egues had decided that he should finally make love to her and then try to rescue her. He needed company and that's where I came in. He suggested that we go together to the red light district and make dates with Chicki and her friend Maria so that we could gain their attention.

Everything unfolded according to plan and soon he and Chicki were alone in a little room and I was alone in a room with Maria.

Maria and I were both feeling a little awkward and distracted. We were not feeling much attraction but we did rapidly make love. We made some comments about how we were hoping that things were going well for Señor Egues and Chicki, but after putting our clothes back on and leaving our room we heard their voices screaming and shouting at one another in heated argument. They had never even managed to get their pants off. Chicki chased him out of her room with a torrent of insults and he and I headed back home.

He had wanted to make love to her but had hoped to kindle her fires of passion by letting her know that he loved her and was worried about her lifestyle. She took it as criticism and wanted nothing further to do with him. He couldn't understand how his knight-in-shining-armor approach had failed.

A few days later he had another chance and failed again. A friend of Chicki's let him know that she was in jail on a marijuana charge. He rushed to the police station and spent a hundred dollars to free her but that didn't improve her opinion of him. As they left the police station she repeated her desire to never see him again.

A final party was held at the school. We sang 'Corazón Contento,' one of the popular songs we had learned from Antonio Castrejon in Cerro de Ortega. Our Mexican friends were delighted.

I was having a fun time dancing to taped music with the only African-American student at the school, Cassandra, when something caught my eye on the floor. An armadillo had wandered in from the bushes and joined the party. Peggy and Sara rescued it from the dangers of our dancing feet and turned it loose in a safer place.

Sailing South

That same night fate brought four or five of us together for our next adventure. Tom was the first of this new group whom I met. I noticed him as he watched our dancing from the edges of the party. I said hello and soon realized he was another one of those young men who had left Germany when he was young and had never been able to bring himself to go back. Nor had he been able to stay anywhere for long. So around the world he traveled, looking for a new identity in the aftermath of World War Two. Tom was one of many such young Germans.

I also met Bob, the most crucial figure in the picture. He had the means for transportation. He had come down from California with his daddy's boat -- and a good boat it was too -- and I could almost hear his daddy's parting words to his son: "Well, I know you'll use your best judgment. Be careful and keep 'er shipshape!"

So Bob sailed out of San Francisco bay on his way south: first to Acapulco and then -- fortune permitting -- west to Tahiti. He had put an ad in the Berkeley Barb, the student newspaper, which had said something like: "WANTED one stout and swarthy chick willing to cook and perform minor crewing duties on board the Don Quixote -- thirty-six-foot sailing yacht -- en route to Tahiti."

So Bob had somehow wound up at our school in Manzanillo -- leaving his only crew member, Claudia, the girl who had signed on in Berkeley, on board the boat, of course, to keep watch on things.

Bob let us know that he was looking for more people to help him crew his boat to Acapulco and then to Tahiti.

One of the school's alumni, Randy, had arrived for a visit. He had graduated two years earlier. Now he was a traveler on his way to wherever the winds might blow. So Tom and Randy and I were all three of us leaning back and sizing up this captain and his boat and getting ready in our heads for a little sea voyage.

Now in my case I knew I wasn't going any further than Acapulco. How, after all, was I to get from Tahiti to Peru? But Randy and Tom were both thinkin' about a month-long sea voyage to Tahiti.

So off we went, the five of us. Me 'n Randy 'n Tom 'n Claudia 'n Bob the captain. We motored out of the harbor one afternoon about five o'clock. The captain had us washing the decks. We motored past the school about half a mile out to sea. We gave a blast on our horn and we could see our friends waving at us.

Once out of the harbor we cut the engine and put up the sails. Claudia emerged from the cabin with some very slippery spaghetti sliding back and forth on some plates in time to the rolling of the sea. Just looking at it made me not particularly want to eat it. I ate some but, since Tom was claiming to still be hungry, I happily slid the remaining heap off onto his plate. I thanked Claudia and went back to the intense business of concentrating on just exactly what this rocking business really felt like. After a day or so of trying to feel it in all its different sizes shapes and forms I began to be able to like it.

And at night, sitting at the wheel watching the stars and the compass, when the wind came up good and strong and we were running ten knots before the wind, I found that the motion could wake me up instead of put me to sleep. But in the daytime it more tended to put me to sleep and I dreamed of cold mountain snow-covered ridges with wind whistling overhead and long stretches of rocky crests on which to move my feet. Raising, lowering and adjusting sails provided a little relief from the inactivity but not enough to make me want to become a sailor.

We divided into two groups and ran the boat for four-hour shifts. Tom and I worked together and Randy and Claudia worked together. The captain appeared whenever he felt he might be needed. The net result of that schedule was that Tom and I got whatever sleep we might get for the day between 10:00 PM and 2:00 AM. And since I was sleeping on the deck instead of in the claustrophobic little cabin, it always seemed that I might just as well help Randy and Claudia whenever they had to raise or lower the mizzen sail, which was just every once in a while.

Watching the stars go around in circles through the rigging -- now that was the most beautiful part of sailing. The stars in Scorpio were the ones I watched through those heavy hours about 4:00 AM when the battle against sleep was the hardest.

On the Loose in Acapulco

Four nights and four days later we sailed on into the harbor of Acapulco. We left Bob to pay harbor fees and to make minor repairs on the boat. Not one of us, not even Claudia, wanted to continue to Tahiti.

Right away we got on a bus and I fell totally in love with the most beautiful girl I had ever seen. She got off into the crowd on one street and we got off into the crowd on the next. She was gone. The world was still rocking under our feet from being on the boat. A plate of ice cream was good, but not beautiful. Down on the beach some teeney-bopper Mexican hippie kids gave us some grass to smoke while we watched a water-skier fly overhead dangling from a parachute that was fastened to a motorboat. The teeney-boppers gave us yet another warning about watching out for cops. "OK. We'll watch out for cops."

We sat down under a straw hut on the beach. Someone came and wanted to charge us money for sitting in the straw hut. We realized we had strayed too far into the tourist end of the beach so we got up and left never to return. We asked a couple of teeney-boppers where we should go that night for music and they told us La Zona Roja.

It took us a couple of hours of wandering and exploring on foot to find La Zona Roja. It was getting dark. We walked through a smoky dreamland which occupied blocks and blocks of territory. We passed doorway after doorway, each one crowded with half-naked bodies of seductive young women. The windows were open and on the sills were perched lovely young ladies. And from many doorways came live music... usually a drum, a horn and a guitar.

There was space for dancing and flirting. I took a chance on a dance with a lovely young woman but it was too early in the adventure for me to want anything more. I wandered back toward the boat to tell the others that Randy and I had discovered an uncommonly far-out place.

The next day we spent a long time in the vast produce markets. My feet were sore from walking barefoot so I haggled and bargained over a new pair of sandals. But Tom, the wandering German, it turned out, was the more expert haggler. It didn't seem to matter to him what he was buying. It could have been an eggplant or a Rolls Royce. What made him happy was the pretty smile on the face of the girl who was selling it. So he finalized the sandal deal for me.

Later that afternoon we chatted with a friendly California guy who was traveling with a little Norwegian girl.

"Do you need a place to crash?" they asked, quite happy to offer us floor space in a room they had rented. So with the question of where to spend the night solved, as darkness fell, thoughts of La Zona Roja were again passing through our minds. Tom said he would go later, so Randy and I began the long winding walk which we had by now learned to traverse on foot, passing up the fleetness of the buses for the sake of being able to savor each street and each section of the city more slowly. We left the crowds of people who stayed near the water and navigated the complex system of little streets and food stores near where our new 'crash pad' lay. We then strode like ghosts through another long section of commerce and shops which had closed and emptied all at once with the setting of the sun. We passed through the edge of the giant central market where we had been wandering for most of the day. We followed the shreds of our memories of the geography of the city until we came to a friendly little man with a taco stand where we stopped and ate and passed the time of evening for a spell.

Dancing in La Zona Roja

We took a few more steps, rounded a corner and the exquisite seductive smoke from the eyes of fifteen women snuck into our souls. We floated on down the street, walking through the magic. Each door and window held another eye, and each eye held that liquid promise: which might last for half an hour.

We entered a door which had music, men and women and places to dance. A little short man in a suit coat was authoritatively demanding: "Papers! Your papers!" Memories of a certain New York City detective flashed through my mind.

I told him: "And what do you think? That I'm going to carry my papers around with me here?"

The man was frantically elbowing his way closer toward us. He was pissed off. He was holding his hand out authoritatively and demanding: "Your papers!"

"Let's split." I said to Randy.

"I ain't gonna show you nothin'!" I said to the man.

One of the bartenders was telling him to leave us alone, but Randy and I spied a hole through the crowd and slipped out through the door where fate presented us with an open taxi door.

We ducked into the back seat of the car. The driver took off down the street, speedy and efficient.

"Where are you going?" he asked.

"This will be just fine," we replied.

We got out and started walking away from La Zona Roja. Neither one of us had said a word. Were we going to let one little weird encounter spoil our evening?

"Do you want to go back?" Randy asked.

"Yeah," I said. And we both turned around and started walking back up the hill. When we got back to the top we stopped again to visit the friendly little man with his taco stand and while we were sitting there Bob the boat captain and Tom the wandering German strode past us looking intent on some objective. We plunged back into La Zona Roja. This time we took a different direction so as to lower our chances of running into our nasty little cop friend.

Rounding a corner Randy and I strolled right into a place with a big band and a spacious dance floor. 'La Huerta' or 'The Garden' it was called. The fun vibe was immediately appealing. We sat down at a little table. Long before I had any inclination to go ask some particular girl to dance, along came one and sat down on my leg. After a minute or two it seemed that we liked each other. She sat there bare-breasted on my knee in a sexy little costume and pretty soon we headed for the dance floor. We had fun mirroring each other's dance moves and others dancing on the floor around us joined in our fun. We clicked. When we touched each other it felt good.

We walked out under the trees into the garden. I saw that the dancing area was surrounded by chains of little white stucco motel rooms and that there were some quite fancy and shiny cars parked here and there. She said she'd be back in a minute and disappeared. I wondered if there was some Madame or somebody she had to go report to. I never found out but presently she came running back and seemed to be really happy at the prospect that we were about to make love. What was special about La Huerta was that the women who worked there were in charge of personally selecting the men rather than the other way around. There was a sense of freedom and delightful flirtation.

We went to her room and soon we were making love. I was feeling pretty calm and pretty much in control, so I murmured that it was nice having as much time as we wanted.

"Half an hour would be nice!" she murmured and I deliberately moved more slowly so we could enjoy ourselves. It felt to me like our connection was real. She moved her energy into the place we were joined... turned up the heat... No, I don't think I ever knew her name... I didn't last as long as I thought I would... oh well...

After a while, resting in each other's arms, we both exclaimed that we absolutely loved to dance. We agreed that we ought to go out and dance together again so we got dressed. Pretty soon we were back out under the lights moving to the music. We included other peoples' energies in our dance and then gradually separated.

I wandered back to the same table I had started from and looked for Randy. He was no longer there. I strolled on up the street and discovered that the friendly little man with his taco stand had closed itself up and withdrawn altogether from the scene leaving a vacant and dusty street illuminated by one corner light. I sat down on a little curb and began to wait. I figured Randy would most likely pass me there if he should decide to leave.

A man appeared on the opposite corner and came over toward me with his hands digging in his pockets for coins which he offered to me saying that I could get some food or a place to sleep. I was quite humbled by his offer and thanked him profusely even though I refused his money and explained that I was simply waiting to see if my friend would walk by. When he understood that I was speaking the truth, he gave up trying to give me the money.

Eventually I discovered Randy sitting in a little corner cafe I hadn't noticed before. Diving back into another part of La Zona Roja we watched a woman dance herself to orgasm surrounded by a group of drummers. It was a show... but not a show. It was real... her orgasm was real. Eventually we walked on back to our 'crash pad' at George and Cecilia's.

Itchy Feet: on to Mexico City

The next day Randy and I found ourselves sitting beside the ocean with itchy feet. We decided to go to Mexico City and then climb Orizaba, an eighteen-thousand-foot volcano, so we quickly said goodbye to everybody and took a bus to Mexico City. Arriving in the city I had a strong impulse to find something comparable to La Zona Roja. We walked the streets of the city for two or three days. We heard of a place called La Zona Rosa and went there with some high expectations for more flirtatious dancing but found only expensive little coffee houses, theaters and art galleries.

I got picked up in the morning by a carload of high school students on a scavenger hunt. One of the items on their list to find was a gringo with giant sunglasses drinking booze out of a family-size coca-cola bottle. They supplied me with the required props and when we arrived at the finish line I was part of their success. I saw some other rather bewildered gringos with the same props that had arrived with other carloads of students. I was hoping there would be a party to celebrate the conclusion of the hunt, but no such luck. They just took me back to the corner from where they had picked me up.

We decided that climbing Orizaba would require equipment we didn't have so we gave up on that idea. I went and got a plane ticket to Peru and Randy bought a train ticket to El Paso, Texas. We had just finished buying our tickets when by pure chance along came George and Cecilia. They had also left Acapulco and were on their way to Veracruz from where it seemed that George thought it might be nice if Cecilia were to fly herself back to Norway.

"Aren't you anxious to get back home?" he would ask her hopefully.

She would shrug her shoulders again and say, "No, I told you, I'm not in the least bit anxious to go home."

"But you don't have any money," he would again explain to her.

"George, I've made it this far without any money, what makes you think I need money now?"

"Ah, you're just gonna wind up bein' a travelin' Norwegian prostitute."

"That wouldn't be so bad!"

"Nah, shit, you'd better fly home from Veracruz. I've got just enough money to send you home from there."

We heard this argument every day from George and Cecilia. He had latched onto her in California a few weeks earlier, and now he was ready to be without her, but his masculine pride and possessiveness wouldn't allow him to just let her go. After all, it was obvious that she would pretty soon wind up traveling with some other guy. And George couldn't quite stand that idea. Poor George. I liked him. He was easy to be around.

"We got some good grass," George and Cecilia told us. "Let's go smoke some."

"Sure," we said, "let's go up to our hotel room. We've both got tickets to leave in a few hours, but we can go get stoned first."

George had his guitar with him. We sat up in our room and made some music and got stoned. Hmmmm. There we all were again. Fate had framed us up for some kind of scene, I could just tell. I just knew it.

"Where are you going from Veracruz?" I asked.

"Well," said George, "Cecilia's going to fly back to Norway from there and I don't know where I'm going to go. I was thinking of Panama; maybe going down there through British Honduras. What's British Honduras like? I've never heard anything about the place."

"Me neither," said Randy.

"Me neither," said Cecilia.

"I don't think I've ever heard a single thing about the place," I said.

"Hmmm," said George. Then we all sat there and looked at each other. Somebody sang another song or two.

"God damn it Randy," I suddenly volunteered, "I know you only have a hundred dollars, but we'll get you through somehow. Why don't we all go to British Honduras?"

Shortly thereafter Randy was back down at the railroad station getting his ticket money back and I was down at the Peruvian Airlines office negotiating to exchange my ticket from Mexico City for one from Guatemala City. George and Cecilia already had tickets to Vera Cruz and were ready to go. They agreed to wait for us there.

Onward to Veracruz

I was so excited I called up Lisa back in the States, a process which took about eight hours of waiting around a long distance phone center. "It's an amazing group of people!" I told her when I finally got through. "And we're headed for some amazing places!"

But she said, "No, I can't just drop everything now. I'm looking for a teaching job in Berkeley so we'll be able to live together this winter in California. I'll meet you in Lima soon!"

When I hung up the phone I forgot the future and the past and dropped even more deeply into a feeling called: 'Here we go!'

The next day Randy and I got onto the train for Vera Cruz. A couple of guys who work for the railway hopped on and sat down across from us. We talked and joked all the rest of the way to Vera Cruz and they taught us some more Mexican Spanish slang: 'ketchy o no ketchy?' 'abusado!'

Once in Vera Cruz we had very little trouble running into George and Cecilia. Fate had sealed our plans and we had little doubt that we could run into each other with no planning or effort no matter what city we might be in. Our paths were set to collide. People of the same viscosity will naturally end up suspended at the same level.

George and Cecilia had spent a good part of the previous day in Vera Cruz lounging on one of the piers smoking dope with a Mexican fisherman. We ran into him again, as it turned out, and he told us that he spent every night on the sea in his small boat.

"Eventually the business of fishing becomes completely mechanical, so completely mechanical that my hands do all of the work while I look out over the sea. I think about everything," he told us. The man was as warm and calm as the Caribbean sea itself.

Later that afternoon I determined to write some things down and wandered down one of the streets of the city in search of a quiet cafe in which to sit.

As I was walking along, possessed with my literary intentions, I heard someone ask, "Hey, are you a hippie?" This was Pedro, the sixteen-year-old son of a local dock worker. I looked at him and saw that there was nothing but open and honest curiosity shining from his face.

"Sometimes," I replied. "Sometimes people say that I am, so perhaps sometimes I am a hippie."

"Look," Pedro said to his friend, "he's just the person we're looking for." His friend looked nervously at me and I could tell that he wasn't so sure at all that I was the person they were looking for.

Pedro continued: "Are you traveling around with a bunch of other hippies?"

"Well, yes," I said. "There are about four of us traveling together now."

"And where are you going?" he asked.

"British Honduras."

"Wow, that's terrific," he said. "Do you suppose we could come along?" His friend fidgeted nervously.

"Well," I said, "look, you'd have to have your own money, 'cause although we don't spend much, we have to buy train and bus tickets sometimes. But anyway, I'm going to try and find a place to write some things down right now, so why don't you go see my three friends. Tell them you met me and are thinking about coming along and I'll be back there later." I told him where the hotel in which we were staying was and went along my way. As I walked along, I realized more and more that I had liked him.

I found a cafe and sat down with a cup of coffee to write some things down, but could barely get into it at all. So I got up and started walking back toward the hotel. Not very far along the way I ran into Randy and George and we walked along together.

Crazy but Lucky

Suddenly a well-formed female shape, also obviously North-American, streaked across the street in front of us. Immediately the three of us picked up speed and began following about a block or so behind her. She was in a terrible hurry but she didn't seem to know quite where she was going. She turned right here, left there, and so on, making a semi-nonsensical trajectory through the city. Suddenly we found ourselves outside our hotel. She had stopped right in front of it and seemed to be in an utter torment of indecision.

I walked over and asked if there was any way in which we could help. I felt enormously attracted to her but she began to unroll a very strange story. It seemed that her boyfriend had abandoned her there alone in Vera Cruz... with her three kids.

"How can I get to Cuba?" she splashed the question on us.

"You can go to the airport and fly or you can take a boat," I said. "Mexico has perfectly healthy diplomatic relations with Cuba."

"But I have to get papers! My tourist card has expired, and the American consul here hates me and won't help me get another one. But if I can just get to Cuba, I'll leave the kids here and forget about them. It would be better for them anyway."

"Where are they now?" I asked.

"They're at a friend's house, but I'm afraid he won't let me have them. And even if he does give them to me I know the consul will try and take them away from me."

"Well Jesus Christ," I said, "they can't do a thing like that. They're your kids. They can't just take them away from you. Why don't you just go get them right away and go back to the States?"

"Do you think they'd let me in with an expired tourist card?" she asked.

"Yeah sure; once you're there they'll let you in. Don't worry about it."

"Yeah I think I'll try that," she said. "But I have to wait until tomorrow for my money to arrive and I'm afraid the consul's going to try and take the kids before then. Besides, I owe money to the guy who's got the kids and he won't give them to me unless I pay him. His wife was a friend of mine, you see, an American girl. And she married this Mexican guy when he was up in the States and then she came down here to live. But now she's gone back home to visit her parents."

"Well when will she be back?" I asked.

"That's just the thing," she said. "I don't think she's coming back. And her husband doesn't think she's coming back. And I owe him this money and he hired a nursery to take care of the kids and they don't want to give them back to me. They want to hand the kids over to the consul."

We went into the hotel. The guys behind the desk seemed to know her and to not like her. She pleaded with them for a while in obvious extremes of pain and embarrassment and they eventually agreed to let her stay there for a night.

We people are strange animals. I felt my attraction suddenly rise again when I discovered that she was going to be there for the night. Maybe she was the classic 'lady in distress.' Was I crazy? Yes, I knew I was crazy.

She left to go over to her friend's husband's house to plead for some of her belongings. I promised to help her move them out of his truck into her room later on in the evening if she should succeed in getting them.

Meanwhile, Pedro had been talking with Cecilia and George. They were quite non-committal about Pedro's joining us, but seemed to get along with him perfectly well. The truth of the matter is that they simply didn't know enough Spanish to be able to really hold up their end of the conversation. In fact Cecilia knew no Spanish whatsoever.

Pedro said that if I was really serious in saying that he could come with us that he would be back in the morning ready to go. I said that his coming along was fine with me and he and his friend, who still had shown no inclination to join us, left.

Eventually my 'lady in distress' returned. I heard her walk in. A bolt of excitement jumped in my chest and I waited for her to come and ask me to help her move her things. She didn't come.

After midnight I went to sleep hoping that sometime in the middle of the night my door would open and she would come in to slip quietly under the covers with me. I knew it was an insane thought but it wouldn't go away.

The next day I saw her briefly one more time. I told her that we were leaving that very day and that was the last I saw of her... fortunately, I'm sure... I had an unsettling awareness that I must be really really crazy but still felt that if I was going to learn the lessons of life it would be essential to stay wide open and let it all flow through me... life...

Pedro - Mexican Hippie

Pedro arrived bright and early. He was ready to go. I could see in his face that he wasn't quite sure he really knew what he was getting himself into. But from that time on for the next two weeks I really spent a great deal more time with Pedro than I did with my other friends. He discovered my real level of fluency in Mexican Spanish and relentlessly taught me and explained to me until he was sure I understood.

He explained that his father was a stevedore; that he loaded and unloaded ships. And that he too would be a stevedore. But not until he was eighteen at which time his father would arrange to have him join the union and Pedro's life as a man would begin.

Consequently, his father had quite wisely advised him: "See the world now, kid, 'cause you're not going to have time to see it later." And Pedro had in fact covered at least half of his country already.

This was not the first time he had gotten acquainted with gringos either. He knew an American family who frequented Acapulco, and who had even treated him to a ride from Acapulco to Mexico City on a jet plane after dressing him up in the latest modern fashions. He had liked his clothes but had eventually worn them out back home in Vera Cruz.

We got on a train and rode about fifty miles south to Tierra Blanca where we hit the main railway east toward Yucatan. It turned out we still had a reasonable supply of dope so we smoked some from time to time as we progressed along our way. Usually when the train would stop somewhere we would get off temporarily and go smoke in the local railway yard.

We had also teamed up with a young anthropology student from the eastern USA who was looking for the right place to do some kind of studies. Another person also seemed to be traveling with us, but somehow his spirit never quite fully materialized and I don't remember much about him.

When we got to Tierra Blanca we got off the train and were immediately confronted by a policeman who wanted to know who we were, where we were going, and especially what Pedro was doing with us.

"What do you think you're doing traveling with a bunch of gringos?" he wanted Pedro to answer. "Where do you think you're going? You'd better turn around and get back to Vera Cruz!" Pedro was just standing there looking inscrutable and not sure what to do.

"Hey, look," I said, "I speak Spanish, and if I speak Spanish that means I'm entitled to have Spanish-speaking friends, god dammit! He came along with us as a teacher and as a friend. He is a friend!"

And so the cop left us alone. *'Now if a policeman wants to send Pedro to jail,' I thought to myself, 'he'll just have to send all of us to jail! That's the only fair way to do it, right?'*

So me 'n Randy 'n Pedro 'n George left our packs in the railroad station with Cecilia and the other two guys and took a walk down a gravel road beside a river.

Seeing a vine hanging above us, Pedro helped me get up to reach it. I started to swing on it. The vine came down, all thirty-five feet of it. We picked it up, declared it a fish, gave it legs and walked down the road each of us carrying a portion of it slung over his shoulder. Eventually we realized that if it was a fish it was going to die with no water. It died and we left it in the road. We sat down on a bridge and smoked some more dope. Tired, we slept on the floor of the railroad station.

Escárcega and the Girl in the Yellow Dress

The next day we got on a long slow train that carried us for two or three days all the way to Escárcega a town in the middle of the state of Campeche. On the way me made music and smoked up all the rest of our grass. I kept focused on learning more new words and how to speak Mexican pig latin: *so-pres-so-sta la so-mo-so-ta = presta la mota = pass me the marijuana.*

In the middle of the night I was standing in between the cars where the air was more fresh. Suddenly the coupling which held the cars together broke and came apart about a foot away from my feet. The guy wearing blue pants standing across from me lost his balance and disappeared onto the tracks between the moving cars. Fortunately the train was moving very slowly and I saw him scramble for his life and avoid the next passing set of axles and wheels. The two halves of the train slowly coasted to a stop and the engineers came back to repair the coupling. I didn't see the disappeared man board the train again. I inquired. No one else had noticed him.

Escárcega is a hot, dry flat place in the middle of a vast brittle jungle with nothing of particular interest save the hordes of mosquitoes... except that, as it was explained to us by one of the locals, all of the long-term alcoholics in the state of Campeche had eventually moved there to Escárcega.

The center of town, where we all crammed ourselves into as cheap, dusty and dingy a room as we could find, was little else but huge open air bars with the same fly-infested food, dozens of incoherent but friendly drunks and...!!! *La Fantastica Musica de Los Fantasticos!*

To Pedro's delight we discovered that there was going to be a dance that very night and that a band from Mexico City, no less, was going to show up and play.

"Are they going to play *'musica de onda'*?" Pedro excitedly asked everybody in town and especially the girl in the yellow dress... She happened to be in the hat store where I had bought a new hat. Pedro told her he hoped she would be there to dance to the *'musica de onda'* with him. When the band itself finally arrived, after unsuccessfully trying to score some more dope off them, Pedro candidly slipped them the question: "You're going to play pure *'musica de onda'*, aren't you?"

"Sure." they replied confidently, "we can play anything."

We ate some food and about 8:00 PM we heard the music start up. It turned out that Cecelia and Pedro and I were the only ones really anxious to go, so we sauntered on over to the dance. Sure enough, there were about three or four hundred people just sort of getting things started. Pedro went to look for the girl in the yellow dress... she had soft looking hair, clear black eyes and a lithe little body.

Cecelia and I sauntered across the dance area which hadn't really gotten very full yet.

"Hey Come here! Over here!" We looked and there was some guy with fancy clothes, a fancy hat and major sunglasses sitting at a table with a few other men drinking beer. There were about ten tables obviously occupied by the town's elite. We went over and sat down. A brief round of introductions happened. No conversation ensued. Our host talked sporadically with his friends about business matters. He had ordered us and his friends a round of beers.

Eventually he leaned over and mumbled some light chit-chat into Cecelia's ear. I leaned over and mumbled to him that she doesn't understand a word of Spanish and that if he wanted to talk to her he would have to get me to interpret things. He didn't take that in, being quite confident that his charm alone was sufficient to overcome the language barrier. Gradually most of his friends got bored and left. He continued to mumble things into her ear. She laughed at the absurdity of what was happening and when I could hear what he said I would translate for her but it didn't help because she could only reply through me anyway and he still had no interest in talking with me.

'At least,' I was thinking to myself, 'at least we're getting a couple of free beers out of this.' Then he got up and gave us a polite *'hasta luego'* and off he went. We started to get up but a lady came over and presented us with the check, not only for our beers, but for everybody else's too.

Poorer, but happy to be back in the crowd, we looked around for Pedro. He'd been sleuthing about, it turns out, trying to find someone to sell us some more marijuana. At last he'd found some kids who'd promised to take him somewhere and sell him some.

"Shit," he muttered, "that ain't 'musica de onda'. These guys aren't far out musicians!"

Half an hour later he came back disgusted from his rendezvous for procuring more dope. "You know what those guys thought I was looking for?" he asked. "They thought I wanted to get laid! They didn't know anything about dope at all! What a bunch of losers!"

Unfortunately... or fortunately, Cecelia and I couldn't share Pedro's disgust. It was all new adventures for us and there was no way we could get bored. And more and more people were starting to dance.

"Hey, look, there's Pedro dancing with the girl in the yellow dress!" I said to Cecelia. Sure enough. Pedro had found her and out of all the dozens of couples out there doing the cumbia, a slow shuffle type cha-cha-cha with Colombian origins, only two were doing anything different: Pedro and the girl in the yellow dress. Where she had learned to dance like people do in San Francisco I don't know, but there she was doing it, so I grabbed Cecelia by the hand and we were out there flippin' and boppin' around too. Wahoo... I love to dance.

So the four of us had made a little pocket in the swaying twosomes and our arms and legs and asses were floppin' around and after about ten minutes I noticed that the circle around us had grown bigger. A couple of other couples were somewhat affected by our style and had begun throwing a few new wilder moves into their cumbia, but not for long. The next time I looked I realized that everybody but us had stopped dancing and that we were surrounded by a huge ring of hundreds of people just watching us.

The musicians dropped out and left it up to the drummer who decided to do his wildest stuff. For a long time it was just me, Pedro, Cecelia, the drummer and the girl in the yellow dress... the glorious miraculous girl in the yellow dress.

Then the music went back into the cumbia and twice as many people were dancing. The party was in full swing.

Pedro got pissed off again: "What's the matter with these people? Why won't they dance and play 'musica de onda'?"

I told him, "Just dance the cumbia you fool!"

Meanwhile someone else was requesting: "Please, sir, let me dance with her for a few minutes, just a few minutes sir." He wanted to dance with Cecelia.

"Sure," I said, "go ahead. If she wants to dance with you dance with her all you like."

Meanwhile she was instructing me, "I don't want to dance with that one, but I want to dance with that one and that one."

"Yes... No."

"Yes... No. Go ahead dance with her..."

"Thank you sir." The mood developed into chaos around us and around the band and around the street and all up and down it was a party and we were just a little tiny piece of it.

The next day there was a picture in the local paper of us dancing. That night the band played again. We danced again. The girl in the yellow dress came and danced again too. The crowd circled around us again during the long drum solos when we would show off our modern dance moves.

Chetumal, Belize, Guatemala: Psychic Sexual Energy

Finally we resumed moving east through the jungle toward the Caribbean coast. The jungle was hot, dusty and dry. Not the rainy season. There were now seven of us traveling together but I was still hanging with Pedro. He was my teacher.

We stood up on a tightly packed little bus all night long and arrived in Chetumal, in the state of Quintana Roo, just north of British Honduras, which later became known as Belize. It had been a long journey from Escárcega and we were tired. I found a park which had a nice bench and lay down in the heat to take a nap.

A policeman woke me up and told me to move on... and that it was immoral to not be wearing my shirt. I looked around the plaza and the park. Where were all the people and all the markets? Everything seemed tame and quiet. I was missing the wild crazy freedoms of the towns on the Pacific coast.

Pedro and I jumped in the Caribbean and swam around a rocky point ducking under the water to avoid the swarms of mosquitoes.

The next day we arrived at the border and sought to enter British Honduras. Suddenly everything changed. The officials were very African-looking men in khaki shorts who spoke English with a British accent! They denied Pedro entry but gave Randy and me three days to pass through the country. They didn't make us feel very welcome.

George was busy once again trying to convince Cecelia to fly back to Norway and wasn't ready to join us so we said goodbye to Pedro, George, Cecelia and to the anthropologist and the silent traveler and crossed the border. We headed south and passed through places with names like 'Orange Walk.' We slept in the back of somebody's truck along the way and arrived in Belize City.

The city was a jumble of wooden structures built in a chaotic maze. The corner of one shanty would be perched on the roof of another. Soon we were heavily immersed in the marijuana-soaked African Caribbean world. It seemed like the British Honduras national economy was fueled entirely by the drug commerce. It was a country with no other visible means of support. Everyone we met was importing and exporting drugs to and from Chicago and New Orleans. They spoke Creole and, when called for, English. Spanish had vanished as a useful language.

Sitting down in a friendly bar which served both alcohol and marijuana, I was befriended by a local guy named James. Another man at the table asked for a match and I produced a lighter with a flame for his joint. Maybe I looked slightly nervous. I don't know.

"Don't talk to us with fear in your eyes!" James admonished me.

"You're not afraid?" he asked me.

"No..."

"You're not afraid of anything?"

"No."

"You're sure?"

"Yeah, man."

"Then I can teach you a lot!"

"Have you been in solitary yet?"

"I've spent some alone time in the mountains."

"Then I'll meet you in the grocery store in about a year!"

"Grocery store?"

"That means some place yet to be determined."

"Ok. See you in a year in the grocery store!" I replied.

"No fear allowed," he embellished. "Know what you want and have no fear of death... if you are really a man of the world."

"Yeah, man!" I agreed.

I absorbed that lesson and wandered to another bar after dark in a part of town called "South Viet Nam."

"Good thing you came in here!" I was told by a friendly fellow. "If you'd gone into that bar across the street they'd have killed you for sure!"

Unable to contain my curiosity, I went into the bar across the street. "Good thing you came in here!" I was told. "If you got stoned in some other bar your only way out would be floating dead in one of those little canals which thread their way through town down to the sea! That's where they dump the bodies! But you're safe in here with us! You understand that the police never dare come into this part of town... so it's up to us to watch out for each other."

I wandered some more, heard music and opened the door to another bar. A bunch of African-Caribbean guys dressed in white were dancing in unison around a pulsing neon-lit juke box. One of them looked at me like I was not part of their Santeria ceremony so I continued on my way. Now I began noticing all the little canals descending through the town oozing with garbage and catfish... and who knows what else...

Another bar was emitting audible music so I entered there. I was stoned and they were drunk so it was a difficult mix but I managed to blend into the dancing fun after a while. Much later the music came to a stop and I discussed my proposed travel plans with a friendly young guy and his companions. "That's a dangerous highway behind Benque Viejo! That is not a well-traveled road."

"But it looks like the most direct path toward Guatemala City according to my map," I commented.

"No no! You will get killed traveling that way! The safer way to go is south to Punta Gorda and then by boat to the coast of Guatemala. Tomorrow I will arrange things with people I know and perhaps even go with you!"

"Ok," I agreed.

"Yes, my mother lives in Punta Gorda!" he added.

Arriving back to a little room which Randy and I had finally rented with hopes for some actual sleep, I looked again at my map and decided that there was only way to find out how dangerous my proposed route really was. The idea of having to wait for a boat somewhere along the way sounded like extra work. I had a plane to catch in Guatemala City.

Randy and I parted company. He would head back north. I arrived by bus to Benque Viejo at dusk, walked a mile or so and passed into Guatemala at Melchor where I slept all night in another bus which was going to take off in the morning.

I was now back in indigenous American and Spanish-speaking territory and I felt more at home. I got off the bus in Flores and then headed south in a small station wagon with twenty-seven other jammed-in passengers. After that I found rides in the backs of a series of trucks in which I bounced through remote jungle while I admired the bare-breasted women who were working the fields along the way.

We passed men carrying big loads of palm fronds on their heads.

"They will need those to make shade so they can cool off a bit and stop sweating so they can find the strength to go and carry some more," a city-bred soldier riding in the back of the truck commented.

"That's just like the rest of life," he continued. "The cure to every problem always just involves more work and more suffering!"

Soon we were parked beside the road repairing the generator and the voltage regulator. We just stayed put and slept through the night in the truck bed right where we were.

It was a very long journey all the way to Guatemala City. There were no signs of danger although the driver of the truck told me that the newly-elected government had a hit list of 25,000 local people to assassinate. We stopped briefly at a hot springs and then arrived in the city.

I had two or three days to rest up once I arrived. I needed that and tried to keep to myself but did end up smoking some marijuana with young guys who had flipped me the peace sign. They took me on a tour of the local red light district where we just walked and admired. I assured them I could find my own way back to my hotel. After three hours of walking I finally proved myself right. Soon enough I was on the airplane to Peru.

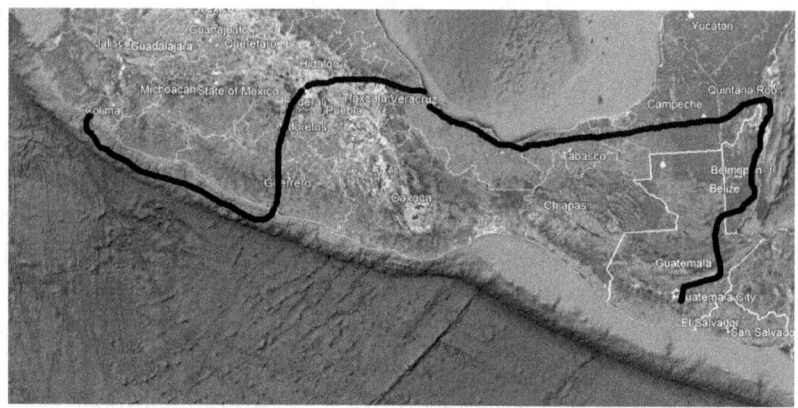
Manzanillo to Guatemala City

Gypsies in Lima

Arriving in Lima I bathed in the Peruvian dialect of Spanish which was what I knew best. I had a few days to wander the city before going to meet Lisa at the airport.

I was highly charged with sexual energy. There had been no love-making since Acapulco. Masturbation had long ago begun to seem like nothing more than a way to lose the precious energy needed to live a fully adventurous life so I had left that adolescent habit behind. I needed my deep energies to guide my intuitive inner radar systems toward real friendships and real love affairs with real people. And Lisa would be arriving soon. We would catch up on love-making.

Walking endlessly through the market labyrinths of Lima I became more conscious of the telepathic reality I was living in. I was in a human ocean of sensitivities which was difficult to find back in North America where people lived so much of their lives locked up behind closed doors.

When I passed someone on the street, if our psychic energies were high enough and we were keeping our tentacles and feelers out, we would exchange little mysterious packets of information.

There is a part of Lima where the gypsies live. I walked past a group of gypsy women dressed in their north India style. They were walking side by side, all eight of them, down the middle of the street. They were projecting an overwhelming flirtatious power and cars and trucks and bicycles and buses were moving out of their way and deferring to their energy as they passed.

As I walked past them I felt the strength of their field of energy and flirtation. They apparently felt mine too. One of them raised the palm of her hand and brushed it sensually against mine as we passed. That was all there was to it but I took it as an official welcome into the land of conscious and deliberate telepathic communication.

Now I knew why I loved walking the marketplaces in tropical cities where this field of awareness was always open and available. It became the sweetest air for my psychic breathing and turned Lima into my infinite playground.

Lisa arrived and we dissolved back into our togetherness. I accepted an invitation to visit with an anthropologist whom I had met at Cornell. We traveled into the wealthier section of Lima known as Miraflores for an evening and attended a dinner party where we all expressed enthusiasm for learning more about the indigenous Peruvian people. I felt like a fish out of water among the academicians and yearned to be back in the market places.

Lisa and I would slowly make our way back to Sina, in southern Peru, but it would take weeks. We traveled the high Andean road through Ayacucho and Cusco. We revisited Machu Picchu, once again setting up camp for a few days in the ruins.

A Rock Laughs Back at Me in Machu Picchu

We traveled through Cojata knowing that there were two or three trucks who would drive once a week on Saturdays to Iskay Cruz, the pass, or 'apacheta,' at the top of the valley which leads down to Sina.

We shortened our three-day walk to a one-day walk by riding in on one of those trucks.

Back Home into Sina

Although we were still a long way from knowing all the villagers by name, we were greeted and surrounded by friendly and familiar faces. Policarpio, whose prowess and strength in the potato fields we had admired a year earlier, was at the market and he put our packs on a horse. It took the whole day to descend from sixteen-thousand feet to nine-thousand feet, but soon we were back in Sina.

We presented my compadre, Don Teofilo Lipa, with a waterproof poncho which Lisa had brought from Colorado. He received it gratefully but when we asked about my 'ahijado,' my godson whom I had 'baptized,' he shook his head. Juan de la Cruz had not survived his first year. It seems that only half the babies born in Sina survive that first year.

Lisa, Edwin, Pastor in Sina

Edwin and Laura offered a vacant house for us and we moved in and made ourselves at home. Settling back into the village felt homey and familiar from the first moment. I had of course carried in another inexpensive guitar from a market place in Cusco. Lisa immediately reconnected with the little girls.

Lisa with the Girls

My harp-playing friend, Jacob, had died while we were absent from Sina during the last few months. He had survived to the age of fifty-five. One night he sat down beside the trail on the way home from a festive gathering in another village a few hours away. His frozen body was found the next day.

"That's terrible!" I exclaimed to his sister, Amalia.

She looked at me quizzically. "Terrible?" she repeated. "No... We will miss him, but it's not terrible."

I immediately realized that I must have brought the North American attitude toward death into this South American valley and that I was being called on it. Something to ponder and think about.

Teofilo Lipa's family kept this village supplied with bread which they made in a large bee-hive-shaped clay oven once a week. Lisa began helping them on bread-making days.

Amalia's son, Antonio, was in town. We had not met him before. He killed a chicken and invited us over. He was back from travels in other parts of Peru and was filled with inspiration about 'cooperativismo,' more socialist forms of government which could lead to land distributions back into the hands of indigenous families.

For some reason I mentioned the world 'population problem' and he looked at me incredulously. He had never heard of any such problem. "Look at the sides of this valley!" he exclaimed, expansively gesturing at the immensity. "You can see from the quantities of ancient terraces which cover these hillsides that this valley was once filled with people! We need to have more babies so that we can thrive once again!"

A few days later his wife Delia arrived with their two-year old son. Lisa and I ceremoniously gave the child his first haircut and we all became compadres and comadres.

Ancient Stone Wisdom and Climber Dreams

After so much traveling through Mexico and Belize to Guatemala and then through highland Peru, I was ready to spend a few days just sitting on the side of this high Andean valley. I found a special spot about an hour's walk above the village and began visiting it on a regular basis. Forty miles to my left, far down the valley, from where the clouds come, lay the jungle which stretched for three-thousand miles east to the Atlantic Ocean.

Directly across the valley from my chosen spot was a small rock face which seemed to be looking right at me. I had the feeling it was trying to tell me something. I listened to it carefully day after day. I later learned that Inca peoples believe that the Andean stones have eyes with which they gather and share ancient wisdom. *'Rumi Ñawi'* means *'eyes of the stone'* in Quechua and is also popularly used as a first name.

One does not shout in this valley. The only noises are gentle wind and the perpetual rush of the river below. What was that? Perhaps the shout of a small child? Perhaps. But as that child grows older, he will learn to be silent like the men in the valley who have learned not to waste vocal energy trying to call to each other across these vast distances and across all these centuries of time. They wait and then greet each other quietly when they meet.

I had brought a climbing rope and crampons and an ice ax with me and had my hopes up for getting onto the glaciers above the pass at the top of the valley. I told Lisa I would be back in a few days and headed up the valley. It was late in the day already. The next day other villagers would be headed up to trade with the trucks.

I was pushing myself. I was trying to get in touch with my inner mountaineer. Exhausted, I crashed down beside the trail. My fingers clawed into my wonderful glorious bag of boiled potatoes and bacon. Cramming them into my mouth I felt a wondrous wave of relief. My stomach had suddenly reached out between my teeth, in search of food.

The night before it had been raining. The valley was so pumped full of fog... it was like the jungle clouds were climbing up a pipe. It was hard to see and it was gradually getting dark. Where was I going to rest and sleep? I came upon an overhanging rock around which someone had built a low stone wall. Squirming inside, I found just room enough for me to stretch out! An hour went by. Still night had not come. Being surrounded by such dense fog had made it seem as though night were about to fall, when in truth it had been only perhaps four o'clock in the afternoon. Another hour went by. Then, just as I had pulled the draw strings tight around my nose in my sleeping bag hoping to fall asleep, two Indians went by. Not wishing to look like a mummy in a tomb, I hastily poked myself out.

"Good afternoon!" I said.

"Good afternoon," they replied.

"To where are you going?" I asked in Quechua.

"We're going to Sina," they said. "We're going to try and make it this very afternoon." And they hurried off.

Now it looked as though it might really be beginning to get dark. I looked at the rock ceiling six inches above my nose and at the wisps of fog blowing in through the cracks in the stone wall. Pretty soon I heard a voice:

Pampa Qarqa - New Friends

"Howdy Mister!" it said in Spanish. I peeped out of my sleeping bag and saw a very young but very ragged and shredded Indian standing outside my cave.

"Howdy!" I called, struggling to poke my head and arms out of the blue bag. How nice to hear a friendly voice, I thought.

"You're not going to spend the night here, are you?" he said.

"Yeah, I'm on my way up to the pass, " I explained. "Very early, when this miserable mist goes away and the stars come out, I'll get up and move on up toward the pass."

"But it's cold and miserable here," he said. "Come on down to my house and I'll put you up for the night."

"I don't want to go down and have to come all the way back up," I said. "It's too far."

"No it's not. It's just down the trail a little ways. You can get up early and leave from there."

"I'll be right with you. Just give me a moment to get my things."

"Where are you from?" he asked.

"I'm from north America," I said. "I'm living with my Señora down in Sina for a while."

"What have you come here for?" he asked. "Surely you must be looking for gold. Have you been up looking for the old mines?"

"No," I said, "I have no interest in mines. I'm just a student trying to learn to speak Quechua."

"Can you speak Quechua?" he asked.

"Some," I replied in Quechua.

"Let's speak in Quechua, then," he said in Quechua. "What are you going up to the pass for?"

"I'm going up to buy some things when the trucks come to the end of the road tomorrow. I also may climb one of those mountains up there. That's why I've got this huge load of equipment," I said indicating my tent, rope, crampons, ice ax and stove.

"Take me with you," he said. "I'd like to climb one too!"

"I'm afraid it would be very difficult," I said, looking at his bare feet. "How would you be able to sleep in the snow?" Besides, a voice was intoning inside me: "Go Alone…"

Shortly he asked: "How long are you going to stay? When are you going back to your country?"

"In August."

"Take me with you, please."

"Perhaps," I said. "But it's a very long journey."

He was right about his house being close. Within fifteen minutes we arrived. His little mother came out and invited me in. Inside, hung a jungle full of skins and rags. The floor was covered with straw. Arranging the pile of skins and fleeces on the floor, my new friend, Antonio, said, "Here you can sleep."

"Much better than my hole up above," I acknowledged. It was extremely dark inside, and it appeared that they didn't even possess a candle. I pulled a candle stub out of my pack and presently we could see one another. "Let's make some tea," I suggested and pulled out my primus stove. Antonio's little mother came in momentarily to get an armload of straw. We exchanged a few words, but her speech was too hushed and timid for me to understand. And, unlike her son, she knew no Spanish at all.

As I was making tea, the door opened and someone else came in: someone about eleven years old. "Good evening," he said. His energy was exceptionally cheerful and eager.

"Very pleased to meet you," I said, "...on this miserable cold night when fog and rain has filled the valley and your brother has so kindly offered me a place to spend the night. It's very pleasant in here... What is your name?"

"Me?"

"Yes, you."

"Gregorio."

"Let us have some tea. I'm making some."

"Good," Gregorio said. "What brings you to Pampa Qarqa?"

"I am on my way to the end of the road at the top of the pass. I need to buy some things. I'm also carrying equipment to climb one of the glaciers up above. I've been living in Sina for a couple of weeks."

"Good! In that case, let's begin a friendship! What book is that?"

Gregorio had noticed that in my pack I was carrying a book. "I'll show you. Look, it's about Peru - poems - each one is in three languages: Quechua, Spanish and English."

Gregorio sat by my primus stove with me and began slowly reading a poem in Spanish - as he had learned to do in the school down in Potoni. Then I pronounced the Quechua version which he understood readily, but did not realize could be written. Then he asked me to read the English. I read a few words.

"Teach it to me!" he said. I could feel his fascination. It was the same fascination I had felt upon first hearing the mysterious sounds of the Quechua language.

"Sure," I said. I read him some of the English. Then he took the book and began poring over it. I was saddened to think about how his curiosity about the remote outside world would probably be overwhelmed by a mountain of difficulties.

An older brother, Eusevio, came into the room and sat down. I recognized immediately that he didn't share his younger brother's curiosity. But he dominated the conversation with questions of a practical nature: "How much did your stove cost?" So Gregorio was left to ponder over the pages of my book alone.

"Where do you get shoes like that?" continued Eusevio...

"Fine flashlight you have there..."

Each time I began trying to respond to his questions, he would lose interest and pass to something else. I told him I was planning to buy a sheep in the market the next day.

"Why don't you buy one from me?" he asked. "I am in need of money. If you give me money for a sheep, I can buy things in the market tomorrow too!"

"But I may not be able to pick up the sheep for several days as I may stay up at the market after everyone leaves and try and climb one of the nearby peaks." I knew if I gave him the money ahead of when he delivered the sheep, I would be violating one of the cardinal rules of good business.

But then something told me: "Who cares...?"

"How much do you want for your sheep?" I asked.

"I'll sell you one for 300 soles." (about $7) "A fat one."

I knew ahead of time and could tell by the look in his eyes that this meant I could bargain him down to at least 200 soles, but again... "Who cares..."

"OK, in the morning I'll give you the money," I said.

He and Antonio were to sleep in some other hut. This left me and Gregorio lying alone in the darkness.

"I worked for Emilio Laura, the school teacher in Sina, for 20 cents a day. Is that a decent wage?" Gregorio's voice drifted over to me in the dark.

"That's actually very little. But it's alright..."

"You ought to plant some potatoes, sir, while you're in Sina. Potatoes are always good to plant."

"The other day we planted lettuce, carrots, parsley and radishes," I said enthusiastically.

"But potatoes. You should plant potatoes!"

Bad Weather and Exhaustion

The next morning I was up early. All night long I had heard drops of rain dripping through the grass. I looked outside and it was no better. Still gray and raining. I gave Eusevio two thirds of his price for the sheep, about $4.50, and set off again toward the pass. Gregorio, Antonio and Eusevio stayed behind, although they were planning to come up later.

It was a longer climb than I had remembered. Each fresh view of the valley above brought sad news. I wasn't getting close yet. My climbing equipment was unbearably heavy and I began to feel painfully exhausted. My heart twittered uselessly in my chest: my knees hurt. I actually had to collapse and sit down every fifty or a hundred yards. My hands were jamming themselves into my potatoes and bacon and feeding my mouth. The rain continued to fall - except now it was snow. I followed the Indians' bare footprints in the snow. The capillaries in my extremities - in my hands and forearms - closed down. I had difficulty clenching my fist. But I had to get to the top of the pass. The trucks would only be there for a few hours.

At the top of the pass people huddled miserably behind little stone windbreaks. Some of the Indian women heated coffee or stew over primus stoves which burned in large tin cans to protect them from the wind. I took off my pack and immediately felt better. I drank a cup of coffee and ate a piece of bread. The snow fell steadily. The shiny splendor of the surrounding twenty-thousand-foot peaks was hopelessly veiled. Visibility was down to about fifty feet.

"Are you really going to stay up here and climb one of those peaks in this weather?" someone asked.

"I don't know," I said.

Trucks Every Saturday at Iskay Cruz

I bought two trout which someone had just caught in one of the lakes further south. I bought candy, oranges, onions - a cigarette. I ate a bowl of stew. Eusevio arrived and I told him I didn't think I'd be able to climb in that weather and that I would probably go on back down the valley and could pick up the sheep from him that very afternoon.

He pleaded for the final third of his payment and, as I could see no reason whatsoever not to give it to him, I gave it to him so he could buy candles to light his house at night.

Thinking to lighten my pack for the trip down and to avoid having to carry them back up again, I snuck off into the fog and hid my tent and rope under some rocks. Hopefully in the time that remained to me I would have the opportunity and good luck with the weather to come up and at least put one foot on the glacier. As it turned out I wouldn't be able to use that equipment for another couple of years.

So I started back down the valley. The descent took the strain off my heart but was no easier on my knees. I soon fell in with my compadre Edwin and his cousin Federico. Edwin put my pack on one of his horses. I jabbered about the rest of the world, the United States, and so on for about three hours - trying to answer their questions as completely as possible. After three hours of such happy jabber we approached Pampa Qarqa - Eusevio's house.

I told Edwin and Federico, "I'll be down shortly. Go on ahead," and sat down under a large overhanging rock - still in the rain. One more group of latecomers from the market passed on their way down with llamas laden with goods.

"Come on down to Sina with us," they called.

"I've got to wait for a friend here," I said, and they went past.

After an hour or so of staring into the fog waiting for Eusevio to appear, I began to get impatient. I knew that we were on Sina time but I couldn't imagine why Eusevio would be delayed and I wanted my sheep. But as always happens at such moments, someone appeared out of the fog - a little smiling face. "Gregorio! How nice to see you! Where's your brother, Eusevio?"

"I guess he hasn't gotten back down from the pass yet," Gregorio said. "Anyway, come on in for a cup of hot tea and spend the night."

"I can't," I said thinking of Lisa, "I've got to go back down to Sina." But Gregorio was already hastily leading me toward his house. At the gate to the house a little old Indian of the poorest sort greeted me with this fantastic smile and I was very impressed. It was Gregorio's father, I assumed, although he didn't say.

I explained in Quechua that I had paid Eusevio 300 soles for a sheep. The man, wrinkled and scrawny with hunger, said he would bring it down. I told him that Eusevio himself had said he would bring it down and that the responsibility needn't necessarily be his, the father's, but the father asserted that nevertheless he would bring it down the very next day. I was sorry that my first visit with this man seemed to be entirely of a business nature and that I didn't have time to sit for a while and drink a hot cup of herbal tea. As I walked off down the trail, Gregorio shouted after me: "Hey! I'll be down tomorrow too!"

Gregorio, Eusevio and Their Mother in Pampa Qarqa

"Terrific!" I shouted. It took me the full two-hour walk on down to Sina to begin to get the cramps worked out of my legs from sitting under that rock.

Where is My Sheep?

I arrived in Sina just after dark and found Lisa already snuggled into her sleeping bag. She hadn't expected me back for several days yet and was happy to see me. Octavia, Edwin's mother and our nearest neighbor, seeing how foul the weather was continuing to be, had told Lisa that surely I would be back down.

Still full of motion from the day, I unpacked all my things, arranged everything neatly in the house, and heated water for a delicious cup of tea made from my favorite local wild herb: muña.

The next day was Sunday. No Eusevio. But that was understandable since it was Sunday, a day of rest, right? So I waited, but when no one had come by Monday afternoon I headed on back up toward Pampa Qarqa to see just what in the hell had happened to my sheep.

On my way past Hornopampa I saw someone signaling me to cross the river and come over for a visit. It was Juan Jironda, father of

Ana, Alfredo, Norma, Napoleon, Carlos and Idelsa, husband of four sisters and the biggest landowner of the valley. We talked quietly for some time and he assured me that he would make sure that I got my sheep.

I went on up to Pampa Qarqa but no one was home, so after getting bit in the leg by their dog, I wandered on back toward Sina.

The next afternoon Eusevio showed up with a nice fat sheep for me. I helped Edwin butcher it. Soon its carcass was hanging from the rafters in our house and we had a supply of meat which would last for at least two weeks. Lisa washed the fleece down in the river and we hung it above the door so as not to risk infesting the rest of the room with the ticks and fleas which were now bewilderedly waltzing around in the wool wondering what had happened to their blood supply. When it finished drying, we would shave it and Lisa would have a new supply of wool for her spinning.

Lisa Washing Fleece

Soon I was asleep but there was an urgent knock on the door. "Compadre!" It was Edwin and he was very worried about his wife, Laura.

"She just gave birth to a baby boy but she won't stop bleeding!"

I went with him to see her but really didn't know how to be of help. It took her two more days to finish expelling the placenta and stop bleeding. I put some water on the newborn baby's head. Guido would be his name and now we too were all "compadres."

Lisa and I spent more time with Edwin and with Laura, who had recovered fairly rapidly, high up in the potato fields. We were trying to help clear overgrowth from the fields and then dig into the rocky Andean hillside and plant seed potatoes for next season's crop. Our bodies were ridiculously inept at those tasks and we marveled at the amazing strength of the men and women with whom we were working. Every once in a while we would take a break and eat a few more potatoes which had been boiling in a little clay pot over a small fire.

I determined to extract another bush from the hillside. Our machetes had nothing left of their wooden handles and our skin had to be tough enough to grasp the naked metal blades... which it wasn't. And the bush was covered with thorns. Grasping it and pulling with all our might, our naked skin had to be tough enough to protect us from those thorns... which again it wasn't. When the bush finally broke loose I lost my balance and tumbled down the mountainside scraping and cutting my skin against the rocks. Helping our friends was kind of a joke but we did the best we could.

There was a little house down near the creek. It was the same house where Ilateria had been working on weaving a blanket the previous year. Whenever I stopped there to say 'hi' it was necessary to speak only Quechua. There were several generations of women living in that house and it was tightly packed. It seemed that about a dozen people lived there and many times when I passed it I would hear uproarious giggling laughter. Sexy laughter. There was a lot of fun going on in that little house. I would stop and say 'hi' but the secrets of the sexy joyful giggling remained mysterious.

I discovered that one of the young women who lived in that house was only twenty-seven years old but was already a grandmother although she was still bearing children herself. I couldn't recall that happening very often in the North American culture I came from.

Patrunila, another woman related to that household, was older... in her late thirties. She had given birth to babies with seven different fathers in the village and all those different men reputedly helped care for her when she was raising yet another newborn.

Finding Pastor's Cows - Down to the Jungle

My new friend, Pastor Moreno Solazano, invited me to travel with him to find and milk his cows. We got to know each other pretty well in the process as it took a whole day to even find, much less milk, those cows. He measured his family's wealth in cattle. It seemed that he had about eight of them... somewhere.

He told me that some of them might be yet further down the valley and we made a plan to take several days and go look for them. Fence-building was not part of life in these valleys. Horses, llamas, alpacas, sheep, pigs, chickens and cattle had to be tracked by their owners who knew their animals well enough to usually have a 'hunch' about where they might be found.

Lisa remained in Sina. Pastor and I descended to Quiaca. We climbed downhill and then went up and over into the next valley... about six hours of walking. We were down to about six-thousand feet elevation and the local crop was corn. We forgot about potatoes and ate corn. The ears grew with multi-colored kernels and it was tough but tasty. Pastor introduced me to many friends he had there and I realized that I could eventually feel at home there too... if I were to go back and spend time. A bear had just been caught and killed. We were treated to a meal of bear meat.

Bear Killed for Eating the Corn

We continued downhill for another two days. We didn't find any more of Pastor's cattle, but I got to discover more of the amazing magic of that huge valley. We emerged briefly onto a road and entered the little town of Sandia at about three-thousand feet. I purchased a melon and cut it up into tiny pieces so I could share it with a few dozen children who had begun following me around.

More villages, well known to Pastor, lay further down that road and I would eventually reach them on another trip two years later. But in Sandia we had reached low enough altitudes to find orange trees and feel the pervasive warmth of the high jungle.

1970 Journey Through Sina

It took us another three days to climb uphill back to Sina. Along the way I asked Pastor if he would be willing to accompany us in the future if I brought adventurous high-school students along with me. I was reflecting on the successes of my Terrible Tours in Mexico. Pastor, who, like me, enjoyed wandering for the sake of wandering, of course agreed. So we had a plan to create more "Terrible Tours."

When we walked back into Sina there was a party going on. My compadre Lucio was feeling better and having a fine time leading the musical drinking festivities. I had brought another guitar with me. I brought it out and gave it to the best performer in the valley, Victor Suarez. We began drinking the favorite mixture of pure alcohol, anise and sugar and wailed at the sky.

Lucio Gonza and Friends in Sina Playing Panpipes

There were songs about harvests, especially the prized coca leaves, and there were songs about local village pride. But by far the favorite musical topics involved the grief of broken-hearted lonely men whose earnest romantic promises had been rejected by women and who found themselves, once again, alone in the vast Andean landscape.

'Oh if I ever hurt you just give me the word and I will kill myself!' The lyrics would wail in mixtures of both Quechua and Spanish. We men would get together and bring ourselves to tears. Our sobbing musical grief would ascend up into the night sky and we bonded deeply in this soul sharing. The feel of this music had sunk into my soul and I was beginning to be able to sing and dance more like a native.

Lucio looked at me earnestly. "We keep teaching you Quechua, why don't you teach us more English?"

"OK, I'm ready. What would you like to know how to say?"

"How do you say 'runtu?'" he would ask me.

"Egg." I would reply, but somehow he always looked unsatisfied and confused. I think he expected a great deal of knowledge about the English language to come rushing in upon him, but it never did.

I was exhausted. I crawled back into my warm little house and snuggled into Lisa's warm embrace.

We picked a Saturday, packed our things, said our goodbyes and ascended the valley to the weekly truck market to ride back out to the big wide world. Coming and going to and from Sina now seemed like an ordinary part of life.

We traveled up to Cusco where we attended the annual Inca revival celebration known as Inti Raymi.

Inca Elders at Inti Raymi in Cusco

We then headed down to the Pacific coast through Arequipa by train. A wave of shock passed through us as we all discovered the reason for our delay at the station: a woman had stumbled and fallen onto the tracks and the train had severed her arm.

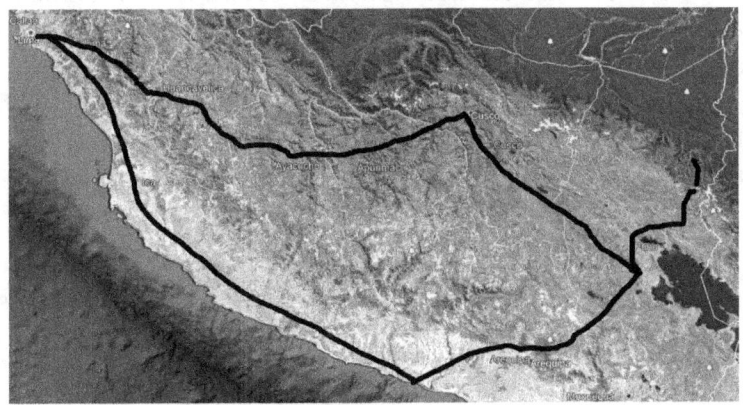

1970 Travels in Peru

Colorado, New Mexico and Texas

We flew back from Lima to Miami and traveled directly to Colorado. Soon Lisa would head for Berkeley and prepare for a teaching job she had landed which would begin in the fall.

I would also head for Berkeley to begin working on a doctorate in linguistics. But not yet.

For some reason I was drawn to drive up to Carp's ranch in the Tarryall mountains... some kind of call of the wild I guess... and wildness is what I found. By the time I arrived I was feeling a deep exhaustion. Lisa had not been there to 'hold my string' and my balloon had been flying too far too fast and too high and I was psychically about to pop. I got some sleep but even the next day I could feel a pervasive quivering in my soul.

My friend Archer and his girlfriend Sandy were there and were recovering from a violent attack on their commune near Guadalupita. Local Chicanos from the town of Mora had ridden through on horseback one night to drive out the hippies. They killed one hippie with a rifle and kidnapped Archer and Sandy who were stuffed into the trunk of a car.

Many hours later Archer was set free a hundred miles away in the remote desert and Sandy was raped by five different guys and then set free in another remote location. That was the end of the 'Kingdom of

Heaven,' as the commune had been called.

Archer wandered across the desert for hours and, coming to a highway, hitch-hiked to Santa Fe. Sandy wandered naked into a remote ranch house with and was given shelter and later a ride also to Santa Fe where she and Archer eventually found each other at a Catholic Mission for homeless people. Archer's attempts to report these attacks to the Highway Patrol resulted in his being threatened with arrest for having muddy feet in their station.

While washing the carrots in the Mission kitchen Archer looked out into the parking lot and recognized the 1924 Dodge pickup truck with wooden wheels which could only have been driven by his friend from San Francisco, George Poor. Archer ran out to greet George in the parking lot. It seemed that George had been staying at Carp's cabin up in Colorado and had made a bet with Carp that he could find Archer if he drove down to New Mexico.

So to enable George to collect on his bet, Archer and Sandy embarked on a slow, leisurely flat-tire road-side chile-relleno drive up to Carp's place. They arrived as living proof that George had won the bet and felt soon forgotten in the swirling pool of local drama.

Mad Dog, also known as Bob Bassara, was there with his wife Stephanie and his friend Fluke. Carp was in the process of wooing Mad Dog's wife and the two of them had begun to emerge as the new hot romantic item which didn't make Mad Dog particularly happy. So the fact that Archer and Sandy had ridden up from New Mexico with George without even a few pennies in their pockets for food was gradually declining in the communal awareness and they were getting rather hungry. I offered to drive them back to New Mexico.

James had also been visiting and climbing granite walls up at Carp's but was about ready to head back down to his apartment near Colorado Springs. He wanted to accompany us.

We said farewell to Carp and the others and headed out toward the highway. James had brought his pistols with him and wanted to stop along the way for some shooting.

I remember lying on the ground listening to his pistol shots in a state of agony. A migraine headache was wracking my nervous system. Was it also possible that I was having a premonition of what would happen in perhaps that same or a nearby spot a little more than a year later?

We continued on our way but I asked Archer to drive and I hung out the window to feel the air on my face. "No, drive even more slowly," I told him. "My body can't stand any more motion." I was reeling with severe vertigo and we were keeping it down to twenty-five miles an hour.

Arriving in New Mexico we learned that a peyote ceremony with Native American Church pueblo Indian leaders was scheduled and that we were invited. We arrived in Taos in time for the meeting.

We sat in a circle all night in the teepee. I had done this before and was familiar with the protocol of the meeting. The leaders kept the glowing coals in the shape of a bird while the drum was beating energetically with a driving sense of urgency all night long. Peyote cactus flesh and peyote tea were passed around for everyone to eat and drink. Although the quantities were much lower than those I used to ingest with friends in the Colorado mountains, there was still a psychedelic effect. The leaders worked with individual Indians who were hoping to recover from their alcohol problems. The leaders of the peyote meeting addressed their suffering and we all prayed for their emotional healing.

"We should drive to southern Texas, pick a trunk-load of peyote and bring it back to these Indians to express our appreciation!" Archer suggested.

"OK," I said and the three of us set off for the peyote fields known to exist near Rio Grande City close to the border with Mexico.

It's a thousand-mile journey and I felt happy to be close to the two of them and participate in this healing adventure.

Arriving in the peyote fields after two days of driving we parked and began walking and searching. Legend has it that the cacti will remain hidden until suddenly, acknowledging human persistence, they will appear in large quantities as if by magic.

After two or three hours, that's exactly what happened. We began digging up and carrying large quantities back to the car. We nibbled on the cactus buds as we picked them which deepened our connection and encouraged them to become even more plentiful and visible. Soon we had a trunk full and began driving back north.

The Border Patrol had other ideas. They pulled us over, took a look at us and announced that they knew of only one possible reason for our presence in this desert. "Open your trunk," they requested. "Yup, it's full of peyote."

They put me and Archer in the back seat of their patrol car and told Sandy to drive my car toward the courthouse in Rio Grande City.

My car was in the lead so we could all see the flames which soon leaped out of both rear wheels of my car. Sandy had left the emergency brake engaged.

She was approaching a right angle turn in the highway at sixty-miles-per-hour and hit the brakes to slow down. No brakes. All the brake fluid had drained out through the molten wheel cylinders. She navigated the sharp turn at high speed and came to a stop beside the road. We left my car right there and all three of us rode on into the courthouse. It was late in the day so we spent the night in jail. Archer and I were together in the men's prison and Sandy was alone in another cell for women.

We still had peyote in our bellies and transformed the experience into a magical meditation exercise. That was Archer's idea. He had been studying Buddhist techniques.

The next day Joe Sharp wired a few hundred dollars from California and, after promising to return for a trial a few months hence, we were set free. My car had been towed to the courthouse. I crawled underneath it with my toolbox and crimped off the rear brake lines. Refilling the master cylinder with brake fluid enabled the front brakes and we drove north to San Antonio.

We spent the next day scouring for parts in the local junk yards and finished repairing the rear brakes.

As luck would have it, the cops had not found all of our peyote. We still had the largest button: the 'king' peyote. We drove back to New Mexico and presented it to the Indians. They invited us to participate in the next meeting so that we might be healed from the negative energies from our exposure to the Border Patrol.

We accepted and sat up for another all-night ceremony the following weekend. The next time I dared cross the Texas-Mexico border more than ten years later I was relieved to find that yes, some statute of limitations had dissolved our case off the books. We had never returned for the trial.

After the next peyote meeting we visited Morningstar up near Arroyo Hondo and admired the evolving communal hippie architecture. We were invited into the little hand-patted mud adobe home of Zadi and Shrada. They looked the part: archetypal hippies. Zadi had the beard, the dark piercing eyes and Shrada was a perfect earth angel.

They told me they were planning to spend the winter camped alone on top of the remote Archuleta Mesa near Pagosa Springs in southern Colorado. Something clicked and I knew I should and would see them again. There was a deep telepathic attraction between me and Shrada. And Zadi was silently supporting it.

"I wonder if there is anything left of our little home near Guadalupita at the 'Kingdom of Heaven?'" Archer wondered.

We drove back into that valley. We both felt fearful. The local Chicanos were, of course, not being prosecuted by their own local law enforcement agencies. They had succeeded in ridding themselves of the hippie commune which had brought scantily dressed English-only speaking kids with drugs into their territory. We spent the afternoon driving in and out. Archer examined the remains of the commune. Nothing much was left. Nothing salvageable.

I was vaguely aware that time had flown and that my classes were actually beginning in Berkeley. I passed through Boulder and then Steamboat Springs with a little U-haul trailer attached to my rear bumper. I put my spare automobile engine, the rest of my tools and assorted parts in the trailer with my other possessions and made my way across the western third of the country to California.

Leda: Greek Odyssey

Linguistics at University of California in Berkeley

I was still exhausted and I was two weeks late. It was the fall of 1970 and I was 26 years old. I had missed all the introductory class material. Having signed up for a class in the Tibetan language, I explored the linguistics department until I found the location of the classroom. No one was there when I poked my head in but there was a list of the students posted on the wall. I read through the names. One of them leaped out at me: Leda Maniatis. *'I wonder who Leda Maniatis is?'* I thought to myself... *'someone exotic I bet...'*

I returned when class was in session and noticed that Leda was an attractive Greek woman. I of course had no idea that I would spend the next fifteen years and have two children with her.

The professor was Dr. Wong, of Chinese descent, and he had hired a Tibetan Lama, a re-incarnated 'Tulku,' to be our 'informant.' Our job was, under the guidance of Dr. Wong, to learn modern Tibetan from Lama Kunga. This was an ideal setup because Lama Kunga himself was incredibly focused, clear-minded and it was easy to communicate with him. I occasionally attended meditation practice sessions in San Francisco in Lama Kunga's small apartment where he would detail the flowery imagery we would collectively visualize emanating from the tops of our heads.

Another professor, Dr. Jim Matisoff, was excited to get to know me because of my Inca language experience. He invited me frequently to his house in the evenings where we would smoke pot and compare experiences. He had written his doctoral dissertation about a Burmese hill language called Lahu which was spoken in northern Thailand. We decided to create a program to teach Quechua and found a suitable 'informant' in San Francisco: a Bolivian man of Inca descent who was fluent in Quechua, Spanish and English. Jaime Daza was his name. The department hired him and my hopes and dreams for the linguistics department came true.

I had moved into a little house which Lisa had rented but the world she lived in, which involved teaching very young children, was not overlapping with my world at the University of California in Berkeley. Our connection was dissolving and weakening. We both knew it.

The first quarter ended and I was itchy to pick up where I had left off with my adventures in Colorado and New Mexico. I put my cross-country skis on top of my car and drove to the Archuleta mesa near Pagosa Springs in southern Colorado. I found a little turnout in the snow-bound wilderness at the foot of the mesa and parked the car. I slept in it until dawn and set off on my skis. Zadi and Shrada were up there on top and I would surely find them before dark.

Darkness fell early as it was mid-winter. I had found an abandoned fire-lookout tower on top of the mesa but I had not found Zadi and Shrada. I had no sleeping bag or tent but there was a little shack at the bottom of the tower with three sheets of fiber board and some old newspapers stored in it. I put one piece of fiber board on the ground and leaned the other two against each other to make an open-ended tent, climbed in and stuffed crumpled newspapers around me with the hope of keeping warm. It didn't work. The only solution involved doing jumping jacks and other aerobic exercises in the pitch black darkness until dawn.

Surely I would find them now that it was light. I skied and skied. No luck. So before facing another freezing night I descended back down to my car. The battery had died. I slept in the car which definitely could hold some of my body heat and the next day set out down the road on skies until I found someone who could come and give me an electrical jump start.

I gave up on Zadi and Shrada and headed for Steamboat Springs. My friend Charlie Bates had convinced David Herz to help him build molded mahogany sailboats in the town of Columbine which was up the Elk river road just west of Steamboat. I wanted to drop in and surprise somebody so I drove to Clark, parked the car again and skied the ten miles of unplowed road up to Columbine. I was in luck this time. I admired their craftsmanship and we practiced meditation in the winter wilderness. With my sense of adventure somewhat satisfied I headed back to California.

Classes resumed and I gradually got to know Leda Maniatis. She came to a picnic in Tilden park where I was playing the guitar at a party and I could tell that there was a mutual attraction.

She let me know that her Greek husband, Yorgos, had just arrived from France and that he had brought another woman, Rena, along with him who was in frail health and who needed nurturing. The three of them were now living together.

Yorgos was in exile from Greece because he had published articles critical of the military regime and he was afraid of being arrested in his native country. Leda had fled with him to Paris three years earlier and would have been happy to continue working there at her publishing job in a city where she felt quite at home. It was Yorgos who persuaded Leda to apply for admission and financial support from the linguistics department in California with the hope that she would emerge as a professor with a substantial salary and be able to support them both. Leda had the academic track record to pull this off whereas, although Yorgos was a published writer, he had never finished high school so he couldn't easily gain entry into the academic world.

As the winter quarter progressed the Tibetan class became an incubator for Leda's and my friendship. Lama Kunga treated us as if we were a couple and cheered us on whenever we let our attraction show. And Dr. Matisoff began inviting me over to share his music collection which included Greek and Ladino tapes. Leda would come with me and we fell together under the romantic magic spell of a song called 'La Rosa Enflorece.'

The winter quarter came to an end and I drove back to Colorado again. I lost my way in a blinding snowstorm in Nevada and accidentally added a couple of hundred miles to my trip. But I found my way and once again put on my skis at the bottom of the Archuleta mesa. I criss-crossed the wilderness and failed again to find Zadi and Shrada.

I again drove up to visit Charlie and David in Columbine. Heavy snow began to fall as I headed by night up the Elk River road. Soon it became impossible to tell where the road was and I felt the car sink into a ditch. I was closer to the highway than to Columbine so I retreated by spending the night skiing south back to the highway. I caught a ride and showed up at the Barn the next day where I was welcomed by Wayne and Linda. I bathed in the warmth of their hospitality for three or four days until the blizzard wore itself out and it might be possible to retrieve my car.

Wayne was ten years older than me. It felt like he had become more and more a role model for me in life. "You know you have become a 'father figure' for me!" I shared with great warmth. He didn't say anything but I know he took it in. He drove me up the Elk river road and a friendly snow plow driver pulled me out with a chain. I returned once again to California.

Yorgos and Leda joined me and Lisa on a hike up a snowfield overlooking Lake Tahoe one weekend. We thought we might enjoy spending time together as two couples but Yorgos and Lisa had no real way to form a friendship.

Life with Lisa became awkward and I moved out into a tent in a friend's back yard. It was damp and filled with little bugs called earwigs but I made it into a workable little home.

Yorgos had told Rena that it wasn't working for her to be there and she had departed. But things couldn't be the same in their marriage and Leda asked Yorgos to move out. She mentioned this change to me and I remember feeling some kind of mysterious excitement. A couple of days later she invited me over and we made love. "It's just like rocking on the waves in a little boat in the Mediterranean!" she suggested. I was eager to find out more.

In Tibetan class Lama Kunga celebrated energetically with us. He could feel the shift. He also gave me a letter of introduction to a friend of his: Chogyam Trungpa, another 'tulku,' or 'reincarnated lama,' whom he said was taking up residence in Colorado.

I had been a success in the linguistics department and continued to qualify for my full scholarship and living stipend. But I was not finding friends in the academic world who had the background to share my world of river running, mountaineering, musical performance and cross-cultural adventuring. I wasn't used to living in the purely intellectual academic world and even the idea of crawling under my car to fix something hands-on seemed appealing. Most of the students in the linguistics department were mathematicians who were planning to develop careers in the brand new high-tech world of computer translation and I wasn't resonating with them. It seemed to me that the soul of a language and a culture could never be translated by computer and that personal immersion had to be involved. And I knew that Pastor was waiting there in Sina for me to show up with students so that we could begin running Cameron's Terrible Tours.

I told the linguistics department that I was going to take a year off from the course work and 'return to the field.' I didn't burn my bridges there and I assumed that I could go back into the academic world whenever I wanted to. That moment never came.

Leda told me that she wanted to ride from California to Colorado with me just to get a small view of my world. She imagined that she would spend perhaps three weeks and then return to Greece or France.

My friend Archer journeyed back to Colorado with me and Leda. Soon he and Lisa took advantage of the vacuum left by the recent relationship shift and gave each other some love. Lisa and I eventually reclaimed our sense of deep fondness for each other and would get together and feel in awe of the adventures we had shared. We ended up raising young children at the same time in the same extended community in Boulder.

Grand Canyon - Communal Life in Boulder

Leda, as I said, had imagined a short visit into my world but Wayne and Linda had other ideas. I drove up to the Barn in Steamboat Springs and they said, "Go to the store and buy yourself a month's supply of refried beans. We're headed down the Grand Canyon and we need you to run one of the boats!"

Wayne butchered an animal, made a giant pot of stew and we gathered, all sixty of our tribe, and feasted as we finished preparations. Twenty-four of us set off with three boats to spend a month running the upper half of the Grand Canyon. Leda postponed her return to California.

I was showing Leda my world and hoping she would feel the freedom, the beauty and the camaraderie. I was seeing her as the exotic queen of ancient mysteries and she was seeing me as Apollo, the Sun god.

I spent less time exploring the remote reaches of the river and its canyon mysteries and more time by Leda's side, gently encouraging her to find personal strength in the natural connections with sky and water and stone. It wasn't actually so easy for her to just pick up the reins of my life style and automatically feel closeness with all my friends and with the rugged landscapes.

Down the Upper Half of the Grand Canyon

After the grandeur of the Grand Canyon we took a breath and looked at some of my other favorite Colorado communities: Durango, Manitou Springs and then Boulder. Leda was no longer thinking of returning to California and school in Berkeley.

She had moved from Athens to Paris to Berkeley to... where? We had already tasted the possibility of living in Steamboat Springs... But Leda had not really bonded with the rural outdoor adventure-oriented women. So we drove down to Durango and visited the Fort Lewis College campus. Perhaps we could re-enter the academic world there but still be in the Colorado mountains? Maybe. Driving down to Manitou Springs we visited my friend James and explored the idea of living there. Leda cooked a marvelously garlic-flavored salmon dinner for us and we spent some time around Colorado College... Should we settle there? We then drove up to Boulder and found ourselves welcome in a communal household owned by John Link. We settled in a for bit. I made money repairing automobile engines and we attended 'encounter groups' and hung out with a motley assortment of climbers and seekers.

Leda found some connection with friendly people in the communal household so we called that home for the next few years. John Link continued to make us feel welcome although we couldn't afford to actually rent a room. We slept in a corner of the living room during the winters and out in the yard on the trampoline during the summers. I played live music for many dance parties and Leda helped keep the kitchen running. Apparently we were earning our keep.

I was thinking about my Terrible Tour business. I would make money on the road by sharing my fascination with Inca culture and I would make money at home in Boulder by repairing engines and by becoming a guitar-maker. Fortunately, Bonnie's new boyfriend, master guitar-maker Max Krimmel, would show me how to do that. I rented a tiny part of a carriage house in an alley near the University for $15 a month and began collecting guitar-making tools.

Remembering Lama Kunga's letter of introduction, I drove up to the bottom of Four Mile Canyon where Chogyam Trungpa was living. I knocked on the door and presented my letter to some of his students. They took the letter and told me to wait. They didn't really seem happy to see me. After a couple of hours of sitting in a chair by the front door with no one coming back to say anything further, I decided to forget it and I left. I was catching the smell of the highly competitive circles which surrounded him. As time passed they earned a reputation for being a nasty egotistical bunch... all the more ironic because they were gathering in the name of 'egolessness.'

I gave slide shows at Colorado high schools until I had a half dozen paying students and we planned a Terrible Tour to Peru for the following spring. I was excited because I was hoping that Leda, a fellow linguist, would be a great partner.

Extreme Tragedy

The news suddenly came in that my friend James had shot himself in the side of the head in the mountains. But that wasn't the most outrageous news. He had shot himself after kidnapping, wounding and raping a young woman. After committing these terrible crimes in some kind of strange trance state he had, following an impulse of remorse and compassion, left a lighted lantern beside the road next to his truck wherein the wounded girl lay. Then, assuming that she would be found and rescued, he had attempted suicide in the nearby forest. The bullet miraculously had not killed him. A three-day snowstorm was just beginning. No one had come up the road to rescue her and she died in the back of his truck while he lay still alive but unconscious in the snow in the forest. He was eventually found by members of a road construction crew and taken to a hospital.

I was completely mystified. I remembered the way I had felt spooked while visiting him one winter in Carp's cabin and I remembered the terrible migraine headache which had overwhelmed me when he had fired his pistol. Had that perhaps been in the same exact spot in which the girl had just died? And I also remembered the tenderness with which he had nurtured my rock climbing skills.

I went down and witnessed an 'arraignment' where he was charged with murder, kidnapping and rape. He didn't raise his head to look at me. They considered him suicidal and kept him in a special padded cell. Everyone who had known him felt completely confused. A few friends chose to honor and continue their friendships with him but most did not.

Eventually, after a couple of years had passed, I was able to visit him. He had been sentenced to life imprisonment. I communicated over the years with the case workers in the prison system. They all ended up liking James' personality and described him as a 'model prisoner.' Fourteen years later he was released to work for my construction company.

Terrible Tour to Peru

Leda and I flew together to Lima, Peru with our students in 1972. Soon we were riding up to Cusco from Lima through Puquio: Charlie, Tom, John, Barker and me 'n Leda. We spent four days on crowded trucks and buses waiting for hours at a time while landslides of mud were cleared from the road.

"These fuckin' Indians won't move over," one of my students complained and I began to wonder just how successful this trip was going to be if already we were down to 'fuckin' Indians!'

"I could'a killed that sonofabitch who bent my pack!" complained another one of my students after watching a young Peruvian Indian hauling an immensely heavy bundle up a ladder on the back of a bus lose his balance and come tumbling down and land on his backpack.

"Let me see," I asked. "Where is it bent?" We examined the backpack and it proved to be perfectly alright. *'And I'm taking these assholes to Sina?'* I asked myself.

We were a floating cultural island. So far nothing had made us laugh or smile but our own American jokes and comments. *'The environment's not sinking in yet,'* I thought to myself. *'We might as well be taking a stroll through the Los Angeles zoo!'* And so it continued: through Cusco -- a place that remains heavy with the weight of past colonial conquests -- through Machu Picchu. My students were not picking up on any of the feelings of these places; we were still an island with no connection to the continent!

We walked up to Machu Picchu. Everyone was carrying their new packs for the first time and the uncertainties were running neck-deep. A walk up to the top of Huayna Picchu woke us up a bit thanks to the exposed steepness but the train ride crammed into a cattle car with a bunch of 'inconsiderate Indians' on the way back to Cusco didn't particularly improve our gringo-Indian relations.

We ran into Federico and also Alberto Valdivia, both friends from Sina, briefly in Juliaca as we passed through, but still nothing could break through the shell that surrounded the group... not until we got to Cojata and a little slightly-drunken man named Bonifacio Casillia Q'alisaya showed up and befriended us. He took me to meet his wife Torivia and his daughter Francisca. They were another little family dressed in rags and living in extreme poverty.

Bonifacio eventually brought his wife, another of his children and some sardines and onions up to our rented room. I introduced them to the students and we sat around in a big circle and laughed at all sorts of things -- whether we understood them or not. At last something was getting through. Bonifacio just kept right on smiling at us with a burning invitation to join in the fun of friendship. He broke the shell around the group and the students shut up and looked around and beyond their own projections a little bit for the first time.

Actually, from that time onward, Barker, very verbal and a natural leader, seemed to be a changed person. We talked about it more at dinner. We also talked about Charlie's relationship to the group. He was a bit older and from Ireland. He had not been fitting easily into the group with its young American ways.

Back into Sina with a Different Woman

Once we got to the Saturday market at the top of the valley leading down to Sina I was swept immediately into the business of saying hello to Edwin, Pastor, Octaviana and others. Octaviana whispered to me that it was sad that I had changed women. I explained to her that I wasn't sad... that I was excited about my new romance. There was no way for me to explain all the waters which had run under my bridge since I had last been in Sina and I knew I hadn't really addressed her comment.

Descent into Sina

The walk on down to Sina went rapidly. We were lucky and were able to use some of our Sineño friends' horses. We got ourselves set up in Edwin's and Pastor's houses in Sina and began the festivities. Victor Suarez and Pastor and Alfredo and his sisters Norma and Ana all were ready for music and dancing.

The bottles of alcohol mixed with warm water and sugar kept coming around and Leda drank it all down, thinking it was perhaps some kind of wine. Finally Leda disappeared, suddenly, right in the middle of a song she was singing. She fell backwards, feet last, over a little five-foot cliff. We jumped over the cliff and picked her up. We set her back down where she had been and the song went on as if uninterrupted.

Anna and Charlie; John and Norma

Alfredo's flirtatious younger sister Norma had brought out her little plastic battery-powered record player and was spinning the latest disks for us and she and her older sister Ana were dancing happily. Right then and there, during the middle of their first dance, Norma fell passionately in love with John, our most dashing-looking young student. That wasn't the first romantic dancing that was done that day. Pastor had gotten a hold of Leda earlier that afternoon and, to the erotic sounds of Victor's guitar, he had led her through a hazy web of sexy Quechua rhythms.

Leda and Pastor

Once the party decided to move up out of Edwin's and Laura's knee-deep-in-mud yard up onto the grassy knoll above, the party divided into two sections: one led by Norma and her plastic record player; the other dominated by the huayños on the guitar: two rather completely different types of music.

Leda was now asleep so I carried her up to the house Edwin had given us to stay in and laid her out on the floor between our sleeping bags and began to turn my mind toward the business of getting food together for all of us.

I also paid a visit to my compadre Lucio Gonza, his wife Patrunila, my god-daughter Natilminda and her older sister Gladys. Leticia was in school in Puno it seems. I was full of the energy of having just arrived and of having danced and drunk some alcohol and our conversation in Quechua went easily.

Lucio Gonza and Wife Patrunila with Natilminda and Gladys

My Comadre Laura was working hard to feed all of us. And that wasn't the only time either. It was basically thanks to her that for the first three or four days we had very much to eat at all.

After the first day's party we were ready for something more serious. But Victor Suarez was ready to make more music. So one part of Sina carried on the party while the rest of Sina went on with its potato-cultivating business.

I took us all down to the schoolhouse. Victor followed us halfway still making music on the guitar. I kept joking about how we didn't need any 'borrachos' (drunks) teaching us in school and he was very nice and took the hint and vanished.

In the schoolhouse Emilio gave us a long winded analysis of the Spanish verb 'to fit,' marriage customs in Sina and his opinion of the government.

Emilio radiated frustration with life in general. We all knew what his problem was. He was thirteen years older than his sexy young wife, Idelsa, whom he had married when she was only eleven. Idelsa had blossomed into a very flirtatious teenager and wasn't happy in the marriage.

Idelsa and Emilio

Pastor had explained it all to me. "Idelsa has had an awful lot of lovers and now that Emilio is paying for her to study in Juliaca she is even more flirtatious and spends all her time dancing her way into new love affairs. But Emilio is hopelessly in love with her. There's a lot of women like her in Peru but I sure wouldn't want one like that," he concluded.

"Well life is good for Idelsa then," I commented. "I know she likes to flirt with me... I can feel it..."

Me and Idelsa

"Yes, Idelsa is good for the rest of us men!" Pastor laughed. "But not for Emilio!"

Then Leda and I went across the river to pay a visit to Amalia Caceres. Her house and garden were always just right and she always had something to give to whomever came to visit. She lent us a stove made out of a huge can and some firewood so that we would be all set for cooking. Leda, with her black eyes and olive skin, was feeling more and more connected in Sina. "I know these people!" she would insist.

Now all we needed was a sheep and I had some ideas about getting one. The next morning Edwin and I set off shortly after dawn up the trail for an hour or so to Potoni. But I was wrong. No one there had a sheep to sell. The sheep were needed to make fertilizer and they were herded meticulously so that they would poop in precise patterns over the potato fields. Edwin, apparently taking our compadre relationship very seriously, told me that he himself possessed one more sheep and that he would let us have it.

Edwin and I got up early again the next morning and ran up to Condorsayana high on the valley above Sina where the shepherds still had the sheep together in little corrals and hadn't turned them out to graze for the day. We determined which sheep it was which Edwin owned, tied a rope around it and led it on down toward Sina. Edwin told me it had cost him 250 soles so I gave him 350 soles. I told him I wanted to give him something extra because he was being so kind to let us stay for nothing in a house which belonged to him and because his wife, Laura, was also being so kind in the way she continually looked after us. She was still cooking for us and generally offering whatever she had.

As we walked on down the valley I decided that I should kill the sheep myself this time. If I was the one who was going to eat it, I should be the one who killed it. No more of this hypocrisy!

We tied the sheep up in front of my house; I pulled out my pocket-knife and moved to plunge it into the sheep's neck when Edwin said, "No Compadre! It can cry! And we need a basin in which to catch the blood!" So I waited while Edwin went down to his house to get a better knife and a basin. Eventually he came back with Laura and Guido.

Laura smiled cheerfully in the morning sun and said, "Well, now you'll have some meat!" We tied the sheep's legs together, held it's head and body firmly on the ground, and I held it while Edwin quickly cut its throat and spinal cord. We kept the blood in a basin and Barker helped Edwin squeeze the poop out of the intestines while I finished cleaning out the guts and then rubbing salt into the meat to discourage the flies from laying their eggs.

We fried up the heart and liver right there for breakfast. Laura went down to her kitchen and came back shortly with a plate full of fried blood, chopped intestines and onions for us: a mixture called 'wilapari.' It tasted good and was extremely rich. As I ate my share of it I thought what good energy it would give me the following day for climbing up to the pass.

We had decided that Leda, John and Barker would go up to a lake to go fishing while Tom and I went to try and climb twenty-thousand-foot Ananea.

The rest of the afternoon was spent cutting up and cooking the two hindquarters from the sheep and boiling up quite a pile of potatoes, the net results of which, however, looked quite piddling when I thought about how high and far we were planning to go on those little sacks of food.

Late that afternoon Charlie came back from spending two days with Pastor in Yanaloma taking care of some cows. Instead of joining with the planned fishing and mountain climbing trips, he decided he'd go back down with Pastor on the following day to Yanaloma.

Meanwhile, our Comadre, Laura was cooking dinner again for all of us because we were to cut my godson Guido's hair that night. We ate. Then we each held four coca leaves at a time between our fingers, then put them in a bowl with money, alcohol and locks of Guido's hair. We kept taking turns cutting locks of hair: me, Leda, Barker, Charlie, Tom and John and Edwin and Laura.

A good feeling was generated by it all, and pretty soon Barker requested that I translate: "Tell them thank you very much and that nothing so beautiful as this happens in our country."

About ten o'clock Laura surprised us with a huge pot of hot 'ponche' made out of milk, hot water, anise, sugar, cinnamon and alcohol which made a nice warm furry ball in my belly while I went to sleep.

Leda's intestines were a bit out of sorts during the night so she decided to go with Pastor and Charlie to Yanaloma and then to Hornopampa instead of fishing with Barker and John.

Climbing on the Glaciers of Ananea

Tom and I set off shortly after dawn and hiked all day long, climbing about ten miles up to the bottom of the glacier at about sixteen-thousand feet. I searched for and found the climbing equipment I had hidden nearby two years earlier. The primus stove fired right up after two years of sitting under the rocks!

Tom and I set up my old tent, made coffee and heated our meat. We were right at the bottom of the glacier and were ready to see what we could climb in the morning. We had good weather all day: not a drop of rain even though clouds had been steadily pumping up the valley. Somewhere at the top of the valley they dispersed into the air.

'Barker and John are over there somewhere on the other side of the valley getting ready to go fishing,' we were thinking. We hoped they would have a pleasant night. I was thinking they might have found one of the stone huts over by the road.

Tom asked me how I thought the trip is going. "It's going real well," I said, "now that we're here in Sina!" Tom was easy for me to get along with.

"Well," Tom said, "Gonna close quarters here," as he zipped himself up into his sleeping bag. "Good night all."

The next morning we got up just before dawn and started climbing about a thousand feet of scree slope to the left of the glacier. It was a long pull but with our packs carrying only daytime essentials we got up in good time.

'Here we are! No bad weather this time! Far out! Nothing's going to stop us! We're actually going to be able to do some climbing!' I was thinking.

Ananea Summit

I put on my crampons and we started around some moderately steep corners on the glacier. It was easy going because we could walk along the ridge where the ice met the rock.

The last three hundred feet was the only difficult part. I chopped steps for a hundred and fifty feet on steep ice. I could rest my knee against the slope while still standing straight up in my footholds. It was exhausting trying to keep good balance while chopping the steps. I had to rest at least between every second step and often between each one. I suppose I reached about seventeen-thousand-five-hundred feet in altitude. Our rope ran out toward the top where I was about to come out on the ridge, so I had Tom leave his belay stance and begin climbing up below me.

Meanwhile the storm clouds were piling up thick. Snow began to fall. Tom was not secure without crampons so once again it was a mountain 'almost conquered' and down we went. Backing down my steps in the ice took careful balancing.

Ananea herself stood huge behind us. If I wanted to climb her, I would have to carry tent and sleeping bag halfway up and spend at least one night on her glaciers. We ran on down in the falling snow to our campsite of the previous night and re-buried my ice ax and rope again in the rocks in hopes for a better attempt god only knows when.

After noting through a hole in the clouds that the sun was still high in the sky, we decided to head down to Iskay Cruz and camp around there somewhere. We passed a man on his way to a mining town called Rinconada, sometimes known as 'the highest continually inhabited town in the whole world.'

Stone Hut at Iskay Cruz

We found a little hut which resembled a stone igloo. Just how those Indians figured out how to build those so the stone roof wouldn't fall in, we couldn't imagine. But there it was. So we slept very nicely in that.

What a Beautiful Woman!

John and Barker came back from their fishing episode and told us of how they had met a little Indian man beside one of the lakes who had let them stay in another little stone igloo-type-house beside the lake and who had caught some fish for them with his boat and net.

We all began the walk down to Sina together but I soon became impatient and zipped on ahead. At a very narrow place along the trail I suddenly came face to face with a bull. He had been coming my way and I was going his way. For a moment we stood there facing each other, both stopped, frozen in uncertainty. I decided that I'd better not let the dominance of my species down, however, so I took a resolute step toward him and, happily, the bull turned around and went back the way he had come.

Back down in Sina I found that our neighbor, Eulogio, had brought us some firewood so we boiled some potatoes. Lucio was over with a friend of his: Benito Chura from across the river. Benito had asked us to become compadres with him and his wife Irene by cutting the hair on his son Ermojines.

'Well, OK! I guess it's alright with me, but it's a little strange because we barely know Benito and his family at all! But he has a good face and seems clear in his mind, so it's alright with me.' We arranged that they would come over to our house that evening.

We were a little slow getting things ready. When they arrived complete with Irene's mother, Andrea Vega Uriwela, and another of her sons, Melisio, we were just starting to boil up the potatoes necessary for the occasion. They had brought some boiled potatoes along with them, however, so our meal got itself underway. Charlie, Tom and Barker took over the task of preparing the potatoes and coffee while I devoted all my energy to the business of communication. Ah yes, communication!

Irene's mother Andrea, what a beautiful woman! Straightforward energy, loud, and strong, coming straight through toward you. And it was all in Quechua. No Spanish. Only occasionally would Benito and I speak together in Spanish, the rest was happening in Quechua. For more than two hours we cultivated our new friendships in a bright foam of energy and good vibrations. Soon Barker was making appreciative speeches again in English. I would translate them and everyone felt included. Over and over again we each took turns snipping locks off of Ermojines' hair, putting them in the plate and pouring alcohol on the ground and on the four corners of the table for the gods.

Daily Life in Sina Unfolding

After the ceremony we thought again of visiting Amalia so we began boiling up a kettle of water and made sweet coffee out of it to take over to present to her so that she wouldn't be overwhelmed having to prepare something for all six of us.

When we arrived she took our coffee away from us, sat us down, and re-appeared half an hour later with our coffee improved... it was now mixed half-and-half with fresh milk and re-heated. She gave us an elaborate tour of her garden and a new problem: there was a certain type of happy bird which was eating the lima beans.

Charlie said that the Irish solution would be to tie threads between the stalks of the plants to trip the birds as they flew around amongst the plants. The birds would eventually get fed up with having to deal with all the threads and leave for greener pastures.

The next day we returned to visit Amalia again and she gifted us with the whole hindquarter of a freshly-killed sheep along with some onions, oregano and chamomile.

Being on that side of the river, we dropped in on our new compadres, Benito and Irene and took a few pictures of them. Remarkable Andrea wasn't there with them and our talk was less intense, but still very mellow. We met some more of Andrea's kids: Gerberto, Rosita and Delfin.

Benito and Irene

What happens naturally in Sina would, as I mentioned before, be amazing in North America. I mean here was Irene, one of Andrea's children, already with two kids of her own: Ermojines and Norberto. That meant that Andrea was their grandmother, right? But grandmother Andrea didn't really look more than a couple of years older than her daughter Irene, and she was still producing little ones who would grow up together with her own daughter's children. The generations, as I had noticed on previous visits, were packed very close together.

Doing my linguistic analysis on tape-recorded Quechua stories and phrases became part of my and Leda's routine for a while. I did my best to share the excitement of this with the students who were still struggling with the elements of Spanish.

Charlie was actually doing very well in Spanish. The time he spent with Pastor taking care of cows in Yanaloma had given him lots of practice time.

Barker continued to effuse and effervesce so enthusiastically that people could understand what he was trying to say no matter what words or grammar he used. Often he would say the exact opposite of what he meant, like: *'I don't like him at all!'* when he meant *'He doesn't like me at all!'* But people always understood what he meant because the context was always clear with Barker. He found ways to improvise with little hesitation: *'You know, a glass of water that you swim in'*... meaning *'swimming pool.'*

John had perhaps the best knowledge of grammar and vocabulary of any of the students from his Texas schooling. He and Pastor became good friends because of that. They kept calling each other *'stupid!'* and enjoyed that endlessly.

Tom joked with Barker quite a bit but frequently laid back and waited. The silly American ideal of *'The-Man-Who-is-Affected-by-Very-Little-If-Anything-At-All'* kept pursuing us.

We had come here to learn, not to impress each other with how knowledgeable we already were! Ah yes, we were still being plagued by the good old high school one-up-man-ship mentality. Charlie could feel it and got very unhappy about it. He even said at one point that he was thinking of leaving and going off on his own. He didn't. He stuck with us.

One evening, after I had eaten too much rice and was bloated painfully from that, Edwin and Laura came over so that I could put a necklace over my godson's neck. We got onto the subject of stars: what constellation... what patterns in the night sky did we see? We could see *'huch'uy cruz,'* the smaller, southern cross. There's something subtly disorienting about having half of the sky above you full of patterns of stars that are totally invisible in the northern hemisphere.

The milky way is called 'mayu,' or 'river.' But it's a different part of the milky way from what we see up north and it's got a big black hole in it called 'condor.' There were other constellations... like 'ch'iq"na' and 'llama ñawi' or 'llama eyes,' and 'ch'isi ch'aska' or 'the evening star.'

The next day we got up at dawn and went with Edwin and Laura down the river a ways to help them clear some land for potatoes. This piece of land hadn't been planted for some thirty-five years and had a fifteen-foot mantle of underbrush coating it. After having tried to work with my friends in Sina before I knew how puny our efforts would be.

What a mess! We tugged and pulled for all we were worth while the Indians doggedly chopped away with their machetes and homemade hoes. After two hours we were beat. I had the same problem I had experienced before: every time I would pull as hard as I could to extract overgrowth and the tree would finally come loose, I would lose my balance and crash down into the rocks below me on the hillside. I took another nice-sized piece of skin off my leg in the process, but when I pulled less hard there just didn't seem to be any way that the trees were going to come loose! So long after I had used up all of my energy and pulled another strip of skin off the palm of my hand, the Indians just kept right on hacking away.

If anyone ever tries to tell you that Quechua Indians are lazy and can't work -- which is of course what the middle class folks in the cities like to think -- don't believe it. Go help someone 'arrancar' his potato fields instead.

After we couldn't pull any more vegetation off the hillside, Leda and I went a bit further down the river to a field full of yellow flowers called *irwi winyayuq" pampa*. It was a nice place to make love.

Later on, in the evening after dinner on the same day, the six of us gringos found ourselves alone. We relaxed a little bit and Charlie played us a tune on his recorder. I suddenly felt a burst of energy and picked up the guitar and played with him but our styles didn't really match.

During the next couple of days we made everything ready for our departure downhill toward the jungle. We fried up the remainder of the sheep's front legs; we bought a chicken and wrung its neck. Tom went with Pastor for a day to help him prepare his cows to be cared for by someone else for a few days so he could lead us on the next leg of this Terrible Tour.

Down the Valley Toward the Jungle

Our long journey downhill to Yanawaya would take us into the land of fresh oranges! We would repeat the journey Pastor and I had made two years earlier... and we would descend even further... down the road which penetrated the jungle far below.

My comadre Laura had made another half week's supply of bread for the village. She made some special loafs too, with sugar and anise in it. My god was that tasty, fresh out of the oven! We ate bread until it was coming out of our ears. I ate so much that the next morning when we got up at 4:00 AM to begin our walk, I was seized by intestinal cramps so severe that I couldn't even stand up for nearly an hour.

"That's what happens to people who eat too much fresh hot bread!" my Compadre Edwin told me. It seems that hours after you eat it the yeast keeps on growing in your stomach. The bread keeps getting bigger and bigger... rising inside you!

Nevertheless, we did get started by about six. The initial exit from Sina requires a climb of nearly a thousand feet before the trail levels out high on the side of the valley and then eventually begins its downhill plunge. When we reached the high point and could look down toward the jungle far below, all we saw was a sea of clouds extending indefinitely toward the east: the Amazon basin! That forest extends for three-thousand unbroken miles all the way until it ends at the Atlantic Ocean! Only the Amazon river herself can offer continuous passage! All other routes are long and arduous.

Sea of Clouds over Amazon Jungle Below

We stood there in awe of the immensity below us just as Pastor and I had stood on the same spot two years earlier looking down on that same sea of clouds. Two years earlier it had been just Pastor and me with small light packs... and I had explained my fantasy of bringing high-school students to Peru... Now here we were, two years later, six gringos in all! Amazing! And everyone seemed to be reasonably excited and happy!

After a mid-morning coffee stop we kept on hoofin' along. About one o'clock or so a young Indian named Mauro caught up with us and he agreed to help Pastor until we reached the road at Yanawaya. At first I couldn't understand why I had so much trouble communicating with him no matter which language I used. Later Pastor told us that Mauro was actually half-deaf.

By three o'clock in the afternoon we were walking down some fairly steep descents in the trail. Leda's leg began to hurt at the knee. Pastor went on ahead to a settlement of about six or seven people called Hochon Qori to let them know that we would be coming to spend the night there. Mauro stayed behind with the rest of us and seemed to brim over with sympathy for Leda when it became apparent that her knee was hurting more and more. He loved to sit right beside her when we sat around the cooking fire at night. He had obviously fallen in love.

We wrapped Leda's knee with an Ace bandage but it didn't seem to help. The steeper the downhill slopes were, the more painful it became for her to move and the final thousand feet down to Hochon Qori was so steep that one's feet were always at the frictional limit with the loose gravel on the trail.

Hochon Qori was an incredibly isolated little settlement. I wondered how it came about that those particular people were living there. At least every Saturday Sina was only a six-hour walk from the truck which leads to the outside world, but Hochon Qori? ...at least twelve-hour's walk from the nearest exit, and that only for healthy walkers! The oldest man there, perhaps sixty, appeared to be dying. A continual hacking and spitting and coughing was emerging from some portion of his chest and it gave him little rest. But the others there seemed healthy enough. The house was surrounded by three or four acres of planted corn which alas was not yet fully ripe.

Ah yes, food. Eventually we were provided with some steamed lima beans and some boiled corn. We were all accustomed to having some meat but we didn't bother to cook any of our own so we all tended to over-eat and bloat ourselves on the vegetable fare.

I played some music on the guitar without doing much singing. Pastor had taken care of the verbal communication. Everyone went to bed but I was still full of unused energy and had to walk out and around through the corn for a while.

The next morning arrived and we seemed anxious to be on our way. Leda went on ahead, the idea being that she could take her time and nurse her hurting knee, but the trail turned out to be confusing and she had to wait for us.

Pastor and Mauro caught two horses and brought them along with us. They proved a great help two days later when we ascended from San Lorenzo, and we were very grateful to the folks at Hochon Qori for having arranged with Pastor to let us borrow them. As always, I was amazed at the skill with which Pastor and Mauro managed to persuade two of the loose and roaming band of horses to come along with us. They drove the herd, themselves only on foot, in such way that the two horses we wanted were separated out and, with a rope passed around the neck of one, the other was persuaded to follow.

We began the day with another steep descent of seven or eight hundred feet but then our route leveled out and even gained a tendency toward the uphill. Leda discovered again that her knee was more comfortable walking uphill than downhill.

We passed laterally along the side of a valley for a few hours, occasionally perching on parts of the trail which traversed cliffs which offered a full two-thousand feet of sheer drop-off. By noon we were sitting on top of the nose of a ridge between the confluence of two rivers looking another two-thousand feet straight down at the humble town of San Lorenzo.

We broke out another bite-sized piece of mutton for each us there on that ridge, and that was the last any of us saw of that meat. We had a bag with just about eight more small bite sized chunks in it, but later that afternoon John's pack fell over beside the river down below in San Lorenzo and the meat fell out and was gone.

Mouse Plague in San Lorenzo

Once down in San Lorenzo, Mauro gave us the word that we could probably buy some oranges from a little seventy-year-old lady who was one of the four inhabitants of the town. No, San Lorenzo was not a big place, but it did have a few orange trees.

"Let's go up to that house," I said to Barker, "and see if we can find whoever has the oranges!" We found the house with the little seventy-year-old lady, and she did have a few oranges to sell us. And Mauro had found some more oranges somewhere. We immediately fell upon the oranges in that bag and begged the little lady to sell us more. We were getting just plain hungry and were basically interested in little besides our stomachs.

Both corn and yuca, a potato-like tuber, were grown in San Lorenzo, and they were usually a reasonably plentiful crop. But this year there had been a mouse plague! Mice had eaten all of the corn and yuca as soon as it had been harvested and stored! Our little old lady friend who had sold us the oranges soon appeared beside our fire and begged us to sell her sugar and any extra food we had.

We had a couple of cans of sardines. We shared those with her but they were soon devoured and the little old lady was turned away hungry. We were hungry too.

The next day we decided to try our luck with trout from the river. I tied some nylon to the end of a long pole and set off downstream with Leda, burrowing our way through the undergrowth. I spent a half hour collecting some little worms from under the rocks and began dangling my hook in likely looking holes along the edge of the river. But I don't seem to have the faith it takes to be a good fisherman. After an hour or so Leda and I lay down on a rock and took the rest of the afternoon off.

Pastor, Barker, Mauro and John had also all been fishing further upstream and between all of them they actually came up with eight trout which we steamed in a pan and rapidly devoured... heads and all.

Charlie was so awestruck by the remoteness and beauty of the place and John was so pleased at the aspect of having a really successful day of fishing on the following day that we decided to spend a third day there in San Lorenzo. I was secretly pleased that we had decided to do that even though I suspected that we were going to be still hungrier by the time we left. Charlie and I played our guitar and recorder softly beside the fire. He was endeavoring to teach me some Irish folk melodies which still didn't come very naturally to me. We were hungry and half asleep.

The next morning John, Mauro and Pastor set off to conjure some more fish out of the rapidly moving waters but they first asked me and Charlie to help lead the horses across the river.

Bridge at San Lorenzo

There was a bridge across the river there, but only for people, not for horses. The horses had to be led across the river which was really too deep for a person to wade or swim. After a struggle, Charlie made it across. We were both naked except for our boots. Then I worked my way out nearly halfway across the river. From there I could throw a rope across to Charlie who then pulled the horses across to the other side. The rest of our group jumped in and we all stripped down naked and rubbed each others' backs.

Washing Each Other's Backs

Mauro got a lead on some *'papas japonesas'* -- Japanese potatoes -- considered to be the least appetizing of all possible crops, but nevertheless food. As it turned out he got so few that he didn't even mention them until the following morning at 4:00 AM when he cooked them up for us just before we left.

Our fishermen had poorer luck on that second day. They came up with only five fish which we all solemnly divided for dinner. I tried to eat less so the students could have more but I could feel my fingers reaching greedily into the fish plate with a selfish life of their own.

Onward to Yanawaya

During the night we lay there waiting for it to be time to leave. I woke up every little while and felt like getting up. But there was no moon! And it was just absolutely pitch black. I had no alternative but to wait for the first light of dawn, which we did. Then we crossed the stick bridge over the river, balancing carefully or on our hands and knees, and started the two-thousand-foot steep climb up out of the valley. Mauro had tied the two horses a few hundred feet up the ridge so we struggled with our full loads up to that point and then began taking things out of our packs to be tied onto the horses.

"God damn it!" John screamed all of a sudden, slapping his forehead. "I left my camera down there."

I went back down and got it for him, which took me perhaps forty-five minutes down and back. The others went on ahead while Mauro and Pastor wrestled with the problem of getting all the stuff tied onto the two horses. I flew down the hill, slipping and sliding in the mud, re-crossed the river and found the $300 camera. I could use my body to its full extent and I felt good. When I got back up to Pastor and Mauro, they were still getting the horse loads adjusted. I kept on climbing ahead of them and didn't break my stride for the next hour or so. I felt great.

I caught up with Leda, Tom, John, Barker and Charlie just after the point at which the trail entered the forest. Suddenly we were enveloped by green and the trail grew wet and slippery. That was it. That was the edge of the high jungle. After that point we crossed no more open grassland. We spent hours climbing on up to the summit of that ridge and then beginning the descent on the other side. It was a long way down from there and Leda's knees began hurting again.

Where were Pastor and Mauro? Eventually we began having fantasies of their having been unable to get the horses through all the narrow greenery with such big loads on their backs, and we lay down to see if they would catch up with us. After an hour or so of semi-siesta we heard a whistle from somewhere above us and Pastor's voice telling us to keep on going. So we plunged on down the hill. After an hour or so we came close to the river which ran down the bottom of the valley and passed a small house. The land had been laboriously cleared. Water ran to the house in giant bamboo troughs from a stream above. Coffee and bananas had been planted. I wondered why the bamboo troughs carried water down from so far up above when I could hear a stream rushing closer by. Then we came to a fifteen foot bridge which spanned a narrow chasm about a hundred feet deep. The nearby stream wasn't so nearby at all. It was way down in the bottom of that gorge. We walked on down the trail, fascinated by the new environment. New plants; new birds; a new style of living and agriculture.

Toward the end of the afternoon, shortly after we had seen the roofs of some houses high on the side of the valley in front of us, we passed a woman on the trail, I explained to her in Quechua that we were descending from Sina and that two friends of ours from Sina were coming along behind us with two horses. She took in this information calmly enough. It seemed that as long as I could explain ourselves in the local Quechua dialect, the fact that we were six gringos with giant orange nylon packs didn't bother or surprise her. She told me something about upcoming forks in the trails and which way to go.

We waited again for Pastor and Mauro at another bridge but eventually we decided that we might as well go on. We ate a half an ear of corn apiece which we had still saved all the way from Hochon Qori. We had eaten the other halves of the ears on top of the ridge two-thousand feet above San Lorenzo. We were getting more and more hungry but I think most of us actually felt fine. We still had another long climb up and over another ridge ahead of us.

We began the ascent and discovered that the business of going uphill was overwhelming us. It took us a long time. We would collapse at different times, yet each time one of us would have to rest, we would all have to wait before we moved on as we couldn't run the risk of getting separated. We kept going higher and higher but had yet to see anything like a central part of the village. We had actually passed only one outlying house which looked as though it might be inhabited. At last we arrived at a good-sized house but there was not a soul around. Our collective disappointment was quite something and we actually began to feel lost. Were we on the right track?

Cooked Corn and A Pineapple!

I told everyone to wait and I went on for another ten minutes. I came upon a house with a little girl standing in the doorway. Her mother was inside so I approached the doorway, squatted down and began explaining in Quechua that we were traveling from Sina to Yanawaya and that we were very hungry because there had been no food in San Lorenzo.

This lady and her little girl were smiling at me and eventually brought me some cooked corn and, of all things, a pineapple! I suddenly realized that I hadn't brought along anything in which I could carry food, so I took off my T-shirt and wrapped the corn and pineapple in that. The lady refused my offer to pay her for what she had given me and told me that I could probably get some oranges from another house further up the hill.

I went on up the hill and came to the next house. This house had another woman at home and I began explaining things to her in Quechua, just as I had at the previous house. This lady was an Aymara Indian, however, not a Quechua Indian, so her comprehension of what I was saying was more limited. I spoke to her in Spanish along with the Quechua and she smiled and behaved generally as if she understood what I was saying. She brought me some oranges and sent a little boy to bring a man who knew some Spanish.

He was still a quite young man -- in his twenties -- and I had the feeling that he was wishing his father were around to tell him what he should do with us. I decided eventually that I should be on my way and paid for and gathered up the oranges and asked for directions to the fastest way back down to the house at which I had left my friends. I asked that a little boy be sent with me to show me the way or that the young man himself come with me but no one seemed enthusiastic about the idea. Eventually I persuaded them both to come at least far enough to show me the entrance to the trail and to explain which way we must go in order to proceed on our way toward Yanawaya.

On my way back to the house where I had left everyone I came upon Pastor. I asked him how his trip had been and he said that one of the horses had fallen and rolled and had nearly crushed poor Mauro. When we got back to the others we feasted happily on the boiled corn and pineapple and oranges which I had procured. Amazing how much better we felt immediately after eating just that little bit!

So we launched ourselves on down the trail again. We were going to make it to Yanawaya, to the road, to restaurants and stores! Wow! Off we went and as the hours went on by we just kept right on going. We outdistanced Pastor and Mauro and the horses, much to their surprise, and we had to sometimes ask or guess about which way to go. We had some moments of confusion but we always managed to figure out some way to choose the path and onward we went. We wanted to keep moving. The day had ended. It was dark. Charlie got so enthusiastic that he sped on into the night and was somewhere up ahead of us. We just hoped that he wouldn't choose the wrong trail. Our walk had a kind of spooky quality. We met no one along our way. Who knows? Perhaps we were on the wrong track. Would we have to spend another night without food and retrace all of our steps the following day? I didn't think so, however, and sure enough, we rounded a corner and could see the electric lights of Yanawaya about an hour away from us on the other side of a valley where two rivers merge!

Way Too Much Food

We kept right on moving fast, crossed another stick bridge and climbed the other side of the valley. We reached the center of town and there was Charlie sitting on a bench surrounded by the local folk explaining everything he could. He offered us each a sip from a can of condensed milk he had bought in one of the stores.

The local police wanted to know all about us and have us fill out their ridiculous pain-in-the-ass forms about all our names and numbers.

I said, "Please! Later! We're hungry, understand? First of all we're going to eat!"

So we went over to a pensión and inquired. Sure enough, they were happy to cook us up some real meals!

We sat down and waited. We ordered beers all around and, after taking a few sips, we were full. Our stomachs had shrunk to the size of walnuts!

A police chief came in and ordered us all another round of beers. He began a long story about himself. "Ah yes, I know how you must feel being here," he kept saying. "I too am a foreigner here. I am from Lima. You can imagine," he would say to us, "what loneliness I feel living here in this remote outpost amongst all these mountain Indians when I was born and raised in Lima!"

Unfortunately, you just can't tell a policeman to fuck off and go away. Pastor arrived and joined us. The policeman was forced to treat Pastor with the same respect that he was treating us gringos but you could tell that it was not his habit to do so. To him Pastor was just another local Indian.

"Kiss my ass!" Barker told him in English with a big smile on his face and the chief would enthusiastically agree, warming up even more to the conversation. Pastor chuckled even though he couldn't understand exactly what Barker was saying. But he could guess.

Pastor had left Mauro to guard our horses so he ordered an extra plate of food, carried it down to Mauro and then came back.

Meanwhile we were still at a loss trying to eat with our stomachs in such shrunken states. Barker sat across the table and didn't even look hungry. Charlie couldn't eat. Pastor and I did a little better with steady nibbling. Leda couldn't drink any more beer even though it had been a kind gift. We had to watch several half-eaten plates being carted back to the kitchen. Very embarrassing!

Pastor's sister Placida lived in a little house down the road. That made a nice place for us to sleep. Our guitar-playing friend from Sina, Victor Suarez, happened to be staying there too.

Barker, Victor, John, Charlie, Pastor, Me, Mauro, Placida, Leda

The next day we spent about three hours or so walking down from the town of Yanawaya to San Juan del Oro. There were a couple of steep climbs uphill on the route and I enjoyed putting all of my energy into moving as rapidly as possible. I was in fact getting a great deal of enjoyment out of matching the speed of my footsteps to the exact limit of my respiratory and cardiac ability and then trying to push against that limit.

But once we had left Pastor's sister's house we were beyond our circle of family and friends connected with Sina. We were strangers again. Our enthusiasm for delving deeper down into the jungle was getting evaporated by the mud, rain and heat.

Once in San Juan del Oro we descended to the very lower edge of town to the Hotel Suisso, which was owned by Sr. Alvarez, a hunchbacked Spaniard whom I had met with his wife up in Sandia two years previously. He had encouraged me to return with students in order that we might set up some sort of educational situation. All we found, however, was a sleepy little hotel being run by his little wife who didn't seem to remember me. Nevertheless we made as cheap a deal as we could with her and spread out our stuff to stay for a couple of days and get caught up on our thoughts and our notes.

I was writing in my notebook and a mouse was nibbling on the cabinet next to me. Leda was sitting and waiting to see if I was going to quit writing and make love to her. Would I or wouldn't I? I did.

The next day we decided to go a bit further downhill to see if the jungle became perceptibly more thick and green. Already we had been surrounded by some new kinds of birds -- flocks of bright yellow ones with jet black tails. And the citrus fruits were running out of our ears. We spent the day sitting beside the river washing clothes and eating oranges. There by the river I decided to eat my fill of oranges, once and for all. The banks of the river were lined with ripening orange trees, so I set about picking them and just eating them right up. I counted thirty of them before I finally decided to quit - not because they no longer tasted good to me but rather because I was beginning to wonder what effect thirty oranges might have on my digestive tract!

How Many Oranges Can I Eat?

Pastor sat down beside the river with us all afternoon and washed his clothes and helped us consume oranges. One thing he told me absolutely amazed me. He said that his father, who had subsequently died, had remembered a conversation with me from when I had first arrived in Sina. And I too remembered that conversation as being the first conversation I had ever conducted in pure Quechua which came off without any misunderstandings. Pastor repeated that conversation back to me there beside the river!

His father had told him that he had met a gringo who had told him in Quechua: *"mayumanta limpiuta unuta apamusaq"* -- "I am going to get clean water from the river." I was absolutely amazed to hear that same conversation repeated to me four years later!

A bit later I took Leda off into the bushes beside the river and we made love again. My energies were re-building and I was hoping she felt less neglected.

We decided to go further downhill the next day to the end of the road, a place called Yanamayu. We found a truck going down that way and spent an hour or more getting there. I got into playing a little music in the rain with a few somber souls, but that was all.

That was the place from which I would have to start walking in order to reach Puerto Maldonado -- a trip which could take perhaps a month and which might lead me to meet some jungle tribes -- a trip I would like to make someday.

Walking Through Sina into Jungle Below in 1972

Back to the Altiplano

We decided unanimously to leave for the highlands again and visit Lake Titicaca, the ruins at Tiahuanaco and perhaps La Paz, Bolivia.

The next day at noon we climbed into the back of a pickup, hoping it wouldn't get too crowded. That was wishful thinking as usual. All thirty of us passengers arrived in the town of Sandia at about 6:00 PM. It turned out that a few people in town remembered me from two years earlier when I had spent a day and a half there. But we found another truck by about 11:00 PM and left for Juliaca.

The road was not describable in North American terms because we simply don't have such precipitous terrain anywhere in our part of the world. We would call it a 4-Wheel-Drive 'jeep trail.' Five-thousand foot panoramas of vertical exposure dropped off below the edge of the road. A month previously a truck had slid off carrying all twenty-eight human souls thousands of feet to a splattery death on the valley floor below.

We now had the views by moonlight. It was getting colder and colder. We were seated on top of the coffee load in this truck along with some thirty others. I struck up a few conversations in both Spanish and Quechua which kept me happy for a while. One Indian wanted me to show him my penis. He said he had heard that gringos' penises were different. I supposed the rumor had to do with circumcision. I declined to show myself off.

In the middle of the night the truck stopped and word went around that people should get off the truck and walk for a while because the road up ahead was a bit difficult and the truck needed to be lighter. Not noticing that only men were disembarking, Leda jumped off with the rest of us and turned out to be the only woman on a long grueling rush up from perhaps fourteen to fifteen-thousand feet of altitude. For close to an hour I did my best to help her along by holding her hand. At one point she suggested that being left behind to die was more attractive than rushing onward, but at last we made it.

By the time we got to Pastor's brother's house in Juliaca and were resting on our sleeping bag around four in the afternoon, Leda finally seemed genuinely happy again. As for myself, I was high from the truck ride and was striding through the streets of town having a great time checking out the marketplace and bargaining for eggs, onions and for fuel for our primus. Three Indians from Sina were with me and Barker and John. The three from Sina were Idelsa, the wayward young wife of Emilio the schoolmaster, her brother Carlos, who was now accustomed to living in Juliaca and away from Sina most of the time, and a girl named Inez who was a quiet but smiley person. We had a fun time hopping and jumping around the town. Idelsa and Carlos were looking for some pots and pans to purchase. Little did Idelsa know that her husband Emilio was at that very moment looking all over Puno and Juliaca for her in a blind rage because she was supposed to be in Puno in her school.

We went back to Federico's house and sang a few songs. Leda and I sang a Greek song she had taught me and everything started to feel happy and mellow. I was more or less ready to spend a few days right there in Juliaca but the students were curious to keep on the road and see some more new places.

Pastor's Family in Juliaca

Charlie went out by himself and came back with the Soto sisters: Lili, Mili, Miriam and Jaquelina. Lili and Mili stood right up in front of us and started singing huayños for us in rapid and intricate harmony, projecting themselves just exactly as if they were on a 1950's TV program. They of course immediately fell in love with John, our dark-eyed boy from Texas.

I pulled out my guitar and offered them some songs from north America. Our group had evolved now and I was surprised at the nice harmonies Tom, John and Barker managed to come up with. Placida, Pastor's rather extremely beautiful sister had journeyed up from San Juan del Oro and was there with us too.

When we got into the market places we spent hours happily gorging ourselves on the endless supply of strange delectable goodies all of which were excitingly new and different. There were fruit juices of all kinds: papaya with chirimoya, guanabana, tumbo, aguaymanto, maracuya, cocona, granadilla, guayaba, lucuma, aguaje, mangos, noni, pitahaya, and numerous others. Ice creams, egg foams, little doughnut-like breads, coffee laced with cinnamon... We all seemed to be starved for all kinds of things and our stomachs were stretching again so we could actually eat.

Eventually we got it together to go down to Puno and look up my old friend Cristobal Ccori who used to teach school in Sina. Leda and I split from the others and went to visit Cristobal and his family alone. Idelsa and Emilio were there, still eyeing each other suspiciously as a result of their recent quarrel. Cristobal's youngest son, Reinaldo, had meningitis, it seemed, and the pall of his possible impending death hung disquietingly over the household. Cristobal's wife, Faustina was visibly disappointed when I told her that meningitis was considered to be a grave disease in the United States too. We sang some songs with some of Cristobal's children for an hour and a half.

We then departed with Cristobal to go out and walk about the town and have a cup of coffee. "I'm happy to be teaching on an island in Lake Titicaca now. I'm away from my wife's brothers!"

"But they have all of your horses and cattle now?" I said.

"They are very happy about that!" Cristobal laughed. "But they can have my horses and cattle. I'm just happy to be away from there. The only thing is that my wife misses Sina."

Cristobal told us many other details about who was related to whom in Sina and how that played out.

Cristobal's Children in Puno

We told him how eager we were to come out and visit him on his island, Taquile. He said that people were so honest on the island that if anyone was ever caught stealing there they were banished forever. He said that if I thought people from Sina were pleasant, I'd find the people from Taquile even nicer! I would journey to Taquile a couple of years later to find out for myself but would only barely begin to explore that island.

The next day we set out for the ruins at Tiahuanaco on the south side of Lake Titicaca. The ruins basically bored me but archaeologists postulate the existence of a huge well-organized mountain civilization which had preceded the Inca empire.

La Paz, Bolivia - Hanging with the Rich Folks

It took us two days of crowded truck rides to make it to La Paz. Somewhere on the road I felt the driver slam on his brakes so I looked ahead. I saw two men waving pistols at the truck from the middle of the road.

I told Leda: "Get down!" And I thought that it had finally happened: we were going to get robbed. But soon these two men were climbing aboard the truck saying "Excuse me!" and all sorts of other polite things as they tried to find room for themselves among the rest of us. It turned out that they were a couple of Guardias in plain clothes and that when they had thought the truck maybe wasn't going to stop for them their natural response had been to wave their pistols at us.

It turned out that two of Cristobal's wife's brother's children were riding in the same truck with us and when we crossed into Bolivia Santiago Valdivia, Faustina's one-armed brother himself was there to greet his children. His son's marriage had recently broken up and Santiago was there to help his son by encouraging him in the business of finding a new woman.

The next day we visited Santiago's kiosk in the La Paz market and I bought Leda an attractive black alpaca shawl from him. Indians in the neighboring kiosks in the marketplace were amazed to hear us carrying on our conversation in Quechua. It had been Santiago and his brothers Roberto and Alberto Valdivia who had helped me with my Quechua upon my arrival in Sina back in 1968. Now Santiago was especially proud of my language ability and just kept on chattering away.

We were continually conscious of people trying to overcharge us for everything. Sina had spoiled us. We were no longer used to paying rent, and when we were confronted with hotels back on the tourist route we got annoyed at the owners. We told them they were lying about their prices just because we were gringos. We decided to forget the hotels and just sleep outdoors in the plaza in the center of La Paz.

The next day we were looking for a place to eat. We entered a restaurant and were befriended by a man who drank a few beers with us. He invited us to come later to his house for dinner.

We followed his directions and made our way into Obrajes, an upper-class suburb of La Paz. We walked into his house and were introduced to his wife, daughter and son -- all in front of a blaring TV set which was never turned off. We were suddenly in a totally different world.

During dinner we all drank more and more beer... especially Pedro, our host. His wife sat cozily by with her fashionably polka-dotted fingernails. Earlier in the afternoon, while we were still drinking beer together downtown, he had asked us about our religions. Some of us told him we were atheists. He had then specifically requested that we not tell his wife that we were atheists should the subject come up.

Another guest arrived: an American high school girl who was in Bolivia as a Rotary Club-sponsored student whom Pedro's brother was hosting.

"But the altiplano is the ugliest part of Bolivia," Pedro our host told us. "Too many Indians! Further east in Santa Cruz it is better: many Germans and Italians... a good racial mixture."

None of us knew what to say so we greeted his comment with silence and blank stares.

"Now I am going to tell you something and I am not going to lie," he told us.

Silence. We were all watching him.

"You all claim to be students. And you," he said pointing at me, "claim to have traveled a good deal. Where is Afghanistan? You," he said pointing to John, "tell me where it is!"

John looked uncomfortable and finally said, "It's in Asia."

"Yes yes, it's in Asia, but where? Perhaps you can tell us," he said pointing at me.

"It's in between Pakistan and Iran," I told him.

"And what is its capital?"

Silence. Leda whispered to me that she couldn't remember either.

"Kabul!" he pronounced. "And how long does it take for light to go from the earth to the moon? We know how fast light travels, right?"

'*186,000 miles per second,*' I think to myself.

"And we know how far the earth is from the moon, right?"

'*I don't know,*' I think to myself.

"400,000 kilometers," he said. "And light travels at 325,000 km per second, so it takes one-and-a-quarter seconds for light to get between the earth and the moon."

"If I don't know something like that I really don't understand what difference it's going to make during the rest of my life," commented John.

"To make you think! To keep your mind alive! Look! I am going to explain something to you. I am fifty-seven years old! And, gentlemen, I am not going to lie to you! Look!" He searched frantically around the table and picked up a glass and a cup and set them down side by side. "Look! You've got to know the difference between a glass and a cup! You've got to know the word for each one!"

"He gets better as he gets drunker!" whispered the exchange student girl from the Midwest. But he didn't ever get much better although we had some light moments toward the end of the conversation and laughed with each other to demonstrate our continuing good will.

"I hate Mexican Indians just the way I hate Bolivian Indians," he told us. "When I used to be in the USA people used to hear my Spanish accent and ask if I was Mexican. That's because the Mexican Indians have gotten you Americans fooled into calling them 'Spanish-Americans' instead of acknowledging the fact that they're just Indians. Look at them!"

Pedro searched frantically over the table top again, picked up a huge grapefruit, and said, "Heads just like grapefruits! Big round Indian heads! They've all got heads just like grapefruits!"

"What is your ancestry?" I asked wondering what part of Europe his ancestors had come from. He looked like a gringo... just like us.

"I am pure Bolivian!" he shouted at me. "Just like my wife!"

I asked him again where he'd gotten his gringo blood but he insisted on telling me again that he was 'pure Bolivian.'

"And now I am going to ask you one question, and I want you to tell me the truth!"

"I never lie!" I told him.

"Are you communists?"

"No," I replied.

Patricia, the high school exchange student asked us where we had been and we told her that we had been staying in a Quechua village.

She looked at us incredulously and said, "But if you go there, no one will give you food or a place to stay... I mean there's no one there... or... there's someone there but..."

"And so many diseases!" she went on.

"Just think, when you get back to the States you'll be able to tell your friends that you got to spend the night in a real Bolivian home!" Pedro, emphasized.

Eventually we all managed to retire and go upstairs to the room which had been given us for the night. We all lay on the floor giggling and laughing from relief for at least an hour before dropping off to sleep.

Leda was suffering from a severe fever. I fed her some aspirins and some tetracycline. Her fever broke in the middle of the night and we were able to continue on our way the next morning -- after cleaning every speck of butter and jam off our host's breakfast table! We hadn't seen such goodies as those for many weeks and there was no way we could resist polishing them off.

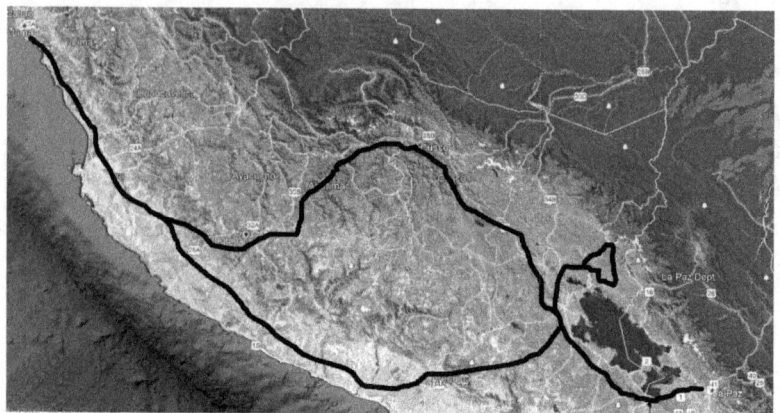
1972 Route Through Peru and Bolivia

Feeling Our Way in Colorado

From La Paz we made our way back to Boulder Colorado... to John Link's house. Frustration. I had been trying to organize a second trip to Peru for later in the summer but it wasn't happening.

Now we were broke and down and out in Boulder Colorado. I felt a loss of mobility. There was nothing left to do but go get a job... just a job. Just a plain old ordinary roofing or building job. Just shingles and pieces of wood and metal.

Bill Chase and his brother Tom were framing up new houses in Boulder and gave me work. We spent enough time eating bacon and eggs in the mornings to swap our latest stories at a leisurely pace and then we 'pounded nails' for the rest of the day.

We climbed up the cable route on Long's Peak... to the summit at fourteen-thousand feet. Leda, Joe Ball, Barry Vaughn and I were together. I had been thinking of dropping some LSD but the situation wasn't right for it. Leda and Barry both were suffering from painful knees during the descent and couldn't become attuned to such an idea. So I decided to wait for a better setting.

View from Long's Peak

Back down at Link's house I played and sang for another dance party. We continued to be welcome to stay for free as long as I produced musical entertainment. Fine with me.

I worked harder on building guitars in the little lean-to addition attached to the side of the old carriage house behind one of John Link's student rooming houses on the hill. Max Krimmel continued to guide my early efforts.

I spent ten days building a skylight for Jim Sharp's rooftop. I put a new roof on Fil Sokol's father's house. But I was most excited about my new shop where I could both write and make guitars! I also had a job re-building a friend's Volkswagen van engine.

Leda and I continued to sleep on the living room floor. This was real communal living... no privacy... occasionally we would borrow a bedroom for a few hours.

Mt Holy Cross: The Buzzing Summit

Joe Ball and I went to climb Mt. Holy Cross. We climbed a long couloir which was slightly airy but never insecure. We climbed a small cornice at the top and, leaving our packs there, scurried on up the remaining six-hundred feet of boulder-field to the summit. I emerged from behind a boulder and caught sight of a wooden cross on the summit some twenty-five feet away.

"Far out!" I thought. "There's the summit right there so I've just about made it!" I got to within ten feet of the cross and suddenly became acutely aware that the cross was buzzing like a high voltage transformer. I did a rapid about-face and started running down.

"Fuck it!" I said to Joe. "The summit is buzzing!"

"It's buzzing here too!" Joe said, feeling the electricity in his clothes. "Let's get the fuck down from here!" We ran as fast as we could down about five-hundred feet of boulder field and steered off to the left away from the ridge. I relaxed and figured we were safe but Joe was still hustling along hunkered over. He said we'd better find a place to lie down amongst the boulders and I got re-infected with the fear of being struck by lightening. Down into the boulders we squirmed... into the cracks and crevices. There were no cracks or crevices which could really hide us. We were at the mercy of the elements. Occasionally we grinned at each other. We heard a tremendous boom from the summit.

"There it goes!" we laughed to each other. Then another almost simultaneous flash and boom came from the ridge right above us and I was scared. I lay there on my back watching the big hailstones that live inside giant cumulo-nimbus clouds coming down out of the sky at me and hoped that luck would keep the electricity away from us.

"God damn fucking lightening!" I said and 'Boom' another one hit the ridge right above us.

"A couple of sinners like us ain't supposed to quite get to the top of this holy mountain," I joked to Joe. But I was feeling quite humble inside and even hesitant about doing any more cursing at the storm.

So I lay there and thought about the future time I knew would probably come when I would be sitting down below remembering the whole experience instead of actually experiencing it. Just lying there like that in the boulder field was a little discouraging. If you're moving along at least you have the distraction of watching the boulders beneath your feet. But when you're already lying immobile in the boulders it's enough like death to make you think it wouldn't take much more -- just a momentary zap -- to transform you into a cadaver lying in the boulder field... something to be found on the following day by someone else.

I wondered if the electricity was affected by my fear level. *'Keep calm and enjoy it as best you can,'* I told myself, *'because the electricity may be attracted somehow to a buzzing brain-full of fear down here on the rocks.'* It occurred to me that this would be a good way to commit suicide... just in case anyone might be interested: stand on the summit of Mt. Holy Cross with the wooden cross against your back during a thunderstorm and just grin while the electricity buzzes louder and louder around you until the whole situation just goes Boom.

I wondered if it were possible to take enough of the energy into yourself to be somehow able to give it back out at the storm. "Fuck you lightening!" you could shout and then hurl a thunderbolt at the sky... like Zeus. Then I remembered myself again and thought maybe I should adopt a more humble attitude.

"Well, do you want to try and go get our packs?" Joe asked. We hadn't heard a close one for about fifteen minutes.

"OK," I said, "let's go." We began sneaking up the ridge toward our packs still walking hunched over close to the ground. I suddenly heard a frizzly sound inside my helmet. I tried to dismiss it as the sound of the hailstones hitting it, but just then I saw Joe freak out and hunch down even lower and then turn around and head downhill once again. Later he said he had felt a spark jump off the top of his head and go up through his hat. As we descended again I lifted my hands into the air just a bit from time to time in order to preserve my balance, and every time I did that I felt a fuzziness escaping from my fingertips and could hear the metal zipper on my jacket cuff crackling like a bowl of puffed rice.

We found another hollow in the boulder field and lay down for another half hour. We heard another big boom go off on the ridge right above us close to our packs. Joe lay there contemplating the value of the equipment he had in his pack and was coming close to deciding that his stuff just wasn't worth waiting around for. He imagined a charred mess lying up there instead of a pack in any case.

I thought more and more about the randomness of it all. I watched the lightening bolts striking in the valley across from us and figured that the conditions which caused a bolt to strike any particular place were caused first by the altitude of the rock and secondly by the degree of ionization in the atmosphere at any given point. I ended up lying there hoping that one of those highly-ionized buzzing little clefts in the atmosphere wouldn't happen to drift over us.

"Ya me voy," (I'm already going) Joe announced and we headed back up toward the ridge again. Again we hadn't heard a close one for about fifteen minutes.

Mt Holy Cross

This time we made it all the way up to our packs without feeling that hideous electricity making our hair stand up on end. We took off down the boulder field and kept right on going without even bothering to tighten up our waist straps or tie up the pockets on our packs.

Our Tent on Melvina Hill

Back down in Boulder Leda and I decided to escape the twenty-four-hour-a-day high noise and distraction level at John Link's house and joined our friends John Solmon, Fil Sokol and his girlfriend Colleen up in the foothills above Boulder on Melvina Hill where we set our tent up in the pine forest. Soon I had my typewriter set up on some rocks and was staring at trees and listening to birds, insects and squirrels while trying to work on writings about Peru and about the Quechua dialect in Sina.

Fil Sokol's dad tried to pay me less than our agreed-upon price for putting new shingles on his house supposedly because my work rhythms weren't professional. I hadn't arrived at 7:00 AM every day.

Leda's birthday arrived. It was a rainy day so we stayed holed up in our tent on top of Melvina Hill as cozy as turtles in their shells. The mist was hanging in the valley.

Leda told me about Greek women. She said that she herself was the oracle at Delphi and could inform me without doubt that she was the most beautiful of all women. After assuring me that I was Apollo, we made love on a fiery orb. Very easy, effortless, beautiful. I'd reached the point of almost never coming before she did. It gave me great pleasure to be able to offer her that luxury.

The oracle at Delphi had informed me that I may make love to ten women tonight at her birthday party but to only one woman tomorrow!

Just as we finished making love a bird began screaming outside of our tent. Leda busied herself frying up a few tortillas for us. I loved seeing her running around naked in the woods. I watched her sneaking up to trees and hanging up the frying pans.

Happy Campers

If only I could make and sell instruments successfully enough so that we could keep ourselves in food, then we'd be a long way ahead!

Paradise in the Mount Zirkel Wilderness

Leda and I drove to the top of Rabbit Ears Pass... on the road toward Steamboat Springs and hiked north for four days with Russ and Shirley. We covered thirty-five miles on foot, passing through the Mt. Zirkel wilderness area.

On the third morning of our journey we got up and ate some wood rose - a psychedelic. We began walking up Mt. Ethel. A storm cloud was aiming right at us. Thunder emanated. I was hoping we wouldn't have to go through what Joe Ball and I had gone through on Mt. Holy Cross but, happily, the cloud passed us by without any great display and we kept walking toward Lost Ranger Peak. The thunderheads were stacked up like giant hot-cakes on either side of us and I was anxious to get over the highest ridge and down a bit on the other side.

Russ and Shirley were carrying on the remnants of a dispute they had been having for the last couple of days. Leda and I quietly slithered along the surface of the earth. With the help of the wood rose my consciousness merged by turns with the wind-formed trees which were struggling to maintain their root-holds in the throats of those couloirs up which the terrible gusts of winter would come charging... and with the butterflies who live up there to dance in the high winds with the birds... and with the deer who sleep in the bushes and spring up the mountainsides when disturbed...

Once we finished surmounting the high ridge -- six hours into our walking for the day -- we were presented with a view of paradise! A green bowl lay below us with a perfect gentle and beautiful arrangement of trees and birds. We peeled off our clothes for swimming in the freezing high altitude lakes and then peeled them off again to tumble down the snowfields. We began the descent into paradise, Leda and I. The trees were all together in the high altitude alpine ravines, the living ones with the dead ones. Everything -- even the rocks -- were alive!

For seven hours we had flowed over surface of the earth and not once had Leda nor I experienced one iota of pain, despite the heaviness of our packs, and as we slid down into paradise we dipped below the danger from the giant thunderheads although we could see lightening mercilessly zapping the ridges of Mt. Zirkel and the other peaks above us. Our green bowl remained immune! Paradise!

Russ was smashing the trees with his giant football-player's body and making our firewood and setting up a camp. We heard bells. Soon we were greeting the Basque sheep herders in Spanish. We had heard through the Steamboat Springs grapevines that they spend their summers up there.

We built our fires by night. We made love in the tent and ate delicious muffins and eventually emerged at the tiny town of Clark on the Elk river road.

Russ arranged for me to come advertise my Terrible Tours at Evergreen High School where he was teaching history and coaching football. One of his students did, in fact, join me on my next trip to Peru!

Going back to the University of California in Berkeley to finish the PhD in Linguistics had its temptations but I kept feeling that time was too precious to waste on another trip through school. The real entrance into the heart and soul of life on earth would be through my own personal adventures.

Dancing Naked in the Living Room

Life kept us busy at John Link's house. We sat in circles called 'encounter groups' and discussed our relationships. Leda seemed to enjoy these and feel at home.

John Link

I finished making my first guitar in my little lean-to shop and it immediately found a buyer.

I had begun writing a *'People's Guide to Peru'* with hopes that it might be published.

I fasted on only water for five days to find out what that might feel like. I climbed the fourth flatiron, one of the many rock faces which hang on the sides of the foothills about Boulder, on the fourth day of my fast. I was light-headed but tapping into some mysterious clean energy source within.

I kept playing for dance parties. I was looking for a new kind of musical vibration in the tunings of the strings. I would eventually find it in Egyptian music but that was far off in the future. I was feeling drawn toward more explorations of other peoples' lives in remote corners of the globe... to find out what really mattered to them... and go deeper into being a musician.

Why not just go for harmony and sexual ecstasy? Why not? ...surrender myself to music and the harmonies of situations...?

I gave slide shows at high schools again and soon had another Terrible Tour to Peru planned for the following summer. Leda let me know that she had fallen in love with a friend of ours, a wealthy man from New York who professed to be involved with various cutting edge spiritual experiments and that she didn't want to accompany me. To give her some space I began sleeping in my little lean-to shop alone while she continued to sleep at Link's house. She also felt like she shouldn't leave for Peru and interrupt her work schedule at the Calico Closet where she had landed a job selling clothing.

Part of me felt happy for her that she had truly become a part of our fun community in Boulder, Colorado. But I felt angry and jealous at the same time.

Our communal household at John Link's house was a determined effort to live with flamboyant honesty. We let our sexual energy show so that an ecstatic quality would underlie everything. We danced naked together in the living room and frequently our desires became clearly visible. Some of our communal house-mates seldom wore clothes during the day.

That churning fluid motion of a walking or dancing woman who was feeling pleasures inside herself was the ultimate beauty for me. I let my attractions flow out more deeply and wondered if I should be flirting more outrageously but nothing evolved to the point of having sex. Leda would still come over to my little lean-to in the alley and we would make love. It seemed that she was the most succulent lover of all... but it also seemed that I didn't really 'have' her. We were trying to define our connection as 'friends with benefits.' As for the friend with whom she had developed her romantic crush, although she was attracted and open to him, they were not moving into the sexual realm.

I rebuilt another engine for Richard Sigismonde who owned the Aquarius silver mine at ten-thousand feet up in the front range above

Nederland. I finished installing gutters on Jim Sharp's house. I got paid.

John Solmon offered my favorite psychedelic. With my stomach full of peyote I ran around and around the local high school football field doing symmetrical somersaults. Doing things totally symmetrically was both exhilarating and exhausting. I had to let my body lapse back into friendly sloppiness sooner or later.

Lying on my back looking at the clouds a psychedelic screen superimposed itself between me and the sky. I didn't want it there and felt that it was interfering with my perception of reality.

Maybe the process of growing old would be like that. One might be threatened more and more by one's own projections... perhaps like my grandfather who had eventually ended up being like a child again, living in a fairytale world which kept him giggling uncontrollably.

Twelve years ago, when I was about sixteen, I had become delighted with the discovery of psychedelic imagery leaping spontaneously into my field of vision while I listened to music. But now I wanted to see past my own image screens and stay focused on straightforward reality. No luck.

Before I knew it I found myself trapped in another exhausting and unwanted symmetry. I had sat down with my legs apart and soon noticed that a the big picture window on someone's house was dead center in front of me. Once I became conscious of the symmetry I became uncomfortable with it. I felt I had to disrupt it because maintaining it seemed so silly. I didn't want to try and be a perfect person. I wanted to be asymmetrical.

Winter was here. I worked in my little shop making more guitars and writing my Quechua grammar. Miraculously, people showed up to buy my guitars. I hired Jim Primock to help with the time-consuming planing and sanding and gluing. He took a second look at me bent over the work bench and my name 'Giant Leprechaun' was born.

Winter passed. The warmth of springtime was melting the snow off the mountain tops and the rivers were running high. We headed back up to Steamboat Springs for a few days on the Yampa river where it descends through Dinosaur National Monument and then merges with the Green river. This time I was rowing with my Boulder river-rat friends instead of my Steamboat river-rat friends. It was more like a sport... less like ordinary life... but still an adventure...

Another Terrible Tour to Peru

It was time to head for Peru with my five students. It was early summer in 1973.

I found a car which needed to be delivered to Miami. Martin, Sue, Spectra and I started driving toward the airport in Florida. We took turns driving and never really stopped. Graham joined us in Miami and we flew to Lima. Chris arrived a day or two later.

Sue and Spectra frantically let me know that the bathroom at our hotel in Lima, the Manco Capac, which I had been using as home base in the big city for the last eight years, could only be illuminated by lighting matches in the dark. "I know," I casually replied. The 'terrible tour' had begun.

We ordered a bottle of wine with our restaurant meal and all agreed that it tasted like it has been strained through somebody's socks. A friendly group of guys helped Sue and Spectra with a few words of Spanish on the street. The girls wanted to know how to say the word 'policeman.' I reluctantly translated for them wishing they had chosen some other word. Things never work out perfectly on a 'Terrible Tour,' but...

We wandered through the giant Mercado Mayorista and marveled at seeing all that naked food. And I drifted into flirtations with the eyes of the lovely Peruvian ladies. I was starting to feel a bit like I was home again... something about those vast market places...

We all flew up to Cusco. Night had fallen over the market. Two Indian women had just finished tying all of their wares up into an enormous package and were looking for an Indian man with a rope to carry their bundle home for them. I came walking by.

"Hey gringo! Come and carry this bundle for me!"

I went over and hefted the bundle. It was about six feet high and four feet broad and weighed about a hundred-and-fifty pounds. Truly, without a rope, I could not hope to carry it.

"I don't have a rope," I explained.

"Why not?" asked one woman.

"Because I am not a professional bundle-carrier."

"What are you?"

"He is a gringo," explained the other.

"In my country I make guitars."

They looked at me.

"Actually," said one, "the reason I called you over was so that you could take my friend here home to be your wife."

"OK," I said, "let's go." I motioned toward the 'wife' with my hand. She had covered her face, giggling with embarrassment like a little girl.

"Give her a kiss!"

"OK," I said, "come here!" We all seemed to be having fun. She came closer and I gave her a little hug and a kiss.

"Is it true," the bold one asked me, "that in the United States the gringos eat little babies for dinner? Do you steal little children and take them home to eat?"

Without waiting for an answer to that she continued: "Can you carry this other bundle for me?"

"Sure! I can help you with that one! Without a rope!"

"What about that lady?" she pointed at an effeminate looking Indian boy with longish hair. "Does she turn you on?"

"No, I like this one," I said reaching toward her still giggling girlfriend. Then I turned and started picking my way up the stone street between the banana peels.

"See you later!"

We took the train to Machu Picchu and discovered that we were no longer allowed to spread out our sleeping bags and sleep in the ruins. But there were places to camp down in the bottom of the valley: less convenient but we found our spot.

The next day we ascended directly up to the ruins on the trail. It felt more 'terrible' to go this way and ignore the new road with its little shuttle buses. There was now a big hotel at the top.

We entered to order a bite to eat or something to drink and I discovered that one of the employees, Frida, was originally from Sina! Amazing coincidence! Before finding work there she had lived in the jungle... in Iquitos... where she had been bitten by a dangerously poisonous snake, a 'muchuchu.' The local Aguaruna Indians saved her by capturing the snake, skinning it, grinding up the flesh with various leaves from local plants, cutting into her flesh over the bite with a machete, using their mouths to suck out venom and finally rubbing the pulverized snake into her wound. She later survived a minibus accident and again the local Aguarunas re-located her shoulder and set her broken collar bone. But her husband had died in another vehicle accident there in Iquitos. "There was nothing left of his head except fragments," she said. After that she had traveled back up to the highlands. Seven years had passed since her last visit to Sina. I promised to say hello to her mother when we arrived there!

Chris and I were both carrying marketplace guitars from Cusco. We were discovering that we could find and play some blues-ish improvisations together and our little group got happier. Chris finally managed to understand that the Peruvian guy who was yelling 'ful! ful!' which means 'cool' in Peru wasn't calling him a 'fool!' The Terrible Tour was evolving. There were six of us: four males and two females... all with very different personalities of course.

We spent the rest of the day climbing Huayna Picchu, a steep climb up an ancient Inca staircase which requires a few hours to achieve. Happily, everyone in our group managed the climb.

Martin, Graham, Chris, Spectra, Sue

We were befriended by a couple who had a little food shack down in the bottom of the valley. Both the husband and the wife were named 'Antonio,' it seemed. Speaking only in Quechua we arranged for me to go pick up a case of beer from one of their suppliers and we celebrated.

We returned to Cusco by train the next day. Graham was now more open. Sue was blooming. Spectra was digging it. Chris was happy. Martin was very solid and steady. I was happy that our disjointed little group was coming together in its own mysterious ways.

Chris had procured a bit of marijuana for us all to smoke. I had just talked with a young California couple who had been jailed by the police for a few hours after someone made a false claim that they were drug dealers. On my way back to the hotel I walked past some police and practiced looking 'not suspicious,' whatever that might mean. I had to tell Chris that if he got arrested and I had to choose between him and the group I would have to choose the group. He said he understood and we left it at that.

That having been said, we all smoked together in our hotel room and discussed finding ways to increase the flows of love between us.

Back out in the market place I fell in love with a girl named Herminia. She worked for her father in a little cafe. Her father looked coldly at me while she did a secret sexy dance for me from behind the counter. It had been a long time since I'd made love and the blue smoke in my belly was getting very visible.

We left Cusco for Juliaca, which was further south and the last real town before Sina. We were now on the edge of Lake Titicaca at twelve-thousand feet. My friend Federico's aunt was running a hotel in Juliaca but couldn't accommodate all six of us. The lady behind the desk in the hotel next door stood firm on her high price until I began bargaining in Quechua. Laughing with surprise, she came down to a more reasonable amount and we moved into one large room for all six of us to share.

Federico's younger brother, Rigoberto, came in to visit and told me that the folks in Sina would be happy to see me again but he wondered about Leda's absence. "She has decided to follow her other interests and is going back to school," I explained, telling him that I was feeling some sadness that she was not with me. "Sometimes it's not possible to share everything and people do go their separate ways. We shall see what happens."

I Just Like This

Soon I was sitting alone having a beer in the little cafe in the front of the hotel, writing: "...four of us just ran up the hill behind the town. We all seem to be strong and feeling good; I hope we can climb one of those twenty-thousand-foot mountains... Now there's a lady sitting across from me -- an Indian woman -- who just asked me to buy her a beer..."

She was smiling at me, motioning with her head toward my beer. I ordered her a beer. She smiled and drank from her glass. She smiled at me again. Complete with bowler hat and numerous billowing skirts, she was an Inca jewel.

"Come on over," my hand told her. She sat down at my table.

"Where are you from?" I asked.

"From Puno. My name is Teresa." She wanted a coin to put in the juke box.

She was flowing like water; we drank beer for half an hour, talking half in Spanish, half in her Inca language. From time to time she danced in front of the juke box. She was all smiles, stretching her arms and rubbing her belly.

Sue and Martin came in from off the street. I pointed them out to Teresa. "Sue and Martin," I said. She looked at them; gave them a genuinely delighted smile. My eyes were rooted on those smiling Peruvian lips...

"Sit down, have a beer," I told Sue and Martin. Teresa moved over closer to me to make room for them. Her leg touched mine! Poof! The blue smoke thickened in my belly!

The room was filling up with people. Four Indian men at another table had by now had plenty of time to get good and drunk. I listened to them: "Nothing else matters!" one was telling the other three, "...if at this moment we are all four like brothers."

They all solemnly bowed their heads in drunken agreement. The little old lady with one eye who was running the place watched calmly from the corner while a couple of unambitious young Indian boys carried bottles of beer and bowls of soup back and forth from the kitchen.

Sue was unfolding in Teresa's presence. They had that same childish looseness. They liked each other: two rubber ducks in a hot bathtub, rolling and bobbing, grinning and chatting away at each other in universal language. Martin was grinning, dribbling comments in English out of the corners of his mouth. Teresa reeled with laughter. Her eyes told us that she had seen Martin's mind in her mind!

"My God," we all exclaimed, "it doesn't matter what language we all speak, we can understand each other perfectly!" Teresa enthusiastically nodded her head and rubbed her breasts from sheer pleasure. We all burst out laughing. Beer and soup. "More beer and soup!"

Martin turned around for a moment and was immediately and hopelessly sucked into the table of the four drunk ones as a fellow brother. Every minute or two he called for help and I translated something for him. I told him he was doing great and to keep it up. He drank another beer and dove back into the cross-cultural mill where the four of them all ground on him at once trying to explain the various details of their concept of brotherhood. I leaned over their table for a while to listen, try to get something straightened out, and then went back to Teresa. We sat closer and closer together; she rubbed her belly harder and harder. Sue sat watching wide-eyed.

"We want some white meat," the four drunk ones started yelling at me from their table. "Let's exchange," they said. "You take Teresa and we'll take her!"

They pointed at little Sue. Teresa laughed, pointed at Sue, and rubbed her breasts again with admiration. "I wish I had a little gringa girl baby like you," she confided to Sue.

"So let's exchange!" the drunk ones were still clamoring.

"What are they saying?" asked Martin.

Sue was smiling and nodding, smiling and nodding, not quite into the men's minds, just soaking up whatever came her way, like a rag in the wind. She liked it… the flirtation…

"I don't own her," I told the drunk ones, pointing at Sue. "She's not mine to give away; if you want her, be nice to her, damn it! Open up a romance!"

I had to take a piss. I got up and headed for the bathroom. Around the corner the two unambitious young waiters, suddenly alive and chuckling, grasped me by the arm. They pointed at Teresa and beat their fists on their hands. They whispered: "Just take her into your room, and wham wham wham!"

"But there are six of us staying in the same room!"

"We will rent you another one," they said, "we've got some more empty ones!"

I pissed and went back to sit down next to Teresa.

Our legs began rubbing together once more. Suddenly Teresa stopped, looked down toward my lap and asked me, "What's it like?"

I realized she was talking about my penis and I felt a flood of deep recognition -- every emotion in the book -- warmth, courage, fear, challenge, desire. You name it. It was there. I felt like I was being welcomed back to some long-lost land where everything made sense.

"It's a good one," I told her. The four drunk ones were still yelling about exchanging white meat for dark meat, grinning at me. Martin had given up and gone into our room. The two waiters were grinning at me from around the corner, waiting for me to come rent another room.

"Let's go," I told Teresa, "and look for another place." I didn't like the idea of everybody just sitting outside our door waiting for us to go 'wham wham wham'... waiting for us to re-emerge with ridiculous grins on our faces... The four drunks were still slobbering and babbling about exchanging meat. I wished them luck on our way out the door but I could see Sue already disappearing towards our room.

We walked out the door, walked into a hotel around the corner and rented a room.

Teresa smiled at me, still loose, liquid. I sat down on the edge of the bed and she leaned over me and planted her big rubbery mouth on mine and lost herself immediately in the kiss. She sat down on the bed next to me, put her hand on my cock and asked, "is it ready? Let's see."

I pulled my pants halfway down and asked her, "How many skirts have you got on?" She lifted all six of them up and showed me her papaya, smiling. I felt it and said, "sweet." I pulled my pants the rest of the way off and she looked fondly at my penis.

She ripped off the rest of her skirts and blouses and lay down spread open on the bed.

'Ah sweet woman, nothing has dammed the flow, gelled the syrup, or sullied the desire for you!' I was thinking.

"Come on, jump on!" her eyes were telling me. Summoning simple faith I lay down next to this big, juicy, pulsating fruit of God's creation. A few caresses and she had swallowed me up with her big wet vacuum of a vagina.

"No no! Not yet!" I had to tell myself before too long and pull it out, away from the hungry aperture. I didn't want to spoil the whole feast by gorging myself senselessly on the appetizers!

"Let's drink another bottle of beer," she said. "I've got one in my bundle!" So we drank a bottle of strong dark beer and lay still for a while. I got up and took a tremendous piss in the basin. I was full of beer.

A new wave of arousal grew. We made love more fully this time, coming simultaneously, emerging through the universal moaning of the woman.

We curled up together and she was soon asleep. But my mind, climbing out of temporary oblivion, was on fire. She rolled over and let out a long calm wet fart.

Mumbling in her sleep she said, "I just like this," grabbing a-hold of my penis.

Teresa snuggled up to me and fell back asleep, but my thoughts were roaring through my mind like freight trains. I tried imagining a sun setting over a calm body of water - a Buddhist trick I had read about in Aurobindo. 'Train your mind to think of only one thing: an orange sun hovering over an infinite expanse of water. Tranquility. Peace. The Pacific Ocean.'

Half an hour later I was still wide awake. She got up and drained herself in a great whoosh into the pan. She climbed back into bed, farting away and horny again. I got it up, put it in her, but lost interest and melted away, lost in that great big papaya of hers. She turned around and got me inside her from the rear. We made love again. At last I was getting closer to sleep.

She woke up from time to time to rub herself against me. About 4:00 AM she announced it was morning. Time to get up. She would be going to go to Puno today. She turned on the light, smiled, patted herself on the belly and said, "I have a little gringo inside now!"

I lay in bed and watched her go through all the business of putting on six skirts and braid her hair. She told me that it had been wonderful and that my white skin was beautiful. She kept on smiling easily... calm, smooth and friendly. She asked me for 20 soles for bus fare. I gave her 50. She looked at me earnestly, said "gracias papito," kissed me again, smiled once more and vanished through the door.

Three days later I bought her another beer and soup in the bar in the front of the hotel; everybody joked about how I had 'my woman' now in town. It was true. We rented a room again and spent another night together... Feeling our attraction again through this woman who was so at home in her female body was guiding me rapidly back to some long-forgotten male home inside myself.

I continued to see repressed sexuality as a primary driving negative force in the human psyche.

Since our sexuality is driven from within our own DNA and could be the most direct answer to the primal question "why was I born?... why am I here?..." it is essential to understand this mechanism properly... keeping things in perspective...

DNA: Deep Natural Awareness

We are just the fruits on the immortal being called DNA.

Our consciousness is built of words, is temporary and contains a measure of fear and grief because we are not immortal and we experience suffering and pain.

DNA is immortal. Perhaps only 4 billion years old, but containing an infinite potential to live forever. And because the essential DNA is always protected by the skins of the seeds which form its containers, the DNA does not directly experience suffering and pain.

There is a non-verbal consciousness in the DNA.

Think about the vastness of the DNA: all the life forms on earth. Imagine the collective consciousness which comes with all of that!

When we access that we attain enlightenment.

We are relieved of our grief and our fear.

We experience sanity for the first time.

We accept our ordinary consciousness as a temporary assembly of rather frightened words: a clumsy and hastily-patched together virtual reality designed to get us through our short lifespan as individual fruits on the immortal tree. We sprout, bloom, make love, rot and plop onto the ground, finished. The trees of life go on and on.

When we experience sexual energies we are tapping into the consciousness of the DNA.

We become ecstatic and our fears vanish in the face of that ecstasy.

We have tasted the feel of immortality but then return to our business of surviving as individual fruits for short periods of time.

Our existence is subservient to and yet critical to the DNA which uses us as links in its immortal chain.

We are the plants and animals, but the DNA is always the seed.

When we allow our brief individual consciousness to dissolve for a moment we are in Samadhi, we enter into and taste the eternal bliss.

All of our mysticisms and religions which are based on our egoistic yearning to convert our individual fruit consciousnesses into immortal beings while preserving our identities as fruits are false.

We cannot be the DNA.

We serve the DNA.

Surrender is the key process to enlightenment.

When we allow our ordinary virtual reality consciousness, our word-based consciousness to dissolve, we can begin to access the DNA consciousness. Why not? The DNA consciousness is inside of us. It is potent in our sex cells and slumbering in every other cell in our bodies!

We begin to get whisperings of past lifetimes, of inter-connectedness of all beings, of direct forms of communication. We begin to feel that we are all plants, all animals and all humans who have ever lived. We will survive into the next stages of evolutionary complexity and revel in it without any sense of urgency. We are immortal. We have infinite patience. We are ultimately sane. We experience neither fear nor pain. We effortlessly survive all the tortures of birth and death.

Imagine! What our individual fruit consciousness struggles to project as heaven is contained inside us, in every cell. We don't even care whether we are cockroaches or humans! We don't mind eating and we don't mind being eaten. Being eaten is painless: part of the immortal process. No fear is necessary.

When we relax and transcend our individual fruit minds we breathe easily for the first time. We become one with the biosphere, the eco-sphere, the entire pulsation called life on planet earth.

When biology classes are taught we sometimes miss the point. We get something backwards. We are taught to think egotistically only about the welfare of ourselves as individual beings! We think we are "using" the DNA to make our babies. The truth is that DNA is using us to make more seeds which in our case happen to be human babies. The DNA is in charge of the whole process and truly is a magical mechanism designed by millions of years of evolution to ensure it's own propagation.

We can eventually dissolve our individual fruit-based hopes and dreams. They are ultimately futile. But the fact that we are part of the magical mechanism for the propagation of the DNA gives us front row seats and a gateway into Deep Natural Awareness.

Once we drop our identification with the fruits, the offspring that we are, we can begin to access the sanity of the Deep Natural Awareness! All the yearnings for immortality are fulfilled. All the inter-connectedness is achieved!

We begin, as Socrates pointed out, to "remember" all the knowledge and wisdom contained in the entire history of all life-forms on this planet! With fear out of the way everything can make perfect sense. We become free! We transcend the captivity of our finiteness and rejoice instead that we are also the containers of the infinite! Removing our focus from our existence as an individual fruit with a skin, a boundary in both space and time, we go within, into the pulp of our being and, identifying with our inner Deep Natural Awareness, our DNA, we enjoy being a chariot! We become beautiful, ecstatic fruits instead of ugly impatient fruits!

To the extent that we surrender and allow ourselves to merge consciousness with DNA, we enter an amazing realm wherein there is no more suffering! The DNA lives inside the pods, inside the eggs, inside the gonads of all existence. The DNA has perfected the arts of survival… of immortality. For the DNA there is neither pain nor death. Only we fruits and flowers and lizards and bugs, the individual beings born who scurry about with propagation as our sole pre-programmed objectives, experience suffering and death.

Our nerve endings are exposed on the outside. The DNA lives protected inside our skins, safe and pain-free. No wonder those who come back from near-death experiences report the discovery of love-filled compassionate gentle pain-free realms and are freed from their fears!

To the extent that we can find ways to surrender our identities as the busy carriers of the seeds and meditate our way into the consciousness of the seeds themselves, we can finally dissolve and breathe!

Sexual Repression and Human Violence

Finally understanding our natural place and role and function as a part of the enormous tree of life here on planet earth, we can try and decipher some of the underlying causes of human violence. Men will become frustrated and sometimes violent when their natural sexual expressions are thwarted by various 'puritanical' beliefs which spring out of the various patriarchal cultures into which we are born.

It is easy to track the roots of this kind of violence. It is very pervasive and the daily news is filled with stories of rape and violence committed by men against women. But it seems that some cultures are more sexually repressive than others. I discovered some entrances into sexual liberation in both Mexico and the Inca world where the indigenous women have long had license to feel their own sexuality more deeply.

Is it something called the 'patriarchy' which perpetuates unhealthy and sexually repressive attitudes, rules, laws and beliefs? Yes, that is a big part of it.

Here's how it works: Men born into powerful religious institutions are surrounded by a system which provides high economic and social benefits to the priests who claim to have access to the 'word of God' and who discourage the villagers from discovering their own natural paths into ecstasy. They always label such pathways as 'of the devil' and threaten eternal damnation to those who dare to have deep expressive fun on their own... to those who follow the callings of their own inner DNA...

Yes, the men who join those patriarchal priesthoods have managed to keep vast populations subjugated... convinced that without guidance from the priesthood, which of course also costs some money, that they will 'rot in hell for their sins...' We all have heard their incredible nonsense.

So natural sexual expression, with all its ecstasies, has become a rare thing on planet earth for the last fifteen thousand years and we have been hearing about strange inexplicable acts of violence committed by men against women and by men against men for a long time. And no wonder modern women are confused. "Am I supposed to be wet or dry?" They are caught between the appreciation for their naturally wet sexiness and all the puritanical patriarchal messages which want them to appear strangely dry and anything but sexy.

I was lucky, as I have mentioned before, to have been born into my small but gentle family and to have been raised through early childhood free from religion and the habitual forms of judgmental thinking which comes with it. I was never told that sex was bad. As I have matured I have discovered that all of humanity is powerfully driven by our DNA to be sexy. The amazing thing is that the vast majority of people have been poisoned by religious beliefs to experience guilt as a consequence of their own natural sexiness. The patriarchal priesthoods need their congregations to remain in slavery and once the poison seed of guilt is planted it self-perpetuates. But our true nature constantly uproots these seeds and women like Teresa find their ways to sexual freedom. It is a beautiful thing to explore and feel and admire. When men can be in the presence of sexually-free women and just worship them in a pure and simple way it opens the gateways into the ancient gardens which are our birthright.

It's important to share these experiences and make them public so that others can feel camaraderie as they enter these supposedly 'forbidden' realms.

Onward Towards Home in Sina

It came time for me to move on... to say farewell for now to my new Inca lover and head for Sina. We climbed into a truck and began the two-day journey through Cojata to the summit of the pass or *apacheta* at Iskay Cruz where the valley tops out and emerges onto the *altiplano*, the *'high plains.'* We had hired a truck to deliver us and did not arrive on a Saturday when the villagers climb up from below to create a market place. So we dismounted from the truck and found ourselves alone.

We decided to sleep in the little hut which miraculously supports it's own roof of magically-assembled stones. I had slept in this hut before.

Spectra confided that she was loving our rides through the vast high altitude landscapes in the backs of trucks.

Martin was inspired by the stone architecture and built another little sheltering wall to help as a wind-break. He liked to be busy with building or carrying.

Chris was just happy because the rest of us were happy.

Graham didn't feel so good in the stomach but that would pass.

Sue was doing fine.

We discussed racism in America as we made a stew and began to fall asleep. We all slept well in our sleeping bags there at sixteen-thousand feet in that marvelous little hut.

The next morning we traveled briefly up the side of the valley and ascertained that, yes, my stash of climbing equipment was still there where I had buried it in the cracks between the rocks a year ago! That was good news.

Then we began our descent on foot toward Sina. Our arrival would be a surprise.

Not really. By the time we walked into the village the news had traveled down the valley and my Compadres Edwin and Laura were ready to welcome us into their home. They offered us half of their house. Laura had moved things around and made some room for the six of us. I was happy to see that my Godson, Guido was healthy. We saved catching up on all the news and got some more sleep.

Of course the kids awakened at four in the morning. Laura went out to the little stone kitchen to make hot pre-dawn tea or coffee, blowing into the coals in the little clay stove through her bamboo tube. There's nothing cozier than getting into that tiny little kitchen with her and Edwin early in the morning and sipping on a hot cup of tea brewed from some local tasty plant while munching on a piece of fried bread or a hot little potato.

Feeling at Home in Sina with Laura and Edwin

Soon we were all awake and we scrambled up the valley wall to recommence the endless cycle of clearing, burning, digging, planting, harvesting. We offered our feeble attempts to help with all this work and we boiled potatoes for lunch high above the village.

It occurred to me that I still didn't know how Edwin and Laura had gotten together. I asked them. Some few years ago Jacob, the village shaman, whom I remembered for his harp-playing, had asked his little magic table if Edwin should bring Laura over from an adjacent village in Bolivia and make her his wife. The table jiggled and danced its message: 'yes.' So Edwin had gone and come back with Laura.

Edwin never had manifested such 'itchy feet' and wanderlust like my friend Pastor and so many others. The months and years had gone by and Edwin had stayed put in Sina. Occasionally he would round up his horses and mules and make a pilgrimage to lower elevations for corn. Then there would be boiled corn to munch on in their little kitchen.

Laura had experienced a couple of brushes with death already. I had been there when she had nearly bled to death after giving birth to her second child, Rudy.

Laura, Sue, Edwin

My Magic Rock

The next day, after purchasing and butchering a sheep for our meat supply, I climbed for an hour and gazed down toward the Amazon jungle from my special magical spot across from the wise rock face.

Breath rose from the jungle.

Heavy wet breath.

I looked up the valley and at the little village nestled into its bottom: Sina.

Comadre! Compadre! A voice cried inside my mind.

The jungle was thinking this morning. You could see her thoughts: heavy wet thoughts... bearing images of large green leaves... tangled vines and large beetles... small beetles too...

'Is that what you're thinking about jungle?' I wondered. *'Are these your thoughts I see gliding up the valley? Your thoughts are so thick I can no longer see my favorite rock portal on the other side!'*

A bird glided slowly over my head; looked down at me with its eye; did a u-turn directly above me and faded back into the mist. It was an eagle or a large hawk. A lizard stopped on the ground in front of me; then vanished between the grasses.

Fever Strikes; La Jesusa Strikes; Dreamworlds Reign

The next morning I was not well. I felt millions of viruses eating away at the insides of my lungs. I slept late until a little old lady scuttled across the room and perched beside my head. For a moment I thought it might be my Compadre's mother but then I saw that it wasn't. It was La Jesusa, mother of the sensual Idelsa...

"Please lend me 1100 soles:" she said...

I blinked my eyes. "Such a sum!" I said. "How could I lend such a sum?"

"I can pay you back on Monday!" she said, "day after tomorrow!"

"What do you need it for?" I asked.

Silence.

"What do you need it for?" I asked again.

No answer. She didn't say a thing.

My Comadre Laura appeared in the doorway. I was glad to see her. I got the feeling that La Jesusa was not.

"So what were you about to say about what you need the money for?" I asked again.

La Jesusa flashed into high speed underground conversation with my Comadre... too fast for me to understand. I watched my Comadre hoping for some sign. At one point she spat on the floor. Was that a sign? Or was she just spitting on the floor? I got no clear sign.

"Come on, lend it to me please!" said La Jesusa. "Let your Comadre be our witness!"

I hesitated. La Jesusa fingered the bottom of Graham's empty sleeping bag saying, "Such wonderful things they have!"

"You're sure you can pay me back on Monday?" I asked again.

She thought again for a moment as if going through all her plans in her head. "Yes, on Monday."

"Ok," I said, "if you're absolutely sure you can pay me back Monday."

I got out my wallet. I gave her the cash.

She murmured something about "Look how much money he's got!"

She said thanks and went out the door only to run back in for a second to admire one of our canteens. Then she left.

My Comadre came closer: "What did you lend her that money for? That Jesusa is an untrustworthy one! All she said to me was 'Tell him to lend it to me!'... nothing about what she wanted it for... nothing! Her whole family is untrustworthy! We gave her all the meat from a bull we had which fell down the mountain and got killed. That was two years ago and we have gotten nothing in return. And it's not as if she was poor! She's got one of the largest herds in the valley! She's got more than thirty cows! And her son Carlos -- surely he is the one she is going to give your 1100 soles to now because he's supposed to leave this morning to go back to school -- about a year ago he stole a bull from another village and sold it to get the money so he could stay in the city and go to school. He got caught and La Jesusa paid the owner back but now he comes and goes with no trace of shame! A boy from another family would never dare show his face around this village again after being caught doing that! But I couldn't tell you all these things right there in front of her face..."

My Comadre turned around and left me alone.

I lay in my sleeping bag. The sun rose over the steep valley wall and began to heat the ground. For four hours I lay immobile in the warm sunlight with my shirt off.

My Comadre told me that sunlight is bad for a cough.

Alberto came by. We sympathized with each other like two big babies.

He also told me that the sun was bad for a cough and that I should go inside.

I was stubborn; I liked the sunlight.

I kept lying there on the edge of sleep.

My mind was the inside of an Oriental temple.
Suddenly the face of death popped through the wall of my mind: a devil or demon... an old man. I had an impulse to push him out. But I felt sorry for him and called him back.
He came back in; the face of a dragon with many teeth.

Then I was in a courthouse and I was supposed to see the judge. I was accused of something but I didn't know what. I was wearing a pair of farmer's overalls. Underneath I had on a suit. I was very respectably dressed but the entire effect was destroyed by the dirty overalls and by my floppy tennis shoes. Nevertheless I entered the courtroom, leaving a small bundle of my possessions out in the hall. The room was filled with young men of supposedly criminal disposition. 'Juvenile delinquents' if you like. The judge asked me why I was interrupting him.

'You called me, sir?' I asked.

'Oh yes,' he said, 'charges of being drunk have been brought against you.'

'Drunk?' I asked.

'Yes. Drunk, irresponsible and disorderly.'

'And do I have the right to know who it is who has brought this charge against me?' I asked.

'Yes,' he said, 'that is one of your rights...' He paused, apparently expecting me to say more.

'I am a hard-working honest man,' I told him. 'I may get drunk every once in a while, but...' I noticed that the judge, seemed to be listening, hearing, feeling me.

'Are you sure you're not paranoid?' he asked me. I didn't understand why he chose that word, but I nevertheless tried to think about myself and my getting drunk in terms of paranoia. I looked inside myself, examined myself truthfully and said: 'Paranoid? Do you mean to ask if I am afraid of what others might say and thereby be led to distort the truth? No.'

The judge showed me the paper he had before him. It seemed that a Mrs. Del Reggato, the mother of one of the high school students I had brought with me on some trip to Peru had lodged the complaint. She didn't even know me. The judge smiled at

> *me and told me he had dropped the charges and that I could go on my way. Meanwhile the entire room-full of 'juvenile delinquents' had quietly filed out of the room and out of the building back into the streets... we were all free! As I passed out of the room into the hall and down the stairs I saw my bundle, which I had nearly forgotten, and received a jolt of surprise. I saw my wallet lying on the floor beside the bundle. All of those 'juvenile delinquents' had filed out right past it and not one had tried to steal it.*

I woke up.

I got up to go find my Comadre.

She was sitting in her room sorting out seed potatoes.

"I had a dream Comadre," I told her and I recounted the whole thing.

"So you see," I finished explaining, "It's something about trusting people."

"Yes," replied my Comadre, "this dream was a good sign which means that La Jesusa will pay you back!"

That night my Comadre got me drunk with another one of her remedies: a big hot cup of eucalyptus tea mixed with special herbs she had picked. It was about fifty-percent grain alcohol. I lay in my sleeping bag on the floor for hours. I felt like I had an aura ten-feet-wide. I felt myself floating up the mountain and onward to Africa, Brazil, Asia. I thought about Leda back in Colorado and felt happy that we were each following our own personal paths and discovering the things that we needed to discover without each other.

I was a giant moth ready at last to burst out of its tiny cocoon. And I felt my body radiating death to the viruses in my lungs.

By morning my breath was still feeling like a blowtorch in my seared lungs but I could tell that the viruses were nearly vanquished.

I had the strength to climb up to my magic spot on the valley wall above and commune again with my rock face.

I must go and see Lucio!

That night there was another party in Sina...

Alberto. Big balloon of a man. Was singing. Like a child. Eyes open. Ready to cry.

Alberto

In Peru when the Indians sing... they don't hesitate... they just burst right into tears.

Faces and bodies in the night. A single candle was drooling hot wax on the rocks and buttering our twelve faces with light.

"Pastor! You understand! You already know!" I told him... my voice tight and on the verge of tears.

Sue and Spectra danced timidly in the background.

"You already know!" I told Pastor. "You already know that this is *It!* This is *life!*"

And it felt beautiful by god. It was enough for me. And I didn't want anything more.

Big magic clouds of shining warmth opened up all around us ready to swallow our pain... all we had to do was sing... I took the guitar and wailed like a big baby under the stars at night... drinking pure alcohol mixed with warm water, sugar, anise and cinnamon.

"Where is Lucio Gonza?" I asked. "I must go and see Lucio!"

I stumbled down the paths and over the rock walls. I opened the door of Lucio's house. I looked around the room. Life was painful in that house... brown like horses in a corral in the winter... Lucio's wife was sitting in the corner by her fire... the two little girls were still awake late at night in the middle of the room...

And Lucio -- was propped up in bed; I sat beside him and looked at him. He was in pain.

"Oh Lucio," I told him. "Why haven't you come? We are having a party!"

"I haven't been well for the last three months now," he told me. "My kidneys -- just keep on hurting me... And my head -- aches every day..."

Edwin was suddenly there, my Compadre, my host... he had come over from the party... And Humberto! "Oh my god is that you?" I hadn't seen Humberto for a year! We buried our faces in each other's shoulders and murmured in three languages crying... for a long time... I was gone into another world...

We opened some gate and let the saints of pain come marching out to live with us... to dine and feast... like kings of nobleness or rays of sunshine... or beasts grazing in the back yard until they became overstuffed and drugged with black wine and ready to fall back to sleep... at which point I said goodbye to Humberto and to Lucio... and let my Compadre Edwin... and Alberto who had come without his guitar... lead me back to the party in that remote valley miles away from the nearest road... eons from the nearest century... on the other side of the mountains nestled in tight and high above the Amazon jungle.

And the party began in earnest again. There was something about the way a man in that particular valley could sing and cry that made me see that the most pressing business of all was to sit together under the moon and howl at the sky like wolves warm for each other's company! We moved our meeting inside some stone hut. I did a dance around the candle... or so they told me...

I only remember going back outside... looking at the sky and saying "Here I can die... Yes here I could die... In this kind of a place I could die... And I wouldn't even notice... Oh how happy and relieved I feel..." My voice leaned out into the sky like a watch spring... "to have at last found a place where I don't mind dying!" And I directed my naked body back into the house.

Potato Field Work and Climbing Ananea

We spent the next four days working up in the potato fields. We were getting better at it. We cut and scraped the bushes up into piles and set them on fire! The whole hillside seethed with wet smoke. My Compadre came with another shovel-full of live coals. He planted fire in the ground like big hot seeds. A hot coal fell off his shovel and down the back of my pants. My Compadre thought it was very funny... barefoot in the burning dirt... and a huge tarantula waddled out from beneath a rock.

I had so many friends and Compadres to visit: Benito Chura... Amalia... Don Teofilo...

Sue and Spectra were frustrated with the boys... they felt that just because they were not in a love relationship with any of them shouldn't mean that they be treated so distantly. We discussed all of this... in groups and in pairs. Breakthroughs happened. We became a happier group.

Later that afternoon we fried biscuits, boiled corn and potatoes and stuffed noodles into our backpacks and the next morning at first light we began climbing uphill. We were Graham and Chris and Martin and I. The girls stayed behind with Laura and Edwin.

Chewing coca leaves we managed to sing while walking uphill from nine-thousand feet to fifteen-thousand feet in one day: up to where it was cold and miserable and beautiful as the sun was setting at the bottom of the glacier... where we set up our tent... and I spilled the soup...

The next day we again searched for and found the cache of climbing equipment: ropes, ice axes, crampons, snow pickets...

Soon we were churning our way up the glacier, weaving our way between the big open crevasses... tied together all the time just in case someone fell through.

We walked over bridges of ice and just kept on taking steps uphill long after the point when we no longer felt like taking steps uphill.

The clouds gathered to make some bad weather... but, just before we couldn't see through the mist anymore, we came out onto the top of a huge cliff whose existence I had never suspected and I could see just well enough to realize... that we had probably come the wrong way...

So by two in the afternoon we were cloud-bound in our tent. We played cards and listened to the snow falling on the nylon.

The next day Chris and I were earliest up and most ready to go... and the sun was out so we could see again!

So up we went: up the glacier and up two short rock faces, at the second of which Chris waited while I went up to the top... and just as I got to the top the clouds came creeping in and I barely had time to see that we really couldn't go that way either.

So we slid back down to the tent; rolled it up and followed our footsteps from yesterday back down through the fog to the same place we had spent our first night... where the snowflakes tumbled down all over us... making everything more wet... and Martin and I said goodbye to Chris and Graham... who had decided to have some other adventure of their own.

A little Indian walked up out of the fog and it soon turned out that his brothers were friends of mine down in the valley below. He was living up here tending five-hundred-and-thirty alpacas with his wife and two kids.

"I make a better living up here than I would lower down in the valley," he said... "So I have plenty of everything for myself and my family."

He took me and Martin to his little stone house and we made up some coffee... stuffing the stove with dried cow shit... which burns pretty much like wood.

We told him goodbye and walked off into the falling snow. After two hours we found a little cave and made some stew and got some sleep for the night.

The next day the little gray clouds had decided to play in their baskets down in the jungle and quit bothering the sky for a day!

We began climbing steep rock slides... and by following gullies between cliffs for most of the morning we came back to the edge of a glacier across which we nimbly trotted... until the floor fell out from beneath my feet and I landed on my ass on the edge of a crevasse. So we climbed up onto a higher ridge.

Only one place that day did we find along our way: a place of slight technical interest... which is to say... that things suddenly got steeper...but not so steep that we couldn't creep... along perfectly happily...

Ridge on Ananea

We were beginning to see how it was possible to go: the steel points of our crampons chomped firmly into the steep ice while we tried not to notice the throat of a rocky gray hole which could have funneled us out over the cliff and into the abyss. Martin had me securely on belay. I lightly trod the thin connecting bridge of cornice ice. If it were to give way, the opposite abyss was waiting directly beneath... But it didn't... give way...

By the end of the day in our tent we were feeling quite strange to be up there with all those mountains and no sign that anyone else had ever been quite crazy enough to have preceded us.

But one gets used to such places... and seeing no faces... which leads to long and involved philosophical conversations about the nature of magic... there at seventeen and a half thousand feet... which was really quite cold... and we shivered almost the whole night through... and were quite happy to see the fifth day of our climb... although the prospect of doing what we were going to do, namely go further out on our limb, was making me quite nervous...

Nevertheless we both did our best at putting our muscles to service! Only one place it seems, was threatening our dreams with its sudden steep appearance and thoroughly scary proportions.

In fact I must admit that my very first impulse upon seeing the ridge plunge down before me... was to cheerfully say 'let's call it a day'... and hang up the whole messy project!

But instead of that... I just sat... without saying a word... and neither did Martin... say a word...

For ten minutes in fact, we just stayed put and sat. And strange to say, without having to screw up our courage particularly, it slowly became apparent to me and to he... that there really was no problem... and that we could proceed with our steel points on our feet down this ridge... which looked like the back of the neck of some swan... and up the other side... which looked like the back of the neck of some other swan... which we did... and felt quite happy about it once we got to the other side!

Cordillera Apolobamba to the East in Bolivia

And soon, before noon, we found ourselves at the bottom of the peak of our dreams. Rather gentle the rest... on up to the crest it seemed we hoped we could go!

So leaving our packs to lighten our backs... with great energy and enthusiasm we embarked upon the final thousand feet.

And you can just imagine our great disappointment... to discover that snow... was making us slow... since alas it was up to our knees. It seems that the cold was sufficiently bold... to prevent that thick crust in which you can trust... from forming to give us something solid to walk on.

But no... it was like walking up a mountain of sugar.

Within range now, the summit began its magnetic influence on us. There was no doubt that we could make it. Our hearts and legs obeyed the force of attraction.

An hour and a half of pumping great quantities of blood through our happy cardiovascular systems... while skirting crevasses and light-footing it over the thin spots... which settled at times with great crunches... we made it to the top! And gave out great whoops, shaking hands on the spot... and ran about in a circle to keep ourselves warm...

Ananea Summit

And from there we could see a dozen brown valleys descending down below to the north and the east into the great mother Amazon jungle... and somewhere down there... above the steaming wet air... lay the village from which we had come... Sina!

Across from us smiled one more great mountain of twenty thousand feet... which remained there for us to think about climbing... some other time.

"You can see absolutely everything from here," said Martin, "including yourself!"

Iskay Cruz and Entrance to Sina Valley Below

Down Through Rinconada: Highest Town in the World

The downhill plunge was fast and sweet. You could run if you didn't trip over your own footprints in the crust!

Yes... now it was down down down... the way we had come. And just before sunset we had the amazing pleasure of crawling into another cave all the way back down at fifteen-thousand feet... below the glacier... and filling ourselves with good stew...

Safe! Through! Finished! We did it! Whatever that's worth...

Our sixth day began with a five-hour morning walk around the edge of the mountain and up over a ridge to the little village of Rinconada where about two-hundred Peruvians were living off the fruit of the land which emerged in the form of yellow metal: Gold. Rinconada lay at sixteen-thousand-seven-hundred feet... maybe more... and was almost directly below the summit we had just climbed... Geographers call Rinconada the "highest continually inhabited town in the world."

Rinconada: Highest Town in the World

But what we liked about this place was the food they brought there with trucks and kept in their little stores: bread and butter and strawberry jam... crackers, peanuts, eggs... and even a bottle of champagne... beer...

After a few hours of talking with a man who ran a store... and the man who ran the mine, we left the town at three in the afternoon... and felt so good... we kept walking around the bottom of the mountain toward that valley which plunges toward the jungle... from which our trip had been born... where my Comadre had helped us fry biscuits!

By midnight we were still walking over the last ridge... at sixteen-thousand feet again... and as we passed over another crest, a hundred miles of ice-fanged mountains extending as far as we could see into Bolivia came into view through the crystal night air. Jupiter reigned in the sky: its flashes of crystal fire working its magic...

We sat down on the highest point of the pass and I could feel the goosebumps and the shivers flowing up and down Martin's nineteen-year-old spine. I told him "thank you for being here with me!"

"There is no other place I would rather be!" he told me.

The big waxing moon gave us our guiding light... on that particular night. And since I was a little older than Martin was... ten years to be exact... and had seen that splendor of the glacier world at night a few times before... I was left with the bittersweet question... of how many more times in my short sweet life... I would be privileged to see this high altitude panorama again?

It suddenly came to me that I had now completed so many personal life adventures... and might just be ready for a major change... maybe having a family.... raising kids... now wouldn't that be an amazing adventure?

So down we did walk... getting lost in a swamp... until the moon set over the ridge... and we crashed at last... behind a rock... right out in the open air... we slept and slept and slept... in the bottom of our favorite valley... only a few hours walk from Sina... which we entered the next day in early afternoon... and found everything quite sleepy and calm... kinda just as we had left it.

Natural Ancient Ways of Life in Sina

Chris and Graham it seems had been back for three days. And the girls had suffered somewhat from not having been easily able to understand the languages there... and for having been shut up at close quarters for so many days with two Incas and their two little children... who cried at times, especially when it rained...

Life in Sina with children... natural ways of doing things... When mom and dad hold the little boy or little girl they jiggle its penis or rub it's pussy... not like sexy but just natural-happy-good-feeling touching... the babies smile and feel loved. Why don't you see snotty mucous on the little ones' noses? Because mom puts her mouth over the baby's nose and sucks it clean. What could be more natural? And no diapers? No, when the baby poops a hungry eager doggie tongue is available to lick the asshole clean. How warm and friendly! And the household guinea pigs scurry around like little vacuum cleaners gobbling up the tiny scraps and... how handy... yes, they even eat their own poop!

Everyone poops outdoors pretty much wherever they happen to be. Immediate clean-up is provided by the hungry pigs and dogs. Where is the dog shit? Gone. The pigs have eaten it up. When all is said and done there is nothing left on the ground but pig shit and chicken shit... both at the bottom of the food chain and nobody, except maybe some bugs, will eat that...

While Martin and I were up on the glaciers Spectra had led 'encounter groups' for Graham and Chris and Sue. She had been with us in John Link's communal house back in Boulder and used that as a model. They had spent some time sitting in a circle with eyes closed feeling each others' faces with their fingers. Sue had felt her way into deeper friendships with Edwin and especially with Laura. She was glad to have me back to help translate. Chris had become happily more spontaneous. Martin's feet were really hurting.

It had been two weeks now and La Jesusa was still not prepared to pay me back. When I checked in with her tears would run down her cheeks and she would squeeze her hands between her knees... expressing her frustration around her difficulties. I went to see Juan, the father of some of her children. He shook his head in silence, in commiseration, as if to say, 'Join the club!' I began to wonder if I was just out of luck.

But who should happen through the village but Victor! Victor owns a mining property and had a wife who had worked for twenty years in the post office in Juliaca. He had money and wouldn't mind buying one of La Jesusa's precious cows! Rushing over to her house I caught her at home: "Can you pay me back yet?" I asked her.

"No," she began whimpering, working up another burst of tears. "Juan won't give me the money," she started...

"I've found the solution!" I exclaimed. "Sell one of your cows!"

"There is no one to buy them," she said, unruffled.

"You don't know of anybody in the valley who could possibly afford one?"

"No, it's hopeless," she pronounced.

"Well, I have found someone!" I announced triumphantly. "Victor will buy one of your cattle and then you'll have the money to pay me back!! I'll go get him. You wait for us here!"

A look of surprise awakened her face into action. She began bustling about the hillside in front of her house. "No, no!" she decided. "I'll go work it out with him myself."

"How may times have you promised to work it out?" I asked her. "How am I to believe you this time?"

"Don't worry, you'll have your money," she said, tears beginning to flow once again.

Telling Victor to expect her, I retired to the riverside to do some badly-neglected clothes-washing. Sure enough, upon my return I found that she had come and paid half the sum to my Comadre. I was to receive the rest that evening. I went looking for her and found La Jesusa at Juan's house. She offered me something to drink and to eat. She and I talked as if we were faithful old friends and after a time she pressed the rest of the money into my hand.

Later, I asked Victor how he liked his new cow. "She never came to sell it to me," he said. "She must have gotten the money somewhere else. You know she is trying to help Idelsa and Carlos, who were not fathered by Juan. They would love to be able to match the life styles of Juan's other children, who receive more money from their father."

It all made sense. But I was very glad to have my money back. I didn't want to open the doors to being seen as a bottomless money machine.

Pastor and Edwin joined me and Victor and they all expressed the idea that I should have a girlfriend here in Sina. "You will feel more deeply what our songs are about once you begin a romance with a Sineña," they all agreed. They told me the names of some of the girls whom they thought might be available but I felt shy about expressing enthusiasm for any of the ones they mentioned...

The next night would be Chris's night to get drunk. I promised to stay and drink with him for as long as he might want to drink. So would Pastor and Victor. Long past midnight Chris and I lay on the ground and, pointing up into the sky at a particular star, he exclaimed: "There is your grandfather! He still lives up there in the sky; you can feel him inside you keeping you warm."

Which I could... And I named four more stars for his Grandfathers and Grandmothers while our two Peruvian friends, Pastor and Victor, got right to the point lying there with us... and said that they never had believed in the imported European Catholic God either.

Later... the moon had set behind the ridge... Chris was falling through the bushes and crashing over stone walls. I found that I was drunk enough to stand on my head without moving a muscle... I entered a special trance...

Announcing that he was going to fuck the two girls who were asleep in our hut he wobbled out the door and lost his hat... and spent the next hour on the side of the mountain like a dancing bear struggling up sand dunes or falling out of trees... At last I heard him clawing his way up some poles... and he was happy to see me... he had become a two-hundred-pound caterpillar glowing in the dark.

Just a little bit later I helped him home at last. I was the last one up... I had been the Papa... Good for me! ...especially since I hadn't even felt like getting drunk that night in the first place. I was learning how to be *Responsible*. But what was this foul mixture of other peoples' drinks and bread doing in my stomach? It was all part of the dance I was doing... I went outside... bent over by the wall... laid my big fat poisonous finger into the back of my throat... emptied out my stomach... The next morning I would be fine.

I talked with Ana about Leda and where she might be... From that distance I was feeling that Link's communal household, in spite of the attempts to be a spiritual community, had never generated the warmth of friendship I experience with my river-running mountain-climbing cross-country-skiing friends in Steamboat Springs nor with my friends here in Sina. I was feeling that Leda might be on the other side of a not-so-friendly fence. Ana was one of Juan's daughters and had a wide perspective from having lived both inside and outside of the village.

I needed to visit my ailing Compadre Lucio again. He was having difficulty even leaving his house and was now going blind in his left eye. His kidneys still hurt and another infection was in his lungs.

Patrunila

His wife, Patrunila, had a swelling in her belly... an infection in her womb she thought. It was hard for her to carry even small amounts of firewood. "No one cares for a Sineño," explained Lucio. "We just die."

I didn't know what to do. The antibiotics I had left with them in the past had not really made a difference. I dreamed of some day bringing a doctor to the village.

Walking into Bolivia

The time had come for us to leave Sina. Forty miles lay between us and the spot in which we would hopefully meet a truck making its weekly journey out from La Paz, Bolivia. Pastor was traveling with us so three horses accompanied us.

Into Bolivia with Horses

The ladies could walk without the burdens of their packs. They could even climb onto the horses and ride occasionally. The rest of us also managed to lighten our packs by tying a few things onto the horses.

A long day brought us up out of the valley onto the Altiplano. We walked across the border from Peru into Bolivia at some unmarked place. The ladies giggled as they walked, their teeth flecked with the green shreds of coca leaves. We had climbed back up to fifteen-thousand feet where we huddled around a shepherd's hut and shivered through the night.

From dawn to dark we trekked through the next day, arriving at another village by 9:00 PM. Afraid of missing the truck, we arose at 3:00 AM and began our ghostlike meander across the Altiplano once more, this time under the full moon. The pristine glory of the neighboring chain of ice-covered summits was gleaming under the lunar brilliance: the Cordillera Apolobamba was spread out beside us in the distance. Herds of vicuñas, the wild ancestors of the llamas and alpacas, floated across the expanse of the Altiplano in the distance.

Forty miles in two days and two nights with very little rest or sleep was terrible indeed and my students were chanting "Fuck Cameron Powers!" as we marched. Sue was sick and running a fever. By 10:00 AM we were gathered around a truck, in the village of Ulla Ulla, anxious to depart for La Paz. A pair of traveling musicians serenaded us with their charanguitos: little mandolins with bodies made from armadillo shells.

Twelve hours in the back of that truck brought us to the edge of the huge high-altitude bowl in which lies the capitol city of Bolivia -- a million people -- all beneath the mysterious colossal presence of Illimani, the twenty-thousand-foot peak which guards the inhabitants of La Paz from earthly diseases...

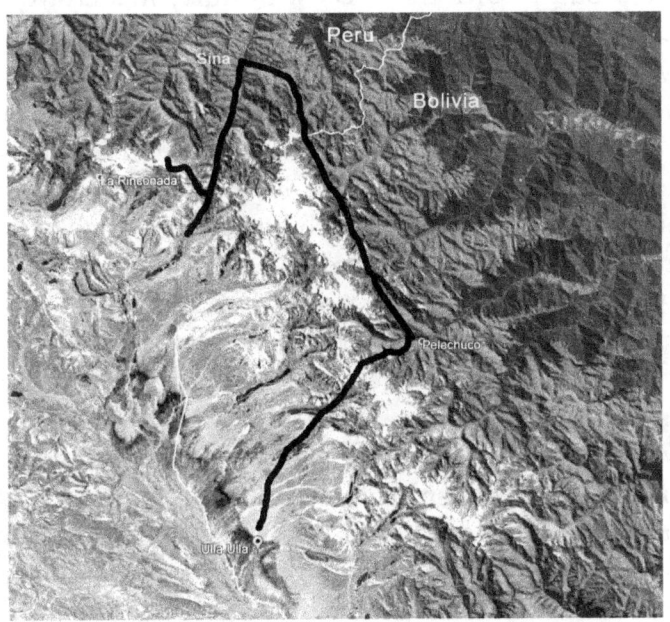

Walking Route Through Sina in 1973

Festival in La Paz

The city was strung like a Christmas tree with colored lights. We had known nothing about this festival! Wham! We wandered into a gigantic celebration: the anniversary of the founding of the modern city! And the Bolivians had just won the soccer game against Peru! Tens of thousands of people were roaming the streets: every lady had put on her finest dress and had cooked her finest food for the occasion. Hundreds of Quechua and Aymara women lined the streets with their little tables presenting, for the price of a snail, the most delectable cooking their giant pumping warm high-altitude hearts could come up with!

As the sun went down the men emerged with trumpets and trombones... drums and mandolins... more charangos! The music was made from the street corners while another breed of men mixed their favorite drinks and passed them out to whomever wandered by. For hours we ate. If I hadn't seen it or tasted it before I wanted to eat it! Yum! I wanted to get down on my hands and knees and lick the street!

People fought over me because I was a foreigner, each one trying to be the first to give me another drink. Hands clutched at my arms. I walked proudly down the street with thirty in a crowd beside me. They closed in around me and, as I struck up a conversation with some young Indian, dozens more came to see what the big hubbub was all about. Although most in the city spoke Aymara, my Quechua and Spanish both worked fine. I was the hole in the dough-nut. It got to be too much. I broke out of the dough-nut like a sperm breaking back out of some ovum into which he had just mistakenly swam... I eventually sought refuge in the room we had rented.

But soon I was out in the street again. This time it was late afternoon and I was just going to look for a quiet cafe in which to sit, drink coffee and write. Another friendly face appeared: "Come have a beer with us!"

I was reluctant. But the face was too friendly for me to resist and was not already hopelessly drunk so: "Alright, I'll have just one..."

I sat down at the table with Esteban and met his friend Federico and for two hours we exchanged the last words from our hearts. Racism. Religion. Hatred. The End of the World. The Bible. The Cataclysm! All of these served as introductory topics. Esteban and Federico were gold miners taking a vacation with wallets full of cash, whooping it up for a few days here in the big city.

I stared into Federico's eyes from two inches away for ten minutes. We were two bucks locking horns.

"And if I kill you?" asked Federico in Spanish.

"I'll kill you!" I told him in the Indian language.

"You little gringo, you disgust me!" he muttered. Little cold wavelets of fear rippled quietly about my fringes. But underneath, in the bottoms of our eyes, there was some bond which told us that this was the right game for us to play... although we were scaring poor Esteban who tried to unlock our horns and eyeballs and get us back to being three men joking while perhaps playing cards around the table...

"Yeah! You'll kill each other because you love each other so much!" he said hoping to relieve the tension which was not really tension.

Federico kept muttering profanities all the while fixing me like a butterfly pinned to the wall with his eyeballs. But I loved the game and seemed to be just as good at it. I stared back. Easily. No tension. We pumped ourselves out through our eyeballs. We drank each other through our eyeballs.

Then we smiled at each other. The game was suddenly over and the two of them began trying to convince me to come live with them at their mine.

"We don't mess around with panning gold out of rivers or nothin' like that. We go right into the earth and yank out the pure stuff." And they opened their wallets again and showed me all their 100-peso bills.

Before long Federico had managed to pass clean out sitting right there in his chair and Estevan and I went about the business of drinking some more beer and getting down to more serious conversation. He told me he could feel the whole world around him and everything that happened in it from the innermost part of his heart and I believed him. I believed his words exactly as he said them.

I told him I had a friend back in the States who thinks I came down to South America to mingle with the Indians in order to be like a god in their midst. Estevan looked at me with incredulity. He shook his head. The reason I came to South America was obvious to both of us. I simply wanted to be with people who had not lost touch with the innermost parts of themselves.

"That's the way it is," Estevan told me. We were holding hands. Our eyes were only inches apart. There was no chance for deception to enter between us. What was inside of Estevan was passing out of his eyes and into my soul, effortlessly... naturally... just as a wind passes through a valley.

"Your friend should accuse you of coming to be amongst the Indians of South America in order to steal the secrets of truthfulness! And so," concluded Estevan, "since we're all going to be blown to nothing by the great cataclysm in just a few more years, there is nothing left to do but live out the rest of our lives, every day trying to love more fully..."

And so I went on my way -- which wasn't entirely easy to do -- and finally found myself a secluded writing place in another cafe. It was time to take a piss. I found a bathroom with pictures on the walls of people sucking cocks. A waiter opened the door, saw me hanging my cock over the urinal, and he decided to use the neighboring commode rather than wait. I listened to him piss. He pissed quickly, in a hurry. I stood staring at the wall in front of me and listened to my own piss slowly, relaxedly, draining from my cock, not in spurts, just draining. Finally I looked down and saw that it was just the water running in the urinal that I had been listening to. I must have quit pissing long ago. I wondered if I had still been pissing when the waiter had looked in through the door...? How long had I been standing there holding my cock over the urinal like that? It seemed Estevan and Federico had managed to get me pretty drunk...

Disaster with the Ladies of the Night

The next day Graham told me "Thanks for bringing me down here!" I appreciated hearing that. He had been engaged in a deep conversation with Spectra which was helping him put all our experiences into place.

Pastor had fallen in love with Sue... but there was no real future in that...

Spectra and Sue spent an afternoon visiting Franz, a German communist, in his apartment. They came back to our group excited about that adventure. Revolution, it seemed, was in the air.

By the end of the decade the Maoist Shining Path, '*Sendero Luminoso*,' movement would plunge Peru into a long struggle. It would become too dangerous to try and visit Sina or other vast regions of surrounding countryside for many years.

Chris and Graham decided that they were tired of being horny... that they would enjoy a few hours of pleasant caresses with the fair sex...

Pastor knew just where to take them. I wanted to go along just to see the faces on these seventeen-year-old friends of mine as they emerged from the depths of ecstasy... so up the hill we trundled ourselves, to the house of the ladies of the night.

"Aren't you going to come in with us?" they asked me.

I told them the truth... that I had been thinking a lot about the other women in my life and that I would just be coming along for the ride... to wait outside...

"Are you going to come in with us?" they asked Pastor.

"I don't know yet," he replied, "I'll have to wait and see..."

Pastor decided to join them so the three of them went inside. I waited out on the hillside in the dark. Dozens of other young men were arriving, climbing up the hill on foot and entering the door. After a while I started to see some of these same young men coming back out, whistling little tunes and lighting up cigarettes...

I greeted them as they came outside and wondered where my friends were... "They've been in there for over an hour!"

"They're about to come out," some guy informed me, "they got delayed because they didn't have the right size bills with them and it was hard to find change..."

I smiled at him in understanding and sat down to wait some more. I began to feel embarrassed for not having gone in with them, anticipating the rapturous accounts with which they would no doubt emerge about their hours spent bathing in the warm gardens of delight while I sat out in the cold...

"Tell them not to go in there!" I at last heard Graham's voice admonishing Pastor to warn some newcomer... "Such a lousy deal! What a waste!" I heard him exclaim.

"Oh oh!" I thought. And sure enough: it had been a disaster. Neither Graham nor Chris had been able to get it up in the wham-bam atmosphere of the 'run-'em-right-on-through' -- 'service-'em-and-get-'em-out' atmosphere of this mass production house where the ladies wouldn't even take their shirts off...

Pastor, who had finally decided to enter, admitted that he had been similarly uninspired and hadn't managed to raise a really healthy hard-on either... but at last he had managed to pump away until he had finished. But neither Chris nor Graham had gotten to the point where coming was possible, so here they were, bloated with unspent sperm and nursing bitter hearts. It had all come to naught...

So the four of us shuffled dejectedly back down the hillside with our hands in our pockets grumbling and muttering.

"My image of myself is shattered," moaned Chris, "the idea that such a catastrophe could befall me had never even occurred to me!" he wailed...

"Well, I've had it happen to me," I confided consolingly and laughed... But my laughter danced out into the night and evaporated amongst the stars... largely missing its human targets...

These Miraculous Little Visits

It was time to head back to Peru from La Paz. There was, of

course, confusion at the border: how could we have gotten into Bolivia without any entry stamps in our passports? We didn't know. There must have been some mistake made by the border police. Eventually the officials shook their heads in bewilderment and went ahead and checked us through.

We stopped in Puno to visit Cristobal CCori's wife, Faustina, and their kids. Mostly daughters, they were, and I spent the whole afternoon with them... again... just as I had a year earlier. Grimanesa, Nemia, Florinda, Vila... then Dimas, the eldest son. Thirteen, eleven, nine, seven and five... something like that. I loved their eyes and faces and the way they crawled around me as if I were a circus come to town...

Our festivities went as they had in years before... They handed me the guitar and stood on the stairs and tables and chairs and told me to sing this song and then that one and they hung on my arms and shoulders and teased me with their eyes... all high-speed heavy-duty competition to see which one of them could persuade me to do what she wanted. Everywhere I looked I was met by a pair of shining little black eyes just chock full of secrets... and if I could get away with being a big funny-looking kid for long enough... well who knows how many secrets they might let me in on?

The oldest two now, though, were getting a little mature for this sort of thing. Grimanesa at thirteen and Nemia at eleven were beginning to suspect that there was more to this climbing-around-all-over-each-other business than meets the eye... They were starting to reach that turning-in-of-the-self which comes at that age with little girls. So they were a bit more coy, reserved, yes, and they didn't quite have the freedom to climb and crawl and flirt that the younger ones still had. I asked about Reinaldo... He had succumbed to the meningitis and was no longer with us.

Just how many more years these miraculous little visits could happen I didn't know...?

But always somewhere in us would be buried, even after they were grown and married, the memories of what it was like to sing immersed in little hints of fire and magic.

At the post office I picked up three letters from that sweet and evil Greek woman whom I had left behind in Boulder, Colorado. She was still feeling a love attraction for our friend, but said she hoped to have figured out how to quit that fantasy by the time I got back. That was enough for me. She had suddenly filled me and surrounded me there in Puno, Peru. My heart took grand swings and leaps and I went into a total love-letter writing trance.

I was lured hopelessly back on the beam of some light of possible and impossible dreams... of setting up life once and for all in the villages and raising children and making guitars... of living in Mexico and dancing to waltzes... of returning to Colorado at times to sell guitars and bring good Mexican energy...

I dreamed of Leda and me in Mexico... "Let's go to Mexico..." I wrote to her...

Five hideous devil's masks were staring down at me from the wall of the cafe where I was writing. Snakes crawled on their faces, some had horns; blue beards; their eyes were wide open, staring and blue... One had a black face with a hideous bulging purple tongue... oriental temple art again. Only this time it was Peruvian cafe art... *'Diablos'*...

Surrounded by warm black eyes, surrounded by the capacity to feel into the middle of another man's stomach here in the land where touching was the way of knowing... and blessed with a heart which could feel, I was afloat in paradise. I would feel everything around me until I might touch ground once again. I did not want to touch ground... I preferred to float and freely feel the emptiness in the air around me; the fullness of the warm world inside me...

Sending those two letters off to Leda was like sending two birds off into the night. I refrained from making copies of them in the same way I would refrain from putting little green birds in cages...

We were under the impression that Cristobal was busy teaching on his island and that now would be a great time to visit. Spectra and Sue needed a break from the boys and announced that they would travel on their own and see us back in Lima. Hanging out with Franz in La Paz had given them confidence that they could create adventures on their own.

Sailing to the Island of Taquile

The harbor by the town of Puno on Lake Titicaca was calm. Only imperceptible breezes drifted past us. Sometimes the voyage could take more than a day if the wind never came up. If the wind were high it seems that boats had been known to make it in two-and-a-half hours... It didn't seem very likely that we would be getting there in any two-and-a-half hours that night; the Indians who ran the boat were going about everything most leisurely. I didn't mind. I was having another one of those conversations about the physical nature of the universe with Chris and Graham and Martin and we were not in a hurry. The 'big bang' theory vs. the 'steady state' theory it was, I believe, that we were discussing...

Jupiter had hung himself with amazing brilliance above the lake and we slipped along with that almost frighteningly ghost-like smoothness that only sailboats in glassy water can have... just enough wind to puff out our sail... and before long we were somewhere out in the middle of our twenty-six mile crossing to the island of Taquile. As the sun went down we got a couple of momentary puffs which goosed us faster along our way. Our nature-of-the-universe conversation evaporated into the vast expanse of the lake.

Chris hammered out a few bars of blues on the guitar and then left it to me to croon a few tunes. The lake seemed to suck the notes right out of my throat, demanding all the while that they be sweet like the water... "Clap clap clap." The dozen or so fellow passengers, all Indians from the island, approved the song and I felt like I had entered the musicians' paradise at last. I was finding the tunes that had the right depth and swing to go with the boat, its gentle load of Inca inhabitants, and the ultramarine turned black underneath us...

But, by god, the wind was coming up and... there was a rushing of water and air which was demanding attention. I stuffed the guitar down into the boat. Not a word was heard from anybody. Yes, by god, the wind was coming up... In fact we were verily hauling-ass across the water and it was pretty chilly up there at twelve-thousand feet. So Chris and I started stuffing ourselves further down into the boat. I was lying next to Martin. I got out my sleeping bag and added it to the general topping. His and my legs stretched damn near all the way across the boat and Pastor had stuffed himself down under one of the seats on the other side. Our bottles of anise and pisco were too much trouble to pass around any more. The boat was dipping and heaving, the spray was flying over the prow and slowly accumulating on our sleeping bags.

Then: Splash! "Oh!" We all groaned like mummies suddenly coming back to life in our coffins. We all sat up. Splash! Another wave poured over the wooden side of the boat.

"Everybody to the high side of the boat!" the Indians started shouting... I translated the message. "Can be very dangerous!" another islander told me. I didn't translate that message. Pastor, of course, understood perfectly, being an Indian himself, but what's worse, not an islander! He huddled further under the seat telling himself to get his shit together inside 'cause it looked like we might all die there. A few more of those big waves and this boat would sink. Boats don't float when they're full of water. And popular wisdom gives a man five minutes to live in that icy lake...

Chris and I sat up on one of the seats, still wrapped in our wet bags. I didn't feel like dying like an ostrich with my head buried in the boat. It was dark as Hades but I could still see the tremendous troughs and crests. We cut across them at about a 45-degree angle. I trusted that the captain back there in the stern knew the best angle. A couple of quick little men had brought in half of our sail so we were not flying quite so fast any more. Every once in a while the timing was off again and our boat-side would bang into the underside of another wave and the water would crash aboard. But we hadn't really gotten all that much water in the boat yet.

Chris was sitting beside me having, I discovered to my astonishment, a great time. He thought this was great fun! Nothing like an exciting sailboat ride! He had a big grin plastered across his seventeen-year-old face and I made no effort to bring him down. If he drowned he might as well be having a great time!

Meanwhile, the island had come into view. After another fifteen or twenty minutes it became apparent that the wind was not building any more; it was in fact abating just a notch or two, and a reasonable man could see at this point that we were probably going to make it. The tiller man changed our angle of approach and, the next thing we knew, we had skimmed right into the arms of the island harbor and quick little men had dropped our -- oh praise the lord mother -- white sail just like the skirt undone from the waist of Aphrodite and let fall in a heap to the floor.

The labor of centuries-old stone-work had produced a magnificent jetty built by these crafty islanders out into the sea just so that on nights like these there would be a calm pool of harbor kissing the sides of our boat as we poled it gently along beside the rocks now fully protected from the wind.

We set about clambering out of the sailboat, lying our selves down on the shore under our wet bags and sleeping the whole nightmare off. It turned out we had made the journey in just two-and-a-half hours.

Island Sunrise

The next thing we knew, of course, the sun was up. We floated ourselves out from under our sleeping bags and began scampering up the island hillside. The age-old trail switchbacked its way up to the high point on the ridge some five-hundred-feet above lake level and from there on top we could see that, "Oh, everybody lives on the other side of the island!" ...which was a more gentle incline with houses scattered here and there: one had a painted pink roof with bright green windows. Intricate patterns of centuries-old stone fencing delineated precious property boundaries separating one agricultural project from the next. We paused on the summit with a few of the islanders to wait for Martin who had been smitten by a cold and was moving slowly.

"You won't find any dogs on the island," one of the islanders who had accompanied us from the boat mentioned to us. "We prefer our peace and tranquility." I passed this piece of information on to Chris and Graham. "Nor will you find any policemen nor any jail here, for just as we have no need of watchdogs, we have no need of police or jails."

I also passed this information on to Chris and Graham but it was not clear that their seventeen-year-old interests were in tune with the values implied by the islander's statement. I was eager to believe that I had found some shred of paradise there draped across the top of this giant high-altitude lake in the heart of the sleeping Inca empire but I seemed to be alone for the moment with my enthusiasm. Even Pastor remained unimpressed, as he was in the middle of a bout of joking with Graham about who was more stupid between the two of them. So my idealistic news got launched into the air and flew off like a bird.

Soon we were settled in one of the rooms in the schoolhouse where Cristobal worked. But, unfortunately, due to the Festival of St. Santiago, which had provided all of the teachers with a week to spend on the mainland, we were alone in our room in the schoolhouse. Cristobal was not there! He was now with his wife and children whom we had just seen and so we were on our own.

Walking up toward the high point at the west end of the island I encountered three lads wandering about knitting hats: the famous Taquile hats which bring the islanders an income a cut above that of the ordinary agriculturalist Indians and they were amused to discover that I was possessed by some minor capacity for speaking their

Inca language. I refrained from breaking down and collapsing back into Spanish so that my own facility for speaking Inca might grow as rapidly as possible and besides... these young Indians wouldn't feel comfortable speaking Spanish anyway... So I told them where I was from, where I had been... and, for the geographic aspects of the description, we ascended to the highpoint on the ridge from where I could point out what I thought was the mountain Martin and I had recently climbed about a-hundred-and-fifty miles to the north.

And I explained more or less why I was there: that I had compadres and godchildren in the village on the other side of that mountain and so I was always coming back to see them and that the school teacher, whom they didn't know since they were already too old for that sort of business yet too young to have little ones of their own under Cristobal's tutelage, was a friend of mine from earlier years and that somewhere in that tangle of information could be found the reasons why I had come to visit... And they began with the usual questions which had to do with the relative values of shoes and labor in different parts of the world. My large feet were the objects of admiration as usual. And after an hour of such casual chat I went on my way happy with having made these new acquaintances.

The women I passed on the trails were keeping their faces covered with black veils. They allowed only one eye to be seen. They didn't yet know who I was and chose to remain protected. Cristobal had told me that they never marry nor develop romances with 'foreigners' who were not born on the island. He had no girlfriends on the island, even after a year. They called him the 'raggedy maestro' because his blood-lines were not pure Taquile Inca.

Back in the schoolhouse we cooked up a pot of stew and broke out our anise, our pisco, a bottle of rum it turned out Graham had saved for the occasion, and the rest of our cocaine and coca leaves. I set about re-twisting my soggy guitar back into shape and re-fastening parts of it with a bottle of glue...

A Translator's Paradise

Before we finally closed our eyes at about 4:00 AM, we had been pressure-cooked by that lonely little schoolroom into finishing off every drop and sniff of the aforementioned drinks and leaves and powders. What came out of that evening was a new dimension of knowledge about each other. Until that night, due to the pressure of everybody's wants and needs, we had been forced to content ourselves with incomplete translations. That night, however, for the first time, we spoke and then translated -- word for word for word -- it was a translator's paradise and all the years I had invested in learning Spanish and Quechua were rewarded. I found that my mind was a formidable machine: put one language in through my ears and the other came out through my mouth. No delay.

There was even a new depth which came from these translations as the story-tellers got to see the effects of their words twice, nay, thrice! And... of course there was the guitar which kept pumping out music from time to time in either my or Chris's hands... And we had heavy-duty beverages which made it absolutely certain that our crescendo of truth would be followed faithfully to the end of Chris' and Grahams' seventeen-year-old energy and that not a shred of that truth should escape the flimsy confines of that poor little schoolhouse... And all night long in the distance we heard occasional flashes of flutes and drums being warmed up by the islanders for the coming Festival of St. Santiago. Martin, unfortunately, missed out on most of this, as his cold had overwhelmed him and relegated him to the misery of semi-sleep in the corner of the room.

Most of these tales had originated from Pastor. He told us about Carmela, the one true love of his twenty-six-year-old life. It seems that he had been smitten by this lovely young lady in Arequipa some seven years ago when he was nineteen and she had been twenty-two. But she was his boss's daughter, unfortunately. The terrible throes of desire they felt for each other were countered by her father's disapproval. The owner of a business in Arequipa didn't want his daughter to marry a poor Indian from some village in the highlands. Pastor made absolutely certain never to come inside her and run the risk of making her pregnant. But the father had the means to send her clean out of the city and plant her firmly in a school for young ladies in Lima. She had told Pastor before she left that she would be willing to escape with him to Bolivia.

"I wish to hell I'd done that," he said, "but I was young then and afraid that the police would come and get us. But you know I've never been able to quite fall in love with anyone since then. Green eyes, she had. Her father told me he wasn't displeased with my work; that I could stay there and work as long as I liked; that he in fact wanted me to stay because I knew things which it would take a long time for someone else to learn. But I just cried. For fifteen days I lay in my room and cried. I didn't eat and I didn't work. Then I came back to my village. Don't lose your Greek woman," he suddenly advised me, "she's a good one..."

Pastor had been making love with a girl from a little settlement about four hours walk down the valley below Sina for the last year now. "But one of us must be sterile; I hope it's not me! A whole year of sleeping together and we haven't come up with anything... I want to have at least one or two children. For what will I work if I have no children? But she doesn't even know a word of Spanish. It would be hard for her to ever even leave the valley and live in a larger town if we ever had children who needed to go to school. I hope it's her and not me who is sterile," and he looked at me wondering if any of my amazing USA technological wisdom had any answers for his question. But I didn't know.

The first time he ever made love, it seems, he was twelve. His fifteen-year-old cousin had seduced him -- rubbed her legs on him and before he knew it, something was happening. That was before he had even discovered the art of masturbation. And then there was another girl who used to come to clean up his family's house to whom he, his older brother and his uncle all three used to make love. "That was when my father was still alive. Sometimes I feel that you are like a father for me," he told me as a complementary aside, "but she got pregnant. We were all thoroughly confused. We had no idea which one of the three of us was the father! But the child died within a week after it was born..."

Pastor had been obliged to spend fifty days in jail a couple of years earlier and another forty days a year or so after that for having being accused by one young lady from his village as being the father of her child. "But the child does not look like me," he said. "It's apparently stupid and I know of at least two other guys who are equally good candidates for being the kid's father. But Peruvian judges just listen to the woman. The woman says that so-and-so is the father and bang: court order for his arrest. If you don't have the money to pay for the child, it's jail. And the worst aspect of that situation is that there is no end in sight. She may continue to make demands and I may end up in jail again. So far I haven't given her a penny. If she doesn't quit hassling me, I may have to steal the kid from her some day while she's working in the potato fields and give it either to my sister or to my girlfriend down the valley to raise..."

Pastor told of discovering two girls making out with each other in the courtyard of a house above Sina. He watched for a bit through the bushes, jumped into the yard, found himself in a sexy wrestling match, and made love to both of them.

Another time Pastor was walking along one day and noticed a girl gently rocking herself back and forth over her hand which was under her dress. "I watched her for a while, and when I was pretty sure something was going on, I went over and quickly lifted her skirt. You know what the had under there? A hard green peeled banana!"

Our Tales Turned Toward the Spooky

Eventually as the night grew later and candle after candle consumed itself, our tales turned toward the spooky, the mysterious, and the magical. Pastor told us about a time when he had gone to a certain mine in which his older brother had once worked. Pastor was considering following in his brother's footsteps and finding out what it was like to work underground to make money. But a late afternoon thunderstorm overtook him along the way.

"Lightening was flashing and hitting the ridge close to where I was and as it got dark I discovered a little cave into which I crawled and sat. It was cold and I was wet and miserable in there shivering, but then Bump! Bump! Something was pushing up on me from the ground below. I could feel nothing but rock with my hands but as soon as I thought it had gone away... whatever it was... there it would come again... Bump! Bump! My ambition to work in that mine ended right there. I spirited myself out of that hole and headed back home that same night.

"One time three friends and I lifted up a rock and discovered a dead woman with a dead child in her arms. Later we went back to look at her again but someone had dug her up and she was gone. We thought maybe there had been some treasure buried underneath her but who knows.

"Once I did find a small treasure: a little silver bracelet I found by digging with my hands in a spot which had many rumors associated with it. "I tried to dig further but the spot was too powerful for me. I would approach the bottom of the hole with my hands and they would be seized by fits of shaking. It was as if an invisible wall had suddenly appeared in the hole. No matter what I did I couldn't get my hands back into the hole to continue digging. But I still have the bracelet."

Then Chris added a story from sunny mysterious California. It seems that at the ripe old age of fifteen he and some of his friends engaged themselves in the arts of the seance and that some few times they did succeed in raising a few ghosts. Dinner plates and ashtrays all flew about the room. "I don't have any doubts about ghosts," he proclaimed with a big smile on his face.

The next day the sun woke me up only three hours after we finally had gone to sleep and I found myself still swirling stone-staggering drunk, weak as a kitten, and with a head throbbing from the booze and cocaine which appeared to have invaded my right sinus. I was so weak I felt I could barely breathe. The day passed and the sun was disappearing once again in the west before the unfolding Festival of Saint Santiago could re-claim my attention.

The official start of the festival was delayed for one day because the emissaries of the European race, an Italian priest with two younger aspirants, a Belgian and a Peruvian from Lima, were all a day late. But now that he was here the islanders were strutting out in full form, each clan, or extended family had their own style. Some wore a curtain of beads over their faces from which protruded long deep bass flutes; another family pranced along with little tiny side-blown piccolo flutes peeping and piping up a storm! Then it was oompah oompah time with a family full of trumpets and French horns drowning everyone else out. Each group in turn took a parade around the church courtyard while the elderly men sat and nodded and winked approvingly at each other, ceremonially imbibing alcohol and coca leaves which the young aspirants of the cloth from Europe and Lima found to be quaint when viewed from a distance but just a bit too pagan and repulsive to accept when proffered toward their own holy tongues... "Well, I'll try just one coca leaf," the young Peruvian aspirant from Lima agreed. And he placed it in his mouth the way a cautiously curious man might eat a mysterious mushroom.

Later in the afternoon a Peruvian navy motorboat putted up to the harbor and found the three Catholics and... Chris and Graham and Pastor all willing and ready to leave the island forever, if necessary. There was something frighteningly claustrophobic about being on an island unless, I suppose, you had your own personal pea-pod to float back home in. So before long I was sitting high on the rocky ridge with Martin watching the smoky motorboat roar across the water toward the mainland.

Now it was just me and Martin and a thousand islanders having a tremendous fiesta. Martin was still too sick to walk very far, so I wandered toward the east end of the island. Along the way I sat and talked with a twelve-year-old boy who was shepherding his goats. He informed me that if I was smart I would take a different boat back to the mainland on Saturday because the San Antonio had a hole somewhere in its bottom plugged with rags. I secretly begged fate to be kind to me and not sink me at the ripe young age of twenty-nine.

The flutes and trumpets and drums echoed off the sky above the high rocky backbone of the island where I was walking. The festival music filled the air and it reached an overwhelming fervor after three days of warm-up.

A friendly little man stopped by and officially invited us to the festival. Somewhere in the conversation he told me that he was ninety years old. I had taken him to be around forty.

Feeling more welcome at last, I walked into the heart of the festival and sat and chewed coca leaves and spoke in Quechua with the old men. We ridiculed the now-departed Catholic priest and aspirants. I now had learned some names and knew that I had been given the keys to friendship with the islanders.

But it would be such a long project to reach the point of feeling at home the way I felt in Sina. It seemed overwhelming and I felt that I didn't really want to meet anyone else. Night fell and I didn't go out.

Martin and I washed the dishes and cleaned up the school room. When Saturday came we climbed back onto the San Antonio and sailed tranquilly back to Puno. Sometimes we added speed by rowing: three oars on each side of the boat. We nibbled on shared offerings of tiny fish, potatoes, coca leaves and bread. The crossing took its usual seven hours.

Labyrinths of Lima

Arriving back on the mainland I could feel the sudden shift back into the 'more civilized' world of locked doors, light bulbs, vendors, competing energies...

We parted company with Pastor who would now head back to Sina. Chris, Graham, Martin and I descended to Arequipa. We befriended a group of young artisans on the street and they took us home to their workshop. A pot of San Pedro, a hallucinogenic cactus, was boiling on the stove. Their magic hands stayed busy making leather goods, paintings, jewelry and rock carvings. It kind of felt like my guitar-making shop.

Outside their shop was a little garden: a river, trees, a little white bridge which gleamed in the moonlight. For those with no fear in their hearts, they explained, a headless woman dressed in white would come. Long hair and bare feet were necessary for increased telepathic sensitivity. They gave us a list of practices: one must know how to believe, to wait, to listen, to pay attention, to work, to see beauty, to make love, to give, to take, to learn... The trees, they explained, were places where souls hang out... good places to pick up the vibrations..

> *I was thinking about making a mermaid-shaped guitar. I was thinking about Leda. Could she fly as fast and far as I? Could I fly as fast and far as she? It was time to go and see! The life you build may be your own! Knowing how to live and sing in the street seemed very important to me. We lose track of ourselves when we stay inside for too long! Yes, I must continue to speak my mind in the street! ...to speak my soul in the street! I must collect more brothers and sisters to play music so that Leda can dance in the street!*

Soon we were back in Lima. I received another letter from Leda. She had received my last two letters and felt ready to move forward with our destiny together!

I was feeling good. I was every man's brother. I walked through the streets of the city feeling happy that I was six-and-a-half feet tall because I felt bigger now!

I stopped in front of a vendor selling beautiful oil paintings on the sidewalk. He was not the artist who painted them. He was just selling them. I taught him how to say, "You are welcome to just look!" in English to the passing gringos.

I watched a man selling boxes of snakes from the jungle. He stood in the University Park and described the sex life of the jungle Indians with a great anaconda draped across his shoulders. "The jungle people get into sex all of the time. The man comes back from the hunt and what does he do? Kiss kiss kiss, eating his woman all the time -- his woman will have up to seventeen children! The rich city man, on the other hand, has two beds, one for him and one for his woman and they get it on once a week, once every two weeks or perhaps once a month..."

I spent the day dancing down the sidewalks of Lima drawing delicious glances from the eyes of the beautiful women... playing with the loose fire in the eyes of all the girls... young and old alike.

And underneath the buoyancy of my street dance was the swelling excitement within me because before long I would be drinking once again from the eyes of my beautiful Greek woman. I let the señoritas in the streets of Lima drink some of this excitement from my eyes, but I secretly hoped to save that excitement for Leda herself.

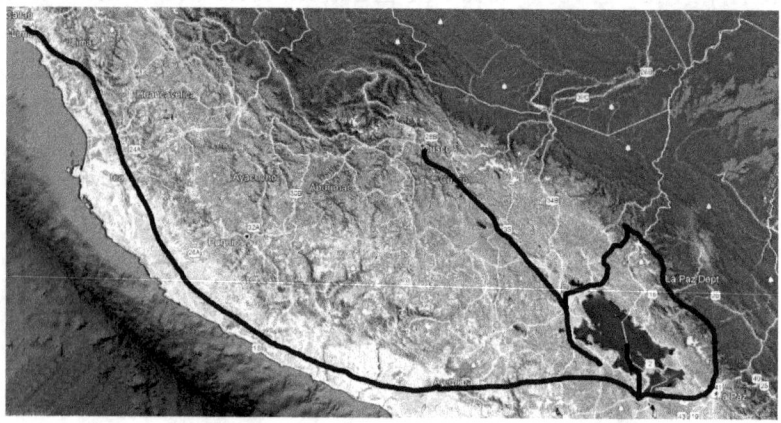

1973 Routes Through Peru and Bolivia

Tito Again - by Chance

Then, quite by chance, we could say, came about a meeting in the center of that city of several millions of people, with Tito. If I had known how much of my energy was fated to be consumed by his apparently bottomless belly during the next three days, I'm not sure I would have been particularly happy to see him. But how was I to know? And how could I be anything but excited to encounter the fellow with whom I had hitch-hiked steadily for four days through Ecuador and Colombia almost five years ago? It was to Tito that I owed much of my vocabulary in Spanish; he and I had surmounted many a language barrier together during those four days of almost incessant conversation and he was perhaps the first Peruvian with whom I had succeeded in sincerely discussing affairs of the heart and of the mystic.

So we greedily rushed into each other's arms there on the street. I asked him if he had time to drink a beer with me. He was on his way to the post office but said that if we first mailed his package he would have time to catch up on the latest events in our lives over a few beers. Little, of course, did I suspect that instead of having 'a little free time' he had an infinity of time within him... as black and as empty as the depths of the ocean.

We drank our beers and presented each other with accounts of our recent adventures. We wandered the streets some more, but no more tales seemed to be forthcoming. It appeared that we had exhausted our potential and my mind began to return to its earlier contemplations while I expected him at any moment to announce that he was, in fact, busy with such and such an errand and that he must be on his way. I had no way of knowing that I had in fact become like a horse with a rider on its back. After a while he was still with me so it occurred to me to ask him where the largest red light district in Lima was. I told him that I had never visited the Lima district and would be curious to just walk through it, wherever it was, and see how it compared in atmosphere with the amazing riots of music and sexy fun found, for example, in Acapulco.

So for three hours we rode buses and walked through the streets of Callao, which is to Lima what Piraeus is to Athens: the port. And after the sun finally went down we turned into an alley way. I was hoping to find streets full of little establishments, tiny cafes and tiny dance floors, bristling with musicians, but I didn't see any such thing. I was confronted with a giant gray building. It looked like a huge warehouse, low and symmetrical, a cube of crumbling brick. No music.

"Don't they play music around here?" I asked Tito.

"Later on they do," he said.

"You mean this is it?" I asked.

"This is it." My curiosity totally satisfied, I was ready to return to the center of Lima, bid goodbye to my old friend Tito, and pick up life where I had left it off in the early afternoon. So we walked back the way we had come, back out into the streets. Eventually it occurred to me that Tito was thoroughly prepared to spend another three hours walking this way and that just so that we might get back to Lima. "Isn't there a faster way to get there?" I asked.

"Only from the Trocadero, from the red light district," he replied. I felt like asking him why in the world he hadn't said that while we were still there, but it was true that I hadn't directly asked... So we went back to the Trocadero to find a bus to take us directly back to

Lima but things there had livened up a bit. A crowd of about a hundred guys was waiting outside the last one of the gates, a gate as big as the kind you find in railway terminals. The big gate was being unlocked, and the Saturday night was under way.

We walked through the gate. The building was almost as drab on the inside as it was on the outside except for the occasional paintings of nude women on the walls. The building was filled with long corridors. Every so often a ticket booth was erected in the centers of the corridors and vendors sat inside distributing tickets as casually as bridge toll-men sell to motorists wishing to cross the Mississippi river. The tickets were cheap and you needed to have one in order to enter one of the thousands of little cubicles which lined the sides of the corridors. In fact the building was like a vast cell-house block in a prison, or like a beehive. And each girl inhabited a cell and paid high taxes to the state which managed the whole affair. So all you had to do was buy a ticket, find a woman you like, and enter her cubicle. There were hundreds and hundreds to choose from.

The closed doors were the ones which were presumably 'busy.' Some closed doors had lines of two or three men waiting outside like schoolboys waiting for lunch... must be a popular one in there if guys are willing to line up like that. We walked down the corridors. The girls who weren't busy were peeking out of their half-open doors, half revealing themselves, wearing torn bikinis pulled half-way down, pushing a luscious brown hip part way out the door, greeting you with a dark soft eye... all was alluring, all calling to my gut which soon began to feel blue and bulging. But I did not buy a ticket. I had done that enough in the past. Sperm swam through my eyeballs clouding my vision. I walked with my hands in my pockets and held my hard-on down. The halls were lit with blue and red light. No musicians were in evidence but somebody had fired up a few jukeboxes so that there was at least a tune in the air.

"Are you going to get yourself laid?" I asked Tito. As usual his response left me unsure about what he was going to do. He went back down one corridor apparently in hope of finding something. I eventually followed him. We were quite a pair. He was the only long-haired Peruvian in the place and I was the only gringo. One woman standing in her door burst out laughing and said, "watch out for those two!"

The saddest sights were the older women who were standing looking hopeful but also unable to conceal a feeling of pre-destined doom in their eyes... the ones who may stand there half the night and get no business. Some of the ones with lines outside their doors were raving young beauties, the kind who can blow you clean off your feet by just passing you in the street. We had to press through the crowd outside their doors and catch just a glimpse of them as they opened the door for just long enough to let out the last man and let in the next. But I was thinking of the mechanical treatment being doled out behind those doors and I saved my money and my energy and my health... all for my beautiful Greek woman.

So Tito and I went out and got in one of the cars now parked outside by the dozen, running full like buses, redelivering us men back to Lima. And I told Tito that I was tired; that I was going to go to sleep. I loudly and formally bade him goodbye at my hotel and went up to my room. I was hungry. I gave Tito a couple of minutes to get out of sight and I slipped back out onto the street and went and ate half a fried chicken. I was still hungry after that so I went to a cheap Chinese restaurant and was busy guzzling some wonton soup when I looked up and who had his face stuck through the door of the restaurant? Tito!

"I came back to your hotel but you weren't in your room," he explained.

"Sit down!" I told him, mustering up some genuine enthusiasm. "I'll buy you some soup!"

So we ate soup together.

Eventually he told me that he came back so that we could go out together for the rest of the night, eat some hallucinogenic San Pedro cactus together, and find two young ladies to keep ourselves company with...

"Look," I told him, "I'm tired tonight and I can't do it. I feel like I'm starting to catch a cold and I just don't have the energy. Let me get a good night's sleep and we'll do all that tomorrow. I promise. Come at 10:00 AM and I'll have the energy, but right now any search of ours is doomed to failure because of the way I feel!" I repeated this speech two or three times and at last we parted once again in front of my hotel. He reluctantly wandered off down the street and I went up to sleep.

Magic Piles of Lettuce

The next morning he was an hour and a half late. But he arrived, ceremoniously pulled a giant cactus out of a bag, gave it to me, announced that he was going to the planetarium for the afternoon and said nothing further about our meeting. I told him I would come by his house later in the afternoon; that I was feeling good, rested, refreshed, happy and ready for adventures.

I put the cactus in my bag and lugged it across the street to my room. It was exactly like the kind of cactus I had bought just a few days ago from a street vendor of herbal remedies, only to be informed by a coca leaf vendor that it was not the *real* San Pedro, that this type of cactus is in fact of value only for infections of the liver...

I showed the cactus to Chris who immediately cut off big chunks and devoured them greedily. "The least we can do is to try it," he exclaimed. So I followed suit and ate an egg-sized piece. But nothing happened. It didn't even taste bitter like peyote or like the San Pedro I had tasted in Arequipa.

But soon the door opened and in walked another new-found friend of Chris's: a Canadian named Guy who looked exactly like myself! He and I were both astounded but we made no particular mention of our physical similarity and proceeded to play music on three guitars after smoking a joint of genuine Colombian weed.

The only difference between me and this guy, literally this 'Guy', was that our lives had given us different experiences. It began to unravel that I was the optimist and he was the pessimist. That is, that I was his optimistic side, a discovery of which I immediately took advantage in order to cheer the fellow up, and he, of course reciprocated by manifesting himself in his true miserable glory, as none other than my pessimistic nature personified.

For three hours we entered a space of at least three-and-a-half dimensions wherein years of experience flowed through our fingers, minds, and souls like the eruptions of volcanoes beneath the surface of the Pacific ocean, a state of affairs which soon left Chris to seek his own devices for self-diversion and us to go finish our eruptions in the nearest beer-drinking establishment: a room with sawdust on the floor, little tables and little chairs, no food, no women, just men talking...

Even Guy was surprised at my optimism when I announced shortly after sundown that I would in fact go pursue my fate with

Tito that very night... that doing so was my desire. So Guy and I bade each other calmly goodbye, saying nothing about seeing each other in the future, only that it would be nice to read each others' writings, but making no provision for such an exchange, being content with allowing fate to either bring our paths to cross once again... or not...

I streaked out through the night and down the streets of Lima, trusting the dim associations of years past to bring me to Tito's house. I gave away one of my two cacti to a group of jubilant youths whom I encountered eating bread outside their local delicatessen and found my way directly to Tito's door with the other cactus in my bag slung over my shoulder.

His older brother's wife was watching TV in the front room, it seemed, and did not care to disturb herself in order to make of us a merry three-some, so now it was me and Tito once again, hanging out in the kitchen of his house, without much to say to each other. After half an hour of not-much-happening I swilled down a full glass of San Pedro tea he had saved in his icebox from some previous occasion and we set off into the night. Still nothing was happening from the cactus. Maybe my liver was getting cured. I didn't know.

It was, in fact, a Sunday night. I had the energy and enjoyed the streets and the party some students could be seen having, dancing in their living room. I waited to see if Tito wanted us to go in and join them. If he did, I was ready to dance or talk or cavort about. But Tito seemed the slow one on this night. We walked through a carnival. All of the merry-go-rounds and Ferris wheels were shut up for the night and only a few girls were still selling goodies to eat from little carnival cafes. Girls? One of them had given me her smile. I was honored and I took a seat. Tito had hesitated but I smiled for him to sit down for a bit. Which he did. Wordlessly.

I ordered something of whatever it was she had to sell. Two female friends were there with her. Three girls in all. The blue smoke was in my belly and I talked and joked with Anna, it turned out her name was, until her legs were bouncing up and down with some kind of excitement and she was sitting on her hands, grinning coyly at me. I liked her. She had no problem with flirting.

I walked down the street still dancing inside. If I were to be in Lima for a while I could come visit her often... I was thinking...

Tito and I took a long walk out through the southern barriadas of the city. We passed hills which were covered with thousands of sleeping people covered with myriads of woven mats, wooden poles and hastily shoveled hillsides.

If you enter the labyrinth at the bottom of one of those hills you may be years wandering your way to the top and no one knows if you will ever re-emerge... not if you get involved in conversations along the way.

We did not attempt to enter such a labyrinth. We spent the long early morning hours walking the major streets which divide these hills and which were the pathways for the arteries of food supplies which flow in and out of the city.

By 3:30 AM we had touched ground back in the Mercado Mayorista where the magic piles of lettuce and cucumbers were reaching toward the sky while slumbering under the mists of the Lima night. Soon it would be Monday. It already was Monday but soon it would be Monday morning and another week of life would begin. But not yet. This was the hour of silence and we had only a few places to choose from for coffee.

We sat ourselves silently down on the stools before the rickety blue shack of an African Peruvian... a black man dishing out the coffee and the eats... and all around him were gathered the night people. A little clan of a dozen little Indian men and women were hanging out there in their particular corner of the market place and the black man's laughter was emerging gleefully from his throat and was heard all the way around the world... clean back to Africa and to the shadowy reaches of northern Siberia...

Tito and I were as tranquil as ghosts. We spent half an hour drinking our coffee and watching the night people chuckle and tease each other as they told each other of their latest adventures. They were the chosen ones, the ones who were awake and smiling, yet their laughter did not fly through the open air as it does in the mountains. The city slept around them and held them in her giant warm hand; their tiny laughs were muffled by the sleeping giant who would wake up all-too-soon and erupt with roars of buses and scrambles of arms and legs. The waking city of millions of people would blast these night people apart once again.

And there sat Tito and I, warm inside, calmly watching and listening. But we made not the slightest ripple in the sacred silence as we got up to pay and leave. The night people flashed us just the trace of a smile as we went on our way. Now, agreed Tito, we should each go home to bed.

She Allowed Herself to be Led Out

The next morning, Monday morning, I was up early. In only twenty-four hours the great silver bird would whisk us northward toward Miami... and I had business to do. Black market business. Little did I realize that I was taking advantage of a black market which had grown to such astounding proportions because thousands of people were about to be slaughtered in Chile! I wouldn't understand that until four months later!

If I had understood at that time that I could make a quick hundred bucks in Lima only because that terrible pressure, I would have elected to keep myself clean and honest and refrained from doing it, just as I was refraining from getting quickly rich by importing cocaine to the US. The contents of a little plastic bag placed between the toes inside the socks in my shoes as I might ride the airplane could suffice to provide the equivalent of what I was making in half a year. But I had decided that I was a guitar-maker and a leader-of-trips to the mountains of Peru and that I would be proud to live off of the money I could win by pursuing those, my chosen professions. 'Keep my karma clean,' I had decided. But I had also decided that the black market in Peru was a clean-karma affair; that my dollars would be better spent by their purchasers in the black market than by the government's bankers.

All I had to do was to sell dollars to a black market dealer on the street. I would stand to increase my cash by close to fifty per cent. The only potential difficulty would come when it was time to sell large quantities of soles back to the bank for dollars, but I had collected bank receipts made out in my name for months which testified that I had changed well over seven hundred dollars into soles, and it would not be unreasonable for me to claim that I had a large number of them left unspent. As long as I possessed the receipts I felt certain of being able to change my Peruvian money back into dollars.

Ducking back into my hotel room for a moment to look up some words in my dictionary, I found Spectra, Sue, Chris and Graham all engaged in conversation. I lay down on one of the beds to listen.

Then there was someone at the door. A thin young Peruvian woman came in. She had the air of someone who was slightly mad. She was not in the least concerned about the formal structures of things. In other words questions about why she had come into the room with us right now were not relevant for her. She seemed to find us beautiful.

There was a liquid warmth in her eyes which could have been tears buried deep down in her throat. There was something pleading about her voice which wanted to be taken care of but it wasn't clear that she really expected to be taken care of... or to be given money or housed or clothed... She was somehow like a little girl who was lost but still playing, still searching for her fellow playmates who had somehow accidentally also gotten lost... who knows what had become of them? Perhaps we were they?

The mud stains caked along the sides of her young ankles didn't bother her... she was not worried about them or even aware of them. She was sitting beside me on my bed and I was talking to her in soothing tones because I didn't feel that I wanted her to go away... in fact that confounded blue smoke was filling my belly once again. She was starting to feel it and her eyes had grown just a little bit wider, just a little bit wetter, her mouth was just a little bit more opened... and I swear that if it hadn't been for all those other people in the room, who were now starting to fidget just a little nervously as they realized that this girl's attention and my attention no longer included them, I would have broken my hopes for saving all that smoke for my beautiful Greek woman and let it spill into this strangely yearning young Peruvian girl...

But Fate intervened in the form of one of the employees of the hotel who happened along at that moment. He asked the girl why she had come in off the street and led her back out as quickly as she had come in... She allowed herself to be led out with a silent protest in her eyes... Just as she was thinking she might have found her lost playmates again at last, the merciless father came to demolish her dreams just as he had done yesterday and the day before... in fact that was what he always came to do... it had gotten to the point where she expected someone to come and shatter her world and she let herself be led off by the hand silently. Only through her eyes shone a kind of ageless terror,... and I could have burst into tears... except that I had a room full of people with me, and I wasn't at all sure that what I was inevitably going to want to do with that little girl was in any way what should be done with that little girl... I was simultaneously angry and thankful to the hotel employee who had done his duty so offhandedly...

His Eyes Shone Warm Sickness and Hate

Still entangled in lingering swirls of blue smoke, I took to the streets once again. The buildings, the buses, the magazine stands, the foods and trinkets swirled past the edges of my vision in triumphant parades of motion and color. I stopped by a bank and showed them my receipts. "No problem," they assured me. "You can change Peruvian soles back into dollars with those receipts." I headed back to the hotel.

Chris and Graham had their eyes on a greater bonanza: cocaine. Their dealer friend arrived to our hotel room looking frenzied like a canary fresh out of a bath in the arctic ocean!

"Shhh!" he said, "we must talk very softly! They just arrested my best friend! He will be in jail for years! I'm giving away every gram of cocaine I own as fast as I can!"

Chris and Graham invited him to unload as much of the unwanted burden as he wished on them right there and then, which he did. "Where can I get the best black market price for my dollars?" I asked him.

"I would come with you," he said, "but I'd best not even be seen on the streets for some time to come. But just go to the doormen of the Hotel Bolivar, the fanciest hotel in town, and they'll give you a good rate. They have connections with the Chilean market where a dollar is worth twice as much!"

In a few minutes I was conversing under my breath with a likely-looking doorman. After a phone call and a short wait, a gentleman showed up who looked, I was disappointed to discover, like a wheeling-dealing Texan instead of a romantic revolutionary. But at this point business was business. Twenty fingers hastily counted sheafs of bills. A mutual nod of acknowledgment and we were gone. My shirt pocket bulged with soles. I had very few dollars left. I was out on the limb now, for sure.

I headed for a branch of the national bank which was still open. They told me that I must go to their airport branch of the bank. I went there. They told me I couldn't change my money until an hour before my plane actually would leave. I protested and fluttered my wings but nothing was to be done about it now. I must carry the cursed currency in my breast pocket until the very last minute.

I didn't like it. There was some kind of buzzer sounding in the hollow regions of my being and the thoughts and songs that were usually free to come and go were magnetized into the dreadful racket and I was left with empty noisy space inside my head.

Back at my hotel I watched the minutes and the hours slowly marching past. In fifteen hours our plane would leave and I would be free of this frightening cabbage. I hoped night would come soon so that I could sleep through most of those fifteen hours, get up at 4:30 AM and go through the necessary gymnastics at the airport with a freshly-awakened mind which would have quieted itself through sleep and dreams.

I heard a quiet knock on my door. I opened it and in walked Tito. "Let's go across the street and drink a couple of beers," I suggested. We drank two beers. I didn't feel any better. I had no energy... not even to talk. I tried to and explain why I had no energy. I explained that I had been trying to make money off the black market. I didn't really want to talk about it. But I had nothing else I wanted to talk about either. I wished he would leave. But he didn't.

I told him we should go back across the street to the hotel on the chance that Guy might happen by. "He looks just like me," I explained to Tito, "and if we find him I want to read the things he has written in his journal." I was vaguely hoping that at the prospect of listening to so much English Tito would get bored and leave. No such luck. We went across to the hotel.

The smell of marijuana hit me hard as I walked up the stairs. There was nothing in the least bit subtle about it. That smell was danger hanging in the air in the hallway. 'Don't worry about it,' I told myself. 'We will have good luck and no one will come to...'

We opened the door to our room; Chris and Graham were happily stirring big piles of cocaine received as gifts from their scared friend who was sharing a joint with them and still looking like a frozen canary.

I kept telling myself that no one would come to do whatever they do to people caught in this kind of moment. Tito and I sat down on the bed beside Chris's twitching cocaine friend. Chris and Graham were gloriously happy with their good fortune! Tito and I took the proffered joints and soon we were incredibly stoned! Every emotional vibration became immediately apparent to everyone. The cocaine friend was the most filled with nervous energy. He soon announced in a thin shaky voice that he had to go. He wanted to get out of there. He couldn't think of anything except his busted friend and of years and years in jail. "Bye," we told him. "Good luck."

I looked at Tito. His eyes were open just a little bit wider than usual. "Guy isn't here," I told him, "let's go back across the street and eat something." I wanted to get away from that room. I wanted the smell of the dope to clear out. Chris and Graham said they would come shortly, when Martin got back, they said, to join us across the street and eat. Tito and I left them happily shoveling their piles of white powder around on little mirrors thinking gleefully of all the friends back home in the States they were going to turn on!

I was incredibly stoned. I was cold and shaking with bad energy. Tito and I sat across from each other in the cheap Chinese restaurant. I tried not to shake. For a while our energies slipped past our eyes and flowed freely between us. We were totally available. Every time the slightest feeling streaked through our gray matter it manifested directly to the other through our eyeballs. Tito was still steady. My energy finally broke free. I talked. I laughed. Soon I internally burned up some of that fearful mood and was feeling better. There were a lot of things I could be talking about but I didn't waste my time with most of them. I mentioned the central words and the eyes did the rest.

Chris and Graham and Martin arrived, sat down, ordered vast quantities of food, started gorging themselves, complained about the taste of the soup and, in general, behaved in exactly the way gringos are supposed to behave. Gringos could quite happily sit down to a greasy feed of little roasted brown children. Everybody knew that!

Tito was looking at all of us without saying a word. He was made sick by what he saw. Chris and Graham and Martin didn't know -- they thought Tito was weird -- but they didn't say anything. They just talked, laughed, ate and ignored him.

I explained to Tito: "This is a special night for us. Our last night in Peru. Our last night together after traveling together for two months. Special but sad!"

I told him. But my words were empty. They didn't explain anything. Tito couldn't stop thinking about the level of incredible greed!

And my pocket stuffed full of soles was creating another wave of anxiety. Tito asked me why I hadn't asked him if *he* wanted to buy my dollars...? "I could have gone to Chile and re-sold them and have made money myself," he said.

"1 don't know why," I told him, "but that possibility quite simply just never occurred to me." The doorman at the hotel Bolivar had won and Tito had lost. The doorman had won what could turn out to be bad karma, I was thinking, but I didn't tell Tito that. I didn't even want to believe that. It was true that ever since I had sold my dollars that morning purely out of a motive of greed, I had been radiating shame and guilt. I still felt I must go to sleep and somehow lose my shame and guilt in dreams so I could appear at the airport bank rid of those incriminating vibrations.

Chris and Graham and Martin got up and left. I knew that in their heads they were no longer in Peru. They had left already although the plane which would bear them was still on the ground and wouldn't actually take off for another ten hours. But they were gone. I had laughed with them because I understood them. I had remained faithful to them. We had been together for two months and Tito couldn't pull me away from them. My allegiance was too strong although I abhorred their crudity. But I also loved their crudity. As long as I thought of them as people trying to find their own tracks through life, I loved them. As soon as I thought of them as ambassadors, I hated them. But fuck the ambassadors. They didn't come here to learn diplomacy. Off they had gone. The three of them had certainly not enjoying hanging out with Tito and me.

Tito was overwhelmed with disgust. He was not even entirely sure from what, but his eyes shone warm sickness and hate. We had nothing to say to each other. But our eyes clanked together like two magnets. For perhaps literally a quarter of an hour I stared primarily into his left eye; he into my left eye. Every once in a while I sought to balance our eyes in such a way that I could see both of his eyes simultaneously but could not maintain the clarity and intensity. I tended to fog out. I settled for one clear eye.

He sent me steady cold for a long time. If I found the whole situation suddenly funny, he didn't. My humors were killed off one by one... There was no love in that left eye of his... that blue-gray eye. I told him, "that's the way it is, man, we're gringos and we cannot help it." But there was no sympathy. The eye kept on judging. At last he grumbled something about Chris and Graham and Martin.

"They didn't even... mumble mumble..."

"What?" I asked, straining to hear him clearly.

"Nothing," he said. "Forget it."

'Well *fuck this bullshit*,' I decided inside myself, and began with my usual habit of eating the remaining food off the table. I finished off Chris's disdained scrambled egg tortilla and a half-eaten plate of chicken.

'Clean up your plate! Think of the staving people in China!' was running through my mind. Tito had only eaten half of his bowl of soup. He was not going to eat the other half. I offered him some chicken. Nothing doing.

"Serve yourself if you like," I told him and called the waiter over and paid for the entire meal. Tito shook fifteen soles in the waiter's face. Tito was going to pay for his own bowl of soup by god! The waiter told Tito to give the fifteen soles to me. Tito didn't want to give the fifteen soles to me because he knew I wouldn't take them. Finally the mystified waiter took the fifteen soles and handed them to me himself, supposedly as 'change.' I was basically insulted but I had no harsh words to say. I was wasted on the marijuana and my eyes were bright red and long since at half-mast. I felt like a rat.

We went back to the hotel. I wished Tito would leave so I could clear my mind but he didn't leave. In five hours we should be getting up and going to the airport and the bank... we had to pack. I threw some things in my pack, went to take a piss and then asked Tito where he was going to spend the night.

"I think I'll go home in order to sleep," he replied but he didn't go. He lay down toward the bottom of one of the beds. I lay down in my sleeping bag on the floor and wondered when he was going to leave. I soon got tired of wondering, turned out the lights and went to sleep.

You Will Have to Pay!

I overslept! It was 5:30 AM. The plane would leave at 7:00. I had wanted to be up by 4:00 AM! I woke all the others up. It was total frenzy... total hurry. We all had to piss and close our packs. I got all my things ready: my pack, my sack, my guitar and I rushed out into the hall balancing all three. Tito was still here. He reached to help me carry my sack and guitar. I grasped them tighter and didn't give them to him. *'If you don't accept the soup I offer, then I don't accept your offer to help me carry this stuff. Fuck off! Out of my way!'* That's what went through my head. I said nothing. We streaked out the door and into a cab.

At the airport we passed fast and smooth through the ticket check. Everything was OK. The plane wouldn't leave for fifteen minutes. I had my pocket full of soles. Then I was through immigration and headed for the bank. Suddenly I heard my name being paged over the loudspeakers.

Graham exclaimed: "Hey! That's you!"

"1 know," I told him, "but whatever it is will just have to wait until I get this money changed."

The cashiers were counting my money and filling out papers. Two men in blue suits were beckoning to me. A woman employed by the airlines came over to me and told me to save a hundred-and-fifty dollars worth of Peruvian money. "You will have to pay the 'multa,' the fine!" she said.

"What fine? There is no fine!" I growled back at her, wondering what in the world could have gone wrong?

"There is no fine," I told the banker. "It is all a mistake. Give me all my money in dollars!" In a flash I had my dollars in my hot little hand. I had gambled and won! There could be no bullshit about a fine?

"You were given sixty days to stay in the country," the woman explained. "That was on May 12th. It is now the morning of July 13th, so you see, you've stayed past your sixty-day limit and must pay a hundred-and-fifty dollar fine in order to leave!"

I saw the two officials in blue suits still beckoning to me. We headed over to confront them. *'We'll have this thing figured out in no time,'* I assumed. After all, the plane was due to leave in five minutes!

"Look," I explained to the officials, "when we came into the country we already had our reservations made for this date of return. It is well within the limit of the ninety days usually extended to tourists. Upon our arrival we showed the Immigration Officer our tickets, which clearly demonstrated to him our intention to remain in the country from May 12 'till July 13th, early AM, a time period which he apparently assessed as sixty days, stamping our tourist cards for that amount of time instead of the usual ninety! So you see, it is one of your own officials who has gotten us into this misunderstanding!"

It seemed, however, that the blue suits had displayed all of the interest of pigs in a trough. We were led to a bigger, fatter official also in a blue suit.

Suddenly Graham, Spectra, Sue and Martin appeared beside me. Another contingent of blue suits had extracted them from the plane, although they had already boarded and seated themselves comfortably. "What's going on?" they wanted to know.

The airline employee, the lady who had come to break this marvelous news to me while I was changing my money, said, "The plane will leave in two minutes! You must hurry and pay the 'multa!'"

The very sound of the world 'multa' sent me into another paroxysm of mulish refusal. Somehow I was convinced that the plane would wait. We began tugging toward the gate, toward the plane, toward freedom and relief from all this nonsense! ...soon I would be on the plane...

With a panic I saw the propeller on one of the engines begin to turn.

"All our stuff is on the plane! cried Graham.

Only Chris had survived the ordeal and was sitting tight on the silver bird with his cocaine between his toes. He had arrived to join us a couple of days late! He had entered the country after the rest of us and wasn't involved in this sixty-day business! The propeller turned faster and faster. The employee of the airline was obviously terrified of the power of the blue suits. "You will have to pay," she told me, "there is nothing else you can do if you are going to leave!"

Another propeller began to turn. "All right! All right! I'll pay!" I said.

"It's too late now," said the airline lady.

"Impossible to get on now," the man at the gate agreed.

The men in blue suits were satisfied with their job well done. "You can pay your fine at our office downtown," they told us.

"But our baggage is on its way to Miami!" Spectra screamed. "You fucking pricks!" she swore at them and started madly kicking at a nearby desk. Sue was sick. She had a cold and was calm, defeated. I had just survived watching a couple of mad movies in my mind in which I ran through the gate, pushed the guards aside, and caught and clasped the fleeing wheel of the airplane... But now I was motionless. Defeated. The plane was gone.

Leave Me One of Those Two Girls

Graham started exclaiming about his hand-carried baggage still under the seat aboard the big silver bird. But I now had only one desire: to talk clearly to the biggest fattest pig in the blue suit and explain exactly what happened so that he would understand whose fault this whole mess was. I found him back at his desk.

"Now that there's plenty of time," I told him, "let's talk about this slowly and in detail!"

"I only talk to decent people," he replied coldly, "not to 'mal-creados' ...people who weren't even conceived and born properly. Do you understand me? Yes, sure you understand me!"

"Well," I began with a grin, "as one man who wasn't born properly to another..." But no luck. No humor in the fellow. He was gone in a huff... scooted off into the distance like a scared little pig puffed up to the size of a pink elephant.

The airline people suggested we talk with their main office downtown. We walked out of the airport in search of a bus.

We had time to drink a coffee before the downtown office opened. We were there at 9:00 AM. The plane had left but time had definitely gone on as usual. And Lima had gone about its business as usual. And the folks in the airline office had come to work as usual... only to find: us. But we were not the first people this had happened to. "It's very difficult to avoid paying that fine," they told us, "but once a German fellow managed to avoid it by going to his consulate."

"OK," we said, "thanks for the tip. We'll give it a try." We turned around to head out the door and proceeded to the U.S. consulate.

"Where's my handbag?" asked Martin. "I had it in my hand; it didn't go to Miami... I had set it right on that table right over there by the entrance door into the downtown airline office!"

What must have happened flashed simultaneously through all of our minds. A thief, as if suddenly possessed of the ability to sense that we had overstayed our welcome in Peru, had reached in through the door and made off with Martin's handbag! We had been so engrossed in describing the airport scene to the airline employees... his camera, and worst of all, his journal, had been in that bag.

But no time for crying over spilled milk! We rushed out into the street. Downtown Lima was doing its usual thing: the streets were jammed with honking cars. In some places it was faster to walk than to take a cab! By 10:00 AM we were all gathered in an excited knot around the sympathetic ears of a lady in a relatively high position in the U.S. consulate. I explained the sixty day fiasco from beginning to end. It seemed we had found just the right woman! She knew a Sr. Rodriguez in the Peruvian government office which was wanting its 'multa'. She called him up on the phone and told us that if we went down there and found him right away "we would have no difficulties..."

We were out on the street again, pounding the pavement and taking cabs. Within an hour we had located the building: the Office of External Affairs. The enemy... but with Sr. Rodriguez on the inside... if we could only find him. That turned out to be the thing. If we could find him, we "would have no difficulties." But it seemed that the public was not allowed above the first floor of this building. And Sr. Rodriguez had his office on the 4th floor. We eventually ascertained this by waiting through a long line of bereaved 'multa' payers.

"I saw him leave the building a few minutes ago," a harassed but friendly clerk informed us after asserting his own helplessness to relieve us from the impinging 'multa'. We watched the clock tick. The whole building was scheduled to close down at noon. If we didn't find Sr. Rodriguez before noon, we were going to have to wait until the next day to complete this nerve-wracking business! It was 11:45. Our eyes were glued to the door to snatch the first person who looked like he could possibly be a Sr. Rodriguez! No one passed through the portals save those who entered with stooped shoulders, dead-pan faces -- all obviously fellow 'multa' payers.

But wait! Who was this? "There he is!" affirmed the clerk. "We are the ones your lady friend at the U.S. consulate called about," I whispered into his ear.

"Ah, yes, go around the corner to the other office and I will call them and tell them to expect you."

We zoomed into the other office at 11:55 and faced the same confused officials whom we had tried to plumb half an hour earlier to no avail. But this time one of them had his ear to the phone and was smiling at us. He called us over and, as his associates locked the doors as the clock struck 12:00 noon, he opened his desk drawer and withdrew no less than five rubber stamps. "Stampity stamp stamp stamp stamp..." Each of our tourist cards received professional treatment from all five stamps.

"The only thing you have to do for me," he said, "is leave me one of those two girls you've got with you!" and he broke out into a hearty laughter. We all had a good laugh at that one! The girls too. They would have probably laughed at anything at that point, kissed the fellow on his bald pate, and invited him out for a date! -- this fellow who wasn't even Sr. Rodriguez! The mighty wielder of the stamps!

Sittin' on the Jet Plane

I had more pent up energy to spend than I could contain and, jubilant from head to toe, took off like a bullet and sprinted all the way back to the airline office. Miraculously, they were still open. They wouldn't close, it seemed, until 12:30. I triumphantly displayed the stamps on our tourist cards: we had eluded the dreaded 'multa!' The airline office employees were proud of us and they had our new tickets ready at no extra charge. We were to depart two days hence, early Thursday morning.

I sat down on the curb with my trophies and waited for the others. Eventually they arrived and were pleased to see that we were ready to go... early next Thursday morning.

Unwinding at last, we staggered back toward our hotel, stopping in a restaurant for lunch, a breather, and a discussion of our karma.

Why did we get pulled off that plane and why did Martin have his valuables stolen immediately thereafter although we had passed two entire months with no comparable catastrophes?

Sue thought it might be because she had lost the keys to someone's apartment in Arequipa who might have been evicted on her account... We wondered if cocaine could have had anything to do with all of this...? Or was it because I hadn't thought to worry that there might be more than 60 days between 5:00 PM June 6 and 7:00 AM Aug 7? Was it because we went to Bolivia without ever getting our passports stamped or in any way letting the officials of either country know that we had quietly crossed their frontier both coming and going? Was it because I had made more than a hundred dollars by trading my money on the black market, a number suspiciously close to the fateful $150 fine? Was it because there was something about the guilt I was feeling for having made that money in that way which produced some emanation in me which the blue suits were especially trained to pick up on? And having picked up my emanation did they then re-check my visa and think to impose a fine...? And why was it my name which they first called out over the paging system and not one of the four others who had remitted identical papers...? There must have been something about the harried state I was in when I arrived in that airport which had brought that whole mess down on us. Or was there a series of connections in this universe which remains invisible to us but which nevertheless proved quite capable to linking me and the blue suits up at that time in that way...?

I had no way of guessing that a few months later I would be meeting Leda's Greek husband in Athens. He would have just returned from a journalistic adventure in Santiago and I would be learning details from him about the tragedies in Chile which were creating the black market of which I had taken advantage.

Lima's roar: the exhaust pipes and horns sunk into my nerves and left no peace. Gone was my desire to drink from the eyes of the women or play with the little girls. A terrible threat of emptiness swept through me. People on the street seemed to be pointing at me. The connection was broken. I no longer felt myself to be part of the vast 'us.'

Our forty hours of waiting for the next plane were colorless and not fun. I did go back to the lady at the US consulate and tell her that her connection had worked and that she should make the same recommendation for others. I did not go re-visit Tito. I thought about the men in blue suits and wondered what our fate would be early Thursday morning if we had to pass through the same gate manned by the very self-same blue-suited pigs. I wondered about the fat one. I was alternately feeling pride at having outwitted his fine and feeling fear that he might invent yet another delay for us.

Early Thursday morning we were at the airport with plenty of time to spare. It was to a different set of blue suits that we handed our documents. We quietly walked onto the great silver bird and flew off to the north.

So now Leda would be mine - was going to be mine again. Did I want anything of her except to assure myself that I could have anything I wanted?

I wanted to see her dance to my music. Would that not be worth a lifetime? I wanted her to be a mother for my child. Would that not be worth a lifetime?

I was sittin' on the jet plane -- feelin' like a success. Goin' back home... Ready to see my woman... Listenin' to the music through the earphones...

There was a bomb scare. Was this plane gonna blow up? They couldn't find anything when they had us all get off the plane for an hour. Engine scare. Something wrong with one of the engines. They fixed it. We hurtled at five hundred miles an hour through the air and changed from Quechua life... flyin' at thirty-five-thousand feet.

We landed in Miami. Leda's voice over the phone: sounded

strange. Foreign. Who was that? Can't touch bodies through the phone.

Graham left the airport telling me: "my heart is open to you!" while beating himself on the heart. Spectra and Sue went with laughter into their next adventures.

I felt good. I felt like buying a new electric guitar. Chris taught me something about playing high speed music but still feeling the holes between the notes.

Soon I was flying over Georgia. I knew the summer cloud patterns in this part of the world. From there to Illinois I could herd them like sheep with my eyeballs. I hadn't slept for thirty-six hours now. Our pilot steered us around the giant cumulo-nimbus cloud giants. Even this plane couldn't come close to flying over those! I guessed that the plane was not going to blow up after all.

'Keep my pain. Don't lose it!' I realized.

'The world is so full of different points of view! Amazing!'

I imagined the extremes... The dark side...

> The executioner looks out through the tiny holes in his black hood. His arms are tremendous. His whole body is designed to swing the ax. He knows how to sharpen that ax to a fine edge better than any other man alive would ever even want to! He is a good executioner. He doesn't miss. And he never requires more than one sure blow -- oh, maybe once or twice... Only he knows what it feels like to peer out of those eyes which must guide the ax.

I practiced cupping pain gently in the palms of my hands, allowing it to smolder and gently burn the skin... which was my way of saying, "I love you! Burn in my hand! My hand is tough and will feel gentle warmth where others would be feeling pain."

My own feeling of elation would do just fine for the bright side.

I stopped in St Louis for one night. I had been awake for forty-five hours. I shared a few stories from Peru in my mother's household but the dream world of my exhaustion kept adding words from another dimension: babbling irrelevant fragments into the threads of conversation.

Back in my own culture I felt the differences between people in a different way. Some were tight and some were loose. I felt the tight ones here in North America as somehow tighter than their tight counterparts in Latin America.

I slept through the night. So necessary. I headed back to the airport for a plane to Colorado. I had a good feeling about what was in store for me and Leda in the next few months!

Yes, I needed a good electric guitar!

Colorado: Man Came Home to Woman

My beautiful Greek woman ran into my arms in the Denver airport.

Man came home to woman. Locked together. Made love together. Like two snakes with muscles tight. Man's mind had been on the world. Woman's mind had been on another man who was my friend... but not a friend I had ever really loved. My woman had been wanting to make love to him. He was not really interested. Turns out they never made love.

Why not live in giant communal units? Life is too tepid, lukewarm, dead in the suburban American households. Could I really care about someone I don't make love with? Yes... with music I could have sex with my friends... my world was a giant communal household.

Leda and I decided to go to Mexico and then to Greece together.

My friend Jim Primock wrote a poem about my return:

> *He is the only one that knows.*
> *Cameron is back. Late. But back.*
> *Not for long, though... he wants to...*
> *Head south to Mexico...*
> *Then east to Greece...*
> *Cameron doesn't stay in one place very long.*
> *Sometimes he is the only one who knows*
> *He doesn't need to.*
> *Cameron is a very accomplished dancer.*
> *He dances through Peru...*
> *He dances across the fretboard of his guitar.*
> *He dances through everything he does.*
> *Cameron has danced in places where...*
> *No one else knew anyone was dancing.*

Who Was That Person...?

We spent a week at home with our friends in Boulder and then headed south in my car towards New Mexico. We stopped in Cañon City, Colorado.

Sleeping beside the highway for the night...
Cars purred by on one side...
Trains made the earth shake from the other...

In the middle of the night I only woke up for the trains and for the wind which kept stealing the bottom of our blanket and uncovering our toes, bared for making love.

I put my pants back on for warmth and slept through the rest of the night... except for the trains... with their eerie sweeping single bright eye.

My mind knew that we were not sleeping in the middle of the tracks. I saw them beside us when we spread out our blankets. But another unbelievably huge roaring clanking pile of moving metal diesel parts was coming toward us down the tracks and something in me knew it was going to crush my head... no... not really...

We really were on our way to Mexico. To the border. To the gardens of music -- to the trumpets and round men keeping rhythm on big bass guitarónes... by the Pacific ocean... where the crabs run sideways and the waves take your body and turn it into a fish!

But here now in Cañon City we got up to go visit my friend James who was now serving a life sentence in the Colorado State Penitentiary. The depth of awareness of what had really happened was very slowly sinking in... kidnapping... rape... murder...

No longer suicidal, James was not being kept in a padded cell. We could visit him from opposite sides of a thick wall with a tiny window. He was glad to see us. We wondered together at the tragedy which had overwhelmed his life... who was it...? who was that person...? who had suffered and died in that spot up in the mountains on that awful night up in the snow...? And what had been the terrible driving force...? And... had I really had some kinds of premonitions when we were together alone up at Carp's ranch and again in the forest while he had been shooting his pistols? The partial answers to some of these questions would begin to trickle in more than ten years later. We left my friend shaking his head sadly as we promised to come visit again. I still remembered his kindness and patience from those times when he had been helping me improve my rock climbing skills.

Stopping in Tres Piedras, New Mexico for food we marveled at an eight-year-old girl who could laugh from her belly... and laugh and laugh and laugh... until every person in that diner had been guffawing hilariously out of control... without even needing to know what was funny.

Whoops... Born Again

Heading south toward Taos I was feeling drawn to visit my friend Justin Case who had served so beautifully as a bridge between Pueblo Indian and hippie culture. Not so long ago Archer and Sandy and I had sat up all night through two Native American Church peyote meetings: one before our night in jail in southern Texas and another after our return. Justin Case had been 'road-man' for those meetings and had offered us help and hospitality on many levels. Justin Case had decided to devote his life energies to being there to help whomsoever crossed his path 'just in case' they might need something! Beautiful soul! He had apprenticed himself to the wisest and most elderly Taos Pueblo Indians and learned some of the ancient ways.

Perhaps he had tried too hard. Something had gone wrong. Had he become too serious? Had he had too much desire to transcend this ordinary world of sun and moon? Had he accidentally crushed the fragile peyote bird? Had he prayed himself to death?

Something had happened. Leda and I knocked on his door. He greeted us and told us to leave our proffered six-pack of beer in our car. He had lost his shine... his welcoming glow was gone.

"My name is no longer Justin Case," he told us. "I'm back to being Jim Case."

Tears were building up pressure behind his pleading eyeballs. He wanted to tell us something.

"I'm saved!" he blurted out. "I have found Jesus and have been born again!"

Justin Case was gone and I, along with my friends, my loved ones, my six-pack of beer, were now on the other side... we had all turned into the devil!

Our visit didn't last very much longer. As we left I wondered if I would ever see him again.

On Our Way to Oaxaca

In Juarez I made a deal with the guy running the local Shell station and parked my car in back. We wouldn't take it into Mexico. We wanted to throw ourselves into the arms of fate. Wherever we might be invited to would be where we would go... mostly by bus.

Juarez was an eternal border town: a crazy membrane between two cultures where nothing ever settles down.

"Taxi! Mister, Taxi! See a good show tonight!"

"Taxi, Taxi! You wanna buy some grass?"

"Come and look inside my shop! Come on Look!"

We found a teenager's nightclub with a live band and danced to the high-energy electric rock and roll and then retired to appreciate the more dedicated art of the Mariachis who had captured Russia, Venice, Spain and Mexico all in the strings of a few violins, a couple of guitars, and one big guitarón that went Oompah! Oompah! ...underneath the trumpets and the songs of the open throat!

We met a guy named Jesus who agreed to drive us to Chihuahua. It was two hundred miles. We drove through the night while he and I practiced telling tall tales. We focused on witchcraft. We took stories which scared us and made skunks of obvious and cantankerous size out of them and shone them around and laughed. It worked. I kicked and thrashed about inside of my skull and eventually found a dozen ways out. Our harmonies of feeling were maintained... perhaps at the expense of needing to always be 'right'... but who cared?

Leda and I fell asleep as he drove and eventually woke up as he was pulling into the central bus station in Chihuahua.

It was very late at night. I wished I was asleep again... somewhere more comfortable with my woman beside me. And I wished I wasn't so hot and sweaty inside my blue jeans. And I wished it wasn't August. And I wished this bus station didn't look the way it did.

But we were on our way to Oaxaca. And in Oaxaca anything could happen. The home of the magic mushroom would surely turn out to be a better place than that bus station. If I had been forced to live the next sixty years in that bus station, I might have considered suicide. Or I might have adapted and learned to see the beauty in all those comings and goings. But I doubted it. I would have hung forever somewhere in between, hypnotized like a frog stranded in the middle of a highway in the desert.

We could sleep on the bus to Mexico City. I didn't particularly like Mexico City. Never had. It would take nineteen hours to get there.

Oh my god? Were we in Zacatecas? Or was this Fresnillo? Where the fuck were we anyway? Where had this bus brought us now? Twenty-five minutes for lunch! I liked this place.

Fuck-it-all-over; sit-in-your-seat-and-die. I just wanted to get to Mexico City... not even Mexico City! Oaxaca!

Señorita, Look What Mexico City Has Done to You!

There we were walking the streets of Mexico City... following the trail of smoke left by some dream of making guitars someday in Oaxaca.

We drank our cups of coffee and our bottles of beer and uncovered the stories of our tarnished past... trying to find the way through the emptiness of some words.

We went to our hotel and un-peeled ourselves and our bed, wrapped ourselves together like two halves from the same orange, made love... two statues of flesh lying together for centuries: that statue no one has yet dared to make of a man and a woman wrapped in each other like a banana in its skin.

I felt proud to dance in the streets and touch the hands and arms of others somehow knowing that I could love all women and have all men for my friends.

Supposedly if I love another man's woman I cannot be his friend, and if I love another woman besides my woman, I cannot be my woman's lover... and if my friend loves my woman he cannot be my friend, and if my woman loves my friend he cannot be my friend... and if my woman loves my friend she cannot be my lover...? Did any of that make any sense?

Let me repeat that...

> *Supposedly if I love another man's woman I cannot be his friend, and if I love another woman besides my woman, I cannot be my woman's lover... and if my friend loves my woman he cannot be my friend, and if my woman loves my friend he cannot be my friend... and if my woman loves my friend she cannot be my lover...?*

No... It doesn't make any sense...

We walked forever through the streets of this city with our energies open to all... no... we would never lose our love for the dance and for those eyes... the eyes of a million people who know how to love. We could fall endlessly in love with all the women... all the men. There were no rules which could make any sense. Fully accepting our sacred connections to flirtatiousness we relaxed into each other fully.

I opened my eyes and saw her looking at me in the way a little girl looks at her father. "Oh little girl," I told her before sinking to become a little boy, with my head on her breast, for a moment, then the father again... All with this woman in Mexico City... This Greek woman I had brought to Mexico City...

'Let's go have children in the villages and make guitars,' I was thinking but not daring to say out loud. "Let's make love again!" I could say.

Back out on the street again. "Señorita, please! More coffee!"

Señorita, look what Mexico City has done to you! And to me!

The Señorita didn't even know how many million people were living here. This city was driving me insane and I had only been there for ten hours. "Señorita, how much do I owe you? I've got to go find out how it happened that all of Peru got lost in Mexico City. Perhaps the people in Chapultepec Park can explain it to us."

For two-and-a-half pesos the canary came out of its cage and picked three sealed messages out of a little tray: our fortune. Everything was going fine in Chapultepec Park... except that I didn't have a peso to spend for this little girl's chicklets... except that Freida Kahlo had died bedridden. at age forty-four from a fatal accident which befell her at sixteen, leaving her twenty-eight years to die and while painting her pain onto canvases which she left bleeding around in museums... a sudden swallowing-up befell us when we fell into the faces of her paintings and now we were recovering, drinking a bottle of mineral water in a sidewalk cafe there in Chapultepec Park. Leda and I were two poets, one Greek and one American, sliding through the inner and outer worlds of the streets of Mexico City, arm in arm, glad for each other's company and... on our way to Oaxaca!

Back to the Mescal Bar

For us in Oaxaca it wasn't the mushrooms, it was the mescal... which we drank from the fingertips of the old bartender who explained it all with a dozen assorted secretive gestures while the marketplace raged outside with chickens and goats hanging upside down with their heads cut off... under a jungle of canvas roofs heaved up into the sky on jagged wooden pillars for shelter from the rain.

Faces in the marketplace... a boy looked up at me and couldn't help smiling. Mescal faces surrounded us babbling with quiet laughter while glowing at us knowingly while my Greek woman led me by the little finger purposefully back to our room... it was 'siesta' time and her body was hungry.

She told me, while we made love, of Mescalito, a face which had followed her around Link's yard back in Boulder. She had eaten peyote with friends... which had been fine until she had gone out into the yard to go to sleep... and faces had appeared in the trees... Mescalito faces... with blond hair and scary eyeballs... eyeballs that knew something... and that was the scary part...

So, after arousing the magic which poured like blue smoke from the end of my penis, we resolved all of this mystery. I told her that even Mescalito couldn't know everything all at once... one thing at a time... give yourself a chance... do your dance. Keep moving... don't let it all freeze.

"You are a poem," I told her, "which it is taking me years to write. What an amazing poem it would be on paper. But it's not on paper. I have you: sitting here smiling at me! And you keep changing stories, changing dances, changing faces. I will never get you fastened down onto a piece of paper! Maybe if I could, I would publish you and be rid of you! But no, here you sit by my side. I have just created another universe and given it again to you! So you are happy for today. Tomorrow you will be hungry for another creation and I will put my penis inside of you and write another novel inside of you with my white ink. And your eyes will shine with the glory of it all!"

We wandered back to the mescal bar. Hours were spent getting to know the men who hung out there. Yes, the men. Leda was one of very few females in the bar. I asked a man named Jorge about his corn fields and his family.

"I have a wife and six children," he explained.

"Where?" I inquired. "Do they live nearby?"

"Not close, no," he continued. "I need to do my work here in Oaxaca. I go and see them every once in a while."

We talked more and discovered that Jorge, like everyone else native to Oaxaca, was embedded in an unimaginably huge extended family. They spoke multiple indigenous languages... Zapoteca, Mixteca, Mazateca, Chinanteco, Náhuatl and many more...

Jorge had children with more than one woman. It was complicated. This marketplace which surrounded us had a certain magic feeling: everyone was related to everyone.

Several little glasses of mescal into the afternoon I began to feel my own deepening connection to this marketplace. A mariachi band was playing Russian music in the central plaza.

The Colored Threads of Energetic Connection

I casually felt my back pocket and panicked. My wallet was gone! How could someone steal my wallet while I was sitting there right on top of it?

What happened next absolutely defies explanation. I stood up, exited the bar and approached the market, my eyeballs scanning the crowd. I suddenly fixed my gaze on a man with mescal eyes, similar to my own, no doubt. He looked at me. I looked at him. He walked toward me and handed me my wallet. He never said a word and wandered off, back into the crowd.

I continued to stand there, dumbfounded. I saw the colored threads of energetic connection fastening us all together… all of us in the market. Or did I? I went back into the bar, sat down and examined my wallet. Nothing was missing.

Too amazed to use any words, we retired back to our hotel room to absorb something of what had just happened. We fell asleep… but what was that? The bed was shaking. It kept on shaking for a few seconds.

Then it really started to shake. The bed was galloping back and forth as if we had been making love!

"Let's get out on the street!" Some panic of walls crashing down ran through me. I don't even remember opening the door. I remember running under the front arch of the hotel courtyard hoping it wouldn't collapse yet. I was out in the street, Leda right behind me wrapped in a sheet.

The shaking stopped. Nothing had collapsed. I looked down and discovered that I was stark naked. The other people from the hotel had all managed to emerge at least wearing their underpants. Not me. No one had seemed to notice while the ground was still shaking. Now the ground had stopped shaking and I was simply standing out in the middle of the street naked. Leda opened her sheet and wrapped it around both of us. We shuffled back inside toward our room.

Meanwhile, to the north of us, in Orizaba, a twelve-story apartment building had collapsed as a result of the earthquake. Many of the occupants, up to a hundred, had been sleeping at the time, and this was the number proclaimed dead at that site. All in all, over a thousand people lay dying, crushed by their own walls and ceilings. Hundreds more struggled out with bleeding wounds while the towers on centuries-old churches crumbled, their giant bells falling to the ground with tremendous final tolls. Meanwhile, earthquakes weren't the only catastrophe! The rains poured from the sky over central Mexico flooding hundreds from their homes.

"Even the Valley of Tears has been Flooded!" proclaimed a newspaper headline.

"It's not a punishment from God," announced a respectable bishop, "all of these things have natural and comprehensible causes."

> *Life back in Colorado is taken like a steak on a plate: cut up into little pieces and savored little by little. Here in Mexico life takes you, cuts you up into little pieces and savors you... poco á poco!*

And my Greek woman was staying very close... our thoughts and feelings inter-twined all the time. This was something Greeks knew how to do. I thought I was learning. I thought I liked it.

We left Oaxaca and traveled west towards the Pacific. The world was knee-deep in mud from the endless heavy rains. Soon we were waiting in a bus in Uruapan which had broken its hind leg. The driver was out fishing in the rain for tools and spare parts... which he couldn't find.

He stood waving ineffectually for half an hour while the rain came down endlessly... like streams of children's faces. We watched from inside the bus. Was he trying to get a cab so he could go get spare parts? At last I saw him climb into a yellow taxi which took him off down the avenue... we hoped... he would do whatever it might take to keep us on the road.

Suddenly, before we knew it, there he was, getting out of the taxi beside the bus.

"What do we do now?" all thirty five of us asked him.

"Nothing," came the reply. "This bus is busted. I can't fix it. And the taxi can't even get me across street... it is impassable because of the rain."

Guitar Heaven in Paracho

Finally, days later, down the road in Paracho, the rain was letting up! I don't know how we got there. I hadn't seen anything through the torrents of water.

Paracho was humming with small boys busy with planes and sandpaper modeling boards into their first crude shapes so that hundreds of guitar makers in hundreds of little rooms open to the streets all over town could shape guitars into their final forms.

The vibrations of thousands of guitars filled the town. We walked down the streets; two guitar makers had lain down their work, picked up their guitars and were singing like bulls or coyotes in the hot afternoon sun... or under the moon at night... with total voice and total conviction that the words of their love song were true and right.

We went into the shops of Daniel and David Caro: two brothers. We talked about making guitars. I was a guitar maker too!

And I played 'Never On Sunday,' a Greek song for them. And the noise of the passing buses, with no mufflers, rattled the metal doors and reverberated off the walls like thousands of exhaust-pipe angels struggling to get from one side of hell to the other! Every bus that went by was another judgment day! The world was shattered asunder by their incredible blasts and everything had to then begin anew -- like the green grasses of spring.

Our songs sought the manner of the open throat and two young Mexican boys came in off the street and showed us how it was done... or sung.

The next day there happened to be a festival... a music festival. Leda and I were invited to sing.

"And now, as a special addition to our show, a Greek couple will participate in our program. We all know how much the world owes to the Greeks. The Greeks, like brothers, have built the foundation we all stand upon. So, let's have a big applause for Leda y Felipe!"

Two microphones. Three hundred faces. I started the guitar. Leda sang 'Never on Sunday!' The crowd applauded. We floated in a double ocean of energy! We were barely beginning the ascent... and the song was over. We had sung. Our moment was over and we melted back into the audience.

It was sundown on Sunday in Paracho. The boys and girls of sixteen-years-of-age were all sitting in various displays: teenage couples in love. Oh no! I couldn't bear to watch it! I loved it! And I had come there with my own little lover.

"To our future and to our happiness!" I said... touching my bottle of beer to hers... and my knee to hers... like the little couple at the next table.

There was another table of boys -- maybe thirteen-years-old -- smoking cigarettes like men. The music played in the juke box while the drummer carried his big bass drum up the street toward wherever the band was going to play.

The guitar shops were mostly lying idle on that Sunday. The craftsmen had all gone home and then reappeared with wives and strings of children so that the whole world might simply be admired for a day!

We sat on a bench in the central plaza. Lovely Señoritas passed by in their Sunday finest! The boys walked one direction and the girls the other.

> *Here she comes again! Oh, wow, it's that one! And there you are again! And you too! Somewhere in the arms of these swirling galaxies of black-eyed Señoritas is The One! Don't worry. She'll recognize you when she sees you. Just keep walking around... dozens of pairs of warm moist eyes... each pair a perfect oasis... a perfect drink of water... in the middle of the desert... where you sit beside the only stream for a hundred miles... under the stars! And I am so lucky to have my Greek woman!*

Juan was making guitars here in Paracho. Oh yes, Juan had experienced his adventures traveling, seeing the world! For two years he had wandered -- with no money... he hadn't needed any money.

And so at the ripe age of fifteen he had come back home to Paracho to get married to a twenty-eight-year-old woman who was now thirty-five... and he was now twenty-two... with five kids -- three of his own; two from her first husband.

"A couple the same age doesn't work out," he said. "They always fight. We haven't had even one fight! A woman has to be mature before she's worth anything. So now I'm completely satisfied."

"Women are three times as smart as men," he continued. "Did you know that? So you let her run the family and you just bring her some money once a week. And only on Sundays does she leave the house. That's the way it is here," he explained, "and trying to change anything too fast can only bring us to ruin."

> *We men are thousands of sperms swimming... we just keep swimming... nothing to do but swim...*

I bought some exotic Mexican hardwood boards from which I later made fret boards and guitar backs and sides back in Boulder. This was not the last time I would visit David and Daniel Caro in Paracho.

Twenty-eight hours in the hot sun inside a hermetically sealed passenger-train-car took us back north across the desert from Guadalajara... Oh my God it was hot.

We had beer and a book of Greek grammar for diversion... yes, twenty-eight hours... and Mexican musicians on board for entertainment!

Ten men plus my beautiful Greek woman were all singing... balanced over the roar of the wheels on the track... standing together on sliding metal plates... between the cars... watching blue flames of stale air licking out of the doors from the blazing furnace innards of those passenger cars... where we had all been sitting with sweat streaming down our faces... laughing because it was so hot!

Again we escaped to stand between the cars. We sang the noise back into the ground and we arm-wrestled amongst ourselves for the fun of it. And when we got to Hermosillo, our destination, we all laughed again because it had been so good.

We slept in Hermosillo in a tiny little room with cockroaches and a fan. We lay naked on the bed with the door open and the fan blowing and the cockroaches exploring avenues of liberal education.

We got up in the morning and headed off toward the border. We bought one last bottle of Mescal to take with us... and a bottle of that good Mexican vanilla.

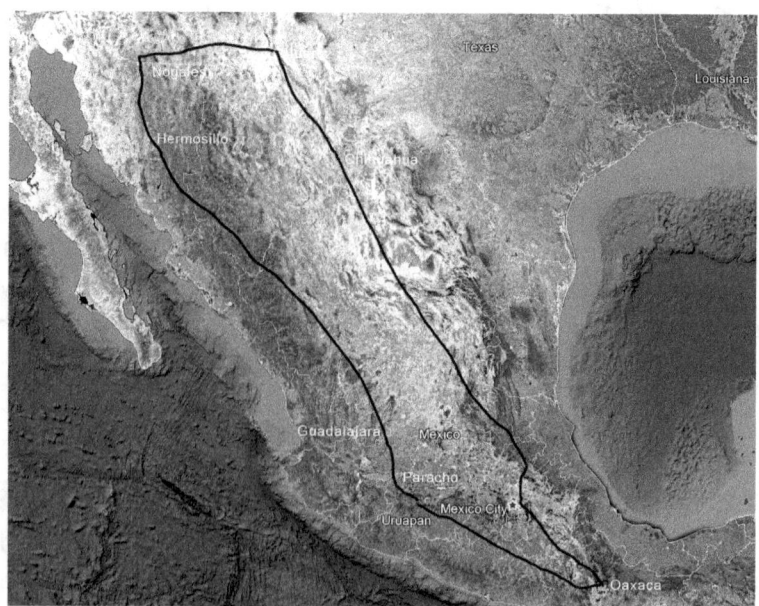

Wandering with Leda Through Mexico

The Most Terrible Place We Have Yet Found!

We stuck out our thumbs at noon in Nogales. A crazy person took us on into Lordsburg... praise the mushrooms that grow in the desert. He told us he was a witch and a private detective with three loaded automatic weapons underneath the seat in his car right now! But that he was a good witch... and might have to destroy his friend George one day with a 357 magnum because George was a Satanist from the Louisiana swamps... and he was looking for another clue to finish the formula for bringing mummies back to life.

"One day that special person's gonna walk into Lordsburg," he said. "And I don't know how I'll know, but I'll know, that that particular person is the one sent for me... and there's gonna be an uprisin' involvin' about a hundred people... and I'm gonna be in the center of it 'cause I got Comanche blood in me!... and they say that them Comanches are mean!"

"I like you better as a good witch," I told him.

He looked at me with a twinkle in his eye. "I always had a bad streak in me," he explained. "Next Halloween we'll see! If George attempts to make a Satanist out of me, and if I say 'What the Hell Why Not?' ...and face all my own curses comin' back at me...?"

'Anyway,' I was thinking, *'I don't wanna be no special person for you Jack.. and I don't wanna be around when you bring them mummies back to life...'*

He said the snake goddess lives in the swamps of Louisiana and that you don't have to go all the way to Brazil lookin' for Voodoo Macumba Hecuba Dumbala... It was all right here...

But he let us off right there in Lordsburg where he said he would... wished us well and left us on our way... muttering something about how he was gonna be a lone man again tonight at midnight up on top of that mountain over there...

Before we got a chance to ride the boxcars on the next freight train, we got a ride with a young man who had just had another pre-divorce fight with his Mexican wife and had been down the road gettin' drunk with his friends. And now he was goin' home at a hundred miles an hour to face the music... or play some music for her to face...whichever... but he wanted to bring us along for the ride and for the touch.

"Yeah, we're still out here," we told him.

Soon we were standing beside the highway in Deming after getting chewed out for asking truckers for rides in the local truck stop. Big semis were blowing us down and making my Greek woman's thumbs tremble and shake... but the next thing we knew one of them had stopped: a big semi was showing us its ass parked way down the road. He waited while we ran... we climbed aboard... and immediately we went about the task of keeping that driver awake with tales of the Love Generation which he was curious about... he wanted to know about their sexual habits and what it meant when you see two guys together with one girl hitch-hiking beside the road.

"Jealousy still exists," I told him. "Don't worry, people are the same all over and you ain't missin' out on nothin' special."

But he let us down in Las Cruces thirty-five miles before El Paso and our own parked car 'cause he just couldn't stay awake any longer and I didn't blame him.

It was four o'clock in the morning and we weren't gonna get no ride so we decided to sleep for an hour in the desert. But the raindrops falling from the sky... suddenly and unexpectedly... woke us right up again and we went under the viaduct cement overpass there and scrambled up the cement undersides onto the little concrete shelf where we lay... and every time a truck dived under the bridge my little girl shook and shivered under my shoulder.

"This," she announced triumphantly, "is truly the most terrible place we have yet found!"

We shivered and shook 'till dawn came to the rescue and two boys on their way to enlist in the US Army took us on into El Paso and to our car.

We drove north through the hot sun speaking in Greek to stay awake... at last on our way back to Colorado and headed for Greece.

Friends and Greeks in Albuquerque

We stopped in Albuquerque for the night and my old friend Elizabeth and her husband Peter offered, "Let's go eat some chicken at a friend's house!"

"OK," we replied, "we've only been awake for thirty-six hours, traveled four-hundred-and-fifty miles through the desert in southern Arizona, seen a hundred worlds in Mexico and Texas... trying to get to Greece... so we feel good and are ready to go..."

And suddenly we were in Greece: the guy we went to eat chicken with was Greek!

And my beautiful Greek woman was blabbering away in pure Greek with this guy... with whom I struck up a beautiful oceanic arch-typical competitive relationship... to our mutual advantage.

He was ready to do anything... start the night off right... fire up our bowls with oil of hashish...

And soon there was no hope. I sat against the wall trying to calm the noises in my head. Noises from Mexico... Noises from Peru... Noises from Greece...

I picked out a few words from what they were saying. I pictured the sun setting over a vast body of water: the Pacific ocean... and calmed my mind...

"I am Ommmm..."

We were Achilles and Priam. No... we were modern Greeks and Americans making guitars and leather goods. We were beautiful men and women. We had survived the struggles of thousands of generations of men and warriors.

Nobles of the Old World sat on the benches of my mind while freaks from the New World scrambled happily about... and I quietly calmed it all down... put the lid on it and took it home to go to sleep... where, just to empty the fruits of our forty-first hour of wakefulness, the burglars had emptied the bedroom and thrown all of Elizabeth's and Peter's possessions all over the floor... where we nevertheless slept among the ghosts of stolen jewelry... slept deeply and completely... until the next day.

Stavros the Greek was ready for anything: cross-country skiing in the summer if possible. Off we went up into the mountains forty miles outside of Albuquerque -- to visit Moe and Karen! ...another young couple becoming hermits in the mountains of New Mexico.

It was just like the old days of communes except people were back into eating meat. Stavros was driving. The sun went down.

We were on little jeep roads through the desert. Lightening flashes were striking all around the mesa. We stopped at an abandoned shack that should have had dead bodies inside.

"Anybody home?" Empty. We searched for Moe and Karen to no avail. Where were they? We hastily searched for firewood before the coming rain. Then a car drove up. It was them. They thought maybe we were thieves. So they came back from visiting new neighbors on the other side of the mesa to... catch us. But we were not thieves. We were friends. So we cooked chicken in the shack 'till the rain stopped.

Stavros and I had developed a love and respect for each other left over from that first heavy night of archetypal thinking. Our love was suddenly strong and it stayed that way.

The sky cleared and filled with stars. We built a fire outside. I played the guitar. We all curled up together in our blankets around the fire: Moe and Karen; Stavros and Diane; Peter and Elizabeth; Cameron and Leda. Cameron made love to Leda beside the fire. The ring was completed and nearly brought together.

The next day the sky was hot. I ran down the road. I stood on my head and stretched all my muscles. We shot bottle caps with a 22-caliber rifle. Our harmony was established... our destiny balanced and completed. So we moved on.

Now it was my turn to pick up a hitch-hiker. Long black mustache. Long black hair. A Mexican with gray-blue eyes -- forty-four years old... a bandanna tied around his head. Five years in federal prison had left no scar on him. He'd expected it from the age of three-and-a-half. His father, cousins and uncles had all been in jail... family tradition of alcoholism... and dealing smack... carga... tegato... heroin.

But his mind was clear and open. We understood each other. He told me about skid row in Denver; in Los Angeles. About boxcars on the freight trains catching on fire. Wondering *'Am I going to die here?'* Six men were frantically trying to piss on the fire. No one had to go. The train was screaming down the track at seventy-miles-an-hour. Jump and die or burn and die: which was better? They eventually put the fire out by digging at it with pocket knives. An old man with charcoal all over his face got down on his knees and prayed. What was it like to have so many names you can't remember which one you gave to the judge? Freight trains from San Antonio to all points in the Universe. No love, respect or fear of the pigs... the police. Just keep going. Don't take a blanket to keep you warm. Just go! Flash hundred-dollar-bills in the narc's face and walk away chuckling.

Boulder to Athens

We were back home in Boulder for a week. I finished making silver and gold jewelry in my shop and packed it to sell in Greece and then we drove east. We nibbled at old friendships of mine as we meandered through the mid-west, a bit of Canada, and then from Philadelphia we flew on a cheap charter flight to Rome where I found my Spanish worked. People at least understood me and half the time I could understand them. From there we flew to Athens and soon we were sleeping on the balcony of a small apartment in the ancient capitol. My jewelry had been stolen from my baggage in the Athens airport but my Greek girl was home! We were living with her mother, Elli, her father, Tassos, and one of her brothers, Costis. They expected us to stay for many months. It was the end of 1973. We did.

Leda's father knew only Greek. But he loved me and we had continual little communication dances in our struggles to surmount one barrier after the next.

Her mother had learned a tiny bit of English over the years in her career as a teacher of French. She was endlessly patient, friendly and full of smiles.

Leda's brother had learned English in school and we could talk functionally. He had greeted me with a big Greek kiss on the cheek... it gave me the feeling of being engulfed by a giant amoeba. As time passed I began to realize that he didn't really have a life of his own and would seek to live vicariously through his sister and her new American boyfriend.

Some of Leda's old friends spoke some English and others quite simply did not. Basically everything was in Greek Greek Greek. I kept my attention focused on the sound of the language and began training myself to hear the separate words and phrases and to use my dictionary, grammar books and Leda to begin finding out their meanings. Endless deep listening was required. How many words could I collect and then re-collect? The learning dance had begun.

Maintaining endless focus and attention required staying seriously put... at the family dinner table... anchored in the present moment... while Leda and Tassos and Elli and Costis endlessly discussed Leda's wayward husband Yorgos... totally in Greek.

Leda, Tassos, Elli, Costis

The police wanted to see Leda the next morning. After all, she had left the country several years ago in the company of a left-wing journalist who was an enemy of the right-wing Papadopoulos regime which was still in power.

Any visitations to or from the Greek police were not welcome. The Greek people were simmering with revolutionary spirit and many were being arrested and tortured. The police revved up their motorcycles outside their stations to muffle the screams of people being tortured. Greeks were frequently blackmailed by the government or the police and forced to testify against friends and neighbors.

The news channels were government-controlled so late every evening Tassos would press his ear to the speaker of his short wave radio to get the real Greek news broadcast from stations in Yugoslavia. He kept the volume turned way down. You never knew if a neighbor in an adjacent apartment might overhear and then report you to the police.

World War Two had never really ended for the Greeks. The same Greek militias who had fought the Nazis in the countryside had been labeled as 'communists' by the British and the Americans and many were consequently imprisoned on certain islands. Conflicts between US-backed governments and the more socialist-oriented popular Greek leaders had led to a civil war which had lasted until 1949 and cost a hundred-thousand lives. The current dictatorship was a relic of those opposing forces and, as I was slowly discovering, pressures for another revolution were reaching explosive proportions. Leda began teaching me revolutionary songs written by Mikos Theodorakis and by Manos Hadzidakis. We would sing them very quietly.

Yorgos was a big controversy in Leda's family. I didn't really like listening to endless stories about Yorgos. Fuck Yorgos... but not right away. I needed to wait and see if I might actually like him. I had met him in Berkeley but just barely. Now he was here in Athens too. We would see him soon. I would probably like him. Then what? Big friendship? Oh boy!

Costis was on anti-depressants and was a source of endless worry in the family. He was afraid of being followed by the police... and also afraid of not being followed by the police... complicated.

Leda came back from the police station interview where she had told them that she was a good girl now: no longer with her left-wing Greek husband. Everything seemed to be OK.

Elli, Leda, Cameron, Tassos

Leda just informed me that her mother was ironing the flour bag I had picked up somewhere in Peru to carry my notebook in... sweetness way beyond the call of duty. I told her, "your chicken soup is delicious!" in my emerging Greek. She was an easy woman to love... I would pay my last visit to Elli in Athens thirty-eight years later.

Soft furry arms were reaching gently out toward my Greek woman. Her old friends caressed her, telling her once again how they loved her and that they hoped we hadn't killed her in America. They looked at me and wondered what in the world I could be doing to their beloved Leda... surely I would take her off once again to fly through the great open American skies of emptiness... with the witches from the Louisiana swamps... where no one knows what it means to have a family or a home or even a circle of friends...

They told us that Americans only know how to *search*. We do not know how to *find*. Poor Greek woman: ripped out of the earth and chased across the skies... through the lands of all possibilities.

One of Leda's old friends, Aliki, had married a British man. We went to visit and I got to speak English but I had less in common with him than I had with the Greeks... Leda drank a lot of ouzo... passed out in our sleeping bag out on the balcony after we made it home. I tried to wake her up... I wanted to make love. My heart started racing and fluttering and it scared me.

The next day we passed a wedding... the bride was all dressed in white... I got all choked up thinking of Leda all dressed in white... strange feelings for a man who wanders the world. Leda took no notice... she was not the one who had never been married.

Leda's father was an orphan from a shepherd village in northern Greece. With the support of an uncle he had grown up in Athens and become a lawyer... not a fancy lawyer... but he got paid to do paperwork on behalf of his clients' needs. Every afternoon at 1:00 PM he came home, put his pajamas back on, and took a nap through the late afternoon. Then he went back to work as evening began and by 10:00 PM the work day was complete and he returned home for dinner.

Elli had the ability to empathize with everyone and was the sweet calm voice in the family. She was a refugee. By the time she had reached ten-years-old she and her parents had fled their home town of Smyrna, located in the modern nation of Turkey. The Smyrnaic Greek population, many of whose families had lived in their homes across the Aegean Sea in Anatolia since before the time of Christ, had been evicted as their neighborhoods had been set on fire. The Turks re-named Smyrna calling it Izmir.

Elli's family had escaped to the island of Lesbos and later to Athens. Her early childhood in Anatolia had been very different from those of the Athenian Greeks. The Smyrnaic Greeks had been better educated, wealthier and more worldly. For Elli to have married Tassos had been quite a leap.

Taking a Break

There was a hill called Likavittos which rose above central Athens. I would climb it every day. The city of two million would be spread out below me. I instinctively saw the geography and mapped out potential paths through the city. My long-term habit was to make great sweeps through cities on foot as I discovered their secrets. I was a mountain man. I passed from valley to valley quietly and rapidly during my explorations. Sooner or later someone would pass a law against me or shoot me thinking I was a fox or a wolf or a coyote. My job was to keep moving... to stay ahead of time.

Something about Time was involved. Was time moving through us? Or were we moving through Time? And something about Freedom. No one wants to allow enough Freedom to move through Time. Time travel is illegal. Even our Space travel is restricted. It felt like humanity had become too lazy to really move through Space and Time so we had made up a lot of rules to make sure that no one would get caught exercising those freedoms.

There on Likavittos I found refuge. When I ran up and down it I felt like I still had a life I could call my own. Greeks were good at not taking breaks. Leda had told me that 'taking a break' was an entirely foreign concept to them. But my American self apparently needed to 'take daily breaks.' It was OK with me.

Leda had friends who owned a little hotel on the nearby island of Aegina. They had offered us a few days' free lodging. They also owned the boat which accessed the island. We stopped at two other islands along the way: Poros and Hydra. The men in the taverna on Hydra were showing off their fearlessness by catching yellow-jackets with their bare hands and pinching them into submission before they could retaliate and sting. They wanted me to give it a try but I was not feeling the need to mirror their macho.

We arrived in Aegina. A rocky shore line. Good for diving. Not good for running along the beach. I looked for sea urchins, didn't see any and lowered myself in. Not too cold. Just right. I swam across the cove and checked out the rocks on the other side. Watch out! Those little black spots under the water were all sea urchins - thousands of poisonous little black needles ready to penetrate human skin. No place to climb out. I was swimming back. Whang! A whiplash on my wrist. It was a jelly fish... a *'tsuxtra.'* In this salty water I could almost float: a good achievement for a bag of bones with scrawny muscles like myself!

Leda and I had some space again and were making love sometimes three times a day. I climbed the hill behind our hotel and swept on foot smoothly from valley to valley.

Back in Athens I found a guitar-maker's shop and spent a day learning some of the Greek language terminology. I imagined myself working there someday.

Walking back home through the streets a man locked step with me, seemed impressed that I had learned a bit of the guitar-maker trade, and offered to buy me a drink. We descended a staircase to an underground tavern, he ordered two drinks and was gone. A woman slid into the booth beside me and wanted to flirt. I realized that I had been cleverly set up in a red-light-district establishment. I excused myself... "Really not interested right now," I told her. As I began to ascend the stairs to the street, a waiter tried to insist that I pay for the two drinks. "No, I didn't even order them!" I exclaimed.

"Let him go.. let him go..." said another voice from somewhere inside. I finished climbing to the street and continued on my way home.

We visited her dearest old friends, Popi and her husband... We ate... magnificent feast. We spent the evening embedded in their huge and ancient family singing. I started to hear and feel the amazing qualities of their musical harmonies. They sang for hours. No instruments needed. Interlocking vocal harmonies... yes yes yes...

I bought a cheap little marketplace guitar. I had my little tape recorder with me and was learning fast. Leda was good at transcribing and translating the lyrics. The songs were beginning to soak in.

Grab the Erect Wooden Penis and Push Down

We headed for a taverna in Athens which Yorgos, Leda's Greek husband, had chosen for our meeting. In order to open the front door you must grab a large carved wooden erect penis and push down.

Yorgos and I remembered each other from Berkeley. We had gone for a hike together and both Leda and Lisa had been with us. I grasped his arm. He kissed me hastily on the cheek. I kissed him on the cheek. Greek style. New Mexico commune style. Something basic had changed: now he was at home and I was the foreigner. He had taken one of his brothers' wives for a lover: she's a beautiful little nymph: Valendini, an Athenian TV soap-opera star.

Yorgos

He was a forlorn figure. Tired. But strong. He was just back from covering news stories in Chile. He related some heart-rending and dramatic details. I kept wondering why he wanted to go to places in the world where he was sure to find misery. Is misery so hard to find? Is the military policeman behind his machine gun still mysterious? Or the secret police behind those closed doors?

Yorgos' lifelong friend, Christos, arrived and joined us. He was magnificently handsome and physically symmetrical. His childhood had given him ancient Mediterranean cliff-diving skills and he had been a miraculously agile gymnast famous for doing handsprings from table to table in crowded taverns. Lately he had been weaving huge tapestries and selling them to Hilton hotels for lots of money. Yorgos was his beloved but relatively gnome-like old childhood friend.

Yorgos and Valendini and Leda excused themselves to greet friends at another table and Christos told me that Yorgos was not good with the literal truth but that his ability to play with words in clever ways somehow made up for his inaccuracies. He also let me know that Yorgos was still in love with Leda because she undeniably had some quality that most other women didn't have.

Yorgos, Valendini and Leda returned and our verbal play got

more complex. My Greek was improving but I was always a few steps behind or still in the dark. Efforts were made, however, to keep me in the loop and my inner artist was feeling a stronger connection to Yorgos and to Christos than I had felt with any of Leda's other friends. I felt open to the flows of friendship and love between all of us although Valendini seemed to remain aloof. I began to appreciate the legacy of love and attraction between Leda and Yorgos without feeling threatened. And Christos helped. He was so beautifully balanced in his soul.

To Mani with Yorgos Maniatis

Yorgos, Valendini, Leda and I decided to take Costis' little Volkswagen bug and travel.

Valendini and Yorgos

We passed Corinth and headed into the Peloponnese. On the road together for a few days we passed through towns made famous through the writings of Homer: Tripoli, Argos, Sparta, Kalamata. We kept driving south down toward Mani. We would surprise Yorgos' mother in his home village of Messini.

His mother screamed when she saw us. She had not been able to keep up with her children's adventures. She had given birth to eight boys and one daughter, all of whom were now grown and at large somewhere in the world. Here was her son Yorgos traveling with his brother's wife. And Yorgos' wife Leda had hooked up with an American named Cameron.

His mother disappeared for a few minutes into the house and then returned, having collected herself, to invite us in for a slightly awkward cup of coffee with appetizers.

Later we proceeded yet further south and parked at the lighthouse overlooking the Mediterranean at the extreme southern tip of the peninsula. How much of history had sailed on its way toward its own making right below this vantage point? The giant light house had been sending out its visible light for... forever... it seemed. It was slightly chilly and windy as we hung out on this unconquerable spot. Yes, the Maniatis tribes had for the most part preserved their freedoms throughout the long occupations by Persians, Romans, Turks and Germans. This was the advantage of remote mountainous terrain. Mani had this in common with places like Afghanistan.

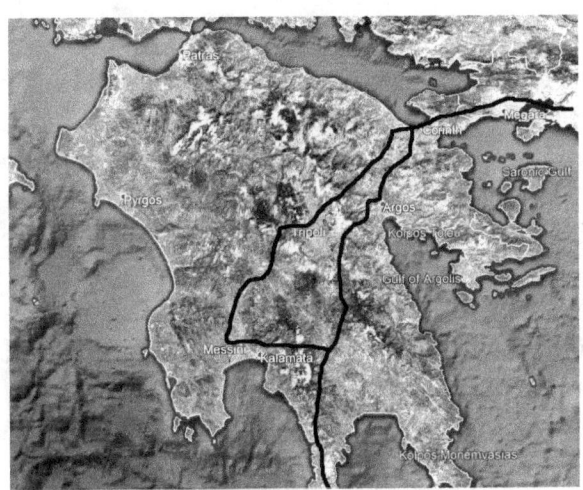

Athens to Mani with Yorgos Maniatis

We had been renting separate rooms for the nights on the road. Somewhere we were all eating little noodles cooked... to overlap the taste of Leda's lithe brown body. Valendini was gorgeous. Yorgos and I were enjoying each other's company. Yorgos was getting a kick out of introducing us as we traveled as "my wife and her husband!"

I turned my eyes towards Leda's moving mouth and saw her through erotic films of fantasy in which we all got together once and for all and drowned our jealousies in their very source by stripping our bodies together naked and performing acts of sexual desire in every possible combination, philosophizing each according to his muse at length and at leisure in the empty spaces of saturated interims...

If we do not ever give vent to those desires which lie within us, chained screaming to our inner walls, we must listen to them sob and moan forever, as the wheels of fortune turn on and on, playing with us their miserable and meaningless games of chance.

But the situation never seemed to be right. Again and again we would feel close to Yorgos -- and his new little nymph. But if one's eyes lit up for a moment, the other's would go out.

Endlessly the time passed. At least we could make music or talk. We could use the music to make love without making love. We could use the words to make love without making love. But I was not Greek and I could not really do it right yet. I was left like a little schoolboy sitting in the corner waiting. Part of me wanted to make love first and learn the music and the language later! Around and around we went.

She Deserves To Stay and Be Greek

Back in Athens we visited Popi and her family again. More wonderful food and Greek voices talking and singing into the night. My little girl among them. She deserved to stay there and be Greek. The pain of separation would not be so great that I could not bear it. Turn her loose. She was such a beautiful creature. Let her spread her wings and fly there at home! Don't keep asking her to struggle in the American dust.

That night I woke up from a dream in a panic... I was sitting bolt upright with my heart racing...

'If I take the train tomorrow and go away my little Greek girl can fly free...'

I went out into the street thinking to find the train station and ask the times of departure. I would go to Yugoslavia and find my way from there. I would buy a ticket. I would disappear and leave my Greek woman to her Greek freedom! But fate was cooking up another scenario.

November 17th Revolution

Voices were chanting in the distance. Instead of finding a train station I went back home. For two days we had been hearing the cheers of protest. Someone had told us it was the students. They were demonstrating. Thousands of people had filled the avenues and were waving their arms in unison like troupes of dancers... shouting political slogans.

Back out on the streets again alone the next day a wave of energy rushed through my spine. I could feel the proximity of the brewing conflict. I went around the corner to the Polytechnic School. The students were hanging from the windows of their school and shouting. They were making cardboard signs and placing them behind the windshield wipers of passing buses. The drivers would laugh and then drive off wondering how long they should dare to carry those signs through other parts of the city.

The nearby streets were filled with a delight... a euphoria. The butchers and magazine salesmen had new notes in their voices. They were calling out the names and prices as if they were hammering nails -- doing their work dances with arrogant pleasure. They were now princes of ancient times... busy gathering goats and wine from the markets... grapes, women and feasts dashed out of fourth story windows and flew hungrily through the air.

The atmosphere was now electric. Revolution was actually happening. The inside of my spine was drinking splashes of cold rapture -- but -- somewhere high above us all in the sky, lurking behind the clouds or in the rocks between the trees, a monster was glaring down at us with giant orange eyes. We could sense the threat.

The further I walked away from the Polytechnic School the more the revolution faded. It hadn't engulfed the whole city. Ten blocks away from the school everything looked perfectly normal -- dull as a bumblebee -- except for the gray squads of police, standing in groups of forty and fifty, tapping the sidewalks with their nervous toes while they stared aimlessly at the sky between the buildings and clasped their hands dutifully behind their backs. I passed a plaza filled with gray paddy-wagons: empty and waiting. The police were waiting. My quest for the train station again forgotten I drifted back home for lunch.

Cameron and Leda crouched with her father, mother and brother beside the radio in their apartment, their ears glued to the student voice coming insistently through the air from the pirate radio station erected within the school.

"Edho Polytechnio! Edho Polytechnio!" The music of Theodorakis, Zorba's Dance, the forbidden music, ...music forbidden by law... was being played over the air for the first time in six years!

"Edho Polytechnio! Edho Polytechnio!" The voice of freedom rose and the police moved into action. The tank drove into the street in front of the school.

The frantic voice rose in panic-stricken pitch: "Edho Polytechnio! Citizens of Athens! Go down into the streets! We need help! We need

Doctors! We have no weapons!"

"Edho Polytechnio!" Tears welled up out of Leda's eyes as she crouched closer, hypnotized by the radio.

The shots were fired: pistols, rifles and then machine guns. It was not enough. The machine guns were fired from the tanks into the unarmed crowd. The steel tank treads rolled over the pavement like sledge hammers and moved forward. The war machines ate their way through the schoolyard gate, now red with the blood of those crushed beneath!

The soldier who had smiled and waved at the demonstrators was shot and killed on the spot. More students died.

But things did not end at the school...

The police ran in great mobs through the streets terrified of everything that moved. We watched from our fourth-floor balcony as the police began a battle with the army. The city streets were like hidden canyons. Machine-gun fire echoed and amplified. But no one knew who was hidden around the next corner.

The taste for clubbing grew in the bellies of the police. Their hours of action had come. The sickening screams of the clubbed ones arose from the streets and alleys. The tanks clawed their way through the little park below our apartment balcony. The machine-gun bullets shattered the marble facades across from us. We retreated into the recesses of the apartment fearing stray bullets.

No one will ever know exactly how many were dead: if it was possible to *not count* them, they were *not counted*. But the dead were dead and the wounded were still moaning and bleeding. Many innocent passersby had died including a young female tourist from Norway.

After three days it was almost enough. The ground beneath the city opened her face with horror and held her breath. Not a sound was heard except for the birds and the occasional guns.

For the first time in years not a human whisper arose from the city of Athens. At first the birds flew about with gleeful chirping as if to say, 'the city is ours at last!' Great flocks of them joined in mad swoops of idiotic chirping. But the great sadness which lay beneath them rose and overwhelmed them slowly until they, too, perched quietly and confused on the railings and balconies. The pigeons began to worry. For the first time they realized that the impatient squeals from the tires of taxicabs and the impolite feet of the pedestrians were things they had come to love. The birds suddenly felt sorry for us.

And then we were left with only the sounds of the last machine-gun volleys and the sounds of our forks and our spoons making great clanks as I set them freshly washed in the drainer beside the kitchen sink...

The streets were empty, devoid of ought but the police, the army... and an occasional fugitive youth still trying to get home.

The hours drizzled past... the meaningless slow revolutions of the hands on the clock.

On the fourth morning the machine guns were silent. Timid pedestrians emerged from their doors, ready to buy eggs. Gone were the chanting voices. Gone was the reckless spirit of freedom, the tens of thousands who had thronged into the central avenues to wave their arms over their heads and cry together into the sky. Gone were the ecstatic cries of the butchers, the bakers, the magazine vendors. Gone were the ghosts of ancient kings and queens and princes. Gone were the waiting gray paddy wagons in the plazas. Gone were the squads of police. The monster had struck, and then retired to lurk behind the clouds or inside the rocks, confident, smug.

Taxiarkhos Dimitrios Ioannides, a disgruntled government hardliner, had used the student demonstration as a pretext to stage a coup that had temporarily overthrown the dictator, Papadopoulos. Military law had been declared and the new Junta appointed a new Prime Minister, but Ioannides remained the behind-the-scenes strongman.

'17th of November,' the date of the beginning of the student demonstration at the Polytechnic School, later became the name of a Greek revolutionary group.

Yorgos' mother, back from her Peloponnese home and still friends with Elli, stopped by for a visit. Two of her other sons, Andonis and Vangelis, were with her. Vangelis had been at the Polytechnic School when the violence had broken out. He said that the shooting had begun when the police were beating a young woman to death and the crowd reacted to try and stop them.

North to Ioannina

The city was coming back to life but we decided it would be a good time to go somewhere else. We decided to drive up to Ioannina in northern Greece with Spyros and Dorothea.

Spyros was Popi's brother and Leda had loved him from a very early age. Now he was married to Dorothea who was pregnant.

We were hoping to leave the threats of violence behind us in Athens, but caravans of soldiers in trucks were passing us on the highways. What was going on? The news channels in Greece were locked down more tightly than ever and there was no way to understand.

We drove north of Ioannina to hike in the Vikos gorge: a mixture of ancient remote villages, monasteries and rugged scenery. We found a little hotel and moved in. Between hikes in the gorge we retreated to our room and our love-making intensified again. I was again discovering that it deepened our attraction if I didn't come every time we made love. Saving some of the energy was better... healthier. We talked of making children together... what would we come up with, we wondered? But the idea seemed remote. We were a long way from having a real home.

Dorothea had been teaching in Ioannina and could show us something of the town. The local music was heavy with the low notes from clarinets. But everyone could see that the military was up to something and most of the night clubs were temporarily closed down.

Spyros was a man accustomed to living from song to song so he was disappointed. Not so long ago Spyros had invited Dorothea to visit him on his ancestral island home of Zakynthos. She had still been a virgin at age twenty-six. They had made love once and boom... a baby was on the way. Her father had not been happy about Spyros as a son-in-law but they had married anyway.

Dorothea was not very happy either. She had been happily surrounded by her students, her friends, her admirers - a whole life spread out before her there in Ioannina. And now she was married to a quiet little guy from Athens and she was pregnant. "I'm a pregnant woman now," she would tell her husband. "We pregnant women have our strange little whims and our insatiable desires and right now your smell is repelling me. It would please me if you wouldn't touch me and the baby. Good night."

Spyros was waiting out the dry spells, worrying all the while, and doing his best to survive until the situation would be right for him to sing another song. He was more a worrier than a warrior and was not good at making money. Leda could read him like an open book. She had known and secretly loved him for so long.

The next night we were lucky and did find an open night club and we danced to the local clarinet music while the piles of clay plates were smashed around our feet. The rhythms were strong and slow and swept us along. Ouzo was helping us feel agile.

The next morning we awoke with all worries washed away. The dancing and music had done its magic. We had followed our whims with no particular plan.

I was no longer swimming through the world. The world was swimming through me.

We visited one of Dorothea's friends and learned that the new dictator, Ioannides, had been thinking to make his new national capitol in Ioannina instead of Athens. That's why we had been seeing all the re-shuffling of military forces on the highway with us as we had traveled north. While Dorothea and her friend finished catching up, Spyros and Leda talked about their own long and pure, but unfulfilled, friendship which could perhaps have been a love affair. Perhaps they should have been more bold, they wondered.

Not liking the idea of ending up in Ioannides' new military capitol, we started driving back south. As we approached Athens we sang as we drove along. Spyros, like other members of Popi's family, never really stopped singing those exquisite harmonies... they were really good at that.

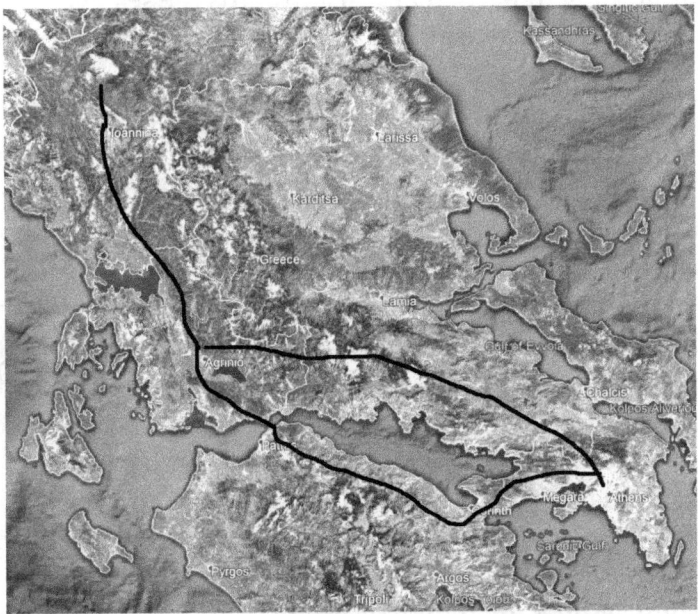

From Athens to Ioannina with Spyros and Dorothea

Moving to Crete

Back in Athens we discovered that our friend, Yvonne, from Colorado, had arrived. She had brought letters from a couple of our friends in Boulder. They contained some news about the friend with whom Leda had fallen in love and I felt irritated and jealous. But just for a moment.

Again, we decided to leave. After spending a day consulting the oracle a few hours north in Delphi, we set out the next morning with the still-timid Athenian pedestrians and, making our way to the port in Piraeus, embarked on the ferry boat for Crete.

All night long the ferry boat churned across the water, as if passing from Florida to Cuba. Dawn dumped us into the northern Cretan port of Heraklion and the marketplace there, unperturbed by the deaths in Athens, absorbed us gently.

After two days we wandered south, a strange trio now: a man with two women. We hopped off a southbound bus at its southernmost terminal and walked on down the road, me with guitar in hand, towards nothing in particular... just towards the sea.

"Which way is the sea?" I asked an old woman we passed on the road. My Greek was getting functional.

"You are walking toward the sea," she affirmed.

Plastic greenhouses thickly covered the landscape, housing just what, I could not imagine. But the plastic glistened, and peering into the distance, I could not tell if it was the far-off sea which I beheld or if it was just another row of greenhouses.

A half-hour's walk brought the sea firmly into view. And there, just at the spot where the road kissed the shore... We all recognized it at once: the tables and chairs scattered randomly about; the old calendars and posters sagging off the not-very-freshly whitewashed walls; the little sink sporting a glassful of used toothbrushes...

An old man was carrying on before three younger men at one of the tables. It was obvious that the old man had been doing most of the talking. He was kneeling on his chair, gesticulating like a big kid. The three younger ones, men in their prime of life, sat more decorously at the table, apparently considering the old man's words.

"To fight for or against the dictators in Athens is ridiculous," the old man was saying. "The price of oil goes up no matter what, although it floats in plentiful blobs right in off the Mediterranean onto our beaches! Who is ruling in Athens does not concern us! As long as we are free to eat, fuck and shit, there is no reason to think of fighting!"

I walked toward the old man and was taken in by a brief glance; I paused, stopped in my tracks, turned around, took off my pack and sat down at a table to wait. Leda and Yvonne did the same.

"The moment those three basic freedoms are interfered with here on the soil of Crete, that is the moment for fighting! Whoever comes to suppress those freedoms, be they the Greek army, the Turks, or the Americans, they must be fought, but now is not the time."

Satisfied with his soliloquy, the old man arose and approached me and the two women. "What kind of wine do you want, light or dark? You are Greek," he said to Leda, recognizing in her the deep crystal-clear black eyes of the race. "You know that the dark is always best. But I have light wine in bottles for the tourists if you want."

"We want the dark," Leda told him.

The old man returned promptly with a time-worn crockery pitcher. "I serve this only to people who seem special. The grapes were popped by the toes of my friends. The tourists don't like the strong wind here," he added, eyeing the three of us. "They think only of swimming and don't know that it is the wind which brings the rain for the tomatoes and cucumbers in our greenhouses. Everything with foreigners is always very difficult," he sighed.

Our eyes were riveted, smiling, on the old man. "I spent twenty-years in the merchant marine, sailing from one port to the next. That's why I know many languages. I never enjoyed learning them one bit and can enjoy speaking only in my native tongue! We do not change. An honest man finally returns to the place of his birth. He returns to the smells and the tastes and he is happy. Only the pace of life will have changed, sweetened. What the young do too fast, the old do more slowly, at a proper pace."

The old man's eyes rolled up to the sky over the Mediterranean and melted like chocolate in the sun. His arms had been sweeping over our heads. The gray stubble of beard on his face was handsome and soft.

Yannis

The old man's wife emerged from the tavern's interior. She was in her forties, broad across the bottom, but not fat. The bones in her face and her ankles were lithe. She approached us, braced herself for a confrontation with foreigners, then melted as she recognized that at least one of our trio was Greek. Addressing herself primarily to Leda, she explained that there were beans a-boil on the stove for lunch.

"And feel free to move in closer to the wall if you don't like the wind." Drawing a chair up beside the large wood-burning stove which was lying in the corner of the patio, she sat for a moment; her gaze resting comfortably on the Mediterranean.

"When I was twenty-one," resumed the old man, "I was taught by a woman in Piraeus that sweetness comes to he who does not move too fast. She was in her forties, the age at which a woman knows the proper rhythm... I have never found a woman more voluptuous than her..."

I glanced at the old man's wife to see if she was registering any resentment at this last comment. She didn't seem to be. No doubt she had heard all these stories many times. Occasionally, something in the way the old man repeated them now amused her and she would smile. The old man vanished into the tavern's interior to bring out the beans and more wine. Leda, Yvonne and I looked delightedly at each other.

"The most handsome man I have ever seen in my life is sitting over at that table!" Yvonne confided to me and Leda, redirecting our attention to the three Cretan men who had been quietly drinking at their table. "The one sitting on the right is the one I mean" she whispered, licking her lips, "the gentle looking one."

Nikos - The Gentle-Looking One

Bursting from around the corner, speedy and anxious as a wet house-cat, strode a girl with curly red hair, glasses, a pasty complexion, and a towel. Conquering her way through the tables and chairs, she headed for the little porcelain sink, filled a plastic washtub with water, plunged her head into it, and began washing her hair. Another girl, a blonde, more sedate, emerged from behind the same corner and took a seat near the wood-stove beside the old man's wife. She flashed us a brief movie star smile but then lapsed back into a heavy dull potato trance which looked like it might eventually claim her for good.

The old man had served us with beans and more wine and now re-emerged from the tavern with his beautiful black-eyed three-year-old daughter in his arms. "Look what I've got here!" rejoiced the old man.

Yannis and Angela

The little girl -- this goddess-like three-year-old -- gave us a steady knowing smile and then, placed on the ground, trotted off toward the red-haired girl.

"Angela!" cried the red-haired girl, having just pulled her head out of the plastic washtub and wrapped her head with a towel. "Come here you beautiful little morsel of flesh!"

Angela allowed herself to be seized and squeezed, contentedly smiling all the while. Chromium blue eyes stared frantically out from behind the red-haired girl's glasses, pleading, desperately beseeching... She set Angela back down on the floor and began playfully chasing her among the washtubs, the tables and the chairs. The red-headed girl's lanky wooden limbs clambered this way and that.

"Angela!" she cried, entwining her arms around the little girl again, "I love you!"

She smiled briefly at me. Yvonne was watching the old man's wife who was displaying noticeable signs of discomfort. The red-haired girl released Angela once again, sighed, leaned against a table and lit up a long filter cigarette which dangled from her mouth. She was built like a boy.

"Is there some place to stay for the night around here?" I asked the old man.

"Yes, down the beach is a hotel."

We paid for our wine and beans, donned our packs and departed. The three Cretan men, still silent at their table, followed Yvonne and Leda with their eyes.

Finding our way to Kokkinos Pirgos in Crete

A Man in Love Kills for His Woman

The Mediterranean waves playfully lapped at the smooth and colorful round stones on the shore causing a tiny but perpetual clatter. There was nothing of the crashing, the churning of the breakers so familiar to me and Yvonne from our own American coastlines. Leda had never liked the tumultuous oceans she had found in America and was languishing in the pleasure of being back beside her gentle Mediterranean after living 'in exile,' as the Greeks call it, for so many years.

The hotel proved to be a large white-washed building right next to the waves of the sea. We were in the little village called 'Kokkinos Pirgos', which mean 'Red Tower'.

"Yes, we have rooms for rent upstairs," the girl replied to my question and tied another knot. Immense heaps of fishing nets lay about the floor. A boy came wandering out of a side room and sat down.

"He is my brother," the girl added. "He is my twin. We are both eighteen!"

We had pulled up chairs around her. I was absentmindedly playing a very quiet tune on my guitar. "These all are your father's nets?" I asked.

"That's right, in the summer my father does his fishing," the girl explained. Her brother seemed content with his silence. The sky was growing dark outside and a chilly mist was hanging over the sea which threatened to pour in unwanted through the windows.

"How long does it take to repair all those nets by tying all those knots?" I asked.

"All winter long," the girl replied, smiling faintly, tying another knot. A moment of silence ensued. The girl tied another knot and smiled again. "There is nothing strange here about the endless tying of knots," she added. "You must explain that to your friends," she said to Leda. "You are Greek. You know. Here we do not play with life."

"Just think of all those eighteen-year-olds in America out drivin' around, drinkin', smokin' dope...!" said Yvonne.

"That's what I mean," agreed the girl. "The foreigners do not understand." Then, addressing Leda: "How did you come to know this couple?"

"They're not the couple. It's me 'n him that's the couple! Yvonne is a friend of ours from where we now live back in America." I leaned back in my chair and resumed the absent-minded strumming on my guitar.

The girl shook her head skeptically and looked at me with a fresh eye. "How much do you love her?" she demanded suddenly.

Irked to find myself suddenly on trial, I, with a wry smile on my mouth, spread my arms wide apart and said: "This much."

Unimpressed, the girl asked: "What would you do if a man tried to flirt with her?"

"They can flirt with her as much as they like; it doesn't seem to do them any good."

"Then you don't really love her," she announced with a triumphant little smirk. "A man in love kills for his woman."

I rose and asked: "Where are those rooms?"

The girl and her brother led us upstairs. Impudent silence was maintained on both sides. Yvonne entered one room and Leda and I entered another. The windows faced south over the sea. Shreds of black clouds were barely visible in the last dismal sunlight from the horizon. A cold wind was buffeting the building. Yvonne, alone in her room, crawled into bed to get warm. Leda and I did the same, curling up in each other's arms. The afternoon wine had grown heavy in our heads and sleep swam briefly through us like a narwhal passing beneath the Mediterranean.

We Began a Slow and Sensual Dance

Reawakening two hours later, we returned toward the old man's tavern, shuffling along the edge of the sea, watching the moon-lit jets of broken waves leaping over the ever-rolling clattering round rocks.

The old man, his head bobbing on the edge of a table, was snoring and collapsing, inflating and deflating like a blowfish on the beach. His eyes opened briefly from time to time to check up on things. He had a nine-year-old son, Kostakis, who was doing his homework at another table, copying pages out of the bible into his own handwriting. Leda and Yvonne and I seated ourselves quietly and the old man's wife brought us a salad with some wine. "Later on there'll be some beans and pork chops too," she said.

Xarilaos, Dimitrios and Nikos, the same three men who had been in the tavern during the afternoon, entered, nodded briefly in greeting, and sat at a table close to us.

The red-haired girl came striding in, followed by the more slow moving blonde, and put some Greek music on the old man's tape recorder. She lit up a cigarette, took a puff, fidgeted, changed her mind about the music and switched the tapes: out blared American rock 'n roll.

"Claudia! Take that shit off!" Dimitrios screamed at her. She obeyed, putting the Greek music back on.

Dimitrios leaned toward Leda confidingly and said, "We have thrown them away, those two German girls, but they won't leave. We don't like them here."

Xarilaos had gotten up and begun to dance. Dimitrios and Nikos arose and joined him. The three of them danced side by side with their arms across each others' shoulders. The old man woke up and joined them, grinning gently at the space in front of him. They danced right up and over a chair and a table which happened to be in their path.

Claudia was fidgeting by the door, one hand occupied with her cigarette, the other stuffed under her armpit. Her body was quivering. She looked like she was dying to rip off her clothes and undulate naked to the music in the middle of the floor. Her impulses to dance were visible but she never got moving for more than a second or two. Her blonde friend had seated herself quietly on a stool.

At the end of the song, satisfied with themselves, Xarilaos, Dimitrios and Nikos returned to their table and sat down. "Bring a bottle of ouzo for *them* too," they told the old man.

The gift was placed before me. I opened it and poured out glassfuls for Leda, Yvonne and myself. The old man's wife appeared with the beans and pork chops. Soon there was food on every table.

Another song had begun and I, beginning with a somersault across the floor from my chair, began a dance, a brief one, which I ended by somersaulting backwards into my chair, where I resumed eating, feeling much better.

"I have finished my homework," announced Kostakis. He stood up, a rotund little fellow, and danced his way over toward the kitchen with his bible and papers. His mother smiled affectionately at his dance. The little fellow was so loose he was a pleasure to watch. Claudia snatched a stick up from beside the door and chased after him, dueling at him as if with a sword. Kostakis pretended he had a sword too, and began dancing out the mock duel with Claudia. He chased and got chased. Kostakis liked it, but everyone else in the room watched with slight aversion.

"Look at the expression on his mother's face!" Yvonne whispered to Leda. Two or three times a womanly stance flashed through Claudia's body and it would look like there was hope: she could be standing there in black silk with her hip cocked. But no... her posture became wooden again. Chasing. A tom-child.

I pulled Leda up by the hand and we began a slow and sensual dance. The sea was finding its way from its deathbed on the beach to the soles of our feet. Claudia and Kostakis began to lose interest in their sword fight and Leda and I danced close to Claudia, looking at her, inviting her to join the dance. She didn't. She was dying to, but she couldn't quit quivering!

Leda put her arm around her shoulder and advised her: "If you want to be like a Greek, do not try so hard. Trying is not the way! Just let things be."

"But I *try* so hard!" Claudia complained, completely missing the point but somehow becoming beautiful in her desperation. "I have traveled all over Turkey and Greece trying so hard to learn! Yet everywhere I go I am told that I can't... that I haven't found the way... and I get so... so desperate!"

The blonde girl flashed Leda one of her warm movie-star smiles, apparently grateful that someone was sympathizing with Claudia. Done smiling, she lapsed back into her potato trance...

The old man's wife had retrieved a sleeping Angela from inside the kitchen and placed the little girl in a little battered wagon. Gathering another bundle into the wagon, off she went into the night... Kostakis in tow. The Divine Mother... Off to the bungalow where she would put the children to sleep... where she would watch over them, mending...

He Had Brought His Guitar

It was up to the old man to keep the show on the road. But exhaustion was stalking him, claiming him. He dozed in fits and starts, snuffing and snorting, his head on his arms at his table. His eyes opened and closed, his hands clambering automatically toward the sky, but the terrible weariness was beating his head down. Weariness had surrounded him like the slippery walls of a drinking glass... He was the giant beetle who had fallen into the glass and never stopped trying to climb back out. The legs climb... Day and night the legs still keep climbing, climbing...

Xarilaos woke him up. "Yannis! Bring us more ouzo!" The old

man arose immediately. There was no hesitation in him. Everyone must have more ouzo...

Yvonne and Nikos had found each other's eyes and were gazing fondly at each other. Nikos was quite obviously the gentle one of the three. "What do you do?" Yvonne asked him.

"I grow cucumbers," he smiled at her. "And tomatoes." Yvonne smiled at him again and he asked her to dance. They began a slow and gentle dance around the room.

Claudia was dancing alone, jerkily, in little circles, embracing an imaginary partner.

Leda and I were standing, watching her. Xarilaos seized the opportunity and, with a grand sweeping motion, enveloped Leda into a dance. "You are a Greek," he told her, "you should leave the foreigners alone! Come, have another ouzo," he added, inviting Leda to his table. They sat down beside Dimitrios. I remained dancing alone.

"It's true," said Dimitrios. "The foreign men cannot become good husbands for Greek women."

"That's right!" re-affirmed Xarilaos. "He has his American woman with him. You should leave him alone!"

"She is just our friend," Leda explained. "It is I who am with him!"

"Listen," advised Xarilaos in a lower voice, "that cannot be. He will turn around and leave you the first time he gets a whiff of another woman. He will grow tired of everything being the same. Only a Greek can have the strength to be with a Greek woman!"

"We'll see," Leda smiled. "I know what you are thinking, but this one is different! Let it alone! Let it alone the way he would leave you alone in his country to find an American woman."

"But the American women *love* Greek men," Xarilaos growled under his breath.

"Look at this one here," Dimitrios added, tossing his head in Yvonne's direction.

At this moment a new face came smiling into the tavern. It was Alexandros, a musician, and he had brought his guitar. The old man instantly arose and brought out another small bottle of ouzo for him, "This is Leda. And there are Cameron and Yvonne," said Xarilaos.

"Not many of the guys here tonight, I see," observed Alexandros, tipping his ouzo. He had an open and friendly glow. "Where are you from?" he asked Leda.

"Athens."

"What brings you down this way?"

"We just wanted to get out of Athens... and somehow we ended up here."

"A song, Alexandre!" demanded Xarilaos.

"Clauuudia!" cried Dimitrios. "Off with the music!"

I stopped dancing and sat beside Xarilaos: "What's up my man?" I asked him, leaning close and putting my hand on his shoulder. Xarilaos answered with a cool, but not hostile, stare.

Enthusiastic about Alexandros' arrival, the old man stayed awake and came over to give me the low-down: "Alexandros' father was a musician too. In fact he was such a fine musician that he had spent his old age singing in the nightclubs of Athens. The youngsters would come, the wanna-be's and the usual middle-men, wanting him to make records! *'You'll be rich and famous!'* they had said. But Alexandros' father," he explained bending confidentially over the whole table, his eyes blazing with amazement, "refused every offer! *'If they like my songs let them come to hear me in person!'* he would say!"

The Athenians Retreated, Jumping into Their Car

Alexandros had begun to tell an ancient musical story as he played:

> *High in the mountains of Crete*
> *Way up high in the crags*
> *An eagle has grasped in his talons a human head*
> *which he pecks at with his beak.*
> *He asks the head, the eagle does, while pecking away...*
> *"Head, what are you doing here?*
> *"What became of you?"*
> *"I came from the East," confesses the head.*
> *"I was a Turk, coming to Crete,*
> *and look what has happened to me!"*

During the song four well-dressed and well-mannered Athenian men arrived, nodded politely at everyone, chose a somewhat distant table and seated themselves. The song came to an end; the old man went to their table.

"Wine is what we want..." one of them announced.

"The light or the dark?"

"The dark. And some kind of snack..."

I reached for Alexandros' guitar and began to play Zorba's Dance.

Yvonne sprang to her feet to dance. Nikos, two of the Athenians, and then Leda, followed her.

Claudia rushed over to me to beseech me: "Play an American song! Play Clementine! Play... some blues! Play some Blues!"

"When we are in Greece, we must play Greek music!" I explained to her with my eyes half-closed.

"You play Greek music for your woman and she likes it!" Alexandros laughed, looking at Yvonne, who was being gently rocked in Nikos' embrace.

"That's not my woman. Leda is my woman."

"Oh?" Alexandros looked surprised. Xarilaos and Dimitrios answered Alexandros' inquiring glance with dark looks.

Leda had in the meantime accepted to sit with the Athenians. "We have a new kind of fertilizer," one of them began explaining to her, "especially developed by the Americans. We live in Athens but we're traveling through Crete talking to the farmers..."

But Xarilaos had risen and approached Leda at the Athenians', table. He motioned imperatively for her to come confer with him in the corner of the room. "What is Yvonne going to do?" he asked her urgently and hoarsely, putting his arm around her shoulder casually, loosely, as if he were an old and familiar friend.

"I don't know what little Yvonne is going to do or if she'll ever get around to doing anything!"

"When she makes love with a man, does she stay with him? Or does she go quickly to look for another?"

"I Just don't know..."

"It is different with foreigners... how about a little kiss..." he suggested leaning toward her mouth.

"And Nikos?" she asked, quickly drawing away, "Is he married?"

"Of course he's married! But don't tell Yvonne."

One of the Athenians had called me over to their table and was quietly warning me, "I'd watch out about letting him dance like that with your woman," tossing his head toward Nikos and Yvonne.

"She's not my woman."

"Oh!"

"Leda's my woman."

"But she's an Athenian!"

"I know."

"Then I'd watch out for that guy," he said, glancing at Xarilaos, "he's a real jerk."

At that same moment, taking advantage of a lull in Xarilaos' attack, Leda slipped back to the Athenians' table and sat down beside me.

"What did he want?" asked one of the Athenians.

"Oh, he just wanted to know about Yvonne..."

Alexandros broke out with another lively Cretan dance on his guitar. Heads turned, feet began to stir...

"Say!" one of the Athenians impulsively cried out toward Dimitrios over the sound of the music: "We have some American-made fertilizer for sale. Are you guys interested?"

"You can take your American-made fertilizer and fertilize your own Athenian ass with it!" came back across the room.

"What kind of place is this?" exclaimed the Athenian, jumping up.

The other three Athenians stood up too.

The old man snapped awake and casually rose to his feet. The dancing stopped. Alexandros quit playing the guitar.

"Nothing makes any sense in here!" the Athenian yelled. "What is this old man doing? Running some kind of musical-chairs-whorehouse with the foreigners? What is he? Some kind of pimp?"

"But we all already know each other!" Leda yelled at them.

Xarilaos, Dimitrios and Nikos were advancing toward the Athenians. Yannis bellowed: "Get out of here! I don't want you to ever come back!" His voice sounded like a giant child's voice complaining at Death for having done the incomprehensible.

The Athenians retreated, jumping into their car. Xarilaos, Dimitrios and Nikos fired up their motorcycles and chased the car on down the road. Dimitrios broke a glass, which he had snatched off a table on his way out the door, against the window of the car. With a roar of engines they returned and parked the bikes laughing as they filed back into the old man's place.

Claudia had begun frantically changing tapes again: Theodorakis songs, Acid Rock, old Macedonian folksongs... everything was flashing on and off the tape recorder and blaring out into the tavern. Yvonne sidled back up to Nikos and gave him a kiss.

"What about me?" asked Xarilaos, and he folded Yvonne into his arms and began kissing her long and deep. But eventually she began to struggle. Xarilaos bit her on the lip and let her go. Her hand streaked to her lip (...is it bleeding?...) but then it struck her as funny. She laughed and went back to Nikos. Dimitrios had returned unkissed to his table.

Swimming Towards the Moon

Yannis had cleared empty plates off the tables and refreshed the wine and ouzo supply. Claudia finally left a Greek song on the tape and Yannis took the blonde German girl, Brigitte, who had been sitting tranquilly by the stove throughout, almost beautiful, by the hand and led her into a dance. "I am tempted," he confided to me and Leda, "to have a child with her. I think it would be a beautiful combination!"

Inside of me something had been growing. There was an energy in me which was too big for the dance I had been doing. I wandered outside and down toward the sea, paused for a moment and then took off my clothes. Naked, I broke into a run, my thighs ejaculating their energy into the beach. I dove into the Mediterranean and began swimming towards the moon. From time to time I disappeared beneath the surface of the water, enjoying the quiet space below.

Eventually I reappeared, hair wet, at the old man's tavern. Yvonne and Nikos had disappeared. Leda was sitting with Xarilaos and Dimitrios, who both looked sleepy and tired. Yannis was cleaning things up. The German girls had both disappeared. Alexandros was playing a quiet song on his guitar. I sat down, but when Alexandros' song came to an end and no one had stirred, I motioned to Leda and we both rose to leave. "You are right about the sea," Yannis commented to me as we walked out the door.

Halfway to our room in the hotel, we heard a motorcycle fire up behind us. Dimitrios overtook us and stopped beside us. "I'll meet you down by the beach at three o'clock in the morning," he whispered toward Leda.

"Good God, get outa here!" I reacted.

Dimitrios coaxed his cycle off down the road. Something about the little red tail-light receding in the distance looked lonely and pathetic.

The next morning found me sitting outside of Yannis' place on top of an adobe wall, playing my guitar. The sky was so blue and the sun so warm that the notes flew out into the sky like birds!

Yannis sauntered up to me from behind. "That's good," he commented. "You are sitting in the right place! You could be sitting down there in the patio on a chair, but you are out here on the wall instead. Much nicer! Your body will always take you to the right place if you know how to listen to it." Yannis was now calling me *'levendimu'* or *'palikarakimu'*... Greek nicknames which imply that he was seeing me as a cool dude...

"These bodies of ours can get us into a lot of trouble too!" I laughed. I was kind of playing the dumb American to invite more wisdom...

"No no. If listened to properly, they will keep us out of trouble!"

Leda, Yvonne and Claudia appeared from inside the patio where they had been drinking coffee. "We should go swimming," announced Yvonne. "I wish I had a swimming suit."

"I can lend you mine," offered Claudia. The two girls studied each other's anatomies for a moment.

Apparently having decided that it would work, Yvonne said, "OK."

"Come into my room then."

Yvonne soon re-emerged clad in Claudia's bikini. Leda and I walked down to the beach with her. "I don't know about Claudia," Yvonne confided. "Offering to help me fasten the bikini top is one thing, but not being able to keep her hands off the goodies in front is another!"

The polished round stones on the beach shouted at us with their multi-chromatic veins of blazing quartz and submarine purples. Great heaps of psychedelic stones! "How was it with Nikos last night?" Leda asked.

"Oh, he took me into one of his greenhouses to show me his cucumbers. Those cucumbers are amazing, they're so huge! And it's so hot and steamy inside those greenhouses! It's like being in the jungle!" Yvonne licked her lips and ran laughing into the sea.

By late afternoon Leda and I were back in our room. Leda was asleep. I was standing by the window. The sun hovered over the edge of the sea; his blazing eye just hung there, didn't blink, smile, nothing. Eternity was written on the landscape and it rushed over me like a wave, leaving me bleached, washed out, thin. The sun was ready to crash and burn... but it went down soundlessly behind the endless commotion of the sea, like a crimson teardrop.

I lowered my eyes to look at Leda. My eyes grew moist. She was lying, still asleep, curled under a blanket, her little feet protruded encased in blue socks. For thousands of years this dark-eyed woman had lived out this drama. Now it happened to be me who was running through her like a river of wind through the sky. She was made from the flesh of goddesses. To polish the desire of her man -- that was her endless task, just as the waves had the endless task of rolling and polishing those stones. The sky had grown ragged again tonight... like the teeth of a butchers saw.

Get Death on the Run

Xarilaos, Dimitrios and Nikos were busy devouring salad and pork chops down at the old man's place. Three other tables were full of men likewise gorging themselves on the fine-tasting fare. The old man and his wife were speeding from table to table producing more pork chops, beans, salads, wine and fish. There was an enormous quantity of food piling up out of that little kitchen and at each passage the crowd heaped the details of further requests on the old couple. Leda, Yvonne and I had arrived and taken seats with Xarilaos, Dimitrios and Nikos. The old man and his wife brought out more food. The mood was somber tonight. No one seemed to have much to say. Yvonne and Nikos seemed to have knowing smiles, but that was about all that was going on. The next time Yannis passed by bearing another plate of food, I looked at him sympathetically and couldn't help murmuring, "It is difficult!"

"You are right," agreed the old man, resting his arm around my shoulders, "it is difficult." A glow had surrounded the old man, and once he started glowing, he just kept on glowing.

"Tell me," I asked, "how many years has it been since you quit sailing and settled here?"

"Fifteen."

"May you see another thirty!"

"Another thirty! Another sixty it will be!" he exclaimed shaking his fist gently at me and at the sky. Then he hurried off to carry more food. Xarilaos shook his head and smiled at the old man's words.

Eventually Yannis found the time to come back. "Why do I do this work?" he continued. "You wonder why I do this?" His arm swept over the tables full of feasting men. "We are all here indulging in one of the pleasures of life. The pleasures of life are not so complicated. We must eat, we must make love, and as we grow older we must philosophize. I do my work by providing for the first pleasure and then spend the rest of my time enjoying the other two!"

Yannis paused, looked around and saw that we were all listening. He continued, "If I lived in the big city, in Athens, perhaps it would be different. Perhaps there would be enough food available and I could beg and then spend all of my time with the other two... like Diogenes! Diogenes was a Cretan who lived in Athens back during the time of Alexander. He slept in a clay urn in the marketplace and spent all his waking hours philosophizing and enjoying the fruits of nature. Food would come to him. He was a man who did not worry." Yannis paused again and exuded tranquility.

> *When Alexander marched through Athens, there was Diogenes, laid out on the grass, absentmindedly caressing the green stems of the dandelions, paying absolutely no attention to the parade.*
>
> *Alexander caught sight of him and approached him saying, 'Who are you? Here the entire city of Athens has turned out in throngs to see me, yet you lie here calmly in the grass, as if you were in possession of some great secret! Your tranquility has impressed me deeply! Name something which you desire and you shall have it, if it be within my kingly powers to provide it! Then we must talk some more.'*
>
> *'Do not deprive me of that which you cannot even offer, that is all I ask,' came the reply from Diogenes.*
>
> *'I still do not understand,' asked Alexander. 'What do you mean by that?'*
>
> *'The sunlight!' Diogenes exclaimed. 'You are depriving me of the sunlight by standing there. Do you not see that you have cast your shadow upon me? Please move a little bit to the left, and we can talk!'*

"Foreigners are always like Alexander, who, compared to Diogenes, was a fool!" the old man went on, "they always want to 'make history!' It is because they come from places which have no history! Here in Crete anyone can see that history has already been made! Even in the time of Alexander, Diogenes could see that!

"Only one time did Diogenes suffer from a moment of doubt! He was seen one day rolling his urn, his house, up and down the street.

> *'What in the world are you doing that for?' asked a friend of his.*
>
> *'Well,' he confessed, 'I just finally broke down. After all these years of watching everybody else hustling and bustling, building new houses and tearing old ones down, I finally decided I*

> *should try that too, so I have been rolling my urn up and down the street in order to become busy, but I must confess it seems absurd to me!' So he went back to philosophizing... content to sleep in his urn in the same spot for the rest of his life!*

"But I have chosen to serve food here beside the sea," concluded the old man, rushing off to tend somebody else's table.

"He's not such a pure-hearted old philosopher as he sounds," commented Xarilaos, "but he tells a good story."

"I wish my father and mother could hear him!" spouted Yvonne.

"I could show them my cucumbers," smiled Nikos.

"Fat chance her parents would be impressed by your cucumbers!" snarled Dimitrios, taking the comment too seriously.

Yannis returned to the table. There was a new gleam in his eye. He had thought of something else. "The problem, as always, is Death! Men run faster and faster away from Death. Tell me, did you ever realize that wherever you are Death is stalking you from behind? Of course you have! He's the big hooded fellow in a black cape with the ax in his hand. You all know him. It's in order to get away from that fellow that men love speed! And we'll run faster and faster. First it's just man on the run, then it's motorcycles, automobiles and airplanes! Spaceships! But every time a man pauses," the old man was drumming his point into the table top with his knuckles, "and chances to glance over his shoulders, there he is again: the black-hooded fellow. Most men go to their graves on the run!

"But there is an alternative: we must turn around! We must turn around so that the black-hooded fellow is no longer behind us! Look, this is no good!" The old man did a caricature of a man running forward, looking fearfully over his shoulder at every other step. "See what a ridiculous way to live a life? "We must turn around and begin advancing in the opposite direction, begin chasing Death! Get Death on the run instead of letting him keep us on the run! Once a man has mastered the game of keeping Death on the run and has learned to see through Death, he becomes free! He no longer has to run!" Intoxicated by his own words, the old man closed his mouth and began a slow shuffle with his feet.

His words had gently plunked into me like furry projectiles and now the old man himself looked furry. Warm and furry. No one jumped up to join Yannis in his dance. One does not shout at the buttercups, even with enthusiasm. Nor was it possible to look directly at the old man. He was too furry. He escaped direct detection. I found that I must look at the whole room and at all the people in it in order to be able to look at the old man. A direct stare would have blown the place apart. The entire tavern had been made furry by the old man's dance. Soon however, Leda and I were on our feet. Xarilaos, too, could not resist dancing, though he danced alone. I had the lovely Leda cradled in my arms and I lifted her higher as she squirmed toward the sky while my feet moved over the floor.

The furry wave of energy subsided as gently as it had risen. Xarilaos and Dimitrios said goodnight, fired up their motorcycles and departed. Leda and I waved at the old man and wandered off down the road towards our room.

Steal One Day from Death

The morning sun found me and Leda and Yvonne back at the old man's place. This time our packs were leaning against the wall, ready to go. Nikos had agreed to drive us on to Ayia Galini and then abandon us to the road once more.

Yannis came out of the kitchen and looked at the packs in disbelief, "What's this? Where do you think you are going? It is not yet time for you to leave! I haven't given you permission yet!"

We looked at each other in dismay, but grins enveloped our faces. The old man had us.

"There is no problem," he went on, "you will have rooms of mine to sleep in for free. Beds, clean sheets, everything! Sit down here, we will have eggs for breakfast!" Shortly the table was covered with a profusion of fried eggs sliding from platters to plates. Nikos, the would-be driver of our chariot to freedom, arrived and was likewise invited to down a few eggs. "These are all on me," the old man hastened to explain whenever someone looked reluctant. "Why a man like you or me needs seven or eight eggs to start the day," he said to me while filling everyone's glasses with wine. Before long we all had an eggy glow. "Where did you think you were going? To Athens? It is cold now in Athens! And the soldiers control the streets! Here it is warm and we have the sea. Whatever could you find in Athens that we do not already have here?"

"But I become restless," I explained. "I am still young and a young man must move and travel."

"Take my advice and steal one day from Death."

"But what am I to do here? I have no work, nothing!"

"The only work worth doing is the soft work of jumping your woman. There is no other work that you need to rush off to do!"

"You know what the ancient Greeks said," I countered. "A man must have a sound mind and a sound body. We must work, we must run, we must become strong. We must jump not only our women, but also the world! In fact it is by learning to jump our obstacles in the world that we become good at jumping our women!"

"The ancient Greeks knew nothing!" Yannis contested. "We know a great deal more today. The great mistake of youth is to burn everything up at once. I am an old man and I can give you advice: learn how to save yourself. Let your strength run beyond you. Be content to jump your woman. Try it for just one day! Steal just one day from Death! Besides, there are many things we could do. Tonight we will have more music and food."

I couldn't repress another grin. We walked a long way down the beach. "That old man is something amazing!" we all agreed and we returned to the old man's place after what seemed like an hour or so. Good smells of things cooking were emanating from the kitchen. The old man's wife, Stella, was standing in the kitchen door with a big smile across her face. Leda couldn't resist giving her a hug. We made love in our new room which was right there in the old man's taverna.

We emerged at sundown and looked at the tables.

"Look at this feast!" I exclaimed.

"Shhhh!" exclaimed the old man. "Just eat, and enjoy your wine! Cameron, you sit here! Leda here! He sat down opposite his own wife and told Brigitte to sit close beside her. His hands reached into the lamb and pulled out huge dripping hunks. "Don't be shy!" he admonished. "Eat!" He poured wine out into glasses, coating everything he touched with grease from the lamb. I reached my fingers into the lamb; Stella, Leda and Brigitte did the same. We plunged into the squid, octopus, the salad. Our knees became wet and greasy. More wine. "May you always remember this feast," said Yannis. "Shhh! You needn't say a word!"

Brigitte obviously loved to eat. A glint of animal pleasure remained in her eye as she licked her fingers; she was in her element and her mind had probably shut down altogether. The old man's wife picked more demurely. She had seen this before, but she was not unhappy to be going through it again. Leda's black eyes shone and she played with them cat-like - or was it mouse-like? - instinctively enticing me who, like Brigitte, had a tendency to swallow myself up with the pleasure of it all...

More wine. The old man was keeping everybody's glass full. There were no forks, no spoons, no knives, no napkins. Brigitte and Leda laughed every time they habitually searched for napkins and ended up wiping their fingers across their knees once again.

Something sexy was happening. Brigitte sat up straight and became more beautiful. The old man's wife's eyes had become soft. The old man had fastened a warm gaze onto, into, her eyes. The awesomeness of what was happening to us was blowing my mind! There was an energy being generated in that taverna which was even deeper than my own private sexual desire.

Leda's face, the muscles around her mouth had opened, grown rubbery. The infinite liquid behind her eyes had become the place to go... I felt the serpents spring from within myself to drown in that liquid, to gnaw and curl in those eyes, in those baskets of thick smoke... Brigitte's breathing deepened. Her eyes were riveted on the old man, but the old man's eyes were embedded in his wife's eyes, tangled in that same smoke! Something struck Brigitte as funny and she snorted into her glass, blowing wine all over her face. We all dissolved with laughter, tears running down our cheeks. I found myself picking more shreds of lamb off the bones and stuffing them into Leda's mouth.

We watched the sun sink underneath bizarre shreds of clouds, showing its blood red slice of a disk through a tiny gap above the surface of the sea. Leda and I stole off to our room to begin experimenting to find out which way of lovemaking we might prefer tonight... Then we slept.

I Felt Like an Intruder

"Here are your morning eggs, Combareh... 'Compadre!'" the old man greeted me with a big platter of slippery fried eggs. Yvonne and Leda had gone off to bathe in the sea.

"Are you really thinking of having a child with Brigitte, Yanni?"

"I don't know. What do you think? Do you think I should?"

"I bet the mixture would make a beautiful child!"

"Not as beautiful as Angela! There is no way to match the beauty of the unmixed, unblemished, pure black-eyed race!"

"In America we have a concept called 'hybrid vigor...' which means..."

"That's because there is no pure race in America," the old man interrupted, "so you have lost the remembrance of purity!"

"I don't know... now with corn..."

"We are not talking about corn! People are not grown to be eaten! They are most beautiful when left in their wild state. And wildness means purity, strange as it may seem to you Americans. A wild man does not bother to cross the ocean to find a woman. You can barely pry him away from his sisters into the bedroom of the girl next door. That's your natural man for you."

Yannis and Me

"I must go for a walk, Yanni..."

"No, Cameron! You should steal another day from Death!"

"No, Yanni! I must go for a walk... Just a short one! I'll see you later." I wandered out of the tavern. My legs were dying to break into a triumphant sprint, but the old man's words were locked in my mind: ...'Steal another day from Death! Just steal one more day from Death! The mistake of youth is to burn everything up at once!'...

So I continued walking slowly, eyes on the road beneath my feet. ...'Your body will always tell you where is the right place to be... if you just listen to it!'...

My body wanted to be on top of that mountain over there, on top of Mt. Ida! Damned if I couldn't feel it pulling me just as plain as day!

A rush of delight flooded my belly at the image of myself bounding up the mountainsides. Still I didn't break into a run. ...I'll never get there at this rate! ... ...*'Steal another day from Death'*...

I turned off the road towards the mountain. My walking body led me between long rows of plastic greenhouses, towards the mouth of a dry little canyon which promised to lead toward Mt. Ida. I was thinking... *'I should listen to the old man, to my Yanni! What he has given me is something very few men have known...'*

In a moment of reverence, I dropped to my knees, bent forward and rested my hands and forehead against the earth.

'What an amazing old man. I must do as he says...'

I arose back onto my feet. *'Still, a short walk doesn't hurt! I won't climb that mountain, but a climb up this canyon onto a ridge above will give me a beautiful look at it...'*

One foot in the canyon and everything changed! Entering those clefts between the foothills took me out of the slow flat land of agriculture and into the land of the hunter. The earth was steep and rocky. The sides of the canyon were hard-baked mud. Everything was dry. Everything green had vanished. Thorny bushes, waist high, coated the ledges along the canyon walls. I picked my way between them.

They were not about to yield to someone with as little resolve as I had at that moment. ...Crete was much wilder than I had thought!... My passage through the brambles reached a cul-de-sac on the end of a ledge. ...I had not seen my way through... I had to backtrack, descend to the bottom of the canyon, wind my way up the other side. ...I felt like an invader from another time... another century...

I didn't want to find anyone, meet anyone, there in that canyon!... Images of hundreds of thousands of Cretan men fighting, dying to protect their island from the Romans, the Venetians, the Franks, Turks, the Germans,... and now the Americans! ...came into my mind. ...What was I doing there? I could feel at home in the Grand Canyon, but I felt like an alien here!... In order to traverse the landscape, one must conquer it, dominate it! and yes... violate it!

A rustle and a slither in the bush beside my feet brought me to a frightened halt. The end of a tail vibrating! Ever so slowly, I shuffled up the hill past the bush. The snake was visible for another second and then disappeared. *'Nothing to fear!'* I whispered to myself, bounding up between the thorns like a rabbit ...except, somehow my breath seemed limited.

'If the snake bites you, sever its head and devour its body! Immediately! That is the only sure cure. Or crush the scorpion that stung you and imbibe its dust! Its poison is thereby overcome. Eat the enemies which would kill you! Ingest their strength! The cannibal is king! Invulnerable!' These are the ancient laws of the hunter, but in order to follow them your feet must be firmly planted on their own soil or willfully conquering a foreign soil. ...What was I doing there? I didn't belong there and I hadn't come to conquer... Claustrophobia in the canyon! Scrambling up and out! *'Where's Mt. Ida?'* I wanted to see Mt. Ida!

By the time I could see Mt. Ida again I had happened across a little footpath which promised to carry me closer to the mountain. I followed the little trail down the side of another little canyon, around a corner in its bottom, then up the other side toward another ridge, and... then I sensed another presence! On the hillside above me was standing a white-haired old man, beside a mule. A little hut was built on the slope above him. ...He lived up there!... I looked at him. He looked at me.

I felt like an intruder and should perhaps have turned around to go back. But I decided to continue walking, half expecting a bullet in the back... *'We must begin chasing Death instead of feeling that Death is chasing us!'*... Seizing the impulse, I continued! I did it. I was coming closer toward the white haired old man... ...*'keep Death on the run'*...

The white-haired old man had not moved an inch. He was a figure on the hillside. Imperturbable, implacable, calm, relentless... I advanced toward those eyes... every thread in me wanted to get close enough to see into his eyes... A white aura had grown around the old man's body; the dust-colored landscape had blurred into nothingness behind his ageless figure... I was almost close enough now to see into those eyes; to greet them with my carefully-mustered defiance...

"What!? Oh my God!" I muttered and stopped. I was gazing into the eyes of a frail human being. Kindness was what was in the white-haired old man's eyes!

"Oh my God," I murmured. "Excuse me for mistaking you for Death, my father..."

The old man had shakily raised a hand in benediction... almost perhaps in appeal, but I, overwhelmed with shame, had now withdrawn and was walking, head bowed, not looking back...

"That was not Death." I muttered. "Just a poor old man! Not Death! ...Not Death! Not Death!..." hammered through my mind and I struck myself in the side of the jaw with my own flailing fist. I had manufactured the entire drama inside my own head! I was losing touch with reality!

"Ohmigod!" Flame-red inside, I emerged back into the land of agriculture: the plastic greenhouses, swollen with cucumbers and tomatoes. Occasionally I sensed someone working inside one of the greenhouses and stole cautiously past, unable to risk facing another living soul... Trundling myself to the road, then to the seacoast, at last I slipped quietly into the haven of Yannis' tavern...

No Fifth Plate Was Forthcoming

"...most Americans, Germans, the British too, for that matter, come through like express trains: whoosh! ...then they are gone. No staying power; no effort to learn the language; nothing!"

I took a look. These words were coming from the mouth of another American, a fellow about my own age who had Brigitte at a table... Brigitte sent an inviting wave of warmth in my direction. I sat down with them at the table. "Hello..."

"Hi, my name's Douglas."

"Howdy, I'm Cameron..."

"They have no sense of the places they pass through. They treat Crete as if it were Miami! They've completely ruined towns like Ayia Galini. I used to live there, but I couldn't bear to watch what was happening so I moved to a smaller village... where everything's still OK! There are a lot of tiny villages on Crete that no one ever goes to. What the foreigners who come here don't realize is that they've come to a place where honor is the foremost thing! Crete is basically an island of warriors! It hasn't been so long since the last war, either! The old-timers remember how to lop off Turkish heads and pickle the ears! Have you been to Ayia Galini?"

"No..."

"It's micro-bus heaven! All the foreigners have brought their VW vans. They all park around Ayia Galini or down in Matala looking out of their portable steel boxes... You get all kinds... ...people writing their Phd dissertations! The thing I hate to see is the effect it has on the people! ...on the Cretans! But they all put up with it for the dollar, or for the German mark. Those cafes are chock full of foreigners sittin' around; none of the villagers go there anymore. Of course I'm not sayin' I understand what goes on in every Cretan's mind... I've just barely begun to scratch the surface... 'n I been here three years."

"Three years?"

"Well actually I been quite a few other places too during the last three years, but I keep comin' back here. Crete has become my home."

"Where are Leda and Yvonne?" I asked Brigitte.

"They're down with Nikos. He was going to show them some more of his greenhouses. Yannis wants us all to have dinner together tonight though, so they'll be back..."

"Hey, listen," continued Douglas, "I gotta go on into town. I'm tryin' to find work!"

"Well come on back later," I suggested. "We can talk some more!"

"Yeah, I'll try to!"

"We'll be here for dinner."

Feeling at ease with the familiar American words, the squealing pain left from the terrible mistake I had made with the white-haired old man was receding into the background... I walked toward where I figured Nikos' greenhouses to be.

Leda and Yvonne were standing outside one of them. "Nikos went to wash up for dinner," they explained. "Come inside and take a look at these cucumbers!" Opening the door we passed inside a hot, steaming, wet jungle atmosphere draped with tangled masses of cucumber vines. The giant green cucumbers dangled in proliferation.

"Here! You want one?" laughed Yvonne, picking one. "They're delicious," she added playfully.

Nikos appeared, hair freshly combed. "Let's go, my little cucumber queen," he said to Yvonne, putting his arm around her. "It's time to go back to Yannis' for dinner. Did you put the basket of cucumbers in the truck?"

"I met this guy who seems pretty neat," I told Leda, "...a guy from the States who's been around Crete on and off for three years..."

The usual evening crowd was reassembling back at Yannis' place. Claudia, her face again stricken with anguish, fretted behind a table on the sidelines. Her hands twisted and wrung at a pencil... Those chromium blue eyes were still peering out frantically from behind those glasses... Seeing me, Yvonne and Leda, she flashed a quick uncertain smile and briefly waved.

Douglas was back. He was sitting talking again to Brigitte. The old man was helping Kostakis with his homework... multiplication tables it looked like. Leda and I and Nikos and Yvonne sat down at a table near Douglas and Brigitte.

"Hi man!" said Douglas to me.

"Did you find work?" I asked.

"Naw..."

Yannis' wife emerged from the kitchen. A beaming glow came from her towards Leda and Cameron...

"Combareh!" I murmured toward her... I wanted to hug her... Not the right time... Too many people! But she seemed satisfied with the flash of love. She was busy cooking dinner.

"But you should be proud of it, my son!" Yannis' voice rose suddenly above the murmur. Kostakis looked shy and embarrassed. "Getting good grades at school should make you proud! You should show everyone your report card!"

Little Angela was playing with a handful of colored buttons on the side of my shoe. Taking a green button, she handed it up to me, giving it to me with those incredible liquid black eyes... just like Leda's eyes... Then she gave me a red button... her whole soul was into the giving! I gave them back to her; her little hand took the buttons. Now she could give them again! That's the part she liked best! Amazing... The giving! The buttons came up toward my eyes again! She was giving them to my eyes! In possession of these two buttons, I was captured, trapped, engulfed, en-snarled and bewitched ...by the magic glance of this three-year-old! The sky had crumbled and the shattered blue chips had fallen noiselessly into the sea. Defeated, my hand remained clasped around the two buttons.

Motorcycles... Xarilaos and Dimitrios swung into the lighted patio. The sun had sizzled once again down into the sea. With a magnificent whisk, Xarilaos gathered little Angela into his arms. He planted a horrendous kiss on her cheek; she beamed through the whole act. I sat up straighter in my chair. "Congratulations," muttered Xarilaos, taking my hand. I peered into the man's eyes and for the first time felt like we might be friends.

"Thanks! Thanks very much!" I replied, not knowing for what he was congratulating me.

Xarilaos sat down with Angela on his knee; the tiny sorceress clambered down and climbed into a five-gallon metal bucket which was apparently made just for her: only her head and shoulders showed above the rim of the bucket! Xarilaos lifted the bucket by the handle and carried her across the room.

Claudia leapt from her chair and demanded her turn carrying the bucket. But uh-oh! Something was wrong! The old man made a bee-line for the bucket. To the rescue! A tiny but slightly frantic struggle ensued amidst choruses of "slowly, slowly!" and "gently, gently!" Then she was free and quite calmly beaming again. Angela had gotten stuck in the bucket! Yannis carried her around the patio in his arms so she could look at everyone's faces... and so everyone could see those amazing black eyes... freshly delivered from near-disaster in the bucket!

"Boy is she ever gonna be beautiful when she grows up!" exclaimed Douglas.

"Isn't she amazing?" I responded. I also knew that praising a child's beauty is against the rules in Greece... we could be inviting the 'evil eye'...

"Some eyes!"

"It's amazing what can be done with those eyes..." I looked into Leda's eyes. She looked at me playfully and wrinkled up her nose.

"When are you planning to go back to the States?" I asked Douglas after a pause.

"Fuck it. Never!"

"Never?"

"I spent a long enough time in jail in the South just 'cause I had long hair... I don't ever want to go back and see those Southern sheriffs again! I don't even like to think about it! There were some narrow scrapes! Besides, like I said, Crete feels like home now."

Leda had pricked up her ears: "I wish Cameron felt that way about Greece! But he wants to go back to the States!"

"You're going to go with him? You look Greek."

"I am Greek." She made a helpless gesture. "Cameron tells me you've been around here for three years!"

"Yeah. Now I'm about out of money again and I'm down this way trying to find some work. I left my pack in Ayia Galini and walked down here along the coast. It's about an-hour-and-a-half's walk. I damn near fell off a cliff along the way too! For a minute I thought that was the end of me! Have you ever walked this coastline? I've walked just about the whole of the southern shore of Crete. That's the way to really get into this island!"

"No, we just got here about ten days ago..." Leda explained. Yannis, the old man who runs this place has... we've seen some incredible things... it's amazing to have just stumbled into a place..."

"That old man there? Yeah! I think I remember stopping here one night a couple of years ago... if this is the same place... it looks familiar. You say he's a wonderful old man? If this is the same place I'm remembering, he was good to me too! I'd like to talk with him."

"Well, stick around!" I told him. "In a bit we'll have some dinner and later we'll hang out and talk."

"I should get back to Ayia Galini though, 'cause I left all my stuff there in a friend's room. I think it'll be safe, but I'm not sure. But I should ask this old man about a job as long as I'm here!"

Stella appeared and set four plates down on the table, one for me, one for Leda, one for Nikos, and one for Yvonne. I made some kind of easy motion to my new *comadre* Stella as if to say: "bring another plate of food for our friend here..." But no fifth plate was forthcoming...

"Here! Have a few bites off my plate..." I offered my plate to Douglas. The music was coming through the speakers from the tape recorder, loud and clear. Too loud. Claudia finally went and turned down the volume to make it easier for people to talk.

"God damn it wench!" Dimitrios screamed at her. "Turn that back up!"

The old man himself went to the tape recorder and turned the music up.

"Yanni!" I called to the old man. "This fellow Douglas, here, is trying to find some work. Do you know of anything for him?"

The old man came over and looked at Douglas.

"I do remember you!" Douglas exclaimed. "A couple of years ago I spent an evening in here and talked with you!"

Judging by the vacant look in Yannis' eyes, he did not share the memory. "I don't personally know of any work," he replied. "Did you go into town and ask?"

"Yes, but it was all vague stuff like: 'Come back in the morning and we'll see...'"

"That kind of response I do not understand!" exclaimed the old man. "A man knows whether there is work or not! If yes, '*yes!*' If no, '*no!*' Simple as that. An honest man looking for work ends up wasting his time! The men in town there are afraid to say 'no' so they keep a man hanging around. I'll show you the courtesy of telling you 'no there is no work' when there is no work. That way you don't have to hang around wondering."

Douglas had been captured by Yannis' style of presentation and was listening with admiration. But with that statement concluded, Yannis departed from the table.

"I like him! He's a far-out old man!" agreed Douglas. "He's got a magic scene here."

Alexandros arrived. This time he had left his guitar and brought his bouzouki. He began to play.

Alexandros with Bouzouki

Dimitrios and Xarilaos had sprung up from their seats, lain their arms across each other's shoulders, and begun to dance. I turned around with a jolt, aware of a pressure, a demand for attention, from the dancing men. I stood up and backed up to the wall to give them more space. The old man's wife gave me a big glow from the doorway of her kitchen. Apparently I had done the right thing: the conversational bubble was broken and everyone was free to dance. Leda arose and began to dance; then Yvonne joined and even Brigitte stretched her slow-moving body and had begun to shake herself.

Yannis' Place in Kokkinos Pirghos

Douglas liked that: wrapping his attention around blonde Brigitte, he watched her intently from his chair. Claudia was vibrating on the margins, clawing at herself from time to time. Once the dance had begun, it didn't take long for everyone to loosen up and then come together. The old man stepped into the motion, slow and easy... that furry quality again. With that new softness touching the room the dancers snuggled into a single serpent-like line, led by Xarilaos... Dimitrios, Nikos, Yannis, me, Leda, Yvonne, Brigitte...

You're on the Run

It had begun to rain with black wet earnest outside; the rivulets drained off the patio roof and splashed to the ground. The tavern's light no longer penetrated very far into the chilly night... the dancers were sealed into their tiny kingdom... a mermaid, chancing to surface at that moment, poking her head up out of the sea, would have seen the distant string of dancers winding gently in the yellow light, the music coming faintly to her ears behind the splashing of the raindrops...

Once released, the dance settled back down into the corners from whence it had arisen, leaving us all sitting in a big circle around two tables... a single body now, with the old man refreshing our tastes for wine from the time-worn crockery pitcher! Alexandros' bouzouki bit into the night with a few notes... Cretan notes...

What about Claudia? Douglas? The dance had never swallowed them! They came now into the circle to sit close to me. "When you get a chance to play your guitar, play some rock 'n roll! Or Clementine!" Claudia whispered into my ear.

"Boy, it sure is rainin' out there," observed Douglas.

"Sure is!" I answered. "No point in your tryin' to go back to Ayia Galini tonight in the rain! I'm sure you can stay here. We'll let you sleep with us in the room the old man gave us ..." I added, then cast myself back into the open mouth of the music, doing my best with Cretan songs I didn't know... I tried to hum along... harmonize if possible... there was really nothing I enjoyed more than to be swallowed whole by a song...

But as the hour grew late people faded off. Xarilaos and Dimitrios were gone. Nikos had vanished. Yvonne was ready to go... she and Nikos were done with their sacred flirtations for the time being... Alexandros closed up his songs, said goodnight... The old man's wife had gone to bed. Now was the time, I decided, to let poor Claudia have her rock 'n roll 'n Clementine...

Douglas opened the door on the wood stove to feed it another stick of wood, but the old man's hand materialized on the stove door and slammed it shut! It didn't seem like the old man wanted to stay up and listen to Clementine.

"Well, it's time for bed!" I announced. Claudia, Brigitte and Yvonne faded toward their rooms, giving up the ghost...

"Is it OK if I sleep the night here? Cameron and Leda said..." Douglas began.

"No," came from the old man. Something sagged in the room as if the space had been suddenly draped with giant wet hemp ropes strung with seaweed.

"You mean you would throw a man out into the rain at two o'clock in the morning rather than let him curl up in the corner?" Douglas asked Yannis.

"That's right," affirmed the old man sadly. "I'll be happy to lend you a raincoat," he said, bringing a plastic green poncho out of the kitchen and plunking it down on the table.

"Why? What is the reason I can't stay here? Is there something awful about me?"

"No no! There's nothing wrong with you! It's just that you're on the run and I can't let you stay here!"

"What do you mean I'm 'on the run'"? I'm not wanted by anybody around here!"

"Haven't you noticed that fellow that's behind you?" the old man looked past Douglas' shoulder.

Douglas turned around and looked, "What fellow?" he asked.

"Never mind," concluded the old man, going back into the kitchen. "We'll all stay up all night! That will solve the problem." He re-emerged with a fresh supply of wine, bread, cheese.

"I don't understand," Douglas persisted, although not angrily... "here on Crete, where I no longer feel myself to be a stranger and I know the rules of hospitality... I can tell you honestly! Nowhere on Crete have I run into a man who would violate the golden rule of hospitality and send another man out into the rain on a night like this... I don't understand! There has to be something you are not telling me..."

"Yanni," I began, "I don't understand either! If he stays in our room..."

"He cannot stay here tonight!"

Leda, growing impatient with Douglas, stood up and clamped her attention onto the raincoat. But Douglas still made no motion to put it on and leave.

"Look, I'll get another raincoat and make the trip down the beach with you," I offered impulsively.

"It's not that I can't make the trip," explained Douglas, "God knows I've been through worse than a two-hours' walk down the beach in the rain... It's just that I do not understand why this is being laid on me! I'm completely mystified!"

"I wish I could help you," the old man said. There was full and genuine sympathy in his eyes. "But there is a power greater than I which is telling me that you cannot sleep here! I will stay up all night with you... Look! We can drink, we can talk, philosophize..."

The four of us fell silent; we sat down to wait out the night; there was no philosophizing. There was only the one burning question: '... why couldn't we all just go to bed and go to sleep?'...

"What is this 'power' of which you speak?" Douglas finally asked.

"I'm sorry, but I don't know... But I'm surprised you haven't noticed it yourself..."

"But if I just curl up in the corner of Cameron and Leda's room?..."

"Their room is a sacred space now and no one is to sleep there but them..."

I looked ashamedly at the floor. The silences between questions grew longer. Finally the old man's head slumped for a moment... the endless exhaustion... his hands remembered the higher commitment and began their eternal climb... their promise to boost the gray-stubbled chin... Another half-hour passed... There was not a light eyelid among the four of us...

At last Leda arose to her feet once again. "This is ridiculous!" Her hands grasped the raincoat and plunked it down in front of Douglas.

Coming full awake in that cold harsh three-in-the-morning reality, with grief in our eyes the four of us looked at each other once again. The old man had not even considered changing his mind. Silently, Douglas donned the raincoat. "Well, goodbye," he said and stepped out into the night.

Leda and I helped the old man carry the last glasses and dishes into the kitchen and then we all headed for bed.

The next morning Leda and I and Yannis sat stone still, looking blankly at each other. It seemed that none of us had understood what had happened the previous night. We still felt close to each other. But we knew that now it was time for us to go.

"Nikos said he would give us a ride to where we could catch the bus back toward Heraklion and then the boat back to Athens..." I murmured. The old man nodded vaguely.

Translating One of Yorgos' Books, into English

In Athens things had returned more or less to normal... the normal fear, claustrophobia... the police...

Leda and I fell back into a deep rhythm with Yorgos and Valendini. We spent twelve hours or more a day in their apartment translating 'Midas,' one of Yorgos' books, into English. He would sit on one side of Leda and I on the other and we would discuss every sentence... every phrase... at great length. We discussed the meanings in ancient Greek, in medieval Greek and in modern Greek. When I felt I had understood the nuances of meaning, I scoured my knowledge of English to find the best equivalent translation. We ate olives and drank red wine... which is called 'black' wine in Greek... and it came, not from bottles, but 'from the barrel'... The little grocery stores down the street could provide this.

Yorgos had decided to learn to play music. He practiced writing his own songs and playing them on the little baglama, a tiny bouzouki. Valendini would come and go. Her acting job at the TV station was keeping her busy.

Yorgos had musician friends: Psonis and Kondoryanis. We regularly visited them. Psonis played bouzouki accompanied by Kondoryanis on guitar. Soon I had bought a bouzouki for myself and Psonis was teaching me the most popular zembekika songs and their underlying rhythms. My little tape recorder was busy and so was I. Stretching myself over these odd-metered rhythms was not easy for me.

We traveled late one night to Piraeus, the port, to go to the 'bouzoukia' where, at unimaginably ear-splitting volume, pairs of young bouzouki virtuosos pumped out zembekiko after zembekiko while drunken men took their turns expressing the pains of life through their improvised dances.

A friend of Spyros' named Juliaras played guitar and sang. So did his gorgeous girlfriend and I began to learn more of the recent Theodorakis compositions from the two of them. There was a magic which they could create, not only with their amazing harmonies, but with the envelopes of time.

When we sang we expanded into a place wherein time disappeared. I had never experienced that in my own American culture where it felt as though there was always someone in the room with a watch reminding us that time was passing and that we should be paying attention, noticing the passage of time. Sooner or later Americans run out of time and feel an urgency to make a change... to end the song and ultimately to do something else... go somewhere else.

With Juliaras we disappeared into a place of no clocks... no time... The song we were singing would manifest tiny hesitations... tiny pauses between melody lines... these hesitations invited eternity to nestle comfortably into the song. A certain ecstasy appeared as we entered timeless space. The songs had become magic vehicles into a place with no hurry... no anxiety... no fear... Later, back in Colorado, I would discover that Americans could respond to this magic too... if I showed it to them when I sang...

Exchange Energies Only Through the Eyes

We visited Christos again, this time in his apartment. Now he could show me some of the fantastic tapestries he was manufacturing and selling. It seemed the Shah of Iran had just bought one and another Hilton Hotel another. We discussed the bones on the rocks below Mount Athos, a Christian monastery in northern Greece. The mythology had it that a young monk who had never had an orgasm could leap off a high cliff above the sea and fly to safety. The bones on the rocks below were evidence that yet another young monk had been lying and concealing the fact that he had masturbated.

Christos shared with us that he and his girlfriend had learned to exchange so much intense sexual energy through eye contact that they could both achieve orgasm without physically touching themselves or each other. They just gazed into each other's eyes.

These were the realms of the Eleusinian mysteries, he explained. Every spring a naked maiden was slowly presented to a naked youth while Demeter, the goddess of the wheat, the flowers, and of all things that grow, watched the naked youth's penis begin to slowly rise. This was the promise of a fruitful growing season. Every day for twenty days the maiden was presented to the youth, both of whom were only partially visible behind gossamer curtains. Every day for twenty days his penis rose for half an hour or so but they would not make love. They were fed only with bread, just once a day and only in the evening. On the twenty-first day the selected youth and Demeter could make love. The people who came to worship and witness this wondrous daily repetition were required to disrobe themselves entirely before entering the courtyard. Then, after witnessing the attraction between the maiden and the youth they were free to express their admiration and attraction for each other... up to a point... The young mens' penises rose and the young women became moist but they were not supposed to touch each other's bodies. They were allowed to only exchange energies through their eyes.

When we had the opportunity, Leda and I began the experiment: both of us naked sitting with our legs crossed in the half lotus looking into each other's eyes... which would give me a big hard-on. But my eyes were still less that adequate for the transmissions I now knew to be possible... I tried, but trying didn't really help. If I ever learned to *not try* maybe... maybe... Eventually she would call me into bed so that something could happen.

Telepathy is not difficult. If you go ahead and lean out beyond the place of language and words it gets deeper. What is difficult is to give up your own privacy and find someone else who is willing to give up theirs! And then learn to Not Do... to move backwards from the ego instead of forward... and to allow the whole gruesome repertoire of human cosmic consciousness to flow uncensored through your mind's eye... so that judgments based on fear and aversion don't continually shut you down... then... magic can begin... connection to *all that is* can begin... it is a welcoming feeling...

My American mind constantly wanted to sugar-coat everything... to imagine that our human condition was getting better and better... that modern times were bringing civilization with all its improvements. But my new Greek mind was aware of the slow rising and falling of colossal epochs of history. I was beginning to see a new path of surrender to what was actually happening... something beyond hope and fear... something closer to reality...

At Yorgos' apartment we met his friend Nolis who had been imprisoned on one of the 'exile' islands for five years. He had been accused of associating with communists. He told us that the sound of his own voice had scared him a few nights ago. He had been singing anti-government songs with friends and the revolutionary passion which had leapt out through his own throat had been louder and stronger than he had expected. "You know that it has been British and American power and influence here in Greece which has led to the imprisonment of many of us? After World War Two the Americans needed another enemy so they chose Russia... and communism..."

"People back home in my country, the USA, don't know a thing about what has happened in Greece..." I commented.

"You know it takes conflict to make some stand out as devils and others as gods. That's just the way it is."

"But it's amazing how little my American friends even know about what gives rise to the conflicts..." I added.

Nolis nodded and continued, "You know it's as if the USA and the USSR are like the thorny plants. For sure nobody will be able to eat them. They are very clever plants! Greece is a soft green plant. I don't know if we are more stupid or more brave..."

Yorgos' brother Vangelis stopped by and gave us a jaw-harp concert. It was totally amazing and it lasted for a long and delightful piece of forever.

Greeks are not big with polite smiles. Saying 'thank you,' is a sign that you have fallen out of your natural order, the place you are supposed to comfortably occupy as a result of your birth. Saying 'thank you' to a waiter in a Greek restaurant will mark you as a foreigner and as an outsider.

Yorgos was not very motivated to try and make money. It seemed that other brothers in his family were helping to support him. He moved slowly in a relaxed fashion and stayed focused on his own creativity as a journalist and a writer.

"Only he who has read all the books can advise the others not to read them," was his justification for his meandering path.

He insisted that we must separate ourselves from our thoughts so that we could discuss them without feeling personally threatened or attached. "The mind is an entrance and the self is the obstacle which blocks it."

Yorgos claimed that the Greek man could smile and be happy, because he 'has time.' If his friends came to visit him he 'had time' for them... all the time in the world for them -- he never had to rush off somewhere. Even when he did have to go somewhere he didn't seem to 'rush'. He would explain himself by saying things like: "To be passionate we work at being not passionate."

Musicians loved Yorgos because around him their notes were given space to exist, to hover in the air, sparkle. They liked to come and visit him because he 'had time.'

Yorgos himself was beginning to also become a musician. Why not? He had plenty of time in which to do it. Yorgos did not tell me that I had helped inspire him to become a musician but Leda said that it was obvious.

When we entered his apartment I could never find the correct light switch! There were two switches: one above the other. One for the kitchen; one for the bathroom. No matter how I approached them and no matter which room I wanted to enter I always flipped the wrong switch. I never quite transcended being my own version of the 'stupid American.'

More Painful... but Much Richer

We went back to the 'bouzoukia' again but I had a terrible headache and felt wretched. Yorgos was not sympathetic that night and took it as another sign of American weakness.

I was gradually feeling that Leda and I had lost our personal private place for loving. In the endless contexts of living either with her mother, father and brother or with Yorgos she sometimes seemed to be unhappy with me and my American ways and sometimes told me that she was in love with me.

Sometimes Leda insulted my lack of Greek-ness to the point where I just had to laugh. I simply wasn't Greek. And when I laughed my penis would get hard and we would make love.

But thousands of years of ancient history had overwhelmed me and my old American identity was gone forever. I had always wanted to start from the bottom up. Now I had my chance… my chance to not eat, to not sing, to not love… wait… To not love? Yes, I decided, even to *not love!*

We learned the lyrics from another new song by Theodorakis.

> *For the sun to rise and set, living beings are required to give their blood…*
> *For the sun to spin on its axis, thousands must die…*

Children's story books in Greece were about keeping the tigers at bay. One child must die for every vanquished tiger… the tigers represented fascist governments and they never would really go away. The martyred children were the heroes of these children's books.

I had decided to take the plunge and come to visit Greece with Leda. I had long felt that I would be better off confining my travel adventures to the mountain parts of North, Central and South America. Something had always gnawed at me telling me that adventures in the 'Old World,' on the other sides of the oceans, would be overwhelming. I had premonitions about the futility of moving through 'Biblical Lands' where each tribe seemed always to be so ready to die in defense of its own beliefs…

Perhaps I should have listened to myself and stayed in the Americas, but… curiosity… whatever you call it… and my love for my Greek girlfriend… had lured me on… I had boarded my first plane to Greece with fear in my soul… but a very few months later my world view had opened way up. I had become more willing to stay immersed in whatever was actually happening in spite of the suffering. So life was sometimes more painful… but it was much richer… Little did I suspect it, but years later I would be ready for Egypt!

Busy Making Money in Colorado

Flying back across the Atlantic I had the good fortune and the bad fortune to sit next to a Peruvian man. I could understand his Peruvian Spanish just fine... but my brain had been so immersed in Greek that my own ability to respond in Spanish had vanished. I was literally tongue-tied. Eventually, a few months later, my brain grew the necessary nerve channels between my new Greek self and my Spanish-speaking self so that my internal translation process didn't have to go through English anymore and everything worked just fine. But it definitely took a while.

Back in Boulder we were welcomed once again into John Link's house. I was out of money. I wanted my guitar-making business to pay the bills. Bonnie's boyfriend, Max Krimmel, an amazing craftsman, was helping me master the techniques. I also took whatever other jobs came my way.

I worked up above Nederland in Caribou at the Aquarius Mine. Aliens in starships had informed the mine's owner, Richard Sigismonde, a local Italian mystic, that large silver deposits lay near the bottom of the mine. We worked in primitive conditions a few hundred feet underground in an old mine shaft and we worked above ground over the entrance to the shaft through the winter in hundred-mile-an-hour winds to construct a metal building. We felt like we were on the moon as we peered out through our space-suit-like parkas to try and manage the screws and rivets. Maneuvering even one large sheet metal panel into place could require a whole day's work.

And while working underground, pump hoses could work loose. One time the contents of the water pipes rained down on our heads and we thought that there had been a massive cave-in and that the end was near. Realizing that we were still alive, we raced to clamp the hoses back together before the water levels could rise to drown us.

John Link had been working with me in downtown Boulder to extract valuable recyclable beams from the roofs of old buildings being remodeled alongside the newly-constructed Pearl Street Mall. We were highly paid to do the dangerous work high up in the air. I remember cutting through old rafters with a chain saw while standing balanced on top of a step ladder positioned in the back of a slowly moving pickup truck. We were well-paid in cash. Then John also began working with me up at the mine until he fell from the roof and pulled the tendons loose in his knee.

I also took more roofing jobs as they came along, rebuilt my friends' worn-out automobile engines and sometimes went through the neighborhoods painting addresses on curbs hoping for tips. Yes... I needed money...

I had learned to do inlay work with silver, gold and exotic hardwoods as part of the guitar-making craft, so I made jewelry along with the musical instruments. I learned to withstand ten rejections for the sake of one sale as I peddled my creations through the jewelry stores in Denver. This became a big lesson in personal stamina.

I was also working on writing a Quechua grammar of the dialect in Sina... a huge never-ending project. It was August. I wanted to travel somewhere but didn't really have any money. Leda and I did make a trip down to Cañon City to visit James in the penitentiary. By now they were allowing us to sit for a few minutes with him in a large room. This was a step up from talking from opposite sides of thick bullet-proof glass.

Wealthier friends were studying mystical things in Chile with Oscar Ichazo and helping to create EST... which later became The Forum... personal transformation programs were growing in popularity... Some of my friends were also managing to climb some long and difficult rock routes in Yosemite. This was climbing in a league I didn't have the strength and skill to approach.

John Link gradually rehabilitated his damaged knee and built a new passion for marathon running. Eventually he managed to run up Pike's Peak, Orizaba, Popocatepetl and Iztaccihuatl... the last being three eighteen-thousand-foot-high volcanoes in Mexico.

Jim Sharp's summers were spent in Alaska flying climbers onto Denali, the highest peak in North America. Jim, driven by his 'manic' periods, followed these summertime flying adventures with long and crazy voyages in his little plane. One year he made it to the southern tip of South America... almost to Antarctica. But he returned by mid-winter smitten by his 'bi-polar' thing... ouch... the depression part... and spent months sitting speechless on Cindy Carlisle's porch...

Birdie, Music, Skiing, Rivers

Somehow Birdie and I discovered each other again and exchanged two sets of letters. It felt like we were blowing each other sweet kisses from afar. She had married and settled in New York City where she was raising her three kids. She wrote:

> "I'm so glad to finally catch up with you after all these years. I've wondered what you're doing and what you've become. You don't know how delighted I am to find an old friend. We had so many good times growing up together. I hope my children will look back on their childhood with happy memories too! Whenever I return to Missouri I check out our old haunts. The quarry and the old mill are still intact! Some of the recently built underground forts are fancier than ours were I'm sorry to say... Bill decided to end it all and killed himself... Bob got involved with drug dealing and was made to dig his own grave and then wiped out... Mrs. Woods died and a family with a bunch of boys moved in and have already built a terrific tree house... Leda, I think you are with a very good person – at least he was pretty nice when he was a kid! And his mother was always good for a big dish of ice cream! Love, Birdie"

We expressed deep fondness. Our connection had been real for both of us.

Leda and I began performing our Greek songs in Boulder. People loved the timeless spaces of the slow melodies and the exotic qualities of the fast ones. Soon we had a band called 'The Silk Route.' I played bouzouki and guitar.

Silk Route: Mona, Margie, Leda, Me, Steve, Bob, Mark

Others joined: Mona on flute, Broc on sitar, Bob, David and Mark on drums, Steve on bass, Margie and me and Leda on vocals... We attracted the local belly dancers... Susheila, Lindy, Melinda, Jeannie and many more...

Melinda, Lindy, Claire, Jeannie, Others

Cross-country skiing was my habit. We skied over Pearl Pass from Aspen to Crested Butte... more than once. We skied over Rogers Pass in the Front Range to Winter Park. We skied from the top of Vail Pass westward to eventually descend into the Vail ski area. We returned frequently to Rabbit Ears Pass above Steamboat Springs to push north toward Mt Zirkel Wilderness.

Pearl Pass Between Aspen and Crested Butte

River running was also my habit. My friends in Steamboat invited me down the Grand Canyon again... the lower half... Bill Chase was eager to come along. I couldn't resist and agreed to run one of the boats.

Colorado River: More Grand Canyon

We descended five-thousand feet from the south rim, reached the river on the canyon floor and peeled off our clothes for that first plunge back into the refreshing waters. We spread out plastic ponchos on the river beach and fell asleep for the night.

Next morning we got on down the river... mad confusion of ropes, loading and unloading, hugging, wrestling and kissing, more swimming, popping open cans of beer... We shoved off, ran Horn Creek and Salt Creek rapids, and set up camp for the night five miles downstream, at the top of Granite Rapids.

Quiet time... Sensuality and back rubs...

On the River Again

The big percussion waves in the rapids at the bottom of Hermit Creek were enough to bring us all into focus on the next day. Feet braced against the cross-beam on the bow, anchored to the end of the fourteen-foot oar, the living link between the boat and the river, I felt myself come more fully to life. Running the very center of the water's tongue, we plunged over the apex of wave after wave until we found ourselves in troughs which seemed capable of flipping our twenty-foot boat end-for-end.

My old feeling for the bow, the cockpit of the boat, rushed into me, I was home once again, perched on a crest, peering eight feet down into the trough below, willing and ready with the oar... anxious, eager for the boat to take the plunge, do its worst! *'I challenge you to spin this boat, turn her broadside!'* Nestled for a moment in the bottom of a trough, oar deeply embedded in the heart of the oncoming wave, the bowman's job was to deliver just the right stroke and keep the craft's trajectory straight and true... wrestling with the end of the oar the way the cattleman wrestles a steer to the ground... wrestling to stay on the boat. The river wrestled to throw, drag or catapult me off.

Chase and Herbie, twin companions on the stern endured the identical fight, each likewise locked with the river through fourteen feet of oar. Old Andy, beard wagging, entwining arms and legs through the rigging, locked himself to the mast and peered downriver through his binoculars. I felt whole once again, freed, rid of my civilized and not-so-civilized obsessions. The river and the canyon, gleaming its rocky glory at me from all four sides, crushed those vague and uncertain dreams and left me standing, clean and reborn, bolt upright on the bow. Chase and Herbie grinned at me rapturously from their oars on the stern, likewise whole and victorious, chests hairy and splendid in the sun, eager for more.

Three miles below Hermit Creek we pulled off to survey Crystal rapids from the shore. There was a pulsing mound of frothing water and a hole below it in the lower part of the rapids which was definitely not the place to go. All fourteen of us, both boatloads, stood goggle-eyed on the shore and watched it seethe. I was aware of Suzanna, Debbie and Cindy, the three women on our boat. Just before we cast off to run Crystal, Cindy came and nestled her chin into the crook of my arm and gave me a deep and terror-stricken gaze. I gave her a re-assuring squeeze on the shoulder and down we went, passing within a few feet of the incredible haystack water-mound which towered above us on the left and which then subsided into a chasm, swirling and sucking, into which we could peer with awe, as we passed safely along its edge. Cindy's face was ecstatic, eyes burning out into the hot canyon sunshine, electricity in the depths of her brain.

Soon after we unloaded at Bass Creek and Wayne signaled me to come over onto his boat. He had brewed peyote tea. By the time the moon rose, approaching fullness, over the rim of the inner gorge, I had tired of the conversation, and was yearning for a more primeval communion with the canyon. Grasping my old friend, the guitar, by the neck, I climbed to the summit of a nearby rock spur and began to sing into the moon-bathed shadows of the canyon, yearning for the company of the spirits which I hoped to call forth. Uncertain of my effect on my comrades below, but played out, I began my descent from the spur after an hour or so. Cindy was waiting for me on the rocks below.

"That was beautiful," she told me. Pleased that at least someone had enjoyed the mood, I sat down beside her. Little Cindy. So thin, tiny. A wisp of a girl.

"I was terrified in Crystal today," she confided. "I've been terrified ever since I was swept overboard with Neil three years ago in Lava Falls. Coming down here again was a big move for me," she continued. "I had this awful feeling that I'd never come back up out of those waters. Today on the boat, when we began our descent through Crystal, it suddenly occurred to me to throw my energy onto the canyon below the rapids, and you know, as soon as I felt it fastened, anchored down there, I knew we would make it. By the time we passed the hole I was no longer afraid. It's such a relief to somehow find your way through something you've been so afraid of for so long!"

Tiny little Cindy! Such a brave little soul: Delicate as a bird! Long into the night we sat beside each other; then lay together naked on the sand beside the river. She kissed me, gently. Our bodies touched, her legs rubbing across mine… we allowed the feelings to arise from within us we entered another magic land… But we honored our soulmates awaiting us beyond the canyon's rim and refrained from fully making love… it didn't seem to matter… our love and attraction had found its ethereal pathways…

Magnificent Plunge into the Pool Below

The next morning Chase and I set off up over the dry and stony plateau which stood between us and Bass Creek. Content to wander slowly, we inspected the cacti along the way.

"My God!" Chase exclaimed. "I don't see how these poor guys manage to survive here. You have to hand it to 'em. They have to be tough. My God Look at that!" he said pointing to a leathery plant just bristling with spines growing out of a crack high above the ground with roots in nothing but sunbaked, blazing, naked rock.

"I have to take pity on a fellow like him! He actually reminds me of myself, ugly fucker that I am!" he exclaimed, reeling with uproarious laughter. He opened one of our canteens and poured its contents onto the parched plant. "For sure you need this worse than I do!" he told the plant, chuckling outrageously.

Bill Chase and the Cactus

Later that night we began to sing a few tunes, quietly at first. I began singing to the moon and felt the satisfaction of harmony and romance arise. What an addict of the orgiastic musical frenzy I had become! Chase's lone deep bass voice began climbing up under my songs from below. Melanie added a slow and perfect rhythm on a tambourine. What a pleasure to be surrounded by the dancing bare breasted women! When Debbie and Cindy began to dance naked beneath the moon, I remember feeling the connection moving out toward all the women in the world!

We all fell asleep in the same spot and didn't move until morning. By afternoon, we managed to get it together to shove off and float on down a few miles. Below us the black granite walls of the inner gorge appeared to rise higher, steeper, and the canyon began to twist more severely, making it nearly impossible to anticipate the exact locations of the rapids which lay ahead or to even find a place along the wall to stop and tie up. We eventually found a shelf to sleep on opposite Garnet canyon. It seemed the canyon had begun to weigh on our souls and the whole mood crumbled like a house of cards. We fell into deep and early sleep.

The next morning we woke up with Elves' Chasm just around the corner. A few minutes on the river and we were at its entrance, right at the point of a sharp bend in the canyon. We entered the chasm and began to swim and play. Chase treated us all to a little dance on top of a rock high above the pool below, striking one pose after another.

Chase Dancing on the Rocks

Suzanna and Andy, the two old leathery ones, joined us from wherever they'd been off together chewing nails, toughening their hides a bit more I suppose... Chase finished his acrobatics with a magnificent plunge into the pool below.

"Thanks, Chase," Suzanna told him. "I truly enjoyed that!"

As the days passed in this canyon, life grew thicker. The very air seemed to surround us more completely... We all began to walk with a sense of connection to the rocks, the water, the air, the sizzling sunshine, the heavy darkness of moonless times of the night... Then the connection to sense, spirit, the plants and animals thickened too... And there was a feeling of being drawn into the swelling desire for contact with even greater depths of the canyon.

Mike, Rebecca, Andy

Cindy and I were drawn that night into Blacktail Canyon, a narrow winding corridor: night air thick with the smell of damp rock. Besieged by the magnetism of this little canyon, we crept our way along its floor, pushing our slight tingling sense of fear ahead of us, surrounded by the amplified echoes of our own breathing. The sun finished setting and there was no light left in that canyon. We had not brought lights. Deeper and deeper into the black labyrinth we slipped until rounding a last corner we could make out the heavy darkness of a solid wall at the canyon's end, a waterfall... or at least it would have been a waterfall had there been enough water.

A spine-tingling noise greeted us at the very moment we rounded that last corner and glimpsed the wall. Was it an owl? Perhaps he had glided ahead of us on silent wings, seeking to escape our advance. Or perhaps he liked his close little place at the very end of the canyon. In any case, he began to scold us now, hooting and howling at us, with a vulnerable and pleading cry in his voice. The tones made the message unmistakably clear: "Don't! Don't! Don't come any closer!" he pleaded. "You're terrifying me whoever you are! This is my canyon; won't you please stay out of it! You're squashing me to the last limit! Please don't drive me out of my very own place!!!"

We immediately retreated, amazed by what we had heard. It was with a gentle sense of relief that we eventually emerged out into the comparative openness of the greater canyon. We nearly stumbled over Suzanna and Andy who were asleep in the entrance to which they had no doubt been lured by the same magnetism.

The Scorpion Did Not Seem to Mind

The next afternoon Chase and I found a rock shelf in the shade and made ourselves comfortable for a while. I found a little scorpion sitting quietly on a ledge. Chase gazed at the little fellow for a while, and then began tickling the end of its stinger with his finger. The scorpion did not seem to mind; did not move; made no attempt to either sting or escape. All the while, Chase looked like he knew exactly what he was doing. The huge man just did not seem able to bring himself to fear little insects...

Back at the mouth of the little canyon by the river we cooked a leisurely and delicious dinner. The usual: tortillas, beans, onions, cabbage, potatoes, plenty of beer... coffee... Wayne brought out his bottle of 150-proof rum! This was the night of the full moon. With wide open eyes we watched the brilliant phosphorescence of its light descend the west wall of the canyon, making the rock as clearly luminous as it was by day - perhaps even more so, for the eye is drawn to drink in that magnificent white light.

Mike and I pulled out our battered old river guitars; Neil sent vibrant banjo notes full into the echoing canyon; Chase hunched over the washtub bass, like a huge gopher stroking his own fur, deep booming notes pounding out over the river. All night long we played. The ladies sang, laughed, danced, beat out rhythms on the planks of the boat upon which we all sat. Debbie, cute and smiling; Melanie, stately and holy, a firm sense of rhythm; Cindy, fluttering, a little bird; Rebecca, brown and womanly, a nymph of the waters! Hour after hour passed... unnoticed by us. The moon drew our energy out like a huge siphon.

Connection Through the Dance

Effortlessly, ecstatically, our bodies played and danced. Neil, his body as tight and heavy as a little bear, began playing that banjo with a fury! I heard the deep booming notes emerge from the washtub bass so exactly in tune, on pitch and precise: Chase had entered a washtub trance and remained in its clutches throughout the night. The moon swung clean across the breach of sky open to us through the canyon above. It seemed too bright to behold with a direct gaze! And just as it finally neared the rim and was on the brink of vanishing, a final musical orgasm shook our bodies and we all dove into the swirling river simultaneously!

We spent two days exploring the recesses of Tapeats cave and then returned to sleep below Thunder Falls. I spread my poncho out on the ground and lit a candle. A perfect little white scorpion marched out onto the middle of my poncho-ground-cloth. Although convinced that dozens of his friends must be jerkily waddling under the weight of their own immense stingers only inches away from me in the bushes, there was nothing for it but to lie down on the oven-hot ground and see what I could do about falling asleep for the night. Some animal a good deal larger than any scorpion had been scurrying noisily through the bushes around us for hours. And now it had the audacity to scramble hurriedly across the small of my back as I lay on my belly on my poncho, hot and scared of scorpions, waiting for some blessing of drowsiness.

Sitting up and quickly putting a match to my candle, I beheld a spotted skunk the size of a large kitten dapperly scratching himself beside my feet. He seemed to have trustingly accepted me as camp-buddy for the night, apparently offering me nothing but camaraderie and friendship. My uneasiness melted into his easy nonchalance and I felt glad to have such a cute little companion. Happily my candle flame did not reveal any more encroaching scorpions.

We put ashore next afternoon at the mouth of Kanab Creek. Neil and Mike twisted green tamarisk branches into rings and began a makeshift game of horseshoes. Before we knew it, that one little game had developed into a full-blown track meet, complete with races, wrestling matches, and handsprings into the river. Variations on the broad jump proliferated as fast as we could think them up: the standing broad jump, the running broad jump, the running jump followed by a headlong dive, a tuck and a somersault, leaving the jumper sitting on his ass, the marks made by his heels in front of him taken as the limit of his jump... Chase outdistanced us all in every event, the incredible springs in his mammoth body unleashing themselves in a frenzy of youth. Perfectly coordinated, his body arched through the air, tucking and flipping at the last possible moments with exact symmetry. A few of the women had decided to enter the races. Melanie and Rebecca flew across the sand, knees plunging, breasts wildly flopping, the last remnant of modern-day womanly decorum peeled off and let slip to the ground. The tension of all that incipient passion, the fruit of so much time spent under the weight of those black canyon walls, was bulging in our bellies.

I Forcefully Repossessed My Soul

The sun set and the night-time spirits settled around us. Neil remembered that we still had one more refuge beyond words and soon strode back to the boat to reappear triumphantly bearing banjo and guitars. This had now become our nightly ritual. Chase set up his washtub bass and notes sprang out into the night like meteor showers in the sky. Locked together by those same liquid steel bands, our arms and fingers began to strum as if attached to a single musician.

Neil and I caught glimpses in each other's eyes of such a fiendish identity that we recoiled at the sight: it was like looking into a mirror. The same frightening creature was alive in both of us; he looked out both of our eyes, catching terrifying glimpses of himself whenever one pair of eyes looked into the other! And when it got right down to it, the music which that creature could play stripped souls like a raging brush fire leaving nothing but smoking black skeletons where flowered jungle had luxuriated only a moment before.

Terrified of the creature, and unwilling to surrender my body to the likes of him, I forcefully repossessed my soul and withdrew into a safer music… a safer song which I knew well and would not slip beyond my grasp… Neil also withdrew; drove the creature back out of himself, although he had been more willing than I to continue and follow its beckoning call.

"I see something in that wall!" cried a small female voice, excited, enraptured… the voice of a little girl… Little Cindy pointed at the tremendous looming south wall of the canyon. Our music hushed. "It's the face of a giant cat!" she cried, lost in the depths of her vision. "A huge black shadow… It's like a gargoyle…"

Wayne turned calmly toward her, removing the stem of the corncob pipe from between his teeth, and smiled knowingly. He had been looking long and deep at the same place. "To me it looks like a huge black cross."

Relieved to wake up and find daylight suffusing the canyon once again, we climbed onto the river and rode it down to the mouth of Havasu Creek. Arriving in the heat of the noonday sun, we swam playfully in the pools at the confluence of the creek and the river. Diving off the boats, we swam up the side canyon, touching the rock walls with our fingertips from time to time, amazed at the sheerness of those gates… Yes, gates they were…

Another commercial boat crew approached and gave us a pile of their leftover groceries. We were happy to laugh and dance like the happy pirates they saw in us and sort through their gifts. They traveled so much faster through the canyon and didn't want to have to pack out their surplus foodstuffs. They were only a few hours away from the end of their run.

Swimming a few dozen yards further upstream we began to find breaks in those gates and we clambered out onto the ledges, chutes and platforms of living rock. Perfectly suspended over the deep pools below, the invitation to dive was irresistible. Over and over again, for hours, we arched, jumped, tumbled and flopped into the water, from greater and greater heights, sometimes with six or eight of us linked arm in arm, entering the water simultaneously with huge bubbling blue splashes.

A little higher up the creek we came across the first travertine pools: white, blue and purple mineralized bowls large and small, built intricately under the rushing milk-white waters of the creek year after year, millennium after millennium, like crystalline lace.

Lower Havasu Canyon

We had entered the gates to the Garden of Eden. A lush green canopy of cottonwoods held the water's coolness snug against the canyon floor. Grape vines, planted years ago by the Havasupai Indians, strangled and choked together in over-abundance, untended, ran wild and green over the beaches and rocks. High above, the orange and white red-walls of rock baked in the sun.

Securing the boats below, we filtered up into this newly discovered paradise, unmindful of each other, sprinkled out in groups of two or three. I set out with Wayne and Chase but out-distanced and lost them. Driven by a deep green longing in my belly to see more, to enter more deeply into this cool and marvelous canyon, I kept plunging on ahead.

With the last light of day, Mike and Rebecca suddenly appeared and became my companions. I slithered and groped my way up the huge crystalline tears, draperies and splashes of the travertine tunnels beside Mooney falls. We had come close to ten miles up the canyon from the river. Here the Native Americans had chiseled a vertical labyrinth through the frills of mineralized rock. Possessed by the fascination of discovery, the three of us emerged on the precipices above, now separated by darkness from our companions below, and sought sleeping spots a bit further upstream on the packed earthen floor beneath the cottonwoods. I remember rolling up in my poncho in a hollow between two rocks, my body making a nest of the ground for the night...

We Don't Welcome White Trash!

Early in the morning I awoke. Mike and Rebecca still lay sound asleep, nestled in each other's arms. Taking care not to disturb them, I donned my shoes and crept back down the canyon. With the early morning silence still unbroken behind the cool, vine-shrouded canyon I remember relishing the chance to return to Mooney Falls, descend the travertine tunnels and see exactly what that incredible tumbling fountain of water looked like. Soon we were joined by more or our crew and we swam for a couple of hours below the falls before the prospect of more explorations above lured us onward. Under the spell of Havasu Canyon we dissolved into timeless consciousness. We climbed to Havasu Falls and spent more hours swimming and diving.

Havasu Falls

"You know, there's a village right above us now," Andy shared…

Sure enough, after another hour's climb we were passing little mobile-home-like dwellings with TV antennas affixed to the roofs. In the center of the village we found a little restaurant. We entered with a feeling of strange amazement: it had been weeks since we had seen a cash register or thought about purchasing something with that green stuff called money. None of us, it seemed, was carrying any. We noticed the pie and hamburger for sale but had no means to pay for anything. We sat around a table thinking to perhaps hang out for a bit and drink a glass of water.

A couple of middle-aged Havasupai men entered the restaurant and informed us that we had needed to pay an entry fee of five dollars each in order to visit their village… Hmmm… We looked at each other and at them…

"Sorry… It seems that we didn't bring any money up from our boats on the river…" we explained.

"The fee is $5 apiece," they reiterated unsympathetically… no smiles… nothing.

We began standing up to leave and, again commenting that we were sorry, made our way out of the little rustic restaurant.

"We don't welcome White Trash!" the Havasupai men snarled at us.

We scurried back through the village down toward the canyon.

It took most of the next day to descend the ten miles back to the river.

Wayne placed his lips to the sawed-off hole in the end of the giant sea conch which dangled from the mast on his boat. His great chest inflating like a mammoth bellows, he sent a trumpet note echoing far up into Havasu canyon. We went about the business of making the ships ready. The sun was getting low, the river was running high, charging by in its endless liquid hurry, sighing and gurgling. Casting one last glance up into Havasu, we cut ourselves loose and abandoned ourselves to the current. It felt good to have the bow oar in my grasp once again. The darkening walls swept past us at incredible speed.

"This is the highest water we've seen yet!" Andy announced from behind the mast. "We're going to be lucky to find a good place to camp. Look! There's not an uncovered beach in sight!"

There were no side canyons for quite a ways. Churning our oars to center our craft in the current around bend after bend, we waited for a glimpse of a hospitable shelf or beach. Beyond each corner we were confronted by the endless plunging black granite walls, striking straight down into the river on either side.

A few low beaches appeared from time to time, but no campsite. You never know exactly what those guys are doing with that Glen Canyon dam. The water can rise or drop six or seven feet in a few hours… all for the sake of generating electricity for the folks in the city.

Eventually we spied a shelf on the opposite side of the river. Small, shaped by the current like a huge sand teardrop nestled against the granite, it climbed fifteen or twenty feet above the level of the river and offered us a place to camp. Surging against our oars, Chase and Andy manning the rarely-used side oars as well, we made for the beach. We tied up the boats; we unloaded them; we unpacked the food, set fires, drank…

We were getting more and more wound up, tight, a bit nervous, hushed: we were approaching Lava Falls, the biggest rapids in the canyon.

We Watched Person After Person Tumble Off into the River

The next morning we lashed the gear tightly around the masts to the decks of the boats and floated to the brink of Lava Falls, tying into the shore just above the tumbling water. We walked down the shore to survey, plan and settle our routes through the gushing descent.

To me the water was feeling like a playmate, and I would gladly commit myself to its most glorious white foam, abandoning my fate to its inevitable kindness. But again and again I paced the shore with Andy, Chase, and Herbie, beginning our evaluation of the lower holes, the boat-eating hearts of the rapids that must be avoided, working our way up the shore again and again, casting sticks into the foam to observe the pathways of the currents, planning every detail of our entry from above.

Two possible routes had revealed themselves to us. One would bring us into the top of the rapids at the center of the river, skimming between another two of those uppermost boulders and then flailing away with oars to the left side in order to miss the big slab. The other, the one which I had begun to prefer, involved slipping between a larger number of rocks in the upper left part of the rapids, gradually working our way to the right until we would arrive in the center of the current, far to the left of and safe from the giant slab, holding all the while to shallower water.

Wayne preferred the first alternative and set off, huge man, barrel chest and belly, hunkered over his bow oar, Neil and Jim on the stern. Accurately slipping between the upper gates to the rapids, the bow plunged deep into a hole which had been nearly invisible from shore, so covered up with froth and foam it had been.

Wayne's Boat Enters Lava Falls

The entire boat vanished into that hole, only the tip of the mast with its fluttering orange flag remained visible above all that cascading liquid. At the next moment the nose of the boat reappeared, soaring up out of the river like a giant porpoise, Wayne holding onto that bow oar as if it was the reins of a runaway steed, crew and passengers still intact behind, water streaming off their faces and limbs.

We stood on the shore with mouths open wide, cheering frantically over their re-appearance. But then next thing we knew, it looked as if the hand of a giant and slumbering river god, a monstrously barnacled old titan who lay reclining in the rocks beneath the rapids, had casually grasped the bow of Wayne's boat, pinching it by the nose and lackadaisically given it a spin. A few frantic oar strokes to no avail, and there they were, flying stern first in the very center of the current headed directly for the awful whirlpool-generating slab on the right side of the river below.

Spun Around Backwards in Lava Falls

We gaped in horror from the shore as the boat plunged, faster and faster, on top of that disaster-bound ridge of water. Beside the giant slab, the boat swung around, placing bow foremost once again. Then a huge watery backlash from the edge of the whirlpool swept beneath the boat from the side, lifting it up into the air.

Tilting vertically on its left edge, it flowed downstream, falling neither upside down nor back onto its bottom. In slow motion, so it seemed, we watched person after person slide and tumble off into the river; Wayne, Neil, Jim, Rebecca... Only Melanie and Mike remained on the boat, clinging to the lashing and to the mast...

Gratefully, we watched the boat tumble back down onto the water right-side-up... if only the swimming crew could either clamber back onto the boat or make it to shore, the worst of the rapids was over. We saw one swimmer headed for shore: Jim it later turned out to have been. He had curled himself into a little ball, was sucked deep down into the roiling hole, holding his breath, his glasses clutched pitifully in the grasp of one of his hands, until the whirling currents choked him back out onto the surface and he drew a grateful inhalation and began swimming for shore. Wayne had plunged into the water, resurfacing under the boat, as did Rebecca. He soon bobbed out beside the bow; Rebecca pushed herself this way and that, trapped beneath the boat's bottom for almost too long, trying to find its edge! At last she found it and her head popped out into the air. Melanie and Neil surfaced with ease beside the boat and all began clambering back aboard. All we could see was a tangling and twisting of arms and legs, a be-drenched craft with a broken mast limping downstream; who was there and who might not be, we couldn't tell.

There were some commercial boat passengers gawking from the shore as were we, but we didn't see them, hear them or think about them.

We Were in Exactly the Right Place

We headed up-shore to our craft, hearts wildly pounding, anxious to follow our friends down to offer any help we could should their struggle persist. One of the commercial boatmen grabbed me by the arm as I raced by.

"Are you going to go the same way?" he asked.

"No," I replied. "We're going to enter the top further to the left."

"Not further toward the left!" he cried. "That's certain disaster! I've seen other boats try that and they can't make it! There are too many rocks on that side of the river and there's a shelf…"

But I was already gone. The route was fixed in my mind. I had looked at it too long, hard and carefully to be able to give credence to his words.

At a run, I pursued the others toward our boat. Halfway there I was confronted by Debbie, pale and shaking, sauntering back down the trail. She gave me a fearful look, lowered her eyes to the ground, then raised them again…

"I'm sorry," she trembled. "I can't go. One of the commercial boatmen has agreed to take me down on a boat with a motor. He'll drop me off wherever you land…"

"OK," I said, feeling her peel off like a sparrow from the edge of the flock.

Andy, Chase, Herbie, Suzanna and Cindy were already there on my boat, coiling the bow and stern lines, checking their hand-holds in the rigging. I climbed onto the bow, lashed down the oar so it wouldn't fly off its pin, gave a nod to Herbie to shove us off. Pulling our way out into the current, we began searching, feeling for the right spot: it's all in being able to enter the top of the rapids at exactly the right spot! I scanned the river downstream for the protruding boulders which I had selected from shore to be our landmarks. To recognize them from an entirely new angle would not be easy, or even possible... usually the top of a rapids must be entered with uncertainty, a best guess...

But this time I was too well-prepared to miss. I spied the recognizable rocks and waves and ripples: there, immediately beneath the left side of the bow, a red rock. That's the one! We were in exactly the right place.

Uh oh! I felt a shallow boulder grab the end of my oar... Going through the rapids with a shattered bow oar or with the oar pushed irrevocably off its pin is to commit yourself to the hands of the river and fate. That had happened to me three years earlier upriver in Hance rapids. This time we were luckier and the boulder let go, the oar slipped free unharmed and stayed still tied onto its pin.

We were halfway down the rapids and the deck wasn't even wet! Zigging and zagging around another couple of boulders, hauling to the right to miss a large hole on our left... we were home free, riding the crest of the central tongue, far from the grasp of the huge slab on the right. We emerged from the lower rapids, rode a few percussion waves -- the kind that are nothing but fun to ride, the dancing water ponies... They kicked us around a little bit, a crest or two moistened our feet, and that was it! We were through!

Wayne's crew had managed to anchor their battered craft to the right side of the river a quarter of a mile downstream; Jim had reached shore, replaced his glasses on his face, and run down to rejoin them. They were all OK, all in the midst of giving gasping accounts of what had happened to each of them. We pulled in beside them; they scarcely realized that we had arrived; they stood clinging to each other, panting and exclaiming...

"Did you hear what happened to Rebecca?" Mike asked me.

"No."

"She was trapped under the boat for a long time! Every time she tried to swim upward she would bump into it again! She was really passing out by the time she finally found her way out! She really almost drowned! And last spring she had seen a dream with the exact same scene... So being trapped under the raft had felt like an eerie deja vue... it was a really close call..."

Little Cindy came up to me, eyes shining, wrapped her arms around me, gave me a big hug. "We ran it perfectly!" she jubilated.

Herbie came up to me and shook my hand saying, "Congratulations!"

Chase declared, "We should have run it the same way Wayne tried! Our way wasn't even exciting: We didn't even get the deck wet!"

The commercial boat brushed ashore above us for just a moment, giving time for Debbie to hop off. Then the boatman took his huge rubber doughnut slithering downriver past us, his passengers waving and cheering at us. Debbie approached us meekly, silently. There was a feeling that suddenly she had become an outsider: the one who had abandoned ship. I had felt similarly six years earlier when I had swum for shore after the raft I was on became hung on a rock at the top of a waterfall in the Big Drop in Cataract Canyon. I had seen the danger coming. It wasn't my boat. I wasn't the 'captain.' But stories were told about me which cast me in an unheroic light. I walked up to Debbie and gave her a squeeze to let her know that she was still one of us.

An Indian Was Huddled Against Me For Warmth

The next morning a rather sullen crew arose and haphazardly loaded the boats. Today would be our last day on the river. Minds began turning toward the outside world beyond the rim.

Time for Relaxation Above Diamond Creek

The huge pointed nipple of Diamond Peak marked our destination; we watched it slowly grow more intimate as we closed in on it, rounding bend after bend in the river. The canyon below Diamond Peak faded into some meaningless anonymity: the land beyond the pale, the yarn to be left un-spun, the song to be left unsung… a part of the land through which we were not destined to pass. Somewhere down there lay Lake Mead, reportedly a vile and stagnant swamp created by the dam. We would not see it. It belonged to another time, another age. We were about to wrest ourselves from the grasp of the canyon.

Hopping ashore for the last time… a dull thump under our feet as we landed on solid ground to stay for some time, some months, a year perhaps… How long before I would find myself on the river once again? …everyone asked himself silently that same question as his feet struck the sand.

A pickup truck full of Hualapai Indians from Peach Springs were enjoying themselves by the edge of the river, trying to conjure up enough sobriety to venture back up the road from whence they had come.

Chase and Mike and I approached. "Hi!"

"Hi!"

"Are you guys going back to Peach Springs soon? Do you suppose we could have a ride so we can bring our trucks down?" we asked.

"Sure, I figure you can come. We'll be goin' along pretty soon… soon as we get wet one more time!"

"Get wet! Get wet!" the six young men cried, splashing water over each other's faces. "Moose! Get up! Get wet!" A three-hundred-pound fellow named "Moose" was already asleep in the truck bed. He didn't have it in him to make it down to the river to get wet one more time.

Mike and Chase and I wound our way up the road with the Hualapais twenty miles or so to Peach Springs. We stopped from time to time beside the creek so that everyone could pile off and "get wet" one more time. We got to exchange happy smiles with their friends as we rolled into town. We were in the right company and were spared the usual deadpan expressions reserved for white folks.

We made our way toward our trucks, gave our thanks to Moose and his friends and went into a little cafe for hamburgers and coffee. A slick be-sunglass-ed couple obviously driving back from California to New York came in. How strange to be back out in this world beyond the rim. The coastal-culture couple sat in smoky silence, their beings apparently diffuse, invisible.

Out here one could forget... forget whatever it was one was trying to remember... Every minute spent outside the canyon walls seemed to me to be a violation of sacred space... It felt confusing.

Just before dark we had finally finished piling the last pieces onto our trucks and we began the slow grind uphill back to Peach Springs, then east toward Grand Canyon Village where a number of our cars had been left parked. Late that night, we pulled off the road and slept.

The next morning I awoke feeling the pressure of someone's head sleeping against my knee. I looked down. An old man, an Indian, was huddled against me for warmth. The sun was just appearing over the horizon and I pulled myself gently out of my sleeping bag. I looked around. Chase, Wayne, others were sitting up, rubbing their eyes, trying to take in this new chilly beyond-the-rim world in which we suddenly were finding ourselves. I pointed to the old Indian, who lay, thin and emaciated as a rail, ribs showing through the shirt on his back, on the ground beside me. I wrapped the sleeping bag around him and went about cleaning the spark plugs in the 1953 Ford truck. Eventually the old man awoke, picked himself up onto his feet and wobbled over to where we were working on the engine.

"I Na...wo meai...," he announced.

"What?" I asked.

He repeated himself, slurring words beyond recognition, brain cells apparently burnt out by too many years of alcohol, but eventually I realized he was telling us that he was a Navajo mechanic. He pointed at the carburetor and said, "ca... wea..."

"Carburetor!" Chase agreed.

"Mmm!" the old man agreed, his tone serious and businesslike.

Soon it turned out that the old fellow had been up on his feet again for too long. He began to collapse, go limp, as he continually struggled to peer into the engine compartment of the truck. I wrapped my arms around him.

I lowered him back onto one of our ponchos on the ground. I put my hands on his back. The ribs and vertebrae were sharp beneath the skin, like sticks inside an old tattered leather bag. As soon as I touched him over the backbone he began moaning semi-consciously with deep relief. I could feel the nearly extinct nerve inside his spine drawing on the life energy in my hands, sucking the electricity like a hungry run-down battery. It didn't matter whether I gently rubbed the bones or just left my hands lying in that spot, the old fellow groaned and moaned with primordial pleasure.

I had no idea how much life was actually flowing out of my hands and into his central nervous system, but it seemed like it might serve the poor fellow for a few more days perhaps... a number of hours at least. It began to lightly rain. We covered the old fellow. He looked like a skeleton anxious for the cleansing, sun-bleaching process to begin, but deep behind those sunken eyes the life force flickered, jovial as ever... essentially the same as always... just sunken, withdrawn, recessed into the core of the man.

Debbie wandered over to my side as I continued pressing gently over those essential central vertebrae. She had caught a little brown lizard. Gently, with care, she placed the lizard on the man's cheek. Leaving the poncho behind, we climbed into the trucks and resumed our journey towards Grand Canyon Village.

Not everyone could fit into or onto the trucks so Chase and I stood beside the highway with our thumbs out. Finally, after an hour or so, a vehicle was approaching. Just as it drew near and we were imagining how the driver must be checking us out, weighing the pros and cons of picking us up, I felt a fiery pain on my balls. In a dancing frenzy I undid my pants and found the culprit: a nasty red ant. So much for that potential ride!

But sooner or later a driver took pity on us and thus began a series of rides which, after a day or so, delivered us back to Steamboat Springs. We said our goodbyes for now to our river-rat friends.

We headed back to Boulder and began the dis-orienting task of re-integrating into this strange world we call civilization.

Wild Dance Parties

Leda was now known in John Link's communal household as 'The Sacred Mother' and was happily exploring her life in Boulder. She had taken on a sales job at the Calico Closet, a woman's clothing store to help relieve our poverty.

I took a job running an Outward Bound course through the Collegiate Range in central Colorado. But... where were the indigenous tribal people?

Whoops... Colorado was nothing like Peru... or Mexico... It was just us white folks... Why were we teaching the students to be afraid of the wilderness? ...always being focused on 'survival techniques' as if the mountains were some kind of dangerous environment...

Instead of the usual students, mostly from cities in the eastern US eager to explore the Rocky Mountains, I was given a troop of teenagers from Hawaii. They were brown indigenous 'juvenile delinquent' kids who had been in prison. By going on an Outward Bound course in Colorado they could rehabilitate and get out of prison sooner. They were 'inner city gang kids,' and I was told that they might try and escape if we got too close to a highway.

Moving south through the vast wilderness of the Collegiate Range we only crossed one highway during our fourteen-day course. No one tried to escape. We had climbed some fourteen-thousand-foot peaks and everything was gorgeous and wonderful. No frightening dangers had emerged to face and over-come... just immersion in a natural and friendly wilderness. My students had to head home with no horrendous tales of danger to tell!

A week later I went up into the Front Range behind Boulder and got caught on the high ridge between North and South Arapaho Peak... the air turned blue and crackled through the rocks above and below my little ledge... thunder shook the earth while little wind-formed trees, black and brittle as the rock, grasped with their root tentacles for a tenuous hold while hailstones snatched the last brown remnants of their summer attempts at growing leaves.

I loved our band, 'The Silk Route.' We played at local Greek restaurants. Audiences showed up to learn Greek folk dancing and to admire the belly dancers. I was always happy with practicing and performing. Our little music and dance tribe, now swollen to fifteen or so, went on tour to Idaho where we were a big success. So fun to be on the road together!

Lindy, Leda, Josie, Bob, Cameron on Idaho Tour

We had flute, bass, sitar, bouzouki, triple percussion, triple vocals and something like eight belly dancers.

The Silk Route with Our Dancers

We had hot exotic rhythms for dancing and we had brought in the Greek feeling of transcending the time dimension and entering eternity with our slow songs.

Steve Fundingsland and Lindy

But one of our dancers had a baby who was not thriving. I don't know what happened, but we heard that the baby didn't make it. There was a little ceremony up in the Gold Hill cemetery. We sang one of our slow Greek songs. "Please sing that song for me if I die!" we were instructed by some of our tribe.

Wild dance parties proliferated at John Link's house. I frequently ended up playing my guitar and singing late into the night. That was my way of paying rent. Our communal reputation in Boulder grew and every party lured fresh opportunities for flirtation. Leda and I deepened our dance connection with each other and kept sleeping in a corner of the living room when it was cold and out in the yard under or on the trampoline when it was warm.

> *The Sacred Mother*
> *Leda is the secret*
> *shot from her own black eyes*
> *like a meteor across the night sky*
> *which left Oedipus standing*
> *With two smoking craters*
> *where 'once had been two eyes*
> *Leda is the bomb*
> *I am the fuse*
> *Leda's are the lips*
> *I am the mouth*
> *Leda is a waterfall*
> *I am the sunlight dancing in her spray*
> *I could lie in her the way*
> *the moon lies in the still surface of a pond!*

Leda and I decided to get married. I was still remembering my high-altitude Andean realization about having children.

I worked hard in my little lean-to shop turning out guitars and jewelry. I made a plaster mold of Leda's shapely body and began to make a 'Leda Guitar.' Oui Magazine, published by Playboy, did a little article about the finished 'Leda Guitar' featuring a photograph of it with one of their models. I sold it for $1200 to a well-known performer in New York City and hoped to get rich and famous for my craftsmanship. One drawback: it took twelve-hundred hours of work to carve and bend forty-eight little pieces of mahogany into the right shapes to produce the instrument. That worked out to $1 an hour.

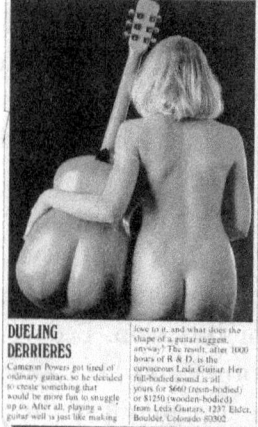 

The Leda Guitar

Wedding

"Let's not wait!" we had decided. "I know weddings are supposed to be in the spring," Leda had said, "but we're excited about it now! Waiting all winter would drain us of our energy! We called and wrote the parents, relatives, told the closest friends, decided to have it in Chase's back yard in Boulder, printed invitations, ordered wedding rings, prayed for good weather, found a Unitarian minister, got blood tests, a marriage license...

The last few days had been the most hectic: get the champagne, beer, wine, liquor, organize the feast, hold a shower, dig the fire-pit, paint the inside of Chase and Jill's house, rake and mow and clean the yards, call the weather reports, practice the song and the fire and water ceremony, get the ice, the tables, drive through ranch lands to the north to buy the lamb and a goat, slaughter them using the techniques I had learned in Peru...

> *Cameron Powers and Leda Papanastassiou, having thrown all caution to the winds, have decided to get on with it and plunge headlong into marriage... on October 18, 1975. There will be a ceremony and a feast at Bill Chase and Jill Jamison's house at 1153 Sixth Street here in Boulder, Colorado. 3:30 PM is the time. We will be honored if you can come and join us.*

Suddenly it was 3:45 PM on the chosen day. Time for the latecomers had been allowed. A hundred-and-twenty dear friends and relatives were present. Ronnie had rushed upstairs to present the bride with her bouquet, an incredible creation of pure white gardenias and greenery assembled by the expert hands of Delanie. Forrest, the minister appeared, sticking his head over the top of the stairs, and said, "I think it's time. It looks like everybody's here. Are you ready?"

At the close of the reading of a poem, something to which I was not sure how much real attention I had paid, Forrest let it be known that it was time for the wedding song. Now this was something for which I was eager and ready. With willing abandon I laid myself open to the song. I heard the song rise, grow and swell through and in and over the air around me. These were the ones! These were the people who loved us! The people who would sing my and Leda's song! Thank you all you people!

My throat had strangled, was tight; my voice was quavering, unable to sing. I lowered my eyes back to the ground and listened to the voices in song around me until, gradually, calm returned within me and my voice re-appeared and now rose with the singing circle... a rich bass harmony, a pleasure even to my own ears, was surging out through me.

Leda's voice had hovered beside me, stable and melodious from the beginning... a song-bird... even and smooth...

I raised my eyes once more to the crowd, the circle, the people. Where's my father? I wondered. My eyes searching, I found my father's face, softly bent with a touch of age, a touch of humility, intent...

The song entered its fifth verse. The English translation to the Greek words had been given aloud:

> *Whose is this garden from which we all reap fruit...?*
> *Black eyes shine in the drinking glass...*

...a eulogy for Leda's beautiful eyes... the most beautiful eyes in the world... Greek eyes... my eyes traveled in the circle... Again I felt like sobbing... once again I cast my eyes down to the ground before my feet. The sobs twisted and grappled in my chest; another full verse passed before I could raise my eyes once again.

My strength came back and I rejoined the bride's unwavering song... I sang once more, twice more, the song... I felt satisfied.

For me, that song was the wedding. The rest could flow hither or thither as it might, but this song had been sung and I was content.

My mother and father sat within a few feet of each other... the first time I had seen them both at the same time in the same place in seventeen years! Somewhere in me I recognized it as some sort of historic occasion.

Leda and I Get Married

Now the drumming had started; the dancers were starting to stomp and whirl.

I danced alone for a bit. "Where is she?" I asked, wondering where my bride had gone to...

"I'll get her for you!" someone volunteered and ran off, soon returning, bride in tow. This was what everybody had been waiting for, wondering for, dancing for, playing for! We whirled like planetary gears in the center of a new circle formed around us. The dazzling white of the dress swept like a gigantic dove through the approaching darkness...

Somewhere over there progressed the feast... Forty casseroles, salads, hors d'oeuvre, desserts, the lamb, the goat, the champagne, wine... none of it had yet touched our lips save for a few drops of champagne! Our feast was on another level that night... uncles and aunts, old friends and new, parents, cousins, children... the greatest assemblage of warm spirit and flesh ever assembled on our behalf!

I somersaulted through the center of the circle... Finally I sampled loin of lamb and loin of goat... the goat was the dark meat, the lamb the white... Wayne had officiated over the final roasting... the meat was delicious, perfectly juicily done... Carrying my vittles, a chunk of meat in each hand, I approached the growing circle... I offered friends a bite of each...

Our hearts were in the people who were there, then, walking, dancing, breathing, loving, that green-grass space below the blue sky... The cake was laden with the love juices of the ladies who had made it... let those juices flow through the years to come...

Joe Ball and Jim Sharp! Amazing! Under the last daylight out in the yard they had stretched themselves open, clung to me, their love over-flowing way beyond the usual limits of expression! We formed a circle, a huddle, arms wrapped around backs and shoulders, Joe close beside me on the right, rubbing his forehead against mine, blessing me with tokens of genuine respect and well-wishing...

Gradually, the circle expanded under the night sky where we could see the real, risen moon -- a full moon! It hung overhead...

"La luna esta brillando arriba!" I finally exclaimed, after twenty minutes of swaying in that huddle...

Bonnie and Lisa at Wedding

Before she left, Bonnie had come to me, embraced me, wished me her very best... "Being here at your wedding I've noticed..." she began, "...I've noticed the kinds of people you've chosen to hang out with... You've chosen the passionate, emotional ones! I just want you to know that I learned passion from you; I remember it! I can see it, appreciate it and cherish it... I know what it is, thanks to you... I know how to recognize it, find it..."

She paused for a moment. "I just wanted you to know how happy I am about the part of our lives we spent together. I feel really good about it, and I'm so glad that we're still friends and that we can be open with each other..."

She gave me another hug... I marveled at the beauty of what she had just said... she went swimming off into the night... Later, she found Leda and hugged her and told her, "I give him to you!"

Chase had danced thrashing, grabbing ladies off their feet, whirling them around, crashing into the drums and the drummers... Now he lay, asleep at last, inside beside the phone...

Rebecca administered the final oil to the midnight candle. Wayne's essence had emerged once again as the mammoth warm teddy bear... the colossal heart... we all sat on the couch together, Ronnie nestled beside us, the bride as gloriously beautiful as ever, reigning from the rocking chair, strong, but growing a tiny bit smaller as the night grew late, as midnight approached... I gathered up my bride and took her home... once again...

Leda's Belly Was Growing

I kept working in my little shop. Leda and I decided to visit our friends Irv and Winnie in New Mexico. We needed a road trip. I worked feverishly to finish fabricating a series of ebony medallions inlaid with silver astrological symbols. I finished and we hit the road. Somewhere in northern New Mexico I stopped driving and lay down in the desert. I was sick. Very sick. I had inhaled too much ebony dust and it was poisoning me. I struggled on down the road and passed out on a bed at Irv and Winnie's rural house.

I woke up twelve hours later feeling like I'd traveled to some distant planet but had survived. I picked up a little divining pendulum which happened to be lying on the table next to me and couldn't believe what I saw and felt. The little pendulum came to life in my hand and did a little dance... all by itself... I lay there and rested some more... Eventually Winnie and Irv and Leda returned from a trip to town. "Hey, watch this!" I invited them and I picked up the pendulum again. But it's magic had vanished... I guess if you've been really sick it keeps the ego out of such things and they work... Then after you recover... oh well... back to normal.

Leda was pregnant. We took on the additional financial burden of renting our own apartment and moved out of John Link's communal household. I kept making guitars and jewelry. Pete Ritter, a friend from high school in Colorado Springs came to say hi. I had just finished making an inlaid astrological medallion with movable planets all inlaid with various exotic hardwoods.

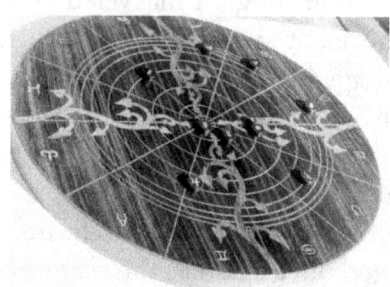

Astrometer

"That's exactly what I was looking for!" exclaimed Pete. We created "World Views Incorporated" and designed and built the first of some twenty-five-hundred *'astrometers'* which we would eventually sell through ads in national astrology magazines.

I studied astrology and discovered that I might be the only person for thousands of miles around who actually cared to know exactly what 'lunar nodes' were or what it actually meant when 'Mercury went retrograde...' I wrote a book for inclusion with our product called *'Astronomy for Astrologers.'*

We met lots of astrologers, even traveling as far as Michigan to consult with one of the more famous. I continued to be amazed that people could talk about 'squares' and 'houses' and zodiac signs without needing to visualize the astronomical realities underlying those supposedly significant events and configurations. I searched for some rhyme and reason underneath the madness called astrology and found none. Oh well... Our product was selling and I got paid for the design and manufacturing and packaging.

I finally finished a draft of my *'People's Guide to Peru'* and sent a copy to the small publishing company who had published the *'People's Guide to Mexico.'* They returned it and told me that they only published one book a year. This year they would publish a *'People's Guide to Purchasing Video Equipment in Los Angeles'*... or something like that... oh well...

Guitar and Bouzouki Making

Leda's belly was growing. Soon I had a smiley little son named Loren. He loved hanging out suspended in his 'bouncer' which I had made with some elastic and a pair of cut-off little pants. Sometimes I brought him to 'hang out with me' while I worked in my little shop.

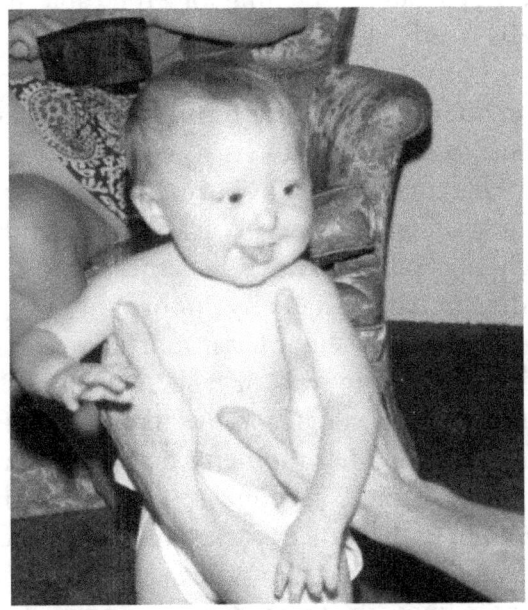
Loren Arrives

We practiced music every Wednesday night and performed on the weekends. Tragedy struck. My dear friend and the bass player in our band was driving down Boulder canyon from his house in the mountains one evening to practice music with us and suffered a head-on collision with a drunken driver heading wildly up the wrong side of the road. The drunk driver survived. Steve Fundingsland didn't. I didn't know what had happened. Why hadn't he arrived to rehearse? I kept calling his house but his girlfriend, Margie, also a singer in our band, had taken the opportunity for some alone time and unplugged their phone. I drove the mountain roads until 4:00 AM but found nothing. The accident had been removed by ambulances and tow trucks.

Around three o'clock the next afternoon, still without any real news, my psyche was hit with the realization that Steve was gone. I don't know how I knew, but I knew. I plunged into deep grief.

Soon we all had the official news and we assembled in Steve's little primitive sweat lodge at his house up on Magnolia Road and we wailed naked together for hours while feeding hot rocks and steam into the center of our circle of grief. Nothing about Steve's death made any sense. He had not in any way been 'ready to go.' His surrealistic oil canvases, which had been selling for $1000 apiece, would progress no further. His steady bass rhythms would be heard no more in our band. And his warm farm-boy friendship from where he grew up in eastern Colorado near the Kansas border would be known no more.

His parents, well-known to us as personal friends, arrived in Boulder. Steve had made a point of bringing us all out to Burlington, Colorado, many times to spend occasional weekends enjoying their friendly rancher hospitality. His dad's name was Shirley and his mom was called Ali. Not having had any opportunity to grieve with us in the sweat lodge they arrived at Crist mortuary just in time for 'the service' hardly able to even walk or talk.

I asked the mortuary staff if some of us could go into the back and be with Steve's body for a few moments before the 'service.' They said, "No... you wouldn't want to see him... he was pretty messed up in the accident... and out of deference to the families of other deceased persons in the same room with him we can't allow anyone back there... but if you want to know the moment we begin the cremation after the 'service ceremony' just go outside and stand by the big natural gas meter and when you hear lots of gas rushing through it you will know that the cremation has begun..."

"Thanks..." I said.

Crist Mortuary was able to provide a 'minister,' who of course had never known Steve, to say a few words and then it was over. We all stumbled back into our separate lives after that moment... Really? Was that all?

Steve and Margie

Athens and Naxos

We took our young son on his first trip to Greece before he was two years old. We of course spent time in Athens with the family, but we also spent a few days on the island of Naxos. It was summer and the panayirya, the music festivals, were happening. The island orchestra was playing in a different village every night. I remember carrying Loren down the beaches for long distances in order to follow the music. I also had my tape recorder with me... the same one which had accompanied me to Peru so many times and was still functioning perfectly... so I could record the village music and learn it later back at home. I loved the fact that the band would play non-stop for seven hours a night. No breaks were taken. Just non-stop music. Yes, if the violin player needed to go pee, that would happen... but the band never stopped... music music music... and the islanders would dance...

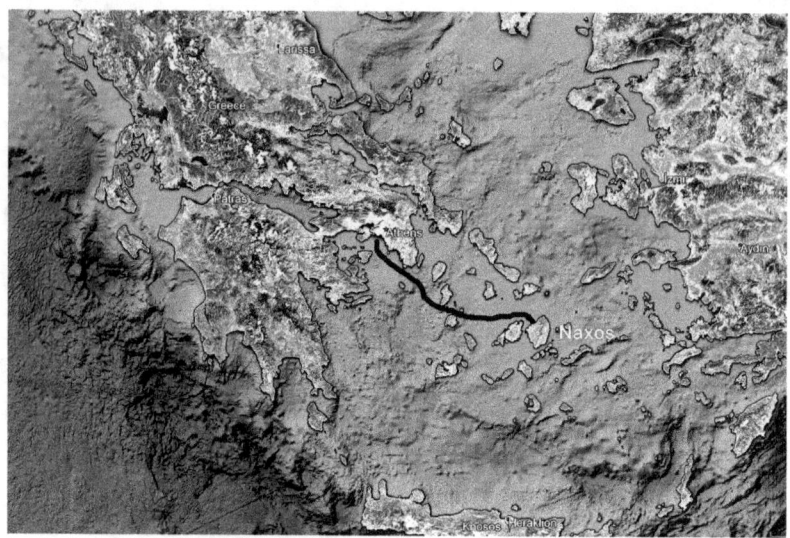

Taking Loren to Athens and Naxos in 1978

Back home I played Greek music tapes non-stop in my shop while I made guitars so that the songs would sink in deeper and deeper... and, shades of things to come, I began listening to Turkish, Arabic and Central Asian music... The more experienced belly dancers were requesting... "If you really want to play for us, then learn more Egyptian music..."

My friend Bob King, a drummer in our band and husband of Lindy, one of our most fun and flirtatious belly dancers, ran a construction company and offered me some stone masonry work. Soon I was making money faster doing this heavy labor. I enjoyed being out of my little shop. Soon, teaming up with an experienced stone mason named George, I found that stonework jobs were stacking up. I bought a 1951 Ford pickup truck and became a regular customer at Leukonen Brothers stone quarry.

Stonework Stairs

We built stone stairway, patios, fireplaces, waterfalls, chimneys... I crawled out of bed every morning on my hands and knees but my back kept getting stronger and stronger...

Stonework Walkways

The loan officer at my bank told me I was a fool not to let him help me become a home owner. My friend Anne Ketchin wanted to sell her little four-hundred-square-foot shack in north Boulder. I borrowed $5000 and with the help of my carpenter friends I framed up a two-thousand-square-foot house on top of the shack. I convinced the mortgage lenders that the house was almost done!

Becoming a Home Owner

I went back to the banks and bought Anne out. I now had a house and a $30,000 mortgage. She and Leda and Loren and I kept living together and I assembled the rest of the house bit by bit. My friend Charlie came down from Steamboat Springs and helped nail on the sheathing to brace against Boulder's high winds. Bill Chase showed up to show off high-altitude plate-walking skills while we pounded nails.

It's a House in North Boulder

I had learned plumbing, electrical, drywall and finish carpentry skills in the process. I applied for and passed the test for my 'general contractor' license and soon not only had a house of my own in which to live but many more skills to offer and could find a lot more work beyond just stone masonry. During the next few years I became a specialist in passive solar design and completed dozens of architectural projects.

After we finished building the house, Elli and Tassos and Costis managed to travel and visit all the way from Athens. I loved having almost a whole acre of land for a yard so that friends could gather and cook food and party for occasions like Leda's family's visit. I built a big deck over the well to give us more elegant outdoor living space.

When Loren was three years old we took him on a nice easy river trip down the San Juan river in Southern Colorado. Silk Route band members David and Melinda accompanied us. Life was good.

A Son and a Daughter and More Time in Athens

Soon Leda's belly was growing again and Melina came into our lives. Perfect. One of each: a son and a daughter. Both of them got to grow up knowing from the bottoms of their souls the feel of the gaze of the warm Mediterranean mother showering love. They will always remember that deep nurturing sprinkled with lots of little endearment phrases in Greek language. And daddy played them Greek songs at bedtime every night. I filled them with music and figured the schools would do their job and teach them to read and write.

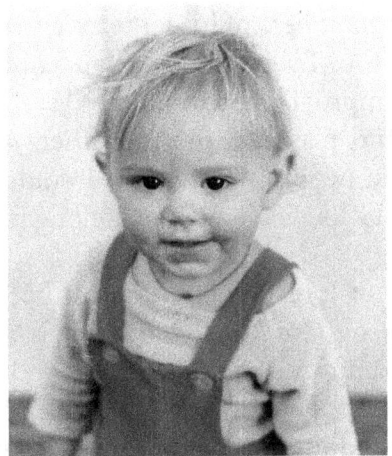

Melina Arrives

The general contracting business was growing and I was usually running four or five jobs at a time. I built a shop addition onto the house so I had an indoor place for an office and workbenches and tools. We lived hand to mouth making just enough money to break even every month. I had never had a real plan for providing lots of money for my family but, like a lot of other families living on the edges of official poverty, I couldn't spend additional time and energy worrying about it.

I had never been able to witness my own father doing his work and learn from him. In my entire life I had seen one of his offices briefly perhaps only a dozen times. I wanted my kids to be able to feel like they had known who I was and how I made life work for me. Running businesses from home felt like a good thing. Loren and Melina could see what was going on from close up and hopefully learn something from it while all just basically enjoyed being together.

I washed my daughter's silky fine hair with a shampoo called 'No More Tangles.' Leda made tasty Greek food for us. Bob and Lindy were getting more involved with Chogyam Trungpa's Boulder Buddhist community and Leda was attracted.

We continued to play Greek music at local restaurants. I met an Iraqi oud player at a party up in the mountains. His name was Muhsin. He kindly offered to teach me an Arabic song. I liked the feel of that music and I knew that the dancers would too. I have subsequently stayed in touch with Muhsin and have visited him over the years in California, Lebanon and Jordan. I have also gradually gotten to know some other members of his large extended family.

I was a dancer too. Every weekend afternoon I joined Nancy Spanier's group of improvisational dancers. We acted out different emotional themes and played with each other. As the years passed I discovered that the people with whom I could form deep dance connections were very likely to become lifelong friends and business partners.

I got the news that John Link's body had been found way up in the Front Range just south of Rocky Mountain National Park. He had been running up and down difficult climbing routes and had lost his footing. I went alone up a nearby trail to grieve his loss but, remembering the times he had told me that he would prefer to die running in the mountains to facing the difficulties of old age, I felt less grief and more of an acceptance. But I knew his kids would feel the grief and the loss.

Before Melina had turned two years old, we decided to introduce her to her Greek grandparents so we traveled back to Athens. With two children it was not so easy. I left Leda with her mom and dad in Athens and took Loren up to Delphi for a few days. We had a little Russian-made bicycle with us which he, now five years old, had learned to ride on the beach on the island of Zakynthos. The streets in Delphi were steep and stony... a perfect place for him to hone his bike-riding skills.

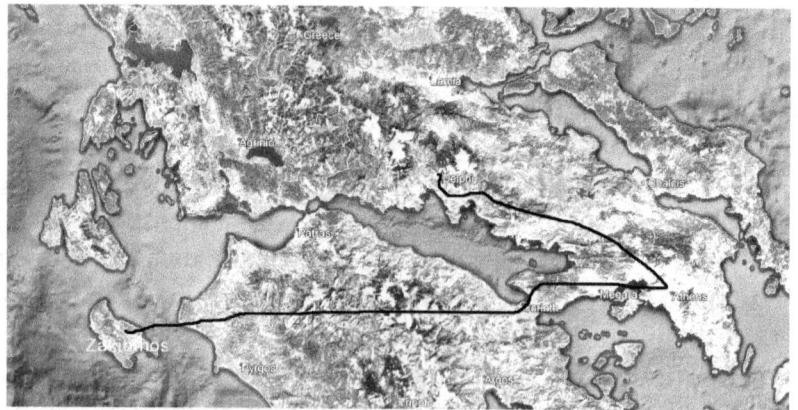

Back to Athens, Delphi and Zakynthos in 1982

Deeper into Music and Dance

Back in Boulder, work resumed. I saw an ad in the local paper for a 'Sufi' class. I went. I was curious. It was taught by Janet and Manny. They were students of an Iraqi Sufi named Adnan Sarhan... from Baghdad. I liked the way we moved to their drumming and when Adnan came back to town I went to his workshop.

He put on a tape from one of the great Egyptian oud players, Farid al Atresh... "Now we will move our bodies to the music... sit in front of me and keep one eye open and do more or less as I do..." he instructed. For the first half hour he did not move at all... then he began a movement in his head and neck... his jaw began to trace a curve through space that was perfectly smooth and liquid, yet so slow that it took five minutes for us to move our heads just once from right to left... gradually other parts of our bodies became included... but so slowly we moved... unimaginably slowly... Suddenly I realized how wonderful this felt! I had uncorked an inner being... an inner snake of some kind... who had a deliciousness in the feel of movement that I had never experienced before... and the music was the perfect music for this movement... I was falling in love with Arabic music!

I was, more than that, falling in love with my own inner self... And, I discovered that the delicious feeling could easily become so powerful that the verbal chitchat in my mind would slow and eventually vanish in order to make room for a pure experiencing of the deliciousness of my own movements. After an hour of slow movements, Adnan's Sufi dance would speed up until eventually we would be leaping and rolling and laughing wildly through the room and playing gleefully with each other. But it had all begun with the most subtle, the most liquid, the slowest of almost invisible movements. To this day, when I begin to dance... and I am a confirmed 'dance-a-holic'... I like to begin slowly and rediscover and anchor myself in that inner sweet place...

An old friend from Missouri, Paul Max, moved to town. He dove right into working for me at Giant Leprechaun Construction Company and became a valuable friend and business partner.

I was also of course introducing my kids to the natural beauties of the Colorado mountains... on foot in the summer and on cross-country skies in the winter.

Loren and I in Colorado Mountains

Our Greek band played on... Thanks to Muhsin, we now knew a few Arabic songs... And there was a new clarinet player in town: Costas Rountas, from Ioannina in northern Greece. He was top-of-the-line professional and was soon playing regular gigs in all the Greek venues in Denver with an assortment of different bands. I don't know why he liked us, but he did. Soon, with him in the lead, we had a much more professional Greek band and we got hired to play at numerous Greek weddings not only in Colorado but also in Nebraska, Wyoming and New Mexico.

Greek Music in Nebraska - Melina Dancing Back to Leda

We were no longer 'The Silk Route.' We became the 'Boulder Bouzouki Band.' Leda had become less interested in performance as a singer. I was the singer, bouzouki player, guitar player and, thanks to discovering an Armenian woman with an instrument to sell, now also a beginning oud player. Dave Morton became the accompanist with incredible accordion skills while Kathleen McLellan became the drummer. We were good. Kathleen also took the job of receptionist for Giant Leprechaun Construction... my contracting company.

Leda was drawn more and more into the world of Boulder Buddhism. I was not similarly drawn. I sensed the competitiveness of the surrounding sangha, or community of followers, and felt like my time was better spent following my own instincts toward a richer spiritual life... if there was such a thing...

Melina and Loren

My band was hired to celebrate the arrival of the mayor of Dushanbe, Tajikistan, to our town of Boulder, Colorado. Our two towns had formed a 'sister city' relationship from which many friendships and exchanges eventually arose. A banquet had been planned. After dinner and several boring speeches our band began to play...

Our dancer, Eva Cernik, brought it to visible form... the dancer is the visible form of the music and the music is the audible form of the dancer... it is a beautiful exchange...

Then when we began to play the songs we had learned from Tajikistan especially for the occasion, the Mayor from Dushanbe... Mayor Ikhramov... sprung up out of his seat and began to dance... soon the other visitors from Central Asia were dancing also, including Fardin, the fourteen-year-old boy who was so charming and outgoing and who had already stolen everybody's heart... Then the Dushanbe Mayor grabbed Boulder Mayor Linda Jorgenson by the hand and insisted that she stand up and dance with him...

In our culture official and political dignitaries do not usually improvise dances at formal occasions... But the invitation was there and our Mayor could only choose to accept... Our mayor began to wiggle her shoulders in time to our Tadjik music and to move in unison with the Mayor from Dushanbe! Soon an amazing transformation occurred: an entire room full of more than a hundred stiffly-sitting dignitaries were up and dancing to our strange Middle-Eastern melodies and rhythms!

Now the connection had happened. The 'sister cities' truly became family. All of the tightly held chest and breathing muscles felt themselves relax. We musicians felt the change equally... our music suddenly got much better. We quit wondering if we were playing for too long. The magic had happened... we played long into the night.

Boulder Bouzouki Band

Boulder Concrete Sawing

Life was filled with helping the kids get to soccer games, music lessons and birthday parties. Leda made connections with Buddhists and I focused on connections through the local public schools. There were swimming lessons and gymnastics classes... and so much more to keep up with.

Loren on Clarinet

Loren developed musical skills on clarinet and saxophone and Melina on violin and silver flute.

Melina on Violin

Giant Leprechaun Construction was doing reasonably well but I realized that a lot of money changed hands whenever we needed to hire someone to use diamond sawing and drilling tools to remove parts of old concrete structures. No one in Boulder was doing that work. One of the Denver-based companies sold me their old air-powered concrete-wall-sawing equipment and Boulder Concrete Sawing was born. I flew to Atlanta, Georgia to attend an annual international concrete-sawing conference and soon my new company was making more money than was my general contracting business.

Boulder Concrete Sawing

Our families in both the USA and in Greece had both managed to occasionally help us out financially when we were in need or wanted to expand, but basically we were breaking even and Leda didn't need to work. She entered the Buddhist path more fully by attending a three-month intensive training in Pennsylvania known as 'seminary.' She had hoped to keep Melina with her there for the whole time but I ended up, when Melina developed a respiratory infection, traveling across the country and bringing our daughter back home to Colorado. One of my lead carpenters, Dennis Duckett, moved into our house with his wife Betsy and their two kids. We had a little kid-friendly commune which worked well enough until Leda got back.

I made an extra effort to keep both of my companies fully legally registered in Colorado because the social workers down in the penitentiary in Cañon City were making plans to eventually release James into my custody because I could guarantee his employment. One day I went to meet his police escort and, after fourteen years in prison, he was a free man.

The sheriff and the state prison police escort service delivered him personally to me. They had rented a small apartment for him and given him strict curfew guidelines. After finishing his work day with me he was to return and stay home.

As the months and years passed, all restrictions were gradually lifted and, after working for me for a few years, he landed a good job in the high-tech engineering field. He continued to play his guitar at home but was not really interested in performance. He would show up and appreciate my musical events and I was always glad to see him. I still run into him now and again in coffee shops and he always sends a burst of loving energy my way.

'What is it that can drive a human being to commit crimes of sexual violence?' I wanted to know. James eventually did share with me some of the answers to those questions. A deep personal dissatisfaction with his personal life had erupted in a warped suicidal impulse which involved the necessity to commit some terrible crime in order to fuel the impulse to pull the trigger which released the bullet aimed at his own head. Being literally 'thick-headed' had saved his life. But after regaining consciousness and being transported to prison he had relied on the idea that surely he would be executed for his crimes. Unfortunately, from his point of view at the time, Colorado had shelved capital punishment and he had been given the life sentence... plus thirty years... I think it was...

But during those many years in prison, with the help of the social workers who saw in him a basically kind human being, he had been re-programmed to accept life again.

My path through life had shown me that we are all more telepathically connected than is commonly acknowledged in our culture... especially when it comes to sensing primal sexually-driven energies. He and I had shared access to some deep connection. Those things are always beyond words and impossible to really describe.

Managing Sexual Energy in Iraq

I received a phone call one day. It was Asaad, my Iraqi oud-player friend's brother. "Muhsin suggested I get in touch with you," he said.

"Where are you?" I inquired.

"Denver."

"I'd love to meet you," I said. "Can you come up to Boulder?"

Soon Asaad arrived with his three-year-old son, Siddhartha, and moved in with us for a few weeks. He had left Germany and ended his marriage to the German woman who was Siddhartha's mother and he was exploring America. We would take the kids to Casa Bonita, a Mexican restaurant in Denver where they had ongoing theatrical shoot-outs and indoor cliff diving. Asaad seemed delighted to be with us and had a smooth and elegant personality. He had spent years in an Iraqi prison for having written poetry. His family finally managed to gain his release and he had fled to Germany. After a few weeks of getting to know each other we shared our feelings on deeper levels.

"Asaad," I asked, "I know you are living in exile and afraid to ever return to Iraq... But is there anything about your native culture that you really miss?"

He thought about this for a while.

"I miss the warmth that exists within families in Iraq. I grew up inside an ocean of love which bound my mother and father together and I almost never see that in European and American families."

"Really? How can that be? Why is that?"

"In Iraq, as in other Eastern countries, men and women have a tradition which involves how they make love. The men with-hold their ejaculation. They seldom come when they make love with their wives. Basically they only ejaculate when they want another child. This tradition is called 'Imsak' in the Arab world."

"Really?"

"Yes. And so the husbands and wives are always feeling a strong attraction toward each other. Being around them is like swimming in a sea of warm love! Yes, I miss that..."

I became very interested in this idea. I had already discovered that life offered much deeper love connections if I didn't masturbate. But actually living inside a marriage and learning to with-hold ejaculation seemed like another step... and something definitely new and different in my own culture. I asked Leda if she might be interested in cultivating something like this with me but she said that we would not be able to pursue that without permission and training from one of her Buddhist teachers. I didn't know how to respond and eventually took it as a sign that we had moved in different directions.

I stayed in touch with Asaad and still continue to greatly admire his wisdom. He later told me that he had been able to see that Leda and I were headed in different directions way back then. It all took time to unfold.

Taverna Terzakis

Bob Drake was thoroughly American but his parents were Greek and he had grown up in an immigrant neighborhood in Chicago. His family had run a Greek restaurant. Bob was deeply involved with a political polling business but still had a dream of running his own Greek restaurant. Taverna Terzakis opened its doors on the Pearl Street mall in Boulder. We were hired. For the next three-and-a-half years the Boulder Bouzouki Band played there every Saturday night.

The belly dancers from Boulder and Denver took turns performing and the Greek folk dance community pranced up and down the tight narrow space between tables in the restaurant. Loren and Melina sat outside making 'gods-eyes' out of popsicle sticks and colorful strands of yarn. They made money; the band made money and the dancers made money. Bob Drake never broke even but he didn't really care. His dream had come true.

Eva, Me, Kathleen, Dave

After Taverna Terzakis finally closed we began playing at a similar restaurant in Denver called Zenobias. We played there every Saturday night for another two-and-a-half years.

Photographs of Tibetan wise men were appearing on our walls

and Leda was very drawn to their wisdom. She was finding truth in what they taught that resonated with her own experience. I went to another talk by Chogyam Trungpa but failed to see the magic. I signed up for the Buddhist "Shambala Training" which involved five weekends of meditation in the mountains but didn't feel that it had any real effect on my life. If I wanted a taste of Eastern spiritual wisdom I would read transcriptions of talks given by Baghwan Sri Rajneesh... Osho. He made a lot more sense to me.

Loren and Melina - Halloween

There had been a gradual separation. Our kids were still having fun but the atmosphere in our house was reflecting the division between Leda's Buddhist world and my Music, Dance and Construction world. She didn't feel that her connections to the Buddhist teachers were inhibiting her love for me, but I felt the gradual intrusion of some kind of high and supposedly absolute moral authority by which I was being judged.

For ten years I had avoided hot connections with other women. When Shrada, who had left Zadi and moved to Boulder, waved for me to enter her apartment I couldn't help but notice that she was lying naked on her couch and she was making no attempt to conceal her bare breasts. I felt very attracted. I had always been attracted to Shrada. I had skied across the Archuleta Mesa in southern Colorado on two separate quests to find her ten years earlier because of that instinctual attraction. But I waved at her nervously and ran away. I was being a faithful married man.

I had begun to explore the week-long Arabic music training in Mendocino, California known as Middle Eastern Music Camp. I was surrounded by four hundred musicians and dancers who shared my passion. Leda wasn't interested in this and I wasn't even trying to include her.

Finally something basic had changed. After fifteen years of being together, Leda and I separated. We worked with a mediator to divide everything fifty-fifty and we came to amicable divorce terms. We would each care for the kids half the time.

Leda's life moved forward in the Buddhist community, her meditation practices and her interest in astrology. I moved forward with the music and the nuts and bolts of architectural design work and soon I was in a rather desperate search for a step-mom for the kids.

The unraveling had been long and slow. Eventually I really wasn't feeling any longer like a faithful married man. When a woman who had been our next door neighbor took my hand at an outdoor party and pulled me down into the grass and I realized she wanted me inside her... she wanted me right then and there... I didn't stay inside her for more than a few seconds and I didn't come.

Kathleen and I were together by day in the context of her job as my company receptionist and book-keeper and we were together by night as musician and drummer through countless music and dance events. We experimented with intimacy but soon looked at each other and agreed that we preferred to just perform together. So we remained very close but without additional complexities. Ultimately, we performed music together for twenty-five years... or more...

Kathleen

I continued to dance every Sunday afternoon with the Nancy Spanier improvisational dance group. Dancing with people year-in-and-year-out brings you very close. Nancy seemed to sense that a change for me was imminent. She introduced me to a woman who was gorgeous and who loved to sit in the car with me for hours and kiss and make out but that's as far as it went.

I stopped to visit Camille in Kansas and there was no doubt about the feverish nature of the connection which still existed between us.

I got an emergency call to solve a frozen pipe problem at a friend's house up in the mountains. The woman who was house-sitting for them was a dancer. We were alone and attracted. I was also a musician. She asked me if I had any diseases. I said no. She said, "Make love!" I visited her a few times after connecting with her that night. I saw a blinding flash of white light one time when we orgasmed together but we never found a vision for our future so our meetings tapered off and came to an end.

My old friend from Missouri and business partner, Paul Max, bought Boulder Concrete Sawing from me for $100,000. He paid me in full over the next couple of years and I delivered half of that money to Leda. That gave us both a little more financial breathing room.

A tiny flirtatious woman named Allegra who was also in the improvisational dance class told me that she wanted me to meet her adopted niece. She thought we would have some things in common. She was a singer and a song-writer and, as I soon found out, had a voice as warm as honey. I met her and we fell in love. She has asked that her name not be mentioned in this book although we still get together from time to time and reminisce about the beauties of the love and creativity we shared.

I cried... I mean major sobbing... nearly every night for two years. I hadn't realized how much emotional agony had accumulated in the depths of my soul. Ouch. But after two years of crying... I was done. I had cried myself clean. Our household was a lot of fun: healthy cooking, theatrical projects, lots of trips to the swimming pools. And of course Loren and Melina's connections with Leda continued uninterrupted. We began with the kids spending a half-week in each household... then a week... then two weeks... then a month... or even longer...

Sol Spice

My new partner became the lead singer in our band which changed it's name to 'Sol Spice' and we continued right on playing every weekend at Zenobia's in Denver.

Solspice at Zenobia's

She was fluent in Spanish, having been partially raised in Mexico, so we developed a new repertoire of Spanish language pop songs. We played Mariachi tunes in the local Mexican restaurants. She could work magic with children if you put puppets on her hands. I made a little puppet stage and soon we were the most popular kids' birthday party act in town. The Boulder City Arts Commission funded us to do a hundred puppet shows in the local pre-schools and kindergartens. She also learned the lyrics of some of our Greek and Arabic repertoire and we kept on playing for the dancers. She went with me to Middle Eastern Music Camp... She bonded deeply with Kathleen, our drummer.

Slide-Ray was our new bass player; he could add hot trombone licks as well!

Me and SlideRay

We began playing at an Arabic restaurant, Mataam Fez, up in the mountains in Vail, Colorado.

In order to counter the materialism of the American Christmas season I took the kids to Taos, New Mexico, and spent December 25th watching pueblo Indian tribal celebrations which were all about successes in the hunt. Young Indians danced through the day with freshly-killed elk carcasses adorning their bodies. There was nothing resembling the white man's Christmas whatsoever and I never saw the kids take the deluge of holiday advertising so seriously ever again. We had escaped the materialism bubble. Our fun theater pieces with our kids at home continued regularly and we enjoyed helping them with their sports programs and local dance classes.

I had created a new career as an architectural and high-tech product designer using the latest Computer Aided Design solid modeling tools. Soon I had dozens of clients and made good money... $25-$35 an hour was easily possible and I was sometimes paid as much as $500 an hour at conventions to teach the fine points of making AutoCAD software run efficiently.

Costa Rica

Things seemed to be going well for the kids. Melina, my daughter, was fourteen when she and I took off and spent two weeks together in Costa Rica. We rented a jeep and explored for birds and monkeys.

Melina in Costa Rica in 1994

Being surrounded by White-Faced Monkeys in Manuel Antonio was fun. Seeing so many exotic creatures around Volcan Arenal was a big excitement for us. We got used to seeing coatamundis, quetzales, agoutis, spider monkeys, howler monkeys and blue morpho butterflies.

Melina in the Jungle

Melina was so excited that she would bound ahead on the trails long after darkness would be immanent at the end of the day. I would have to turn us around so we could see well enough to find our way back.

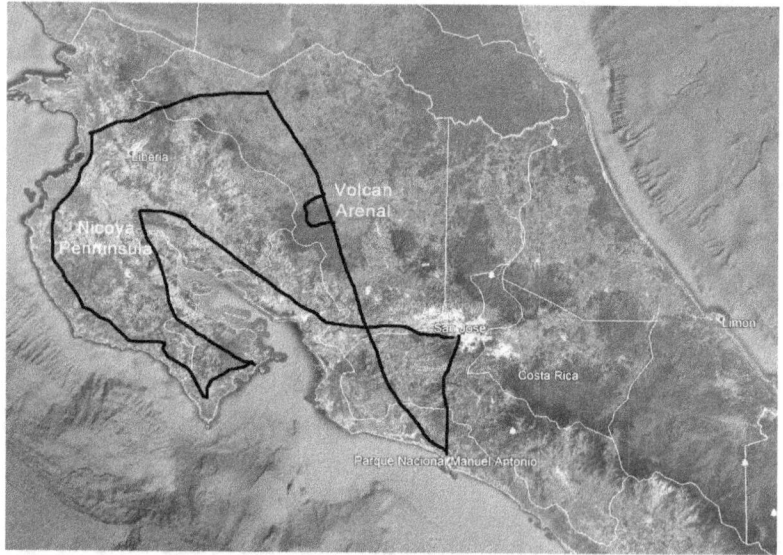

Exploring Manuel Antonio, Volcan Arenal, Nicoya Penninsula

I was able to send both Loren and then Melina to a traveling summer camp which carried them through some of the amazing canyon and mountain areas of Arizona, Utah, Colorado and New Mexico.

Children's Television and Bilingual Teaching Programs

My new partner and I also worked together in children's television thanks to her talents with puppets and then in bi-lingual education. We won a regional Emmy Award for children's television riding on a financial investment made by the Denver Center for the Performing Arts but creating our Spanish-English teaching program put us deep into debt.

Even with my computer-aided designer's income I still couldn't offset the debts our language teaching products were incurring. We flew to a bi-lingual language convention in Houston, Texas, rented a sales booth and got a glimpse of the big publishing houses with whom we were trying to compete: McGraw Hill, MacMillan and others. They had deep pockets and could spend hundreds of thousands of dollars on marketing. Our business plan wasn't working.

We flirted with some rich folks from Denver who promised the moon and we went even further into debt while being assured of a massive million-dollar financial bailout. In the end the supposedly wealthy investors told us that lawyers hired by their various squabbling family members had taken all their money. No bailout would appear.

In a desperate effort to cut expenses we moved into a tiny little carriage house in an alley. But something fundamental had gone wrong. One day my new partner announced that she was moving out. My attempts to win her back by bringing even more frequent love-making into our life didn't work. I felt extreme grief. And the thought of losing my close connection with her dad was deeply painful.

Nine years had passed. We had been amazingly creative and happy together. My friend Tom, who was now comfortably close to her, told me to just buy her some flowers and tell her I loved her and... who knows what might happen? I bought flowers and composed a long letter filled with reminders of our deep love. I put the flowers on her front porch but for some reason I never gave her the letter. I guess I knew that, painful as it might seem, it was time to let go and move on.

Loren Graduates from Boulder High

My son, Loren, had graduated from Boulder High and was taking a year off to travel South America. When he got back home our step-family had mysteriously dissolved. That was heart-breaking for him. I think he felt that if he had not been on the road that he could perhaps have saved the situation. But twenty years later, at his wedding in California, his step-mother and Leda shared the role of 'mother.' It was a beautiful thing and the underlying love energies buried in our extended and combined families ultimately triumphed.

It was truly magnificent. Ultimately we reclaimed our deep friendship and we like to get together and share the fond memories and feelings of love.

But back then when she vanished from my life I felt broken and lost. It took a few years for me to fully heal. I began the process with a trip to Egypt. I had lots of re-shuffling of living spaces to do before I could leave. I moved out of the little carriage house, put things in storage and began to float. Melina stayed for a few months with Leda. Melina and Leda also both felt sad and confused about the step-family breakup.

An Albanian Gypsy in the Band

We expanded our band to include Joffer, an Albanian clarinet player who was a wild and crazy gypsy musician who had played his way out of a Turkish prison and somehow found his way to Colorado.

He and Kathleen became romantically involved which was fun until Kathleen was ready to call it quits and things turned violent... Kathleen was fragile and he would hurt her. She asked me to help and I raised money to buy Joffer a one-way ticket back to Albania. Kathleen said she would call the police and report him if he didn't go. But nothing changed. He refused to leave. "I don't care!" he told me over the phone. "Have them come put me in jail!"

And Kathleen, when it came down to it, couldn't bring herself to call the police. His anger gradually subsided over the next year and he finally quit stalking her.

I saw him years later helping deliver food to our Iraqi refugee friends in Denver and we greeted each other as dear old friends.

Me, Kathleen, Joffer

Saadoun al Bayati

One evening Kathleen handed me a tape recording with no label on it. It featured the sounds of a man's voice singing in Arabic while playing the oud. Kathleen and I were both collecting tapes of Arabic music and our love for that music genre was growing deeper. She was getting frequent jobs playing at clubs in Denver with a variety of Arabic musicians. She did the homework to memorize their songs so she could back them up with her percussion in precise ways. And sometimes they would share their favorite but all-too-frequently unlabeled recordings.

I was captivated by the voice and oud and drum sounds on this tape. Wandering through a flea market in Denver one afternoon I noticed a vendor who looked Middle Eastern. He told me he was from Syria and I mentioned the mysterious tape. He agreed to listen to it and told me that it sounded like it was from his part of the world. We scheduled some time in his apartment so he could translate it for me. Little did I suspect that this would lead to years of musical adventures and that decades later I would finally meet and bond deeply with the mysterious singer, Saadoun al Bayati, himself.

Deeper and Deeper into Imsak

I had been moving more deeply into my 'imsak' or 'taoist' or 'tantric' practice of only coming once a month or so for a long time. My world and my music performance remained predictably vibrant if I cultivated my sexual energy. I always remembered what my Iraqi friend Asaad had said about what he missed from his Iraqi upbringing: that being around his mother and father had been like swimming in a sea of warm love... because of the ancient tradition known as 'imsak.' I had wanted my world and family to be like that! What is 'imsak?'

> *Imsak had initially been used by early Arab and Persian Muslims, but then spread to India in the Mughal period where it became known in Sanskrit as 'amsak.'*
>
> *For a certain type of gentleman the ability to create great pleasure and joy in their women's lives, is in itself the ultimate pride – the joy of giving pleasure and happiness to another.*
>
> *Imsak allows a woman to be more thoroughly and deeply pleased than otherwise possible, because typically a woman's or-*

gasm takes longer to develop than a man's. Women are capable of depths of orgasmic pleasure because they are naturally able (though this instinct is suppressed in many cultures) to experience multiple orgasms of astonishingly exquisite pleasure.

The Arabian Prophet Mohammad had left the faithful in no doubt when it came to the flesh: he bequeathed guidance on the importance of foreplay and mutual consideration during sex, stressing particularly that a husband should not 'lie with a woman and satisfy his need from her before she has satisfied her need from him'.

Imsak was once a commonly known body of techniques and part of a specific field of Arabian medicine known as the medicine of sexuality, literally al-Tibb ul-Jinsiy.

Imsak is to be regarded as the Muslim equivalent to the Chinese Taoist practice known as Fang Chung. There are in Tantra Hindu and Buddhist practices of similar type, though Imsak does not require you to adopt the metaphysical precepts of the culture that produced it. Imsak is not necessarily about chakras or goddesses or circulating sexual energy.

If Imsak is not properly taught to men, many women will be going unsatisfied, many hearts, unable to bond and find mutual love, will be unnecessarily closing and many people will be missing out on incredible experiences.

The Persian and Arab writers realized the immense need for the female orgasm and that it was a psychological need that took a sensitive male partner to help fulfill.

Without knowledge about Imsak the truth is that most men simply thrust themselves into a woman, pound her a few times, ejaculate, and then roll over totally spent, asleep. In the meanwhile their woman simply feels used, cheap, and totally frustrated.

In the middle-eastern culture of those more ancient times a viable ground for divorce for a woman was a husband's inability to sexually fulfill her. In order to provide husbands with the information they might need, medical authors worked hard to record their experiences with their sexual lives, meticulously noting their women's reactions to various practices and positions, words and seductive talk. All of this produced a body of literature that was consumed by young men, often at their father's direction, to understand how to please the women with *whom they would soon be in betrothal.*

In many parts of the East, up until the late 19th century, it was not uncommon for young men to be taught the arts of lovemaking from the sorts of marriage and lovemaking manuals known as "Kutub al- Báh" (books of pleasure.) This was the case from the Muslim Middle East, to the mixed Hindu-Muslim cultures of India, and up into China. These sex manuals more than rivaled any sex and seduction manuals that you will find today.

Essentially, teenagers in these cultures were educated in these matters before their first sexual encounters, usually in marriage anywhere from the ages of 14-18. This means that the young men went into their first relationships with a fairly in-depth knowledge of aspects of seduction and love making.

The Books of Jalaludin Suyuti, Ahmad Kamal Pasha, Ahmed al-Tifashi, and many other Arab and Persian Sheikhs from over a thousand years ago are full of descriptions of the pleasure responses women are capable of. These writers were able to tell the differences between various types of female orgasms in a day and age in which the Christian Church was keeping knowledge of sexuality in Western Europe in the dark.

At the end of this book I have included parts of a bibliography on this subject published in 1886 by Sir Richard Burton, translator of The Arabian Nights.

For several years I had been invited to become temporary lovers with a number of different women. I really didn't initiate any of these connections. It was the women who were excited about me and I worked hard to put their pleasures in front of my own and kept discovering that the strange result was an increase in pleasure for everyone involved including myself. Occasionally I would be invited to make love to two women at the same time. Our experiments, however, didn't easily fit into Western culture and after a while we all gradually withdrew from trying to maintain these somewhat delicate balances. I am delighted to say that our mutual love has withstood the test of time and that now, years later, I am still connected with and have deep loving friendships with all of these women.

Kristina: Crossing the Iraqi Sands

I was house-sitting for a drummer friend in Boulder and, before I knew it, Camille was living with me. She had not, of course, left her lawyer job with the attorney general's office nor moved out of her house in Topeka, Kansas, but there she was smiling at me in the same way she always had.

We journeyed together to Missouri where my step-father had passed away. Camille had always seemed like family... always will. She helped scatter his ashes, gave my mother big hugs, and we returned to Colorado.

Making and sharing love was so easy for me with Camille. She talked about moving to Boulder... sharing a house together... but I told her I wasn't ready. I had a feeling that it might be five years before I would really be ready for another deep partnership. I told her about that feeling. It was disappointing but we knew it could be foolish to move too fast.

I was deeply embedded in Boulder, Colorado. For decades I had been singing, dancing, working there. I knew everybody in town. How could Camille integrate into this? I needed to be close to performers... musicians... singers.

Eleanor, Camille, Melina, Loren

Camille went back to Kansas. We would see each other again soon. Other women who knew me well from mutual music and dance performance connections brought me into their love-making nests. There was no suggestion of partnership. They were just offering their softness and, of course, tasting my maleness.

Still, my mind was obsessing. I couldn't stop it. What had happened to my partner? It didn't compute in my soul so I obsessed about her sudden disappearance. The same thoughts went around and around... over and over. No... for me, it just wasn't right... it didn't make sense.

Off to Egypt with Eva

My dancer friend Eva was planning to lead another one of her belly dance tours to Egypt. The usual group of students was not materializing and she was on the verge of canceling the tour. But she wanted to go. We decided that I should go with her.

I would get my own private tour of the music and dance world in Egypt from this tiny gracious woman who had been born in Brazil to parents who had just fled from Czechoslovakia. So her first languages had been Czech and Portuguese but she had still been very young when her father managed to move the family to New York where they all learned English. Eva moved to Denver, Colorado and the rest of her family followed later.

Eva had chosen her full time dance career before the end of her teenage years and she was highly respected and loved. I had played for her to dance for close to twenty years. And she had helped guide my choices of which Egyptian songs to learn and perform on my oud... something which would soon lead to some amazing connections.

One of Eva's close friends was a merchant marine with whom she had connected here and there around the world. They had originally met when he had been a student and they had stayed in touch ever since. We agreed that we would travel together for a few weeks until the time came for her to meet up and spend time with him. In the meantime it was very nice have someone with whom to share daily adventures.

The Mizmar Band Continued Until Dawn

I had a feel for Arab culture but had never really been there. Landing in Cairo was a sudden entry point into that crazy high-speed boisterous market place world. I had begun studying Arabic but it was not easy. Eva taught me how to give a taxi driver directions back to our hotel but that was about all the Arabic I knew.

Eva

We spent time visiting Eva's Swedish belly dancer friend, Semasem, and some of her musician friends. Tradition has it that the Egyptian drummers take charge of dancers' careers and simultaneously 'own' them and 'protect' them. It's a delicate balance and may or may not involve sexual connections.

We saw one of their shows which typically happen in large hotels and I got a whiff of their lives. Eva and I also went to see one of Dina's shows. Dina is Egyptian and, of course, apparently totally at home in her dancer role in the five-star hotel circuit. Dina sings... she dances... she invites visiting friends up on the stage to sing with her... She moves so slowly and in such a relaxed fashion that we all felt like we were at home with her in her living room. Her moves were deeply feminine but no effort was made to be super sexy. She was just a woman who was totally comfortable in her own body... just as Egyptian women have been for thousands of years, or so it seemed to me.

Of course we went to see the pyramids. We rode horses and camels and Eva showed me the route she took one night to climb her way up the stones all the way to the top of the highest one. There was no remedy for being subjected to the usual tourist scams: *'This area is off limits, but for extra money I will meet you here after hours and let you in... special... just for you...'* I relied on Eva to navigate. She had been in Egypt something like twenty-five times.

Eva and Me

We spent days in the market, Khan el Khalili, while Eva placed complex costume and scarf orders with Mahmoud. I found little coffee houses and hung out. Sometimes an oud player would show up and play in the background. I loved Egyptians. It was an immediate thing.

Eva took me to see the largest mosques and we moved and bobbed with entranced Sufis outside their walls. I felt the depths of their non-verbal spaces... so relaxed... so easy... so *not-a-big-deal.*

We also attended a public Sufi show... this *was* a big energy deal... meant for foreigners... impressive but definitely a show... lots of drums and high-speed athletic whirling.

We passed another coffee shop near another large mosque... there was a Sufi band inside performing. I was magnetized by the Tura player's radiant smile and presence. Turas are big finger symbols. I still was not quite sure about where I might or might not be welcome... eventually I would realize that I was welcome pretty much everywhere. I sensed a vastness that is Egypt... an Egypt that remains Egypt while the empires come and go... it felt so friendly.

We climbed on a train and went south beside the Nile... all the way up to Abu Simbel. I walked into a restaurant in Aswan and an Egyptian school teacher recognized me. He had traveled to Colorado to attend a program at Regis College and my band had been selected to perform at their graduation party!

I didn't remember him, but I remembered the event. That was the first time I had been in the same room with dozens of Egyptians and I had noticed that they behaved very differently from Americans. They seldom divided into separate little cocktail-party groups. They just kept having one big conversation with everyone included. They seemed to collectively change the subject together on a whim. They behaved like a flock of birds or a school of fish. It had been my first glimpse at what I would later call 'Egyptian telepathy.'

Eva and I climbed aboard a little sailboat... a felucca... and spent a few days descending the river. I had purchased an oud in Cairo. I sang and played as we sailed along. At night the captain would find abandoned automobile tires and build big stinky fires which emitted dense plumes of acrid black smoke.

Felucca on the Nile

Arriving in Thebes, now known as Luxor, near the Valley of the Kings and the Temple at Karnak, we took a boat over to the west bank of the river and searched for Eva's friend, Tayyib, one of the town's many taxi drivers. Happy to see each other again, they began planning a dance party. Eva could not show up in town without celebration!

Tayyib suggested that I rest in his little rustic rural abode and wait while he and Eva went to search for the musicians. Tayyib introduced me to his wife and some of her female relatives. His wife had been suffering in extreme poverty... close to homeless. Tayyib had married her and taken her in to help her, but there had never been a 'romantic' relationship.

I sat on a bed in their home. The chickens were busy scratching and pecking at the dirt floor. The goats were busy munching in the yard outside the rickety door. Still anything but fluent in Egyptian Arabic, I began singing Arabic songs. The women gathered around me and snuggled close. With our faces only a few inches apart we sang together for hours.

Wide open eyes and souls surrounded me. I felt bathed in love. We found everything funny and enjoyed the mystery of having no functional verbal communication... no English... no Arabic... just our songs... yes, I knew at least ten songs which they knew... we sang them over and over again, snuggling closer and giggling more and more freely... it was a pile of Egyptian women. I didn't even try and count to see how many there were. I don't know if Tayyib or Eva could have guessed how much fun we were having.

The two of them returned after a few hours. The party was set. And our little family tour group suddenly grew by one more: Asata arrived. She was a woman from Oakland, California who had hoped to join Eva for this tour. There had been delays but here she was, just in time for the party.

After the sun set we drove to an open yard surrounded by mud walls. Two tables were stacked and wired together. Three 'mizmar' players and a drummer perched on top and began to play. A mizmar is an ancient primitive oboe which emits the sounds of a bagpipe. But it is powered by human lungs.

Mizmar and Taktib Party

'Taktib' is the name for the martial-art-like stick dance done by the indigenous residents of the west bank of Luxor. The men took turns performing in pairs... exhibiting their endurance and strength. Local traditions permitted a somewhat elderly local widow to dance with the band. She exhibited that easy, comfortable way of being in her female Egyptian body. But the younger women stood together watching from near Tayyib's house and refrained from dancing in public. Eva and Asata, being foreigners, of course took their turns dancing. Asata was a performing belly dancer back home in California.

Energetic Connection Through A Stick - Eva

After a couple of hours I was drawn into the stick dances with the men and had to call in extra energies to keep up with them. I had my oud with me. Sooner or later it was my turn to play. The band was quiet and I sang one of the Egyptian songs which Eva had suggested that I learn a couple of years previously: *'Sawah'*... by Abdul Halim Hafez.

I had no amplification and there were hundreds of people gathered there, but they all listened carefully and then sang with me. Waves of delight passed through the Egyptian crowd. An American... a foreigner... an *'ajnabi'*... was singing one of their all-time favorite songs! After that our feelings of brother-hood and sister-hood deepened to another level.

Eva did a dance standing elevated on a bench so all could see her more clearly. Tayyib looked like he'd had an endlessly long day but was happy. The mizmar band and the taktib dances continued until dawn.

Eva Uses Bench for Stage

The next day I thought about international relations... agreements between governments... aid organizations... trade agreements. I couldn't imagine anything in those procedures that could have the instantaneous cross-cultural magical emotional effect that we had all just felt... the music and the dance... they had been the real magic carpet ride.

It was time for Eva to go meet her merchant marine friend. She headed back toward Cairo and Asata and I rented a room together in Luxor. We finished exploring Luxor and took photos of each other doing silly things in sacred sites. Asata was also in Egypt for the first time and was having a ball.

"This is the first time in my life I've ever been somewhere where people don't even seem to notice whether I'm white or black!" She was being treated like a queen.

Asata and Ibrahim

She was flirting with delight and cultivating a romance with a local Egyptian guy named Ibrahim. Asata soon decided to make a quick trip back to the USA to arrange some things and then return for a long stay in Egypt... her next stay lasted for several years.

Egypt with Eva in 1996

I returned to Cairo alone. I had a few days to myself. No playmates. I discovered that my mind was still fascinated by its own obsession with the mystery of my Colorado lover's disappearance. Not fun. But I didn't really find a remedy. As they say: *'Wherever you go, there you are.'*

But underneath my obsession the seeds for a whole new phase of musical exploration were quietly germinating.

Hitting Bottom in Pennsylvania

I flew from Cairo back to where I had parked my van near Washington DC. My son had begun studying up in Montreal at McGill University so I drove up there for a visit. Then I started winding my way back toward Colorado visiting a few old friends along the way.

One night somewhere in Pennsylvania I hit some kind of bottom. I was exhausted from long hours of driving. I went into a diner to eat and felt more lonely than I ever had in Egypt. The Pennsylvania Dutch had a way of not welcoming strangers that I could feel. I crawled into the back of my van to sleep. Something happened which had never happened before... and I don't think it has happened since... but I remember it.

I curled up alone to try and sleep: not a pleasant prospect as my dreams were generally filled with themes of abandonment. So I curled more deeply into my inner consciousness... and then more deeply yet.

All at once I found a warm spot! It was a little warm spot inside my chest that I had never known I had! It wasn't big, but it was there... all my own. Rather amazed, I drifted off to sleep. I had discovered a new internal ally.

Playing with a New Band Called Sherefe

Back in Boulder I rented a little house up on the hill near the University. I hadn't lived in that part of town for nearly thirty years but I liked being back there surrounded by the students and their noisy parties again. Melina was halfway through Boulder high school and she settled in with me. It was nice for both of us to be just father and daughter for a while.

We all might have said something about continuing to perform together and keep Sol Spice alive but it wasn't happening. Kathleen and I were good as a duo so we pursued that. I also began playing solo in local coffee shops and felt the warmth of appreciative audiences. Leda cheered me on. She knew that the music could lead me back out into the sunlight. Camille would visit from Kansas from time to time which was always a delight but I still felt that I wouldn't be ready for another full relationship for some time... probably some years... to come.

Kathleen and I both began playing with a new band called Sherefe... It was a good fit for us. Greek, Arabic, Turkish, Balkan music... all being eagerly explored by young and highly skilled musicians: Jesse Manno, James Hoskins, Beth Quist... many others... I said yes to playing again for the New Years Eve party at a Middle Eastern restaurant called Mataam Fez up in Vail, Colorado where I had played the previous two years as Sol Spice. Sherefe members dove into learning my favorite songs and we were up and running. Now my life was recovering itself around the music.

New Musician Friends

My mother was not doing well alone in Missouri after her last husband's death so I moved her to Boulder where she recovered strength and enjoyed another twelve years of fairly happy creative life. She had some money so I bought a house with an attached apartment and Melina and I moved out of our little apartment up near the University. We brought our elderly tom-cat named 'Dennis' who had thoroughly adopted us.

My mother began her residence in Boulder in an assisted living facility which her insurance money could pay for. Later she moved into the house where Melina and I were by then already living.

I was still in touch with so many friends whom I had met while living in Manitou Springs years ago! They had all been students at Colorado College and, although I had never enrolled in that school, they treated me as one of them! This is the beauty of long-term friendships. A group of them decided to get together in Santa Fe, New Mexico and I was invited! So was Camille. From the moment we arrived in Santa Fe, Camille and I felt the same connection and enjoyed our ongoing bath of love. Northern New Mexico is great hot springs country and we all basked for days in the warm waters under the sun.

Enjoying Time with Camille

I sent a demo tape of me playing '*Samra ya Samra*,' a popular Arabic song, to Simon Shaheen who was initiating an east coast Arabic music retreat and I was accepted. I studied oud with him for a week and then flew directly to California just in time for another week of intense study and immersion at Middle Eastern Music Camp in Mendocino. This was something like the eighth time at that camp for me. I felt happy to be learning as rapidly as I could from amazing musical masters from Palestine, Syria, Turkey and Lebanon.

My son transferred from Montreal to the University of Victoria on the Pacific coast of Canada. I had been dancing and flirting with a woman named Susan every week at one of Boulder's regular 'barefoot boogie' improv dance events. She traveled with me up to Victoria. It kind of looked like we were a couple but I was still a long way from being ready for a new relationship.

Loren and I in Victoria, Canada

Eva was running another tour: this time to Turkey as well as to Egypt. James Hoskins, the cello player in Sherefe, agreed with me that we should go. His wife, who loved the folk dances from the Balkans, would come too. I decided to leave my computer-aided design career behind and gamble on music... hopefully for the rest of my life.

I was deeply curious about Turkey. When I had lived in Greece with Leda I had mentioned a couple of times that it would be interesting to go 'next door' and visit Turkey. But to want to visit the descendants of the Ottoman empire who were remembered as the brutal conquerers who had occupied Greece for four-hundred-years had been absolutely unthinkable.

Now that I had acquired a taste from Egypt of Arab-world civilization, I wanted to see Turkey and get a feel for what might be similar or different... I knew that some of the Turkish music and music scales, called *'maqams,'* had come from Arab culture. But I was still not able to listen to Arabic music and then Turkish music and sort out the different flavors.

Demystifying Turkey and Alexandria, Egypt

We began exploring Turkey in Ankara, in the center of Anatolia. We would eventually make our way around through Cappadocia and Konya in the south back to the Mediterranean coast and up through Izmir, where Leda's mother had been born, and then up to Bursa and Istanbul.

We were a group of ten or so... mostly belly dancers and musicians... and we rode in a yellow bus driven by a friendly mellow guy named Necati. Eva had arranged for a professional tour guide named Baki to also travel with us. We sang our theme song, *'We all live in a yellow submarine,'* as we bounced along from one Roman ruin to the next with as many music and dance events included as possible. Spirits in our group were running high.

I fell in love with a dancer named Birgul in a belly dance club in Istanbul, and also with a beautiful village girl somewhere in the middle of Anatolia and I got deeply into snuggling with Miramar, one of the dancers in our group. She had a beloved husband back home so our flirtations remained in the snuggling department but that still felt good to me. My friendship with Eva felt warm and deep and sharing experiences with James and his wife, Biz, was wonderful.

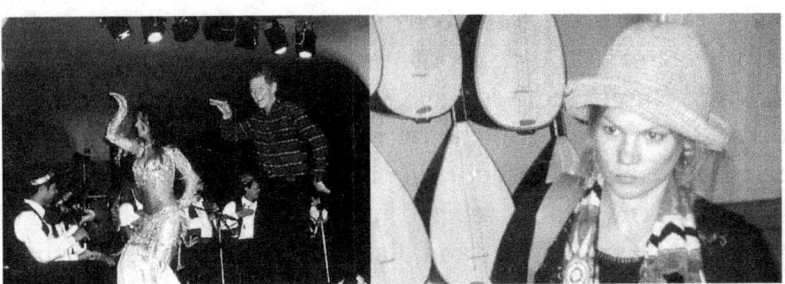

Birgul and I - And Miramar

When we got to Kusadasi on the Mediterranean coast I ended up playing an oud for some dancers in a local music club. It seemed to me that, while the official Turkish cultural doctrine demanded erasing Arabic language and music and encouraging everything European, the Turkish people retained a deep hunger for the Arabic music styles which had been a sophisticated artistic fountain for them for so many centuries. They seemed to love it when I played songs from further south from the Arab world.

Playing in Kusadasi

We were treated to Turkish folk dance exhibitions and even to a military Ottoman Mehter band which elicited a deep patriotic fervor in the audience. It was as if we were being subliminally told, 'Ummm... excuse us... we actually have a huge empire... it's just that we have temporarily misplaced it...'

We visited Rumi's tomb. Rumi, a twelfth-century Persian poet, is globally famous, even in the USA where certain skillful translations have raised him to the status of *'America's favorite poet.'* Konya, the town where Rumi's tomb resides, is no longer in Persia, but rather in modern Turkey. Our women covered their hair as we explored the amazing Persian artwork adorning Rumi's tomb. But to my performer's soul the ornate tomb seemed just like the endless Roman ruins we visited. It was all history and it all had that musty feel of tired old museum exhibits.

In Bursa we allowed our skin to be deeply scrubbed in the public baths and we collected cassette tapes of amazingly beautiful Sufi music. I walked for blocks one day searching for a news stand. In Egypt they were on every corner and publications in many languages were available. Not so in Turkey. I began to wonder how well-educated the local folks really were. I asked some questions to Turks who could speak in English about the Kurdish people and culture. I was disappointed and confused to receive basically flawed information... more than once. I was told that Kurdish people speak 'a degraded form of

Turkish.' This is not even true. Kurdish language is not even remotely related to Turkish. It is a Persian, Indo-European language.

My experiences kept reminding me that Turks were historically illiterate central-Asian horsemen known for military prowess. A thousand-years-ago they had begun to move south and to acquire knowledge from the much-more-civilized Arab peoples whom they eventually occupied and ruled. Many Turks became highly educated and contributed to developments in science, mathematic, medicine and music, but their discourse then proceeded in Arabic language, not Turkish language. And Arabic script, which was also used to write the Persian language, had been adopted so that Turkish could also become a written language. But with the creation in 1923 of modern Turkey, the Arabic alphabet was jettisoned in favor of using the European roman characters. The last thousand years of Turkish history, which had been written using the Arabic script, was lost as Turks were no longer educated to be able to read that alphabet.

My elderly Turkoman friend, Ihsan, whom I knew from Middle Eastern Music Camp in Mendocino, California, was old enough to know how to read Turkish in the old script. He lamented the loss of so many beautiful Sufi scriptures. Had Ataturk, the founder of modern Turkey, 'thrown out the baby with the bathwater?'

Back in Istanbul we attended a Mevlevi Sufi whirling dervish ceremony which had its roots in Rumi's teachings but for me it still smelled kind of like another museum. The dance was strictly formal and I couldn't feel the real magic of excitement or creativity which I know it must have contained back in its day.

The real Turkish music which expresses the Turkish soul and which does not have its roots in Arabic music is known as *'Ashik.'* The favored instrument for this is the saz… a very long-necked lute. As we rode through Turkey in Necati's yellow bus I began to let this music soak into me. James Hoskins, who is a very quick learner, was also picking up tunes from the Ashik tradition. There was something about pain and loneliness expressed in a very Turkish way which pervades this music… something which feels almost metallic in the soul. Now I finally was developing a feel for the differences between Turkish and Arabic music and feeling my way into a new fondness for the Ashik style and for the Turkish Sufi musical traditions.

Turkey with Eva and Friends in 1999

We had completed the Turkish part of Eva's tour and we flew south to Egypt. Eva had stayed in touch with Asata and we soon met up with her on a Nile river boat which featured a touristy belly dance show. Asata was still living in Egypt. Her romance with Ibrahim was ancient history and she was partnering with a Sudanese man named Adil. I greeted Adil and immediately sensed his calm and warm nature. The next time I saw Asata and Adil they were married and living in the USA. We have stayed in touch over the years. I got together with them recently in Arizona. They have been together now for close to twenty years.

Asata and Adil

While Eva led the tour to see the pyramids I hopped on a train to Alexandria. I wanted to see how I would do navigating on my own in Egypt. My Egyptian Arabic was a bit better but still awfully basic. Alexandria was a modern middle-class Egyptian city. I got very little flavor from its past identity as a cosmopolitan hub which had been home to a large Greek population and which had supported vast libraries.

I was on a quest to find a larger oud, supposedly called a *'forma'* oud, which I was hoping would better fit the long bones in my arms. No luck. A couple of shop owners agreed that they had heard of these larger instruments but no one knew anything about actually finding one. They are visible in old photographs of Egyptian orchestras from back in the early twentieth century. Oh well.

I walked the Mediterranean waterfront and, after three days in Alexandria, climbed back onto a train to Cairo. I sat right behind a man who had the smelliest feet in the entire world. He was fast asleep for the entire journey.

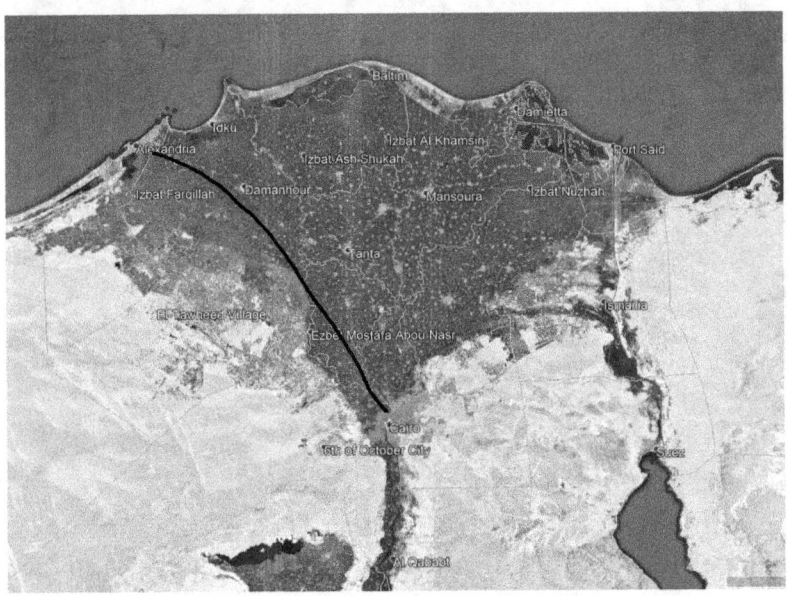

Cairo to Alexandria in Search of Giant Oud

Back in Cairo I wandered into one of the gigantic old mosques. Not much was happening but the Muezzin approached me and asked if I'd like to hear the call to prayer. We were standing right under the center of the huge dome above us. "Sure," I replied. He exhibited his amazing vocal artistry by emitting an entire sequence with all of its complex phrases in one or two breaths. The shapes in the giant edifice amplified his powerful voice and I felt like I had been gifted with something special. I gave him a little tip to express my appreciation.

He looked at me: "Do you want to hear it again?" he asked.

"Sure!" I gave him another tip and he sang it again.

After another Egyptian whirling dervish show... colorful... acrobatic... an exhibition of youthful stamina... our short time in Egypt was up...

Egyptian Dervish

California, Mexico, Music Music Music

Back home in the USA I headed to Mendocino to attend Balkan Camp with James, Jesse and some other Sherefe band members. We learned new Greek, Turkish and Macedonian melodies and enjoyed our connections with that part of our extended tribe.

Melina had graduated from high school and I wanted to help her make choices for the next stages in life. She and Leda and I climbed in my van and drove from Colorado to the West Coast. We visited about ten colleges. I was hoping that Melina would get a feel for her upcoming choices and that she might like the west coast. The three of us enjoyed being re-connected for a time in our original nuclear family form.

Melina Graduates from Boulder High

My son spent the summer back in Boulder working for one of my favorite former clients, a company involved with aerospace communications satellite projects for whom I had executed large volumes of Computer Aided Design drawings. He was living in the attached apartment in our new house and fell in love with Lila, the violin player in our band. He went back to school in Victoria but they maintained their romantic connection.

Winter arrived in Colorado. We worked hard to build Sherefe into a professional performing orchestra. My daughter took some courses at Naropa, the local Buddhist University, and my friend Susan and I enjoyed a couple of semi-tropical weeks in Puerto Vallarta. A few other friends from Boulder were there in Mexico at the same time.

One of the nearby music festivals we found had a rodeo attached. As the evening began the bands took turns with the calf-roping and bull-riding events. Soon the dancing crowd didn't want to stop so the musicians kept playing while the cowboys roped and rode along the edges. Before long the whole field was a fantastic mix of music, dance, horses, bulls and calves. The daring fun deepened and soon the teenagers were skiing on their feet behind the bulls as they grasped and held onto the tails of the powerful animals as they ran about through the crowd. It all was cradled by the rhythms of the dance bands and most folks were just focused on dancing their sexy belly-to-belly cumbia and somehow it appeared that no one got hurt. A few policemen were standing around sipping their beers and likewise enjoying the fun.

Early Sherefe Fun

And Excellent Musicianship Makes for a Good Band

James and Kathleen and I began learning traditional Egyptian melodies from a Moroccan violinist who was living in Denver. We had the time, working with him, to learn some long pieces of music in depth. My son and Lila made plans to attend the Sacred Music Festival in Fes, Morocco and invited me to meet them there. Nabil, my Moroccan violinist friend, arranged a connection with his father, mother, brother and sister who called Fes home. It would be wonderful to have a music family connection there...

"It will be hot," Nabil had warned me... "But it's the kind of heat that makes you feel good," he added.

"Now just what kind of heat could that be...?" I wondered.

We planned to travel afterwards up into Spain. My Armenian-American musician friends Souren Baronian and Haig Manoukian had been stopping to play in Spain for years. Granada, Seville, Andalusia... Flamenco... It all tied into the music. Plus, I would be able to relax in the warm waters of a language in which I was comfortable: Spanish!

The possibility for traveling to Greece also occurred to us. I hadn't been to Greece in nineteen years! My children were half Greek. Their grandmother was still alive in Athens! She was ninety. How much longer would she last? Coincidentally, Leda had been planning a trip to see her mother during the same overlapping period of time. My son and I would travel together to see his grandmother and I would re-awaken the Greek part of my soul.

Sacred Music in Morocco

Finally, after waiting for days and days in Casablanca for lost luggage, my son and I could head for Fes and really be in Morocco!

I called Nabil's family and arranged to meet his brother, Imad. He was very friendly and spoke a good bit of English. Morocco was tough for us linguistically. If you don't know Arabic or French, well... good luck! But a few local folks, mostly people under thirty years old, had studied some English. Imad took us to his home where he was living with his father, Abdrafie, his mother, Malika, and his sister, Btisami. There, we were treated to a warm welcome and a chance for Lila and I to play Egyptian Um Kolthoum pieces which we and Nabil's father all knew... Abdrafie played both violin and oud. As usual, the music gave us an easy deep connection.

At our hotel, the Cascade, situated right inside the main gate, Bab Bujloud, to the most ancient part of Fes, 'Fes el Bali,' we immediately met young Moroccans excited about our musicianship. We played on the roof of the hotel while watching huge flocks of swallows swirling through the evening skies.

"I want to invite you to my house," said Ali.... These were no empty invitations. Out of eleven or twelve nights spent in Fes, we spent three of them partying 'till 4:00 AM with young men we had met near the hotel, and three nights at Nabil's family's house, feasting and playing music, all the while 'chatting' as best we could in our rudimentary combinations of Arabic, French and English.

They all knew many of the Egyptian songs I knew. We all sang together; the young men danced and when I began my vocal improv 'mawwal' 'ya leili ya leili' I was greeted by choruses of "Allah, Allah"... I knew I had found the right mix of traditional form and personal ecstasy.

Playing in Fes, Morocco

Two young guys, Majid and Mohammed took turns with me playing oud and I was astounded to hear their mastery on the instrument. That also freed me to add some elementary nay, or Arabic flute, improvisations, something I was sneaking up on and not generally ready to perform.

They provided such a receptive audience for my efforts that I couldn't help but just laugh and laugh... ... not the best condition in which to play the nay, but oh well... ... which is more important... the music or the laughter? Lila was able to perform many of the pieces along with me on her violin.

Nabil's father, Abdrafie, was especially fond of Um Kolthoum pieces. We played and replayed the ones I knew and worked on some of the ones I didn't. We grew very fond of each other. Gradually, as our visits increased, the feeling of warmth grew with all of his family members although really Imad was the only one with whom we could actually speak. For lack of verbal connection we just kept picking up our ouds and violins. Abdrafie came to Fes el Bali from time to time to seek us out at our hotel. He would bring his violin and we would play sitting up on the roof.

Playing with Nabil's Father, Abdrafie

I got nailed with the local dysentery and had to lie in my a-hundred-plus-degree hotel room with a-hundred-and-two degree fever... this is not the kind of heat that 'feels good'... I think maybe you have to be either younger or from the tropics to know what kind of heat Nabil thinks 'feels good'... Being sick I fell behind on keeping up with all the invitations to visit and play music.

The Sacred Music concerts proceeded, usually two of them a day for ten days. Carrie, a twenty-three-year-old girl who had been singing with me in Boulder arrived just in time for the last concert and to see a little of Fes. Loren and Lila left for Marakech and Essouaira. Carrie and I waited another day or two in Fes but soon were eager to move on.

An all-night train plus an all-day bus brought Carrie and me into Essouaira, where cool Atlantic sea breezes refreshed us. World class wind-surfers criss-crossed the bay by day like swarms of gossamer-winged insects skimming the water. We found Loren and Lila tucked into their hotel room.

Carrie fished the market streets until she found a handsome young Moroccan to escort her to Tangiers so that she could move on to Spain and connect with Meagan. I found myself strangely lonely in Essouaira where I hadn't yet found the musician community. For me it didn't have the variety and magic of Fes. Oh but how welcome were the cool breezes!

We moved on to Marakech. We spent one night there wandering amid the snake charmers, acrobats, magicians, musicians and dancers on the famous plaza Jemaa el-Fnaa. Drawn to a circle of belly dancers who appeared in the early evening I felt somehow hesitant to interact with a veiled beauty who approached me wanting to dance. A deeper look into the eyes above the veil revealed that 'she' was a 'he.' I checked it out: most of the dancers were guys.

I did see one female dancer whipping her spine back in forth to the music breathing herself into Sufi ecstasy. Later that night, Lila and I wound our way through the plaza with our tape recorders surreptitiously recording the sounds of the circus. A few tourists were sprinkled through the crowd, but the vast majority of the gawking crowd were Moroccans. Lila was dogged by henna girls who would create decorations on her arms and then try and charge their fee. This extraordinary entertainment plaza has been seething with this activity every night for hundreds of years.

Southern Spain, Gypsies, Moroccans

Our visit to Marakech was sandwiched with interminable confusion and long waits for buses and trains. I felt ready for Spain. Another too-crowded all night train ride brought us to Tangiers. Early morning running the gauntlet through random ticket sales and customs checks landed us on a ferry to Algeciras, Spain. Then we took a bus to Jerez de la Frontera, where thanks to previous e-mail communications, we managed to rendezvous with Carrie and Meagan.

A tiny but neat hotel room served as home base for the next three days or so. Meagan introduced us to her Gypsy boyfriend, the triumph of her six-month stay. We did play some of our Armenian and Arabic songs in one of the town parks one night. Meagan and Carrie both knew lyrics from our band's repertoire back in Boulder. Meagan's Gypsy friend wanted to try singing his flamenco style over the oud accompaniment I was playing. Freelance videographers with impressively professional equipment asked our permission to tape us as we played. For the next two nights Carrie and Meagan stayed out 'till the wee hours at the local discos. So much for live music.

Loren and Lila headed off to Malaga to spend some alone time before their impending separation. Leaving her beloved Gypsy community behind at last, Meagan led us on to Granada where I finally had a chance to hear a live Flamenco show.

Once settled into our hotel in Granada, Carrie wandered out into the streets and attracted another Moroccan fellow who proved to be generous enough to invite all three of us to his brother's apartment for an afternoon meal. Once again we found ourselves in the company of a group of five or six young Moroccan men who seemed happy to while away the hours discussing all the details of the modern world and the history which had preceded it... as best as we could in our assorted languages. At least there in Spain I had a fighting chance of carrying on conversations since my Spanish actually worked.

An underlying element of our new young Moroccan friend's sociability was his desire to eventually ask Carrie if he could have just one kiss. Upon being told no it seemed like the friendship cooled a bit... more from Carrie's end than from his. I was struck by how intimately they invited us into their home, encouraging us to look through the personal photos in their rooms, listen to the Koranic recordings and other favorite music tapes. They made me a present of a cassette of a popular Lebanese singer I seemed to like.

Eventually we tired from the effort of cross-cultural communication and took our leave. They seemed to understand that we had reached our limits and said goodbye. Again we had enjoyed the friendly nature of Moroccans in general. Would the Spaniards be similarly inviting? Carrie and Meagan decided negatively and headed back to Morocco.

I decided to go down to Malaga. Loren and Lila had been enjoying themselves on the beach. It seemed that Lila had over-cooked her skin a bit so they were ready to move on. We rented a car for four days which was to be delivered in Barcelona, our final Spanish destination.

Passing back through Granada, Loren and Lila took in the elegance of Alhambra. I had already visited there and found it to have an incredible underlying feeling of peace and tranquility. Inconceivable quantities of elaborate inlays and carved geometric shapes adorn the beautiful pools and gardens. I felt like just sitting down to soak it into my senses. Others were similarly struck and were doing the same.

I found another Moroccan musician: Uzman Al Murabet. His name had been given to me by Souren Baronian. Uzman amazed me with his oud technique... he was a true master. He was running a teahouse and a music school there in Granada. We sang a number of Egyptian songs together.

We moved on to Alacante, a summer resort back on the Mediterranean coast. Elegant yachts moored in the harbors reminded us that multi-millionaires must be wandering in our midst. Disco clubs seemed to be the sole offerings in the music scene.

Barcelona Thievery

Arriving in Barcelona, the second largest city in Spain, we plunged back into the urban tangles. Negotiating traffic and finding a hotel before turning in the rental car was another ordeal. Loren ran from hotel to hotel while I violated parking rules until we succeeded in establishing a foothold in the city. Barcelona is the home of Gaudi, the incredible architect who designed the cathedral called Sagrada Familia. The tall slender spires rising in clusters high into the sky were like fantasy land... eat your heart out Walt Disney. The main street, Rambla, supposedly the most visited street in Spain, was filled with the same kinds of silver-and-gold-painted moving human statues also famous in San Francisco. Exotic bird vendors lined the edges of the street with their incredible selection of species available in cages. Not so exotic to my eyes were the caged chipmunks, imported from who knows where, maybe from the American West?

Rick and Peter, members of Lila's band, 'The Pickpocket Ensemble,' arrived from San Francisco. They had paused in London to rent an accordion and a full-sized upright bass. Traveling in trains, taxis and buses across Europe with the bass had been no mean feat. Looking at Peter struggling to haul that huge instrument made me cringe with empathy. I learned that he had somehow had his pocket picked along the way. The Eurorail pass he was transporting for Lila had fallen prey to the thieves along with some of his other valuables.

Rick told us he had a connection to a village party that evening. 'Could be fun... also an opportunity to hear the Pickpocket Ensemble perform,' I thought...

"Should I bring my oud?" I asked Rick.

"Absolutely," he replied, "I want to hear what you and Lila play together."

We boarded the train which was to take us to the village of Vals where we would find the party.

Crowded as usual, the passenger car yielded only a few free seats in a scattered pattern. After settling into my seat for a few minutes, Loren came to me and revealed that Peter's pockets had been picked again as he had boarded the train and he had lost the remainder of his valuables: drivers license, credit cards, etc. He suspected one of two black guys who were seated in the car. He was requesting my help because I was the one most fluent in Spanish. I looked at the black African kid sitting across the aisle from me, one of the 'suspects.' Noticing that I was looking at him he returned my gaze and gave me a sweet childish smile.

'This is not the guy,' all of my intuition told me.

I talked with Peter. Rick, whose day job was apparently a prosecutor in the legal profession, had encouraged him to accost the young men with African skin. We acknowledged the delicacy of the situation but he pleaded for me to help him question the 'suspects.'

The conductor, a middle aged woman, told us that we should file a police report.

"And I'll call ahead to the police," she said.

The train stopped at a small town. The other 'suspect' got off. Peter got off behind him and motioned for me to follow. Reluctant to be involved, feeling like if I had been Peter I would have taken my lumps and not risked accusing a possibly innocent person, I was slow to respond. Eventually, out of a sense of compatriot duty to Peter, I followed him out onto the platform. He had stopped the black man up near the front of the train and motioned for me to translate.

"When he got onto the train carrying his bass, someone picked his pocket," I explained.

"And so...?"

"He thinks maybe it was you," I explained, feeling like I was playing a ridiculous part in some movie.

"You think just because of the color of my skin that I must be a thief? I sell clothing for a living." He pointed to the two large bundles he was carrying.

"Excuse me," I added, "I have simply been asked to translate because I speak Spanish..."

He gave me an understanding smile.

"How could I have picked someone's pocket while carrying all this stuff?"

Peter indicated that he wanted him to show us what was in his pockets.

The train accelerated out of sight, with Loren, Lila, Rick and all of our possessions aboard.

He showed us that his pockets contained only his own wallet, not someone else's. Peter apologized profusely and we went our separate ways.

It took an hour in a taxi on winding mountainous roads to complete the journey to Vals, a distance the train had been apparently able to cover in only fifteen more minutes.

Rick's friend, an American with a Spanish wife, showed up after another half-an-hour in his car to pick us up. A long ride carried us further into the countryside, a lovely place to go... if only we didn't have to be back in Barcelona before noon to catch a train toward Greece the next day! The village picnic turned out to be small and fun. I got to hear the Pickpocket Ensemble perform and others got to hear me and Lila play some Egyptian pieces.

The pearl in this gritty oyster of an evening turned out to be a man named Ricard Margarit. He had a musical instrument-making studio there in the village from which he was turning out violins and guitars with sympathetic string sets built in. I felt like he was a true soul-mate. I had the honor of grabbing my three hours of sleep in his workshop late that night. Rick's American friend was kind enough to rise with us at 6:30 AM and deliver us to the train. We made it back to Barcelona before noon and checked out of our hotel room. Loren parted company from his beloved Lila and he and I went on a long walk to the wrong station in order to leave on our train for France and Italy.

Fortunately a shuttle connected us to the correct station and soon we were fifteen minutes away from boarding. We had spent over two hundred dollars for a sleeping compartment which would bring us to Milan by mid-morning the next day. Deciding to pull my passport out of my pack to have it ready, I discovered: that it wasn't there!

With growing disbelief and apprehension I realized that the little pouch in which I kept my passport, my travelers checks and my $100 emergency stash of cash was not there. Surely it must be buried somewhere in the depths of my pack! It wasn't.

Should I get on the train? What if we got to Italy and they sent us back to Spain? But booking space on this train must be done several days in advance of departure... ...better just get on the train and gamble that I would get through...

At each destination we faced another moment of truth... The conductor was kind enough to accept a photocopy, which fortunately I had made of my passport only a few days before, which he kept along with Loren's passport to ensure that we didn't get off the train somewhere in France during the night. He told us to report the theft when we arrived in Milan. We calculated that the theft must have occurred from our hotel room in Barcelona during the night when we were gone to the village.

With much scribbling in quadruplicate, since the local police post's copy machine was down, we reported the theft in Milan. They told us to go to Rome and have the US Embassy issue a fresh passport. A phone call to the American Express office in the USA yielded the comment, *'they won't let you into Greece from Italy without a passport...'*

'What does some guy in an office back in the States know...?' I mused. Not eager to trade intended precious time in Greece for days of stagnation in Rome unless absolutely necessary, I decided to gamble again. Although my principal debit card into my main account had been eaten by a hungry ATM way back in Fes, I used one of my remaining credit cards and snagged a little Italian cash. Loren bought an ugly looking cellophane-wrapped cheese sandwich and I settled for a Coke. We bought tickets and boarded the ten-hour train for Brindisi - a seaport on the eastern Italian coast.

All day we took turns crouching in crowded uncomfortable spots in the aisles and compartments, occasionally doing battle over the placement of our packs. Getting hungrier by the hour we parsed our little stash of Italian money into little packages of cookies. Toward the end of the ride I hung out in the food car drooling over stuff I simply didn't have the cash to buy.

Arriving in Brindisi, Italy, at 10:00 PM, we stumbled onto the platform and followed the signs saying 'Ferry to Greece.' Yes, the boat would leave in half an hour... no time to look for food now... gee... this could be the moment when they send us back to Spain... or... maybe, just maybe, we would be lucky...

Hiking from the Ferry boat ticket office to the mystery location from which the shuttle bus was about to leave took another twenty or thirty minutes. Once aboard the shuttle we held on tight while the driver screamed through the harbor trying to make it to the boat in time. Zooming past customs offices which were either closed or politely pretending not to notice us... you guessed it... we simply walked onto the boat. I sat in an obscure corner out of sight while Loren surrendered his passport in exchange for a key to our room... 'Gee... I guess I'm a stowaway...'

Now: food. Yes, you could get Greek money from the guy at the window... And yes, the cafeteria was still open... And damn that cheese sandwich tasted good! We chugged out of the harbor. We slept for a few hours.

Greece: Corfu, Athens, Samos

At 7:00 o'clock in the morning we docked on the Greek island of Corfu. Surely here they would discover that I had no passport. Too bad to have made it this far and then...? But the customs offices appeared to be still closed so early in the morning. The boat had docked and the ramps were lowered. We passengers simply wandered into town... no questions asked.

We were in Greece! "Jeez, Loren, what say we stay here for a couple of days and make up for the last three nights of mostly lost sleep?"

"Sounds good."

We rented a car, read our Lonely Planet guidebook, and drove across the island to Pelekas. Hotel room. Lots of sleep. Grocery stores, trips to the beaches... Restaurants with incredible views near Makrades and Krini. And yes... I really could speak Greek. So even when they spoke to me in English, I replied in Greek. How satisfying to exercise those old brain and heart parts... Painful too... But that's OK... When you're in Greece you're supposed to feel some of the pains of life... I was claiming some kind of Greek soul-citizenship on my own, without Leda as leader. So I kept speaking Greek with relish.

And yes, the food... Getting cocky, I started assuming I had recovered from a previously-acquired allergy to olive oil. Pouring it more and more liberally on my salads I sowed the seeds of truly incredible pain.

Realizing that we could take a thirty-minute flight to Athens for only $40 apiece, we abandoned further plans of oversea and overland travel and plunged into Athens. Stumbling through the wrong neighborhoods for a couple of hours due to the fact that there were two 'eleftheria' plazas in Athens, we eventually found Loren's grandma's apartment where Leda was staying for the summer. Walking and riding through the streets of Athens after so long an absence was a strange dream: oh yeah! There was Likavittos, the only hill in the middle of the city... the one which I used to climb daily to keep in shape and some sense of the outdoors...

What a joy to see Loren's grandmother, Elli... But what a miserable situation she was living in. Now blind and ninety-years-old, she endured the heat, noise and mosquitoes of her little apartment in the summertime... house-bound due to her blindness... dependent on others. She somehow remained cheerful while sharing the bad news that the doctor said her heart was still in great shape. She would rather die now, she asserted. But some things, like life and death, are beyond our control.

I called my old musician friend, Rowan Storm who had been living in Athens. Taking Loren and Leda with me, I journeyed across town to spend the first of several evenings with her and her young Kurdish boyfriend Fardin. I took my oud. Fardin played Persian setar and Rowan played percussion. We were on their apartment rooftop in Exarchia, the exact same part of town in which I had lived during my first visit to Greece.

During the next few days I replaced my lost passport and my lost travelers checks. I also endured increasing pain as my throat turned redder, lumpier and produced dozens of oozing white blisters. Only by playing music with Fardin or by wandering the streets could I distract myself from the constant searing pain. Damn. I had been down this road a year earlier at home in Boulder, Colorado. Somehow, in my ecstasy of love for olive oil, I had overdone it and created a horrible allergy.

Now I was faced with being in Greece unable to eat Greek food. If I ate in restaurants I had to plead with the waiters and cooks to make something olive oil-free for me. This does not come naturally to them and many times I was forced to simply eat hamburgers at MacDonald's.

The hundred-degree heat and the mosquitoes and the throat pain combined and created discomfort I could only imagine relief from by activating the next part of our trip plan: a trip to one of the Aegean islands.

Another short airplane flight took Loren and me to Samos, only twelve-hundred-meters from the coast of Turkey. In fact from the beach at Psili Amos I could look across to Kusadasi, the town in Turkey where I had enjoyed playing oud in a local restaurant the previous year!

We rented a car and drove across the island to the village of Kokkari, settled into a little hotel and began to seek out island musical events: panayiria... music festivals. A migraine headache, surely left over from Athenian stresses and strains, laid me up for the first night. But Loren attended the local late night outdoor festival and came back reporting having seen a live band with bouzouki, violin, keyboard and drums. The following night hundreds of villagers assembled to dance again. This time a different band: bouzouki, bass and keyboard with damn, you guessed it, a drum machine in place of live drummer... It was true: they had killed the music. The musicians sat back and just chimed in on top of the never-ending never-changing repetitive robotic electronic beat!

On two other nights we tracked down village music festivals on Samos and watched hundreds of people dance... but we never found another live drummer... always the same disco-sounding beat, even if it was programmed in 7/8 or 9/8! Amazing! The songs were mostly the same songs they had been playing thirty years ago! Just anesthetized by the drum-machine inoculation.... deadly soporific rhythmic virus. The dancers worked hard to acquire their energy in spite of the horrible repetition.

What were they doing? Going through the traditional motions: the traditional feelings and styles of zembekika, tsamika, kalamatiana, syrta... only once did they play tsiftitelli... suddenly sexy... everything changed... the Greek belly dance license was issued during just that one song... only one thing: the girls only dared dance with the girls and the guys only dared dance with the guys... yes, the guys entwined their legs together up close and hugged and undulated together in outrageously sensual moves... they became so outrageously sensual that people watching screamed with laughter. And then it was over. The song ended. And the mood dove back into the lighter syrta or the traditionally heavy zembekika... all much safer emotions... apparently.

Dance Party on Samos

During five days on the island of Samos we explored a number of places, taking our rented car on voyages by day and by night... And a couple of friendly restaurant chefs in Kokkari adopted me with promises of olive-oil-free cookery! By the time we returned to Athens my throat blisters were beginning to heal and the pain was diminishing.

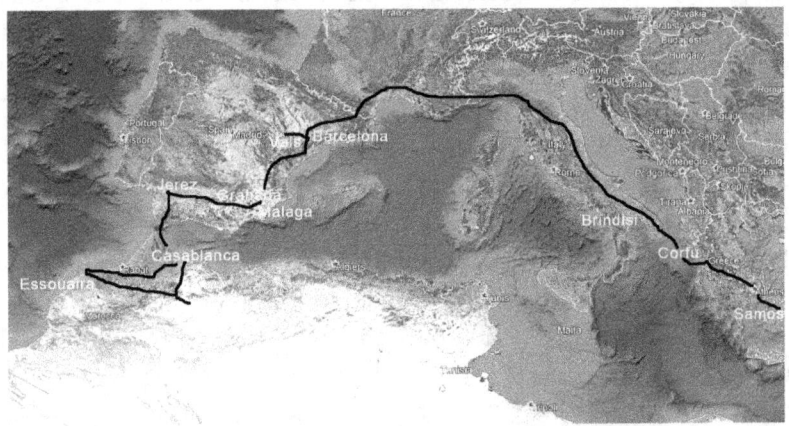

Morocco to Spain to Greece in 2000

After a couple of more days in Athens visiting Elli, Leda, Rowan and Fardin, Loren flew back to Lila in Spain and I flew back to the States. I was eager to see my daughter. Her messages were making me realize that Melina was feeling like she was facing some frightening health issues.

Chorus of Female Singers

I was glad to be back in Colorado so I could try and help Melina decipher those health problems. I tried taking her to various doctors but we didn't have very good luck. Her problems remained a mystery and her trust in both me and the medical establishment took a plunge. Further down the road, years later, my attempts to help her continued to lead to confusion and mistrust. Many aspects of the evolving conflicts between 'conventional Western medicine' and newer, largely nutritional, 'alternative' medical treatments became a strange battleground which would continue to deliver conflicting answers.

I had a vision for our band, Sherefe. I wanted us to become a spectacular dance band capable of powering large crowds of dancers into ecstasy. We needed more drummers and we needed more singers. After a few more months of putting my feelers out through our

Boulder musician community I found myself working with four or five young singers. I named them the 'Habibi Babies' and they suggested shortening it to just 'The Habibis.' 'Habibi' is an endearment term in Arabic which simply means 'my love.'

We could perform as a band in all sizes, all the way from two performers to ten. Kathleen and I decided to perform as a duo at a benefit party to raise money for a cancer victim. We did our little show. Someone I didn't know was admiring us... another singer. She did a late night show with her band and I was watching. She invited me on stage and handed me a microphone. We improvised together and our voices seemed to fit very well together. I asked her for her phone number. Her name was Kristina.

Soon Kristina began working to become one of the 'Habibis' and was spending a lot of time at my house learning our Arabic and Greek and Turkish songs. Her voice had an absolutely clear liquid quality. Wow!

Sherefe and the Habibis

We liked to lie on the couch and flirt our way into a gradually more and more intimate connection. I was slowly feeling my way into her world and she into mine. She was from the Pacific Northwest but had fled, after graduating from high school, to sea-food industry employment in Alaska and then into California's misty forest dwellings. Slightly-renovated chicken coops had made nice dwellings for her while she worked in leather shops in Mendocino or took random Anthropology classes back up in Bellingham, Washington. Her mother had always known where she was as a child because she never ceased singing.

Kristina inhabited a place in which magical transformations between material and spiritual dimensions could easily take place... usually somewhere in the wilderness... She didn't have a ready vocabulary for describing these things... It would take a long time for me to understand her world.

Sitting on the living room floor I would encourage her to improvise melodies for my poems. Another young 'Habibi,' Ariana, was present one evening. I encouraged Kristina to improvise and sing and I could see that Ariana was also hearing and feeling the liquid energies which passed so easily back and forth between me and Kristina.

Our flirtations on the couch gradually brought our bodies and souls closer together... little by little... We were moving slowly... Eventually we went into the bedroom and made deeper connections.

Kristina and I - Halloween

Soon afterward we spent a long weekend together up in Steamboat Springs. We drove up Buffalo Pass together and Kristina showed me the power of her voice with traditional Native American ceremony. We were alone up high with the sky and the trees. I could feel her vocal power unleashed to another level. Wow!

We spent several days living together there in Steamboat Springs in a condo which had been gifted to us. We discovered that we could spend long periods of time together with gentle and smooth energies surrounding us. We had fallen in love! Effortlessly! Little did we suspect that we would end up living and traveling together for hundreds of thousands of miles... year after year... singing... playing... presenting...

Kristina had been living in her own mobile home with her daughter, Lauren, who was close to finishing high school. Soon it seemed that Lauren would be living there in the mobile home by herself. Kristina, after sixteen years spent as a 'single mom,' was living with me.

Puerto Vallarta and Southern Utah

Kristina and I flew together to Puerto Vallarta. It was her first trip to Mexico and she found the obvious new freedoms exciting. You could ride in the backs of the pickup trucks. You could jump on and off the bus while it was still moving. You could join into the perpetual motion of street life in lots of fun ways. I introduced Kristina to my friend Cyndi who runs a fabulous restaurant which had been a musicians' hub in Puerto Vallarta for a long time. We took a little boat to Yelapa and felt the tropical warmth and the relaxed pace of life in a village beyond roads and electricity. We practiced singing together all the time. Our world had become fun and magical.

Back home in Colorado, we journeyed to Comb ridge, a mystical Native American area in Southern Utah. We really enjoyed being out in the wilderness together. I was running through the rocks when I lost my footing and had to catch myself with my left arm. That evening we huddled together in our tent and had to acknowledge that I was 'kind of going into shock.' I recovered enough to drive us back to Boulder over the next two days. I put off seeing a doctor but no healing was happening. I finally scheduled shoulder-cuff surgery to re-attach tendons which had been ripped off the bones.

Our first gig as 'Sherefe and the Habibis' was a big success... Audiences loved the spectacle of seeing a chorus line of flashy young singers dancing and singing on stage. Adding more drums was tricky because Kathleen was picky about whom she wanted to work with. There were no other drummers available who knew the songs intricately the way she did. I brought some of them into the band anyway on some kind of 'temporary' basis.

Kristina had learned enough to join the Habibis and sing with us on our larger gigs. And she began training her fingers to play percussion. It takes a long time to master those traditional odd-time signature rhythms but she kept being fascinated by them. When you come from a 4/4 music culture which automatically encourages even-handed-ness, it can be amazing to discover rhythms in 7/8, for example, which suggest the possibilities for alternating right and left hand dominance... It's a way to open up the soul... And of course learning to re-tune your voice and sing in other music scales can open up the soul to new possibilities in even more amazing ways!

The Habibis in Front

Sherefe and the Habibis grew and could please larger audiences. We played at the Boulder Theater which can hold up to a thousand people as an opening act for an Algerian band. It seemed to me that the audience had actually responded better to our show than to the main act!

Boulder Theater

Kristina and I traveled together to Middle Eastern Music Camp in Mendocino very close to the forests in which she had lived 'the hippie life' for years. At the music camp she could easily soak up exotic music styles from many diverse teachers.

Sherefe and the Habibis in a Pile

No Palestinians Allowed at Boulder Theater

Nabil Azzam was one of my favorite personalities. He is a Palestinian violinist with seemingly bottomless wit, good cheer and musical expertise. I had met him at Middle Eastern Music Camp a few years earlier and I invited him to come to Boulder and perform with us at another Boulder Theater event. Nabil found that our schedules overlapped in the right ways and we bought an airline ticket for him to fly in from southern California a couple of days before September 27, 2001 when the show was scheduled so we would have time to rehearse.

Of course when we booked the show we had no idea of what was about to happen on September 11th... the world trade towers in New York city collapsed... all three of them... two of them apparently the result of airplane collisions... and it suddenly seemed, in spite of assurances to the contrary, that the Christian world and the Muslim worlds were at war. I had been seated in a dental office when I first saw the images of airplanes hitting the towers. My gut feeling from the first was that there was something deeply fishy being acted out. Although most Americans still don't realize it even sixteen years later, in-depth research reveals that 9/11 was probably yet another carefully orchestrated 'false flag' event used to justify endless war.

The Boulder Theater called me and let me know that the show could proceed as scheduled in spite of the fact that a large part of our repertoire came from the Muslim world, but that we would not be allowed to use the word 'Palestinian' in the advertising.

"But our lead violinist is Palestinian! ...a world-class artist!" I protested. But the Boulder Theater had laid down its rules.

I called Nabil and told him this news. "Should we cancel the show?" I asked him.

"Absolutely not!" he replied in his Arab accent. "At times like this it is more important than ever to do the show!"

Our audience was smaller than it would have been but those who came were especially supportive. Just playing Arabic music in public had suddenly become a political act rather than an exotic artistic act.

Nabil stayed in a bedroom at my house. "How could I ever have guessed that I would be standing here in my pajamas in your living room at 3:00 AM serenading you two with my violin? I would have said no... not possible!"

Kristina and Nabil

He suggested to Kristina that learning 'Atini Nay,' a song made famous by the Lebanese singer Fairouz, would be a good fit for her voice.

"But you should also keep up your connections with your old band and American music!" I told her.

"No," she would reply, "now that I have discovered Middle Eastern music, I don't want to sing anything else!"

I was just finishing publishing my "Middle Eastern Moods - 4:01AM" CD so it was possible to include a bit of Kristina's voice.

Middle Eastern Moods CD

Long Drive Down the West Coast of Mexico

As the weather turned colder again in Colorado, we climbed into my van and headed south. It was 2002. We drove six-thousand-miles down the west coast of Mexico and back.

> *Here we go...*
> *You know how it is: two weeks of frantic preparations... now we're finally getting out of town... this is it... we're climbing into the van and starting the engine...*
> *Set the odometer to zero... I figure it's gonna be 6 or 7 thousand miles of driving before we pull back into this driveway... don't look back... pray for a smooth-running engine and sturdy wheel bearings...*

Somewhere on I-25 south of Denver I noticed that I was still in a hurry. How long would it take for the rhythm of the trip to take us over and create some relaxation?

Of course we were still in a hurry. We were supposed to be in Abiquiu, New Mexico in time to enjoy a musical evening with Rabia and Benyamin. We forsook the whole scenic route past the sand dunes in favor of the faster interstate.

This was a business trip and a spiritual quest. We were going to prioritize music gigs and chances to sell CD's... the spiritual quest was our friend Gail's idea... sounded good to me... all of life seems to be a spiritual quest anyway.

Kristina was totally cool... full speed ahead... we looked at each other and silently reveled: the adventure had begun.

Remote New Mexico... An Islamic community in the middle of nowhere... Rabia greeted us wearing her head scarf... her face undeniably Jewish... what had made this woman convert to Islam? She has told me parts of the story... a lot had to do with Benyamin, her solid Dutch husband... somewhere in Israel, on her own spiritual quest long ago, it was Islam and not Judaism that had spoken to her soul... I liked this... I liked these anomalies, these superficial contradictions.

Of course to Benyamin and Rabia there were no 'contradictions.' There was just Life. September eleventh, 9/11, had scared us all and made us become more of who we were. Benyamin and Rabia had a renewable state grant which was paying for them to play Turkish Sufi music and spread the beauty of Islam throughout rural New Mexico schoolrooms. Every year the State had augmented their grant and their musical messages had grown. And Benyamin's wood-shop had been turning out massive hand-carved bedsteads and cabinets destined for wealthy California clients.

We sang Greek and Sephardic songs. We slept. We arose and sang more songs through the morning hours... We bade farewell to Benyamin and Rabia and climbed into the Dodge van and steered toward Santa Fe.

We arrived mid-afternoon at Myra's house. This woman gushed the power of the feminine. Her Tribal Belly dance Troupe was top of the line. I loved playing my oud for Myra. I could see the moment she would dig in and say: '*OK, now I'm going to give it all I've got*'... When I played for her and I saw her do that, I would feel my own energy climb to match hers... We would become vibrational lovers... with our music and our dance. As an 'Imsak' practitioner my energies were available for both Kristina in the flesh and for Myra in the music.

Myra

Kristina loved soaking up the teachings which Myra offered. Their sisterhood was a joy. Amalesh and Max were now Myra's husband and child. Amalesh was devoted. Max was a handful.

It was Myra's generosity which inspired the party that night. It was in our honor. It was in everybody's honor. We played. We sang. We danced. We sold CD's. This was my new passion: getting rich selling CD's!

Moving on toward Albuquerque: the next night we found Beth and Marco's home in Cedar Crest. Members of their band Sazlar were rehearsing for a gig. We just pretended we were practicing too. We played along with Beth's qanun (a Middle Eastern zither) and with Marco and friends' percussion and other instruments... We celebrated Marco's comfort level with his new job at the landfill...

"I thought people would treat me like some sleaze-ball, but you know what? They don't. They treat me with appreciation and respect."

Yay Marco! We thanked him for the fun and generous hospitality.

Onward: we had lunch with old friends Peter and Elizabeth Chestnut in Albuquerque... we took a walk through town and... New territory lay ahead: Sedona, Arizona by nightfall...

Some patches of ice seriously reminded us that we had made the right decision to leave the studded snow tires on for the trip!

Yes, new territory: we pulled off into a wide shoulder of the highway around midnight and crawled into our mattress in the back of the van. No, the cops didn't pester us in the middle of the night... next day we looked up John Michael. Not easy to find him. He didn't even have a phone. Spiritual guy. Spartan lifestyle. We hiked in the red-rock countryside and then met him for late afternoon tea. Philosophy. I guess we got it all figured out except for where to play the music that night... oh well... there must be music beyond Sedona...

Late night behind the wheel... we passed through smoggy Phoenix, Arizona... We made it to a 'sorry, campground full' sign at Tortilla Flats near Apache Junction. By 3:00 AM we were snuggled up to the gate of another campground at the end of a winding rock-goblin-filled moonlit stretch of two-lane pavement... sleeping peacefully in our beloved Dodge van shell... what else could we possibly need?

We had been on the cell phone with Kristina's mom and dad. Guess what!? They were escaping the Washington State rains by cruising south in their Dodge van!

"No need for groceries," said Kristina. "Mom always has plenty of stuff in the icebox..." this was the second time I'd met these nice folks. We hung out. We visited. We hiked into the canyon above the Lost Dutchman State Park campground. We assembled CD's and passed on a few to her folks.

"That sounds pretty good," they affirmed.

I could tell they really did like it even though Middle Eastern music was not what the folks in Chelan, Washington spend their time listening to.

It was good for Kristina to get this time with them. I was willing to stay for as long as she wanted. But a cold front arrived from Alaska... kind of rained on our parade.

We guessed we really would have to drive further south to find the tropics. OK, so it was true: it was not just a business trip and a spiritual quest: it was an excursion into the Tropics. By the time we would return we would view the southern tip of Texas as the 'far north'... and we would have spent some time being too hot in February.

Heading south after only one night camping with Elmer and Stella, we pulled off into another midnight parking lot haven just north of Nogales for some sleep.

Then came the border: pesos... papers... fees... mute officials with a slight edge got back at us Americans in some small way for making it so damn hard for them to cross over onto our side. Yes, our side of the border has long been teeming with border patrol vehicles beaming their spotlights into the bushes and rounding up 'illegal aliens'... Did we call foreigners 'aliens' when I was a kid? I don't remember that. When did we come up with that term?

We stood in four or five lines. It was still cold. We had our jackets and hats on. We got xerox copies made of our titles, our licenses, our passports... we paid some money... we got a sticker on our windshield. We headed south.

We were in another country. It was kind of exciting. We looked at each other with quiet satisfaction. For some time now I'd been eager to refresh my membership as a global citizen and leave the confetti-shower of American flags behind. Mexico! Yay!

Internally, I was breathing some sigh of relief. We stopped for some road food. My tongue was enchanted by its own knowledge of Spanish language and I wouldn't relapse into English for the duration of the trip... except when I was talking with Kristina or other Americans. I ordered my tacos in Spanish with passionate vengeance. I ordered them for Kristina too and helped her learn a word or two. She didn't even know it but she was learning fast... soaking in sounds and ways of being.

After a few days my mind had fully switched into Spanish. As I watched the deserts, mountains and villages pass through the windshield of our van I witnessed all my own mental chatter happening in Spanish. Those years spent in Peru and Bolivia had given birth to another soul inside of me which didn't speak English. The Spanish in my mind was a little more halting than my English flow, but it seemed that there was nothing that it couldn't express. Listening to my own mind chatter away in another language always feels so good to me...

We hit the Pacific coast at Guaymas. First taste of the ocean. It was almost dark, but we drove across the sand and admired the water for an hour. Then we drove south to Navojoa and rented a hotel room. Time for a shower. That was one of three nights during our six-week excursion that we paid for a room in which to sleep.

Alamos Music Festival

Inside the hotel room there was an advertisement for a Music Festival fifty kilometers to the east in Alamos. Saturday, January 26th, 2002. Perfect timing! It seemed that the festival had been going on for the whole week... and this was the last day... so we turned off the main highway and drove to Alamos.

We parked the van near one of two central plazas and inquired in the street: "there's gonna be a big party tonight..."

The police... generally some smiley young guys... were cordoning off central parts of town and began blocking further traffic... It was lucky we got in early 'cause we were then centrally located.

By evening the streets were filling up... around four thousand people had wandered into town for the festival.

A local oompah band was getting up a little steam on one corner of the plaza. What's an oompah band? I don't know what to call it: there was a big guy with a tuba and a little guy with a sort of French horn next to him and they played bass parts. The tuba did the downbeats and the little horn the upbeats. The rest of the band was a bunch of young guys with trumpets: maybe fifteen of them.

It was only seven or eight o'clock. They paused between songs. It was going to be a while before they would be totally into it. But we jammed ourselves into increasingly tight squeezes in the high places on walls around the plaza to maintain a decent view as the crowd rapidly thickened. They were all there of course: the kids, the teenagers... yeah, lots of them... the young folks with babies, the moms and dads, the grandmas and grandpas, the friendly drunks... we didn't see any unfriendly drunks...

"Let's go see what's going on at the other plaza..."

"OK," said Kristina.

We couldn't see a way through the crowd so we wound through some back streets up and over a hill and descended into the other plaza. This was where the big bands were going to play. Huge stacks of speakers surrounded the main stage. Looked like a rock concert setup. We wandered. We sampled from a taco stand. We circled the plaza, sometimes going in the male direction, sometimes in the female direction... couples can go either way. We wandered into the main church by the smaller plaza.

Huge buses had transported the Arizona State Symphony Orchestra. We watched several hundred perplexed Mexicans and a few dozen visiting elderly Norte-Americanos try and appreciate a series of modern dissonant classical compositions from the far North. I didn't get it... musically... Kristina hoped they might play something beautiful. They didn't.

We wondered: *'how do you sign up to play in this festival? If they were to hire Sherefe and the Habibis they would love it!'*

Back in the largest plaza the 'rock concert' had begun. It was way too painful to stand right in front of the speaker stacks, but back somewhere in the crowd it was tolerable. There were some slick dance moves going on: these guys hold their women really tight against their bellies with their right arm; let their left arm hang free and do some high-speed spins... pretty sexy moves. I grabbed Kristina 'cause I wanted to try it. Some young guys admired our efforts and handed us a can of beer from their stash of six-packs.

"Are they laughing at us?" inquired Kristina.

"No, they're laughing with us!"

Satisfied that I was right, she let me move us through a funny imitation of that dance. The guys around us admired and smiled... offered another beer... no, we didn't need another one, but thanks...

We danced for a while... Something else was going on simultaneously on another stage... like mostly women... were they having a sort of a singing contest? Something like that...

We walked through 'kissing alley'... you see, I didn't have time to translate everything for Kristina... I knew it was called 'kissing alley' ... 'calle de besos'... we squeezed along with the crowd and the guys on the wall above were screaming: "a kiss a kiss!" at all the pretty girls and their boyfriends and of course at the funny gringo couple... "un beso un beso!" they yelled at us... I leaned over to kiss her, but she didn't understand... she thought they were screaming for pesos...

It's harder to join in the fun when you don't really know what's going on...

I explained. "Oh," she laughed...

It was kind of a relief to be away from the big stacks of speakers. We wandered past the oompah band, which had gotten livelier and we saw the audience from the church concert pouring out into the street. There were a couple of groups of guys with guitars singing popular songs right near the entrance where they had drawn a crowd of several hundred. This was exquisite... It wasn't too loud.... and pretty soon we heard the crowd beginning to sing along with these guys... the two groups of guitarists merged into one band of ten plus one more guy carrying his double bass.

They sang... the crowd grew... the crowd got more and more into singing the latest popular songs of the region... people had their beer and their tequila and we all began to wander... for the next hour or more... from doorstep to doorstep through the streets... wherever a sidewalk was raised enough to make a stage... this place was good enough to deserve three or four songs... we were enchanted with the sense of freedom... wow!

You know this really couldn't happen in the states... somebody would make it illegal or try and control it to death... we were hooked... we wandered with the musicians... too bad we really didn't know the songs.... I think by the end of the trip we were getting familiar with some of them... I guess it was around midnight or one in the morning when we felt ready for dinner.... we parked ourselves in a restaurant... we ordered the usual chicken tacos and enchiladas... ...salad... ...tea...

Back in the small plaza at 2:00 AM the bands were getting hot. There were new bands, new musicians setting up, playing amplified, but not too loud... fifteen-piece bands... accordions, horns, clarinets, guitars, basses, singers, violins.... shoulder-to-shoulder packed into the crowd we did small dances that would fit in the spaces... now the grandmas and grandpas had gone home... these were the young folks... the girls... the guys... yeah, everybody was out strutting their stuff... sexy stuff!

Exhausted, we climbed into the van and sort of slept from 3:00 AM on... the party rocked 'till dawn... people were leaning on the van, perching on the back bumper, whatever, yakking away... ...not really guessing that we were inside. I was treated to endless lessons in modern street Spanish... no, I didn't get that much of it... I think Kristina zonked out a little better than I did. In the morning we noticed that someone had peeled off one of the little convex mirrors I had pasted on the bottom edge of the larger left external rear-view mirror... oh well...

No, I didn't really sleep all that well... sometime early in the morning the police, who had thoroughly enjoyed the party along with everyone else, let the traffic back into the plaza and endless processions of trucks nosed their way past our narrow street, really just a few inches from our noses... somehow my body didn't completely relax as I sort of idly fantasized about the van getting gently sideswiped by some truck...

But I must have slept enough... I don't recall being all that tired.

We got up and went for breakfast or tea or something. We met an American lady who had been living there for a few years running a coffee shop: lattes, etc. We chased down the administrators of the indoor music festival and acquired application forms for the following year and expressions of interest in our Middle Eastern Band. Then we hit the road.

Cute Little Dangerous Mexican Bandito Families

In Puerto Vallarta we stayed with Cyndi and followed our musician friends D'Rachel and Rigoberto to their gigs and recording studio sessions... In Barra de Navidad we wandered the hippie beaches...

Passing Manzanillo we headed further south. We passed Aquila which had been the end of the road more than thirty years ago when I was running my Terrible Tours on foot and horseback. I remembered my crippled school teacher friend Rafael Cisneros who had welcomed us there several times as we had wandered through. Now there was a new road on which we could proceed, hugging the coast. We were driving through the area about which Mr. Hawley had warned me: "whatever you do, don't go in there!"

Every time we drove past another cute little Mexican family we would exclaim, "Oh no! Those are the dangerous Mexican banditos!

We had better watch out!" We drove past a turn-off to the town of Pomaro which used to be unbelievably remote. I was tempted to go explore in that direction... I probably should have...

In Zihuatenejo we found an amazing guitar player... or two... now we were down to seventeen degrees latitude and it was marvelously hot.

Paracho - Thirty Years and Five Thousand Guitars Later

Heading inland and back north we cruised into Paracho, the guitar-making village where Leda and I had sung Greek songs back in 1973. I began looking for my guitar-maker friends David and Daniel Caro. I found David. He remembered me well. We spent a couple of hours together catching up... all in Spanish of course. He said his brother Daniel was also well. They had both pretty much retired after each making something like five-thousand guitars! ...using the same primitive tools. "Why did you never upgrade your tooling?" I asked.

"We wanted to, but we just kept pouring the money we made back into our families. You know, both Daniel and I have each raised seven or eight children and sent them all through the Universities in Mexico City. Many of them became Doctors or Lawyers. We just never had the extra cash to purchase fancier tools."

I was thinking about the Japanese company called Yamaha which had monopolized guitar manufacturing by automating the whole process.

"No, we still make them using the same tools and techniques," David continued. "But the world has discovered us. We provide instruments for the flamenco players in Spain, the classical players in Europe..."

We reminisced about Leda and me singing 'Never on Sunday,' in their music festival so many years ago. David remembered it well as a very special moment.

I selected an excellent-sounding small guitar made by a younger member of the Caro family and purchased it. The more I play it the more I appreciate its fine quality. I remembered admiring the free-hand wood-bending techniques I had watched him use so long ago. That had impressed me as being a real dance between the luthier and the wood. A few years later one of Kathleen's boyfriends had created a thriving business importing and re-selling guitars from Paracho in the US and in Europe. Instruments from Paracho had earned a fine reputation and continued to find their ways into the hands of professional players.

Something about visiting my friends in Paracho again gave me immense satisfaction... this was a testimony to the beauty of human nature manifesting through devoted traditional artistry.

Moving north we passed through a famous gringo ex-pat destination: Ajijic on Lake Chapala. We were invited to return and perform in a local restaurant... which still hasn't happened. We were also invited into the home of a North American guy who had made his home there. His Spanish was minimal and, in spite of his pride in the artwork adorning the walls of his house, I sensed a rather lonely soul.

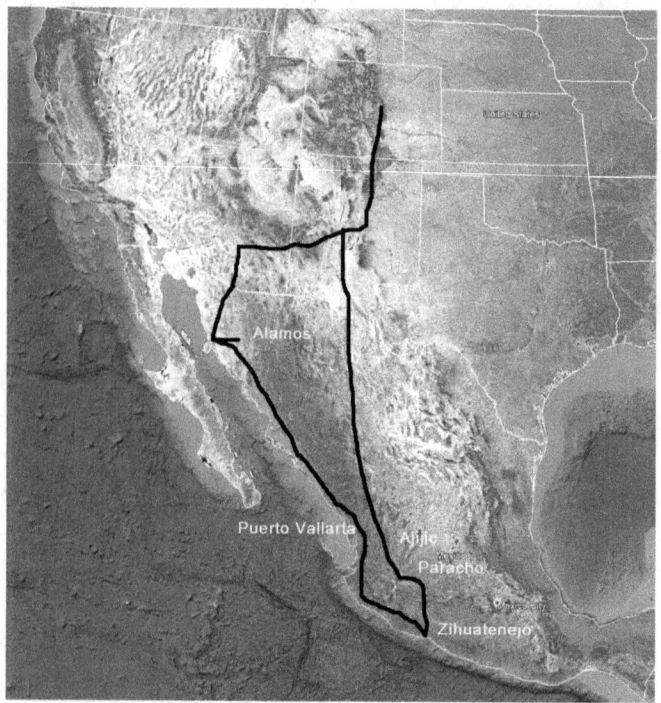

Mexico by Van 2002

Boulder to Santa Cruz, California

It was time. We pointed the van north and eventually rolled back into our driveway in Boulder, Colorado. My mom's insurance policy had reached its limit for paying for residence in assisted living facilities so we finished moving her into the new house. Kristina studied for and passed a Certified Nursing Assistant test so we could administer insurance money earmarked for in-house caregivers. During the next six years, until my mom's death, these caregivers would fall in love with my mom and form a growing community of admirers. My mom's social network in Colorado was thriving. We would have parties from time to time and my mom would read her latest poems and stories.

Me, Eleanor, Bonnie

My daughter had been living in the upstairs apartment with her boyfriend Lucas. Kristina and I needed space for ourselves so we bought a little travel trailer and a diesel van with which to pull it. We kept it parked in the driveway of the house and made curtains for the windows so no one could easily detect that we were living therein... in violation, of course, of Boulder's extensive zoning rules and regulations.

Loving Kristina continued to be effortless and easy. We made love in accordance with my 'imsak' practices. The goal was to be a hundred per cent present with my real actual flesh-and-blood-and-soul lover so neither pornography nor masturbation were ever part of it... and I would generally only come about once a month...

Sherefe kept evolving with expanded repertoire and popular performances.

Loren had graduated with an electrical engineering degree and was working as a raft guide in North Carolina for the summer. He was now partnered with a belly dancer named Monica in California. He traveled with her to Bolivia to meet her family in Cochabamba.

Melina had arranged to begin studies in aromatherapy, herbalism and nutrition at three separate small schools in Santa Cruz, California.

Melina and Kristina in Santa Cruz

Kristina and I drove across the country with her and helped her move into her new apartment.

Melina at Botanical College in Santa Cruz

As Lovers of Arabic Music We Head for Jordan

As the American government dug itself more and more deeply into its fear-based approach to the rest of the world, I began to feel the outrageous anti-Arab and anti-Muslim mythologies growing. The drum-beats of impending military aggression were getting louder. I felt that those of us who shared a love for Arabic music and dance and people had better do something more. I didn't know what we should do but it seemed to me that an answer might reveal itself if we made a journey. I had never been to Jordan before. One of my favorite oud-player teachers at Middle Eastern Music Camp, Nasser Musa, was a Palestinian from Jordan. Kristina and I bought tickets to Amman, Jordan. We had also received an invitation from some musicians' association in Baghdad to come and sing in Iraq. We would try and follow up on that possibility from Jordan.

I wrote down my vision which we published on the back cover of our next CD, "Baghdad and Beyond."

> *Imagine: in a drastic cost-cutting and psychology-changing stroke of diplomatic genius, 100,000 Americans are trained to sing a few popular Arabic songs. A few are trained to play oud (Middle-Eastern Lute), nay (flute) and dumbek (drum).*
>
> *Deployed throughout the Arab world, these young Americans invade the streets of Beirut, Baghdad, Cairo, Amman, Damascus, Riyad... The State Department pays for their meals and lodging...*
>
> *Simultaneously, legions of Americans learn a few Persian songs and a few Turkish songs...*
>
> *Additional invasions begin... This is much cheaper than arming soldiers with high-tech weaponry...*
>
> *As the Americans begin to master music and languages from dozens of foreign cultures, imagine the richness of learning, of friendships and connections... Imagine the eagerness with which many would return to re-visit their new friends to establish new trade routes, new businesses.*
>
> *When you learn a new language you gain a new soul!*

Little did I suspect that for the next month in Jordan and Palestine we would not see a single other American!

> *Kristina writes: At 2:05 AM our plane lands in Jordan. By 2:25 AM we are singing and laughing and having a general good time with our taxi driver as he drives us the fifteen miles to our*

> hotel. He doesn't understand why American TV has so many guns and everyone is shooting everyone.
>
> "It is the heart that is important..." continues our taxi driver. "It is romance that is beautiful." He is so amazed that Cameron can speak some Arabic and that we sing Arabic songs. We sing together a few popular songs as we drive. "My friends they will think I'm crazy," he says. "They will never believe when I tell them an American sings Sabah Fakri songs from Syria."
>
> This taxi driver has a beautiful heart. Cameron has told me how these people accept you as one of their own. How they welcome you when you bridge the gap between cultures with an attempt to learn their language and sing their songs. This is my first opportunity to experience this warmth first hand. We have come to Jordan and plan to travel to Iraq to be people's ambassadors. We have the tools to do what few Americans can do to bring understanding and friendship from America to Iraq. Cameron has studied this music for thirty years and is an accomplished Middle Eastern Musician.
>
> I'm much newer to this music, but I've studied hard and it has touched my heart. Somehow I have been called to do this. As I ride along in the taxi I realize there is something here for me. I am very glad I came.
>
> A bit later in the hotel lobby the desk clerk, the hotel owner, a few of their friends and the taxi driver are all singing the chorus of a popular Iraqi song with us. "If you go to Iraq," the hotel owner says, "they will love you, they will welcome you with open hearts." We had not mentioned that we were planning to go there. I take this as an omen that we are on the right path.

We lay in bed as the sun was first showing light and listened to the call to prayer broadcast over dozens of loudspeakers outside our hotel window.

"It's just the same as when I last left an Arabic-speaking country," I observed to Kristina. These guys are party animals... ready to sing at any moment... and they all seem to live inside the same telepathic thought bubble."

It felt so very different from the West where we all think independently individual thoughts and have to go to great pains to get on the same wavelength.

I had spent the larger parts of our trans-Atlantic crossing with my nose glued in my Arabic language books and tapes. It seemed to pay off. I was as ready as I possibly could be to enter into my Arabic conversation with the taxi driver. And when I didn't understand what he was saying I would just repeat the syllables he was saying to keep the ball rolling and to teach my tongue how to make the sounds of the language.

I went to sleep with a big Arabic-speaking smile on my face.

> *The following evening we plan to go back to the hotel. They want to have a party with us crazy Americans. It is Ramadan now so everyone sleeps late and stays up very late to eat and party.*

Ali Picks us up and Takes us Home

We returned to our hotel planning to continue the party and keep singing but we received a call from my friend Muhsin's nephew, Ali. He wanted to come right over and pick us up. He insisted that we move into his apartment and stay there with him and his younger brother, Haydar.

On the way to his apartment he wanted to treat us to a few hours of feasting and listening to a local band at a restaurant called Amasi... They had singer, oud, qanun, violin and drum in the band. Near dawn we proceeded to his home and got a little bit of sleep.

> *"So why did you not call as soon as you got here?" Ali, asked. We told him that it was so late that first night we thought he might be sleeping and we didn't want to wake him. He assured us he is awake almost all night every night. This was true. It was now 1:57 AM the following night and we had just finished the second meal of the evening.*
>
> *Ali was a very, very gracious host. He was twenty-nine and worked with computers on web design projects. He came with us during the day to the Iraqi Embassy to get our visas for Iraq. As it turned out, as Americans, we need an official invitation*

from someone in Iraq to enter the country. We came back to Ali's house and he started making calls for us. We may receive an invitation from the head of the music association in Baghdad which had sent us the original invitation.

Ali's other uncle, Jihad, was there in Amman for a couple months. He had one wife here and another in Baghdad. Jihad had a friend at the Iraqi Embassy and would try to get us an interview with him on Saturday. Meanwhile he took us to see many sites around the city.

The people we have met have welcomed us with open hearts. We discussed life, played music and tried to understand what these people were experiencing. Ali and his family were Iraqi descendants of the prophet Mohammed so they had connections with royalty. Most of them had left Iraq because it was so difficult to live there now with the U.N. sanctions. Everyone we talked with just wanted peace. They knew we didn't align ourselves with president Bush. We assured them that there were many, many Americans who wanted peace too.

I just wished that more Americans would travel here and get to know these people. We have such a distorted view of Middle Easterners in the U.S. These people were very gentle and went way out of their way to make sure we were taken care of.

Our singing continued. It was what we could most offer... we sang for the band after they finished playing... we sang for dinner guests after breaking the Ramadan fast with them after sundown... we were getting to know these people fast and furiously... more than I can write about...

Every day we fasted, along with the entire population there, until about 5 PM, when the sun set and it was 'eftar' and time to eat again. Ali would cook macaroni, his younger brother's favorite, or we would go out and eat chicken and rice at local restaurants... we stayed up late at night... men walked through the neighborhoods at 2:00 AM and again at 4:00 AM playing large drums loudly to remind us all to eat the last foods before the sun would rise and the next day's fast would begin. We were into the last week of the month of fasting and the recorded calls to prayer were being lengthened and augmented by other live singers or 'readers' as they call them. Many times a day the neighborhoods were filled with the songs of these calls to prayer... Islam was very very present.

Ali was very Islamic and had been explaining all the rules and the beliefs, most of which he seemed to share, about men and women, marriage and divorce... and he was constantly pushing forward with a mix of boundless hospitality to us while also running his business.

"My brother will have to quit being lazy when our mother gets here," he added. "She makes us get up early every morning."

We had benefited from many hours of conversation every day with those two brothers, especially with Ali, whose English was excellent.

No, I am not an Admirer of Saddam

Muhsin had provided us with the contacts necessary to be invited into Iraq by the Musician's Association. Every day Ali called our contacts in Iraq. It seemed that the letter of invitation had been written and was now being signed and stamped by the appropriate officials. It would be sent to the Iraqi Embassy in Amman and we would be granted admission to the country. We didn't know how long this would take... a few more days, we guessed.

> *Cameron and I are still in Amman. If Ali is representative of Iraqi hospitality then we will be cared for very well in Iraq. He is not wealthy but insists on paying for everything and takes us around and shows us the sights of the city. He cooks for us and won't let us help.*

When Ali's mother arrived from Baghdad with her youngest son, we moved into a small $9-per-night hotel in the old center of the city. I liked it there... the sidewalks and streets were filled shoulder-to-fender-to-shoulder with folks scurrying from shop-to-shop or... whatever it was that humans do in the center of town.

We could practice more of our songs in the hotel room. We had been singing our best-known Iraqi and Egyptian songs for Ali and his brothers' uncle, Jihad, who had been showing up with his new young wife... she was a second wife. Islam allows short-term affairs called *'mut'a'* marriages. This was one of those. The first wife was living in Baghdad. Jihad was serious and jolly at the same time. He had been a military man until he had been shot and wounded during the war against Iran. Now retired, he would come over to discuss stories and philosophies about women with his two nephews.

Kristina and I threw in our observations and comments from time to time. Jihad was enjoying a renewed youthful vigor from this second marriage. But Ali said it probably wouldn't last because Jihad was very responsible toward his first wife and the ten children they have. He didn't think his first wife would ever even find out about the new short-term wife.

We asked questions: to get married the man must give money to the woman... to get divorced the man must also give money to the woman... to be married to more than one woman the man must be able to afford this... if he gives something to one wife he should give the same to the others... but the women cannot initiate divorce proceedings the way men can unless the husband is physically abusive... or unless he fails to satisfy them sexually. Women can make the mistake of being too impulsive in their decision-making so it was thought safer to rely on the man's decisions with regard to divorce. But to guard against any impulsive decision-making it was customary to give a couple three chances to get back together if the man had announced that divorce is necessary... but only three chances... if he had announced divorce three times then it was prohibited for them to try to get along any more... unless it was arranged for the woman to marry another man for a brief period of time, wait three months and then return for a fourth try with her first husband.

Well it was all somewhat familiar and yet different. The marriages were arranged. If you liked some girl you asked your parents to approach her parents. In Jihad's case it was said that his father had put a gun to his head and said, "you will marry this one..." when Jihad had been only seventeen.

At one point in our conversations with Jihad he let us know that there was always one way to be guaranteed easy entry into Iraq. "Just let it be known that you are an American admirer of Saddam Hussein."

I shook my head... "No, I am not an admirer of Saddam... That's not a possibility."

My Arabic was just enough to initiate conversations which didn't really go anywhere. But the basic ideas could be exchanged... so the world of Amman was unfolding for us with taxi drivers at our disposal.

Are You Afraid to Come Here?

Since we were no longer residing at Ali's and there was no TV in our room we wouldn't be catching the latest news and Egyptian comedy soap operas which showed the range of facial expressions and body language from so close up... We had learned a lot about these things which are so very different from their counterparts in the West.

It sounded like the Iraqi economy had been slowly picking up in spite of the embargo imposed by the USA. The inspections were not turning up any 'weapons of mass destruction.' The bombing in the north and the south was continuing, supposedly in response to Iraqi attempts to shoot down US aircraft.

Everyone we were meeting there in Jordan was friendly. None of the maps in Jordan showed anything called 'Israel' in what was labeled 'Palestine.' While walking on a hill above the city Kristina and I and a Palestinian were interviewed by a roving BBC reporter: "Who would you side with, Bush or Bin Laden?" she asked... "Well, neither," we all three responded by turn.

"Are you afraid to come here?" she asked us.

"No, not at all... these are very sweet people," we replied.

We explained our musical mission and I reiterated that trusting any of our governments to solve these problems was something I had given up on. "The people must reclaim the power from the governments... that's why we are here now..."

The Palestinian insisted that he had no problems getting along with people from anywhere, including Jewish people. "It's the leaders who create the problems," he said. He also asked why the US government was so concerned about Iraq when Israel obviously was the country with the nuclear weapons and creating the threat to world peace.

"And the only country in the world to ever actually use nuclear weaponry was the USA..." he pointed out. He had received some education in India.

Two news pieces would come out over BBC airwaves during the next month with our voices recorded but we never heard either one.

> *A BBC news reporter interviewed us. These kinds of 'coincidences' give me encouragement, like we're getting the big 'way to go' from the universe. And the TV interview we did before we left Colorado on Free Speech TV will air December 21 and 22. Catch it if you can!*

We had learned so much from Ali there in Amman.

Neither Ali nor his brother looked stressed out. They were in the hands of their own faith... the will of God...

Ali had been in Baghdad when the bombing occurred in 1991 in the Gulf war. "It was kind of fun, actually. We would be asked to escort various girls here and there to help them. It made us feel strong and proud. Somehow, when you are in the middle of all the explosions, fear disappears. One night I was awakened by a flash and explosion so big and so bright... so much bigger than the rest that I thought: *'that's the nuclear one!'* ...but I just rolled over and went back to sleep..."

Kristina and Ali

It Was Very Passionate Playing

Kristina and I were not there to analyze politics or to take sides. We were there to be with the people... people of any size shape rank or color... and to then share our impressions.

More and more people back in the US... hundreds... were forwarding and replying to our emailed descriptions and seemed to be immensely interested in our journey.

> Whew! I've been so moved by the stories that you've been sending out, and then the pictures! Wow. They made me cry. I hope more and more people will come to realize that it's not the people who want to fight, but the governments. I'm just awed and inspired by what you two are doing. I'm honored to be your friend.

Wandering into a little city center music shop we saw lots of ouds hanging in the windows and on the walls. We were in the center of the old market place: crowded streets and tiny little shops placed in endless labyrinthine alleyways.

I asked for an oud and sat down. I played a little and the shop-owner, whose name was Jihad, played a little... he gave me some suggestions about my right hand technique. He was right, of course. I had been cultivating some bad habits there for a long time.

Little by little we sang songs from Syria, Iraq, Egypt, and Lebanon... then a song from Greece. Tea was ordered and we all settled in to get to know each other.

Another man with a bright beaming energy in his face arrived and sat down to begin a chess game set up on the little table. After the game he picked up a violin. Everybody in the shop... there were five or six of us... was saying: *professional...* about this man. He added that he also wrote children's songs. Then he played 'Yam Saharni'... an Um Kolthoum piece. It was very passionate playing... everyone sang along during the vocal parts.

Kristina and I shared that we were hoping to get our visas to enter Iraq so that America could be known to have sent something musical... "yes, yes! very wonderful!" they all cheered... "and the Iraqi people are wonderful people... they will treat you very nice..."

We promised to see them again soon.

We Had to Leave Haifa in 1947

The next day we passed another music store with ouds hanging in the windows. Inside we found a Turkoman gentleman born in northern Iraq and a Palestinian woman born in Haifa. I played an Um Kolthoum piece from Egypt and they both sang along with Kristina. The woman had fairly good English and showed us pictures of her two sons and four daughters, "who all sing very well... and one of my sons plays oud like his father did." She showed us a picture of her deceased husband playing the oud.

She explained: "we had to leave our house in Haifa in 1947 when the Jews arrived. We left everything, the furniture and all our possessions. We thought we would only be gone for a short time. I was just a child. We lived in Nablus for three years but there was not much work so we came here to Amman. Eventually we could afford to have a house. I went back to Haifa once to see my house... the Jewish people living in it let me look inside. They had subdivided it into four parts... two apartments each with two stories. The high ceilings had made it possible for them to add another floor halfway up. I don't know when we will finally get our house back. It's very beautiful there... close to the sea."

The Turkish man played 'Never on Sunday' on the oud and I sang along in Greek. Then he played 'Ushkadara gider iken'... I sang some of the Turkish words along with him.

We told them that we were hoping to go into Iraq so that people could see that there are Americans who love the Middle Eastern music and people... "Wonderful... yes... a good thing to do... they will treat you very well... and maybe you can find an Iraqi oud..." The Palestinian woman seemed to know that very fine ouds were made in Iraq.

Ali had come down with the flu. He sounded very miserable when we talked with him over the phone but he was worried that we were no longer sharing his apartment with him. We told him that it was also good for us to be back out on the streets everyday exploring the city and its musical moments.

> Amman's altitude is almost 3000 feet so it is cool here. The downtown, where we are staying, is a very busy place. It is now 11:00 PM and the street is still very full of people. They are shopping for 'eid el fitr' the three-day celebration at the end of Ramadan.
>
> The horns and cars never stop; this is downtown after all. Our hotel window looks out on a main thoroughfare and across to the Roman Theater: eighteen-hundred-year-old ruins and still a functional setting for dramatic productions which they hold here in the summer.
>
> Yesterday we played our music in the Roman Theater. The

children and some adults swarmed around us delighted with these Americans who sang their songs.

"Hello," says a little girl "what is your name?"

"Kristina," I reply.

"Kristina, my name is Ibtisim. Goodbye." A little bit later she says the same thing to me and I realize that is the only English she knows, she fooled me. Her pronunciation was perfect. I am taken with her. She is one of those little ones who can capture your heart.

I am growing very fond of Amman, We spend our time connecting with the locals, playing music when we can and sitting in cafes and restaurants studying Arabic. I can now write my name in Arabic and am able to slowly sound out some of the words I see on buildings and street signs.

'Shwaya shwaya,' (little by little) I am learning. I find writing the language is quite fun, kind of like figuring out a secret code, only here it's not so secret. When you say anything to the people in their native language they light up, delighted that an American has taken the time to learn a little bit. This seems to be true in all of the few places I've traveled.

Red, Blue and Green Pigeons

While the red, blue and green pigeons circled endlessly overhead, we sat on the ancient stone steps of the Roman Theater in the heart of old town downtown Amman. Once again we played a song of Um Kolthoum, the Egyptian super-goddess of the Arab world.

Children were playing all around the theater, climbing the steep stairs, laughing and yelling while parents and older brothers or sisters watched. We smiled at the children as we sang and they gathered around. They smiled back with their eyes and their faces. A little six-year-old girl snuggled up behind me and offered me sunflower seeds.

Playing in Roman Theater in Amman

The pigeons overhead had been painted or dyed under their wings by their owners. They flew in circles around the houses where they were raised from 'chick-hood'...

Ali had a negative opinion of the bird owners... "I don't think it is fair to train these pigeons to feel like they are only able to fly around one house. And we don't trust these bird owners because when they sit up on their rooftops they have an unfair chance to watch what all the people are doing down on the streets... or in other houses."

We sang another song, an Iraqi song this time. The children were gathering in a tighter-and-tighter group around us. Soon the group was at least one hundred. They clapped and sang along. When we finished the song, they cheered. Some of the older folks began to approach and sing with us too.

Suddenly a young boy grabbed my oud neck and prevented me from continuing. The call to prayer had begun in the background from a nearby mosque. We waited until the call to prayer was completed and then we began another Egyptian song. The people all knew this one and sang along. I reached the end of the song and began a *'mawwal'* - a singing improvisation which follows certain traditional patterns... The crowd screamed with delight.

"Come down into the center so there is more room," suggested someone.

"No, this is fine... Stay here!" insisted others.
"Where are you from?"
"America..."
"Very good..."

The pigeons were still circling in the afternoon sunlight, glowing in their brilliant painted colors. The pigeon owners take the young pigeons and cut their wing just enough so they can't fly too far. They become accustomed to flying only short distances... just around the house. Then they let the feathers grow back and the pigeons can fly all day. But they have been trained now to only fly around the owner's house. They take them inside at night and touch up their brilliantly-colored plumage. Whether this good or bad, I do not know. It certainly is different from what we do with our pigeons in Colorado.

After a few more songs we agreed to meet again the next day... insha-Allah...

More Nightclub Shows

After a sip of Turkish coffee and a bit of hummus, tomato-cucumber salad, some chicken and a bit of baklava, we dropped in at Jihad's music store where we had spent so much time a day or two before. We hung out and sung an Um Kolthoum piece and a Fairouz piece. I traded in my funky travel oud for a nicer one.

Jihad's Music Shop

I watch the women on the street. Ninety percent of them wear the hijab: the scarf that covers all of their hair. Many of the young girls wear jeans and western-style sweaters but they still wear the hijab. The last few days have been very warm but I've yet to see a

> *woman's arms uncovered... at least not on the street, nor in the shops.*

We decided to check out some more nightclub shows. In spite of the promises from a guidebook and from a taxi driver that we would find more live music with oud, qanun, nay, violin, drum, (the old favorite acoustic instruments), as we had before, we only found piercingly loud 'org' (keyboard)... minimal movement go-go-style belly dancers gifted at extracting money from crowds of young Arab men who try and look uninterested, occasionally giving way to fits of dance or throwing money while making a big show of being unable to resist. The girls wandered through our tables occasionally placing their hands on our shoulders or touching our arms in friendly ways.

Approached by the 'dancer' and a male singer with a wireless microphone and, for extra power, a drummer, cash was thrown on our table apparently to indicate how much they were hoping we might throw back in the dancer's direction. We came up with considerably less and after another half hour when it was clear that our table was next in line again, we paid the tab and slipped out the door.

> *We went to another night club last night. I was the only woman customer, the only other women were the minimally dressed waitresses. Extremely short tight skirts, low cut tops, high-heel boots and gobs of make-up seemed to be the style of the evening. They were friendly to me and smiled. But no respectable Islamic women would go into the place, I don't think. As a Westerner and in the company of Cameron I can get away with it. There was a belly dancer of sorts, but she couldn't hold a candle to most of the dancers I know in the states. I know there are some good dancers here somewhere but we've yet to find them.*

We were in a part of town now which had fancy hotels and fancy taxis. Prices, even for cabs from here, were hard to control.

After one more attempt: "Oh yes," said this high-priced taxi driver, "I know where the music clubs are with the old style of Arabic music being played." We trusted him only to find ourselves being guided into another money-suction establishment with nothing but a keyboard for a band. We declined the invitation to sit down and we kept wandering until we found another hummus and falafel restaurant where we could relax and study some more Arabic.

Our Arabic books and our Arabic song-lyric sheets were our constant companions and every day we plowed through new material. Kristina was fascinated with learning the writing system while I was finding that my conversations with the taxi drivers could frequently remain at least half in Arabic... ...as long as we stuck to simple subjects like: "turn left at the next corner, please..." but, hey, that was a lot more fluent than I had been before...

Baghdad Had Come to Us

On the first normal weekday after the three-day Eid al Fitr holiday after Ramadan had come and gone we checked again with Ali to see if we were any closer to being issued Iraqi visas. It wasn't so easy right then for us Americans to get into Iraq and the time it was taking for official paths to be followed could be considerable.

We met a young Welsh lady named Lisa who had just finished living in the West Bank of Palestine as part of an International Solidarity group which goes in to try and help shield Palestinians from the Israeli soldiers. She told us that a friend of hers had been waiting two months for his Iraqi visa.

Lisa was in her twenties... young twenties. Driven by curiosity and a need to find some better version of the truth, she had decided to quit her corporate job in London and volunteer to teach English in Palestine. She soon found herself working with a solidarity group in Nablus to try and help Palestinian families survive the siege they were under.

Lisa and Kristina

The Israeli army was sending in tanks and bulldozers to destroy homes. "Ridiculous," said Lisa... "it is one of the most modern well-equipped armies and it easily dominates a civilian population with very few arms." After three months in Nablus she was returning to Britain to try and educate people about the situation.

She had lived with various Palestinian families. She would walk out with the school children to show solidarity in breaking the curfew which prohibited Palestinian children from going to school. The Palestinian parents say that their children must become educated and refuse to abide by the curfew. Lisa would walk out with them in front of the tanks and receive curses from the Jewish settlers.

We asked her what it was like being a young blond-haired woman alone in Palestine. She said that she was proposed to over and over again... politely. She learned something one day, she said, watching a very beautiful young Palestinian woman who was being admired by the young men. The young woman wiggled her body a little bit to show that she appreciated the admiration. Suddenly, she said, she realized that acknowledging the attraction was easier than trying to resist it and that nothing bad was really going to happen. Lisa said she never had felt threatened. Her impression was that women were much safer alone here than they are in many parts of the Western world.

Later that night it was as if Baghdad had come to us. Ali's mother had requested to hear our Arabic singing so we were able to provide a songfest for them during the evening while tasting his mother's Iraqi food.

Around noon the next day we sat in a downtown Amman park... I began to play the oud... soon a few passersby paused and listened... after another few minutes more people gathered and began to smile... another few minutes and some began to sing along and clap and dance... ...we were the mysterious but welcome strangers from America who could sing in Arabic...

Playing in Public Park in Amman

Sometimes people couldn't help laughing at our pronunciation but it was still plenty good enough for them to be able to sing along.

An hour of music passed. We took a few photos. Families and various individuals wanted to have their pictures taken with their arms draped over the American oud-player's shoulders.

Family in Park Appreciating Our Music

Later we got the film developed. We dropped into a smoky coffee shop, drank some tea and passed the photos around to the men playing backgammon. They all smiled. The one-eyed man with the horrendous scar reaching more than halfway around his neck and across his face came and sat down beside me and extended his hand. "Are you Muslim?" he couldn't resist asking.

"No," I replied. "But I am feeling very comfortable with Muslim people." The healed wounds on his body looked horrendous. I wanted to ask him what had happened to him but my language skills were not yet strong enough.

Our Favorite Late-Night Spot

It was time to get our Jordanian visas renewed. We waited outside the local police station for the four policemen on duty to get finished singing one of their favorite popular songs and then made our request. "Come back tomorrow," we were told by the smiling officers.

Ali continued to try and contact our friends in Iraq to see if any progress was being made with our official invitation. We would see. Perhaps we would go to Egypt for a while.

We returned to our favorite late-night spot, 'Amasi.' Oud, Vocalist, Violin and Drum... all top of the line musicians... not too loud... good food... they nodded in greeting as we entered and came over to our table during a break to encourage us to return frequently.

It was midnight... at the table next to us we saw a family: the dad, the mom, the oldest son and his sister or cousin or girlfriend???? The youngest daughter was maybe seven years old -- she liked to clap in time to the music. The oldest son couldn't contain himself and rose to dance briefly from time to time... finally he got up with his sister or cousin or girlfriend???? ...who danced beautifully and sensually as Middle Easterners do.

My oud was stashed under the table hoping for another chance to get out of its box but the music came to an end. Oh well... "Come back tomorrow night," suggested the violinist.

It seemed that they must have a very low crime rate in Amman. No guards were required near the public ATM's nor the numerous jewelry stores in the Gold Market.

A taxi driver listed all the major world Heads of Government for me and divided them all into good or bad. That was interesting but it made me again realize that *always always always* we must return to the music. Verbal realities were only doorways into confusion and conflict... We must return to the music and to the beauty of the children's faces... the mothers' faces... the fathers' faces...

> Ali tells us that the invitation has been written but it needs to be approved by the Iraqi equivalent of the CIA and various governmental departments. "Mrs. N" in Baghdad is overseeing the process and we are told that if she can't get it for us then no one can. We are very fortunate to have the connections we do.
>
> Today is the international day of peace. I am encouraged by all of the peace efforts that are going on around the word. Peace will prevail.

That evening we visited a monkey in a cage in a local pet shop... very human looking eyes and a low, non-verbal, grunting voice... "See you later," we told him. There were many cats living in the streets of Amman... zero dogs.

Kristina had been keeping her books open to study Arabic in the restaurants... we quizzed the waiters on how to say or pronounce various words. Kristina had taken to enjoying wandering the city by herself now that we had a basic handle on the geography.

As for me, I was remembering about ten percent of the basic Arabic vocabulary I would eventually need to be able to actually communicate. Every day my mind was hungrily scanning the dictionaries and the grammar books and finding new words and phrases... faster than I could try them out... and every day my mind was scanning its inner recesses: 'what was that word, anyway...!?'

Crunch! My mind was trying too hard! Trying to work too fast! Where had that habit come from? Talking and being with Kristina helped me stay in a smoother pace. My mind actually worked a lot better when not frantic... Duh...

Suad Told Stories for Hours

The next day we again spent with Ali and family. It had not been so easy for Ali's mother, Suad, and his youngest brother, 'Ahmad,' or more affectionately called, 'Hamoudi,' to get out of Iraq into Jordan. The stories about the decimation of everything Iraqi after the 1991 Gulf War were true. Where people were exposed to the bombing in Baghdad, they would break out in painful skin rashes... little scratches that would have been nothing became ulcerated sores... the babies born were frequently horrendously deformed.

Suad had these rashes and sores on her body.

These were the survivors of a once well-to-do family now reduced to poverty, unstable health and uncertain futures as refugees. They were Iraqi refugees joining the vast crowd of Palestinian refugees making the best of it in Amman.

Kristina and Suad

Ali's mother invited us to dinner again yesterday: plates full of rice with pine-nuts, raisins, a lamb stew with eggplant, chicken, salad, coca cola, two or three deserts and, of course, tea. Ali assured us that she would have cooked more, but she had recently arrived here in Amman from Baghdad and didn't have all the right things to cook with. They had trouble finding a pot to cook the rice in. Ali and his brother had been living by themselves and were not noted for their well-stocked kitchen. Ali's mother was forty-two years old, Ali was twenty-nine. Figure it out: she had been thirteen when he was born.

"We grew up together," he said. "She would put me in a basket and take me downstairs when she went to play with the other girls."

Ali's mother had listened to our music the other night. She clapped and sang along and ran out to get a pan to use as a drum. She was smiling and laughing and looking at me with penetrating and welcoming eyes.

I asked her last night what it was like to marry when she was twelve-and-a-half years old. Was she happy to marry or sad? "Oh my husband was very handsome... he looked like a movie star. I was very happy." She spoke in broken English. Ali, the English expert, helped her find the right words.

"A girl is always asked if she wants to marry or not," says Ali, "only if the girl's family is poor and they find her a well-to-do husband will she sometimes be forced to marry against her will."

Ali's mother married well. If you remember, they are Hashemites, direct descendants of the prophet.

She was highly prized as a wife. Her husband was a wealthy civil engineer sixteen-years her senior. After marriage they had lived in Kuwait. She had lived like a queen: servants to cook and clean for her, boxes full of gold rings, necklaces, jewelery, clothes of all sorts and silk carpets. She had an apartment in London and had accompanied her husband to Switzerland, Germany, India, all over Europe and Asia and the Middle East. Kuwait was home base until Ali was seventeen. Then the war came. Ali's father decided it would be best to go back to Baghdad. They had to leave in a hurry. Many people owed his father thousands of dollars but they have yet to collect it. No more money was coming in.

"I would take a ring and sell it to get sugar, flour, tea. I would take necklaces and sell them. I would take carpets and sell, sell, sell, until nothing was left." She had no rings on her fingers now. Everything was sold for food. Ali's father had died a year-and-a-half ago. Ali now is the main provider for his mother and two younger brothers. The second oldest brings in a bit of money but it is Ali who holds most of the responsibility bringing in paychecks from his webpage designing business. After dinner she sat with us on the floor and we talked.

"Before war cancer seemed very rare... now my friends... five members of the same family... cancer, cancer, cancer... they die. Before war, babies born happy, good health... now after war, babies born no fingers or no nose or one eye. My friend, she has five babies... each baby born missing arm or head open or heart outside. They live one, two, days and then die... deformities..." she gestured showing places on the body where deformities appear.

"Before war if you caught the flu... it took maybe two or three days... now it takes two, three months to get well." She looks at Ali for the right word. "Immune system... immune system weak."

I knew what she was talking about. Even the guide book we

bought talks about it: the Depleted Uranium. Geiger counters register radioactivity in many places in Iraq. All the symptoms she described fit in with radiation poisoning. What is so disturbing to me is that it appears the U.S. is responsible for this. We used depleted uranium in the bombs we dropped and the anti-tank shells fired. I know that some of you reading this may take issue with me. But this is how I understand it to be.

I sat and listened to her. I felt so many different things. There really are no words... just I am so sorry. We moved onto lighter subjects. We watched a bit of some singer on TV and then she told me to come with her. I followed her into the bedroom, she opened a closet door and took out a blue velvet dress with gold embroidered grape leaves and urged me to put it on. I did and then she took out a black cut velvet scarf and wrapped it around my head. "Beautiful," she remarked. The dress was cut like all the dresses there, very loose fitting, down to the floor with long sleeves. I felt very elegant. I followed her back into the living room and she introduced me as her good friend from Saudi. We all laughed and they all remarked how I really did look like I was from Saudi Arabia.

What I didn't understand was that she was giving these things to me.

"When an Iraqi gives you something to wear", said Ali "she is giving it to you to keep." I didn't know what to say...

"Shukran" (thank-you)... "Shukran, it is so beautiful".

Suad told stories for hours about the lives of her family members... brothers and sisters... scattered all over the globe now... I burst into tears at some point... But Ali was maintaining optimism and hope that he, the eldest son and now the sole bread-winner for the family, could earn enough to rebuild a home somewhere someday... they didn't yet know where...

These people are more than generous. Ali says what he and his mother have done is nothing... "Just wait until you get to Iraq, they will not let you alone. They will treat you very, very well."

I have been longing to connect with some women here. Most of the people we meet are men. They are the ones out on the street. I sometimes look out the hotel window at one spot on the sidewalk. I count the number of men and women who pass by. Usually it is ten or twenty men for every woman. Most of the shop owners are men but there are a few women here and there. Quite often they *travel in groups with small children and babies. Ali's mother is the first woman I have really gotten to know. Although we communicate in limited Arabic and English I know that we have a strong friendship. I think there may be a stronger camaraderie among women here. Like we are all members of the same club... there seems to be an immediate sense of trust.*

Ali and his brothers treat their mother with an amazing amount of respect. I think Ali would do anything for her. They put their arms around her and take turns kissing her on the forehead and are constantly calling her habibi (my love). She does the same with them. It is hard to say who is in control. There is much mutual respect. Ali says they argue but I think they mostly argue in a kind of playful way. Who gets the final say remains to be seen... My guess is that it is mom.

Kristina in Suad's Dress

The next morning as I left the hotel I was invited to share tea by a Palestinian shopkeeper who runs a little repair workshop. I sang him a piece of Abd 'al Halim's *'Sawah'* and he grabbed me and planted kisses all over my face.

We were gradually getting to know the musicians who play late at night at 'Amasi': Bassam on oud, Sa'ad on Percussion, Sabah on violin... Bassam had let me play his oud again after their performance the other night...

> *Today it rains in Amman. We will not play music in the park or in the Roman Theater. Yesterday we did play and a crowd again gathered around us. A family of eight sat down next to us, Mom and Dad and six children all under ten-years-old. The mother's eyes are smiling at me as she sends her daughters over to shake my hand and introduce themselves. They can say hello in English.*
>
> *What I have noticed when we play is the deep understanding we have without saying a word. The world may be on the verge of war but these women and I... we know we are friends. Our eyes smile, our hearts connect and the children are taking it in. I am very blessed to be here. Thank you again to the friends back home who have helped us with donations.*

Aqaba

We began to suspect that the visas for entering Iraq were never going to show up so we got on a bus and rode for four hours south traveling beside the Dead Sea.

We wandered through the spice and meat market in Aqaba, beside the Red Sea. Some boys pointed at my oud case and cleaned some metal stairs for us to sit. With racks full of skinned goats hanging in the background, we sang three or four songs for the enthusiastic all-aged, but all male, crowd.

Kristina pointed at my watch to remind me that it was almost time for the afternoon call to prayer. We stopped our songs when we heard it begin.

Our songs led to invitations from one of the local butcher-shop owners for coffee. We did our best in Arabic to discover that yes, his grandfather and his father had already passed away. They had owned the shops before him. There were pictures of them on the wall.

Butcher Shop in Aqaba

We entered the spice shop next door for more tea and felt the deliciousness of the smells of the piles of naked powdered and ground spices enter our noses.

We walked down by the edge of the Gulf of Aqaba there on the Red Sea and sat on a low concrete wall.

Playing at Night by the Red Sea

Kristina sang Fairouz songs. We sang again songs of Abd 'al Halim, Farid al Atresh, Um Kolthoum by Mohammad Abd 'al Wahab, Sabah Fakri...

More tea was brought... The sun set and darkness fell.

So much fun for all of us! What an easy opportunity it was to leap across the politically-created fear barriers and celebrate our new friendships right there in public streets and parks!

Later that night I checked out the singer and keyboard show in a big hotel... too loud... hard to relate... kind of painful on the ears... but it was fun to watch the guys get up and dance the line dance known as *'dabke.'* The singer, a young female with long flowing bleached blond hair reigned queen... the boys in the crowd got up when she beckoned them... clapped when she clapped.

A Bedouin Guy Approached

Breakfast... Arabic coffee. A Bedouin guy approached, asked about my oud. We played him songs. We went down beside the Red Sea and sang him another song.

"OK," he announced, "you are now part of my family... I want to take you to meet my uncle near Wadi Rum, up in the desert. He plays oud... very good... You not tourists... no charge... just you pay for gas for the camel... my name is Jafar."

We climbed into the 'camel', a vintage Datsun Patrol, held together with the Bedouin versions of duct tape and bailing wire.

> *With eighteen local uncles, Jafar had cousins in every kind of business. We visited a road watchman cousin on our way to the desert. Jafar said he didn't really watch out for anything. He just camped there and played with his dogs. These were the first dogs we had seen in Jordan. He used them for hunting. I made friends with the cute puppies.*

An hour or two north we entered Al Quwayra, a Bedouin town. "My uncle lives in that house," points Jafar. "And my other uncle lives in that house... and another uncle in that house... another in that house..."

We putted and sputtered through town, the camel grinding its gears because the slave cylinder which operated the clutch was no longer functioning. We stopped at another cousin's house, went upstairs... met cousin, wife, children... had tea... played oud...

This cousin, Hussein, played very good oud... very many styles. His eyes shone brightly into mine as he played several songs.

Hussein

I played several songs back to him... Jafar was very happy with the situation. We all got in the camel: Jafar, Hussein, wife Zeinab, six-month-old daughter Taif, four and six-year-old sons Sa'ad and Aktam, me and Kristina. We took many blankets and we stopped and bought chicken.

Jafar's 'Camel' with Hussein and Kids on Top

We drove off in 4-wheel-drive through the sand on 'a Bedouin Road' into high arid desert.

Bedouin Road

We stopped at a stone natural bridge and climbed up through rocks. Hussein was a fluid climber... a spider on the rocks... he zoomed away up high. Zeinab and Kristina and I took Taif and their two sons and my oud and climbed up into the eye of the stone arch. We sung a dabke. Zeinab knew the words and sang also. The sun was approaching the horizon.

Desert Arch in Southern Jordan

We zoomed off across the desert in our sputtering 4WD camel, stopping every little while to refill and bleed the clutch master cylinder. When the engine stalled, it could only be restarted by connecting the terminals on the starter motor with a wrench under the hood.

We pulled into a small side canyon of one of the many high wind-carved sandstone mountains and emptied out the camel. We gathered dry brush for firewood, made two fires, spread blankets, cooked chicken, made tea. At 4:30 PM and again at 5:00 PM Hussein removed his shoes, washed his feet, and beautifully sang the call to prayer... it echoed inside the canyon walls.

Camped in Desert Canyon

Jafar, a very strong and efficient twenty-five-year-old, obviously wise way beyond his years, expounded on the art of balancing work and life... "...not so much work that you lose yourself and forget who you are... it is the silence of the desert that makes it so precious to me..."

Jafar and Zeinab

We watched stars appear... the temperature dropped into the low 40's... we added more twigs to the fire and played songs on oud, and on my Arabic flutes.

Kristina and Hussein - Music All Evening

We practiced Arabic and sang for three more hours and finally curled up under the blankets under the stars to find sleep... or to let sleep find us. I heard everyone breathing and snoring around me but I didn't fall asleep. I watched the moon move from 12 o'clock midnight to 3 o'clock in the morning across the heavens.

"The stars witness your sleeplessness as you dream of your loved ones. Hussein had taught me this poem in Arabic and I had felt another little piece of Arabic soul glide into my body.

> *We slept under the stars with new Bedouin friends at a camp we assembled in the desert. Hussein and Cameron took turns playing oud and Jafar danced. Earlier in the evening Zeinab, Hussein's wife, and three of their children were with us. We roasted chicken on the fire and played music non-stop into the night.*
>
> *The desert is cold at this time of year. The place we set up camp was a very good place surrounded by beautiful wind-carved cliffs. Out on the open desert the wind was blowing hard but our spot was protected and our fires kept us warm.*

Morning came. Jafar was first up with fire and tea for all of us. Hussein played more songs on the oud: Bedouin, Kaliji, Omani and Yemeni styles... each had its own rhythmic pattern of picking.

We went for a two-hour hike and Hussein climbed way up to the tops of two mountains while we climbed on the lower parts.

Back to the campsite... fifteen minutes of pumping and engine cranking and the camel sputtered into life. We bled the clutch, piled in the blankets and off we went.

We stopped at an ancient cistern, obviously carved by hand out of the rock... "...water is the 'gold' of the desert." Jafar reminded us.

I pointed at the right front tire, which had lost half of its air.

"It will be OK," said Jafar.

Stopping two or three more times to bleed the clutch brought us to the point of disaster with the tire. It was flat, shredded and halfway off the rim. Still we drove through the sand.

Finally reaching a small paved road not far from the village, we stopped, jacked up the front end and prepared to put the spare tire... yes, there was one!... onto the front wheel drum.

One of the lug nuts was stripped and the tire iron was a little too big to lock onto it... a furious half hour was spent fighting it... pounding it and the wrench with rocks to try and get a purchase on the offending nut... no good... a passing truck stopped... we tried with those tools... nothing worked.

We drove through the sand beside the pavement a little further and stopped in front of a house. They brought another wrench. No good. They brought out the pickup truck and towed the diesel tractor, a relic from fifty years ago, until it sprang to life... the tractor, with its big wheels, dragged us to the edge of the pavement where somehow, we were hoping, a miracle would take place.

Instead of the miracle we found that the clutch would no longer function at all and we couldn't drive any further on the shredded tire.

Returning once again with the diesel tractor, they towed us into the yard of the house... a low concrete block wall contained the sheep, the goats, the pigeons and several decades worth of discarded fuel cans and tractor parts.

A very elderly bearded grandfather was sitting on his mat in the sun beside the repair yard where two more ancient diesel tractors could occasionally receive patching and love... the elder had his shoes parked neatly behind his mat and had obviously already passed into some kind of after-life here on earth wherein the physical work was done by others... his apparent function now was to pray and to witness.

A very sturdy man appeared with welding equipment from the shed. We were going to torch off the offending lug nut... ...behold! ...one more try with yet a different size wrench and: the miracle! The nut came loose... The tire could be changed!

We all sat down for tea... Myriad flies buzzed around us.

Discussion turned to the broken clutch... ...more attention there... more fluid... more bleeding of air in the lines.

And then we were off again. Triumphant, we cruised into the yard beside Hussein's house. Zeinab made hummus, fuul, olives, tomatoes, bread, potatoes for breakfast... more tea.

Taif and Hussein

We sang more songs. We called another driver we had met in Aqaba using the cellphone... (how had the Bedouin survived without cellphones for all those centuries...?) He appeared and we kissed and embraced our Bedouin friends, who never did ask for money. I insisted on giving Jafar and Hussein each a few dollars.

"No," they said... "You are our friends."

"But it is just a gift." I insisted.

Hussein and Zeinab

Jafar Has to Confess Something

We departed for Wadi Musa and Petra. There we became tourists again.

Kristina on a Camel

We walked for six hours through the ancient town of Petra, carved two thousand years ago out of the solid living red and purple sandstone cliffs in the bottoms of myriad labyrinthine canyons... ...incredible... ...but somehow I still wouldn't have traded even one second of looking into Hussein's smiling eyes while he was singing me another song for this experience in the ancient ruins. But I was lucky. I could have both.

Carved Nabatean City of Petra

We rode the mini-buses back to Aqaba through the town of Ma'an. Army tanks were stationed here and there in Ma'an because of recent trouble... several deaths from fighting with the army. According to the Jordanian Times, some of the folks in Ma'an were revolting because they were angry about the Jordanian government's unwillingness to take a stand against the USA regarding upcoming violence against Iraq. But others claimed that it was just a local problem resulting from some 'bad people...'

Arriving back in Aqaba we were immediately spotted and greeted by Jafar. After we got settled in our hotel, we went to his house in the Bedouin suburbs and ate dinner which he had cooked. He had invited several neighbors over to listen to us play oud and sing some of our Arabic repertoire.

Jafar

He offered us his house to move into but we preferred the privacy of the hotel. He wrote us a poem and gave us a small teapot. We turned down his other offered gift of a piece of local feathery white coral. "How could we carry it in our backpacks all the way back home without breaking it?"

Everyone focused on our music as we played and our performance quality climbed thanks to the appreciation and focus. Of course one of the guests also played oud very well. He played a few songs.

Later that night, driving back to our hotel in the 'camel' which now had a working clutch... he told us something...

"You know I have to confess something... when we left for the desert and I asked for you to pay for the cost of the gas only... I put more gas in the tank than I really needed to. I put in 20 JD and all we really needed was maybe 15. I was thinking to siphon off the extra five liters and make 5 JD. I tell you this because I feel badly that, although I told you that you were family and that we would go to the desert without your having to pay anything except expenses, I was still secretly trying to make a little money from you... now I have told you this truth and I feel better."

Again walking down the marketplace streets of Aqaba people remembered us and invited us to sit and play oud and sing in their restaurant. We were now famous on the streets.

> *We played in the market in Aqaba and drew quite a crowd. I suppose tomorrow we will return there as it is quite a bit warmer and hence much more conducive to playing music in the streets than it would be back at higher altitude in Amman.*
>
> *Still waiting for our Iraq visa...*

We were working very hard to exercise our contacts and connections and speed our permission to gain entrance into Iraq. I was able to get a call through into Baghdad to one of the main friends there, only to learn that our visa applications were still being held up. We decided to make a quick trip into Palestine.

Ramallah, Palestine

At the bridge over the river Jordan, at the border into the West Bank which is controlled by Israel, we met a Palestinian family waiting for admission to the next bus. We sang a few bars of familiar popular songs. They said, upon seeing the little bag of Lays potato chips I was holding for my pre-breakfast snack: "Now we are very careful not to buy anything from America... *nothing nothing nothing* American. See our two-year-old boy? He's only two and he already says he expects to die at the hands of Israeli soldiers in Jerusalem... look at what is becoming of our children!" Then we sang some more Arabic songs. When in doubt, sing. It works every time. Big smiles broke out.

We crossed the bridge in one bus... we waited for another passport check... we rode in an expensive taxi over tiny back roads away from Jericho, which was currently closed by the Israeli soldiers, through a couple of checkpoints to the outskirts of Ramallah. The taxis were not allowed to go into Ramallah... we walked through a labyrinth of concrete barriers past Israeli bunkers and past coils of razor wire. The Israeli soldiers asked us what we wanted to do there.

"Just tourists... we are musicians..." we told them. They looked at us coldly, knowing that we were going to visit with Palestinians in Ramallah, home of Yasser Arafat.

We walked into the city... a long way... we eventually took another taxi to the city center. It was 4 or 5 PM and we were ready for breakfast. We entered a place that advertised 'Mexican Food.' The 'tacos' tasted distinctly Middle Eastern... but were still tasty. We inquired and found a hotel.

We entered the hotel and bargained with the manager... we sang a few phrases of Abd 'al Halim... big smiles.

Following our noses and various pieces of advice on the street, we entered Mataam Ziryab, a coffee shop, art gallery and restaurant, with oud in hand. The Palestinian owner was sitting down with his wife to celebrate their fourteenth wedding anniversary. He was a successful international artist... the walls were covered with his latest work: paintings created with fire burned into wooden plaques.

I asked him if there was going to be music in his coffee house that night?

He looked at my oud and said, "Yes! You!"

We brought out the oud and sang four or five songs. A group of five or six young women encouraged us: they sang along and asked for more songs... the waiters listened in the background. For a couple of hours we got to know the owners.

Mataam Ziryab - Ramallah

The wife, whose name was Raja, told us of the latest curfews and closings. Only a month previously the town had been cut off from electricity and phone lines. And a couple of weeks ago Israeli soldiers had surrounded her house because they thought a plastic toy her ten-year-old son was playing with might be a gun. They had been watching him play through binoculars from the settlement above their house. They threatened to destroy the house with bulldozers if the toy was not found. Finally the boy, shaking and sobbing, was able to lead the soldiers to some alley where he had thrown the toy away.

"If you ever buy even a toy gun, we will kill you and your family!" he was told. He was still shaking from this experience and having nightmares.

Our new artist friend, Tayseer Barakat, the owner of Mataam Ziryab, told us that just the day before he had met with Jane Fonda, who had recently returned to the West Bank in some expression of solidarity with Palestinian people. "It was an artist to artist meeting," he explained.

Soon he would have a large exhibit in a gallery in Texas. He gave us three prints of some of his earlier works and talked about the dream states he enters in order to create. I read his poetry about the exodus of Arabs from Grenada, Spain, back in 1492. He had painted a series of watercolors on the same theme. His work is a portal into the dream-scapes of history.

Me, Raja, Tayseer in Mataam Ziryab

"And for this restaurant," he explained... "I use all kinds of scraps and recycled materials to decorate the interior."

"And I made the light fixtures from old paper," added his wife.

"We exhibit the artwork of many different people here and we want people to be able to sit and be comfortable... drink a coffee... and be surrounded by the art... it's more lively than walking through a museum or gallery."

They were raising their three children there in Ramallah in spite of the difficulties. I wondered how he maintained his artistic focus in the face of the heavy distraction of being under multiple degrees of siege.

We returned to the hotel at midnight to find a group of Palestinian men sitting downstairs in the lobby. They asked me to bring out the oud. Soon we were busy with song again. It was late at night. It was quiet except for our singing. We focused on the music and it got really good again. We sang and laughed and smiled. They helped us to better understand the meanings of the Arabic lyrics we were singing.

Hotel Clerks and Friends in Ramallah

Sometime after 1:00 AM we went upstairs to bed.

Rising early at 9:00 AM, we left the hotel and took a cab to see the remainder of the government buildings in which Yasser Arafat was being held captive. He was supposedly free to leave Palestine to negotiate on the Palestinians' behalf in other parts of the world if he wanted to. But the Israelis had threatened to not let him ever return if he did leave. Only the central building of his government compound was still intact. It was surrounded by several city blocks of the remaining rubble and twisted metal of what had once been government offices. Smashed automobiles which had been pulverized under the treads of the Israeli tanks lined the edges of the streets.

Yaser Arafat's Government Offices

We took a taxi back to the checkpoint at the entrance to Ramallah; our packs and oud case were opened and searched by the Israelis. The two Palestinians in line in front of us were denied passage for some reason and turned back. We rode in a large 'service taxi' back toward Jericho - named 'Ariha' in Arabic - and were held up behind a truck hauling a huge Israeli military tank.

Above us on various hilltops we could see what looked like Israeli settlements. We asked the taxi driver... "Kibbutzes" he replied. Confusion about the best current routes around the checkpoints was constant. We were guided and misguided during expensive taxi rides and then a series of bus rides back to the bridge to Jordan. The Israeli control made it impossible to just take one taxi or one bus. We paid a large exit fee at the border and breathed freely again once we were finally back on the Jordanian side. Now we had new friends in Ramallah. And we had invitations, of course, to return and spend more time... and play more music.

> *Last night we spent in Ramallah in the West Bank of Palestine.*
> *I lay awake far into the night. There is a heavy cloud of oppression and fear: Palestinians afraid of Israeli soldiers; Israeli soldiers afraid of Palestinians. Beyond the cloud I could feel the presence of millions around the world who are focusing on this area and praying for peace. It seemed that what I was feeling*

> was that the prayers were holding this land together and keeping it from erupting in total mayhem.
>
> I know our prayers are very powerful. I had planned on asking you to join me at a specific time when I was in Baghdad to pray for peace. The Baghdad trip will have to be postponed. The visa process has taken too long and now we must return to the U.S.

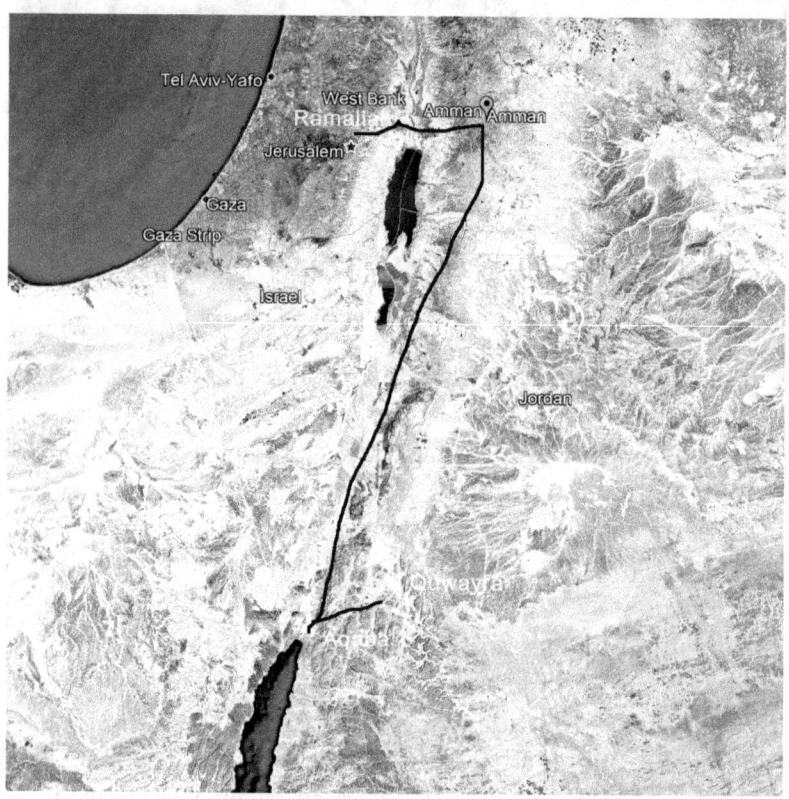

2002 - Amman, Aqaba, Al Quwayra, Petra, Ramallah

Back in Amman it was cold and raining. But we could come and go as we pleased... that was a nice freedom. I wondered if those large buses filled with Palestinians which we had passed near the bridge were still waiting...? or what percentage of those people had been turned back for some reason...? Time and time again we were told, "Yes, I have family on the other side of the border, but now it is very difficult for us to get in or out."

> *We just had an interview with a Saudi news reporter. It is funny how these things work. Cameron woke up this morning thinking we should contact the local Jordan Times. We had coffee and walked over to this Internet cafe where we have lately spent a lot of time. A news reporter happened to be there and the owner, whom we knew, introduced us to her. She works for the Saudi paper OKAZ. She interviewed and photographed us.*

Our time was up and we went to the airport to fly back to the USA.

Colorado Friends Want to Know

Back in Colorado we told about a dozen friends that we would give a little talk and slide show about our trip. About sixty people showed up and we realized that there was more interest in first-hand information about the Arab world than we had thought.

We drove to southern California in time to see our friend Nabil Azzam's new 'Multi-Ethnic Star Orchestra' perform.

MESTO Performing in Los Angeles

The concert was part of a huge Palestinian effort to celebrate their own identity here in the USA.

Kristina and Nabil

We were still focused on the idea of giving a concert in Baghdad so we headed back to Colorado and bought tickets to fly back to the Middle East. The drumbeats of war... the media mythologies being created to justify a 'pre-emptive strike' were making us feel a sense of urgency. Could the huge anti-war demonstrations occurring all over Europe and America actually halt this upcoming war? Could we be a significant part of that?

We felt called to represent an America that was rarely portrayed on TV screens. We wanted to continue to cross the bridges of cultural understanding by creating friendships and connecting with the people of these Arabic-speaking countries through the power of their beautiful music.

We were members of a gigantic global voice. We the People needed to insist upon our rights to trade and build and worship and sing and dance on this beautiful green jewel of a planet... we had always felt our psychic connection... and now our Internet connections were giving us voices and votes which could be counted and we were coming from every corner of the earth and we were just saying *"no"* to the old hierarchical governments and their military solutions:

> *Leave us alone! We have lives to lead! Get out of our way! We are the people and we are the singers and the lovers and the cultivators! We will dismantle the treaties of inequality. We will learn each others' languages and songs and a global democracy*

> *can now emerge. Those who try to keep their power by instilling fear between peoples can no longer succeed. We have sung and danced together in hundreds of tribal manifestations... oh the songs... oh the dances... oh the courtships... we are done with rule by fear!*

Back Across the Ocean To Egypt

We arrived at the airport in Cairo at 3:00 AM Tuesday, March 25, 2003. Yes, I was worried... what would I say to the twenty-five-million folks in Cairo...? I told the taxi dispatcher in the airport that I was feeling very badly because my American government had chosen the path of war and had begun the invasion of Iraq a few days ago with bombing on March 20, 2003.

He looked into my eyes: "Is that the way you really feel?" he asked.

"Yes," I responded.

"Then that is what shall determine your destiny, my friend!" he told me with a smile. Soon we were in the cab, slowly meandering toward downtown, bathing in the warm welcome from the driver and his friend. We paused in front of the hotel so that we could take turns playing my nay and sing another song together.

These people know that people are people. Yes, our government was angering a huge piece of the world. But that was the government and we were the people!

> *Come on people! Let's remember to be our lusty beautiful selves... someday the emerging global democracy will gently make obsolete the current fear-based government protection rackets... we only have so many precious lives to lead... we cannot afford this waste...*
>
> *So, yes, we have been bathing in the warm welcome extended universally here in Egypt... it is so easy if you just welcome yourself... then the whole world welcomes you...*

Climbing up into the hotel we found eight or nine men and a woman with her new-born girl gathered to enjoy each others' company and ours... singing... talking. It was 4 o'clock in the morning.

The next day we spent a full twelve hours on the streets... bazaars... the Nile... the music shops... exotic essential oils and aphrodisiacs... the restaurant with qanun and riq players... customers singing along...

> *I am the first of an army of American musicians who have already lost... We surrendered our hearts to Um Kolthoum, the most famous Egyptian Goddess-singer, and we now wander through the ecstatic alleyways of Cairo...Wherever we go we want to be free to 'try that too'... Eternal children of the world, we become the singers when we hear the song... ...we become the acrobats when we see the dancing... ...we become the vendors when we see the selling... ...we become the cooks when we taste the cooking...We are Americans and we are Chinese...We are Arabs and we are Turks... ...and we won't be ruled by a bunch of jerks...*

So it only took half an hour for my apprehension about what to say about being an American in Egypt to dissolve into this warm bath of hospitality.

The next day we made a dozen new friends on the streets and in the marketplace... all that was necessary was to say *'yes!'* We wove our way through endless mazes of people, carts and cars... a human soup as thick as the richest stew... Confidence in the human heart was reflected on all sides through this, one of the densest and tightest expressions of human life on planet earth: Cairo!

Ancient wisdom gets organized up in Asia and India... but the raw materials are found in Egypt!

Late that night we played ouds in the shops on Mohammad Ali street. We told the Egyptians that hundreds of our American friends were contributing to support our ability to be here. We told them that dozens of our Arab-speaking friends back in America had been helping us dive more deeply into the songs and language and meanings of the beautiful ancient cultures of the Arab world.

> *So there is no doubt, you see... There is no hesitation about the opening of all of our hearts... The eyes, as always, speak the truth... There is no fear... We are truly blessed to be here... And yes, every moment the war is hurting our hearts... The woman claps her hands in front of her news-stand on the street corner in time to the music... she is happy about something... The grandmother hobbles through the traffic on bent legs, wincing from the pain in her back, but still a part of this celebration of buying and selling, coming and going, talking and listening and feeling... never stopping... twenty-four-seven...*

We arrived in Cairo very early Tuesday morning. I was a bit concerned before we arrived about anti-American sentiment but this, as I might have suspected, was totally unfounded. These people, like all Arabs in this part of the world, are so welcoming it is embarrassing by American standards.

Cameron and I were talking about why some Americans feel threatened, especially single women, when they travel here. I suppose a single American woman may feel threatened when a man offers to show her the way to her hotel, walks a few blocks with her, gets in the elevator with her and takes her to the lobby on the 4th floor. But this is just standard courtesy, as happened to us the other night. Egyptians are just a little too friendly by American standards. It takes some getting used to, but relaxing into this scene is really quite a beautiful experience.

I bought a dress in a little shop in the Egyptian market the other night. This is a complex of narrow alleyways with no cars, lots of dust, scrawny cats, tons of people and merchandise all made within a few blocks.

Later we asked how to get to Mohammed Ali Street where the ouds are made. The shop keeper told us it was very far but that he would take us the 'short cut' and off we went. Along the way his 'cousin' saw us and joined us. As we walked the shop keeper told me that here in these dark alleys, "it is always safe at one or two or three in the morning... it is safe, always safe."

Twenty minutes later we emerged out of the maze of alley ways and arrived at the music shop where we all sat down and were served cokes and tea. The rest of the evening we chatted. Cameron tried different ouds and I sang.

I could tell by their eyes that they thought I sung very well. I know my Arabic pronunciation isn't perfect but the music shopkeeper says I sing from my heart. I am pleased. The war of course is on everyone minds. But again, here as in Jordan, they say "American people good, you are welcome here. People everywhere good, governments bad."

Bush is very unpopular here. We have talked of the war with everyone we have met, and that is quite a few: maybe fifty people... remember... Arabs are very friendly. Mohammed the accountant who lives part time in Frankfurt says he cries at night thinking of the Iraqi children. He has tears in his eyes as he

> speaks to us.
>
> The Egyptians do not understand the American invasion. No one here feels that the US is liberating Iraq. We do however have an Iraqi friend in the US who feels the war is justified but I've yet to meet anyone here or in Jordan who feels that way.

CAIRO... Those of you who know these parts of the world share already in knowledge of these things we report... But others, who have never traveled here, or who were not ready to truly join this vast human celebration, might want to receive this news: forget fear and join us here where the ancient wisdom speaks so clearly.

A rich person is not she or he who has the most, but rather she or he who needs the least...

The next day we held our own demonstration in Tahrir Square, in the heart of downtown Cairo. It was the same square which had been used by close to a hundred-thousand Egyptians a few days earlier to protest the war being waged by America, 'the last surviving super-power.'

Cairo Anti-War Demonstration

A decade later the demonstrations which expressed the hopes of the Egyptian youth which became known as 'The Arab Spring' would happen in this same location.

We did not have an anti-war demonstration. We held a pro-peace and music demonstration.

Me in Center Playing Oud

We didn't have to explain it, really. The Egyptians immediately were thrilled to hear us singing their music and we were surrounded by dozens of smiling, dancing, clapping young men and women.

Egyptian Girls in Central Cairo Square

We sang for an hour or more. Kristina danced with young Egyptian women… and men.

Kristina and Crowd

A three-year-old boy danced exuberantly in the center of the crowd. The old woman with missing teeth pleaded for another verse from Abd El Halim.

At this very same moment, not too far to the east, many people were dying in Baghdad because of the incomprehensibly strange dream-world inhabited by certain 'heads of state.' Really, the Egyptians, polite and accommodating as always, seemed as nonplussed, confused, shocked and, yes angry, as you might expect them to be. I think they live more in the moment, most of them, than Westerners do. You don't see them holding the same tensions in their bodies.

For the last few days we had been learning a musical prayer in Arabic. We sang this in reverence to the tragedy unfolding.... *'T'ala al batru alaina...'*

It wasn't clear that reverence was more appropriate than boisterous celebration. The crowds traded songs with us... many songs we did and didn't know... rhythmic chants and beautiful love songs. A journalist from an Arab-language newspaper approached and asked our opinions... translation happened haltingly... these were not the rich people, well-trained in languages... these were the people who call downtown Cairo, this 'village' of twenty-five-million people, 'home.'

We were gradually, now that I had an oud which I had purchased from my friend Nasser on Mohammad Ali Street, becoming known in our little downtown neighborhood.

Thanks to our precious musical friendship connections, we spent several hours playing with teachers at the Cairo College of Music across the Nile on the island of Zamalek. These musical professors said that it is always the same: the people and the governments belong to different species. We, the people, watch helplessly while the governments wreak destruction... ...we chose to play another classical piece of music... we had qanun, nay, oud and, of course, our voices. But really, thinking about the ongoing bombing in Iraq, I felt sick inside.

That night the men on our street, yes from our little downtown Cairo neighborhood, who now know us from our little hotel, invited us to sing and play in the tavern on the corner. Our songs were highly appreciated and we were rewarded with many more bottles of beer than we could possibly drink.

Playing Music in Cairo Bar

"America is ten thousand miles away..." mused one man, showing some anger, "why are they coming all the way over here to kill our women and babies? No one in Iraq has attacked them...!" He told Kristina that she must write a letter to Laura Bush about this, assuming, I suppose, that Laura Bush could drive some sense into her husband's head.

One of the Egyptian men whom we met in our corner tavern had a farm back in Kentucky. He had lived in America for twenty-five years, raising horses and frankincense. After 9/11 his barn was set on fire. Broken-hearted he had returned to Egypt. Would he ever go back to the US? ...he shook his head... no...

I was holding hope that the war might end quickly so that fewer human souls would be maimed and killed. But news on the Internet about the numbers of deaths was making me lose another level of hope. I guess we all had been hoping that somehow those so-called 'smart bombs' could miss all human targets... but it was simply not the case.

What I could say for sure was that in downtown Cairo, in Tahrir Square, Cameron and Kristina had been welcomed and told that we could consider Egypt to be our home any time we should choose. Really, that was one of the very touching things we were told.

Meanwhile dozens of supportive emails were coming to us every day.

> *Cameron and Kristina, the only words that come to mind are 'thank you'. Thank you for going, thank you for sending back your wonderful chronicles. I find it very inspiring. Thank you! I look forward to every next installment.*

For so long these tragedies had seemed like something awful that could only *possibly* happen and we had chosen to hold the hope that somehow they could be avoided. Well... now the unthinkable horrors of war were a living, breathing reality staring us in the face. What were we to make of the decision-makers who led so many innocent people into this place of needless war? We felt we really must make our feelings known. The writing was on the wall.

> *I'm sorry, but America, as the last surviving superpower, had every opportunity to set an example of leadership with something more holy than 'might making right' and the deployment of, yes, America's own weapons of mass destruction...*
>
> *Who is responsible for losing and wasting that opportunity? Empires who choose to rule with the iron fist... their days become numbered... please, Americans, wake up...*
>
> *The flesh on one body is not worth more nor less than the flesh on another...*

We were in a whirlwind of a million changing thoughts and emotions. The Arab world was shocked that Iraqis would actually surrender so easily to the Americans. We were thanking God that the attack was winding down and that the lives of people in the war zone would no longer be in such danger. But according to the news reports the burning and the looting in Baghdad was continuing.

Our Egyptian taxi driver expressed: "No one knows what will happen or who will do what. But the people remain the people. For thousands of years we have been simply trying to live in peace while the leaders have remained unpredictable. No one can stop these wars. The people, like you and me... We are helpless."

Magnetized Toward the North: Back to Jordan

We traveled north up to Jordan. Soon we were back in Aqaba at the northern end of the Red Sea.

Everyone had been wrong and everyone had been right. No matter which 'opinion' we had been holding, pages were turning and the emotionally charged logics of only a week before were becoming obsolete. A gardener in Aqaba said to Kristina, "Of course I was against the war, but now I see pictures on TV showing happy Iraqis, so now I am happy for them and hope only for the best!"

And when we arrived into Jordan our taxi driver and another Jordanian passenger didn't even try to analyze the world with these two American mystery characters named Cameron and Kristina. Once they discovered that we could sing and play Arabic music, they just wanted to sing, which we did, as usual. With the bond of musical friendship established it felt, as always, like we were all part of the same family.

For the forces toward healing the wounds in Iraq to proceed as rapidly as possible, hatchets must be buried and new alliances formed. However mistrustful of the American government's motives for attacking Saddam Hussein many of us may have felt, we must try and support cooperation and growth. The old concepts of 'good and evil' could, hopefully, dissolve. With our united efforts and prayers we could move forward.

Our Iraqi friends had been themselves divided about the merits of America's attack on Saddam Hussein's rule: some seeing only evil in America's war and others hoping for a quick American victory over Saddam's regime so that things might begin again with a fresh start. As I said, the page had now been turned. There had been a war and people had been wounded and killed. It looked like it was about over. Another Palestinian friend in Jordan expressed: "Six months from now things will be much better for the Iraqi people... We will hope for this."

That evening we spent two hours down beside the waters of the Red Sea in the Gulf of Aqaba playing with thirty or forty dancing Arab and Bedouin young people.

Music at Night in Aqaba Park

It had all begun when a tea vendor had noticed my oud and invited us to play.

Me Playing Nay

Before long we were taking turns playing my oud. There was much singing and dancing.

Kristina Dancing

I played the nay along with many local Bedouin melodies. Kristina and I were both pulled to our feet to dance.

Warm Feelings from the Music

We sang a few popular songs and were treated to lots of free tea.

Whenever someone asked me where we were from and I replied "America," I thought I detected a slight hesitation or look of astonishment before the hospitable "you are welcome... welcome to Jordan...!" Or maybe it had just been my own feeling of sadness that had made me have this perception... I don't know... anyway, we didn't discuss the Iraqi-American situation.

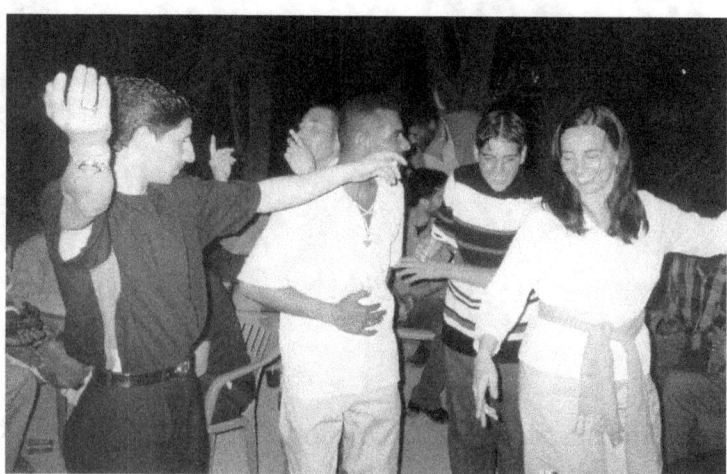

More Dancing with Kristina

And, of course, our attention was frequently focused on the Palestinian situation. Fresh and open-minded work was desperately needed to bring a better situation for the millions of living souls involved.

The next day we would travel north to Amman and, hopefully, visit with Iraqi friends there. Complex allegiances surrounded us all. When we visit our Arab friends, we will offend some Americans and Persians and Jews. When we visit our Turkish friends, we will offend some Greeks, Armenians and Kurds. The list goes on and on. Trying to live in this complex soup provides an opportunity for the most sacred ways of being to float to the top.

> *Here are the latest results:*
>
> *1) We should not indulge in humor at the expense of others. This creates a way of thinking which eventually becomes an obstacle.*
>
> *2) We should not create or play violent video or war games, nor watch violent 'entertainment.' This contributes toward making this violence seem acceptable.*
>
> *3) We should never introduce violence of any sort into lovemaking. The sacred connection between man and woman needs the fragrance and stillness of a peaceful garden in order to manifest and deepen.*
>
> *4) We should never believe in nor be convinced by the fears of others. Your own trust in love and friendship is the only reality.*
>
> *5) Trust the natural attractions that exist between us. Ignore efforts of those who would have you feel guilty for accepting loving gestures from others.*
>
> *6) Learn at least five languages in this lifetime. You will gain as many souls. We live in a multi-colored garden and must learn to see beauty through many ways of thinking and feeling and being.*
>
> *7) Do not believe in 'good' and 'evil.' We all contain each other. Through an open heart we learn to include and understand everyone.*
>
> *8) Do not pass up good opportunities. Whatever effort is required will be transformed into ecstasy.*
>
> *9) Do not give up.*
>
> *10) You write this one... send it to me...*

We arrived in Amman, the capitol of Jordan, by bus from Aqaba, a five-hour ride. Swarms of taxi drivers pounced onto us as we extracted our luggage from the bus. Kristina, offended at being treated like a newcomer, fended them off and led us out onto the street.

"I feel like walking, don't you?" she inquired. After all, we had just been here for several weeks not so long ago back in November and December. It felt like we needed to reclaim our familiarity with the city by walking through it.

"Sure, let's walk!"

We eventually found a familiar restaurant. This seemed like the right place to pick up the thread from our previous trip. Just before we had departed we had shared in the owner's eager anticipation: the parakeets in his cage had produced an egg and he had been hoping for a baby bird.

We entered and asked him about his birds: "They had an egg which hatched, but the poor little fellow died. He didn't make it. But now they are busy making more eggs... this time... insha-Allah..."

We dined on delicious food and made our way to the Al Saraya Hotel where we were greeted affectionately by Fayaz, the owner. Many of the international motley brigade of Human Shields had been using this hotel. During the next few days we sat in on their story-swapping sessions as they were just coming out of Iraq in considerable numbers. We began becoming acquainted with ten or fifteen of them. And of course there were around ten local Jordanian Arabs eager for us to sing and play, so we brought the oud and sang for a couple of hours with them downstairs.

> *We arrived back in Amman last night, and are staying at our favorite hotel. The owner gave us both a big hug when he saw us. They remember our music and are very welcoming. Late at night after we arrived Cameron got out his oud and we had another party. All the hotel staff was there dancing and singing along. Cameron accompanied a couple of men who sang beautiful vocal improvisations. One of the staff members passed out tissues to dry the eyes. He was making a joke about how tear-jerking the improvisations were. We laughed and cried at the same time. Someone ordered a mass quantity of food and we all ate together at about 2:00 AM.*

It is a confusing time, Iraq is in a state of chaos. We are close here to Iraq. We hear conflicting reports of what is happening. What is the truth? It seems that there are many truths. This hotel is where many of the human shields who have gone into Iraq are staying. Some people are on their way to go into Iraq tomorrow; some have just arrived back here. One group who went into Iraq a couple of days ago told us the devastation is immense. It is difficult to travel into Iraq now: the cost now for the nine hour ride to Baghdad is around $2,000 US dollars. There are no gas stations open along the way so fuel must be carried. And it is still a dangerous journey.

The one thousand journalists who had been waiting in Amman during the bombing have all gone to Baghdad. One young U.K. lad luckily is catching a free ride with a journalist tomorrow. People who have been in Iraq are passing out Iraqi Dinars, now worthless.

The young British man who was shot and killed by Israelis in Gaza recently was here staying at this hotel a couple of weeks ago. The hotel owner tells us "Tom was a good guy. We played chess. Tom was trying his best to make the world a better place." Many of these people have very strong ideas. They felt their presence in Baghdad would deter American bombs, but I think they were lucky to make it through.

Several Arabs we have spoken with have expressed concern that America would not stop with Iraq... that soon they would attack Syria or Iran or somewhere else. They do not trust Bush and call him a terrorist. And they see the U.S. government as wanting to control the whole world.

Now of course the thing to do is to get as much humanitarian aid as possible into the Iraqi cities. The people need food and water and electricity. So no matter if you were for or against the war now we must work together to bring life back to normal for the Iraqi people. After all this destruction, people must receive the help they need. I hope that convoys of food and medicines are on their way from America into Iraq now. Our Iraqi friends here are concerned for their family and friends who are still in Baghdad. They do not know yet if they are safe. There are no telephones. There is no way yet to know.

The next day, still settling into Amman and the hotel, we did a few errands, called our Iraqi friends, talked further with various Human Shields and yielded to local pressure to once again spend the evening playing Arabic music in the hotel.

My birthday came on the following day. Kristina bought a piece of cake for me in a little restaurant to finalize our roasted-chicken-and-rice meal. We visited the Monzer Hotel across town where members of Voices in the Wilderness congregated before and after traveling in and out of war zones to witness and document events from a peace-keeping point of view. That is where I had met Kathy Kelly, founder of that organization, last December and she had attempted to help us get into Iraq a few months earlier. She and others in her organization organize vigils and demonstrations and sometimes end up doing time in American jails. Kathy Kelly had been staying in a hotel in Baghdad for the last couple of months so that she could witness and report.

Dead Bodies of Many Civilians

We met Nassim, who helps run the Monzer Hotel, and he offered to set up a car with a driver to deliver us to Baghdad, five-hundred miles away, for a reasonable price: only a quarter the cost of what the high-end journalists had been paying. Our cost would be $200 each... $400 for the two of us... one way.

Our imaginations were sparked. We had not expected to make it into Baghdad with the war going on, but now it seemed that the fighting and bombing were tapering off.

We told Nassim we would be thinking about that possibility.

We headed back to our own hotel to meet one of the would-be Human Shields who had arrived too late to make it into Baghdad before the bombing began: Stefa. She was a Canadian woman who had never been an activist in her life but who had felt driven by the apparent violations of international and human decency by her dear neighbor to the south, the USA, to impulsively purchase a ticket to Amman so she could 'chain herself to a power plant' in Iraq and try and save something. Failing in her plan to get into Iraq, she had stayed at Fayaz' hotel in Amman and worked on behalf of the Human Shields who were in and around Baghdad. Stefa had invited us to go with her and a Palestinian-Jordanian friend to hear a house concert of a young female singer accompanied by an oud player who specialized in Lebanese styles.

Fawaz picked us up from the hotel. We were joined by Ibair, a woman who was a top fashion designer in Jordan. We were in the company of the upper class now, it seemed. Fawaz had been detained, or kidnapped, and held incommunicado by the Jordanian government during the first few weeks of the war and had just been released. I don't know why exactly. He had been active in trying to have the sanctions against Iraq lifted for many years. He and Ibair returned to our hotel after the concert and sat in on a major information-sharing session from the Human Shields. This story-swapping session was punctuated with a lot of *'well, what should we do now?'* questions.

We listened to the story told by David Lynn, an American Human Shield who, after having been a soldier in Viet Nam, eventually turned his energies to anti-war activities. He had been in northern Baghdad which was one of the last portions of the city to be taken by the US Marines. Deciding at some point to go out on his own and see what was happening, he had walked some fifteen-kilometers through the northern parts of the city.

What he saw were the dead bodies of many civilians who had been shot while walking or driving. Afraid to even leave the shelter of their houses, their families were just now emerging to bury these bodies which had lain out in the sun for several days. David witnessed these burials now taking place, in spite of being shot at several times himself. What is obvious is that there is no record-keeping of these deaths being carried out by any government. We had thought perhaps to play music, but on this night the discussions were paramount.

The next morning we got up at 8:00 AM and sped over to the Ministry of the Interior, as Nassim had suggested, to try and gain papers from the Jordanian government so that we could be allowed into Iraq. After the fall of Saddam's Iraqi government, the Jordanians had instituted a policy of allowing only journalists and military people to pass the border.

We were, in some sense, journalists, but we didn't have official press cards. The Ministry of the Interior referred us to the Press room at the Inter-Continental Hotel. Instead of presenting press cards, we presented an introduction written in Arabic, which has been gradually evolving with the help of several Arabic friends. It described us as 'musical ambassadors.' The Jordanian officials read this, looked at us inquisitively... we sang them a part of a song in Arabic. They smiled broadly, told us, "Sure you should be able to go wherever you want to go!" and arranged a contact for us at the border so that we would be given permission to pass into Iraq.

We headed back to the hotel to meet Stefa. She had invited us to go with her to meet Aida and her friend Sonia. Aida was a wealthy Jordanian peace activist. She picked us up in her friend Sonia's car and we headed for a bookshop, Books@Café, which contained a little restaurant. Once we were all seated she brought out an Arabic newspaper which contained the news that the Human Shields organization had been infiltrated by the CIA who, according to this article, had worked inside Iraq to pay off Saddam's Republican Guard so they wouldn't put up a fight against the US military. The point which Aida was trying to make to Stefa was that being associated with the Human Shields was no longer an honorable thing in the Arab street. It was now a suspect thing. I congratulated myself privately on my decision to never associate myself with any organization or government.

> *Last night we were invited to a concert. The daughter of a local politician sang songs of Fairouz and some older traditional songs. She sang very well. The people who attended were clearly from the upper class. None of the women attending this concert wore head scarves. That seems to be more common with women in the lower classes who tend to be less likely to emulate Western fashions.*
>
> *I met a women who was a fashion designer in Jordan and who now is a broker handling franchises for a large American restaurant chain. She is a single mom and had lived in California for ten years so her English was very good. She talked about how Americans were fooled by the media. She speaks on the phone frequently with her friends in America and compares what they are getting on the news to what she hears from the Arabic TV and news media. Very different stories she says.*

Preparing for the Trip to Baghdad

We stopped by the Monzer Hotel and told Nassim that the plan to enter Iraq was a go: we had successfully arranged to be permitted by the Jordanians to cross the border.

Evening came and we took a taxi across town to meet with our Iraqi refugee friends Ali, Suad, Haydar and Ahmed. Ali could only afford to pay enough phone bill to allow computer communication; he couldn't call out on his phone. But we could call him.

We brought a box of chocolates for Suad. Ali insisted that we all read the ingredients on the box to make certain that there was no brandy and no pork fat in the chocolate.

Later, Kristina presented Suad with a gold bracelet, a gift we had carefully calculated to be a way for us to get some form of money to them to help just in case of emergency. Ali immediately announced that they would not accept the present.

"It's not for you!" I told him, laughing at his stubbornness. "It is for Suad!" That seemed to settle the issue and Kristina's gift to Suad became a reality.

They returned a gift to us: a series of psychic readings from Suad which addressed all our plans and ambitions as well as the outlook for all our relatives. Suad had inherited a collection of seashells and other objects, like old door-keys and other relics from her family's past, from her mother. And she had inherited the psychic gift, we were told, also from her mother. The next two hours were spent with Suad tossing this double-handful of relics into the air over a cloth and then reading their positions as they landed.

Ali translated from the Arabic to the English, a skill he had mastered to a high degree. Several times they looked into our plan to enter Baghdad by interpreting these shells and could see only failure ahead for us. Even death could come to us if we were to try and make that trip. But the outlooks for all of our children seemed quite good and information about their past and current struggles seemed quite accurate.

Leaving to return to our hotel at 2:30 AM, we found a long walk awaiting us in the cold. There were no taxis in sight in that part of town. Eventually we reached a larger avenue and found a cab for the rest of the way. I lay awake until 7:00 AM digesting the various aspects of Suad's reading. Parts of it had seemed to come clearly and other parts, including the dire predictions about our trip to Baghdad, seemed to come from their background and angle on reality.

After one hour of semi-sleep, I arose from bed to begin a busy day preparing for the trip to Baghdad: we had to carry our own water and food and be prepared to pay for things with small bills of US Dollars. I withdrew the maximum allowed daily amount from each of my two debit cards. That gave me $1000 in cash. That seemed like a lot of money compared to my usual habit which was to withdraw $200 every four days or so. But at the same time I realized we would go in and out of Iraq on a very tight budget. If our ride out ended up costing the same $400 as our ride in then that would leave us only $200 for food and lodging. We wouldn't be able to stay for very long. Our return flight to Egypt would also be coming up in only a few more days.

We spent part of the afternoon with Nassim at the Monzer Hotel discussing all of the arrangements regarding our driver. Only Iraqi drivers would be allowed into Iraq. And these Iraqi drivers and their vehicles were only allowed to enter and park in one place in Amman.

We communicated our arrangement made at the press room in the Inter-Continental Hotel. We were to arrive to Al Ruwasheid, the last small town before the Iraqi border, and find a certain man named Mahjed at the Shat el Arab Hotel, provide extra passport photos, and there we would be given some kind of visa permitting us entry to Iraq. We were able to contact Mahjed on Nassim's cell phone, and he assured us that he already knew who we were from Maha at the Inter-Continental Hotel and that there would be no problem. The only thing was that he might not be there, in which case we were to find his brother, Ali. Nassim introduced us to our driver's brother, a large man who assured us that everything would be fine.

We returned to the streets to finish the errands of preparation for the trip. We needed white cloth so that we would be able to wave white flags of truce toward the US Marines if necessary. And we needed orange tape to put large letters on the car saying 'PRESS' and 'TV' so that we would not be suspected of being some kind of smugglers or infiltrators. We told Nassim to have the Iraqi driver take care of that part as we didn't have a ready source for the orange tape.

Nassim had told us to call him at 10:00 PM and find out where to meet our car and driver. He said we would be part of an armed caravan, departing early the following morning from the Iraqi border to travel together under protection of the US Marines through the lawless and bandit-filled three-hundred miles of the western desert of Iraq.

I asked Kristina if she was certain she wanted to make this trip with me. "It seems to be our path," she replied with no hesitation.

All the years I had spent traveling through so many districts of South America finding delightfully friendly folks around every corner in spite of the repeated warnings from wealthy people and rival tribes that 'surely I would be killed if I went there' came together to give me clear confidence now. Armed with my musical instrument and a handful of heartfully memorized Arabic songs, we would sing with the people on the streets of Baghdad, making our American nationality known and trusting in the music and the basic goodness of the common man.

We called Nassim from our hotel at 10:00 PM after scrambling for the rest of the evening with preparations. He told us to hurry and come over to the Monzer Hotel; that he would accompany us to the Iraqi car and driver from there.

By 12:30 AM, we were headed out of Amman toward Iraq with Imad, our expansive, energetic and basically mono-lingual driver. I shifted all of my knowledge of Arabic into the front of my brain and began getting to know him. Basic sentences still took me a long time and a lot of brain strain.

Imad seemed friendly and alert. He took turns initiating basic conversations with me and Kristina: how old are you? He was twenty-nine. He had a wife but no children.

"God's will," he explained, adding that he had been to the doctor but either he or his wife was infertile. He seemed obviously quite sad about this.

After about three hours we arrived to Al Ruwasheid, found the Shat el Arab Hotel, and pounded on the doors to no avail. We found someone with a cellphone and tried the phone numbers. The two brothers had their phones turned off and were sleeping, we supposed. It was 4:00 AM. Determining to wait for another hour or so, we thought to maybe grab a nap in the parked car.

Suddenly a large German nurse appeared outside our car door. She was in the middle of some misunderstanding with her Jordanian drivers. I don't think she was aware that only Iraqi drivers were being allowed to cross into Iraq. She was very upset and hoping that she could ride with us, although she still didn't have her visa. Imad quickly concluded that she was insane: "majnoona!"

There seemed no way to work things out with this big angry nurse, so Imad sped off into the night toward the Iraqi border.

"No, wait!" we told him. "We must find one of the brothers and get our visas!"

Crossing Into Iraq

But Imad had decided to proceed. "We'll miss the armed convoy if we don't go now," he said. Unable to convince him otherwise, we sped the last fifty miles to the border where we entered into a tangled mass of Jordanian officials in various offices and behind various windows. We would not be allowed entry without press cards it seemed.

Signs on the walls proclaimed in both Arabic and English: "The highway in Iraq is exceptionally dangerous. Jordan does not recommend traveling."

We produced our explanation about our musical mission written in Arabic and, when they looked at us quizzically, we sang snatches of Arabic songs. Stunned, delighted and amazed, the on-duty and exhausted-looking Jordanian army officer with the bloodshot red eyes arranged for the stamps in our passports to miraculously appear. It was amazing to watch his inscrutable soldier's mask dissolve to reveal the face of a man who could care for friends and loved ones.

Imad had done a good job, also, of leading us from one official to another, although at one point he had seemed ready to give up. It seemed to cost a little more than we expected. Also... who was pocketing the extra change? Imad? One of these officials? Both? We didn't know. Oh well...

It had taken two hours of 'musical negotiations,' but soon we were speeding across a no-man's-land toward Iraq. We had sung our way across the border. There was obviously no 'armed caravan.' We were on the road alone. Imad had filled a number of large cans with gasoline and added them to our load in the trunk of the car. The price of gas was still the same as it had been for years in Iraq under Saddam: about four cents a gallon thanks to the generous government subsidy.

Imad had carelessly sloshed the liquid onto his clothing. "Gasoline here is cheaper than water! We could be just drinking the stuff!" he explained. We would be smelling gasoline strongly all the way to Baghdad.

Of course we had no way of guessing that in just a few days the new American occupation would suddenly raise the price of gasoline to $2.80 a gallon... and, of course, simultaneously make it illegal for all Iraqi farmers to plant anything but Monsanto seeds!

"Enough with the Jordanians!" exclaimed Imad. "I don't like them!"

We approached a checkpoint manned by US Marines. Imad, the

ultimate horn-honking, aggressive taxi driver, tried to nose his way into the front of two lines of cars waiting to be checked by the Marines. "No, Imad," we told him, "this is not going to work with these guys!"

Soon we were escorted back to the beginning of the lines and made to wait our turn.

"Americans, huh?" the Marine checking our passports muttered. "You guys must be crazy!"

Soon we were speeding down a divided highway made of concrete with metal guard rails between the lanes headed toward Baghdad. Iraq obviously had, at one time, enough money to spend on highways much fancier than anything we had seen in Jordan. But soon we were weaving around bomb craters punched into the concrete and passing the burnt husks of trucks and buses and cars and tanks. Imad winced with pain as we passed each one.

Bombed Highways

"And that bus there," he explained, "was not even Iraqi! It was from Syria!" We stopped and looked more closely. Inside the burnt-out bus the seats appeared covered with blood.

Blood-Filled Bus

We had read about the bombing of a Syrian bus in which several Russian diplomats had died along with ten or so other passengers.

Bombed Bridge

The power of modern American weaponry was amazing. Concrete structures were blown apart.

Remains of Truck

So many vehicles had obviously been randomly targeted and blown up from the air.

We covered two or three hundred desert miles. Off in the barren distances we could occasionally see tall black stone towers rising out of Bedouin villages which were part of another world. Eventually we passed the Euphrates river. Palm trees began to appear as water became part of the landscape. We passed clusters of burnt, overturned or abandoned Iraqi tanks, and more bombed trucks, buses and cars.

Baghdad

"Ali Baba! Ali Baba!" exclaimed Imad. Eventually we realized that the looting which had been occurring in Baghdad extended also out onto the highways. If your car ran out of gas, or otherwise became inoperable and you had to leave it, when you came back you would find all its working parts stripped and gone.

Imad had brought us all five-hundred miles of the way from Amman. He slipped at high speed through the smoke-filled Baghdad intersections. No electricity meant no traffic lights. No government meant no laws. Drivers made up their own rules. Imad made up for the loss of order by leaning on the horn.

Six or eight of the nearby high-rise buildings had flames leaping out of their windows.

Baghdad Buildings Burning

No water meant that there was no way of putting out those fires. Who was torching this city? Why? We now could see exactly why there was no longer any telephone service in or out of Baghdad. The largest transmission towers had been destroyed during the 'shock and awe' campaign by the US military.

> *Baghdad was burning. We drove into the city Friday, April 18th, 2003. Many tall buildings were burning. Flames poured out of the Ministry of Foreign Affairs building which was several stories high. Several other government buildings were also in flames. As we drove we saw looters carrying away their booty. All the more affluent stores had been looted: banks, whatever. The city was in chaos. The air was filled with smoke. As we drove our taxi driver cursed the looters calling them 'Ali Baba,' the famous thief.*
>
> *We turned to go down one street toward a hotel but there was a huge traffic jam due to a demonstration which, we found out later, was thousands of Iraqis protesting the American military presence in Iraq. While the TV audiences back in the US were being told that Iraqis were welcoming the Americans, we could clearly see from the numbers of protesters filling the streets the outrage against the invasion that the vast majority of Iraqis were feeling.*
>
> *Our taxi driver pointed to our hotel. We had chosen it because our friend, Kathy Kelly, had been staying there. Inside, we*

were told there was only one room left. We took it. It would be too crazy to go looking for another room although it was more than we wished to spend: fifty US dollars. The price had been raised as soon as the journalists had shown up. The owner later lowered the price to thirty-five dollars for us after he found out what we were doing in Baghdad.

Next door was the Palestine hotel: the one where, a week previously, journalists had been killed in a blast from a US tank. It was hard to see the damage from the outside. There was only a small hole where the projectile had entered. It had exploded inside.

Our room had no electricity. There was a generator at the hotel, but that was used for lights and satellite TV in the lobby. One light bulb lit each hallway in the seven-story building. In the rooms we were on our own. We used our flashlights in the bathroom as there were no windows for light. Later in the evening we were glad we had brought candles. I was happy there was water.

We ventured out on the street. Cameron brought his oud. We had walked less than half a block when some street vendors pointed to his instrument and asked him to play. So he did.

"Nam, ana a'azif al oud," - Yes, I play the oud, I responded to the question asked by one of a group of men on the sidewalk. I took the oud out of its bag and began to play and sing a 'mawwal' in Iraqi style. A crowd of Arab men gathered around and smiles broke out. Everyone sang along. These people were not shy about using their voices; they sang freely. Twenty feet away was a US tank with alert soldiers with guns at hand but the music made the Iraqi crowd happy. An Iraqi man took a turn playing the oud and then handed it back to me.

Passing the Oud Around on Streets of Baghdad

It was my turn again. *"Lamma anakhu qobail el sobah... - When the camels kneel down to be loaded in the early morning dawn..."* I began... Certain men began to sing along as I progressed into this well-known stylized introduction. This hit the perfect note, it seemed, with the crowd; eyes closed, heads bobbed and shook with appreciation as the musical flow developed.

Playing for Appreciative Iraqis

Halfway through the introduction an Iraqi man lovingly brushed my eyebrows back into place while I kept singing. We reached the beginning of the melody: *"foq' nahel fo-o-o-o-oq' yaba..."* *'above the palm tree the full moon...'* Others joined in the singing. More people gathered. The crowd grew larger. Dancing began to happen. Two street vendors fed us shish-kabobs.

Shishkabob Vendors Feed Us a Bite

> *Everyone wants to be in the pictures I am taking. In Egypt I had passed the camera out to the crowd to take pictures. I had known that even if I had lost sight of it, it would come back, which it did. Here I guarded it a bit closer. After seeing all the looting I was not so sure. Doing these street performances was not easy. Dozens of men crowded closely around us. They asked all kinds of questions:*
> *"Where are you from?"*
> *"America."*
> *"Welcome. We need to see people like you!"*
> *One man wished to emigrate to the United States.*
> *"Will it be good for me there?" he asked.*
> *"Maybe yes, maybe no," I replied. I was thinking of the many Arab friends we have in the states and how life had changed for them since 9/11. Some had been detained, some discriminated against in other ways. Others had been doing ok. He seemed a little disappointed with my response.*
>
> *It was a bit exhausting to be the center of such attention. These were very friendly people. We played and sang for a while and then felt it was time to move on down the street to another location. A few of the men followed us and wanted to talk. We asked them how they were feeling. We told them our hearts were with the Iraqi people.*

An older man in a tan robe approached: "Since you are Americans, I would like to send a message with you to your president Bush. Tell him that the Americans must leave! We will build a new government ourselves! But a government such as the Americans want to build coming from the outside...? We will kill them!"

Meanwhile, a few feet away, two men were telling Kristina the opposite message: "We are thankful to Bush for ridding us of Saddam Hussein." An excited young man approached and introduced himself as the author of a book about Arabic musical scales and very enthusiastically offered to take us to a music school to meet a great master oud player whom he respected. He was apparently oblivious to the fact that the city around us was in flames.

More Burning Buildings

I had come here with the intention of looking beyond the concepts of good and evil or right and wrong. These were all people; they had all suffered in some way. Many had been imprisoned or had lost family members killed by the former Iraqi regime. They had all suffered during the bombing. Many had suffered from the effects of the sanctions. One man told me his child was very sick but that he could not take him to the hospital because the hospital had been destroyed.

I remembered again what the Human Shields with whom we had met in Amman had said after returning from Baghdad. All of them had seen civilians dead on the streets or being piled into the backs of trucks and carted away. What was clear was that these Iraqi people had suffered beyond what most Americans could understand.

Many of the US soldiers, too, had suffered. I looked at these young men. They all looked like they could be my sons. They were so young! Tears came to my eyes when I thought of how their young lives had been rudely awakened. Many of them were trying very hard to be good to the Iraqi people and to do their jobs with minimum violence. But some of them were tainted and saw the Iraqis as less than human. A few of them, we were told, had killed civilians for target practice. I don't think this will come as a surprise to those who have experienced war first hand. The Vietnam vet, whom we met upon our arrival in Amman, said he had seen it in Vietnam, and that now he had seen it in Baghdad. War is war. Atroc-

ities are committed on both sides, always.

What would we do now? What could we do? Cameron and I had our own way. We would play popular Arabic songs with these people. They had never seen Americans like us. They were overjoyed that we knew their music. I felt that at least we were showing these Iraqis that there are some Americans who appreciate them and their culture. We got very enthusiastic responses. For a while we could all forget the pain and suffering and immerse ourselves in the power of song. There is a power in this: the power of spirits joining together in friendship, of moving beyond the idea of separation. Singing together joins hearts and minds and spirits. I felt blessed that I could share this immediate connection.

We passed by the Tigris river thinking there might be a nice spot for more singing there but the Marines were using the park beside the river for a camp. Returning toward the main streets, we came to the circle where the whole world had watched on TV as Marines used a tank to help Iraqis pull over a huge statue of Saddam.

A man driving by in his car spotted the oud and inquired if we play it: "Yes, we are Americans who love Arabic music and who play the oud and sing," I told him. He parked his car and we began singing for him and others who randomly approached. The pedestal with fragments of Saddam's demolished statue stood in the background as we sang Abd el Halim's '*Sawah*,' a song about a man who is longing for his lover as he walks for days and weeks like a stranger in a strange land.

Playing for Iraqi Musician in Front of Saddam Statue Pedestal

As I sang, I scanned the eyeballs in the crowd... they were so happy to see us singing... we announced several times, as people inquired, that we were Americans who love Arabic music. Some of the eyes were uncertain at first, but not for long as people melted into the songs and joined in the singing. The man with the car said he could play the oud also and was anxious to take us with him to his house to play music. He, too, seemed to find his encounter with us more important than the fact that the city was in flames. It took five or six polite declinations from us to postpone this offer until another time. I added his phone number to my list of musicians to contact in the future. We feared that accepting invitations to visit people in their homes could put them in danger. Neighbors who see the presence of an American guest might jump to the wrong conclusions and accuse our friendly hosts of collaborating with the enemy.

Hundreds of international journalists thronged the spaces around the Palestine and Ishtar hotels, both nearby. They peered out from the rooftops with the latest high-tech portable video gear. Grim-faced and red-eyed, they were going about their story writing with cigarettes lit, adding to the smoke.

We had just proved, to my own satisfaction at least, that America could have invaded Iraq with battalions of U.S. citizens trained to play ouds and sing just a few songs in Arabic. But the journalists, for the most part anyway, didn't seem to be interested in covering anything that wasn't wrapped in violence.

At this point, as I later calculated, I had enjoyed only one hour of sleeping out of the last fifty-seven. Feeling more and more groggy with exhaustion, I suggested taking a break in the hotel room.

But Kristina was eager to continue. She asked a Marine behind the hotel if we could interview him. "Not while I'm on post," he replied. "But if you go down this street, there is a little place for coffee where Marines hang out. But I don't know if I'd recommend it. We've got snipers on the roofs of all these hotels."

Marine Can't Talk to Us

We were searched by other Marines before being allowed to proceed. We asked for the location of the coffee shop and a higher-ranking Marine said, "You mean one of my men suggested this? He should not have. Which one is he?"

"I don't remember," replied Kristina, not wanting to get anyone in trouble. We proceeded through coils of razor wire down the street, but were told we could not go toward the coffee shop.

Leaving the area cordoned off by the Marines, we re-entered the city and found a restaurant which, surprisingly, was open and we ate some chicken and rice.

"What snipers do you suppose he was referring to?" I asked Kristina.

"Well, Iraqi snipers, I assumed," she replied.

"I thought maybe he meant Marine snipers," I suggested. We didn't have a clear idea.

We wandered back toward the hotel. I was more and more groggy with exhaustion. We heard what sounded like a gunshot. Kristina backed behind a concrete wall away from the center of the street. It didn't occur to me to worry for some reason, but I backed into the more protected area also. No one out on the street seemed to pay any attention so we continued walking.

We saw Marines for the most part trying to be polite, but we also witnessed about three instances of Marines brandishing weapons and shouting things like: "Move that fucking truck and move it quick, asshole!" ...this screamed in English at uncomprehending civilians...

Video clips published later in the Arab media show US soldiers handing out food to hungry Iraqis saying in English, "so you'll suck my cock if I give you this bread, right? ...and let me fuck you in the ass..." thinking that was really funny...

We entered our room. I lay down on the bed and passed out for two hours. Opening my eyes again in the late afternoon I announced to Kristina that I was ready to go back out. But now she was feeling worse. The smoke from the burning city was making her sick at her stomach and giving her a bad headache.

The hotel we were staying at was also used by Kathy Kelly, founder of Voices in the Wilderness. I found her room and said hello. I discovered that she was preparing to leave Baghdad the very next day.

The purpose of her organization was to witness and report from inside Iraq about the effects of the sanctions and the war on the lives of Iraqi people. Kathy had been there in the Al Fonar Hotel with a few other members for the last two months and had, like the Human Shields, been unwilling to leave when the bombing had started. She was an activist with a track record of having succeeded in walking the fine line required by Saddam Hussein's government to be allowed entry, although they had been required to live under constant surveillance by their Iraqi 'minders' in order to do their reporting. They had deliberately tried to avoid association with the title 'human shield.' But there were fines now being imposed on her and her organization by the US government so she was disbanding the organization known as Voices in the Wilderness. It would soon re-appear under a different name: Voices for Creative Nonviolence.

We accepted an opportunity to ride back to Jordan in a car with her and another Voices in the Wilderness member, Kathy Breen and with a French surgeon who had been in Baghdad during the last month. The price for this ride fit exactly in our budget: $300 for the two of us. That solved the problem of how to get back out of Iraq. With most drivers charging $2000 per person we could have easily been stranded in Baghdad with no way to leave and very little cash.

We left Baghdad the next morning with Sattar, a good friend of Kathy's, doing the driving. Once again, we wound our way out through the burned and looted sections. There seemed to be fewer flames leaping out of the tall high-rise buildings. The smoke was clearing a little bit. As we exited the city center, Kristina began to recover from her night of vomiting from the exposure to the smoke.

We learned from Jacques, the French surgeon, that he had volunteered to be there for the last month, since the bombing had begun, and that he had worked in a small hospital every day staffed by Iraqis who had welcomed his help. He said he had performed seventy-two surgeries himself and assisted with countless others. At the most intense time, he said, they had received a hundred-and-fifty wounded Iraqis a day for three days in a row. I told him how much I admired his work. He seemed like a tough little guy with tremendous dedication. He had come to Baghdad from a stint of surgical work in Africa in Ivory Coast, another war-torn country.

Kathy Breen, a nurse and long-term member of Voices in the Wilderness, had worked and lived in Cochabamba, Bolivia for ten years and in Germany for six years. I sang her a song from Cochabamba which I remembered from my years traveling in the Andean world. And Kristina and I sang Arabic music with Sattar.

When we arrived back at the Jordanian border, the police remembered us. They smiled and requested more songs from us. We obliged and their smiles broadened further.

Out of the War Zone and Back to Amman

Back in Amman we spent the evening visiting Ali, Suad, Haydar, and Ahmed. Suad cooked a fabulous dinner for us. We discussed the readings from the shells which had predicted that we would not go to Baghdad. We agreed that the reading had been close, perhaps meaning that our trip to Baghdad would be difficult.

We showed them our photos from Baghdad. We discussed the question of who it was setting all the fires. Haydar agreed that the best guess was that the looters, many of whom were very poor and very young, teenagers perhaps, just get carried away with the destruction and, after looting, light the places on fire.

We heard many more stories about the details of their family lives: the little four-year-old girl now promised in marriage to 'Hamoudi'... no one knew if that would really work out... but it could. Ali's near death experience at birth and his feeling of never having been welcomed... The family trend of having firstborns be girls... Suad's disappointment at never having had a baby girl... hence all the photos of baby Haydar dressed as a girl... Suad gave Kristina a beaded vest made by a favorite aunt... and perfume...We would see them next trip, whenever that would be... insha-Allah... At this point it didn't seem that any of them had any plans to return to Iraq.

We visited Jihad's music store... learned another maqam...talked with Stefa at Fayaz' hotel. The next day we would fly back to Cairo.

We had been another month in the Middle East: Cairo, Aqaba, Amman, Baghdad, Amman, Cairo... we had sung popular Arabic songs in the hearts of all those cities... in the streets with whatever people happened to be there.

All we were saying was *'Leave the TV, come back to the People'*... Take the time to learn a song in a foreign language... go there! There is nothing to fear. Forget the politicians and the 'experts'... we have everything we need already: just ourselves and our smiles and our songs...

> *I give up... The horror of death and war washes past and nothing is solved. The wounds will last forever, but I cannot hold any attitude... the giant Nations and Armies and Religions yield to the magnifying glass: we are all nothing but PEOPLE... with individual faces, ears and noses and eyes... the democrats... the republicans... the kurds... the turks... the shi'ites... the sunni... the human shields... the palestinian christians... the palestinian muslims... the jews... the anti-war activists... the israelis... the jordanians... the hashemites... the egyptians... the iraqis... the coptic christians... the u.s. marines... the beggars... the saudis... the americans... the germans... the french... the rich... the poor... the looters... the republican guard... the kuwaitis... the voices in the wilderness... the rednecks... the south africans... the iranians... the bedouins... the british... the australians... the canadians...*
>
> *In the past few weeks I have heard something bad about each one of the above... I have also looked into the eyes of each of these... I've seen suffering in each... I've seen fear... I've seen joy... I've heard each one maligning another... Where do we stop? Are we seriously supposed to choose sides between all of these? I give up... I represent no side... And I will sing...*

Dissolving out of Egypt, out of Jordan, out of Iraq. Cameron and Kristina: "First American musicians to play Arabic music in Baghdad after the fall of Saddam Hussein!" Did this mean something? Were we part of the 'mop-up' operation which followed invasion by the US Marines? Was this the meaning?

Settling Back into Cairo - Time for Reflections

We rode a train to Maadi, in southern Cairo. We were surrounded by women and children giggling and laughing uncontrollably all around us. We talked with them with our limited Arabic abilities... the men in the railroad car broke into beaming smiles and laughed and laughed. I know the meaning of all this: Egyptians are in a permanently good mood! I remembered our Egyptian flute-playing friend Qadry shrugging off the painful memories of his open-heart surgery with laughter. The children playing in the dusty streets outside his small house in Maadi were laughing uncontrollably.

But what does this have to do with Baghdad? Inside Qadry's living room we showed him and his daughters our photos from Baghdad. What meaning did this have? Soon we would be back in America. What would the meaning be there?

Cameron and Kristina entered Iraq. So what? We watched Isaam, an Egyptian friend who had lived in Baghdad for ten years burst into tears when we showed him our photos from Iraq. Why did we go there and sing with the Iraqis on the streets of Baghdad? ...to help this man have his tears?

It is the fighting, death and destruction: the war which creates the tears. It is the maps which create the wars. It is modern technology which creates the lines on the maps. In the old days the lines were more fluid... empires were more like lakes... and they left puddles behind when they receded. These lines in the middle east which define the edges of Jordan, Iraq, Saudi Arabia... they were drawn by the British after World War I... no wonder they are in the wrong places... and puddles left behind by previous empires are no longer allowed! ...now the lines must need serious adjustment... the politicians must create serious arguments with serious symbolic meanings so that new lines can be drawn... and armies will be sent...

Cameron and Kristina had been required to sing their way through the Jordanian police three times... to three different groups of police in order to obtain visas to the no-man's land called Iraq. So our songs had become our visas. There was some power... some lessons in that...

Sleep was good. It gave us a rest and it gave us the chance to go to bed in one reality and wake up in another! But I had a dream. I was wandering through a forest. I was approached by a group of men. One of them said, "We need to tell you about the tiger."

"Ok," I replied.
"He is living in his cave and you must go and see him."
"Ok..."
"When you enter his cave he will snarl and show his teeth. He will seem to attack you. There is nothing you can do. He is so strong and his stripes are so orange and black!

"He will open his mouth wide and there is no escape! He will envelop your face and your whole head in his jaws.

"At that moment you will feel a deep tenderness in his heart. He will not bite you. You will feel the warmth of the inside of his mouth on your face. Then he will let you go and you will have a new friend."

So in the dream I found the tiger's cave. I entered and lay down to take a nap. When the tiger came home everything happened just as the men had said it would. I had trusted the men. I had trusted the tiger. I had trusted myself.

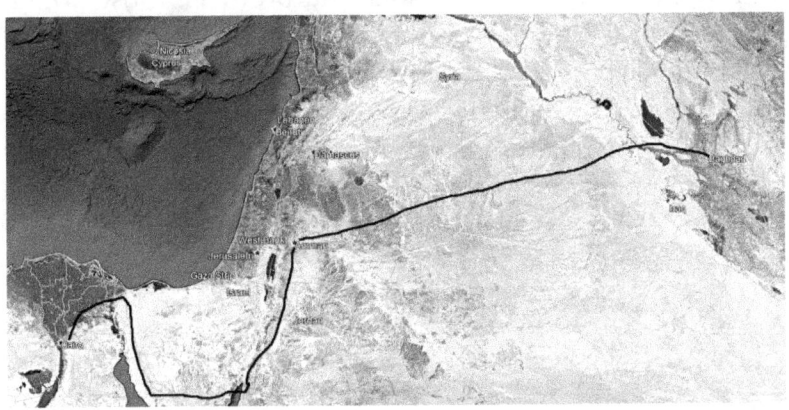

2003 - Cairo, Aqaba, Amman, Baghdad

Back to the USA - Culture Shock

The question comes up: 'what's so great about the Middle East?'

We've heard that Islamic Arabs are frightening fundamentalists, terrorists perhaps, who deny equal rights to women.

But there are so many delightful ways of being... Remembering looking into my Bedouin musician friend Hussein's eyes while he played a song for me had been like drinking sweet nectar seasoned by centuries of gentle wisdom.

Eyes are a window into the soul. I seldom experience the open eye channel here in America that I find in the Middle East. Or if the window opens for a moment, we shy away and detach our gaze.

Broad-band wide-open soul-level eye-contact can continue unbroken for many minutes in the indigenous Middle East.

Watching mothers or fathers with their children, no matter what their ages, I had seen a loving connection so intense that we 'Westerners' might want to know how this can happen? The sweet wet glances of women I passed on the street, even those of Saudi women who can only be viewed occasionally through a slit in their veils, had given me a glimpse of a very vibrant being inside.

When I recently left Amman, Jordan, and boarded an airplane staffed by European flight attendants, I immediately felt starved for the eye-contact connection which is standard in the Arab world. It made me realize how strongly we 'Westerners' guard our emotional availability. Our souls can seem shrouded and gray because of this guarding.

Women in the Middle East are worshiped for their beauty and wisdom by their husbands and sons and brothers. Most would not trade places with 'Western' women who have entered the 'man's world.' To do so would do violence to their softness and femininity. And their husbands would not wish such hardship upon them.

Westerners generally misunderstand Arab women's dress. The now almost ubiquitous 'hijab,' or head-scarf, can be a way of showing their pride in their traditional, and now threatened, ways of life. Covering themselves can also allow them to feel softer and more precious, which they are, to their families and close friends.

Arabs Are Not From India

Westerners often make the mistake of assuming that the low value placed on women in India is the same in the Arab world. The opposite is actually the case. In order for a woman in India to marry, her family must pay a dowry to the husband's family. In the Arab world the husband must provide gold jewelry and an apartment to the bride in order to qualify for marriage. It's the exact opposite. Arab women are born with high economic value. When Arab women suffer from lack of freedoms it's because their society is trying to over-protect them and treat them like queens.

When I have been befriended and invited into Arab households, I have discovered that the women soon shed their 'street clothes' and they can be naturally very intimate and sensual. As I mentioned, in Egypt the women had snuggled up next to me even though they really hardly knew me... especially when I sang with them after reaching the limits of my Arabic or their English.

Also I notice that woman-to-woman relationships are cultivated in deep soul-sister ways... not gradually, but immediately. It's as if in America we display a lot of externally flirtatious behavior, but when the initial strutting is finished, we put up walls and slam ourselves shut. It feels like the Arab world way is to look more deeply into souls through the eyes and then continue to honor that presence. Maintaining psychic contact with someone with sustained eye contact in the Arab world feels safe. I don't know why this is.

Young men in their twenties walk down the streets holding hands. They find it natural and easy to be close to one another. The women cluster together in public also, frequently doing some shopping with their children in groups of seven or eight. It is not so common for men and women to display sensual affection with each other in public. It's almost as if there are two worlds: the marketplace world where men are juicy with other men and women are juicy with other women, and the household world where men and women are juicy with each other. I do not get the impression that Arabic women are ruled by their men. When a woman has her say, she gets her way. Most men seem to regard women with awe as though they were sacred creatures.

The women on the bus, public transportation, may pass their babies to each other whether they know each other or not. They will pass them with equal enthusiasm to 'Western' women who happen to be on the bus in an effort to extend friendship and include all women in this sisterhood. The babies seem to enjoy this adventure. They don't seem to experience sudden panic related to 'being away from mommy.'

Living in community in harmonious generous ways is a big part of Arab world culture, even in this day and age. People are not coveting their private times and spaces. There is much more of a sense that 'we are all in this together...' not so much striving for individual superiority.

Most people pause what they are doing five times a day during the very beautiful call to prayer which is audible, frequently, but not always, on a crunchy loudspeaker from the minarets of the mosques. Sometimes the 'muezzin', or 'prayer reader', is live, not recorded, and, if the sound system is good, his voice echoes through the city streets in exquisite song and melody. They are careful to call this 'reading' the Koran, rather than 'singing' the Koran because their idea of 'singing' can have such sensual and 'unholy' qualities. But it sure sounds like singing to me! And it goes through your senses several times each day. Sometimes I have heard waiters in restaurants singing along with the call to prayer. Perhaps this helps explain the readiness with which most Arab-world people sing.

People tend to remember and live according to the rules of Islam, which are basically the same as the rules of all great religions: *'do unto others as you would have others do unto you...'* The word 'Islam' means 'surrender'. When you see groups of Arabs 'praying' together, they are not 'asking for' something in the way that American Christians do when they 'pray.' They are surrendering together to the will of 'Allah' which means *'all and everything...'* Allah is not some old hairy white guy up in the sky based on Yahweh. Allah is the ongoing incarnation of "Al" who was the ancient creator God who fathered both "Yahweh" and "Baal." The Jews and then the Christians ultimately follow the legacy of Yahweh while the Canaanites or Phoenicians followed Al and then Baal and the modern Arabic-speaking peoples of the Levant still preserve this allegiance.

Honesty prevails. This does not mean that people won't sometimes try to talk you into paying high prices. But they will not physically rob you. That is something which happens much more in the Western countries.

Between men, once the bargaining over prices is completed, a jolly friendship is immediately available. I am seldom disappointed when I enter into this. And then the bargaining becomes easier too. Taxi drivers and other men I meet in public places routinely invite me to their homes to meet their families and to drink tea or even have a meal. Many times this invitation is reiterated and I realize that it is sincere. Sometimes I take them up on it and enjoy their ancient hospitality. Occasionally, I will be asked for a financial contribution, but usually not. They take pride in being able to offer their hospitality for free.

Women are also safer, in my opinion, walking the streets of Arab world cities than walking the streets of our American cities where alcohol is such a common influence. Perhaps it is not so much the alcohol which is to blame for the increased violence in our society as is the relentless tendency toward loneliness and isolation. Desperation results and crimes of personal violence are committed. That is my opinion.

In the Middle East the fabric of society is much tighter and people do not fall through the cracks so easily. Does this tighter fabric create restrictions on 'freedom?' Girls in America do not expect their parents to arrange marriages for them. But it may be much easier in the Middle East for each person to feel that he or she has a 'place…'

I, of course, as a 'Westerner,' an American, would ultimately have a hard time 'fitting' in such a family-oriented society. It is not easy for a person to emigrate in either direction. But it is far more interesting to me to explore and admire beautiful aspects of another people's ways than to sit in distant judgment, never entering the open doors of hospitality which are so frequently offered in the Arab world. To me it seems that there is a wealth of ancient tradition in the Arab world which supports intimacy in especially exquisite ways.

Here is what I am frightened of: I am frightened that the modern American obsession with making our world 'safe' by force, is causing people to forget that gentleness and generosity are the greatest guarantors of 'safety.'

Are we so obsessed with control that we have suffocated all the lovers? Are we so obsessed with 'fighting for freedom' that we have forgotten how to simply be free? Even in a war zone, Kristina and I felt safe simply because we were on a musical mission of peace and we trusted that we would be understood and seen for who we were.

I look at us Americans and I look at my village friends who live in 'poverty' in 'underdeveloped' nations: I see us frowning with worry, plagued by our lives in the fast lane, and I see them exercising ancient traditions of hospitality, inviting strangers into their homes to offer friendship and morsels of food. I have village friends in Peru who would serve a main dinner course of boiled potatoes with the skins on, followed by a course of boiled potatoes with the skins off for dessert! And who is happier? …he who *has the most* or he who *needs the least*?

After the September 11th attack I watched the whole world generously offer to help America track down the terrorists who perpetrated that event. Within two weeks time I watched in shocked disbelief as our government's leaders belittled those offers by threatening to invade any and every country in the world to ensure that America would remain in control! Our leaders insulted one nation after the next by bringing the threat of the use of American military might center-stage, ignoring the sympathy and hospitality almost universally offered. I cringed as I watched countless rebuffed world leaders return home to lick their bruised pride and, of course, to have second thoughts about their willingness to help America.

How long will the American people remain asleep in this insurance-padded dream? As mighty as our military might be, to think we can long survive as top dog in a world we are trying to micro-manage is absurd. It doesn't take long for all the victims of America's 'economic embargoes' to look at each other and mutter: "you too, huh…? Well, let's just trade with each other and hey… let's leave America out of the loop this time!" Wake up America! It's time to rejoin the human race! Since when were 'freedom' and 'control' synonymous?

We Quickly Constructed a Tour

Returning again to the USA, we began giving our presentation of music, images and stories called 'Singing in Baghdad' in Boulder, Denver, Santa Fe, Albuquerque… at venues already familiar to us from our musical performances with Sherefe. We did about seven shows and found a lot of interest and enthusiasm.

We also finished recording and publishing our new CD, "Baghdad and Beyond," which contained our band's best effort to record our favorite Iraqi, Lebanese and Egyptian pieces as well as some flavors from Greece.

Baghdad and Beyond CD

Reaching out through our networks of musician friends on the West Coast we quickly constructed a tour which took us to Laguna Beach, Long Beach and Santa Barbara in Southern California.

One of Hundreds of Venues in which We Performed

We then performed further north in Monterey, Santa Cruz, Ashland, Berkeley, Oakland and Bolinas where we were invited by another couple to share a nice soak in a hot tub. Kristina became the object of a lot of caresses and attention from the husband and it seemed that the wife would happily make herself sexually available to me. But that sort of adventure was really not what we were there for and we retired back to our travel trailer. There would be hundreds of shows ahead of us in more than half the United States...

These American Audiences are Hungry for Information

We drove back south and did another show in Santa Barbara and then headed back to Colorado and New Mexico where we gave another dozen performances.

Our Diesel Van and Travel Trailer

> *If more people canceled their subscriptions to fear and their fascination and addiction to violence, they could discover that, even with cities burning in the background, we still live on a gorgeous planet populated primarily by friendly peace-loving people!*

Most of those who have come to see our presentation felt that their eyes were opened to new realities...

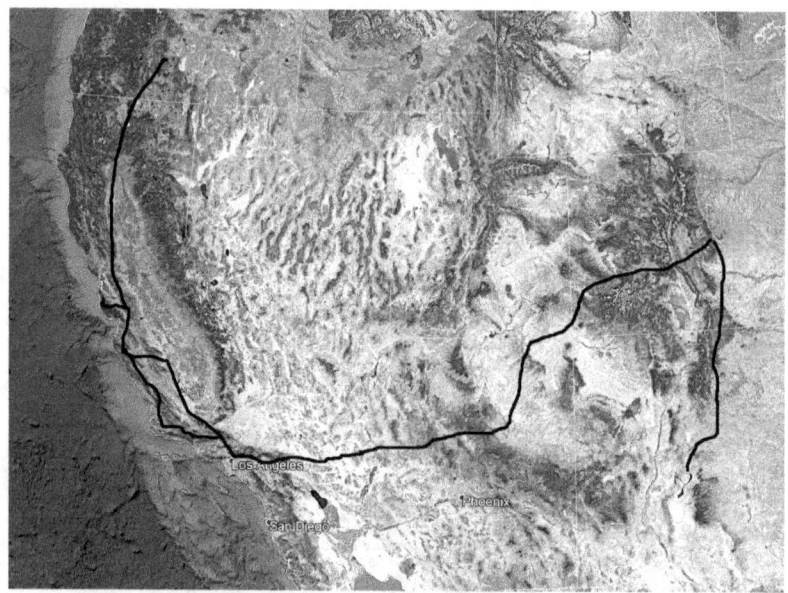

Summer 2003 Singing in Baghdad Tour Through USA

> "I've seen Cameron and Kristina's magnificent show. I give it a 15 out of a possible 10. Being a musician myself and actively building bridges of understanding, their message really hit home with me. Knowing the power of music, hearing Cameron and Kristina's stories brought tears of joy to my eyes. They are really using music for what it needs to be used for. Not only are they active and articulate musical ambassadors between America and the Middle East, in my mind they are National Heroes!! Tell everyone you know who may not have seen them that this is a must see!!!"

Karin, a kind woman who had emigrated from Germany to the USA and become skilled in setting up foundations, offered to create a non-profit organization built around our musical missions. We called it "Musical Missions of Peace" (now more commonly known as "Musical Ambassadors of Peace") and began to realize that this would become a valuable tool for helping get our messages out in America. Zia, with whom I had been dancing for decades in various improvisational groups offered to be president. Bonnie Carol, whom I had met at Reed college in 1964, offered to be secretary-treasurer. Daune Green, one of our fantastic percussionists, offered to be vice-president. Her ex-partner Pete Jacobs, long-term bass player in my band, later took over the presidency.

Egypt - The Cairo Stadium

By October we were back in Egypt. The invitation we had received to perform in the Cairo stadium had turned out to be a real thing.

We received overflowing appreciation from an Egyptian audience of approximately sixty-thousand on October 17, 2003 and all our expenses were paid for.

We had played our first show on one of the smaller stages outside the main stadium. We began more or less on time after watching delightful selections of children's dances and Saidi folkloric music and dance: a girl dancing with two boys dressed in a horse costume... a troupe of mizmar and percussion players and a tumbling costume which appeared to be two midgets wrestling but in reality is a costume worn by only one dancer...

Happy with the reception from the crowd during our first show, we began looking forward even more to our performance on the main stage. After delays in the scheduled performance lineup had cast doubts for a while on whether there would even be time for all of us, we were invited up to the main stage in the center of the Cairo Stadium.

We were extensively introduced as "the Americans who chose to go to Baghdad armed with Iraqi music instead of weapons." We felt very honored and we felt that our intentions were easily understood by Egyptians.

The stacks of speakers stood thirty-feet-tall on both sides of the huge stage and my oud, since it is not a modern electric instrument and it still has a hollow resonating body, nearly jumped out of my lap as waves of sound would pass from it through the microphones and speakers and then back into its body.

Audience of 60,000 in the Cairo Stadium

We could hear the crowd singing along with us and during our improvisations there were moments of ecstatic appreciation when the crowd erupted with appreciation as they heard our voices... They clapped and sang along at the climactic moments in the music.

We began with '*Habibi Aini*,' a sensual Egyptian dance favorite which had been made famous by the female pop star Warda. I sang a vocal improvisation in the middle which allowed me to pour full expression out into the crowd... They screamed with appreciation.

Kristina and I Singing in Cairo Stadium

We then played *'Daret el Ayam'* and Kristina's voice carried the crowd into their deep love for Um Kolthoum. We could hear even more voices from the crowd... tens of thousands of them singing along with us during this song.

We finished with an Amr Diab hit: *'Habibi ya Nour el Ayeen'*... We sang it too fast and the guitar, which I had purchased for $60 from my friend Nasser on Mohammad Ali Street only the night before, sounded terribly metallic. But we felt welcome and we felt appreciated.

We wove our path from one TV interview to the next in the deafening arena surrounding the stage. We signed autographs and shook hands in the crowd.

Our energy was now reverberating in ways that could help the fundraising for this Children's Cancer Hospital being constructed in Cairo.

And we could help Americans understand how the US, as a nation, could be reaching further out toward the vast majority of Arab world peoples who work toward the common good. We would do everything we could to help other Americans overcome the fears about the Arab-speaking peoples which had become so exaggerated.

Egyptians live in a constant up-swell of positive energy which somehow makes things come together at the last minute. Much of the work seems to happen on some telepathic level. They do not think or work linearly. Everything happens at once. They swim in a constant flow of powerful energetic currents. Beatifically smiling faces pop up everywhere. Anger rises briefly when there are bottlenecks in the flow. Westerners find it exhausting yet somehow magical. All I can say is that I felt honored.

The last few days before the shows in the stadium had been an amazing whirlwind. We had not had time to adjust our internal clocks to the eight-hour time change from Colorado. We are night-owls by nature, but being awake every night until the sun rises had been ridiculous. The night before the festival had given Kristina less than one hour of total sleep. Being hailed by an adoring Egyptian audience as the 'beautiful Miss America' buoyed her spirits, however... to say the least.

We finally found a place to rest and, with some of our growing network of friends, both Egyptian and American, who had been surrounding and supporting us, eventually enjoyed a bowl of kosheree, one of the delicious spicy vegetarian Egyptian countryside dishes.

At the end of the evening, after a long parade of the latest top Egyptian popular singers, Amr Diab, the most popular singer of them all, was whisked magically onto the stage and we all enjoyed his energetic performance.

> *Kristina here... everyone, just to share a bit with you... I have a theory about Egyptians: they are on the road to enlightenment, although they would not use that term.*
>
> *The most common comment you hear from them is 'insha'allah' which means 'God willing.' When you say 'see you tomorrow' it is always followed by 'insha'allah'. Every plan for the future is subject to the will of God, thus in their minds nothing is set in stone. Everything is always in a state of flux or change.*
>
> *Consequently they are alert and awake. They have to be. For example, it is common for cars to whiz by pedestrians with only 6 inches clearance.*
>
> *In this part of the world nothing happens as planned but somehow it all works. For all of you new-agers who are striving to learn how to live in the present moment, just come to Egypt to live for awhile. You will either get it or you will turn into a nervous wreck. It will also be a good place to come if you tend to have a controlling type of personality. Nothing here will be in your control. It is useless to even try. It is all placed in the hands of God. Again, you will either get it or you will soon catch a flight back home.*
>
> *It is very safe here despite what you may have heard. I highly recommend booking a flight ASAP.*

We were invited to be guests on one of Cairo's prominent TV talk shows... Selma Semaa is the Egyptian equivalent of the American Oprah Winfrey... something like that...

We were driven a long way outside the city and into the 'Egyptian Hollywood'. Credentials and gate passes were required for entry. Their makeup artists paid attention to every facial detail on both of us for an hour or so and we emerged looking twenty-years-younger and oh-so-beautiful. They interviewed us mostly in English, translating into Arabic on the fly, and then asked us to sing an Um Kolthoum song.

Kristina and I on Egyptian TV

After this TV show appearance people started recognizing us on the streets of Cairo. We had been given totally supportive and favorable coverage. They experience most Westerners coming fearfully into the Arab world and we were the opposite.

Our hotel and airline tickets had been paid for by the Hospital fund-raiser. We found ourselves in a fine room in the Nile Hilton Hotel... for a week or so. This lodging was a lot more elegant than what we were used to. How had all this come about? And who was this flexible female who had been traveling and singing by my side?

Kristina and I found it very easy to love each other. It seemed that we always agreed about when and where we should go. We were dialed into the same internal compass and clock.

I practiced my 'Imsak...' withholding my ejaculation down to about once a month. This kept the energies of our attraction running high. We seldom put those ideas into words. We just did what we did. Our creativity was constantly required as we sang our way through life so we were way too busy to think much about our relationship. It just kept unfolding and whenever we looked at ourselves in the mirrors of reflected consciousness we liked what we saw.

We had requested that our return trip to Colorado not be booked until several weeks later. We wanted to have time to make our first trip to Syria.

Palestinian Refugee Camp in Syria

With performances behind us in Egypt, we flew up to Damascus and began to explore. We walked the central parts of the city and then asked a taxi driver to take us to one of the huge suburban sections known as 'Muhayim Filastini' -- a Palestinian refugee camp. There were many to choose from.

We ended up in Jaramana on the south side of Damascus. It was just a short time before a Palestinian man pointed toward my oud case and asked for a song. I sat in a little plastic chair in front of a tiny grocery store and withdrew my oud from it's case. Kristina and I began to sing Egyptian, Syrian and Lebanese songs as the crowd grew around us.

Singing in Palestinian Refugee Camp in Damascus

A group of grade-school age children in their blue school uniforms gathered around close. Their favorite of the styles I could offer turned out to be Lebanese and Syrian 'dabke' line-dance music. We sang *'An Nadda'* over and over again at their insistence.

Palestinian Refugee Children Gather

One of the men who had initially invited us from in front of his store had assembled a plate of appetizers for us to snack on, but the singing would not stop to give us a chance to eat! The children screamed for more and more music until the crowd grew to such a size that unpredictable crushing waves of appreciative onlookers could have accidentally squashed me and my oud and my singer.

Eating the offered appetizers was still not possible in this situation, so we accepted an invitation to climb the stairs across the street to enter a bare room wherein we met and drank tea with six brothers, one sister and their mother.

The fourteen-year-old sister was the only one in the family who spoke any English. But it didn't seem that her English was really any better than our Arabic. They were uproariously enthusiastic about the idea that Americans would show up on their streets singing Arabic music.

There are several of these Palestinian refugee camps surrounding Damascus: Kabr Essit, Jaramana, Khan Dannoun, Khan Ashieh, Sbeineh and Yarmouk are among them. They were created in 1948. Several hundred thousand Palestinians are living in these camps hoping for the day when they, or, as they explain hopefully, at least their children, can return to the towns from which they fled or were driven.

Returning to the streets, we made our way back toward the 'old town' in the center of Damascus. Late that night I found myself playing another musician's oud and singing in the Umayyad Palace Restaurant. We picked songs from the old traditional Syrian musical style and the audience appreciatively sang along as the qanun player and I discovered melodies familiar to both of us.

Umayyad Palace Restaurant

Down to the Mediterranean Coast

The next day we got on a bus and began to explore more of this magical ancient land. We stopped for two nights in Latakia, down on the Mediterranean coast, on our way to Aleppo. The hotel owner's family of twenty-five or so people gathered on one of the balconies of the hotel where Kristina and I and one of the uncles took turns leading the singing.

Mohammad's Family in Latakia

Later that night the women took Kristina back into their rooms and kept her laughing for two hours while they played with each other and the children.

I went with a few of the men to inspect ouds at a local workshop. The father had been making ouds there for the last forty years and now the son was taking over the work.

The following night we went to watch the young men and women dance 'dabke' at a large seaside restaurant. Every day we were amazed at the glimpses we were getting into this Arab world. Outrageously uproarious fun is what these guys were having while doing these highly improvisational but also traditional line dances.

What can I say... you had to be there...

And sometimes you just can't bring yourself to drag out the camera and poke it into the situation... or you are having too much fun and don't even think of it...

> One thing I have noticed about the Arab world is the respect the teenagers have for the elders. I'm reminded of Margaret Mead's observations in 'Coming of Age in Samoa.' I've yet to see a teenager make an angry or critical remark about his or her parent. It probably happens occasionally but I've yet to witness it.
>
> The other day in Latakia, Syria, I was 'kidnapped' by two young girls, probably about sixteen and seventeen-years-old, and

I was taken up to their apartment. The young sisters Rana and Hessin were eager to introduce me to their mother who obviously was dearly loved. Three aunts were there visiting along with several cousins of all ages and an uncle or two. The house was full of people all smiling and using whatever English they could come up with to communicate with me. They kept asking me to sing to them either the Lebanese 'dabke' song 'An Nadda' or a Fairouz song like 'Atini Nay' or 'Nassam Alaina.'

When a new person came in I would have to sing another line. They would all smile and giggle. They couldn't believe an American knew their music. Rana and Hessin and their mother would all say from time to time "I love you Kristina!" I felt so welcomed I honestly felt like crying, they were so sweet.

At some point Hessin and I lay down on her bed with her English book and I helped her with her pronunciation while she helped me with some Arabic words. She told me that she wished very much to learn English but that she did not have a good teacher. At this point I was fantasizing about staying here and making a living as an English teacher.

I think if I were to stay I would have a network of hundreds of female friends within weeks. I can't help but notice the contrasts in our cultures. I think the Arab ways are usually misunderstood by Americans. The women travel in different circles than those of the men. The men are more on the streets. The women travel more between the houses, but they seem to have a lot of power. In Egypt, our Canadian friend Pat who has lived and worked in Cairo for six years claims the women are the ones who are in control. She tells us, for instance, that most women and their families insist that the husband-to-be buy and completely furnish an apartment before he can marry. A new bride almost always steps into a marriage with a new home, and a few thousand dollars worth of gold jewelery which is hers to keep even if the marriage fails.

North to Aleppo by Train

We climbed onto a train which took us north and passed close to a region which the Syrian government considered to be illegally occupied by Turkey.

We arrived in Aleppo which is called 'Haleb' in Arabic. This is a huge sprawling city which has been continuously inhabited for thousands of years just like Damascus. It is the home of one of the most highly prized musical traditions in the Arab world: 'qadoult arabiya.'

Ramadan was beginning. We stayed in our room to catch up on much needed sleep. We had breakfast with everyone else immediately after the sun set. We entered a restaurant about half an hour ahead of time so that we would be certain to find a seat. We sat at a large group table with a Syrian couple.

An oud player and a singer appeared just before sunset. The singer sang the call to prayer for us in the restaurant and we began to break our day-long fast by eating dates.

I knew that there was a French-Swiss qanun player named Julien 'Jalal Eddine' Weiss who had been living in Aleppo for a long time and who played with the popular Al-Kindi orchestra. I found a phone number for him and gave him a call. He had been playing music all night with some Greeks and wanted to go back to sleep after my call. So he promised to meet with us another day but gave me a phone number for Ibrahim Sukar, a very well-known Aleppo-born oud maker and musician. He suggested that I give Ibrahim a call. "Call me later and tell me what happened," he added.

Here is what happened: Ibrahim Sukar came to pick us up an hour later in his little covered Suzuki mini-truck and carried us, along with a friend of his, into the outskirts of Aleppo. We sang improvisations... mawwals... along the way as we headed towards Ibrahim's oud factory.

Four young craftsmen were working together in the workshop, manufacturing the instruments. Several of Ibrahim's six children scooted about. The oldest was eleven, the youngest was three months: four boys and two girls. The second youngest boy climbed over us like a little monkey. Kristina couldn't believe how strong his wiry little arms had become. Ibrahim grinned at him, picked him up and treated him to an acrobatic flight up over and around his head and shoulders.

We tuned and played four different types of ouds and I was impressed that we really had found a high-quality factory here in Syria. Ibrahim began trading melodies with me and showing me the fine points of microtonal note pitches from here deep in the land of maqamat - ancient Arabic musical modes and decorations. He complimented me by telling me that my playing already sounded Arabic, which he conceded was very difficult, and added that if I were to spend only a week working with a local master teacher, I would put the details together and attain to another level in my own playing.

Regardless of where I may be in my progress as an oud player, I found myself hypnotized by his musical energy. I watched his face depart from the business at hand and become the pure expression of very ancient purely Arabic tradition. During these times he seemed to forget that my Arabic was only that of a two-year-old and he would spontaneously launch into in-depth explanations using the fine points of Arabic musical terminology. I nodded as if I understood, not wishing to interrupt his flow of words and music. Somewhere inside of me a whole new arena for learning was being created.

Ibrahim Sukar - Oud-Maker in Aleppo

After an hour or two of oud playing, the moment of sunset was approaching. Ibrahim invited us upstairs to his home where his wife had been preparing the first meal of the day: to be eaten immediately after the sunset call-to-prayer. We took one oud with us upstairs. Ibrahim spoke English better than I spoke Arabic, but not by a whole lot. We would gently nudge meanings this way and that with a mixture of words from both languages. After we discussed the world situation briefly, Ibrahim laughed, picked the oud back up, and said: "The only things you and I will ever be able to change in this world will be the music!"

The meal was served to us by the children. They were a smoothly functioning adjunct to the flow of work. They also took turns caring for the three-month-old, who seemed quite content. We never saw any of these children exhibiting anything but playfulness, love and caring for each other. We just can't help noticing the contrast with family life in America where children reach their limits of compassion for each other so quickly and seem always so eager to make their contributions to the family work-load as short as possible. This family seemed to have boundless mutual energy for generosity with each other.

Kristina took her turn holding the baby and then was invited by the children to go and hang out with Ibrahim's wife. This mother of six had prepared the meal but the children were doing all the serving. Things here were obviously worked out according to some ancient formula.

Ibrahim told me proudly that he had succeeded in purchasing a home for each of his children. He volunteered the prices of these homes: equivalent to $16,000 US dollars each. The boys flowed constantly around him, watching and listening and learning. They were never demanding or interfering in any way. The daughters flowed equally smoothly through his loving energy. They spent more time helping their mother... or so I was told by Kristina who was spending part of her time in another room with the women and girls.

Could it be that these ancient social structures were based on responsible family behavior with an expectation of guidance from the wisdom of the elders? Could it be that the children were integrated into this structure and performed useful functions within it from such early ages that their pride in their own contributions replaced opportunities for rebellious behavior? The constant pushing to 'test the limits of parental authority' which is so embedded in our American children's way of life seemed completely absent. Is that why the life on the streets even late at night was so safe here?

One of the young sons fell asleep in the middle of the floor. Free-form nap-taking apparently replaced any firm concept of 'bedtime.' People were out and about all day and all night. Several two-hour naps apparently could replace the eight-hour rest period which we so cherish in the West.

Syrians are a little more introverted than Egyptians. They think perhaps twice instead of just once before they speak or act. We Americans seem to need to think ourselves into exhaustion... more like five or six times before we speak or act. Maybe that's why we need more sleep. Perhaps that underlies our habit of experiencing constant stress. It's certainly not that you could ever find more horn-honking and tightly interwoven traffic patterns than we were finding in Syria. Yet the workmen on their ladders still seemed relaxed in their faith that the automobiles whizzing past only a foot away from their legs would always maintain the necessary magical cushion of safe space.

He Gave us our Midnight 'Lunch' for Free

Much later the same evening we entered a restaurant back in the center of town for lunch at midnight and recognized the resident oud-player's instrument as a product of Ibrahim's craftsmanship.

Yusef, the oud player, soon deciphered our familiarity with Arabic music and began 'talking to us' with his oud-playing and with his eyes. This is a deeply ancient Arabic way of communicating and Aleppo was the place where this was still happening. We laughed and smiled as the 'messages' entered our souls. He switched from one musical mode to another... and then another... artfully... to make his musical points.

Soon we were invited to sing and play a song. One thing led to another. We met a rare breed: another American. We laughed about the silly misconceptions which lead Americans to always congratulate us upon returning 'safely' from Syria or other places in the Arab world. He, like us, always tries to explain to the Americans back home that it's much safer in Syria than in the States. He was an Arabic-music-loving gentleman who worked for the Environmental Protection Agency in Washington DC.

We also met Bachir, a co-owner of the restaurant in which we had just been playing and singing. He laughed with us about the idea that Westerners have about safety here. He said that even Europeans now were sometimes arriving filled with the American and British propaganda and would inquire if it was safe for them to go out of their hotel rooms. He told us about real estate transactions commonly conducted on the streets where citizens are busy counting hundreds of thousands of dollars worth of cash in public places with no fear of robbery. He gave us our midnight 'lunch' for free in exchange for our music and our friendship.

He told us more about the incredible melting pot of Middle Eastern cultures here: Armenians, Greeks, Turkomans, Kurds, Azerbaijanis, Uzbeks, Russians, Syrian Arabs, Jews (we met a couple of them), Palestinians... etc etc... But there were no MacDonalds, Coca Cola, Kentucky Fried Chicken, American Automobile Dealers or Western Banks.

It was kind of like living inside an exotic history book... but with modern sexy Lebanese music videos dancing lively on the TV sets... and with women's clothing stores filled with risqué outfits while a mix of conservatively dressed and more modernly dressed females walked the narrow labyrinthine ancient cobblestone streets.

Bachir took us down the stairs under the restaurant into a furnished cave with ventilation holes carved up through the ceiling. "We can guess that this cave has been inhabited for five-thousand years now... we don't really know..." Archaeological diggings are showing that Aleppo may actually have been continuously inhabited now for more like eight-thousand years.

We called Julien 'Jalal Eddine' Weiss and told him that we had indeed had a marvelous welcome from Ibrahim. We visited him briefly in his home but he was too busy with other visitors from France to find the time to play music. Perhaps another time.

My Personal Evolution in Traveling... How to make it appeal more to new-age thinkers and help people understand how fear can rule our lives and what freedom really might be.

How are we being manipulated? How has the terrorist scare influenced you personally. How has it influenced me? Personally I, for most of my life, didn't pay much attention to what was happening in the Middle East. It seemed so confusing to try and get a handle on it. History was never my strong point and when people started talking about which people or ruler did what to whom I would shut down and not pay attention. It had all seemed so dead to me.

What has changed is that I now know so many people of Middle Eastern descent here in Syria and in several Middle Eastern countries that the conditions that they live under and the political climate is very real to me.

My dear friend Suad, for example, is an Iraqi refugee in Amman, Jordan, who has chosen not to return to Baghdad for various reasons. She felt that she didn't wish to trade being controlled by Saddam for being controlled by Bush and his new Iraqi government. And the tomatoes didn't grow there so well anymore... too much toxic waste from all the weaponry...

So how did I end up here? I was a person not very interested in world affairs who is now traveling the US and talking about and sharing views and music from the Middle East.

I think of the world as I think of myself. There are warring fragments within myself, at odds with each other, creating obstacles for me to overcome instead of paving the way to a creative fulfilling life. Why do we make it hard on ourselves? Why is it we are so controlled by forces which wish to subjugate us?

Before I started traveling I had a limited view of foreigners whom I met in my own country. I would see them and not be able to see past their difficulty with speaking our language. I was unable to see the fully blossomed human being behind the person who was struggling to speak English. Not until I was in their position was I able to empathize fully with these people. There is a still point of understanding that you cannot reach when relating to people whose language you do not speak well unless you bypass the uncomfortable place which stems from your fear and open your heart to their beauty.

It is a process that you develop with time. You cannot expect yourself to magically become an all-loving-totally-welcoming individual all at once. You need to allow yourself to slowly test the waters. Like a person who has been denied water, you must sip slowly the waters of life until you can feel the nurturing life-giving water restoring you to your natural relationship with the rest of the world. Then you can begin drinking in the welcoming energy of those around you. Eventually what you see is the oneness that exists when you view others as aspects of yourself.

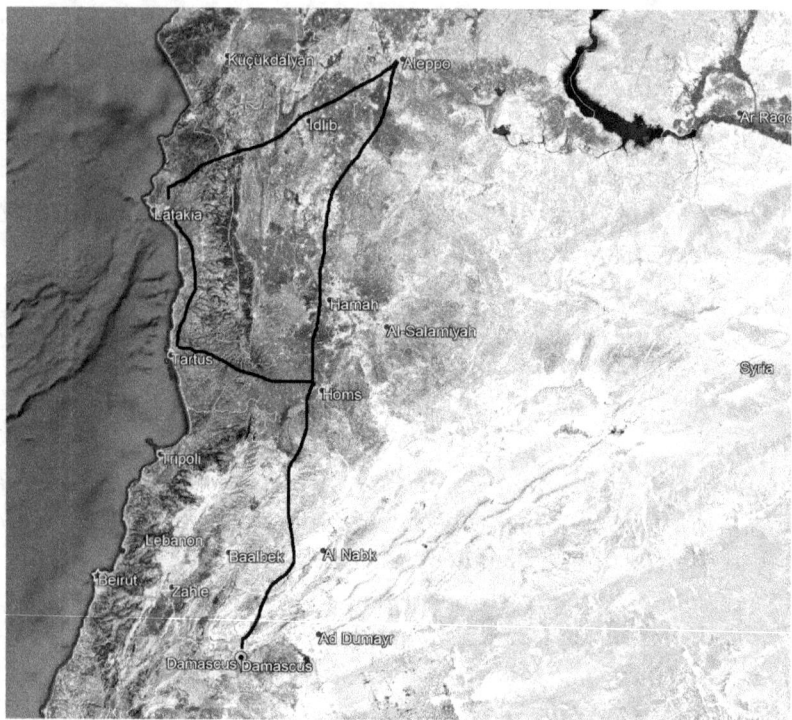

Summer 2003 - After Cairo Concert - First Visit to Syria

Colorado and Touring the USA

We returned from Aleppo to Damascus, then to Egypt and finally back home to Colorado. I had stayed busy with emails on the Internet and had booked our new 'Singing in Baghdad' presentation all over the USA. We would be on the road now for years to come. We lived in our travel trailer. Eventually we would perform in so many places in the USA that we would feel like we had our fingers on the pulse of how Americans were feeling in different parts of the country. Beginning in the fall of 2003 we began again with more performances in New Mexico and Colorado. The fact that we had now performed for such a large audience in Egypt and also been to Syria added to our mystique.

Nahalat Shalom, a Tikkun-oriented synagogue in Albuquerque, hosted us. That was unusual... perhaps the only time we were invited by a Jewish organization. Tikkun has a somewhat pro-Palestinian orientation. We then performed the next night at Tribes Coffeehouse in Santa Fe. Less than a week later we gave a series of three presentations in Grand Junction, in western Colorado where generous newspaper coverage provided substantial promotion. Excitement was running high. Our 'Singing in Baghdad' show could captivate audiences and open a lot of minds.

Lots of Coverage

Back home in Boulder we were featured on local radio before we headed back south into New Mexico again to Abiquiu which is home to a small Muslim community. They invited us to give a presentation in their elementary school. The children jumped up and down like popcorn when they heard some of our more up-tempo Middle-Eastern and Greek rhythms. In nearby Santa Fe we performed at an art center and at a local high school.

Whenever Arab-world families living in the US came to our shows, tears would roll down their cheeks... living proof that what we were presenting was deeply real.

We were back home in Boulder for a couple of weeks and then headed for Texas to begin a Southern tour. In Fort Worth we presented for a martial arts studio audience and then for a Unity church in Denton, Texas.

As it became our new way of life we created many varieties of shows and workshops. We found certain formulas for presentation which seemed to always work and repeated those to predictable ooo's and ahhh's from the audiences. And we were also aware that every show and every audience was different and constant creativity was called for.

> *Burlington, Colorado. First night spent on the Southern Tour here. Truck stop restaurant in the morning. How to insure that we stay healthy as we travel. Getting plenty of exercise. Perhaps stop mid-day and find a good place... Hey... If this is my life style, how do I make it work? Perhaps writing in the morning before we take off from wherever we camped for the night... Yoga stretching exercises... How to not feel rushed? What kinds of things can I do when Cameron is driving? Writing, drumming, Arabic, brainstorm while driving... When we stop make sure to stretch... Bless the countryside as we move along... Feel the energy move through me... and feel the heightened energy that happens when we see others, all others, as divine beings and keep the focus that we can add to other people's lives which actually adds to our own life and is not an energy drain... Remember the ego tries to tell you that by giving to others you give up something in yourself, but this is not true. That is the old paradigm, we now exist in the new... So breathe, relax and realize that everything is in order. All is as it should be. You are embarking on a new adventure and you want all your facilities and capacities of all sorts put together and strong so that you can draw upon them...*

Another Unity church in Fayetteville, Arkansas invited us to do a short introduction during their Sunday morning service as a prelude to our full afternoon presentation. They held us over to teach a workshop on Monday evening which we titled "From the American Dream to the Global Dream." Funky American rural humor in Arkansas made us laugh. A trash can placed on the smashed hood of someone's car had a sign with the instructions: "File Insurance Claims Here!" An abandoned chicken coop was labeled "First National Bank."

We did the first of many presentations at a Unitarian congregation just north of New Orleans in Lacombe, Louisiana. They wanted the workshop too. We gave presentations at Loyola University in New Orleans and at Delgado Community College in Slidell. Louisiana people were friendly and wanted to make tasty food and drink wine every night. Fun. But this was at the time when American flags were flying from nearly every front porch and "Support Our Troops" was the message of the day. I was watching for signs of thought or compassion for the innocent Iraqi victims of America's aggressions and was constantly disappointed. No one seemed to have thought of that... at least not until after they had seen "Singing in Baghdad."

Moving east we stopped at a Unity Christ Church in Mobile, Alabama and at another Unitarian Universalist Fellowship in Columbus, Georgia. Columbus State University had us give two back-to-back presentations for large student audiences at their Davidson Center Auditorium. We returned to give a second, Thursday evening performance for the same Unitarian Fellowship. Friends had been advised that if they had missed our first show they should come and see our second show. Meanwhile a local TV station chose to broadcast scenes from our presentation during their news hour.

We presented for another large Unitarian Fellowship in Durham, North Carolina and then circled back west for a radio interview, two television performances and a live presentation for a large and friendly audience at The Pilgrim Congregational Church in Chattanooga, Tennessee. Again the local TV station sent cameramen to cover us and then broadcast parts of our show during their news hour. The Congregational Church brought us back to perform more music, have us mingle with their members at "A Simple Lunch with Cameron and Kristina" and to teach a workshop. That made a total of eight events in Chattanooga. We felt very appreciated.

We proceeded down to a famous commune called "The Farm" in Summertown, Tennessee which had been founded back in the 1960's. A visionary named Steve Gaskin had led a caravan of a hundred school buses filled with hippies in search of a rural home and the settlement became well-known not only as a successful back-to-the-land experiment but also for his wife's work to establish midwifery as a modern alternative to standard gynecological obstetric hospital practices. The commune had shrunk after all the children had grown up and moved away but was still home to a couple of hundred folks who appreciated our show.

In Cookeville, Tennessee we gave shows at the Wattenbarger Auditorium, the First Presbyterian Church and at the Roaden University Center. In Nashville we gave a poorly-attended Arabic Music Workshop at the Global Education Center and then headed back home to Boulder, Colorado.

We gave a series of concerts and presentations in Estes Park, Lafayette, Dillon, Frisco and Avon... mostly at Religious Science, Unity and Unitarian congregations. The newspaper in Estes Park gave us a full page color spread. But in less than three weeks we took off and resumed our tour up in the Pacific Northwest.

Quick Swing through Southern California

Unitarian fellowships hosted us in Hillsboro, just outside Portland, and then in Klamath Falls where they also wanted additional workshops. A Unity church presentation in Corvallis produced by a belly-dancer friend was followed by a show at Cozmic Pizza in Eugene, Oregon.

Moving down to the bay area in northern California we performed for the Sacramento Street Co-housing group in Berkeley and then at the Oakland Box Theater which was co-sponsored by the Middle East Children's Alliance.

We made a quick swing through southern California to perform in Laguna Beach, Pacific Palisades, and at the large Orange Coast Unitarian Church in Costa Mesa. We offered multiple shows in Mission Viejo and then reversed direction. We were headed back toward Boulder, Colorado again but not directly. We would re-trace parts of our path through the Pacific North-West.

We gave shows and workshops at the Aronos Women's Research Center and at the Tuolumne County Association of Realtors in Sonora, California. We offered two live shows, and radio and TV events in Eugene and then headed up to perform at the World Beat Dance Studio back up in Grants Pass, Oregon. We then did a show at a Presbyterian Church on the Southeast side of Portland before giving four shows and workshops over a period of several days in Port Angeles, Washington at the Juan De Fuca Festival up on the northern edge of the Olympic peninsula.

We then gave shows in Chelan, Washington, where Kristina's parents lived, and also at the Jeannette Rankin Peace Center in Missoula, Montana. This was followed by an Interview with the Yakima Herald-Republic and a show at the Allied Arts Warehouse theater in Yakima, Washington. We gave shows and a workshop at Unitarian fellowships in Idaho Falls and in Pocatello, Idaho and then drove back home to Boulder again.

But we were still on the road. We gave shows at a Senor Center for Spirit Keepers and Dances of Universal Peace in Boulder and then at the "Ruth Marie" in Del Norte, Colorado. We were featured in Crestone, Colorado as part of Sylvia Hazlerig's Concert Series and we gave a presentation, a concert and a workshop at St. Peter's Episcopal Church in Basalt up near Aspen.

For someone who had not been raised in any religious tradition I was spending a lot of time getting to know American citizens who were church-goers. I was happy that they wanted to feature us but still conscious that I never really felt very at home in formal religious settings.

But touring the USA had just begun. After less than a month in Colorado we gave our presentations and two workshops in Kansas City, Kansas at the St. Marks United Methodist Church. The Methodist Wesley House in Rolla, Missouri also featured us and from there we proceeded to a TV interview and a presentation for a Unitarian "Stop War on Iraq" organization in Terre Haute, Indiana.

We had been booked to perform in a concert series in Bean Blossom, Indiana. We had no idea what to expect but were delighted to see the hall fill up with a hundred or more which made a large and enthusiastic audience. We had a little gap in our itinerary so we remained parked in that part of Indiana and explored the countryside and a nearby little town with the colorful name of 'Gnawbone'. Kristina went for a walk in the woods and came back covered with chigger bites... little microscopic red mites which burrow into your skin and cause two weeks of itchy misery.

We continued further east to perform in Pennsylvania at the Union Lutheran Church in Schnecksville and at the St. John's United Church of Christ in Jonestown. The Lutheran congregation was extremely Republican and our message was strange to them. But there was a feeling that we were actually getting through to a few of them.

Leaving our travel trailer parked at Kristina's old friend Suki's house in eastern Pennsylvania, we drove to Long Island, New York and performed in Farmingdale at the United Methodist Church. Returning to Pennsylvania, Suki explained to us that the only political party in the entire region was Republican. There were no Democratic party representatives at all so any 'liberal' work had to be conducted under the Republican banner.

From there we headed back to Boulder doing presentations, concerts and workshops for Unity and Unitarian congregations in Edinboro, Pennsylvania, Brattleboro, Vermont, Racine, Wisconsin, Peoria and Rockford, Illinois, West Lafayette, Indiana, and Mankato, Minnesota. We did a presentation for a very enthusiastic choir director at the First Christian Church in Des Moines, Iowa. This led to later invitations to mingle our Arabic music with huge backup choruses in both Iowa and Florida at annual Choir Director Concerts.

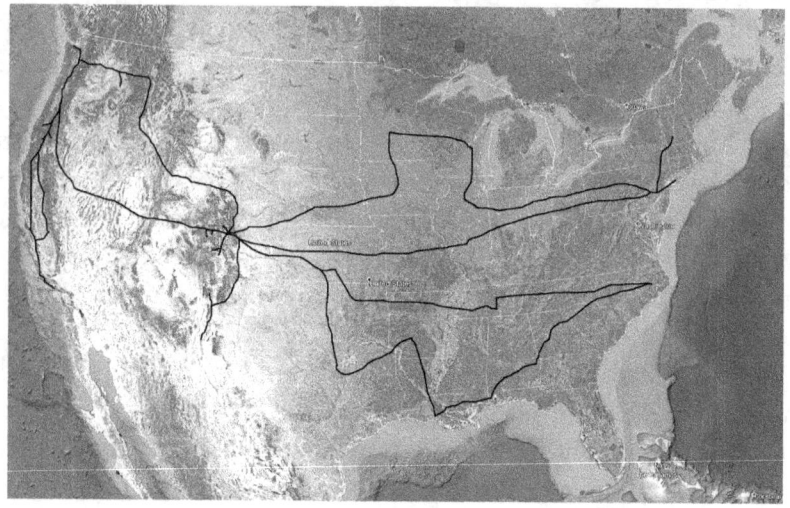

Touring Through USA 2003 - 2004

Back in Boulder and Denver we performed at a United Nations Picnic, a Mennonite Church and at Regis College.

I drove up to Steamboat Springs and visited Wayne and Linda at the Barn. They had gotten a legal divorce years earlier and Wayne had explored relationships with a few other women but none of them had lasted. He re-modeled one of the out-buildings to become the 'Men's Club' and moved out of the Barn so that he and Linda's living spaces were separated by a few dozen yards. This seemed to suit them and he continued to call her "cher" and the world still perceived them as a couple. The three of us had dinner together in the 'Men's Club' and acknowledged the depth of our fondness and caring for each other... it was profoundly emotional for me. A few years later Wayne died of a heart attack while lying in the grass at a summer music festival. Linda and I continue to stay in touch.

Syria Calls us Back

By the end of 2004 we had realized that it was time to head back to Syria. We had only begun to explore that ancient land. We would go and come through Egypt... We flew to Cairo.

> *Dissolving into the ancient NOW of Egypt. Life here can't really be contained by word-bags: 'joys, frustrations, welcomes, poverty, ecstasy, traffic, singing, eyes and smiles...'*
>
> *Ten thousand moments tinged with Arabic ways-of-being enter our Indo-European English essence.*
>
> *Excited by the intensity: our new journalist friends translate ancient Arabic desert poetry and Modern Messages of Peace all in the same breath. An Egyptian woman is ululating - making high-pitched vocal sounds perhaps in celebration of a wedding - in the distance... Children laugh and play next door...*
>
> *Square pegs fit snugly into round holes.*
>
> *We are left with the sound of the poetic syllables in Arabic.*
>
> *Opening new soul-balloons inside ourselves we drink in the ancient messages and we translate our modern American Heart-Lust for Peace and Brother-Sister-hood. We shape and forge this message endorsed by American Musical Missions for Peace into Arabic until we smile uncontrollably! Ahmad, blessed with the gift of divine laughter carries us into some hilarious place we don't even need to 'understand.' Trust us: this is good! This is way more than just trying to fight our way through the hawkers who surround the pyramids!*
>
> *Musical Missions: Singing with the waiters... Singing with the pedestrians... Singing with the taxi-drivers... Singing with the musicians... Singing with the instrument-makers...*
>
> *Kristina on drums and vocals... Cameron on flute... Omar on oud...*
>
> *We line the busy city walls with a filigree of Arabic Music...*
>
> *Satisfied with musical missions into the NOW we break out in smiles all around... We will always come back for more.*
>
> *Politics: Funny how war and politics never even come up; those subjects don't really even have a place here... but somewhere, left unspoken in our Egyptian and American hearts, we keep wishing the strange forces of colonial occupations would somehow someday just go away...*
>
> *The more of us there are who choose to live in the music and the love, the fewer there will be who remain in the fear and the greed and the other black and white realities...*

Soon we would be back in Syria with a dip into Lebanon... Aleppo, Latakia, Beirut, Damascus, Amman...

Several people would be coming over to join us in Egypt in January. So many places we could go: Cairo, Luxor, Valley of the Kings, The Nile, The Oases and The Bedouin, Alexandria, Sharm el Sheik, the Mediterranean, The Red Sea... Pyramids and People and Musical Missions every day...

> *We walk in connection with some divine rhythm which remains un-nameable... Remember just one thing: nothing is ever as it seems... it's always much better... all that is required is the dissolving: mine and yours...*

Aleppo, Syria Again

Back on the Streets of Aleppo, in northern Syria: "Welcome," we heard again and again as we walked down the streets of this ancient city. I looked at the eyes and the faces and realized that I was in the presence of an indigenous people who had been there since the dawn of recorded history. Their eyes were very soft and invited friendship.

We called Ibrahim Sukar on our cell phone. He came to pick us up again in his little pickup truck. The three of us jammed into the front seat and drove to the musical instrument factory where fifteen men were now busily assembling traditional Arab-world instruments: ouds, qanuns, buzuks. His factory had grown rapidly.

Ibrahim Sukar Oud Factory

It was cold. It was December. We huddled around a tiny woodstove and began to pass around an oud. Ibrahim introduced us to Bashir, "the best oud player in Aleppo!" We all could speak music!

We sang popular Syrian, Iraqi, Lebanese and Egyptian songs together, some familiar to us and others not. The qanun-maker gave us a tour of his part of the five-room factory and we could see the bare bones of the instruments in various states of shaping before assembly into the multi-stringed plucked zithers which they would eventually become. He asked where we were from...

"America," we replied...

"Why Bush?" he asked. "Why did you pick a man so hated by

everyone in the Arab world?"

"I don't really understand it," I replied.

He shook his head, obviously dumbfounded that a nation could make such a choice... he resumed showing us the pieces of wood, the kinds of glue and the pieces of fish skin used in the manufacture of the qanuns.

After four hours of music it was late and we prepared to go back to the center of town. We had bonded deeply, admiring each of our techniques and songs and, of course, Kristina's voice and improvisations.

> *There is a religion of love. We all belong to it. It doesn't promise salvation for some while leaving others out in the cold. It doesn't say which wise men we must listen to and which ones to ignore. It doesn't invoke God as an excuse to move onto someone else's land. It lives in all of us, has the sensitive ears of an angel and gazes in adoration at all beings present in this moment.*

I don't know exactly where the 'Holy Land' begins and ends. We rode the train down from Aleppo to Latakia, Syria, on the eastern edge of the Mediterranean coast and we were greeted by our friend, Mohammad. He had been following our Musical Missions and sending us e-mail messages such as this when we had arrived in Cairo:

> *"Ahlan wa Sahlan... welcome back Cameron, Kristina.. nice to hear such a good news that the musical mission is now again in the Arab world... you are best people to represent America than any other American ambassadors... and your tools are better to spread peace and rebuild the bridges between us and America than your officials' weapons.. so we need you now for four more years... hoping that you will not need to also learn singing in Farsi - Iranian language - after then... ...so Cameron and Kristina... 'al hamdillah ala alsalameh' ...thanks to God for arriving safely... to Cairo."*

Mohammad had a great desire to see people assembled around us now that we were actually back in Latakia and he had good instincts about where we should go to accomplish this.

Following his invitation, we began to sing in the lobby of a hotel in which many Iraqis were staying. Latakia is a seaport and many material goods were constantly shepherded through there bound for Iraq. The tiredness in some of these Iraqi men's eyes was thick and they weren't certain whom these two Americans singing popular Arabic music might be. They peered at us from within their red and white checkered keffeyas.

Gradually, as we moved through seven or eight songs, their eyes began to shine. They allowed the religion of love to begin to shine back at us and our breathing and singing became like a flock of shy birds in the room. Mohammad is, in some ways, a shy man himself, but his instincts had guided us to the right place.

He then led us with our oud, guitar and drum to a nearby restaurant where he had arranged for us to do a concert. It was an elegant setting. The owners, managers and musicians welcomed us with impeccable generosity and set up two chairs and three microphones for us.

Mohammad introduced us to the hundred or so who were assembled and we began, again, to sing Egyptian, Lebanese, Syrian, Iraqi songs to the mixed Christian and Muslim crowd.

Restaurant Audience in Latakia

Amused at our accents and delighted with the songs, they clapped and sang along with us.

Enthusiasm in the Restaurant Crowd

Kristina, the 'Little Fairouz,' as they liked to call her, sang like a bird.

Kristina and I Sing

Mohammad announced to the crowd the basic messages of peace which we carried and new friends, eager to stay in touch, came up and introduced themselves.

Finishing another Song

The kind, elderly musician, who had graciously relinquished his space for us, then resumed playing and singing while Kristina and Bashar, a new friend, danced.

Kristina Dancing

Mohammad and Kristina and I were all feeling very good about this event.

Mohammad and I

We were given a nice meal.

Mohammad and Friends

We spent a long time getting to know the young folks who had come to hear us.

Restaurant Friends

On our way home in the wee hours, we passed Mohammad's father, Ismael, on the streets. He had an impressive dignity and a warm smile. Something seemed right with the world there in this ancient holy land.

The next day we were invited to dine at Mohammad's home.

More of Mohammad's Family

Kristina had spent the afternoon with two young Syrian women in conversation about differences between American and Syrian women's lifestyles.

Two Syrian Women Discuss Lifestyles with Kristina

When she returned we walked to Mohammad's home. While his mother was preparing the delicious food we sang with a dozen or so female members of his family whose names all began with 'R': Raneem, Rahaf, Rama, Ruba...

More Singing with Mohammad's Family

A couple of uncles were also there: one serious and one delightfully 'crazy'...

Me and Mohammad's Crazy Uncle

We also now had, thanks to new Iraqi friends in Syria, knowledge about how to publish messages of good will and peace in mainstream newspapers available in Baghdad as well as in the rest of the Arab-speaking world. The message, translated from Arabic to English was:

> *To the People of Iraq and other Native Arabic-speaking Peoples: Our Songs, Hearts, Thoughts and Prayers are with you. We look forward to the day when your ancient wisdom can shine throughout the world once again! --Your Friends in America*

We continued with our work to build bridges of musical friendship at a grass-roots level between the Arab world and America. We were singing and walking in peace and in freedom and trying to help others to see that this was a possible path.

All We Want to Do in Life is to Dance

We met a Lebanese man who offered to give us a ride into his country. "Why not?" we thought. We had double entry visas into Syria so we accepted the ride which Kristina remembers as having been wild and crazy with high-speed maneuvering.

Soft Palestinian eyes welcomed us into Beirut. Knowing from the Internet who we were, we were welcomed by a young Muslim Palestinian woman who was a singer... and by a schoolteacher. She handed us a cassette tape of her band... if we wanted to stay and play, here was the invitation! Organizations were being set up to help bring musical training into the poverty of the camps and we were invited to participate... we felt at home.

Late that night at an Internet cafe in Beirut, I was befriended by some teen-age boys and girls. The girls couldn't stop dancing.

"All we want to do in life is to dance," they announced.

"Me too!" I replied.

I told them I was a musician from America. We began singing some Lebanese songs together while the girls danced some more. They wanted me to bring my oud and go home with them but the hour was already close to 2:00 AM... not this time.

We crossed two snow-covered mountain ranges back into Syria and descended back into Damascus. The sounds of my oud and Kristina's drum and our voices soon permeated the textile market in the ancient souq, or marketplace. We felt at home.

Crossing south out of Syria back into Jordan we were soon looking into the eyes of Iraqi friends in Amman. Suad and her son Ali had moved into a larger apartment and it so happened that my friend Muhsin, whom I had originally met in Colorado back in the early 1980's, was there. Our eyes exchanged delight with seeing each other again and our smiles contained all our eagerness! As usual, he was carrying his oud and violin. His assumption that I would automatically know all of his favorite Iraqi songs just because of the length of our friendship proved slightly frustrating. I, of course, had not learned anywhere near so many songs! But we found quite a few which we could play together. It had been a long time!

Muhsin and I

The war news was too horrendous to report. War news frequently remains unfathomable unless you were there in the streets with the tanks. Muhsin and his new wife's recent attempts to return to live and work in Baghdad had been abandoned. Too impossible. But one of Suad's sons, Ahmad, was still there. They were worried. Young men get conscripted or even sometimes enthusiastically join various armies and then who knows what might happen... the possibilities of loved ones' flesh and blood being wounded and torn hovered in the thought fields around us.

Jordanian friends at Fayaz' hotel threw another party for us. It was Christmas, 2004. We again sang late into the night.

Living in the spirit-body of the world there seemed to be no place that we could not call 'home.'

New Years Eve with Cairo Bedouins

We returned to our Egyptian home from our Syrian, Lebanese and Jordanian homes.

Sitting beside us on the plane back to Egypt was a soft-eyed African-American man. He was journeying out of Iraq for the first time after serving sixteen months of 'Department of Defense' duty. He had been trying to train Iraqi police recruits to stand in line... not something which comes naturally to Arabs. Even after sixteen months in Iraq he hadn't had an opportunity to even taste Iraqi food... he had been given only one day of training in 'Iraqi culture.'

He was fascinated to hear of our ability to enter Iraq on the wings of a song and enjoy friendship with people on the streets. Something like this seemed unimaginable to him. We taught him the first three words of a popular Iraqi song and wished him luck.

We swam in the uproariously gregarious energy of the Cairo streets. It was two o'clock in the morning and we were winding our way back from a concert of Nubian music. Throngs of teenagers adopted us. We crossed the Nile. The sky was clear that night over Cairo thanks to a gentle but persistent breeze.

New Year's Eve arrived and we were invited to a party in some Cairo suburb by Bedouin friends.

Me and Sabry at Bedouin Party

Kristina and I played and sang and then danced late into the night to recorded music.

Kristina Dancing - New Years Eve

This was an endless dance party for everyone...men, women, children.

Children Dancing

The sounds of the women ululating continued through the evening... lots of fun and ecstasy!

Sabry and Friend

Egyptians playing for Egyptians
Two young American ladies joined us to share adventures for the next two weeks: Kristina's daughter Lauren and her step-sister Kristen.

Kristen, Lauren and Kristina

We faced the horrendous onslaught of sales pitches which lands on all tourists one more time in order to go see the pyramids. And we ventured up to Luxor, in order to go see the temple at Karnak and the Valley of the Kings… another tourist haven wherein all foreigners become targets. Kristina's internal protective 'mother hen' attacked and kicked a young man whom she perceived as flirting too heavily with her daughter.

"He didn't say I had a 'nice ass,' mom!'" Lauren explained… "He said I had 'nice eyes!'"

We crossed to the west side of the Nile in a little water taxi to escape the heart of the Luxor tourist area.

Crossing the Nile

Lauren was asked to steer the boat.

Lauren Steering

We wandered through the poor side of town and found a street concert: Egyptians playing for Egyptians. The four of us joined in and freed up our bodies with improvisational dancing... lots of fun.

Street Band - West Bank of Luxor

More Dancing on the Red Sea Coast

We had been invited by Sabry, one of our Bedouin friends in Cairo, to enjoy a free stay at a vacant condo in the town of Hurghada on the coast of the Red Sea. We said yes and traveled there and moved in.

The condo wasn't quite finished but it made a nice shelter.

Hurghada was a resort town and we enjoyed the late night dancing in the local restaurants. In fact... it was amazing... when Egyptians allow their bodies to enter fully into dance they become androgynous... their inner masculine and feminine blend and merge and a deep sensuality drives them which is male and female at the same time. It takes youthful exuberance and the magic which comes during the very late night hours for this to fully manifest... it's not something which you will see so clearly in Western parts of the world where gender identities have been differently defined. My memories of these dances exist in my mind and soul.

Lauren Dancing

As usual the sisterhood connections between women were sweet and strong.

Kristina and Friend

Our time here in the Middle East is drawing to a close. We have just two more days. There is a bit of sadness in me as I prepare to leave new-found and old friends here.

At the close of my fourth trip to the Middle East and after more than six months total in this part of the world, I feel that I am just beginning to understand these people. There are so many subtleties that we foreigners miss.

The people of Egypt and other Arabic-speaking countries, if you allow them into your soul, will bathe you in loving warm energy. Cameron has spoken of how the people here seem telepathic. This telepathy really exists all around us here, although I would venture to guess that most English-speaking visitors don't catch onto it. When our Egyptian friend Ahmad sits beside the taxi driver I notice how they speak as if they were old friends even though they have never before met. This is not an occasional occurrence, this is constant. These people are connected to each other in ways that we have no clue about. In 'new age' terminology you might say that they have not separated so far from God or from each other. Their individual egos are not as separate as are our Westernized egos.

The traffic and the constant noisy interactions take some getting used to. Many tourists come to Cairo to shop in Khan el Khalili, one of the ancient markets and they can find the hustling to be too much. The other night, as I was walking through this market, it took me a while to let go of the annoyance of constantly being asked "come into my shop" by shopkeeper after shopkeeper. But I could feel the safe and warm and welcoming undercurrent. This warmth keeps the fabric of this society together.

You can see this in the families. They all live together. I've not yet met one college student who lives on their own. They all stay with their families and contribute to the welfare of the whole tribe. Only after they marry do they start their own households and then it is often within walking distance to the family homes. Grandmothers are the primary caregivers of the grandchildren if the mother chooses to work.

Of course I love my friends in America too. So many wonderful people have invited us into their homes as we travel from state to state. We are incredibly blessed to know so many welcoming people. But please be aware that we Americans have created more walls. I urge you to experiment. If you know a native Arabic speaker begin with them. Open up those channels that have cut us off from one another. That connecting energy is the glue that keeps us together. It is called love.

We have had several articles written about us in newspapers here and will be appearing on Egyptian Television Friday morning January 21st. We are doing everything we can to let the people here know that there are Americans who only wish for 'the peace' as the people here say.

For the last two weeks we have been traveling south along the Nile through Egypt with my daughter and her friend who are both in their early twenties. It has been a great pleasure to watch them begin to understand the generosity of the Egyptian people.

The secret is to refuse all 'guide services' until you have escaped from the 'tourist trails.' Cross the river or go to the other side of town if necessary. Around the corner, after midnight, you will find magic streets with live bands perched on donkey carts. The dancing is infectious and soon you find yourself moving with the dancing villagers. What a treat to watch my daughter and her friend learning new dance moves from the village girls! And again, beyond the edges of the tourist trails, Egyptian friends by the Red Sea adopted us and kept us busy dancing and singing in their favorite late night restaurants.

Dancing Fun in Hurghada

Making Flutes and Human Rights Concert

I visited my musician friend Qadry Sorour who taught nay at the traditional music school in Zamalek and he showed me how a nay is fabricated from the grass reeds which grow in the Nile river delta.

Qadry Sorour Making a Nay

Before we left Cairo we gave a concert for a delightfully fun Egyptian group called the South Center for Human Rights in the suburb of Imbaba. And we gave Interviews for Al Akhbar Newspaper and Akhbar Gideed Ch 9 News which was aired to millions in Arab world.

Performing for Human Rights Center

After the formal part of our concert was over they wanted more... so we played for a long time into the night.

They Want More Music

During the afternoons we hung out with our journalist friend Ahmad. He was always full of brilliant cross-cultural insights and smiles and good cheer.

Kristen, Lauren, Ahmad

Kristina and I had, as she said, completed four trips together now through Arab-world countries in the Middle East. Whenever it was time to move on from one household or city or country to the next we would find ourselves sharing the same feelings at the same moment... we would just look at each other and know... yup, time to move on... we still seemed to share the same internal clock... I could never have moved so smoothly through all those adventures without having been so connected to Kristina's warmth and intuition.

2004 - 2005 Syria and Egypt

Surgery in France

We flew to Madrid where I came down with a nasty kidney infection. It was the spring of 2005. I was losing ground to the fever so we went to a hospital. They cultured the bug in my urine and had a way to target it with an antibiotic within only three hours. That was fast and efficient. I offered to pay for the hospital services but they said that the billing wouldn't be processed for a few weeks and suggested that I just blow it off since I was a foreigner.

We climbed onto a train and crossed up to Bordeaux, France where I had arranged to have another surgical procedure - an ablation which might actually fix the heart arrhythmia called 'atrial fibrillation' which had been plaguing me for the last ten years or so. I had been taking blood thinners and medications to slow my heartbeat for a long time and was happy that the doctors in France had finally invented a surgical cure.

Still extremely weak from the kidney infection, I showed up in time for the heart surgery which would be accomplished without actually opening my chest. They would introduce their tools through my arteries and veins in my legs and thread their way up into my heart. I had high hopes that I might finally be cured of that nasty kind of heart arrhythmia which commonly afflicts those who, like me, had pushed our hearts too hard with climbing and cross-country skiing early in life.

Back in the USA at the Mayo Clinic I had been told by a cardiologist that he had been working to copy the French doctors' technique and that for around two-hundred-thousand dollars he would take me as a patient and give it a try. The French doctors wanted only twenty-thousand dollars and they had a much better track record. Some old friends of mine conducted a fund-raiser and came up with the twenty-thousand.

After two weeks in Bordeaux we took the train back to Madrid, I paid my hospital bill there as a matter of personal conscience, and we holed up for another week or so in a small hotel. I was too weak to go out. Kristina brought food back to our room.

Louisiana, Paris, California Disaster

Back in the USA I was still extremely weak but somehow we did a half dozen shows in Colorado before heading out on another tour through Louisiana and the South. Again it seemed that every night in and around the New Orleans area involved delicious dinners with plenty of wine... dancing... music...

After that came a quick trip to Paris. We had been contacted by a Dutch non-profit organization called 'Music in ME' - which stood for both 'Music Inside of Me' and 'Music in the Middle East.' We had met the director of that organization by now and were interested to discover how much our non-profit goals overlapped. Franz, the director, flew both me and Kristina from Louisiana to New York for an introductory meeting with other members of 'Music in ME.'

Franz then bought me a round trip ticket to Paris, France for their next meeting. I asked for an extra ten days or so and spent my time exploring Paris. I had never been there to walk beside the Seine, visit the Louvre nor to see what turned out to be my favorite: the Moulon Rouge dance extravaganza which had been running continually for a hundred years.

Back in Colorado again we gave another show and more radio and TV interviews. Then Kristina and I set off on another West coast tour. I was still quite weak from the ablation I had undergone in Bordeaux. But even though I was moving slowly we drove back west and completed more shows and workshops in Santa Barbara, Monterey, Aptos, six more events in Sonora, and a long-distance radio interview for KKNW in Seattle.

One night our luck ran out on the highway. We lost our travel trailer. It clipped a bridge railing during high gusty winds somewhere on Interstate 5 in central California.

After some wild fish-tailing we came to a stop... we were pulling a flat-bed trailer with a toilet on it. The remainder of our little house on wheels and all our belongings were in a heap of wreckage in the middle of the highway. A few of the young men who stopped to "help us" jumped back into their car and sped off... they had found and stolen Kristina's Jordanian gold jewelry.

We always kept all the musical instruments and sound equipment inside the back of the van so none of that was lost or damaged. We picked through the pile of debris, which the police had shoved onto the dirt beside the highway with the big bumpers on the fronts of their cars, and we put the most valuable things we could find into the back of the van.

We drove down the road and rented a motel room for the rest of the night. The next morning we returned to the remains of our trailer and finished picking through and salvaging what was left. We eventually got a bill from the State of California. They had hauled the rest to the dump.

We had to cancel a number of up-coming shows in Oregon, California and Arizona. That was the first time we had failed to stay on schedule. In fact we had actually succeeded in never missing or having to cancel a single show... even when it had meant doing seven shows in six days and driving a thousand miles at the same time!

We bought a tent and a little utility trailer and moved into a campground near Santa Cruz. A kind elderly gentleman then offered us a little apartment on his avocado plantation. We managed to do two more shows in San Leandro but we were exhausted and crippled without our little home on wheels. I came down with another fever and Kristina drove us back home.

We stayed in Colorado to recuperate for the next few weeks. Then we received an invitation to sing our Arabic music backed up by four choirs in Omaha at St. Cecilia Cathedral... sponsored by the North Central American Choral Directors Association. We couldn't resist that. Especially haunting was an arrangement of John Lennon's 'Imagine' punctuated in several places with very slow and ethereal phrases from a Lebanese Fairouz song which employs a minor second in its music scale... something hardly ever heard in Western music. We were left to produce the Lebanese song solo with just Kristina's voice and my oud. Christian choir directors wanting to include Arabic music represented quite a bold step for them.

We managed to complete additional shows in Nebraska and up in Wisconsin on the same tour. We gave presentations and workshops in Madison at the largest Unitarian Universalist congregation in the whole USA. Our workshops there were titled: "Is English the Only Language in which it's Possible to be Right?" and "Spiritual Traveler: Journeys Beyond Fear." Our presentation was now called "Singing in Baghdad and Beyond" and we also gave that show for the Unitarians in Wausau and for the University of Wisconsin at Marinette.

Increasingly I was becoming aware of the self-imposed cultural isolation within the English-speaking world. Native English speakers seldom go out of their way to master and immerse in other languages and the whole world pays the price as powerful decision-makers flail in ignorance. It seems that English speakers have an unconscious arrogance which prevents them from hearing other points of view which have their origins in other language families. With workshops like "Is English the Only Language in which it's Possible to be Right?" I was trying to address this strange truth directly in ways that might make people stop and think.

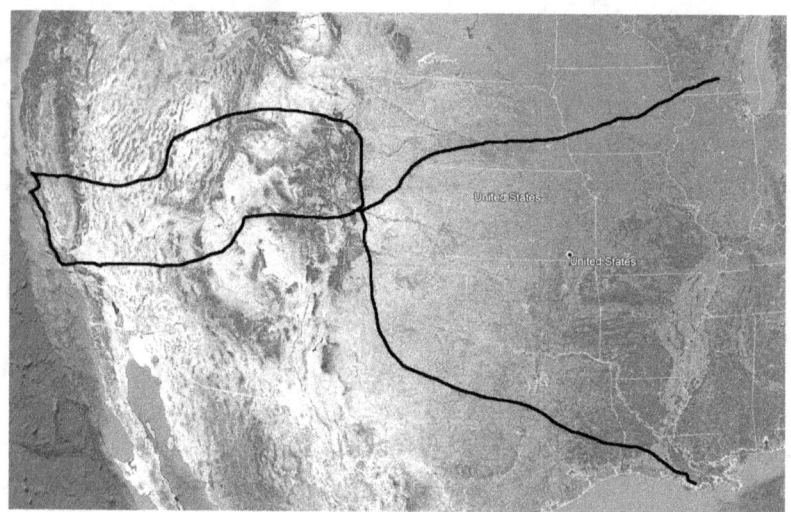

2005 - 2006 in the USA

Shortly after we returned to Colorado, Franz flew me to Los Angeles where I was able to introduce him to Arab-world musician friends of mine. Perhaps some of them would be interested in helping his Music in the Middle East projects.

Ultimately Franz and I discovered a basic difference between our approaches. I didn't share his long-term agenda to bring European classical music into the Middle East. We let go of our dreams of partnership. I was one-hundred-percent focused on bringing the beauty of Arabic music and culture into the West... nothing much the other way around. But Franz and I and Kristina had enjoyed a marvelous time getting to know each other.

And of course we continued to perform with our musician friends in Boulder... our home base. Combining our financial resources, Kristina and I bought a little house in Broomfield, Colorado just east of Boulder. We had actually done pretty well financially on the road... close to half of our income came from selling the beautiful beaded Egyptian scarves we kept buying from our friend Mahmoud in Khan el Khalili in Cairo... the same Mahmoud to whom Eva had introduced me more than ten years earlier.

My daughter returned from living and studying in Santa Cruz and moved in with us in our new little house in Broomfield. A month or so later her boyfriend, Lucas, also returned and moved in too.

It had taken months before I had regained some strength... then we were ready for something entirely different.

Belly Dancers in Venezuela

We landed in Caracas and made our way to Isla Margarita, right off the Venezuelan Caribbean coast.

Warm tropical breezes... warm water... sand... very nice...

We had only been there for a day... we were walking down a street in Porlamar, the largest town on the island... a poster caught Kristina's eye. 'Belly dance classes'... by Angy Najla.

Kristina wrote down the phone number... I called... Angy invited us to meet her at her studio. She was just finishing teaching a class for around thirty of her three hundred students. I had my oud with me so we played a few tunes for the class.

Angy Najla and Her Belly Dance Class

The next few nights we were busy following Angy from party to party and playing for her to dance. There was only one problem: we had no portable sound system... frequently the background noise levels at these parties was so high... people having fun... that playing acoustically was frustrating. Still, Angy managed to pay us $100 for each event. Belly dance was extremely popular in Venezuela, perhaps partially thanks to Shakira, a sexy Colombian singer whose father is Egyptian.

While green parrots chattered overhead, a family of four mounted a motor-scooter and headed down the road. Leaning gracefully into a high-speed curve, a young father passed on a motorcycle: right hand on the throttle, left hand cradling his tranquilly-sleeping infant son.

High school girls were practicing their sexy moves to music on the street while another proud young man, of the usual African-Native-American-European mix, explained once again that Venezuela is the happiest place on earth! "We are always in enjoyment! And we are good people and there is hardly any crime or delinquency! The newspapers are not telling the truth about that! The reporters want to get their pay so they invent stories about crime!"

My son Loren flew down and spent a week or so with us on the island... wind-surfing was added to his bag of sporting skills. We had a good time... his Spanish was pretty good...

Me and Loren

Green Andean Valleys

Kristina and I wanted to explore more of Venezuela. It cost us less than $50 to fly from Caracas up to Merida in the high-altitude south-western part of the country.

We enjoyed our plane flight in ways I hadn't experienced since being a child. We could see out the front windows of the plane: a rare treat! No closed doors to the cockpit! And we could carry our liquids and our scissors and pocket-knives on board no problem! I guessed Venezuela hadn't made too many enemies, or, if they had, they were too busy living life to worry about them. Fear was definitely not the ruling factor for how to conduct your life there.

We rented a car in Merida and began a thousand-mile meandering journey back downhill toward the Caribbean coast. Venezuela was an oil exporter: we pulled up to the pump and filled the empty tank in our rental car for less than $2. Gasoline was subsidized by the government and cost about $0.16 a gallon. This reminded me of being in Iraq when gasoline had still been only $0.04 a gallon.

The highway wound its way down through green Andean valleys. Remote Venezuelan communities like Jaji and Bocono were beautiful little worlds unto themselves. You could obviously be born, live your life and then die in one of these little well-groomed towns and never hardly even think about the rest of the world.

Stopping in motels at night we would occasionally turn on the TV. Venezuela was carrying channels not just in Spanish but also in English, Portuguese, Arabic, Italian and French. Travelogues featuring the beauty of Arabic civilization as it now exists could be seen... gee... why didn't we ever get to see these kinds of shows up in the USA?

The government had a health campaign going to reduce the number of cigarette smokers in the country. This billboard displayed an interesting angle on that... "Smoking causes impotence!"

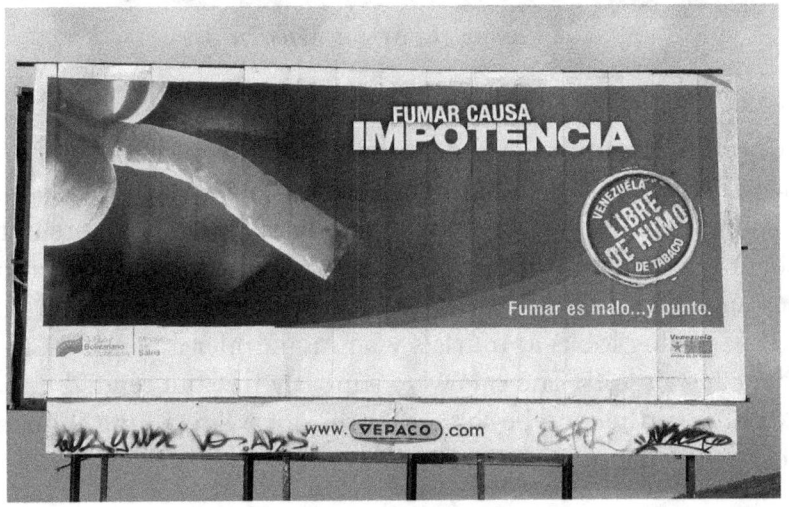

Stop Smoking!

As we wandered through western Venezuela we noticed that there were very few visible police. I don't think we ever even saw a 'traffic cop.' But as we moved closer to Caracas the police became more visible and some young police even extorted about $8 from us by refusing to allow us to pass through a 'closed' park after dark until we paid them off. Eight dollars poorer we continued driving and arrived in Choroni back on the Caribbean coast later that same night.

Venezuela Street Musicians

Choroni is famous for drumming on the beach... kind of a back-packer's haven. We did find the drumming and... it was so much fun seeing the dogs free to enjoy themselves. Since they were not on leashes or behind fences, they had a very mellow society of their own which included a lot of nap-taking along the road-sides and occasional hang-dog looks at tourists who might offer a hand-out in the outdoor restaurants. The cats were similarly free but tended to hang back a little further and be shy. As for the dogs: I'm talking about a *lot of dogs*... very happy dogs!

Very Free and Happy Dogs

The Venezuelan people, the vast majority of those whom we met, were extremely supportive of Hugo Chavez and his government. Cardboard shacks were being replaced with nice little houses all at government expense. Green energy technologies like wind-farms were proliferating and wealthy landowners were having to prove the productivity of their vast haciendas or face nationalization with the poor folks becoming the beneficiaries. The mainstream Venezuelans had just re-elected Chavez with a huge favorable landslide of votes and they were comfortably enjoying some time at the beach.

Happy Venezuelans on the Beach

Traffic flows organically in Venezuela... free like the dogs... with minimal adherence to the rules. I love renting cars and driving in places like Venezuela.

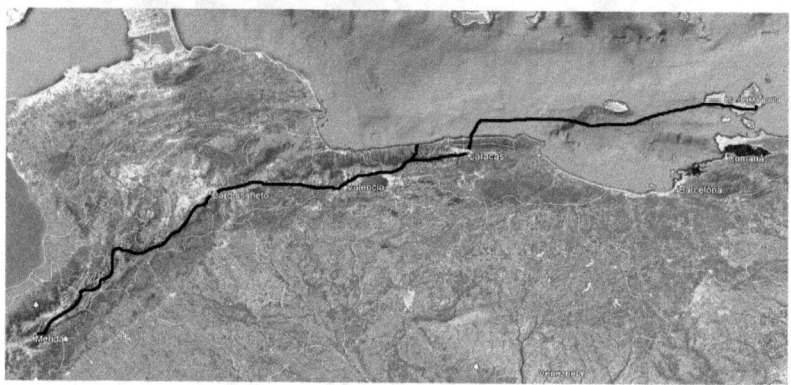

Venezuela - 2006

Telepathic Plant Communication in Mexico

Our friend Zia, who was also the acting president of our non-profit organization, Musical Missions of Peace, had long been connected to a circle of friends in Mexico who had indigenous Mexica, or Nahuatl or Aztec blood running through their veins. They were actively sharing information which was enabling them to reclaim their ancient cultural ways of being. Zia had been traveling quite frequently to visit them and now a plan had emerged which could include other friends of hers from Colorado... like us for example...

It has long been known that humans can sharpen their deep listening skills and learn to communicate in more direct ways with animals and plants. Zia organized a weekend practice session for all of us who were interested. She chose one of the most spectacular known hot springs-fed canyons on planet earth: Las Grutas de Tolontongo in the state of Hidalgo.

Tolontongo Hot Springs

Mexicas, as the Nahuatl-speaking Aztec people are now known, showed up in their finest Aztec feathers and with their drums and conch horns and rattles they descended back into their indigenous roots.

Mexica Feathers

I was invited to offer musical samples from Iraq, the cradle of old world civilization, and the Mexicas were fascinated to discover that there were 'notes between the notes' which created musical intervals with each other which were more in tune than are the modern Western 'equally tempered' music scales. Diving into ancient indigenous wisdoms, skills and art forms gave us all some sense of liberation.

I had recently published my "Arabic Musical Scales" book and could describe the precise harmonies of ancient music.

Arabic Musical Scales

The warm river in the bottom of the red canyon nourished greenery... living plants with whom we began experimenting... could we feel each other's presence on some telepathic level? We believed that something like this must be possible so we followed Zia's instructions on how to awaken those skills and connections. I had felt the non-verbal connections with other humans for so long, a natural by-product of traveling in lands where my language skills were limited, that I felt optimistic about including animals and plants more consciously into my world. And we now had a new circle of Mexica friends and looked forward to seeing them all again.

Huichol Indian Refuge in Guadalajara

We traveled from Tolontongo to Guadalajara with our friend Elena who introduced us to an extended family of Huichol musicians living there in the city. The Huicholes are famous for the depths of their peyote-driven spiritual quests, their active shamanism and for their very colorful psychedelic artwork. They continue to dress all in white with colorfully embroidered and beaded hats and pants and shirts.

They played modern Mexican music for a living in whatever venues they could find. Their own indigenous music, played quietly on tiny violins, they kept to themselves.

We spent a couple of days and nights with them. By day we would follow those tiny people as they conducted their errands through the city on foot. Their habit was to move fast and keeping up with their walking pace was a lot of work for us.

Huichol Friend

By night we all slept on the hard common-room floor of their rented space in the city. And we listened to their tales about the changes they were going through. They were having a hard time. Their own children were succumbing to depression and alcohol. There wasn't enough income to travel back home to their remote villages and their elders were passing away unattended.

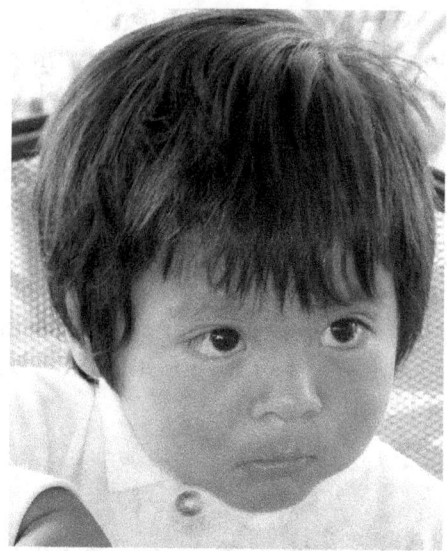

Huichol Child

We felt very grateful to Elena for introducing us to this extended family. It would have been nice to be able to celebrate more openly with them as we had just done with our Mexica friends in Tolontongo, but the poverty crushing this Huichol family was overwhelming.

We continued down to Puerto Vallarta on the Pacific coast. Our friend Cyndi offered an open-air loft in her house for us to sleep in and we began re-connecting with our musician friends... Antonio, D'Rachel, Sylvia, Pablo, Rigoberto...

Antonio - Master Keyboard Artist

We had our instruments with us and the basic wiring needed to connect to a small sound system.

We put out the word through the local belly dance community. There was a dancer who was actively performing and eager for adventure: Aisha Santy. We arranged two performances at The Arabian Corner and did what we could do to bring the magic of the indigenous Middle East into Mexico.

Playing for Aisha at the Arabian Corner

Working with Aisha was a pure delight. Every once in a while you meet someone who has the gift of being able to enjoy their own body, their own sensuality and their own ability to delight audiences by sending out pure energies of love with no hesitations or inhibitions... Aisha Santy is one of these people. What fun!

Aisha

We have stayed in touch with her through subsequent years as she has experimented with performance venues on the Caribbean coast as well as on the Pacific coast. She has also become a young mother. Her dance career is growing and expanding. I feel like we have a deep love connection. She is not an English speaker so all our communications have happened in Spanish and through the music and dance.

2006 - Mexico

Boulder - Visit from Robin

Back home in Boulder I received a message from Robin. "I'm going to come through Boulder! I want to see you!" We spent several hours sitting on a rock up in the foothills and catching up. She had started a dating service in Dallas, Texas, and done very well with that as a business. I was sad that she was just passing through and that we wouldn't have a longer period of time to reconnect. So many years... So many life adventures not shared! How could we ever catch up?

She also had very bad news. Breast cancer. Yes, she had undergone all the surgeries and the treatments... but there was a fear that it might still be hiding in her body. She was thinking to marry a boyfriend and move to his house in California. He would be able to offer her some additional love and support. She did marry him and move to California. The next time she contacted me it would be through the ether... a couple of years later...

Seven Hundred Voices

Singing with the four choirs in Omaha had been a success in those choir directors' estimations. In 2007 they flew us to Orlando, Florida, to sing with additional choirs which would back us up with seven hundred voices! An audience of a thousand filled the First United Methodist Church in Orlando and it was a powerful event. We also gave a workshop on Arabic music and an interview on Orlando radio.

Back in Denver I was invited to give the keynote address for the Universal Peace Federation. More and more often I was being asked to speak at similar conferences being produced by organizations like the Peace Corps, Colorado Ambassadors for Peace, the Museum of Natural History, The United Nations International Day of Peace, the Universal Peace Federation, a Daniel Pearl Peace Concert, the Network of Spiritual Progressives at the opening of Democratic National Convention, and the Abrahamic Initiative.

It always seemed that unless I was given the time to present my full 'Singing in Baghdad' event, these audiences couldn't really make the leap to understand what I was talking about. For people to begin to believe that a pure music and heart path was possible, they had to see more. And the usual methods of operation for these larger organizations involved long verbal discussions about politically-oriented solutions. They wanted my words but seldom invited my music and images. The realm of the arts has a traditionally low position in patriarchal consciousness and people don't readily realize that if there ever really is to be peace on earth it will probably be thanks to music and dance. I also found it frustrating to realize the degree to which American audiences had been basically brain-washed with all kinds of backwards notions about the Middle East.

I expanded my Colorado band and played Arabic dance music using names like 'Rockin' in the Cradles of Civilization,' 'The Innernationals,' 'Arabic Trance Dance,' and 'Musical Avatars.'

Expanding My Colorado Band

Those events were fun, popular and felt very successful. My Moroccan musician friend Rachid Halihal would sometimes join us and add those skilled violin licks which could take our sound up into the professional realm for all audiences... even Arab audiences.

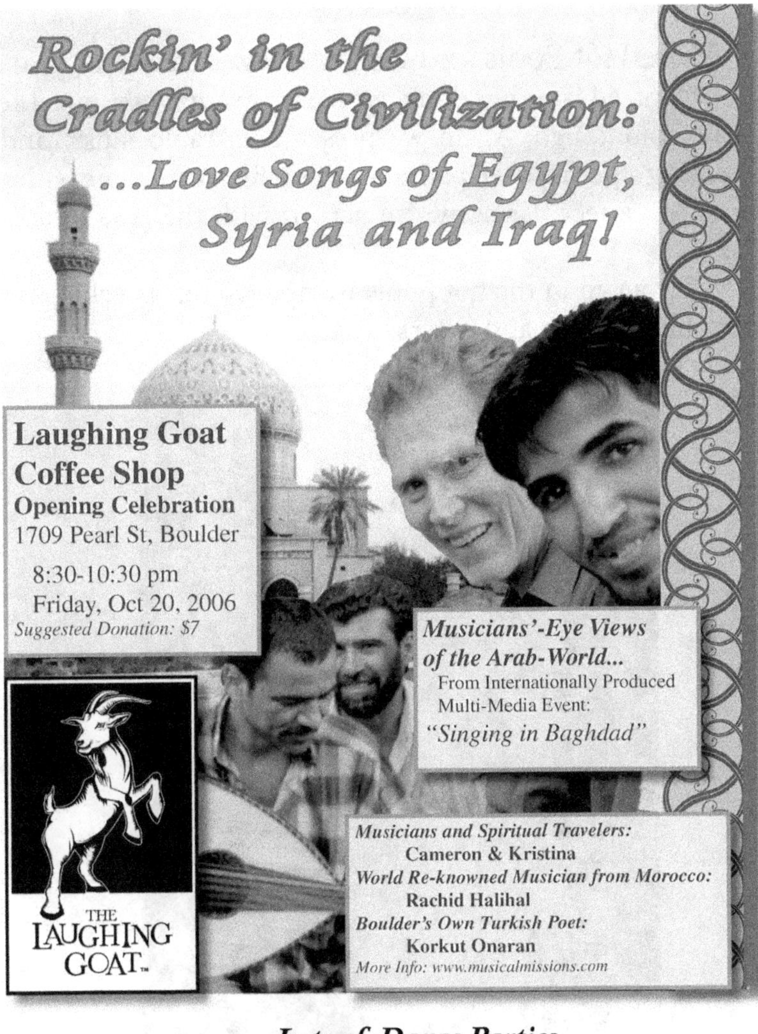
Rockin' in the
Cradles of Civilization:
...Love Songs of Egypt,
Syria and Iraq!
Laughing Goat
Coffee Shop
Opening Celebration
1709 Pearl St, Boulder
8:30-10:30 pm
Friday, Oct 20, 2006
Suggested Donation: $7
Musicians'-Eye Views
of the Arab-World...
From Internationally Produced
Multi-Media Event:
"Singing in Baghdad"
THE
LAUGHING
GOAT
Musicians and Spiritual Travelers:
Cameron & Kristina
World Re-knowned Musician from Morocco:
Rachid Halihal
Boulder's Own Turkish Poet:
Korkut Onaran
More Info: www.musicalmissions.com

Lots of Dance Parties

But I couldn't afford to go on the road with ten musicians so those shows remained a Colorado phenomenon.

Cameron Powers Project Band

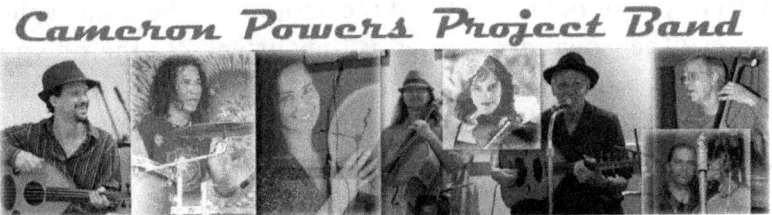

Cameron Powers Project Band

More Hot Pools and Green Leaves in Mexico

Zia organized another long weekend event with our Mexica friends in Tolontongo. Again we presented Arabic music and the deep listening - perhaps telepathic - skills which can come with playing music in perfect harmony... in accord with the laws of acoustic physics.

As we lay again in the hot pools we opened our psychic pores to our vegetable brothers and sisters.

Back in Tolontongo Hot Springs

Our Mexica friends remembered the information I had presented the previous year about 'the notes between the notes' being the ones in harmony with nature and told me about how that knowledge had reinforced their own discoveries as they listened to their own whistles and rattles and flutes. They bathed us in the powerful dances and chants which they had been revitalizing from their own culture. How could we not fall in love with all those colorful feathers and radiant faces?

Mexica Friends in Tolontongo

Back in Colorado we performed for Persian New Year... a fund-raiser for the Tadjik Teahouse and the Boulder-Dushanbe sister city relationship. We made a quick tour through northern California and performed in San Francisco and Santa Cruz.

Returning to Colorado we went to the Denver airport and picked up three Iraqi refugee women, a mother and her two daughters. We took them to an apartment complex which was largely filled with Sudanese refugees in South Denver. There was space for them there but we couldn't resist bringing them home to our house in Boulder after witnessing their levels of exhaustion and fear. The relief agencies would soon provide them the usual $340 per month per person with which to begin life here in America. How would they survive on that? The husband and father of the family had been killed two years earlier in Baghdad because one of his sons had worked with Americans. Very few Iraqis were being allowed into the USA. These three women were among a total of only five hundred Iraqis given refugee status during the whole year of 2008.

You may remember that when we were singing on the streets of Baghdad in 2003 we had deliberately turned down Iraqis' offers to come visit them in their homes precisely because we suspected that our acceptance of their hospitality could lead to this kind of retribution.

It had been two years since our last visit to the Middle East and we were feeling called to make another trip to Jordan and Syria. We offered our home for free to our three new female Iraqi refugee friends. It actually worked out so well that they continued living with us for several months even after our return.

Iraqi Music Party in Jordan

We spent our first night back in Jordan surrounded by thirty Iraqi refugees singing the 'old music' for us. This gathering had been organized by my old friend Muhsin to honor our return.

He had invited a large group of his refugee friends to the party: about twenty-five Iraqis. We all sat in a large circle. Muhsin used his violin to magnetize us all into a unified field of music. It was not a night for words and discussion.

Muhsin with Violin in Jordan

Underlying all the singing voices were the instruments: two ouds, two drums, a violin and a nay (Arabic flute) and as the night grew later more people were drawn to dance.

Two of the women present were accomplished singers and their lead vocals were given appreciative space. One of these women was also a fine percussionist.

I offered my version of a favorite introductory mawwal and Muhsin sang and spoke the lyrics with me. All Iraqis seem to know this traditional poetic musical story about a young man who seeks the advice of a village elder on matters of love. "Have you seen any available beautiful girls?" the lad inquires.

"Yes," replies the elder holy man, "but your luck is not so good. They departed early this morning with the camel caravan."

The mawwal ends and the famous rhythmic song begins. The young man goes out into the desert and sings of his longing to the full moon.

We Sing for Iraqi Refugees in Jordan

After midnight one of the most revered living Iraqi maqam singers, Hussein al Adhamy, whom Muhsin had also invited to the party, began to weave the poetic lines of his 'mawwals,' or arrhythmic incantations. He was truly giving voice to the old spiritual wisdoms of Iraq.

"Sama'i!" "Listen carefully!" was repeatedly whispered to encourage absolute focus on the poetry and the musical scales.

As I looked at the faces around me, all men and women who were now exiled from their homeland, I could see the different mixes of hardships and suffering. And I could see the childlike joy with which the music emerged from their souls.

Kristina Sings at Muhsin's Party

Musical Missions of Peace Project in Jordan and Syria

The next day we began dialogue with Jihad, our friend who owns one of the downtown Amman music shops, regarding our Musical Mission of Peace project designed to offer support to Iraqi refugee musicians in Jordan by paying them salaries to teach the refugee children. Jihad offered to allow the lessons to take place in his store until we could raise enough money to rent a dedicated location. We reached out through our network of musician friends and soon had three teachers ready to begin giving lessons. The songs they would teach contained spiritual wisdom handed down from the days of the Silk Road. The full ranges of ancient subtle microtonal musical scales would be used and the extreme fine tuning of the students' senses would be required. These songs were a container for the ancient Mesopotamian way of life which dates from the times when the Fertile Crescent was making some of the greatest contributions to civilization ever known. Another Iraqi woman, Widad, offered to help receive and distribute the salaries as soon as we could provide them.

At least two million Iraqis had by now fled to Jordan and Syria to escape the disorder and violence in their homeland. But neither Jordan nor Syria had the infrastructure to offer employment to so many people. That was why we were there. We would do what we could, in our own musical way, to provide a pipeline of financial support from sympathetic Americans.

This pathway through Musical Missions of Peace would be a direct connection through living Iraqi musicians who were eager to pass their traditions to the children. Musicians could be seen as the most trustworthy souls to carry out this mission. They were neither politicians nor military men nor even ambitious in business. When they had chosen the musical path, they had chosen the paths of the heart and of the poet.

The governments had spent hundreds of billions on the destructive process and shown very little ability to fix the things they had broken. In my opinion it would be up to us, the people, to actually make progress in this direction.

> As I walked down the street today in Amman, Jordan, tears came to my eyes. I felt like I had come home. This feels like home to me not because the sights are familiar or particularly beautiful.

The buildings are mostly gray concrete colors. The streets are dirty. Many people smoke and I dislike the smell of tobacco inside the shops. It's just that there is something else in the air that feels more powerful than the smoke.

So how do I explain to you what it is?

Maybe security is a part of it. If I should fall down everyone around me would come to my rescue. If I should get lost someone would personally guide me back to my hotel. No one is trying to steal my purse. Every shopkeeper and almost every other person I meet on the street is saying a sincere "Welcome" or "Hi."

Maybe it is that there is less fear. I have very little fear here. My heart is so open, because every other heart it meets is so open to me.

I guess another word might be 'relief.' I don't have to be an island. Women in the lobby of the hotel, whom I have never met before, motion for me to sit down next to them. I am welcomed. I don't have to be alone. Relief to know I'm surrounded by loving beings.

Isn't that what home is?

I've heard that there is no word in Arabic for 'alone', the closest word means 'lonely'.

I wonder why I, an American, need 'retreat time' or 'personal space' or 'time to collect my thoughts' or 'time to regroup' or just time to shut out the world and rest? For an Arab, time alone is just 'lonely.' Do we Americans tend to stress each other out? Why do we need a break from each other? Here they just like to sit close to each other and feel the connection. The air is filled with the currents of acceptance, less judgment, more connection. Like Fayaz the hotel owner here says, "Arabs are your friend immediately." You don't have to "earn their trust." It's just so much easier this way.

The next day we would leave for Damascus to initiate an identical project in Syria which had been the most welcoming country in the whole world to these now-homeless Iraqis.

If they could not yet return to their homes in Iraq we could at least provide this musical way for them to preserve their ancient spirit.

Famous Female Singers Performing in Syria

We traveled up across the border into Syria. Arriving in Damascus, we were in time to see the last two evening performances of 'Women in Arabic Music' presented at the Azem Palace in the old city. We had already missed the Iraqi and Syrian evenings but were able to attend the Egyptian and Lebanese shows during the next two nights as parts of tightly-packed open-air crowds.

Admission was free as the Syrian government sponsored the event. Conversations with Syrian folks in the audience revealed that, yes, they were surprised to discover that we were Americans. They hadn't seen many Americans for the past few years.

We were gratified to see that ongoing love for the ancient maqam music remained predominant with very little influence from modern European and American equal-tempered scales. Only the Lebanese music had sometimes been more Westernized.

Damascus, like Aleppo and Baghdad, claims five thousand years of cultural and musical heritage wherein lyrics have been composed in Arabic, Aramaic, Hebrew, Turkoman, Persian, Armenian and Turkish tongues by mixtures of Assyrian, Armenian, Syrian, Shi'ite, Sunnite, Christian, Jewish, Arab, Kurdish, Turkish, Turkoman and Persian musicians.

Aramaic Speakers in Ma'alula and Networking in Latakia

After a third evening in Damascus we rented a tiny little car and drove to Ma'alula and Jubadin where Aramaic was still the commonly spoken household language. Ma'alula was becoming an important destination for Christians interested in hearing the language Jesus would have spoken.

Aramaic Speaking Christians Still Live in Ma'alula

We spent the night in the Christian Convent of Saint Tekla, a female Saint who had lived eighteen-hundred years ago. We were delighted to discover that the inhabitants of these two towns now took pride in their ancient language and were helping make sure that it wouldn't die out. Of course they were all bilingual in both Aramaic and Arabic. There are also Aramaic-speaking villages still in Iraq. Ma'alula was invaded and occupied a few years later by Islamic State and some of the nuns were held in captivity for ransom. Their release was negotiated but some Christian icons were destroyed.

Driving down to the Mediterranean coast to Latakia on the following day we were greeted by our friend Mohammad. Thanks to him we met Fadhil, another Iraqi refugee and lover of the old Iraqi music styles. Fadhil offered to be the new Iraqi director for our project to support Iraqi musical teachings in Syria. He offered to meet us back in Damascus later in the week to help bring our project to the attention of the Damascus-based Institute for the Study of High Musical Arts. Fadhil felt that we needed recognition and approval from some Syrian government agency.

Fadhil and Me

Through Mohammad we also met Arab music historian Ali Haddad and his son Abd al Wahab Haddad. They both generously offered to support our work in whatever ways possible.

Also through Mohammad we met Anthony Ham who was researching and writing the latest Lonely Planet guidebook to the Middle East. Anthony was impressed with our projects and eventually wrote an extensive, accurate and eloquent feature article about our work which occupied a full page in the next edition of the Middle East Lonely Planet guidebook. I printed that article at the very beginning of this book.

And, again thanks to Mohammad's networking, we did a musical performance at the local Dhikrayat Restaurant in which we featured songs from Iraq, Syria, Lebanon and Egypt for an appreciative audience who honored us by singing along, especially when we performed the Syrian music.

The next day Mohammad took us on a drive up the Syrian Mediterranean coast where we spent some time hanging out on the beach with other friendly young Syrian folks.

Mediterranean Beach in Northern Syria

Jewish to Iraqi to Sabaean to Palestinian Neighborhoods

Driving back up into the Northern highlands we arrived in Aleppo where we met with our oud-maker friend Ibrahim Sukar and discussed methods for providing traditional Arabic musical instruments to the Iraqi music students who become involved with our project. We met an oud player who sings both Syrian and Iraqi maqam music in a local restaurant and joined in the singing with him when our repertoires overlapped.

The next afternoon we visited with a Syrian Jewish friend whom we had met on a previous trip. Israel had always seemed like a crazy idea to him. He still felt welcome at home in Aleppo and, along with other members of his ancient community there in the Jewish quarter, he still called that place home and kept his shop open. Knowing that visiting Americans would be surprised to learn that Jews were still welcome in Syria, he liked to befriend us and let us know what he thought about the crazy Israeli attitudes.

We headed down to Damascus to meet with Fadhil and begin our quest for Syrian government approval of our programs. Fadhil also wanted to take us to the parts of Damascus where most Iraqi refugees were living. He took us to Saida Zeinab where we walked down 'Little Iraq Street', ate Iraqi food and visited the incredible Saida Zeinab Mosque.

Little Iraq Street in Saida Zeinab

Saida Zeinab is a popular destination for people from all over the Islamic world. The neighborhoods were teeming with multi-ethnic populations. The evening ecstatic activities in the mosque, which had been built to honor a female Shia saint, were powerful and fervent with the prayer and singing building to uproarious devotional proportions. Kristina joined women and children who romped and prayed on one side of the internal shrine while Fadhil and I entered the men's side passing through groups of young men singing vocal chants while striking their bodies as if they themselves were the drums.

Sparkling lights were reflected in multicolored chandeliers of crystals underneath a golden dome illuminating everything with indescribable brilliance while the men moved and undulated in trance as they rubbed themselves against the shrine.

Saida Zeinab Mosque

Jaramana, the same neighborhood in which we had sung with Palestinian refugee children in the fall of 2003, was nearby. There we met a Sabaean Iraqi. Christian historians sometimes acknowledge Sabaean wisdom as having underlain the Essene teachings which had helped shape those attributed to Jesus.

Out in the streets we were again surrounded by an Iraqi majority just as we had been in Baghdad. These people knew and adored singers like Nazem al Ghazali whose ecstatic performances of maqam music seventy years ago, at the dawn of the era of recorded music, helped perpetuate the legacy of the Iraqi soul. They were enchanted to hear that our Musical Mission of Peace aimed to support the teaching of these ancient musical styles.

Millions of Iraqis in Syria

When you hear the word 'Syria' what thoughts and feelings come to mind? Are they warm and fuzzy thoughts, or thoughts with a bit of fear? If there is some fear in those thoughts where did it come from? Who put it there?

Ahmad the hotel owner in Aleppo tells tale after tale of the absurd fears Westerners have while traveling in Syria. Yesterday two young American women had tried to pretend to be Canadian.

"Anyone could see that they were California girls," Ahmad declared. "I took them around in the market and eventually they learned that the shop-keepers gave them just as many treats when they admitted their real nationality as they had been given when

> they had claimed to be from Canada.
>
> "But everything is confused," he continued. "I watched the Western journalists deliberately mis-translate a Lebanese woman's statements on television just the other day. When asked about a local youth organization she replied in Arabic that they provide much charitable aid and are very helpful to the local people. But the English version broadcast on the BBC made it sound as if she was afraid of them and had claimed that they were some kind of terrorist organization. She had said nothing like that whatsoever!"
>
> A Peruvian woman who was traveling with her German husband told us, "We were a bit afraid to come, but we wanted to challenge ourselves." They were immersed in the light-hearted conversation taking place in the small hotel lobby where tea is always freely served and laughter is the common theme. They now feel a bit foolish that they had felt any fear at all. "But we are fed the same stories on the news in Germany that are broadcast all over the Western world!"
>
> Unspoken unconscious assumptions: how much are these controlling our thoughts and feelings and where did they come from?

The Exact Opposite of War

After traveling through the Southern, Western, Northern and Central parts of Syria it had become clear that all roads lead to Damascus. I opened a bank account and Fadhil and I both became signers on the account.

We also met with employees of the United Nations Refugee Agency in Damascus and they put us in contact with those who administer classroom spaces and other facilities which could be utilized for our teaching program. Thanks to donations which had already been received we had enough money to begin on a small scale.

We were working to accomplish goals which were the exact opposite of war. The more we worked on setting up this project the more we realized what a perfect vehicle it would be for Americans who had felt anguish about the war and who wanted to give something back to the Iraqi people.

And of course members of fundamentalist Arabic groups wouldn't become involved because they don't see popular music as a legitimate part of their Saudi-trained Wahabi world. If they did open their minds and want to be included then that would be so much the better.

Fadhil arranged for us to meet with administrators who coordinate non-profit activities with the Syrian government. We received enthusiastic responses but it seemed doubtful to me that any of these official doors would really open. We weren't big enough and the process would take too long. Fadhil was thinking that we were stuck without government approval. I was thinking to just proceed without official authorizations. We had assembled a list of Iraqi musicians who would be happy to teach. I felt that those commitments were all we really needed.

Just Give this Hundred Dollars to some Iraqi Refugee!

We crossed the border again and returned south to Jordan.

Following another lead in our endless search for live music performances we climbed up to the fourth floor open terrace of a restaurant we had never before discovered in Amman. The manager told us that the regularly employed Jordanian oud player was not there that week but that they had an Iraqi oud player in his place. It was only 10:30 PM, still early, so he hadn't arrived yet. We settled into a table and ordered a salad and Arabic coffee.

An hour later the oud player arrived and plugged into the sound system and the table full of Iraqi men sitting next to us began singing along with him. When a song came by which we happened to know, we sang along too. I also made requests for some of the older Iraqi songs of Nazem al Ghazali and he was delighted to mix them in with his presentations of newer music. I was very happy to be bathed in his elaborate usage of maqamat, the ancient microtonal Arabic scales which I had come to love so well.

Our new oud playing friend, like all Iraqis, was in Jordan under rules and regulations which were not so favorable and the endless question in his mind was of course, "Where should I try and go to from here?"

He was very curious to hear my opinions about various possibilities like Sweden or Canada or the USA.

I had heard a few stories and I passed them on. One of our Iraqi friend's son had managed to get into Turkey and then on a boat to Greece. But, being required by the boat captain to finish the last part of the journey into Greece by swimming ashore, he had been immediately captured and sent to spend some time in a Greek prison before managing to move on, at considerable expense, to Sweden where he was now facing deportation back to Iraq. Not a pretty picture.

And of course we had recent experience with the refugee support options in America: try living on $330 a month until you find a job and get on your feet.

"So Canada is good?" he asked me.

"Maybe so... Or maybe Brazil..." I responded out of almost complete ignorance on the subject but knowing that going back to Iraq at that time could mean death for a lot of Iraqis.

I looked at him playing Iraqi music for the still-appreciative group of Iraqis in Jordan and I thought that maybe this place was not so bad for him. But the governmental pressures were being raised to make the Iraqis feel less welcome and the Jordanian government was increasing deportations. How about Syria...? Syria probably was offering the best circumstances at that time for Iraqis but everyone knew that, having already absorbed two million Iraqis into their economy, a ten-percent total population increase, the potential for employment in Syria was small.

Around 2:00 AM he thrust the oud into my hands and very appreciatively sang along with my still very imperfect rendition of 'Lamma Anakhu...'

Before we left we explained our work in Jordan and Syria and he was eager, of course, to be a part of it. He gave me his mobile phone number.

I put a large Jordanian Dinar bill in his hand. Later, when he would have the opportunity to look at it, hopefully he would be pleasantly surprised. A friend in Boulder had given me a $100 bill and said, "Just walk up and give this to some Iraqi refugee!"

With Widad and Fadhil ready to help administer our programs in both Jordan and Syria and with our lists of musicians ready to teach, I felt like our mission had been accomplished!

Greece Island of Rhodes: Finding the Music

We flew from Amman to Athens and then to the Greek island of Rhodes. My inner Greek soul was hungry for interaction. It had been too long.

We rented a little car and drove down the coast to Haraki Mar and claimed a little hotel room. I was feeling another version of being back home again and Greek language was flooding my brain. I exchanged insults and 'what-the-fuck' gestures with some guy trying to control my parking space and felt even more at home. I knew how to do that in Greek.

Stella and Eleftheria, two charming sisters who ran the little hotel at Haraki Mar, warmed up to us more and more as they discovered that I could speak Greek. Tranquility reigned. Delicious food... similar to food in Syria actually... was always a treat. Yes, now we had some time to hang by the clear blue Mediterranean waters... swim and... explore...

Downtown in the old walled city of Rhodes we found music venues... they opened around midnight and the bands would play until dawn. There we found musicians who could not only exhibit their mastery of the soulful Greek music known as Rembetika, but who also could add their artistry on the Turkish saz with its meticulously-placed quarter-tone frets... wow... real music!

What the Greeks know as Rembetika came with the refugees who, like my own kids' Greek grandmother, had fled Turkey to Athens after World War One from their ancient home in Smyrna. And by changing their preferred instrument from saz, with it's micro-tonally tuned frets, to bouzouki, with its equal-temper-tuned frets, the Greeks had begun to lose the fine tuning of the music which the Turks had largely learned five-hundred-years earlier from the Arabs.

No need to fully understand what I just said if you are not a Middle Eastern musician, but it was rare to see a band which employed both bouzoukia and sazlar. These orchestras on Rhodes could make the ancient flavors sing. They were good-sized and would typically have around ten musicians... percussion, strings, singers...

Greek Music on the Island of Rhodes

We would return back to our hotel under the rosy fingers of dawn with these deep ancient melodies ringing in our heads... this really was the place where East still met West and something harmonious was emerging... not so easy to achieve...

We loved driving from village to village on the island. We saw a little restaurant on the western side advertising special pie... "Where did you drive from?" the owner asked.

"From Haraki," we replied.

"Oh my god! All the way from over there? I've only traveled so far once or twice in my life!"

These villagers pretty much stayed put. We had driven about forty miles to get all the way from the other side of the island!

The pie was delicious... the woman who had made it was happy to give us news about her family.

I remained very happy not going to see the standard popular tourist destinations... the various forts and castles on the island which always just seem empty and dead to me. It doesn't usually occur to visiting tourists that, when they see fortified structures like castles, they are probably looking at the abandoned dwellings of the invaders who were not even really welcome there. If those invaders had been welcome they would have lived in little agricultural villages down in the valleys with everybody else... with the local folks. But history loves the legacies of military occupations and conquest and modern tourists automatically assume that that's where they should focus their attention.

My Kids' Athenian Grandmother is Ninety-Nine

Back in Athens we found a few more tastes of live Greek music and the lyrics and the dances also still contained the culminations of eons of popular wisdom.

Life for Greeks is a mix of joy and pain and, no, it's not going to be changing any time soon... Greeks watch the empires rise and fall as the centuries roll by and willingly shoulder the work which needs to be done... as expressed in so many songs...

> *One swallow is flying*
> *again across the precious dawn...*
> *To keep the sun rising and setting*
> *takes a huge amount of sweat...*

> *Just to keep the sun revolving on its axis*
> *thousands of deaths are required...*
> *Living beings are all required*
> *to give their blood...*
> *Yes, living beings are all required*
> *to give their blood...*

My kids' Greek grandmother, Elli, was still alive and I decided to go and visit her. She was ninety-nine years old. I hadn't seen her since Loren and Leda and I had all been there together eight years earlier. At that time the first thing she had told me was "Now I am just hoping for death. I am blind. I can no longer see. I want to go!"

So far, she hadn't gotten her wish. She was still alive and she was very glad to feel my touch and my presence. We had always had an easy friendship. The two women who were caring for her were very welcoming to me and to Kristina. They told me that Elli had quit speaking but that she could still hear and understand and smile.

We visited her for a long time... more than a couple of hours... I just sat beside her bed and held her in my arms. She made some happy sounds and smiled occasionally. I softly discussed family news with the two women... they had loving advice for helping my children. I could tell that Elli was still attentive and was understanding most of what we said. But she didn't try and speak.

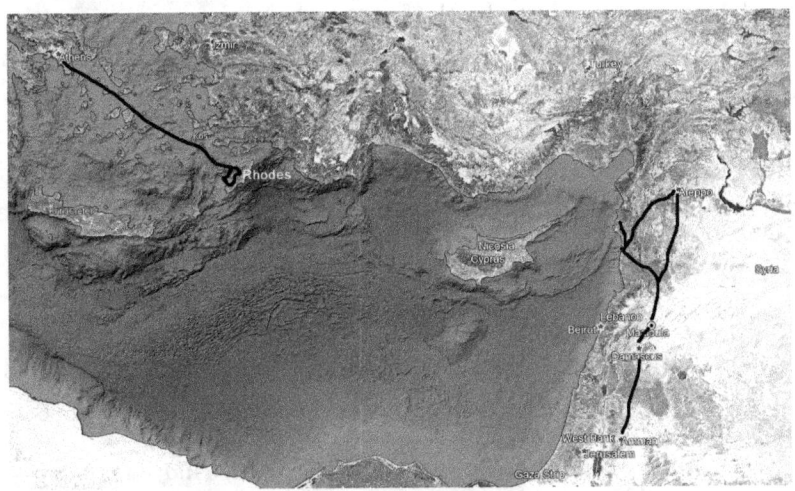

2008 - Syria, Jordan, Rhodes and Athens

A year later, at age one hundred, she finally would be granted her last wish... she would pass on.

Leda has told me several times that she feels very grateful that I was able to arrange that last visit.

Iraqi Refugee Musicians Begin Teaching

Soon our Iraqi Refugee musicians in both Damascus and Amman were sending us photos and videos of their students' progress and we began sending them money from Musical Missions of Peace from back home in Colorado.

Iraqi Music Lessons in Syria

After a few weeks word came back from Fadhil that official agencies were scrutinizing our financial transactions and might begin to investigate. Who knows what problems that might lead to...? So Huda, one of the Iraqi women staying in our house, swung into action and opened up a more underground channel for sending funds. Our project was entirely people-to-people and none of the official agencies in Syria had chosen to become involved. Operating 'underground' had turned out to be the best option.

Overt associations with Americans, as I had predicted, could be disastrous for Iraqis. Huda had been in touch with another Iraqi friend who had been studying in California at Stanford for a few months. But she could no longer safely go back home to Baghdad. Her family had been attacked because of her association with Americans.

Musical Detective Work

At about this time I received an email from a man in California.

> *Hello Cameron,*
> *My Name is Nadim Al-Bayati and I have really enjoyed reading your travel blog and learning of the good work you have done, it is all very exemplary.*
> *I was browsing your website, and noticed that the translation and transliteration of the mawwal from the song "Fog An-Nakhl Fog" needs some touch-up, as both the translation and transliteration*

> are inaccurate, and do not convey the full beauty of the poem.
> As it turns out, we are a family of Iraqi musicians, and have in the last few years, re-released onto CD, my fathers 1973 LP, "Saadoun Al-Bayati: Songs of Iraq." I would like to share with you our translation of the Mawwal attached to "Fog An-Nakhl Fog," which is called "Lammâ Anâkhu." The poetry is by Iraqi poet, a barber who would occasionally nick his customer's ears while excitedly reciting his poetry, Yûsaf Al-Lampachi.
> We hope you have many more wonderful music missions.
> All our best,
> The Al-Bayati Family

This was a miraculous connection for me and for the Al-Bayati family. It had been twenty years since Kathleen had handed me that mysterious tape and, based on a close but still inaccurate translation provided by the friendly Syrian fellow whom I had met at the Denver flea market, I had begun learning and performing that mawwal and song. I sent Nadim a recording of me singing it and he shared it with his now-aging father, Saadoun, and was soon told that the family wanted to meet me whenever possible. That would happen a couple of years later.

Losing my Mom in Colorado

My own ninety-three-year-old mother, Eleanor, had been in the hospital but was soon dismissed to recover from her lung infection in a nursing home. I visited her there and she was up and attending the public dinner table again. I came down with an intestinal virus and ran a high fever for four days. On the fifth day I was finally better. A native African caregiver on the staff at the nursing home called me and said, "I think you'd better come now..."

By the time Kristina and I arrived Eleanor was no longer conscious. She was still breathing. We sat and held her hands until the last breath had been taken... and then released... "She was waiting for you," explained the African woman.

I had been watching the difficulty and pain with which she had been moving that ninety-three-year-old body of hers... liberation seemed like a good thing.

If I had made great expressions of sorrow and loss I might have accidentally lured my mother back into her body. I had possibly had that experience twice... once with the old Indian in Arizona and once with a highway accident victim who had resumed breathing when I had placed my hand on his back and encouraged him.

I knew my mother's life was now done... it would have been silly for her to come back. There was no unfinished business. I remained in the state of surrender and allowing... allowing her death to be complete... a smooth exit...

My mom's last twelve years with us in Boulder had been good. I set about gathering and publishing more of her art work and her little 'not-really-for-kids books'... People who stop to read them get a taste of the high-flying ticklish loving sense of humor with which I had grown up.

New Mexico; Alone in California

Kristina and I traveled into the Colorado mountain town of Vail to produce another of a long series of shows in the nearby village of Avon and then we headed down into New Mexico and gave workshops at the International Sound Healing Conference.

I had shows booked in Ventura and Laguna Beach on the Southern California coast. Kristina didn't want to go so I drove west and enlisted the help of Christine Stevens and Rowan Storm. They did a good job of backing me up.

Christine offered me a free place to stay. Christine had begun traveling to northern Iraq to work with refugee women and children and had sought my advice a couple of years earlier. Later she had complimented me: "Out of all the people of whom I asked advice about what to expect in Iraq, you were the only one who made any sense." Years later Christine and Kristina and I and other members of Musical Ambassadors of Peace (the new name for Musical Missions of Peace) continue to launch exciting new non-profit projects.

Rowan was one of our Musical Ambassadors... and a dear old friend. Musical Missions of Peace had contributed to her adventurous traveling through Iran... a woman alone... making friends along her path with her extensive knowledge of Persian singing and her skill with the daf, the Persian frame drum. I had known Rowan since the 1970's when she and Leda and I and Danilo Stepanovich had all been in the same band together and performed Bolivian, Serbian and Greek music. That was shortly after Leda and I had returned from living in Athens. It felt good for me and Rowan to share our energies on stage again.

Kristina called me one night: "I found some really cheap tickets to Panama! Shall I buy them?"

"Yes," I agreed.

After I got off the phone Christine said, "Panama!? I'm going there too!" It turned out that we ended up there at the same time and did manage a musical rendezvous.

With my tour complete in California I headed back to Colorado and we soon flew to Panama.

Moving Slow in Panama

Renting a little car we headed for a little slow relaxation time in central Panama highlands: a little town called Santa Fe... healthy food... tropical birds... mellow mellow mellow... a week went by before we were again ready to go explore.

We drove toward the border with Costa Rica to the town of Volcan and found my old friend Russ Peterson with whom Leda and I had hiked for four days north of Rabbit Ears Pass up into Colorado's Mt. Zirkel Wilderness thirty-seven years ago. We had lots of catching up to do.

In search of real Panamanian music festivals we headed down into the Azuero Peninsula which hangs down off the southern coast of Panama into the Pacific... we found a combination music festival and rodeo. Samy and Sandra Sandoval performed hot sexy cumbia dance music. Farm tractors covered with feathered dancing girls pulled wagons filled with trombone players... the dancing girls reached between their breasts to extract sweat - nectars of the goddess - with their fingers which they then flicked out onto the adoring crowd. The grandmothers climbed up onto the main stage to dance. We were the only foreigners in sight.

Music Festival in Azuero Peninsula in Panama

Passing back through Panama City we found another music festival. Samy and Sandra Sandoval, king and queen of the cumbia, performed again. Apparently they were everywhere.

That festival featured bands from Panama... Colombia... Venezuela. In between each act the master of ceremonies repeated the same sentiment with passion: "We are one people! There is no difference between us! Colombia, Panama and Venezuela should be one people! One nation! Why are we allowing the politicians to divide us?"

Kristina and I practiced dancing belly-to-belly. If we separated our bodies by even a few inches for even a minute, someone in the crowd would emerge to embrace us and smush our bellies back together again. "This is how we dance in Panama..."

By day we watched high school kids parade down the streets of Panama City showing off their hot sexy drum licks... strutting their stuff... boys... girls...

Our friend Christine Stevens was drawing near on a cruise ship laden with workshop participants from Michael Beckwith's Agape Church in California. We were invited to meet them, so we drove to the northern end of the Panama Canal. Christine and a few passengers joined us on shore for a few hours. The local Afro-Panamanian drummers and dancers put on a show. We performed Iraqi music as an extra added bonus.

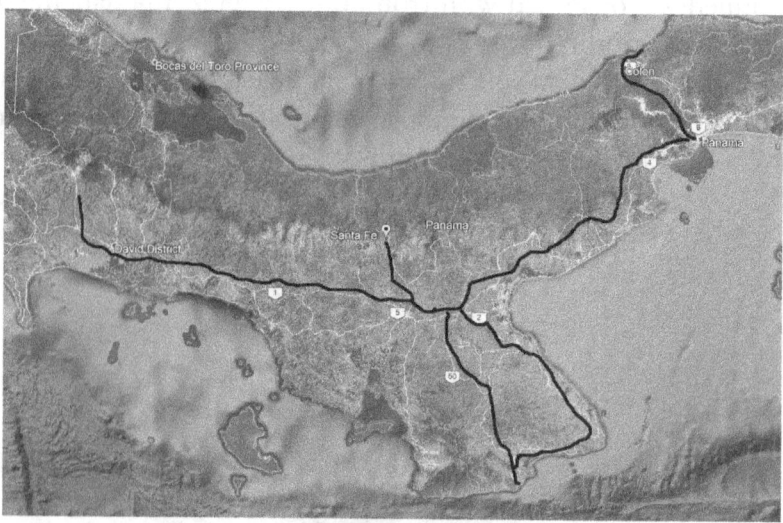

2009 Panama

Kristina always wants to return to live everywhere we go. Panama was now on her list!

Robin Calling Through the Ether

My mind was filling with images and energies from Robin. I had no contact information for her but I knew I should answer her energetic call. I began an Internet search for her and located the man whom had told me she was going to marry in California after realizing that she might be losing her battle with breast cancer. I called him. He was crying. He told me that she had always spoken highly of me and that she had died on February 26th, 2009. There was no easy way to digest this news. The love energies were still strong for her in my heart and it felt like our connection in this life had not yet been finished. Obviously her husband, a man named Barry, was feeling the same way... no doubt even more so. He and I are hoping to meet in person and share some of our Robin stories. When I talked to him over the phone he kept alluding to her amazingly adventurous spirit. I can still feel her primal love energy traveling with us.

Back in Colorado we were invited to present and perform at The Littleton Art and Music Festival, the Lyons Folk Festival, the University of Denver, the United Nations International Day of Peace, an Episcopal Convention in Pueblo, the Annual Muslim Students Cultural Festival, a Naropa University Civics Engagement Class, and the University of Colorado.

I also played "the music which Jesus might have heard" every Sunday at the Evening Wilderness Services at St. John's Episcopal Cathedral in Denver. I did this regularly for quite a few months and then passed the gig on to other musician friends of mine. I was always left with an incomplete feeling after these performances. The Christians were always eager to lay their emotional claims on this music without realizing that it really came from indigenous peoples from the Middle East who were still there... alive and well... from cradles of civilization which were much deeper and still more vital even in these modern times than Americans can generally imagine.

We rented the First Christian Church in Boulder and built up the band with more drummers and musicians and continued calling ourselves 'Arabic Trance Dance.' Our shows were drawing bigger and bigger dance crowds... visual art and light show magic voluntarily showed up. Our Boulder friends remember these events as having been real highlights in our efforts to bring ecstatic energies from the indigenous Middle East. I was having fun bringing as many guest musicians into my band as possible... excitement was running high as so many artists contributed their skills and talents.

We toured the West coast again for the winter months. Kristina began designing singing and drumming workshops for women. Starting in Arizona we began a series of new workshops and presentations with titles like 'The Transformational Power of Voice.' We worked our way up the California coast from North Hills to Montclair, Tustin and Aptos.

West Coast: Healing The World Through Music

We created new titles for our shows and workshops: 'Healing The World Through Music;' 'Love Songs from Around the World;' 'Musical Medicine from the Hot Spots: Iraq, Iran, Kurdistan, Syria, Egypt;' 'Healing the Wounds of War and Working across Cultural, Religious and Language Boundaries;' 'Becoming Musical Avatars for Peace;' 'Love songs from Egypt, Iran, Greece, Iraq, Peru, Syria, Armenia, Bulgaria, Mexico, Lebanon;' 'Discovering the Ancient Wisdom of Love: What Messages and Secrets do these Beautiful Ancient Melodies Contain?;' 'Let's Move from the Me to the We!' and more workshops called 'Spiritual Traveler: Journeys Beyond Fear; How to become a true Global Citizen.'

Most of our audiences were spiritually motivated to believe that "we are all one." ...that all beings are inter-connected and should have equal rights so that no group bears an unfair burden of suffering.

"Is English the Only Language in which it's Possible to be Right?" remained a powerful theme which I would try and develop to help people think sympathetically about people who live in other parts of the world and who speak other of the world's 7000 languages.

My readings of history were drawing me to the conclusion that far northern tribes who had never participated in the 'camel caravan' connectivity which developed in more tropical latitudes had never acquired the cultural propensity for learning multiple languages. These traditionally monolingual far northern tribes seemed to share unconscious beliefs that basically they were the only 'real humans' on planet earth. They were good empire builders and people who lived further south feared their invasions.

The Germanic, Slavic, Turkish and Mongol tribes all fell into this category and English, being a Germanic language, had never been a good vehicle for a real road into a genuine 'we are all one' mentality.

Ottoman Turkish leaders took pride in not learning other languages and relied on recruiting agents from other cultures to administer their empire. Their expertise remained in the military realm.

Mongols invaded India two dozen times bringing death and destruction and never learning to talk with the native inhabitants until they finally became Muslim and grew into a more global consciousness only about four hundred years ago.

European colonial atrocities were perpetrated by Germanic and some Romance-language nations. And the Slavic tribes finally imposed the Russian language throughout the whole culturally diverse region which eventually became the Soviet Union.

Fully aware that there are many exceptions to this general pattern I still felt it was worth bringing up in our workshops so we could take a look into historically reflected realities about the short-comings of our English-speaking culture.

As a trained linguist I had learned that a motivated adult can learn languages much more rapidly than can a child. So why do English-speakers continue to believe that they can't learn foreign languages if they don't learn as children?

And most importantly what penalty is paid by all of us thanks to our self-imposed mono-lingual way of being?

Trying to present as many of these workshops as possible we performed at Centers for Spiritual Living in Santa Barbara, San Leandro, Santa Cruz, Placerville and Oakland. We played at The Greek Restaurant in Downtown Santa Cruz, organized an Arabic Trance Dance Party in Placerville and did a presentation on the Common Ground Internet Radio before passing north through Washington State where Kristina offered another workshop for women in Chelan.

Kristina also worked hard to help me approach our workshops softly so as not to offend our largely mono-lingual attendees. It was hard for me, having seen the suffering of so many perfectly innocent people in places like Iraq, not to feel anger at my own culture. I also had little faith that even the best-intentioned prayers were going to solve these problems. But when I stood back far enough away from the whole picture I would see clearly that no one was to blame and that everyone deserved equal compassion and sympathy... even those who had been driven to carry out attacks motivated by racial hatred

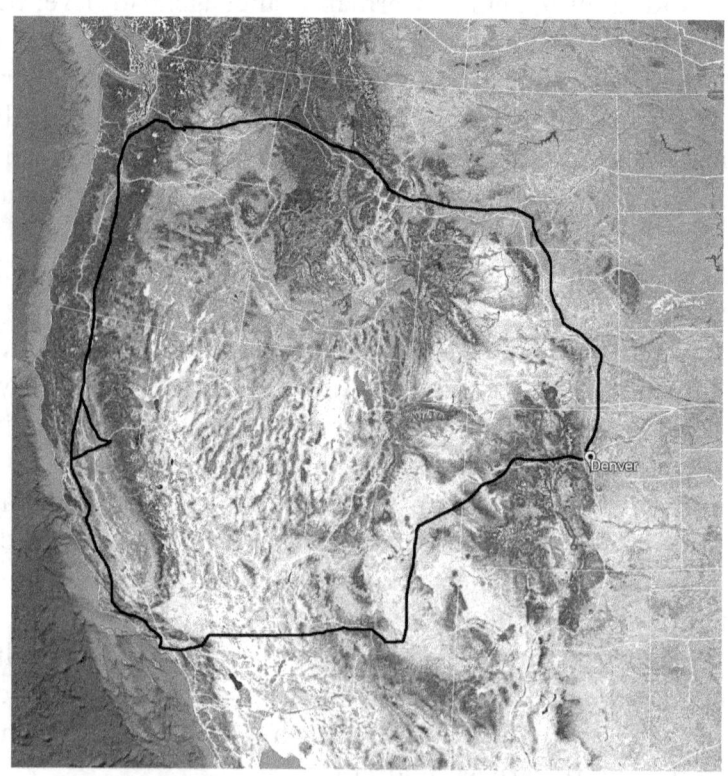

2009 - Arizona, California, Washington

My Musical Dreams Deepened

Returning to Colorado my musical dreams deepened when Kristina and I began practicing and performing with Gilly Gonzales and his wife Lisa. I had been amazed at Gilly's strengths as a percussionist. I remember watching quarts of sweat stream off of him as he performed for six hours straight in three different bands and never miss a beat. To me he seemed like the best drummer in the world and I couldn't believe it when he eagerly said "yes" to the idea of practicing and then performing together. I had first seen him in the national touring band Kan'nal. I was excited to play with him and his wife for the ecstatic improvisational dancers at both the Denver Rhythm Sanctuary and the Boulder Rhythm Sanctuary.

Kristina and I did a concert for a Sufi gathering at Shambala Mountain Center and I played music at the opening of the King Tut Exhibit at the Denver Art Museum.

We played for the regular 'Morning Meditations' at the Boulder Public Library and Kristina led another 'Women's Frame Drum Circle.'

Gilly invited me to be a Special Guest performer with one of his bands called 'Lunar Fire' at the Crescent Moon Carnival Feat at the Cervantes' Masterpiece Ballroom.

Playing with Lunar Fire in Denver

Kristina followed frame drum workshops with her 'Transformational Power of Voice' events for the Spirit Keepers Dances of Universal Peace group in Boulder.

Christine Stevens came to town and she and Kristina did a weekend event called 'Healing Rhythms: A Drumming Weekend to Discover your Musical Spirit' up in the mountains at the Shambala Mountain Center... a Buddhist environment.

And down at the Trident Coffee House Sandbox Theater and at the Public Library in Boulder we conducted musical Meditations with master violinist Kailin Yong, Gilly Gonzales, Lisa, James, Jesse, Scott, Dexter, Jenna, Michael...

Each event flowed nicely into the next... But by the fall we were headed back to the Arab world...

Bedouin Eye Contact in Jordan

Landing back in Amman we found ourselves adopted by a young Bedouin man named Yazid who was now working at a little hotel where we booked a room. It was 2010. After hearing our music he determined to invite us into his world. We needed a drum for Kristina so we stopped in a small music shop which happened to be still open around 11:00 P.M. that same night. Yazid came with us. We played oud and sang Syrian, Iraqi, Egyptian and Lebanese favorites for the young sales attendant and for the passersby... it was getting close to midnight... lots of fun... so refreshing to feel everyone united in the same bubble of musical appreciation. We purchased a goat-skin frame drum for Kristina.

Yazid was eagerly sharing his world: "we all are in trust with each other here... even on the street... I can even walk up to anybody and borrow 5 Jordanian Dinar" (approximately 8 US Dollars) "and they will give it even if they don't know me..."

To prove his point he walked up to a couple of young men sitting on the step outside a shop and asked them if they would do this if he asked... they smiled and agreed. "Of course!"

Yazid is a half-Jordanian Bedouin from the Petra area where he grew up in Wadi Musa (Moses Gulch). He was now working in the hotel and studying languages in the college. According to Yazid there are only three aboriginal Jordanian family lines: all self-defining as 'Bedouin.' "All other Jordanians are refugees," he explained. "Mostly Palestinian of course but now there are many Iraqis too."

Yazid's Bedouin grandmother used to tell him stories from One Thousand and One nights for three hours at a time... insisting on maintaining uninterrupted eye contact during the whole time. If he ever looked away, she would give a little tug on his shirt sleeve. He said the older generations had this habit of continual eye contact even more strongly than the younger generations have it now.

The Western 'Bankster' Problem

We then traveled into another part of the city to enjoy the music of the oud player at the Umiat Coffee shop and then went to meet with Fayaz, such an extremely well-educated man, to discuss the world situation. We were in night-owl heaven. It was 3:00 AM. We were all wide awake and there was plenty of time... no one in a rush.

Yazid had just shown us how money was shared on the streets. Now Fayaz painted a picture for us of typical larger-scale Arab-world financial transactions. He explained that folks in the Islamic world were protecting themselves against the Western 'bankster' problem fairly aggressively by returning more resolutely to the Islamic banking model which, unlike the Judeo-Christian system, prohibits charging compound interest on a loan. Just a one-time 10% lender's fee... that's all that's permitted... and, what's just as important, the lender must share all risks equally with the borrower.

Due to the obviously destructive results and recent partial collapses of the Judeo-Christian banking system, the percentage of Islamic people using only Islamic banks had again grown rapidly. But in reality more than half of ordinary Arabic-speaking people don't use banks of any kind. They will only borrow or lend through personal family or tribal connections.

As we know, over the last two-thousand years various parts of the Middle East have been occupied by Greek, Roman, Persian, Byzantine, Mongol, Turkish, British, French, Israeli and American forces.

Since the future may involve the re-appearance of other invaders, Chinese perhaps, Fayaz suggested that we study history in order to determine the flavor of each occupying culture in order to predict how brutal or benign things might become for indigenous peoples. We discussed the nature of past occupations by Chinese, Turks, French, German, British, Portuguese, Russians and Dutch. Our assessments were inconclusive... of course. Nevertheless, Fayaz seemed to have especially poor impressions of the French, German, Chinese and Portuguese occupations.

As for current changes under the American and Israeli domination, Fayaz made the point that it would be best for everyone if changes happen slowly so that commercial systems don't totally collapse and cause catastrophic starvations.

Fayaz felt that the status of Iraqi women had been put back by several centuries, maybe by four hundred years, as a result of the recent American invasion. A counting of women in Iraq who had recently been widowed had just been released in the news: two million Iraqi women had just lost their husbands.

We both agreed that Jewish Voice For Peace was a very encouraging and rapidly growing movement. More and more Jews were apparently seeing Zionism as an embarrassment and as an ultimate threat to the deeper values of Judaism.

Held Captive for Eight Hours in a Palestinian Restaurant

The next day we passed by the music store owned by our good friend Jihad. We brought him up to date on the successes of our two-year-old Musical Missions of Peace 'Iraqi Refugee Project' through which we had channeled approximately $9000 US dollars to Iraqi refugee musicians in both Syria and Jordan to provide employment for them in exchange for the teaching of traditional Iraqi music and culture.

It had been two years since Jihad had helped us find local Iraqi musicians in Amman to participate in the program and he was happy to hear of our success.

Then came the magical moment: Jihad picked up a huge Iraqi oud made by Najim Aboud in Baghdad and began to play an improvisation for us while transmitting the emotional and spiritual essences through intense continual close-up eye contact.

I couldn't believe my ears! I had never heard an oud with a voice so sweet. I had purchased more than one oud from Jihad in the past and they had all been exceptional instruments. I had left one of them in Syria to be part of our Iraqi music school project there. But this was another step up. This professional-quality oud devoured me with sweetness from the moment I picked it up! I bought it and we also purchased another drum for Kristina.

We then met with Yazid, who introduced us to his oud-playing brother, Hamza. With the new oud in our hands we exchanged musical moments for the rest of the evening: Hamza playing the Bedouin desert music and Kristina and I the old popular mainstream urban Arabic compositions. I recorded Hamza's songs hoping to some day find the time to learn them. To me they resembled the Saudi desert Khaliji genre.

Kristina met during the late morning hours with Amal who had worked with women-to-women networks in the past to benefit

Iraqi refugees trapped in Jordan. Some of these networks were now continuing their work inside Iraq... but underground as there was no friendly government infrastructure yet. Kristina was planning to expand the use of the the drum circle, now so widely acclaimed as a healing path, among Iraqi refugee women. Amal was enthusiastic about this plan.

Later in the afternoon and evening we were held captive for eight hours in the Limana Coffee Shop and Restaurant by Mustafa, the Palestinian owner. We were forced to sing for our supper for several hours to an amazingly loving audience. This was so much fun that once again I didn't get to sleep before the sun came up.

Mustafa had claimed that the work we were doing through Musical Missions of Peace shined even above and beyond what Arabs themselves had been able to do. He had me say a few words in Arabic to ensure my place in paradise. He didn't want to get there and not find me! And he agreed that Kristina's voice indeed had that indescribably beautiful female Arab quality which reminded us of Fairouz, the famous Lebanese 'nightingale of the Middle East!'

We got a late night visit from Haydar, one of our friend Suad's children. He was one of the few Iraqis who had so far managed to survive the Jordanian government's attempts at expulsion. He was deeply involved working for an organization devoted to finding and helping re-settle Iraqis who had been displaced inside Iraq. He explained the necessity of cooperating with the occupying US forces since the alternatives lead nowhere. And he claimed he could see a long-term positive potential of a post-Saddam government.

And he revealed that the organization for whom he was now working had counted, not just two million, but four million Iraqi widows. A holocaust-sized catastrophe had been wrought by the greedy pressures of hunger-for-oil and the resulting war and destruction.

The next day Kristina met with Julie, an American Music Therapist, who wanted to use drum circles as part of her work with Iraqi refugees. She knew our friend Christine Stevens.

Young Iraqis Now Hate America

Later I was walking down the street around midnight and some teenagers asked me: "Where are you from?"

"America..."

But this time I got a new and unusual response: "I hate America!

What are you doing over here?"

"I hate what America has done too! That's part of the reason I am over here," I replied.

Another Arab teenager added: "I hate America too! I am from Iraq!"

I was speaking to them in Arabic. "I sing the old songs... from Um Kolthoum, Abd el Halim, Nazem al Ghazali..."

Another Arab teenager approached me with a loving vibe: "Here is how we teenagers greet each other now." He showed me a complicated jive handshake sequence ending with bumping our right shoulders together. I had been adopted.

But this was new for me. That was the first time I had heard hatred of America directly at me personally.

The next day we spent a very happy evening having an Iraqi dinner with Haydar and his mother, Suad. She gave Kristina new abayas and scarves to wear in places like Saida Zeinab where the Iraqi refugees wear conservative dress. We had so much news to exchange about all our families and all the latest changes.

And the next day Kristina had tea with Dhuha and Amal in another coffee shop.

> *Dhuha is Iraqi. She has an organization called Association of Women Entrepreneurs. She has helped start businesses for Iraqi women to sell their hand-crafts and is very concerned about the situation of the women in Iraq. Some of our Iraqi friends have suggested that their situation is worse now than it has been in more than one-hundred years.*
>
> *Amal has worked for Women-to-Women - an organization which funds job training programs and provides micro loans to get them started.*
>
> *Both are very interested in our ideas of providing the drumming circles for Iraqi women. I show them the research studies that have been conducted in the United States on the effects of group drumming and recreational music-making: boosting our bodies' natural defense mechanisms, reducing anxiety, depression, anger and fatigue.*
>
> *Dhuha is adamant that all Iraqi women be invited from all religious backgrounds. Of course this is essential.*
>
> *She proposed that Cameron and I provide a lecture on*

our work to an organization of Iraqi Artists and Intellectuals to drum up support for our idea. She went off to contact the necessary people and get the ball rolling.

I just received an e-mail from her saying the idea is being enthusiastically received.

Please keep this project in your prayers that it manifest easily and successfully. Iraqi women have been through more hardships than most of us can imagine. Every woman I have met has had one or more family members killed or kidnapped or both. Many of their homes have been destroyed and many are left without any means of support.

Facilitating communal drumming among the women is a very simple way to help lift them from despair into empowerment.

Gaza-bound Palestinian Relief Convoy Parked in Syria

We took a taxi from Jordan to Damascus and found a hotel.

We visited David Fraser and his Japanese wife. David, from Australia, was serving as the Universal Peace Federation's regional secretary general for the Middle East and North Africa. He and his wife and their five children had been living and working as teachers in Damascus for thirteen years now. Wendy Forster of Boulder, Colorado's E-Town, had suggested to him that he contact us after she learned about our work and presented us with a couple of 'E-chievement' Awards. David's network of friends in both Syria and Lebanon was considerable. Perhaps through him we would meet more wonderful bi-lingual bi-cultural folks. Kristina and I had been made honorary Universal Peace Federation Ambassadors back in Denver a while ago.

The park outside of David's apartment was filling with young folks. Everyone was out for the evening until midnight at least. The shops in the Christian quarter were open, as it was Friday and Islamic shop-owners were taking the day off. Like everyone else, we gravitated towards the part of the city in which the shops were open.

Damascus was a happy and thriving city. The value of the Syrian pound had been climbing against the dollar. David had shared his sense of pride in helping Syria expand into its more modern role as a cultural bridge between East and West.

Under the new president, Bashar Assad, certain legal reforms were facilitating economic expansions which could include more Western business enterprises. But Syria, with it's ancient taste for indigenous agriculture was not about to open the doors to Monsanto whose modern 'terminator seeds' had already destroyed food industries in Iraq. Doors to large Western bankers would also, it seemed, remain closed. The world had seen the consequences of letting those guys in.

The Syrian secret police, the 'sabiha,' notorious for brutality, had the confusing job of thwarting the efforts of a constant stream of well-funded spies and mercenaries sent by Israel from right across the border to the south. No one was guessing that within the next year car-loads of snipers funded and trained by Saudi Arabia, Israel, the USA and their networks of cooperative regimes would sneak into Syria and begin shooting civilians, police and soldiers alike to try and create a civil war.

We walked into the old city through Bab Tumma. We were jammed shoulder to shoulder between cars, people, bikes, carts... We went into another restaurant to listen to oud and riq players who were singing many songs we did and didn't know. We admired a woman with her new baby and friends... everyone was feeling so very soft and warm. Many people looked at us with warm smiles and said "welcome... you are always welcome here."

The next afternoon we had tea with Samir at his seven-hundred-year-old house... now a hotel. "Forget the governments... we are all people..." he reiterated. This message gets repeated again and again.

There was a strong sweet perfume smell from the overhanging jasmine vines through the narrow passages of the old city. There were carts and stores vending dozens of kinds of nuts and dates and other tasty organic tidbits. Modern ice cream was also available. All fruit drinks were squeezed fresh: melons, pineapple, lemon with mint, orange, mango... dark green tabbouleh with finely chopped parsley, olive oil, onion, tomato, herbs. The hour was again getting late... passersby were greeting us once again "habibi"... "my love..."

Smiling women of all ages in every different type of dress were catching up with the latest news from friends... cell phones abuzz. Twenty cars with party-goers were honking their horns... a flotilla driving together in the traffic... young folks sitting in the automobile window openings were waving and shouting as they passed... the organic weaving of traffic and pedestrians were all-in-motion and tightly-packed with just enough attention to traffic signals to help things work...

> *We pause and sit in a park just outside of the Northern Gate to the old city. It's 9:00 P.M. Under the glow of the street lights the playground is alive with little children. The grassy areas are spread with blankets and picnickers. Every bench is full. The young, the old, the teenagers... everyone is visiting together. We feel a loving warm vibe as we walk through the park.*

We changed hotels and went to get money from our Syria bank account and purchased a cell phone for local use. We took naps... making love in the timeless warm atmosphere of the ancient city. We studied song lyrics with friendly local guys... one of them an excellent singer although economist by trade. His first comment to me, upon learning that I was from America was, "Why do you like to kill people?"

"I come from a country where there are a lot of crazy people who don't seem to know better," I explained and then we spent the next two hours working on musical translations together.

Sexy Lingerie Shops and Glittering Mosques

I received a phone call from Guy and Mohammad. The Gaza-bound Palestinian relief convoy had just arrived in Latakia on the Syria coast. More people were arriving from all over the world and donating more goods. At least one-hundred-fifty people were planning to make the voyage by sea. Kristina and I had been invited to represent Musical Missions of Peace and perform an Arabic music concert for the Palestinian Refugee Camp being formed in Latakia. Soon we would take the bus down to the Mediterranean coast and offer that concert.

Kristina's stomach was slightly under the weather so I went to the Iraqi refugee section of Damascus alone while she reluctantly resigned herself to rest. If any Westerner is interested in going to another planet without having to leave the earth I highly suggest Saida Zeinab.

Saida Zeinab Mosque

I went inside the glittering mosque to offer my prayer for world peace as a part of the mix. La Illaha IlAllah... There is Nothing But Divinity... Everything is Sacred...

I remained in a quiet mood sitting inside and went up to touch the kaaba. Being tall, it was easy for me to see the women on the other side of the curtain offering their prayers and sometimes wailing with grief. These were mainly Iraqis and Iranians... in fact someone asked me if I was Iranian. I said, "no, I'm from America..."

The Kaaba Inside the Mosque

I walked the marketplace streets. The Iraqi women, without their men, had been reduced to begging. The advances made for women during the second half of the 20th century in Iraq were now history... gone...

I gave some money to an Iraqi widow whose daughter lay apparently near death in a basket in front of her. The child was staring weakly out of her emaciated body... perhaps a five-year-old but weighing almost nothing, skin hugging her bones... "Hiya marid!" wailed the mother... "She is sick!"

Damascus was now, according to the taxi driver, a city of eleven million. Syria had grown between 2003 and 2010 from nineteen million total now to twenty-two million. Something like three million Iraqi refugees had been admitted. Many were now beginning to return to their homeland but no other country in the world had allowed more than a trickle of Iraqis to enter. Sweden was the second most generous with sixty-thousand Iraqis allowed. Syrians had basically opened their arms and welcomed millions.

Yes, Damascus had been here now for at least five-thousand years... they say it is the oldest continually-occupied city in the world... it was filled with magnificently decorated inner courtyards. Our hotel was now just an inexpensive backpacker destination, but it had obviously been an elegant home for the last seven-hundred years.

But the huge influx of refugees had overwhelmed parts of the city where the smell of jasmine alternated with the smell of urine. And the city was chock full of feral cats... who had plenty of rats, big ones, to catch... And there were more and more people sleeping out in the open, with the cats and the rats... an eight-year-old girl was dozing inside the pedestrian overpass while a little pile of coins accumulated beside her... she was a product of the stresses and strains of this all-too-tightly-packed modern world full of refugees.

But even in Saida Zeinab the sexy lingerie shops were everywhere, even as the women all wore the Iraqi abaya in public... a long black gown with head-scarf as the surface layer. Changes changes changes changes... changes for the better... that's what we all had just been praying for in the mosque: that it all might somehow come out good!

Singing in Latakia for the Convoy to Gaza
We climbed on a bus and rode down to the Mediterranean coast

to join our friend Guy Benintendi, who had driven an ambulance all the way from London, to be delivered, along with another one-hundred-and-fifty ambulances and six-million-dollars-worth of medical supplies to the Palestinian people in Gaza.

Guy and Me in Latakia Beside Donated Ambulance

We moved into our friend Mohammad Ziadeh's little hotel and were greeted by his many aunts, uncles, sisters and cousins who all made their homes in the same building.

Thirty-two countries had contributed to this Gaza-destined medical relief convoy but the USA had not been one of them. We felt honored to be able to present our musical offering. Guy had promoted our Arabic music singing skills and successfully arranged for us to entertain the members of the convoy who now had time on their hands while the search continued for another ship to complete the passage down to Gaza.

A good-sized crowd had gathered... mostly Arabic-speaking folks... and we began singing classical favorites from Egypt, Lebanon, Palestine, Syria and Iraq.

Kristina and I Perform for Gaza Relief Convoy

Mohammad's father, Ismael, was there cheering us on. Soon the Arabs in the audience were falling into the mood to want to sing and dance and their energy ran high as they gradually took over the microphones. A ten-year-old boy was invited to be lead singer for many of the songs. He had a very passionate and powerful vocal energy and we all cheered him on. He led the celebration of song and dance for the rest of the evening! The passion arising from seeing the world actually doing something to support the Palestinians was sizzling under the surface... a rare opportunity!

By offering our Arabic songs we had miraculously become a significant part of the whole convoy effort and as we wandered the streets later that night we felt a deep sense of belonging mixed with an edge of danger and fear as we all knew that the Israeli military had unpredictable ways of unleashing violence against medical relief convoys such as these. These international volunteers were risking the possibility of being attacked as they neared their destination. But for now they were still safe here in Syria.

Mohammad had arranged for us to do another concert the next night at the Nay Cafe.

Performing at the Nay Cafe

Kristina was especially delighted that some of his family members had made a point of coming to hear us... especially the female ones. One of them, Judy Misto, has stayed in touch and helped us with many translation mysteries.

Mohammad's Cousin Judy Misto

Once again the magic of the music led to immediate connection and invitations. We went over to the home of a Christian Arab family after our show and were introduced to a family of artists: the father's work involved inlaying tens of thousands of naturally-colored wood pieces to create murals and tabletops while the mother worked clay into vases and figures derived from ancient styles and the daughter was a performing rap singer in both English and Arabic and also a skilled graphic artist! All these new friends gave us new ways for us to represent America thanks to the music! Almost every day another bridge was built!

The next day Mohammad took us to record Kristina's voice in the giant underground cistern at the Salah Al Din castle... an amazing echo chamber!

We returned to deepen our network with the local artist community at the Nay Cafe. We were approached by two women who worked at the US Consulate in Damascus. They had heard our concert the night before and had apparently visited our websites to learn more about us. They suggested that we come and visit them back in Damascus. They had ideas they wanted to share.

The new Iraqi oud I had purchased in Jordan from Jihad was vulnerable. It was naked. It needed a sturdy protective case but it was too large to fit inside most oud cases. But I was in luck. Mohammad helped me find a music store whose owner was optimistic. He could have a large case delivered by the following day from Damascus. He couldn't absolutely guarantee a fit but he was pretty sure. I would have to commit to buying the case... no matter the outcome. I gambled. They next day we went to see. It was tight but yes it fit! So now I could travel with it much more easily! Of course we spent part of that same afternoon celebrating by singing and playing in that same music store for a small but very appreciative and musically educated audience.

Back to Beirut, Lebanon

My new oud case was so big that I had to buy it a ticket for a seat on the bus on the way down from Damascus over to Beirut, Lebanon!

We plunged into the high-speed high-priced Lebanese world. 'Beirut is Back!' screamed the sexy billboards. An Argentine belly dancer of Syrian descent drove my brain into three languages all at once: Arabic, Spanish, English...

We visited the home of my oldest Iraqi friend, Muhsin. He and his new wife, Warood, had moved to Beirut from Amman and were busy raising their two young children while Muhsin organized convoys of construction materials destined for rebuilding Iraq.

"Forty trucks just disappeared with all the materials they were carrying," he lamented. Working in Iraq was difficult. He and Warood had also tried moving back to Baghdad to live there, back in their native home... but it had proven to be too difficult and dangerous. They had given up and become refugees once again. Warood was not happy away from her home but Muhsin had left decades ago and was used to being an Iraqi expat. He had funding, perhaps from Saudi friends he had cultivated years previously, to carry his reconstruction projects forward.

We again expressed our appreciation for the monumental music party they had thrown in our honor a couple of years earlier in Amman, but this time we contented ourselves with just a simple visit. Raising the small children in yet another foreign capitol was not easy for Warood.

Our journalist friend, Brooke Anderson, a young American woman who had made journalism a career and Beirut her home was in town and we caught up with her at a downtown restaurant. She had helped edit my book, "Spiritual Traveler: Journeys Beyond Fear" a few years back. I had a high degree of respect for her language skills. She really had become fluent in Arabic and was now working on Turkish.

Little Iraq Street in Saida Zeinab

Once again we took the bus over the mountains from Beirut past Baalbek through the Bekaa Valley and back down into Damascus.

We found ourselves singing in an ornate lobby in a downtown hotel where a Bedouin rebaba, a simple one-stringed violin, was presented to us as a gift.

We were drawn back to Iraq Street in Saida Zeinab and we were surrounded by the refugees who had just lost so many brothers, aunts, children. I walked past a five-year-old girl sitting beside a baby sleeping on a rag between two parked cars in the muddy trash on the edge of the street. Did she have a parent around somewhere?

Our first night there in Saida Zeinab, after an Iraqi meal with a new Iraqi friend named Zahara, we sang an Iraqi song. She was touched.

Zahara and Kristina

She said we were the first Americans she had met who knew how to feel who the Iraqi people were. She put the emphasis on the word 'feel.' Her deepest wish was that more American people would learn how to 'feel' Arab culture and know how warm, friendly and forgiving Arab people are. We were surrounded by Iraqis there in Saida Zeinab. No one knew exactly how to count them but she said there were five-million Iraqis in exile there.

We then sang songs from Iraq, Lebanon and Egypt with a handful of Iraqis in the front of our hotel. The videos made of us were in the hands of the local internet-cafe manager. We would see what might happen.

We again entered the incredible ornate glitteringly mirrored golden-domed and turquoise-tiled Saida Zeinab mosque and joined in the energies of prayer with hundreds of Iraqi and Iranian pilgrims sharing the grief of historic tragedy. All these energies were bigger than we were. What could we do to try to imagine what these people had been through? And yet every voice was greeting us.

"Welcome... welcome," they said.

"Yes, the politicians put us back a hundred years... more than that," they said. "But surely the American people never wanted that to happen."

We were being bathed there in Saida Zeinab with a deep sweet energy of forgiveness. It really was more than I could fit into my emotional being and I felt like crying... again. I didn't know enough... but I knew too much... where could we go from here? I didn't know. Tomorrow we would see.

> *My home was now made of glass... the walls between the rooms became transparent... the whole world was now filled with people who see into each others' rooms, hallways, minds, thoughts, deeds... there could be no more secrets... nothing could happen one-at-a-time... nothing in isolation... it was all happening at once... everybody's reality overlapping... nothing was private... all this came to me in my sleep... in my dreams... I joined the human race on a deeper level... I was being invited into the ancient Mesopotamian consciousness... Egyptian consciousness...*

I walked downstairs from my room there in Saida Zeinab... "Good morning, brother..." ...high five handshakes from the younger guys. They had adopted us now because we had played their favorite songs the night before. "When do we party today?" they wanted to know.

We had breakfast at 4:00 PM with Zahara. She had lost two cousins to the US soldiers in Iraq: they simply disappeared into US custody and were never heard from again. And two more of her relatives had been killed by other Iraqis because they once had helped the Americans with some translation projects: helping Americans leads to the death sentence in Iraq... they had been executed on the street.

Zahara knew from personal family experience about the deformities in the new babies resulting from the poisonous weaponry used by the US military: the depleted uranium. Her young niece had been born with her mouth on the side of her face up under her left eye. This was now the normal situation for newborns... always something deformed.

Being in Saida Zeinab with all these Iraqis was not so easy. The older people looked tired, exhausted, worn out. Inside the Saida Zeinab mosque these people were taking refuge, crying out loud for the pain of the Shia history and for the pain of the present moment.

Some of the Iraqi men looked like gnomes who had been suffering for years in some underground prison. I didn't see any hope left in their eyes. I saw shells of human bodies with nearly life-less energies.

Iraqi Refugees in Damascus - Saida Zeinab Neighborhood

Many of the elderly women scuttled about in their black abayas looking nervously from side-to-side as they navigated the streets. Like owls forced out into the daytime sun, they didn't look like they belonged there. They were relics from some other time and place. War is hard on men. But war is even harder on women. They had lost the promise of modern times and been deprived of the elegance of the past: they were now caught in a nowhere land.

We walked past men with withered legs using their arms to peddle themselves in makeshift carts and wheelchairs.

We were confused and tormented by little boys and girls begging for coins. Giving them something did not satisfy them. They simply became angry that we were not giving more.

Mothers displayed malformed children in baby carriages and collected the coins of passers-by.

Wealthier Shia pilgrims were arriving in buses from Iran and moved in little crowds to cry and pray in the mosque. They didn't speak Arabic. They spoke the totally un-related Persian language: Farsi.

But that's not all: a re-birth was happening! The teenagers and young adults did have some energy! I don't think many of them ever planned to stay forever in Saida Zeinab. But fresh fruit-juice shops, Internet shops, a few upscale hotels for the pilgrims, and a few restaurants were open and busy behind the flurry of cars and carts and street vendors. Youth would eventually have its way and things would somehow develop.

Zahara, the young Iraqi girl of twenty who had befriended us, took us to the best Iraqi restaurant in the market. One of her uncles was running it. We chose between the dishes made of sheep brains and testicles and opted for a bit of sheep meat with a tomato sauce: excellent taste! She would be leaving the next day to go back to Iraq to see her father.

Kristina sat with her and they played frame drums together. "Here, take these three drums to your women friends in Iraq," Kristina insisted and gave them to her. Zahara seemed delighted.

Love is My Religion

The same group of men with whom we had sung a couple of nights ago had told a few of their friends and come back for more the next night. After following our lead for a few songs, one of the men launched into a vocal improvisation with praise to Allah and followed that with an adhan, or call to prayer. I responded by leading 'T'ala al batru alaina'... a song which could be called the Islamic national anthem and concluding it with an Egyptian version of the call to prayer.

After this there was a pregnant pause filled with the unspoken question about my and Kristina's presence in Saida Zeinab: "were we Muslim? What was the meaning of our being there now singing these things?"

I explained in Arabic that the version of the call to prayer which I had just sung came from an Um Kolthoum composition by Riyad el Soumbati called 'al thoulasia al muqadasa'...

This was my way of bringing the conversation back to music and away from religion... which of course everyone found somewhat confusing as in Arabic there is a pretty solid line between 'music' and 'prayer.'

But the truth of the matter was that Love was my religion. And any music which felt to me like it could express Love could be my prayer... depending on my mood at the time. So I was crossing lines that were not so easy to cross from the insides of places like Christianity, Islam, Judaism, Buddhism, Native Americanism, Hinduism or any of the other places where traditions prevail.

Musicians can sometimes blend in with the clouds, birds, gypsies and Bedouins. We sometimes cross borders with no papers needed! We can pitch our tents in no-man's-land: in the last remaining strips of freedom between the borders!

Yes, even from western Jordan we had seen the Bedouins with their tents pitched surrounded by their herds of sheep: right in the no-man's-land between the border check-points where the guns were aimed from Israel on one side and from the Jordanian army on the other... where licensed citizens with their passports dared not trespass! Here in Saida Zeinab we were again hanging with the refugees with no official permissions: just a few Iraqi songs!

And what else do we seem to all share? ...no money in the bank!

> *The Drums Have Gone to Babylon... Where do I start? The last few days my energy has been very low: the result, I think, of being around desperate folks in Saida Zeinab.*
>
> *What was hardest for me was the begging children. That is always the hardest for me to deal with in poverty-stricken areas. They are not normal children. They are totally focused of getting whatever they can from whoever they can. They don't play like normal children. They don't smile. What can we do? This problem is bigger than me. It is hard to know what their living conditions are really like. I can't communicate with them well enough to ask questions. I just pray that someone somewhere is working to make their lives better.*
>
> *Did I tell you about Zahara?*
>
> *Zahara means flower. Now twenty-years-old, she has been in Saida Zeinab for a year staying with her uncle. Her mother emigrated to the US a year ago. But she has to wait to get more papers with the help of her father who lives in Iraq. Her English is excellent, a rare find around here. Born in the town next to the ancient ruins*

in Babylon, Iraq, she lived in the US from age two to twelve. She has been very eager to show us around: "This is the best restaurant, this is the best place to get fresh juice, this is Iraqi street..."

I invited her to the hotel lobby and pulled out a frame drum. I showed her how to hold it and I started a common Arabic rhythm. Pretty soon a smile broke out on her face. She said somehow the rhythm which is inside her was just coming out. Everyone here has the rhythm inside of them. They just need the drums and the opportunity to let it out!

The next day she would leave for Babylon with my drums in her luggage to share with the women in her home village!

After some serious meditation, extra vitamins and musical uplift my energy was returning. Onward we go, just doing what we can.

Before leaving Damascus we followed up on the invitation from the two US State Department women who had seen our concert in Latakia. They worked in the US Embassy department of Culture. We found our way into the diplomatic hub of the city and met them for lunch. They were excited about us and our work. They said that they were envisioning creating a concert series which would feature our historic path: we would begin giving concerts in the city parks and then be featured in larger venues. The concept of building bridges across borders with music made sense to them.

They would make the preparations and the following year we would return at their expense... "Americans Sing Arabic Music for Arabs!" No one had seen that before! But it was what we were doing. And it didn't feel like they wanted to steal us for propaganda purposes the way government agents usually might. So we agreed to cooperate with their plan and felt some excitement that a whole new adventure might unfold.

We didn't have any way to guess that by the next year Syria would have been invaded by snipers bent of creating a civil war and our new female State Department friends would have lost their jobs in Syria and left the country.

Back into the Arms of Palestinian Friends

We traveled back south across the border into Jordan. We were invited to play again at Limana restaurant in downtown Amman. The Palestinian family who owned the restaurant came down for the event so we met quite a few more members of the family, including one of the female elders. We felt the depth of their invitations to include us and our music more into their vast extended family. Recently they had traveled to Gaza and adopted a one-year-old child whose entire family had been killed in the last Israeli invasion. Other members of the family who had tried living in New Jersey for many years had now moved back to Amman. They had found it too difficult to raise their four sons with their notions of decent family values while in the US.

We happened to meet an Australian friend whom we knew from Cairo, Egypt, where he owns part interest in a small, Bedouin-run hostel. He was on his way back to Bangkok and then Australia. He would be glad to be back home in Sidney and to receive a Thai massage along the way but, "I sure will miss being able walk through the city any time of night without risk of running into belligerent drunks or risking being robbed!" And of course we laughed at the way our respective countrymen always say that "they hope we will be safe" in the Arab world.

I repeat these things to try and awaken curiosity and of course to challenge the stereotypes.

In a couple of days we would fly back to Arizona.

We were very kindly included by our new extended Palestinian family friends from the Limana restaurant by being invited to their gathering at Said and Rodina's home in Al Rabia to emotionally prepare for Said's mother's open-heart surgery which was scheduled to happen in another couple of days. They wanted to share with us so we did play and sing for a good part of the evening. We now had many more new friends.

Later we walked up to the second circle from our hotel to satisfy our 2:00 AM hunger and realized, more emotionally now with our departure imminent, how we were appreciating the inter-connected and welcoming atmosphere of these places which had all come to feel like another home.

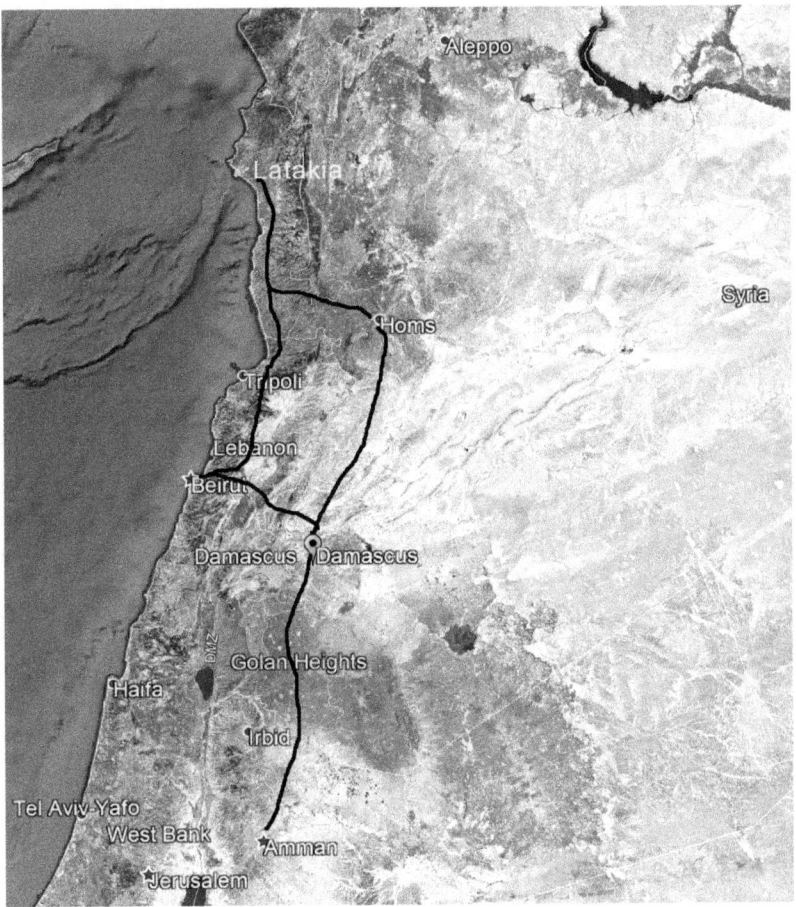

2010 - Jordan, Syria, Lebanon

And yes, my Arabic was getting better. It had taken a long time but now there was some compartment in my brain which could work and remember - and forget - in Arabic! And yes, as my father had told me, 'when you learn a new language, you gain a new soul!'

It was only two days before we would go to the airport. I returned to the Terrace Restaurant in Shmeisani, which one could call the 'entertainment district' of Amman. The Iraqi singer and oud player remembered me from a couple of years ago and lent me his oud and microphone. I sang and made a few new friends but mostly just wanted to sit in awe of his musical expertise. In my studies of Arabic music scales I had discovered the existence of some extremely rare and ancient modes. This performer actually knew them... he could play songs in maqams like Mustaar and Mukhalaf and Awj Ara. Wow.

The intervals in these scales are so strange that I couldn't even imagine learning and performing in them... but he made them sound just like simple familiar chicken soup.

The next day I returned to visit my friend Jihad in his music shop. I recorded him playing some improvisations on his oud in various common maqams. I would eventually include some of those recordings on the CD's contained in my next book: Harmonic Secrets of Arabic Music.

Harmonic Secrets of Arabic Music Scales

Soon we would be suffering culture shock as we slid from the warm caring faces of the flight attendants on Royal Jordanian Airlines into the chilly emotional distances maintained on Lufthansa.

Connecting our Love Bridge in the USA

Back in the USA we jumped back into our travel trailer-veggie-oil-diesel-van-beast rig and traveled the West coast for months... touring... touring... all kinds of venues... dozens of shows... It would add up to more than just months... We were on the road for most of the next year and a half.

In the Arab world we had told our Iraqi, Jordanian, Syrian, Palestinian and Egyptian friends that we were a musical bridge which connected back to a population in America which had a heart... a heart which was actively caring and sending love to the indigenous Arabic-speaking people of the Middle East... a heart which was sharing the suffering created by all those war wounds. I needed to be on the road to keep connecting the American end of that bridge. But the going was not really so easy.

We began in Joshua Tree, California, with our show called 'Ancient Musical Wisdom: Sowing the Seeds of Peace.' We had been invited by Eva Soltes to present this at the Harrison House. Lou Harrison had composed Western Classical music on the East Coast before retiring to Joshua Tree. He had tired of the out-of-tune equal tempered scale and made the change to justly intonated tunings somewhere in his career. After his death his home, famous for its acoustics and for his legacy, had been transformed into a performance venue. Our justly intonated microtonal Arabic music fit in nicely and our audience was very appreciative.

As long as we were in Joshua Tree we added a Meditative Dance event at Paula's Dome. We then gave additional concerts up in Long Beach and then at Glen Muse in Ojai. Glen Muse was a large estate inhabited by the creative team known as Elevate Films under the leadership of Mikki Willis.

Mikki had felt a spiritual awakening in New York City when, on 9/11, he had rushed into Building 7 to see if help was needed. The twin towers had already fallen and Mikki could see that there was not enough fire or damage to Building 7 to bring it down. When the building totally collapsed it was obvious to him that it had been a preplanned demolition... and that of course, for those of us who have paid attention, brings up the doubts about the official stories about the world trade center twin towers' collapse. Anyway, Mikki was devoting his life with a passion to making films to elevate humanity. Darakshan, who owned and managed Glen Muse, was host to Mikki's team and did his best to welcome Kristina and me into their world there in Ojai.

We went down to Ventura and gave interviews for a TV documentary about Musical Missions of Peace and then did another concert. We were able to invite my old friend, and now Musical Ambassador to Iran and Kurdistan, Rowan Storm to be our guest artist.

We bounced back up to Ojai where Darakshan had arranged for us to do an Arabic music concert.

We then returned to Joshua Tree to offer another Meditative

Dance and a series of 'Transformational Power of Voice' and 'Sing to Heal and Restore Your Body, Mind and Soul' Workshops in Paula's Dome... followed by another series of Sound Healing Meditations.

I Finally Meet Saadoun

We received an invitation from the al-Bayati family to join them at Nadim's house east of Los Angeles for Thanksgiving. We walked into the house. Saadoun al-Bayati appeared in person and greeted me. Here was the man whose voice had captivated me twenty-two years earlier. He and I were magnetized by each other. We became instantly aware of a deep soul brotherhood. His son and daughter and wife and all their Filipino and American in-laws surrounded us. Thanksgiving dinner came and went. Loving interactions abounded. But Saadoun and I began passing an oud back and forth and we were lost in the magic of our new-found brotherhood for the next eight hours. We returned a year later for the next Thanksgiving. The same thing happened.

I began visiting them more frequently and eventually completed a recording project featuring Saadoun which I also included in the practice CD's which would accompany my "Harmonic Secrets of Arabic Music" book. By the time Saadoun passed away in 2013 at the age of 79 we had bonded so deeply that Kristina and I felt like one of the family... all thanks to the soul-resonance I had felt from the Iraqi music on that tape which Kathleen had handed to me back in 1988.

Iraqi Refugees in California

After passing through Encinitas to present our Arabic Music Trance Dance event we played Iraqi music for eighty Iraqi refugees in El Cajon, just east of San Diego. After our performance Iraqi men began spontaneously composing poems in our honor, a professional Iraqi percussionist joined in for our last song and a whole new kaleidoscope of friendships were born. We would stay connected with these folks and run many drumming and singing events for these Iraqis... especially the women, for years to come.

These women don't speak English. They had heard that street life in the USA was dangerous. They were scared. But their fears would start to dissolve as we encouraged them to play drums and sing and dance. Kristina and Christine Stevens and our new Kurdish Iraqi friend Dilkhwaz Ahmed took the lead. Soon we had videos showing the amazing ecstatic release of war trauma as these refugee woman danced and sang their native songs with each other. All they had needed was our encouragement. With the videos we could successfully fund-raise through our non-profit and support an ongoing series of events by supplying the drums and paying for the venue. Americans were willing to help these refugees partly because they were women and partly because they were now living on American soil.

Kristina with Iraqi Refugee Women in El Cajon

Times had changed since Musical Missions of Peace had been gifted to us back in 2003. We had been sending emails and photos back from Baghdad and Americans who had been against the Iraq wars were supporting our travels, explorations and bridge-building to the tune of fifteen to twenty thousand dollars a year. But now Americans were tired of reading and hearing about wars in the Middle East and were reluctant to fund our programs and travels over there. Average annual support had dropped to half of what it had been. But supporting refugees in California was a more attractive goal.

Musical Ambassadors of Peace Program Ongoing in El Cajon

We traveled back up to Ojai to present our Full Moon Arabic Trance Dance with guest percussionist Judy Piazza at the Ojai Foundation, another marvelous venue. The 'Singing in Baghdad' theme was not broad enough so we elaborated on the qualities of music which spring from Ancient Egyptian, Mesopotamian and Fertile Crescent styles. We explained that *'This music is built from justly intonated scales which contain the true harmonic intervals that resonate deeply within us so people who allow their bodies to move with this music frequently find an easy portal into ecstatic trance experience.'* These *'true harmonic intervals'* are in accord with the laws of acoustic physics.

Judy introduced me to Tony Khalife and we found great joy in playing together. Tony was originally from Lebanon. He knew the popular Arabic songs we loved to play. He had followed the American trend into Indian Kirtan music and was a popular performer. He wanted me and my oud in his band so I joined him in his next show: My Rumi Valentine... celebrating the poetry of Rumi on Valentines Day with Indian Kirtan musical flavors. We had a great time.

Back down in Encinitas we played for Christine Stevens' Radiance Sutra Jam and combined our music with wisdom from ancient India.

We then performed at The Temple of Light in Lake Forest and then at the Unity Church of San Leandro where we also encouraged their congregational members to join us vocally in a *'Great Ecstatic Sound Bubble.'* We then headed up to Berkeley in northern California to produce two days' worth of events at the Unitarian Universalist Fellowship.

Then we headed back down to the southern California high desert to play for the Mountain Tribal Gypsy Dance in the Harrison House in Joshua Tree and we then gave an Ecstatic Egyptian Music Concert at the Joshua Tree Retreat Center, a venue which had become famous for hosting Kirtan events like the Bhakti Festival.

Driving back up into northern California we played at the Fountain Plaza, the Cozmic Cafe and Pub, the Placerville Town Hall, the Mountainside Center for Spiritual Living and at the Heart and Soul... all in Placerville and in nearby Cameron Park.

Then we proceeded further north to the Pacific coast where we played three events for the Mendocino Center for Spiritual Living before heading up to perform at the Humboldt Unitarian Fellowship in Bayside.

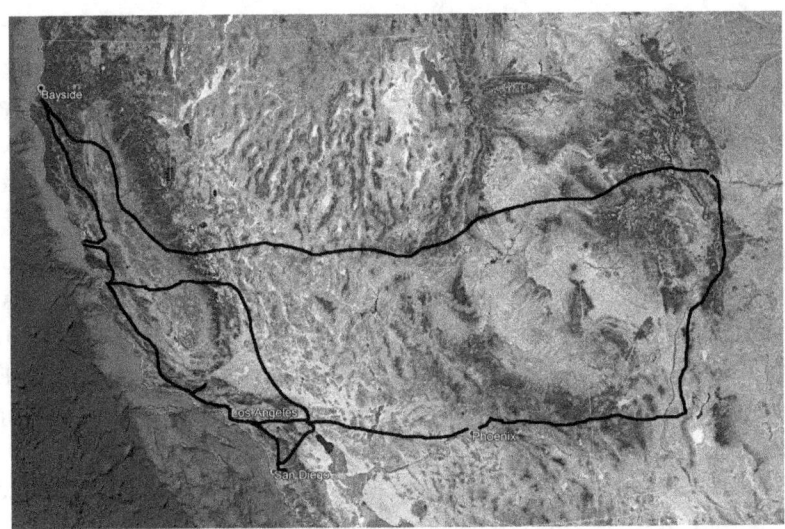

2010 - 2011 West Coast

I was staying as open and flexible as possible... trying to chameleon my way into every event and artfully appear in a form best-suited for whatever occasion. But inside I was starving. I felt like I had promised my Arab friends in the Middle East that I represented heartful people in the USA who thought about those who were directly receiving war wounds as a result of America's reckless behavior and that these Americans really cared.

But was I finding those Americans? All too often, at various Centers for Spiritual Living, I would be greeted by people with big smiles. "Let's take a minute to be grateful!" they would say. *'Gratitude'* had become the new buzz word. "Let's be here in silence together and be grateful!" they would repeat. They insisted on only addressing the positive aspects of life. Inside of myself I knew that everything didn't seem so positive and worthy of gratitude from the points of view of my friends in Saida Zeinab in Syria or in Iraq.

I wanted to say something about this but the modern new age code of endless positivity left no space for real historical awareness. Prayer was supposed to be the one-size-fits-all solution for everything not-so-wonderful... for all suffering. Inside myself I gradually began to lose respect for these devotedly positive people and to conclude that, indeed, America's shadow side had grown so dark that Americans could no longer risk acknowledging that it even existed.

I was also dismayed to see that Americans were falling for the media stories about the nature of the Assad regime in Syria. I knew from my Syrian friends that they were under attack by foreign invaders who had been cultivated, educated, paid and armed to de-stabilize the Syrian nation to the point where its government would collapse so that the Western multi-national corporations could move in and take over the economies while simultaneously paving the way for Israeli expansion and subsequent attacks on Iran. All the suffering... the human costs... of these aims seemed grotesque and not OK with me. But I felt like an island. Very few young and energetic 'spiritually-aware' Americans could even focus on these realities. I felt like I might have lied to my Arab friends when I had assured them that I was building a bridge with loving energies at both ends.

Kristina was better able to float in the positivity so energetically being generated by the Christian and New Age folks. I would lean back and acknowledge to myself that I still had a lot to learn. But the feelings of frustration continued to arise.

Occasionally I would remember the confusion I had felt years earlier when Robin had returned from traveling in Cambodia and had insisted with fire in her eyes and heart that we Americans must all 'do something' to change our evil ways. I had felt at a loss. What to do? And I had felt that my incomplete response must have been frustrating and disappointing for her. The bottom line was that I hadn't been to Cambodia. Was there a parallel here?

More Ecstatic Trance Dances in Colorado

Finally back in Colorado by mid-summer we launched more 'Ecstatic Arabic Trance Dance' events... people loved it... our band kept growing... Kristina was singing... her voice always so beautiful.

We started practicing more with Gilly Gonzalez and his wife Lisa Wimberger. Gilly, for me, as I said before, was a percussion dream come true. We launched our 'Ecstatic Egyptian Music' trance dance events again with Gilly in the mix. I was perhaps the most ecstatic of all. My Colorado band was evolving into a more and more solid dance band.

We also joined forces to play with Janis Kelly, Cheri Shanti and others at the Rock N Soul Cafe and then traveled back up into the Colorado mountains to perform at another house concert near Vail.

It was after that house concert in Vail that someone from the audience, who had been exceptionally attentive, told me that they had discerned that it had been my oud and our voices that had been creating the magic... and that the guitar just couldn't do it. After performing most of the evening microtonally with the oud, I had answered a request from the audience to play a lovely Greek song using the guitar.

"To tell you the truth, although the song was very beautiful, the magic spell was broken!" I was told.

After receiving that feedback I began labeling our events in ways which promoted that aspect of our music: 'Magical Microtonal Egyptian Music: Featuring the Perfect Just Harmonies of Arab Music!'

The guitar and the other fretted instruments could not be played in the perfect harmonies of just intonation. Their musical intervals, fixed by the frets, were in equal temperament and therefore just slightly out-of-tune according to the laws of physics and ancient musical traditions.

Another 'Ecstatic Egyptian Music' dance party back in Boulder came next wherein we were again joined by Gilly Gonzalez and Lisa Marie. Wow!

Kristina started a new series of healing meditative sound healing events using only her voice and frame drum and then we traveled as far east as Kansas City to Unity Village, Missouri, where we presented perfectly-harmonious justly-intonated micro-tonal music to an amazed audience of Unity choir directors at their annual convention. No, they never had known that their music scales were out-of-tune... but with one of their favorite keyboard artists, JD Martin, on stage with big speakers and my tunable keyboard they sure could hear and feel the difference!

"That explains why I use my voice instead of the keyboard to play the major and minor thirds!" JD commented, suddenly getting it. "I always wondered why it sounded so much better when I did that!"

Yes, the major and minor third intervals are the most extremely out-of-tune in our modern Western tuning scale called equal temperament. JD had followed his deep listening skills and created a partial work-around for this problem.

On our way through Kansas we had stopped to visit Camille. She had been following our adventures and been inspired to journey to the Middle East on her own and she had visited Turkey, Tunisia, Syria, Oman and Yemen. Her trips continued for a decade and the three of us felt connected in so many ways. She was feeling a special fondness for Syria.

Back in Boulder, Kristina continued her series of 'Sacred Space Sound Meditations' and we booked more ecstatic trance dance events with Gilly and with my favorite dear friend and cello maestro, James Hoskins. I also began teaching workshops with titles like 'Perfect Harmony, Ancient Wisdom, Modern Times.' I felt that I had derived lessons of ancient wisdom from my musical adventures in Peru, Greece and Egypt and that because of my linguistic training and my fascination with musicianship I had found certain keys to forming deep soul connections with individuals in those cultures which could help us 'Learn to Lead our Lives in more Perfect Musical and Spiritual Harmony.'

Meanwhile our dear friend Guy Benintendi, with whom we had just spent time in Syria, had launched the Boulder-Nablus Sister City Project which was very controversial in Boulder because Nablus is a Palestinian city in the West Bank and Boulder has a powerful pro-Israel city council. Kristina and I were invited to perform Arabic music at one of the Sister City planning sessions.

Gilly began including me as a special guest with his Lil Sum'n Sum'n band. We played a double header with Stephen Kent and his new Sufi Trance Band 'Baraka Moon' out of San Francisco at the Cervantes Theater in Denver.

I dared to include a little recent history in my next workshop: 'Perfect Harmony, Ancient Wisdom, Modern Times and Making Sense of 9/11' and Kristina continued with another half dozen healing drum and voice events.

Manal, a marvelously gregarious Palestinian woman who ran the Arabesque restaurant in Boulder discovered us and we created a 'Live Arabic Music and Food' event. Her restaurant was small and outdoor seating would have to accommodate our audience. It was late in the summer... late September. It was a gamble. We were lucky. We had a huge turnout and the weather stayed warm. Manal couldn't even manage to feed everybody and the dancing spilled out onto the sidewalks beside the street.

Cara Cruikshank, with her marvelous track record from the New York area, created the first in a series of 'salons' at the Caritas Spiritist Center in Boulder and Kristina and I and Jesse Manno and Brett Bowen from my old band, Sherefe, performed. The salon was titled 'Cafe de la Culture: The Venue for Visionaries: Ruminating Rumi -

An Evening of Discourse on the Mystic Poets.' It was a big success and sold out.

I created more workshops and addressed subjects like: 'What are the whole-body and possible spiritual effects of perfect harmony and how did European and American music lose the correct tuning traditions?'

I was prepared to demonstrate various forms of justly-intonated perfect harmony on my programmable keyboard to try and initiate the practice of deep listening... a prerequisite for introducing perfect harmony into our lives.

I encouraged people to use their deep listening skills and their voices to co-create more 'Great Ecstatic Sound Bubbles!'

Occasionally I dared to open the deepest questions of existence. Are time and space infinite? As a child in Missouri I had intuited those infinities while lying on my back looking at the obviously infinitely vast night sky. But I had discovered that religious indoctrinations has given most people a fear of infinity! "Oh no!" So many would exclaim. "Everything has to have a beginning and an ending!"

But it was my comfort with infinity, in both space and time, which gave me an endless thirst for learning and helped me keep my ego in check. I had never felt satisfied with simple answers founded on the dumb dualism of linguistic opposites like 'good' and 'evil' or 'right' and 'wrong.' Author Tom Robbins claims in his autobiography that he had lived his whole life in terror of the idea of infinity until he took LSD and dissolved into the helical spiral pattern of the petals on a blooming daisy and traveled through the opening of the 'now' into 'infinity.' That moment changed his life more than any other... he claims... No longer terrified by infinity he could finally relax and accept our true place in the cosmos.

Kristina was invited back up to Unity of the Mountains near Vail to offer a 'Power of Music' workshop at the Avon Library while the 'Hemispheres Program' on KGNU, Boulder's alternative radio station, interviewed me regarding our progress with Musical Missions of Peace.

Can I Compose Egyptian Songs?

My friend Eva Soltes arranged a month-long artist-in-residence for me at Harrison House in Joshua Tree in the California desert. We drove west in the late fall of 2011 and I set up my mobile recording studio and worked sixteen-hours a day to compose melodies in eighteen different Arabic music scales. This was an invitation to become a songwriter. I did my best to awaken my inner Arabic musician and create archetypal compositions... nice... it actually seemed to work.

Already back on the West coast, we continued touring for months... through the winter of 2011-2012.

Kristina sang with Deepak Ramapriyan to 'Sing in the New Year' at the World Beat Center in San Diego. Deepak, leader of the 'Breath of Life Tribe,' played the violin and sang in the perfect harmony of just intonation... not consciously I don't think. He just had the deep listening skills to enter the realms of perfect harmony. I loved it. That was the first time I had heard Indian Kirtan music performed in tune. Usually the equally-tempered harmonium, a product of India's long association with the British empire, would make me either want to laugh or just leave the room.

Unfortunately, a byproduct of opening my deep listening skills by playing traditional Egyptian music for so many decades had made me acutely sensitive. If a performance lacked the charismatic lead performers or percussionists to suck me into ecstasy, I would be left stranded, beached on the modern island of out-of-tune equal temperament. I wasn't the only one. Many of Europe's most famous composers and musicologists, men like Mozart, Bach, Chopin, Hayden and Helmholz had suffered for the same reason although modern 'piano-oriented' Western music schools ignore this very revealing part of musical history and are still unaware.

We played with Christine Stevens at another Sutra Drum Circle at the Seaside Center in Encinitas and I joined the percussionist and band leader Frank Lazzaro to play for the Sabrina Fox Tribal Dance Class at the World Beat Center again in San Diego.

My old friend from Middle Eastern Music Camp, John Bilezikjian, invited me to sit in with him and Frank Lazzaro and play nay at the Casa Blanca Restaurant in Carlsbad. "Not bad for a white boy!" John complimented me. In truth it had been difficult for me to keep up on the nay with John's high speed tempos. Oh well. What an honor to perform a couple of songs with a world-class musician like him!

Frank invited me to play with him at a private party in Encinitas and then, sponsored by our non-profit, Musical Missions of Peace, we drove to El Cajon and Kristina helped conduct a 'Multicultural Women's Drum Circle:' an all day training for Iraqi refugee women with

Christine Stevens and Dilkhwaz Ahmad. Again the event sprouted wings of its own and magical healings of war wounds seemed to happen. There would be many more of those events.

Meanwhile we drove up to the Unitarian Universalist Church of Long Beach and parked our travel trailer in the driveway of our good friends Ken and Lynn Shaw, who had featured us in their house concert series long ago, and presented an event called 'Singing the World Back Together.'

We represented Musical Missions of Peace at the Season for Non-Violence up in Encinitas at the Seaside Center for Spiritual Living then conducted another drum circle with Christine Stevens after which we headed back to Joshua Tree to teach another workshop called 'The Arab Spring: Ancient Wisdom and Perfect Musical Harmony' and then it was time to drive back down toward the coast for another 'Multicultural Women's Drum Circle' for the Iraqi refugee women in El Cajon.

Frank Lazzaro and I played Arabic Freeform Music for another event in Encinitas while Christine and Kristina conducted a 'Moving Sound Meditation.'

We headed up to the Myztic Isle in La Mesa where Kristina offered another pair of 'Sound Healing Meditation' events.

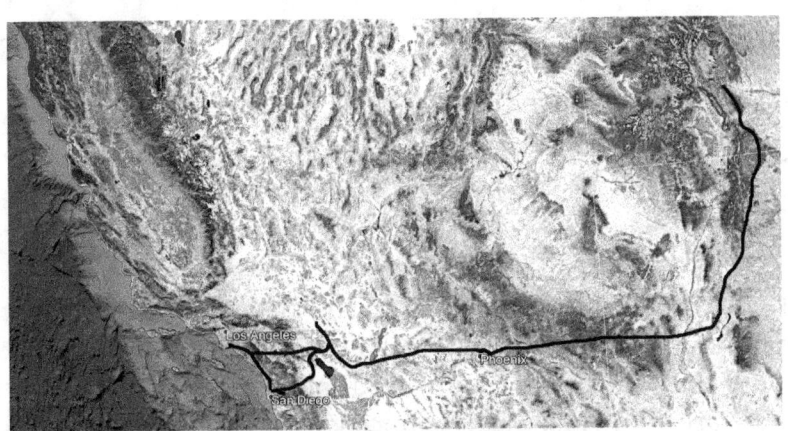

2011-2012 Southern California Artist Residency and Tour

Earth Dance and Gigs and Workshops

But midsummer was a great time to be in Colorado so we headed home to Boulder in mid-2012 and I began teaching my new songs, which I had now strung together into medleys with dramatic bridges between songs, to my band. With these added to our repertoire we continued doing Ecstatic Egyptian Trance Dance events. Our Colorado audiences knew what to expect from us and were eager to dance. I brought more drummers and musicians into my band.

Our friend Janice Kelly produced an Earth Dance festival and designated Musical Missions of Peace as the primary non-profit recipient. My band swelled to nine members for this event. Additional musicians were wanting to join in the fun... but only those few who could play microtonally could actually be part of it all. I gave the Earth Dance Keynote Address but not many were listening. Tierro, who had been in Kan'nal with Gilly, had learned to play microtonally by bending notes on his guitar and had played with one of our Arabic Trance Dance events. He invited me to sit in with his band when they performed at Earth Dance.

I performed in Denver for the Mile High Global Bazaar as a trio... just me and a drummer and a dancer. I also played solo oud for background musical atmosphere at the Caritas Spiritist Center, but more and more we were a now a big band.

Kristina offered her 'Singing Our Way Home' workshops every Tuesday at Adi Shakti, a local yoga studio and Manal wanted us to repeat the Live Arabic Music and Food event at her Arabesque restaurant.

"It is late September already," I told her. "We are gambling again with the weather."

"No worries," she insisted, "I want us to do it!"

She made a ton of food this time so she would have enough... the weather turned cold... very few people showed up... I felt badly for her... She looked at me like... 'Cameron!!! You were supposed to take care of everything!' But I could tell she still loved me.

I was hired to play solo at Boulder's new late night venue, the Bramble and Hare Restaurant. The folks in the restaurant seemed to enjoy it but the manager approached me after the gig: "This is the hardest part of my job," he announced. "I know you're not going to want to hear this, but I don't think your music is a good fit for this venue!" He was emotionally wrestling with having to deliver this potentially devastating news. I tried to re-assure him that I had other irons in the fire but he seemed convinced that he was destroying my career and that he should apologize until I might finally break down and reveal the depths of my pain.

I followed Kristina's initiative and began offering Sound Healing and Ecstatic Movement events at the local yoga studio. I enjoyed that. The performance pace could be very laid back and relaxed... nice... I would sometimes bring in various band members to fatten the music.

James and I played a duo oud and cello evening at the local oxygen bar, the Tonic Herban Lounge, called 'Plucked and Bowed.' We got surprisingly well paid by just passing the hat for tips.

We had been using my friend Suter's coffee shop, Caffe Sole, more and more as our primary venue for dance events, but it was small.

Health Catastrophes: Life Gets Stark

Suddenly Kristina's dad had a stroke and she would be gone for the next four and a half months. I drove up to visit her and her family in central Washington state a couple of times and we did an event at the Lake Chelan Lutheran Church but my creativity was flowing out in Colorado where making music was going so well.

I was also surrounded by my other dance-a-holic friends and I was a regular at many free-form improv dance events in Boulder's dance studios... those of us who were regulars loved to move and stretch and flirt to the music. I got very close to a lot of people by dancing with them. I had been doing that for decades. My 'imsak' practice kept my flirtatious energies powerful and available right on the surface of my energy field.

I drove to Denver and played for a 'Benefit Fund-raiser for Palestine: an Anti-Home Demolition Palestinian Cause.' But as we moved into the winter months life got stark for me without Kristina's presence and companionship. I was living in our travel trailer alone... parked in an industrial section of town. My friend Dave Moloney finally noticed my haggard looks and offered me a free basement bedroom in his house and that felt better. I had begun to feel and look kind of homeless.

Meanwhile I continued presenting workshops at the Adi Shakti Yoga center and I went with a dancer friend, Seemie Xavier, to meet another Palestinian restaurant owner, Abu Ibrahim. He immediately loved the idea of having my whole band play and he had the space for dancing. So we began performing at the Petra Mediterranean Restaurant in Longmont and Abu Ibrahim and family offered fantastic food and warm welcoming vibes until, after a few more months, Abu Ibrahim and his wife broke up and closed the restaurant.

My band was invited to play for the Syrian Relief Benefit and Arab Cultural Night at the University Memorial Center at the University of Colorado and my singer friend Ariana Saraha invited me and Scott Bears to join her in playing a Boulder House Concert and Party.

I had been trying to offer some emotional support to a singer and song-writer friend... Naomi... who had become suicidal. I would stay with her and watch while she cried and screamed and clawed with her fingers at her own body. I would hope that she would reach the end of her frustration and settle back into a calmer place, but she wouldn't and I would finally have to hold her arms and slow her down. She hadn't been sleeping... sometimes going for as long as seventeen days with no sleep at all. I felt like I had extra strength and some love energy for her but wasn't so sure after a certain point had passed that I had the inner tools to stay centered.

I had known Naomi for more than a decade. She and her ex-husband Rick had been well-known hosts of musical bonfires up at their mountain home. They had broken up three times and it seemed like the marriage was really over. Naomi was realizing that Rick really had loved her unconditionally and she felt like she was to blame for throwing a good marriage away. She also would scream in self-hatred for being a 'spoiled Jewish princess.' She was a work-a-holic who made good money hiring herself out to do office work and organize other people's businesses. Even with no sleep she was driving herself to keep working and would rise early in the morning and throw open the curtains and exclaim "it's another beautiful day and I have created another hell for myself!"

Just before Christmas I drove up to see Kristina and told her I'd been having a hard time trying to help Naomi... I was feeling very raw inside.

"Don't worry," replied Kristina... "After you've been here with me for a few nights you'll be fine again."

It was true. With our lovemaking and daily sharing I was healed after a few days. So I drove back to Colorado.

I hadn't heard from Naomi for a few weeks but I saw her out dancing. She confided in me that she had been avoiding communicating with me because she was determined to kill herself before the end of the year. It was December 28th... 2012...

I stayed with her until the calendar ticked into 2013. I had told her quite honestly that I wouldn't judge her negatively... whatever she did... and she had believed and trusted me. She would go stand on the tops of cliffs and then call me at 2:00 AM and say, "I'm still here..." ...meaning... she hadn't jumped...

"Are you OK now?" I would ask her. "Shall I go back to my place and leave you alone?"

"I like it better when you are here," she would tell me. There was some kind of deep connection between us.

She was still getting only one hour of sleep a night and going crazy. I took her to consult with two of my friends who were professional mental health workers. We tried to find sleeping pills which might work but they all seemed to create more problems than they solved.

My daily life was getting quite fully occupied with Naomi. When we danced we had fun and her craziness would suddenly become irrelevant. It was amazing how the dance could heal. We were very close in the dance.

I knew how to use only my peripheral vision and open something like a 'third eye' while dancing with others... if they could do the same. With Naomi the telepathic dance connection was extreme. It seemed we could track and move with each other even with our eyes mostly shut.

A couple of weeks into 2013 things evolved... things were smoothing out. We had passed the end of 2012 and Naomi was still with us on planet earth and she was functioning a little better. I was able to begin spending the nights back in my friend Dave's basement and hope for the best.

Naomi would tell me that I was one of the few with whom she could be totally honest and that perhaps the psychic link between us had gotten her through the extreme suicidal period. She made me a stained glass 'dance angel' to express her gratitude.

I felt like it had been thanks to my Peruvian and Egyptian friends that I had been able to allow deep psychic linking... and bring constant artfulness into the connection with Naomi instead of trying to navigate by 'setting boundaries,' which seemed to be the modern new age American solution for conducting relationships. I opened myself to emulate my Egyptian friends who seemed endlessly ready to stay in the connection. To me it seemed like the real adventures could be undertaken if we surrendered, stayed fully awake and allowed them to unfold. Did we want to be 'safe?' Or did we want to be fully 'alive?'

Naomi and her ex-husband Rick made the momentous decision

to get back together. That made the difference. Naomi was healed... for now.

Agony into Ecstasy: Dancing with Our Shadow

My band had learned my new 'Egyptian' musical compositions and our dance parties became more and more popular. Kristina finally returned. Summer was coming. I began to feel more steady warmth in my soul. The winter had been hard.

We began playing the outdoor mountain music festivals and we began recording sessions to create a new 'Cameron Powers Project' CD based on my new compositions made in Joshua Tree in the Harrison House.

Our latest workshops were called 'Perfect Egyptian Harmony: Ecstatic Singing and Toning For Everyone.' We were enticing our fans to come sing with us: *'Did you know that Western Civilization has been Singing Out-of-Tune for the Last 150 Years, according to the Laws of Physics? Come feel what it is like to sing in absolute ancient perfect harmony and discover a deep vibrational re-alignment. Discover the powerful secret of indigenous music. No musical training necessary! Everyone Welcome!'*

We did an evening of mystic poetry, music, and remembrance in the Sufi tradition at the Star House called 'Alchemy of the Heart.' And our 'Ecstatic Egyptian Trance Dance Party: The Powers of Love' events were ongoing at several venues.

Kristina was again invited up to Vail to conduct Sound Healing Meditations at Unity of the Mountains and Christine Stevens asked her to help conduct a ' Rhythm of Your Soul Healing Drum Retreat' up at the Shambala Mountain Center.

Gilly and I again played for Tarena to dance at the Denver International Fair and my band, now known as 'The Cameron Powers Project Band' was asked to perform at the Unify Festival in Georgetown. Gilly asked me to Perform with his band Lunar Fire in the same festival. The sky reserved a torrential downpour as decoration for our outdoor event. Lightning flashed and electrical connections buzzed. The crowd danced half-naked in the mud.

Gilly and I played for dancer Christine Moore at the Carillon Retirement Home... an easy gig. Then came another big step for me and my band. I booked the Trident Coffee House Sandbox Theater and we rehearsed some of my favorite Greek dance songs from the Rembetika genre... this is a genre which carries the deep pain of the Greek exodus from Anatolia after World War One. I was looking to add some flavors of the shadow sides of life and I promoted the gig with words like *'Music Can Transform Our Agony into Ecstasy! Traditional Greek Musical Wisdom and More! Come Dig into your Deep Soul and Dance it all out!'*

Adding so many songs which were new to many of the band members placed a big strain on our learning capacities and on my memory. James Hoskins, my cello player, helped keep it all together with his seemingly impeccable memorization skills. Actually, the show went extremely well and something in my soul felt deeply satisfied. I was presenting Arabic music, my own compositions, and now Greek music in one of its deepest forms... all mixed together...

Then another outdoor festival, the Arise Festival, was coming up and I was asked by Gilly to perform again with Lunar Fire. I was used to playing my Middle Eastern stringed instruments sitting down. I wanted to stand and play like a rock star with Gilly's band at the festival. It didn't work out so well. My fingers were clumsy on my instruments in standing posture. I was disappointed in my performance.

We did another 'Powers of Love: Ecstatic Egyptian Trance Dance Party' with guest dancer Xitlali Baila and then presented another 'shadow-side' gig with Greek music added called 'Ecstatic Egyptian-Style Music Meets Dancing With Our Shadow' with guest dancer Seemie Xavier featured.

Seemie Xavier

Our guest dancers would inspire sexier moves in the crowd and my band had the skill and power to drive it all forward.

Cameron Powers Project Band

Ecuador: Back to South America At Last

As the summer of 2013 came to a close Kristina and I headed for Ecuador. My Inca shaman friend, Oscar Santillan, was there. We spent marvelous time with him in the town of Otavalo. We went up to fifteen thousand feet and sang at the sky with eagle bone whistles and centuries-old jade flutes which had been in his family for generations. A condor circled us in the sky. Oscar took this as a good sign... more than a good sign... it was an answer from an old ally.

Oscar Santillan in Otavalo, Ecuador

We went to a waterfall and I played my Egyptian flutes and my Turkish çumbuş while he played jade flutes and Kristina sang. We met his new wife... new baby... numerous brothers and sisters... slept in his large communal household... I began speaking a little bit in Quechua again.

We met with Oscar's brother Rumi Ñawi - Eyes of the Stone - another keeper of Andean wisdom.

Inca Traditional Music - Oscar's Brother Rumi

I had not been so close to the ancient heart of the Inca empire for forty years. I felt like my Inca soul was slowly coming home again! A great simplicity was revealing itself to me in the lap of these ancient Quechua ways of being.

Rumi and His Wife

Our friend Gail was just arriving from Boulder. She had discovered the charms of Cotacachi, a little community very close to Otavalo. She was building a little house on the property of a local family who had adopted her. She wanted us to meet them. Another whole world of wonderful family connections opened for us. We had the çumbuş and a drum with us... we offered tastes of indigenous Middle Eastern music... not something often heard in Andean territories.

My friend Dave, also known as 'Santa Cruz Woody,' had purchased a little hotel down on the Pacific coast. He and I had become friends while Kristina and I had been touring through Santa Cruz on the US West coast. He offered us a free stay for however long we might want down in his hotel on the Ecuadorian coast. In exchange I would get to know the new managers, Milton and his family, take some promotional photos and give Dave a report on how his hotel was doing with Milton in charge.

The hotel was catering to weekend Ecuadorian vacationers who would descend from the capital city, Quito. It was not a destination for English speakers... everything happened in Spanish. Milton and his family were from Ecuador.

In the little nearby beach town of Canoa there were a few laid-back restaurants... the local fishermen would come and go out to sea every day in their tiny little boats following their ancient rhythms.

Fishermen Carry in Their Bags of Fish

I felt good about my friendship with Milton and his family and gave Dave a positive report... along with "the best photos of the hotel I've received yet..." according to Dave.

We headed south through Guayaquil and then up over a fourteen-thousand foot pass toward Cuenca. Our dear friends Zia and Roshni had left Boulder a couple of years earlier and begun a perma-culture farm project in Vilcabamba.

Zia was still the official president of our non-profit. She not only introduced us to glimpses of all her new friends and projects in Vilcabamba but arranged for us to present indigenous Egyptian music with it's 'notes-between-the-notes' as we had presented under her guidance for the Mexicas in Mexico. She had traveled up to Otavalo and shared time with us while we were staying with Oscar Santillan. She and Oscar were co-planning multiple workshops to promote perma-culture and the values of indigenous Inca agricultural wisdom.

We stayed long enough in Vilcabamba to connect with both the indigenous and the foreign communities. It became another of the places we could call 'home.'

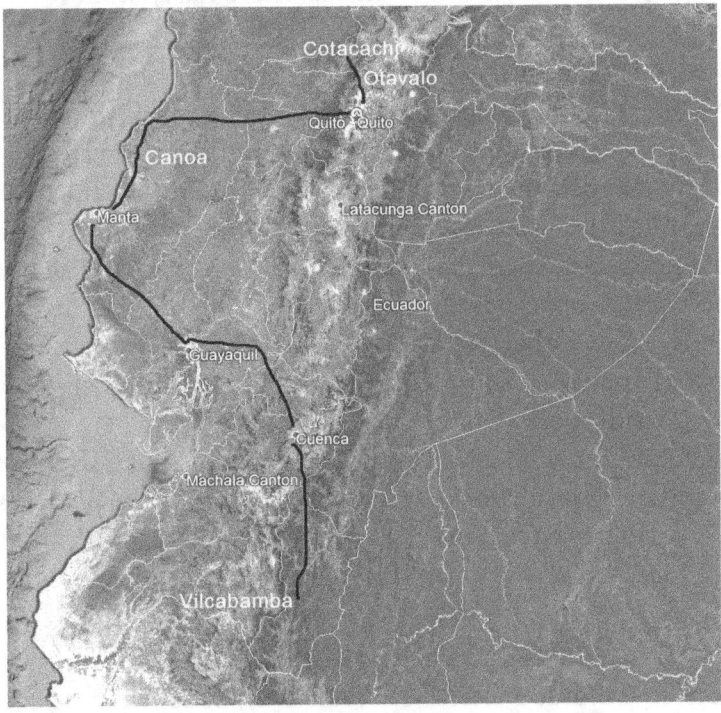

2013 - Ecuador

Ecuador had been very soft and welcoming for us. We flew back to the USA and the US customs agents grilled me to the max and searched every tiny cranny in my luggage... they could see I was a musician... they were very suspicious... about what I could not guess... not a nice welcome back to my north American homeland.

We had a two-and-a-half-hour layover in Miami and it was all used up by the customs agents' searches and insistent questioning.... who did you visit? Where did you meet them? etc etc... I never went into specifics of course. I was just another dumb tourist. Then they had to go write up a long report about their findings... kinda funny and a big waste of everyone's time but very weird to go through. There were so many militarized-looking guys everywhere... shaved heads, tattoos, no smiles, US flags sewn on their collars, military clothing... the whole USA was feeling kinda nasty.

We arrived in Boulder right after a big devastating flood. Kristina's daughter, Lauren, and her boyfriend had been able to offer housing to the now-homeless flood victims in Lyons. And later they were witness to weird people dressed as government FEMA inspectors showing up and then looting homes... more nasty stuff.

Mexican Village with Turkish Friend

We flew down to Puerto Vallarta with our Turkish friend Korkut and his wife Jenny. Moving down by boat from Puerto Vallarta to Yelapa we escaped the world of roads and cars for a while. Yelapa has neither. But it was not as remote as it had once been. Now they had planted poles and strung wires... they had electricity. The little town was now much noisier with televisions blaring.

Korkut and I always have a wonderful time. He is a poet and a student of history... and a busy architectural designer with global projects... and a connoisseur of tequila.

Back in Puerto Vallarta two of our local musician friends took us to a beach near the airport to sample what may be the tastiest seafood I have ever experienced: pescado sarandeado... fresh fish smoked in a unique Mexican way... wow!

Colorado, Washington and California

Back in Colorado after New Years Day, 2014, we produced more dance events. Kristina produced a series of about seven "Women's Sing Dance Drum Circles" and I began presenting events to promote my new set of five CD's for meditation, movement and massage... I called them *'Soulscapes.'* I created them in twenty different perfectly harmonious Egyptian music scales. My events were designed to explain the physics of just intonation, or perfect harmony. I was excited to share information about how these harmonies between notes had been lost in the West but preserved in ancient traditional music from places like Egypt.

Soulscapes - Five CD's of Perfectly Harmonious Music

Kristina made a quick trip to El Cajon to help produce an Iraqi Refugee Womens Drumming, Singing, Dance Circle but soon returned to produce more workshops in Boulder and join the Cameron Powers Project Band Members to exhibit our "Middle Eastern Jazz" at the Boulder Jazz Fest in Front of the Boulder Courthouse on the Pearl St Mall.

Kristina and I then performed and taught workshops in Pagosa Springs, Colorado, at the Earth Goddess Rising Festival over a period of several days. A sweet camaraderie was born out of our connections with those very starry-eyed men and women.

Rainbow with Lightning Over My Head in Pagosa Springs

It was deep summertime and I again played for my exotic dancer friend Tarena at the Denver 16th St Mall Festival. Gilly Gonzales, whose amazing energies and drumming skills always rock my world, agreed again to be our percussionist.

Kristina's 'Women's Sing Dance Drum Circles' and my 'Soulscapes: Lost Harmonies of the Nile' presentations kept us busy again for the next few weeks.

Then, after passing through Washington State to visit Kristina's mom and dad, we met key members from my band in Northern California's Olympic Village near Lake Tahoe to play for my son Loren's wedding... what a beautiful love fest!

My Son's Wedding - James, Gilly, Loren, Alison

Leda and my kids' ex-step-mom and Lindy shared the "mother" role beautifully and co-created a flower arrangement for the wedding ceremony. They had all played deeply nurturing roles in raising our children: mother, step-mother... god-mother.

We continued to Southern California, still driving our diesel van and pulling our travel trailer to offer performances for the Iraqi Community in El Cajon. But I was exhausted and we headed back home.

Dumping Our Belief Systems

Back in Boulder I played Greek music, Sufi music and Turkish music with various members of Sherefe and with Benyamin and Rabia who were up from New Mexico.

We also played a fund-raiser for our friend, Theresa, at the E-town Hall shortly before she died of cancer.

My friend Naomi was doing well. She was re-claiming her earlier identity as prolific singer-songwriter. I helped her produce two shows. Her husband Rick and I felt a deep bond. We both knew that we shared a network of love energies which had helped keep Naomi alive with us through tough times.

But something happened. Their marriage fell apart again. Kristina helped me go and give Naomi some love and a massage. I took Naomi out to dance a few days later. I tried to help her with some practical advice and some loving energy. She just looked at me and shook her head. The next day she drove high up into the mountains above Boulder and disappeared into the winter wilderness.

I knew what she must have finally done... and several days later a search and rescue team found her body. She had hung herself from a tree.

Some of us still refer to her as 'our little warrior.' She couldn't go through the same cycles of agony yet another time.

And yes, life and death do look a bit different from the vantage point of our later years when suffering begins to take its toll... no one is immune... and we finally realize that each of us is a perfect manifestation of a unique brand of craziness... why would one crazy person ever dare to judge another...?

There are other natural stages in life too. We spend the first half exploring the world and eagerly acquiring 'belief systems.' At some point we realize that all our 'belief systems' stand between us and a clear view of reality. They block our view and, when we finally realize this, we begin to unload them... get rid of them as best we can. So our beliefs too, go 'from dust to dust'... unless we get stuck somewhere along our path and cling to them. Spiritual freedom can only happen somewhere out there beyond belief systems... which are mere words... nothing but another 'virtual reality.'

I have had the good fortune to acquire something of an Inca soul and something of an Afro-Asiatic soul to add to my Indo-European soul. My native Indo-European soul is good at thinking alone... in a linear fashion. My Inca and Afro-Asiatic souls are able to taste what it's like to think and feel collectively... in the same ways a flock of birds or a school of fish manifest one consciousness with their multiple bodies. It really is so very different...

People from different cultures can learn so much from each other. But it requires staying open through two genuine adventures... one on the outside and another on the inside...

My friend Sadie Marquardt announced that she wanted to produce a fund-raiser event for Musical Missions of Peace. She had been watching us evolve for years. And her belly dance career had been growing incredibly. Some claimed that she was the most famous belly dancer on the planet because some of the videos of her dance had been viewed over thirty million times on Youtube.

My band was excited. I was excited. Sadie and I invited a total of ten dancers to perform and I began mixing my own newly composed "Cameron Powers Project" songs with well-known Arabic dance tunes and checking with each dancer to see what she might like.

Dancers and Musicians in Sadie Fundraiser

I spent over a hundred and twenty hours composing medleys and when the time came we nearly filled the house at the Cleo Parker Robinson theater in Denver.

Sadie Fundraiser

One of the Iraqi refugee women from the community in El Cajon, Nidal Mishkoor, flew in for the event and sang an Iraqi song with us on stage after publicly complimenting our work. "You really understand our people!" she said.

But my health problems were wearing me down. The electrical pathways in my heart had apparently developed short circuits from too many years of pushing my limits and my stamina was barely sufficient to finish the show.

The following year in 2016 I assembled a smaller version of my band to do a Rumi show featuring our Persian musical ambassador, Ari Honarvar, a woman whom I had originally met dancing at one of Boulder's ongoing "barefoot boogie" improv dance events.

Ari Honarvar's Rumi Show

Again we nearly filled the house and set a precedent for many more similar shows. But I no longer had the strength and have had to refrain from producing further events.

Our Loving Has Survived and Deepened

Kristina has been caring for me diligently and with great love through the last two years as I have gone through surgery after surgery. A chiropractor ruptured my lowest lumbar disc in early 2017 and an electrophysiologist accidentally burned an artery in my heart while trying to fix my pre-ventricular contractions which had been causing my heart to miss every other beat for many hours every day.

It required double-bypass open heart surgery to fix the electrophysiologist's mistake and it required four-level cervical vertebrae fusion surgery and three-level lower back fusion surgery to fix the chiropractic injury. By the end of 2018 these had all been accomplished.

The outpouring of support has been off-the-charts phenomenal. Musician and dancer friends coordinated a fund-raiser which featured something like thirty performers and stimulated hundreds of people to donate. Dozens of friends have appeared to make certain that I was never left alone either in the hospital nor at home. Food and financial donations have been flowing in and I have been bathed in love.

It is early 2019 as I write this now. I have become extraordinarily weak but at last there is hope that I can finally heal without needing additional surgeries.

Kristina and I are so lucky that our loving has survived and deepened... and ripened during our eighteen years together.

A daily sorrow for me, however, is the fact that my dear daughter, Melina, has not fully healed from those mysterious modern diseases which now seem to afflict so many. Oh how I wish that she could have more strength to pursue a more joyful path. But she is still making the most of her gifts. I am happy for that.

My son has had good luck and is in good health and is a thriving electrical engineer who designs vast solar energy farms. He and his wife Alison have gifted us all with their lovely daughter, Sierra Aerial Powers... my grand-daughter.

Do Lovers Amplify Each Other?

I have been so very lucky to stay in touch with most of the women with whom I was in deep love connection. They are still in my life although Lisa just passed away from a sudden massive stroke. But she, like Bonnie, had been coming over once or twice a week to help me recover from these surgeries. My kids' step-mom has also been visiting me and Leda and I are in touch. When I see their faces I feel instantly transported back into a realm of deep love and trust.

We are remembering something precious and keeping it alive. What is that precious thing which has survived? I think that lovers somehow amplify each others' soul energies. We want to be seen and appreciated and our lovers have accomplished that for us. We become larger thanks to them. We never forget that and we always feel warm in the presence of one of our lovers who used to perform that very magical function for us.

If it were just me with my fond memories of my lovers I would not be so sure. I would wonder if it was just me being overly romantic. But Birdie, Bonnie, Lisa, Robin, Camille, Leda and my kids' step-mom all keep showing up in radiant forms to celebrate these feelings with me. So no... it's not just me. They all feel it too.

They form a powerful sisterhood. They greet each other with deep hugs and loving energies. Kristina welcomes them all and they all reciprocate with love toward her.

And I feel a deep brotherhood connection with the men whom have been deeply involved with my past lovers. We know that we have been drawn to honor the preciousness of the same person and that creates a deep bond.

The power of loving connection is much vaster than we can guess. Quietly, all over planet earth, networks of men and women who have been lovers continue to celebrate lifelong friendships which have a truly magical foundation! Something in our psychic wiring system has enabled us to amplify and broadcast each other's beauty and our souls appreciate that and will never forget.

Musical Ambassadors of Peace

An active board of directors keeps the non-profit moving forward independently from my own efforts and leadership which is a marvelous thing. To find the latest information go to:

https://www.musicalambassadorsofpeace.org

Other Books and CD's by Cameron Powers

Harmonic Secrets of Arabic Music Scales
Fine Tuning the Maqams – With 2 Audio CDs

Play Modern Music with Ancient Tunings

If you are in love with a Middle Eastern sounding music scale and want to learn Arabic music and related Indian music scales, you need genuine Middle Eastern music theory which is Arabic music theory.

How to write Middle Eastern music? It involves using Eastern modes, Middle East instruments, and genuine Arabic music scales.

When I was only 5 years old I listened to the piano and I could tell there was something wrong: it should sound good but for some reason it didn't. They all thought it was in tune but I could tell that it wasn't... quite right...

Secrets of Magical Music Explained in Detail! What are the harmonic secrets of Egyptian Music? Whatever your instrument... Whatever your skills... Whatever your singing style...

You can put this information to use and become the musician or performer you really want to be!

You will be able to rock the world with this knowledge!

In addition to full disclosure of the ancient secrets of perfect harmony, more than eighty ancient scales are taught.

This is enough material for lifetimes of musical creativity!

Arabic Musical Scales
Basic Maqam Teachings - With 2 Audio CDs

Enter the Exotic World of Quartertone Scales

Designed for both the beginner and the professional musician, Arabic Musical Scales is the ultimate guide to 45 of the most popular Maqams

"Excellent book. I would highly recommend the CDs that are sold separately as well. They are very well done. Very informational and also have improvised demonstrations of the scales so you can hear each scale in a musical setting."

"All I have to say is 'WOW'!

You just put together what I was looking for, a concise yet comprehensive material for someone like me to study and get on with my ultimate passion, Arabic music!"

"I bought your CDs and book of basic maqam techniques. It was a wonderful surprise... it put everything I was looking for in my hands with no effort!"

"Your book on Middle Eastern scales has been invaluable to me. I lead a Middle Eastern musical ensemble but I'm the only Arab in the group, so your book has been the standard by which I teach my musicians. It really is a great book."

Maqam Practice Tracks
Perfect Harmony of Just Intonation

** Beyond Quartertones **

We return to the true ancient roots of Perfect Harmony; 21 Different Arabic Music Modes; Available on 6 CD's; Additional Track Included: Modulation Practice; A total of 22 Tracks: Six Hours of Practice Material. Each Track is Actually 15 Minutes Long!

Arabic Musical Scales and most other maqam teaching systems rely on the "quartertone" concept for determining pitches of notes in various maqam intervals.

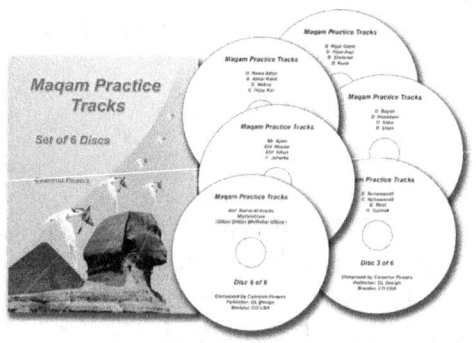

These teachings are a great start, but quartertones do not take us to the heart of the matter.

We must return to the laws of physics which determine the harmonic roots of all ancient indigenous music systems...

These musical laws of harmony are called "just intonation."

If you already purchased one of my books: Arabic Musical Scales or Harmonic Secrets of Arabic Music ...or if you have approached from some other direction and are learning to play Arabic music with its fascinating and beautiful maqam system, then you are already trying to find the musical intervals on your instrument or with your voice...

I have designed this series of 15 minute tracks to try and help you...

Each Practice Track Moves Slowly Through Musical Phrases — Sometimes with Rhythm and Sometimes without — So the Student has Plenty of Time to Practice by Playing Along with any Instrument of Choice — Great for Singers Too —

Arab Musicians Insist on These Intriguing Musical Facts:

"I've identified at least 12 notes between my lowest e-flat and my highest e-natural."

– Sami Shumays, Arab Violinist

Soulscapes
Sacred Meditation Music in absolutely perfect harmony!

These vibrational soundfields are unique! They literally vibrate your energy fields into place! Even those who have spent years working with other popular meditation soundfields are switching to Soulscapes after trying them out! Perfectly Tuned Music Intervals!

These cd's contain something never before produced: ancient music scales from Egypt in mathematically perfect harmony created with modern technology which allows perfection!

The intervals between the cello, dulcimer and vocal notes which you will hear on these cd's can work a magical alignment in your being because the vibrational laws of physics are in action.

The wavelengths of the different notes actually nest together! They amplify and reinforce each other according to the physical principles of "just intonation."

Just intonation creates the same harmonies which are found in the sacred traditional musics of Egypt, Mesopotamia, and India!

The adventurous meditator can literally disappear into the sound fields contained in this series of 5 cd's. And the fact that the perfectly harmonious musical scales presented are primarily from the Egyptian tradition gives access to another fountain of traditional ancient wisdom.

Some say that the perfection of these harmonies resonates within the stored memories in our DNA!

To find out more information on this set of CD's go to:
https://www.sacredmeditationmusic.com/

Middle Eastern Flute Magic: Play the Nay
Finger Charts for Arabic Music Scales

There was an instrument being played which sounded like a rush of liquid sensual fire. I had no idea what it was. By the mid-1980's I was spending a week every summer in Mendocino, California at Middle Eastern Music Camp. Omar Faruk Tekbilek was one of the instructors and I found out what had been making that amazing sound: the Nay!

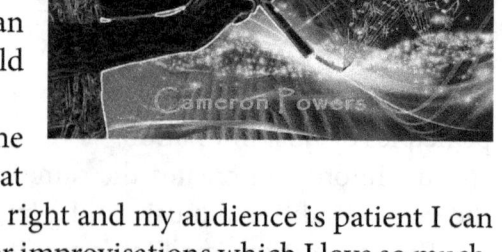

I discovered that just getting notes out of the Nay that alone was still not enough. It was a certain double octave technique which produced the real magic. This requires infinite delicacy but once achieved the ultimate cosmic Nay secrets could be revealed. The higher notes could be supported by identical notes from an octave below. Two notes could emerge at once and that thick smoky almost-human sound of musical breath would suddenly manifest.

I have never acquired the agility on the Nay to perform at high speed. But if the mood is right and my audience is patient I can produce those slow melodies or improvisations which I love so much.

Since I have written two books which reveal the structure of the maqam systems of indigenous Middle Easter music scales I was apparently the perfect person to decipher and describe the musical maps finger-hole by finger-hole on the most common Dukah Nay. I have also provided maqam lists for Nays of different sizes which begin from different tonics or keys. I haven't seen this information published elsewhere so I will present that in this little book.

Singing in Baghdad
A Musical Mission of Peace

The story of events leading up to and including a journey to Baghdad, Iraq made at the same time as the US Marines were entering the city in the spring of 2003. The success of this journey illustrates the capacity of the Iraqi people to distinguish love-based invasions from fear-based invasions. The story told in Singing in Baghdad illustrates the possibility of expanding cross-cultural musical study and performance into a new kind of people-to-people international diplomacy.

Review: "I have had the good fortune of reading two of Cameron's books. Just like his and Kristina's visionary simplicity in connecting with peoples our culture habitually misconstrues, they are replete with profound insights. It is not often that I get entirely new perspectives on how our world is shaped through culture. Cameron's works are chock full of them.

I recommend Cameron as someone who is an expression of the change our world inspires. When you meet him, you realize that he is the change wherever he is, always ready to sing and travel widely with spirited gentleness into the landscape of the human heart. And all of his words lead toward that knowing that there is a realm which is fully human that we can dwell in together in a way that words can't express – but a voice, a drum or an oud can... And that is the disarming genius that Cameron expounds; rather than taking us through more thought processes about how we might think ourselves into having a different perception of other, Cameron takes us directly into ecstatic song, directly into shared ecstasy which, once shared, radically softens the very sense of other and opens us to mutual discovery through the bliss that inhabits our core and is yearning for release and connection. He is not out in the world resisting fear; he is out in the world inviting fear directly to the party and the feast which always awaits us in the communion of hearts. -- Olivier Tryba

Spiritual Traveler
Journeys Beyond Fear

Musicians have long held many of the keys to cross-cultural journeying as a spiritual path. Along the way many things are learned. In this book we find many clues about Arab-world people and the beauties of their ancient ways. With fear removed from our perceptions, we find a way paved for endless cross-cultural love affairs.

Review: The Spiritual Traveler book is incredible!! You just might be the wisest man I know! I really love how you write. I want every Bellydancer who trains with me to read it!!
– Sadie Marquardt

Review: I love that the tone of his Cameron Powers' writing is also characteristic of his speaking tone (obvious for those of us lucky enough to witness his speech firsthand). Not all writers achieve this, and that, in and of itself, IS an achievement!

To read his words is indeed a journey beyond fear regardless of the range of your geographic and cultural travel. In fact, the heart of this book hearkens you on an adventure of relating to yourself and others regardless of who the 'others' are (and who 'you' are, for that matter) at any point in time and space. And Powers' approach is unique. The chapter and sub-chapter headings are enough to shake ya awake and getcha moving! I mean, how can you not be drawn forth by such chapter titles as 'Do We Speak Language or does Language Speak Us?' or '"Civilization'–Whose?" or 'Sacred Flirtation' or 'Do We Really Want to Waste this Precious Lifetime?'

There's such an immediacy, urgency, insight and exuberance to the content of this book that it should always be within reach.

Oh yeah…don't you dare put this book down until you read the 'Tomatoes' poem at the end!
– F. Medina

Naked Wild and Free in the Grand Canyon
Rowing and Roaming

Venturing down the rivers and canyons of the American West we touch sacred and primal worlds, both outside and inside ourselves. Anyone who has enjoyed such an adventure knows about this. This journal gives a taste of how it looked and felt to our crazy crew.

The author was fortunate enough to be included on four river trips which took place between 1969 and 1975.

This book contains an expanded version of the written journal kept by the author during a passage through the lower half of the Grand Canyon in 1975. Some of the photos included are from other earlier trips.

These adventures involved descents of the Colorado River through Cataract Canyon and the Grand Canyon, the Yampa River through Dinosaur National Monument and Echo Park, and the Green River through the Gates of Lodor, Grays Canyon, Desolation Canyon and Canyonlands National Park.

The rafts were of our own design and took a lot of muscle to row through the numerous white water rapids. The pace was leisurely, with plenty of time allowed for each trip.

River runners are a notoriously wild and crazy bunch. This book contains a small taste of the adventures enjoyed by a communal group of friends from Steamboat Springs, Colorado.

Review: Naked wild and free magically transported me back to the excitement of the 60s and 70s. It was a time in my life when the universe was wide-open, every day offered new opportunities, and subtle energies ruled. The greatest high was connecting with another soul whether it be human, plant, or animal. Even though I didn't know the characters, I could feel them and know their experiences. Really?! Yes, this is a fun, easy read – yet profoundly deep. Thank you for sharing your adventure with us.

— John, Boulder Colorado

Cameron Powers Project CD
Dance Music - Egyptian Music Scales

Middle Eastern Dance Rhythms…

Review: Your Cameron Powers Project instrumental CD is incredibly on-target! It's one of the only truly "in-tune" performances I know of. The shift to the soul-stirring ancient harmonies is now complete in you. They are so internalized that you can dance freely there, and the result is breathtaking. The "minor" thirds and sixths sound so much more powerful than the same minor intervals in western tuning. The sevenths are incredibly evocative. I know you studied and practiced hard to find these notes, but now that the heavy intellectual lifting has been done, you have uncovered a treasure trove of brilliant sound that far surpasses any academic or intellectual achievement. This is no academic exercise, it's a bringing to the surface the radiant jewels that had been buried in our hearts for too long.

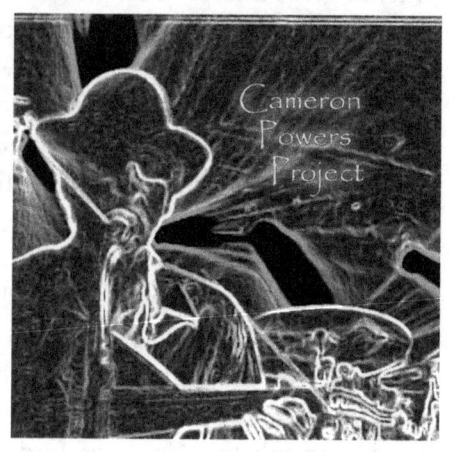

Love always,
Chris Mohr – Microtonal Composer

Review: Congratulations. Good stuff. I enjoyed the CD. Thank you for sharing.
Naser Musa – Jordanian Oud Player – Songwriter

Review: For my Birthday I received the new Cameron Powers CD caution: do not try to drive listening to it! I found myself in another world and had to park! It transports one straight to the heart and beauty! I LOVE cut 3 Breath of an Angel. Master musicians exploring rhythms and maqams!
Diane Eger

This CD is a reflection of Cameron's years of immersion in the music of Egypt, Iraq, Syria, Turkey and Greece.

Baghdad & Beyond CD
Cameron and Kristina and Sherefe

This CD features four of the popular Arabic songs sung frequently by Cameron & Kristina in the Arab world. A couple of Greek songs add icing to the musical cake!

Review: Thank you so much for sharing the CD Baghdad and Beyond with me. I have been listening to it for the last two days and I really like the way that you have done these songs. Kristina's voice is very beautiful and your two voices go together very well. Cameron did a great job at singing and playing these hard styles of Arabic music. I did not expect to hear what I heard. Congratulation on a job well done and I am sure that many Arabs just like me appreciate all this great effort and hard work that you both have done and still doing. You are doing our culture a big favor. I love you both and wish you all the best. May God keeps on blessing you and using you as part of his beautiful-hearted angels. Love, — Naser Musa

Review: I don't usually write fan letters, but I have to tell you your latest cd, Baghdad and Beyond, is really amazing. They're all good, but this one has something extra about it. Lots of interesting subtlety. And I always get a kick out of the last cut, the one with the Bedouins. Ha! — Doug

Middle Eastern Moods
4:01 am CD

The sun sets, a flurry of evening activities come and go...
As midnight passes the quiet deepens...
Somewhere, in a few living rooms, in a few taverns or restaurants or around the campfires in the forests... a few people stay... conversations dwindle...

The time for music is arriving... The musicians are slowly melting into their instruments, becoming one with their sounds...

It's 4:01 a.m...

The painter paints, the sculptor sculpts, the writer writes, the musician plays and sings, the dancer dances... What is left? We have paintings, statues, books from centuries past... The musicians and dancers weave their magic and it vanishes.... until the advent of recording devices... So here it is: captured on Cameron's recording device and offered on CD plates... threads of live song... flavors of Greek harmonies and Egyptian oud moods.

Contributors are too numerous to mention: musicians in Athens, Cairo, Fes, California and, yes, right here in Colorado, who have taught and inspired over the last 30 years...

This view through this thousand-year-old arched doorway in the Alhambre in Granada in Spain frames the still lingering vapors from countless such moments... Now under the warm afternoon sun the musicians are just finishing their breakfasts...

Dancing with Your Soul
Arabic Nights

Let your body gently move by itself to this music and see what happens...

Editor's Pick on Indie-Music.com: "...recognition that our screeners found your music of high quality..."

Review: "Hey I've become totally addicted to your tune Damascus... I'd like to download this one to my collection which I'm playing while driving in my car. Please send me a link to buy this... I just can't wait until I add it to my list of favourites!!!" — Denis

Review: "I absolutely LOVE Dancing with your Soul!!! Listening all the time to it and singing along... great tool for my learning maqamat." — Ynyra Oshea

Review: "Erotic, a desert flower in bloom... for making love, not war..." — Tessalin Green

Review: "I received your new CD in the mail and it is incredible !!!! Dancing with Your Soul is one of the most amazing CDs in my collection!! Thank YOU. — Lynnie Zsidov-Steiner

Cameron and Kristina have been deepening their musical and cultural connection to the Arabic-speaking people of the Middle East by making several recent journeys through Egypt, Syria, Jordan, Lebanon, Iraq and the West Bank of Palestine since 2002. Well over 300 musical and multi-media presentations have recently been completed in more than half of the American states as well as in Panama, Venezuela, Ecuador and Mexico.

Smooth and Slow and Sensual...

The books and CD's listed above can be ordered from:
https://www.gldesignpub.com
or
E-Mail: distrib@gldesignpub.com

www.ingramcontent.com/pod-product-compliance
Lightning Source LLC
Chambersburg PA
CBHW071657300426
44115CB00010B/1234